Peterson's Guide to
Colleges with Programs for Learning-Disabled Students

CHARLES T. MANGRUM II, Ed.D., and
STEPHEN S. STRICHART, Ph.D., Editors

With a foreword by Mrs. Pete Rozelle
Founder and President
Foundation for Children with Learning Disabilities

Peterson's Guides
Princeton, New Jersey

Library of Congress Cataloging in Publication Data
Main entry under title:

Peterson's guide to colleges with programs for learning-disabled students.

Includes index.
1. Universities and colleges—United States—Curricula—Directories. 2. Learning disabilities. I. Mangrum, Charles T. II. Strichart, Stephen S. III. Peterson's Guides, inc. IV. Title: Guide to colleges with programs for learning-disabled students.
L901.P458 1985 378.73 85-3497
ISBN 0-87866-327-4

Composition and design by Peterson's Guides

Cover photograph courtesy of University of Pennsylvania

Printed in the United States of America

10 9 8 7 6 5 4 3 2

For information about other Peterson's publications, please see the listing at the back of this volume.

Contents

Foreword

Peterson's Guide to Colleges with Programs for Learning-Disabled Students brings a ray of hope and sunlight into a field where there has been a serious lack of resources. This new guide is also a landmark symbol that increasing numbers of learning-disabled young people are successfully entering colleges and professional schools.

In 1977 I established the Foundation for Children with Learning Disabilities to help other parents who shared my frustrating efforts to find the right schools for my learning-disabled sons. There were many moments of discouragement, disappointment, and eventual anger that learning disabilities were not recognized. Countless other families all over the United States could not find local resources and did not know how to locate appropriate diagnostic centers. Even good pediatricians and experienced teachers had not been trained to identify and provide remediation for children with learning disabilities. The purpose of the Foundation for Children with Learning Disabilities has always been public awareness, and therefore it gives me much joy to introduce a college guide that brings such current information to young people who are learning disabled.

Readers will find excellent descriptions of programs that have been researched and have proved to be successful. There is wide geographic selection, and details about programs of instruction are carefully annotated in true Peterson's tradition. My congratulations to the editors and all good wishes to every young person and parent who uses this guide. It is a stepping-stone to the higher learning opportunity that will assist every learning-disabled student in reaching his or her potential.

Carrie Rozelle

Mrs. Pete Rozelle
Founder and President
Foundation for Children
with Learning Disabilities

Introduction

Yes! Students with learning disabilities are going to college, succeeding there, and graduating. They are going to all types of colleges and universities, participating increasingly in the mainstream of college life. With appropriate knowledge about college programs for students with learning disabilities, the right preparation, and proper guidance, learning-disabled students can choose a suitable college, major in any area of study, and graduate successfully. Today, learning-disabled students are also going to graduate school. Some are becoming attorneys, others physicians, still others engineers and architects. For the learning-disabled student who receives the proper support and guidance, the world of opportunity is rapidly expanding.

This guide represents a comprehensive attempt to gather and evaluate learning disabilities programs found in colleges throughout the United States. To prepare the book, we mailed questionnaires to all accredited four-year colleges and universities (over 1,800) to identify those with formal and established programs especially for students with learning disabilities. The detailed questionnaires were completed by responsible professionals at the colleges. These professionals were asked to describe special provisions for learning-disabled students at their institutions that are distinct from the services offered to all students. The results are shared through this guide.

Of course, college is only for learning-disabled students who have the potential to succeed, just as it is only for any other high school graduate with that potential. College learning disabilities programs help students who have the basic potential for college achievement to succeed despite the problems they encounter as a consequence of their learning disabilities. The most important thing to keep in mind is that students must have average to above-average intelligence. This is necessary both to enter and to succeed in college. College programs for learning-disabled students can help these students realize their full potential. However, the potential must be there from the start.

Even with the potential to succeed in college, most learning-disabled students take more than the usual four years to complete their studies. Frequently they take a reduced course load of 9–12 credits, rather than the usual 15 credits. The reading, writing, and study demands of a full college course load are more than typical learning-disabled students can handle at first. To help such students make the difficult transition from high school to college, programs for learning-disabled students provide intensive services during the freshman and sophomore years. These services are gradually phased out as learning-disabled students progress through college.

HOW TO USE THIS GUIDE

First read "College Opportunities for Learning-Disabled Students" in this guide, which presents information on what learning disabilities are, what learning-disabled college students are like, why colleges began providing programs for these students, how such students are admitted to college, what services and aids the college programs provide, and how high schools can help qualified learning-disabled students prepare for college. Then read "How to Select a College for a Learning-Disabled Student," which presents a series of steps to help you choose a college. Use the section called "College Profiles" to obtain the detailed information you need to implement the steps outlined in the section on selecting a college. The profiles present comprehensive information on colleges providing services and aids especially for learning-disabled students. General information is presented about each college followed by specific information on the learning disabilities program at the college. The last section of the guide lists sources for additional information about learning-disabled young adults that may help you further in selecting a college.

College Opportunities for Learning-Disabled Students

WHAT ARE LEARNING DISABILITIES?

As long as there have been schools, there have been children who have had difficulty meeting academic requirements. For years these children were labeled "underachievers." It was assumed that the problem was that they were not trying hard enough or perhaps that their teachers were not teaching well. As parents and professionals encountered more and more children who seemed to have the potential to succeed in school but were not doing so, it became apparent that the problem lay somewhere else. Professionals working in the fields of education, psychology, and medicine began to identify a group of children who had problems processing information through their ears (auditory modality), eyes (visual modality), and/or hands and eyes working in coordinated fashion (visual-motor modality). It soon became obvious that many of the children labeled underachievers had perceptual handicaps that appeared related to a central nervous system dysfunction.

During the period from 1930 to 1960, a number of terms were used to describe the problems of children who were not succeeding in school. Some of the most common terms were aphasia, dyslexia, hyperkinesis, specific language disorder, minimal brain dysfunction (MBD), perceptual impairment, and neurological impairment. For the most part, parents of these children were told that the problem was primarily medical. However, most parents kept insisting that the real problem was educational.

In 1963, Dr. Samuel A. Kirk, a leading authority in special education, addressed an organization of parents concerned with the problems of perceptually handicapped children. In his address, Kirk coined the term "learning disabilities." He described a group of children who had disorders in the development of language, speech, reading, and the associated communication skills needed for effective social interaction. He made it clear that he was not talking about children whose primary problems were blindness or deafness, mental retardation, emotional disturbance, or severely debilitating motor impairments. The response of the parents was immediate and overwhelming. The very next evening, the organization changed its name to the Association for Children with Learning Disabilities and has subsequently become the Association for Children and Adults with Learning Disabilities.

Learning disabilities quickly became a popular concept with both parents and educators. For years, educators faced the problem of providing services for children who failed to succeed but who did not fit into any existing categories of special education. These children fell through the cracks and went through their school years without the assistance they needed to achieve their potential. This circumstance, coupled with the emerging learning disabilities concept, quickly resulted in the birth of a new special education category termed learning disabilities. Children who previously fell through the cracks could now be diagnosed as having a learning disability and placed in a program specially designed to meet their needs.

The federal government became involved as an increasing number of children were identified as learning disabled. In 1969, Public Law 91-230 was passed. This law is known as the Specific Learning Disabilities Act. It provided funds for training, research, and program development in learning disabilities.

What followed is unprecedented in education. Never has a new field grown so quickly. In 1969, approximately 120,000 public school children in the United States were identified as learning disabled. By 1970, just one year later, public schools were serving 648,000 learning-disabled children. Current U.S. Department of Education figures indicate that there are approximately 1,750,000 learning-disabled students enrolled in public schools. This growth rate is staggering and indicates clearly the impact of learning disabilities upon educational services. Approximately 5 percent of school-age children are learning disabled, and the same holds true for freshmen entering colleges and universities throughout the nation.

How Are Learning Disabilities Defined?

For many years there was considerable confusion regarding the definition of learning disabilities. Through the 1960s and even into the 1970s, professionals in the field spent much of their time and energy debating the relative merits of various definitions of learning disabilities. The uncertainty was clarified to a large extent in 1975 with the passage of Public Law 94-142 (PL 94-142), the Education of All Handicapped Children Act, wherein learning disabilities were defined. Because the PL 94-142 definition was tied to federal funding of programs for learning disabilities in public schools throughout the fifty states, the definition became widely accepted. It runs as follows:

> The term "children with specific learning disabilities" means those children who have a disorder in one or more of the basic psychological processes involved in understanding or in using language, spoken or written, which disorder may manifest itself in an imperfect ability to listen, think, speak, read, write, spell, or do mathematical calculations. Such disorders include such conditions as perceptual handicaps, brain injury, minimal brain dysfunction, dyslexia, and developmental aphasia. Such term does not include children who have learning problems which are primarily the result of visual, hearing, or motor handicaps, of mental retardation, of emotional disturbance, or of environmental, cultural, or economic disadvantage.

The regulations for PL 94-142 specify that a child study team may determine that a child has a learning disability if he or she does not achieve commensurate with his or her age ability levels in one or more of seven specific areas when provided with learning experiences appropriate for the child's age. The seven areas are oral expression, listening comprehension, written expression, basic reading skill, reading comprehension, mathematics calculation, and mathematics reasoning. A learning disability is determined if a child study team finds a severe discrepancy between achievement and intellectual ability in one or more of the seven areas.

What the Definition Means

The PL 94-142 definition was written at a time when children, up to the secondary school level, were the focus of the learning disabilities field. Since then, the field has expanded to include young adults and adults, so the concept is now used to cover all individuals with learning disabilities.

The first element referred to in the definition is a disorder in one or more of the basic psychological processes involved in understanding or in using spoken or written language. Language is a means of communication. In the spoken form, this means that a child is able to understand what others say and is able to express thoughts to others. In the written form, it means that a child is able to read and to write language using correct spelling and grammar. Basic psychological processes are the operations that occur in the brain when a response is made to a stimulus. When a stimulus is transmitted through the ears and a response is made, this is referred to as auditory processing. When the eyes are involved, it is visual processing. When the hands and eyes are involved in combination, it is visual-motor processing. The effects of deficits in these basic psychological processes become apparent when a child uses language. Depending on the nature and severity of the deficits, problems occur in listening, thinking, speaking, reading, writing, spelling, and/or doing mathematical calculations.

The next element in the definition refers to a number of other conditions—perceptual handicaps, brain injury, minimal brain dysfunction, dyslexia, and developmental aphasia. These terms were used in the early years of the learning disabilities field to describe the learning problems of children from essentially a medical perspective. Because the term "learning disabilities" is broader than these terms and has an educational orientation, it has replaced the earlier terms. While literally thousands of classes for learning-disabled children exist in today's public schools, almost none exist for children labeled with one of the earlier terms. For all practical purposes, if your child is described with any of the earlier terms, think of your child as having a learning disability when seeking services and assistance.

The final element in the definition is known as the exclusion clause. This is because the element identifies problems that are *not* learning disabilities. For example, if a child's primary problem is loss of sight, the educational classification centers on visual impairment or blindness rather than learning disabilities, even though the child may have difficulty learning. The same is true for loss of hearing, severe motor handicaps, mental retardation, emotional disturbance, and lack of exposure to good learning opportunities due to environmental, cultural, or economic disadvantage. By implication, the definition is saying that the problems of a learning-disabled child are not primarily attributable to sensory limitations, physical limitations, lack of intelligence, emotional problems, or environmental deprivation.

CHARACTERISTICS OF LEARNING-DISABLED COLLEGE STUDENTS

There are many characteristics associated with learning-disabled college students. These can be classified and discussed under seven major categories: cognition, language, perceptual and motor skills, academic work, work and study habits, social skills, and emotional development. There is overlap of the characteristics across the categories, and no one learning-disabled college student will have all the characteristics we present. The following list was prepared after a thorough review of published information on learning disabilities at the college level and our discussions with directors of college learning disabilities programs throughout the country.

Cognition

Cognitive characteristics are those commonly referred to under the general heading of intelligence. They have to do with the way people think and reason. Learning-disabled students may have difficulty with some of the following:

- Acquiring a fund of information about the world
- Sequencing events and ideas
- Understanding abstract concepts
- Distinguishing important from unimportant information
- Reasoning in a deductive manner
- Perceiving cause-and-effect relationships
- Remembering things seen and heard (short- and long-term memory)
- Sustaining attention to tasks
- Organizing ideas and information
- Generalizing skills from one task and situation to another

Language

At the core of every learning disability are language difficulties. Learning-disabled college students may have difficulties in both spoken and written language. These difficulties may interfere with achievement in all courses taken. Students may have difficulty with some of the following:

Spoken Language

- Grasping what others say to them
- Using mature syntactical patterns
- Using an appropriate range of vocabulary
- Retrieving the appropriate word for a situation
- Using words in their appropriate context

Written Language

- Expressing themselves precisely and clearly
- Using a variety of sentence structures
- Using mature syntactical patterns
- Using an appropriate range of words
- Using long and/or difficult words
- Organizing thoughts
- Using punctuation correctly
- Using a sufficient number of verbs, adjectives, and adverbs
- Writing compositions

Perceptual and Motor Skills

Perceptual-motor deficits are very prevalent in young learning-disabled children. As they mature, they learn to compensate for these deficits; however, vestiges remain even in adulthood. Therefore, it is not unusual to find that learning-disabled college students have problems in perceptual-motor areas. They may have difficulty with some of the following:

- Perceiving the correct orientation of complex visual figures
- Perceiving spatial attributes
- Dealing with three-dimensional figures and arrays
- Discriminating between similar visual designs and configurations
- Locating specific information on a page
- Discriminating between similar-sounding words
- Performing tasks requiring fine motor coordination

Academic Work

Every learning disability is accompanied by significant underachievement in one or more basic academic areas. Learning-disabled college students may have difficulties in reading, spelling, handwriting, and/or mathematics. Underachievement in any of these basic areas makes it difficult for the student to meet college course requirements. Learning-disabled college students may have difficulty with some of the following:

Reading

- Decoding unfamiliar words
- Understanding what is read
- Knowing the meaning of words read
- Maintaining an efficient rate of reading
- Adapting reading rate to specific reading purposes

Spelling

- Maintaining the correct sequence of letters when spelling words
- Perceiving sound-letter correspondence when spelling words
- Spelling words that have uncommon patterns
- Spelling long words

Handwriting

- Establishing a comfortable style of writing
- Maintaining an efficient rate of writing
- Writing in cursive
- Forming legible letters
- Forming letters of appropriate size
- Producing neat papers
- Writing within the margins
- Gripping the pencil correctly
- Maintaining writing quality when time limits are involved, such as during timed tests or when taking notes from lectures

Mathematics

- Doing computations
- Mastering the multiplication tables
- Reasoning mathematically
- Solving mathematical problems
- Recalling the sequence of operational processes
- Understanding and retaining terms representing quantitative concepts

Work and Study Habits

To succeed in college, learning-disabled students need more than average or above-average intellectual ability and basic academic skills. By the time they enter college, they also need a sophisticated set of work and study habits to handle the many and varied requirements of college courses. Learning-disabled college students may have difficulty with some of the following:

- Organizing and budgeting time
- Getting work started
- Sustaining effort on a task
- Completing work
- Establishing short- and long-term objectives
- Identifying the essential requirements of a task
- Integrating information from various sources
- Using library resources
- Using the dictionary and other reference tools
- Taking complete and accurate notes
- Outlining important information in a text
- Controlling test anxiety

Social Skills

Learning-disabled college students might drop out of college more because of their inability to handle the social demands than because of their inability to handle the academic demands. The social difficulties that the learning disabled experience as children carry over into college. Learning-disabled college students frequently have trouble interacting with their college peers, professors, and counselors and may have difficulty with any or all of the following:

- Establishing good relationships with others
- Making friends
- Working effectively with others
- Maintaining appropriate family relationships
- Reading body language and facial expressions
- Manifesting appropriate social behaviors
- Saying what is thought or felt
- Avoiding saying or doing things that are later regretted
- Knowing what to say in a situation
- Understanding humor and sarcasm
- Engaging in small talk
- Developing and maintaining hobbies and interests
- Maintaining appropriate personal appearance
- Relating to authority figures, such as professors and advisers

Emotional Development

Those familiar with learning-disabled college students are frequently struck by the students' immaturity in handling their emotions and feelings. Learning-disabled college students often manifest personality characteristics that are usually associated with young children. They fail to demonstrate the mature set of responses that typify adulthood. They may have difficulty with some of the following:

- Establishing a positive self-concept
- Establishing a sense of competence
- Developing self-confidence
- Adjusting to new situations
- Avoiding overdependence
- Accepting criticism

- Adjusting to the feelings of others
- Dealing with frustration
- Viewing their life prospects optimistically
- Trusting others
- Clarifying their values
- Meeting responsibilities
- Curbing impulsive behavior
- Working with others in a sharing manner
- Maintaining motivation
- Controlling anxiety
- Interacting with others in a nondefensive manner

WHY DID COLLEGE PROGRAMS FOR LEARNING-DISABLED STUDENTS COME ABOUT?

The field of learning disabilities dates from 1963 and is relatively young by any standard, and the creation of programs for learning-disabled college students is an even more recent development. In 1970, Dr. Gertrude Webb began the first full-fledged college program for learning-disabled students at Curry College in Milton, Massachusetts. Dr. Webb was one of the first to recognize that many learning-disabled students had both the ability and the desire to go to college. She believed that they deserved an opportunity to get a college education and could, in fact, achieve a college degree if provided with the compensatory assistance they needed to meet the demands of college. Since that time, a rapidly increasing number of colleges and universities throughout the United States have begun to provide special services for students with learning disabilities.

The tremendous increase in the number of colleges providing services for learning-disabled students is directly attributable to a number of important events, outlined below.

Extension of Existing Programs

When the learning disabilities field first began, professionals gave most of their attention to young children in the belief that if learning disabilities were identified early and programmed intensively, they could be cured. Consequently, the first programs for learning-disabled students were at the elementary school level. However, it soon became apparent that the problems of young learning-disabled children persisted beyond the elementary school years; learning disabilities do not disappear. As these children moved through the grades, programs had to be developed to meet their continuing needs, providing them with the coping mechanisms appropriate to their age group. Soon there were programs for learning-disabled students at the junior high school level and then at the senior high school level. This extension of special programs has now moved to the college level. The emergence of college programs for learning-disabled students may thus be seen in part as a natural extension of programs that were begun at the elementary school level.

College Becomes an Attainable Goal

For many years, learning-disabled students wanted to attend college, but they did not believe that they had a genuine opportunity to succeed. Once it became apparent that appropriate opportunities did exist, the natural desire of many learning-disabled students to further their education and knowledge led them to actively pursue entry into college. There are studies that show that as many as two thirds of young adults diagnosed as learning disabled have a desire to extend their education beyond high school. As college officials became aware of the large number of learning-disabled students with college aspirations, they looked for ways their colleges could meet the needs of these students.

Pressure from Parents and Professionals

Parents and professionals brought considerable pressure upon colleges and universities to offer programs for learning-disabled students. The work of a number of organizations composed of parents and professionals concerned with the learning disabled has added immeasurably to the impetus of colleges to provide special services. There are many organizations that have worked on behalf of the learning disabled. Some, such as the following, have had particular success in bringing about increased services and opportunities for learning-disabled students at the college level:

- Association for Children and Adults with Learning Disabilities
- Association of Learning Disabled Adults
- Foundation for Children with Learning Disabilities
- Orton Dyslexia Society
- The Puzzle People
- Time Out to Enjoy

Source of Enrollment and Revenue

As colleges experienced a decline in enrollment, they began looking for new sources of students. Convinced that many learning-disabled students could succeed in college and aware of the large number of these students, many colleges began to develop the support services needed to help these students succeed. As it became apparent that learning-disabled students were succeeding in college, the desire of college officials to attract these students increased.

Moral Commitment

The American educational system prides itself on providing for the needs of individuals and giving opportunities for growth and development to all those who can benefit from the opportunity. Many colleges and universities are providing services to learning-disabled students as part of the perceived social mission of their institution.

Legislation

Clearly the most significant factor leading to the development of college programs for learning-disabled students has been strong federal legislation. The two most important laws are Public Law 94-142 (PL 94-142), discussed above, and Section 504 of the Rehabilitation Act of 1973 (PL 93-112). PL 94-142 has been referred to as the Bill of Rights for the handicapped because it guarantees to all handicapped individuals, including the learning disabled, a free and appropriate education through the secondary level. As a result of this law, many learning-disabled students attended regular high school classes with students who were not learning disabled. As they did so, they acquired many of the academic skills that would enable them to attend college. PL 94-142 has, therefore, had an indirect effect on the development of college programs for the learning disabled. It has helped to produce a large number of learning-disabled students with many necessary academic skills and the desire to attend college. As a natural outgrowth, many colleges have responded by developing programs to enable these students to do so.

Section 504 has had a more direct impact on college opportunities for the learning disabled. This law guarantees that no otherwise qualified handicapped individual shall be excluded from participation in a program solely by reason of the handicap. Subpart E of the law applies specifically to postsecondary education; it prohibits discrimination against qualified learning-disabled persons in admission, recruitment, and treatment after admission to college. Because colleges can lose all federal assistance if they are not in compliance with Section 504, the law has had an enormous impact upon college opportunities for the learning disabled. One should keep in mind that the law is a safeguard against discrimination; it does not dictate that colleges must have special programs for learning-disabled students.

HOW LEARNING-DISABLED STUDENTS ARE ADMITTED TO COLLEGE

Most colleges operate with either open admissions or selective admissions policies for all their applicants.

Open admission is typically found at junior or community colleges, although some four-year colleges also use it. To enter a college with such a policy, all a student needs is a high school diploma or its equivalent. When an open admission policy is in force, learning-disabled students, like other students, have no difficulty gaining admission. The question, however, is not whether the student will be admitted but rather whether he or she will be able to succeed. Learning-disabled students interested in colleges with open admissions should be doubly sure to look into the existence of programs established at these colleges to help them succeed.

Selective admission is more common at four-year colleges and universities, especially private institutions and well-known state universities. It requires students to have earned a high school diploma or its equivalent and to submit to the college their grade point average (GPA), their rank in their graduating class, and their scores on such standardized tests as the College Board's Scholastic Aptitude Test (SAT) or the American College Testing Program's ACT Assessment (ACT). When these are the only criteria used in the admissions process, learning-disabled students often find it difficult to gain admission for several reasons. First, because learning-disabled students usually take many regular high school classes with their non-learning-disabled peers, their GPA and rank in the graduating class may be lower than is required in a rigid admission policy. Second, learning-disabled students typically have difficulty taking standardized tests such as the SAT and the ACT because of the controlled time limits. This usually means that they obtain SAT or ACT test scores that are below the established cutoffs used by some colleges.

Some colleges, like many in this book, have special admissions policies that use flexible entrance criteria. Admission personnel review each applicant according to different criteria, as reflected in the following typical questions that would be discussed in an admissions committee session:

Does the applicant have a learning disability? Evidence must be supplied to support the existence of a learning disability. This generally means that the applicant must submit a recent report from a qualified psychoeducational diagnostician that shows the nature of the learning disability and lists the instruments used to determine it. Frequently, transcripts are examined for evidence that the applicant has participated in a learning disabilities program sometime during schooling. The applicant's learning disabilities high school teacher may be asked to submit a letter verifying the learning disability.

Does the applicant have the intellectual ability to do college work? Regardless of the desire or commitment of a learning-disabled student, the college must be assured that the applicant is able to do college work. Most often, this is determined using the results from a standardized, individually administered intelligence test, such as the Wechsler Adult Intelligence Scale—Revised (WAIS-R), the Stanford-Binet Intelligence Scale, or the Ravens Standard Progressive Matrices. Usually the WAIS-R is the required test. It is important to keep in mind that college programs for learning-disabled students are designed for those with at least average intellectual ability.

What knowledge has the applicant acquired? In addition to basic intellectual potential, a learning-disabled applicant must demonstrate acquisition of a sufficient fund of information about the world to serve as a background for college-level work. It is unlikely that learning-disabled students can handle the requirements of college courses without having the background knowledge that they will need to draw upon. Admission personnel may request three indicators of a learning-disabled applicant's general knowledge:

- They may require the results from an *untimed* administration of the SAT or ACT. While the results are not used to establish cutoff levels for admission, they are used to reveal areas where the applicant possesses or lacks information.
- They may request letters from English, mathematics, science, and other high school teachers describing the applicant's knowledge in these subject areas.
- They may request that an applicant visit the college campus for an interview. As part of the interview, they assess an applicant's knowledge of various subject areas.

Can the applicant succeed in college? When an on-campus interview is required, admission personnel ask a series of questions that help them evaluate a student's potential for college success. Questions are asked to elicit evidence of a student's

- Thinking ability
- Motivation to succeed in college
- Productive use of high school years
- Assertiveness and self-advocacy
- General self-sufficiency
- Awareness of academic strengths and weaknesses
- Awareness of the consequences of inappropriate behavior
- Awareness of underachievement in college-prerequisite skills
- Understanding of preferred learning style
- Understanding of the learning disability

It is not uncommon for parents to be interviewed as well. When this is done, college officials are interested in knowing whether the information provided by the student is accurate and whether the parents fully support the goals and direction of the program in which the student will be involved.

WHAT DO COLLEGES WITH PROGRAMS FOR LEARNING-DISABLED STUDENTS PROVIDE?

Because of their varied characteristics and multiplicity of needs, learning-disabled college students require a comprehensive support program. The components of such a program are diagnostic and prescriptive planning, advisement, counseling, remediation, tutoring, special courses, and a range of auxiliary aids and services. If a college program for learning-disabled students is to be considered comprehensive, the program must provide these components in a manner specifically designed to meet the needs of such students and be staffed with personnel with appropriate experience and training.

Diagnostic and Prescriptive Planning

Diagnostic testing is needed to assess a learning-disabled student's cognitive abilities, academic skills, language abilities, perceptual-motor skills, social development, emotional development, and work and study habits. Information from diagnostic tests and admission procedures is used to prescribe services for the student. Following are some standardized tests frequently used as part of this diagnostic and prescriptive process:

- Beery-Buktenica Developmental Test of Visual-Motor Integration (VMI)
- Bender Visual Motor Gestalt Test
- Detroit Tests of Learning Aptitude
- Goldman-Fristoe-Woodcock Test of Auditory Discrimination (GFW)
- Gray Oral Reading Test
- KeyMath Diagnostic Arithmetic Test
- Malcomesius Specific Language Disability Test

- Peabody Individual Achievement Test (PIAT)
- Peabody Picture Vocabulary Test—Revised (PPVT-R)
- Slosson Intelligence Test (SIT)
- Tennessee Self Concept Scale
- Wechsler Adult Intelligence Scale—Revised (WAIS-R)
- Wide Range Achievement Test—Revised (WRAT)
- Woodcock-Johnson Psycho-Educational Battery (WJPEB)
- Woodcock Reading Mastery Tests (WRMT)

Frequently, the diagnostic information is used to develop an individual educational program (IEP) for the learning-disabled student, which specifies the services that will be provided to a student through the learning disabilities program. The format for the IEP varies from program to program, but the basic information included is fairly consistent. Typically, an IEP will include information about the following:

- Academic and learning strengths and deficits
- Effective learning strategies to be used by the student
- Effective teaching strategies to be used with the student
- Areas in need of remediation
- Courses in which the student requires tutoring
- Problems for which the student requires counseling
- Special courses that will help the student develop the skills necessary to succeed in college
- Auxiliary aids and services that will help the student compensate for the learning disability

Advisement

Learning-disabled college students need careful and ongoing academic program advisement for these reasons:

- They frequently enroll in courses that are too difficult for them.
- They tend to enroll in the wrong courses.
- They often misperceive the progress they are making in courses.
- They rarely seek out services they need to overcome academic and social difficulties.
- They frequently are overwhelmed by the registration process.
- They tend to accept poor advice from well-intentioned peers.

It is important for advisers to ensure that learning-disabled students do not end up with overly difficult course loads, courses out of their program sequence, or a poorly planned schedule. It is not essential that a learning-disabled student be advised by staff members from the learning disabilities program. It *is* essential, however, that advisers be familiar with the goals and procedures of the learning disabilities program and the characteristics and needs of learning-disabled college students.

Counseling

To meet social needs, counseling is often necessary. It offers learning-disabled students a sounding board for their feelings and provides an opportunity for them to develop self-understanding and more effective peer relationships. Counseling available may include group counseling, informal rap sessions, individual counseling, and career counseling. The major goals are to help learning-disabled college students reduce anxiety, increase self-confidence, increase socialization, learn life skills, understand their learning disabilities, and achieve a sense of normalcy.

Remediation

Learning-disabled college students need remediation to improve their achievement in the basic skill areas of reading, writing, language, and mathematics. They also need assistance in developing compensatory strategies that will minimize the impact of their learning disabilities upon their achievement in college courses. A student's need for remediation depends upon three factors: the severity of the academic and learning deficits, the level of proficiency in the academic skills needed for success in the student's program of studies, and the student's desire to achieve. Remediation is typically provided in individual or small-group sessions. Those providing remediation should be skilled teachers who are knowledgeable about learning disabilities.

Tutoring

Tutoring is designed to help students understand and master the content of their courses. The major objective of tutoring is to help students pass their courses. Because students see immediate results, they frequently report that tutoring is the most important component of learning disabilities college programs. Tutoring is most often provided in English, mathematics, physical sciences, and social sciences. It is usually given individually or in small groups by professional tutors who are experts in their subject areas. Sometimes, non-learning-disabled students who excel in a subject are used as peer tutors.

Special Courses

Frequently, special courses are offered for students enrolled in learning disabilities college programs.

They provide learning-disabled students with the prerequisite skills and social and emotional awareness necessary to succeed in college. The courses may be taught by staff members from the learning disabilities program or by faculty members from academic departments. They may be credit or noncredit courses and may or may not count in a student's overall grade point average. Examples of special courses are:

- Developmental reading
- English composition
- Fundamentals of communication
- Language remediation
- Study skills
- Note-taking techniques
- Writing research papers
- Speed writing
- Typing
- Memory improvement
- Personal psychology
- College survival

Auxiliary Aids and Services

Colleges with programs for learning-disabled students provide a number of auxiliary aids and services to help them compensate for their learning disabilities. Auxiliary aids include tape recorders, taped textbooks, calculators, typewriters, and word processors. Auxiliary services include the assignment of notetakers, alternative arrangements for taking course examinations, advocacy, and special housing arrangements.

Tape Recorders and Taped Textbooks. Learning-disabled students often have difficulty taking notes from class lectures. The tape recorder becomes a valuable auxiliary aid for these students. They are able to tape-record a lecture at the same time they take notes. Later, they can replay the tapes to check their notes for completeness and accuracy. The use of a tape recorder reduces the heavy demands upon learning-disabled students' auditory memory, language processing, and writing skills. Because of the value of tape recorders, professors are encouraged to allow learning-disabled students to use them in their classes.

Taped textbooks are used by learning-disabled students who have difficulty reading college-level materials. College learning disabilities program staff members help such students to obtain taped textbooks from Recording for the Blind and from the Library of Congress's National Library Service for the Blind and Physically Handicapped. The role of staff members is primarily a facilitative one. They familiarize students with the services of Recording for the Blind and the Library of Congress and help them complete the necessary application forms. They also help students determine the textbooks needed for future courses to enable the students to submit applications for taped textbooks in sufficient time to receive books prior to the beginning of a new term.

Calculators, Typewriters, and Word Processors. Calculators, typewriters, and word processors are additional aids provided by college learning disabilities programs. Calculators are used by students who have not mastered computational skills to an automatic level. Typewriters are made available to learning-disabled students who have poorly developed handwriting skills that interfere with their ability to produce written assignments. Word processors assist in the writing of term papers. Students are able to store what they write and make whatever revisions are necessary. A word-check program may be used to identify and correct misspelled words.

Notetakers. Typically, notetakers are non-learning-disabled students who attend the same classes with the learning-disabled students. They have been identified as good notetakers who are reliable, are competent in the subject, and have legible handwriting. A duplicate set of notes is given to the learning-disabled student through an intermediary member of the learning disabilities program staff. Usually the notetaker does not know the identity of the student receiving the notes.

Alternative Examination Arrangements. Alternative arrangements are provided for students who have difficulty taking examinations in the usual manner. Often learning-disabled students have difficulty completing a test within a specified time limit, accurately reading test questions, and writing answers. Staff members from the learning disabilities program make arrangements with professors to allow students to take course examinations with one of a number of alternatives:

- Extended time limits
- Questions dictated onto an audio tape
- Questions read by a proctor
- Responses dictated to a proctor
- Responses dictated onto audio tapes
- Responses typed rather than handwritten
- Questions presented in a different format, e.g., multiple choice in place of essay
- Take-home examinations or projects in place of written examinations

Advocacy. Members of college learning disabilities staffs also serve as advocates for learning-disabled college students. They work with professors to ensure that students are given every legitimate opportunity to succeed in their courses. Some of the activities performed by program staff members in their advocacy role include:

- Requesting lists of required textbooks for taping
- Obtaining permission for students to tape-record lectures
- Obtaining permission to use a non–class member as a notetaker
- Requesting opportunities for students to take tests in alternative ways
- Arranging for incomplete grades when students need more time to complete a course
- Arranging for withdrawal from a course without a grade penalty when extra time is not the answer
- Helping professors understand the needs of learning-disabled students
- Providing suggestions to professors for modifying their teaching style to enhance the learning opportunities for learning-disabled students

A goal of learning disabilities programs is to have students become their own advocates. Therefore, the activities and roles performed by program staff members are phased out as students develop increasing independence.

Housing. Careful consideration is given to housing arrangements for learning-disabled students. Program staff members ensure that such students have the availability of a quiet, nondistracting environment for study and that they are adequately supervised. Programs vary with respect to specific dormitory arrangements. In some, learning-disabled students live together in special dormitories. In others, learning-disabled students are assigned to dormitories with their non-learning-disabled peers.

HOW HIGH SCHOOLS CAN PREPARE LEARNING-DISABLED STUDENTS FOR COLLEGE

There are many learning-disabled students who have the potential to go to college. These students must be identified by high school teachers and counselors and then provided with the instruction and counseling needed for college preparation. What follows are recommendations for teaching and counseling learning-disabled high school students who wish to go to college.

Teaching Recommendations

High school teachers must help learning-disabled students acquire an education that is consistent with their abilities. These students must be involved in a curriculum that is commensurate with their intellectual ability, rather than a curriculum reduced to the level of their basic skills deficiencies. Following are recommendations that will help high school teachers prepare learning-disabled students for college.

1. Enroll students in college-preparatory courses that provide the requisite knowledge they need to enter college courses in English, mathematics, physical sciences, and social sciences.
2. Provide content area instruction by teachers who have certification and training in the subjects they are teaching.
3. Provide assignments to students that are similar to those they will be required to complete in college.
4. Teach students strategies for reading textbook materials effectively and efficiently.
5. Teach students how to use the graphic aids that appear in their textbooks to increase their understanding of technical materials.
6. Teach students the major study skills that will help them to locate, organize, interpret, and retain information; to adjust their reading rates for different purposes; and to demonstrate what they have learned when taking tests.
7. Teach students how to organize study time and space for maximum efficiency.
8. Provide intensive vocabulary instruction so that learning-disabled students can more effectively handle the listening and reading requirements of their courses.
9. Develop composition and spelling skills through daily writing assignments.
10. Familiarize students with the use of the auxiliary aids they will need to use in college.

Counseling Recommendations

Many learning-disabled students have no idea what college is like. They often have an overinflated estimate of their abilities, unrealistic career goals, and little or no understanding of the impact of their learning disabilities. Following are recommendations that will help high school counselors prepare learning-disabled students for college.

1. Help students to gain a realistic assessment of their potential for college.
2. Help students to obtain information about learning disabilities programs at various colleges.

3. Help students complete applications to colleges with learning disabilities programs.
4. Help students prepare for their college admission interviews by role-playing responses to such typically asked questions as these:
   - Why do you want to attend college?
   - Why do you want to attend this college?
   - What do your parents think about your going to college?
   - In what would you like to major?
   - What are your plans after college?
   - How does your learning disability affect you?
   - What things are easy for you to learn?
   - What things are difficult for you to learn?
   - What services or aids have helped you learn?
   - What help do you need from our program to succeed in college?
   - Are you prepared to spend extra time and effort to succeed in college?
5. Help students develop the interpersonal skills they need to relate to other college students.
6. Help students understand the ways in which their learning disabilities may make it difficult for them to succeed in college.
7. Help students to formulate a realistic career plan.

How to Select a College for a Learning-Disabled Student

Parents and professionals who help learning-disabled students select colleges and universities must carefully examine the programs available to select a number of programs that meet an individual student's needs. There is no one best learning disabilities program for all learning-disabled students. Rather, for each student there are a number of programs meeting that student's needs to varying degrees. Because many programs have waiting lists, it is a good idea to apply in the junior year of high school. The student should apply to a number of desirable programs in hopes of being accepted by one or more.

Following are the steps we recommend for selecting suitable colleges:

1. Look through the profiles presented in the College Profiles section of this guide and identify those of interest to you based on geographical area, size, and cost.
2. Use the Key Features Chart at the top of each profile to compare what is offered to learning-disabled students by each of the colleges you selected in Step 1. This comparison will reduce the number of colleges identified in Step 1.
3. For those colleges remaining after Step 2, complete the Checklist for Selecting Learning Disabilities College Programs found on page 16. To complete this checklist you will need to carefully read the complete entry for each college you have chosen in Step 2.
4. Use the results from the checklist to make a list of colleges that seem to be most appropriate for the student. The more instances of "yes" responses there are in the checklist for a college, the more needs that college is likely to meet. However, be sure to keep in mind the *specific* needs of the student; he or she might not have trouble with mathematics, for example, in which case the availability of calculators would not be important. This will further reduce the number of colleges to be considered.
5. Have the student write to each college remaining after Step 4 to request further, detailed information about the learning disabilities program and the college. A sample letter the student can use is shown on page 14.
6. Using the information received in Step 5, select up to six colleges that the student would like to attend.
7. Have the student complete and submit all applications and other appropriate forms to the colleges identified in Step 6.
8. Visit those colleges to which the student has been accepted; if there are many of these colleges, visit the most desirable ones. Use the sample letter on page 15 to arrange these visits. If the student is not accepted by any of the colleges identified in Step 6, return to Step 4, 5, or 6, as appropriate, to begin the process of identifying more colleges to apply to for admission in the next academic semester. If you have followed the selection process carefully, however, the student is likely to have been admitted to a college in the first round.
9. Select one of the colleges and have the student enroll.

Sample Letter Requesting Information

Student's street address
City, State Zip
Date

Name of Learning Disabilities Program Contact
Name of Learning Disabilities Program
Name of College or University
Address
City, State Zip

Dear (Mr. or Ms.) (last name of contact):

I am a student with a learning disability and am completing my (junior or senior) year at (name of high school). I expect to graduate in (date) and then go on to college.

Please send me information about your learning disabilities program, admission forms, a catalog, and any other specific information that will help me to learn about your program.

Thank you for any assistance you may be able to give me.

Sincerely,

Name of student

Sample Letter Requesting a Campus Visit

Student's street address
City, State Zip
Date

Name of Learning Disabilities Program Contact
Name of Learning Disabilities Program
Name of College or University
Address
City, State Zip

Dear (Mr. or Ms.) (last name of contact):

I have been accepted to the learning disabilities program at your (college or university). To help me make a final decision about attending, I wish to visit your campus. During this visit I hope to talk to you or someone on your staff, see the campus, and meet some of the students. If possible, would you please arrange a visit for me on any of the following dates: (list two or three available dates).

I look forward to hearing from you and to visiting your campus.

Sincerely,

Name of student

Checklist for Selecting Learning Disabilities College Programs

Names of Colleges

Directions: Write the name of each college to be evaluated at the top of the column under Names of Colleges. Review the information you have obtained and answer each question. Write YES or NO as the answer for each question. Do this for each program.

Questions to Answer About Learning Disabilities College Programs

1. Are the following items used to evaluate learning-disabled students for admission?
   — Untimed SAT or ACT
   — Letters of recommendation
   — Autobiographical statement
   — Psychoeducational report
   — Personal interview
2. Is diagnostic testing available to learning-disabled students?
3. Is subject-area tutoring available?
4. Is basic skills remediation available?
5. Do staff members of the learning disabilities program as well as academic advisers help learning-disabled students plan their academic program?
6. Are special courses available?
7. Are the following auxiliary aids provided?
   — Taped textbooks
   — Tape recorders
   — Calculators
   — Typewriters
   — Word processors
   — Others
8. Are the following auxiliary services provided?
   — Alternative exam arrangements
   — Notetakers
   — Advocacy
   — Others
9. Are the following counseling services available?
   — Individual
   — Small-group
   — Rap sessions
   — Career
   — Others

College Profiles

This section contains profiles of 279 colleges and universities that offer programs and services for learning-disabled undergraduate students. Each profile presents detailed factual and statistical information in a standard format with three components—a key features chart, general institutional data, and LD program information—to facilitate comparison among colleges. The material below provides an outline of the profile format, describing the items covered, followed by information on criteria for inclusion and research procedures, explaining how colleges were selected for inclusion in this volume and how the data were collected and compiled. All information in the profiles was supplied by the colleges themselves. Any item that does not apply to a particular college or for which no data was available is omitted from that college's profile.

KEY FEATURES CHART

The chart at the top of each profile enables the reader to see the key features of each college's LD program at a glance and to make a quick comparison of these features among colleges. The first two items show when the college began offering services for LD students and what fees, if any, are charged for these services. In the next eight items, check marks indicate which of the following types of services are offered: special orientation, diagnostic testing, subject-area tutoring, basic skills remediation, special courses, taped textbooks, alternative course examination arrangements, and notetakers. (For definitions of these terms, see the explanation of the LD Program Information section of the profile below and the section entitled "What Do Colleges with Programs for Learning-Disabled Students Provide?" in the essay on College Opportunities for Learning-Disabled Students above.) The last two items show the numbers of full-time and part-time staff members responsible for administering or providing LD services and the number of LD students currently served by the program.

INSTITUTIONAL DATA

This portion of the profile presents information on the college and its undergraduate programs as a whole, divided into the following paragraphs.

General Information

This first paragraph gives a brief overview of the college, covering the following items.

Institutional Control. Private institutions are designated as *independent* (nonprofit), *independent-religious* (sponsored by or affiliated with a specified church or religious denomination, or having a nondenominational or interdenominational religious orientation), or *proprietary* (profit making). Public institutions are designated by the source of funding, as follows: *federal, state, commonwealth* (Puerto Rico), *territory* (U.S. territories), *county, district, city, state and local* ("local" referring to county, district, or city), or *state-related* (funded primarily by the state but administratively autonomous).

Institutional Type. A *four-year college* awards bachelor's degrees and may also award associate degrees, but it does not offer graduate (postbachelor's) degree programs. A *five-year college* offers a five-year bachelor's program in a professional field such as architecture or pharmacy but does not award graduate degrees. An *upper-level institution* awards bachelor's degrees, but entering students must have at least two years of previous college-level credit; it may also offer graduate degree programs. A *comprehensive institution* awards bachelor's degrees and may also award associate degrees; graduate degree programs are offered primarily at the master's, specialist's, or professional level, although one or two doctoral programs may also be offered. A *university* offers four years of undergraduate work plus graduate degrees through the doctorate in more than two academic and/or professional fields. In addition, any of the above types except university may be designated as *specialized*, indicating that degrees are offered in one field only, such as art or music.

Type of Student Body. The categories are *men's* (100 percent of the student body), *primarily men's*, *women's* (100 percent of the student body), *primarily women's*, and *coed.* A college may also be designated as *coordinate* with another institution, indicating that there are separate colleges or campuses for men and women but that facilities, courses, and institutional governance are shared.

System Affiliation. This is the name of a formal administrative grouping of institutions, either private or public, such as a state university system, of which the college is a part, or it is the name of a single institution with which the college is administratively affiliated.

Founding Date. The year the college came into existence or was chartered is indicated, reflecting the period during which it has existed as an educational institution, regardless of subsequent mergers or other organizational changes. If the year an institution was chartered differs from the year when instruction actually began, the earlier date is given.

Degrees Awarded. An associate degree (*A*) may consist of either a *college-transfer* program, equivalent to the first two years of a bachelor's degree, or a one- to three-year *terminal* program providing training for a specific occupation. A bachelor's degree (*B*) represents a three- to five-year liberal arts, science, professional, or preprofessional program. A master's degree (*M*) is the first graduate degree in the liberal arts and sciences and certain professional fields, usually requiring one to two years of full-time study. A doctoral degree (*D*) is the highest degree awarded in research-oriented academic disciplines, usually requiring from three to six years of full-time graduate study; the first professional degrees in such fields as law and medicine are also at the doctoral level.

Institutional Accreditation. Full accreditation or candidacy (preaccreditation) status granted to the college as a whole by one of the six regional associations of schools and colleges (Middle States, New England, North Central, Northwest, Southern, and Western) and/or by the following other recognized institutional accrediting bodies, which are referred to in the profiles by their initials, is indicated: the American Association of Bible Colleges (AABC), the Association of Independent Colleges and Schools (AICS), the National Association of Trade and Technical Schools (NATTS), and the National Home Study Council (NHSC). Program registration by the New York State Board of Regents or recognition under the "three-institutional-certification method" by the U.S. Department of Education may serve as a substitute for institutional accreditation. For more information on the categories of accreditation as they apply to the colleges listed in this guide, see the section on Criteria for Inclusion below.

Program Accreditation. Full accreditation or candidacy status granted for programs in a particular field by a recognized specialized accrediting body is indicated. The following areas of program accreditation and their respective specialized accrediting bodies are listed in the profiles (the accrediting body is referred to by its initials): programs in architecture are accredited by the National Architectural Accrediting Board (NAAB), art and design by the National Association of Schools of Art and Design (NASAD), business by the American Assembly of Collegiate Schools of Business (AACSB), engineering and technology by the Accreditation Board for Engineering and Technology (ABET), funeral service by the American Board of Funeral Service Education (ABFSE), interior design by the Foundation for Interior Design Education Research (FIDER), music by the National Association of Schools of Music (NASM), nursing by the National League for Nursing (NLN), optometry by the Council on Optometric Education (COE), pharmacy by the American Council on Pharmaceutical Education (ACPE), rabbinical education by the Association of Advanced Rabbinical and Talmudic Schools (AARTS), and teacher education by the National Council for Accreditation of Teacher Education (NCATE).

Campus Setting. This is designated as *metropolitan* (located in a major metropolitan area with a population of over 500,000), *city* (population 50,000 to 500,000), *small-town* (population under 50,000), or *rural.* The phrase *easy access to . . .* indicates that the campus is within an hour's drive of a major metropolitan area. The term *barrier-free* denotes that the institution meets federal standards for access to buildings and facilities by handicapped students.

Total Enrollment. The number of matriculated undergraduate and (if applicable) graduate students, both full-time and part-time, is given as of fall 1984. If the institution is a subunit of a university, the total university enrollment is given.

Faculty. The number of full-time and part-time faculty members teaching undergraduate and graduate courses as of fall 1984 is given, followed by the percentage holding doctoral degrees. Whether or not graduate assistants teach undergraduate courses is also indicated.

Calendar. Most colleges indicate one of the following: *4-1-4*, *4-4-1*, or a similar arrangement (two terms of equal length plus an abbreviated winter or spring term, with the numbers referring to months); *semesters; trimesters; quarters; 3-3* (three courses for each of three terms); or *modular* (the academic year is divided into small blocks of time; courses of varying lengths are assembled according to individual programs).

Grading System. This is designated as one or more of the following: letters or numbers, pass/fail, and faculty reports.

Library Holdings. This includes numbers of bound volumes, titles on microform, periodical subscriptions, and records/tapes.

Undergraduate Profile

The fall 1984 undergraduate and freshman (or, for upper-level institutions, entering-class) enrollment figures are listed, followed by the number of U.S. states and territories (including the District of Columbia and Puerto Rico) and foreign countries from which undergraduates come. The percentages of undergraduates who are part-time students, state (or territory) residents, transfer students, financial aid recipients, women, blacks, Native Americans (Indians, Eskimos, and Polynesians), Hispanics, Asian Americans, foreign nationals, and students over 25 years of age, as well as the number of legally handicapped undergraduates, are given.

Expenses

Costs are given as shown for the 1985–86 academic year, or for the 1984–85 academic year if 1985–86 figures were not yet available. Annual expenses may be expressed as a comprehensive fee (including full-time tuition, mandatory fees, and college room and board) or may be given as separate figures for full-time tuition, fees, room and board, and/or room only. For public institutions at which tuition differs according to residence, separate figures are given for area and/or state residents and for nonresidents. Part-time tuition is expressed in terms of a per-unit rate (per credit, per semester hour, etc.) as specified by the institution.

The tuition structure at some institutions is complex in that freshmen and sophomores may be charged a different rate from that for juniors and seniors, a professional or vocational division may have a different fee structure from the liberal arts division of the same institution, or part-time tuition may be prorated on a sliding scale according to the number of credit hours taken. In all of these cases, the maximum and minimum figures are given along with an explanation of the basis for the variable rate. For colleges that report that room and board costs vary according to the type of accommodation and meal plan, the lowest figures are given, followed by the notation *minimum.* If no college-owned or -operated housing facilities are offered, the phrase *college housing not available* appears in the Housing section of the profile.

Some colleges offer a *guaranteed tuition plan* whereby a student's tuition does not increase for the entire term of enrollment, from entrance to graduation. Others may have a *tuition prepayment plan,* which gives a student the option of locking in the current tuition rate for the entire term of enrollment by paying the full amount in advance rather than year by year. Colleges that offer such a prepayment plan may also help the student to arrange financing.

Financial Aid

The first part of this section contains data on financial aid awarded to needy freshmen who enrolled full-time in fall 1984: the percentage of the freshman class that applied for aid, the percentage of those who were judged to have need, and the percentage of those who were aided; the dollar amount of the average financial aid package received by needy freshmen, broken down into the percentages of scholarships/grants and self-help (jobs and loans); and the average percentage of need covered by this aid package.

Information on college-administered aid for all 1984–85 undergraduates includes the types of aid offered and, where applicable, the number of each type awarded and the average dollar amount per award. *College scholarships* are awards for which the college chooses the recipient and uses funds under its control, broken down into *need-based* and *non-need* scholarships. *Loans* are broken down into *short-term loans* from college funds and *low-interest long-term loans* from college funds and from external sources, such as the government-sponsored National Direct Student Loan Program. *SEOG* denotes Supplemental Educational Opportunity Grants, which are federally funded need-based awards administered by colleges. *College Work-Study* is a federal program that enables students to earn money by working on or off campus in public or private nonprofit organizations. *Part-time jobs* are on-campus work provided by the college apart from College Work-Study.

The information in this section is limited to *college-administered* aid for which the college determines the recipient and amount of each award. It does not cover awards from public and private sources, separate from the college, that a student may use to help pay college costs. The largest single source of such outside aid is the federal Pell Grant Program, for which students apply directly to the government.

The supporting data that a student may have to submit in applying for financial aid are grouped into three categories: required for all, required for some, and acceptable (may be submitted in lieu of a required form). The types of supporting data most commonly required are the following: the federal government's Application for Federal Student Aid/ Student Aid Report (*AFSA/SAR*); the Financial Aid Form (*FAF*) of the College Scholarship Service; the Family Financial Statement (*FFS*) of the American College Testing Program; the *Financial Aid Transcript*, a record of aid previously received for college study, required of transfer applicants; the Guaranteed Student Loan form (*GSL*); a college's own financial aid application form (*institutional form*); federal income tax form 1040 (*IRS*); and a state government aid application form (*state form*), such as the Student Aid Application for California (SAAC), Illinois State Scholarship Commission form (ISSC), Tuition Assistance Program form (TAP) for New York, or Pennsylvania Higher Education Assistance Agency form (PHEAA).

The college's financial aid application deadline may be given as a specific date, continuous processing up to a specific date or until all available aid has been awarded, or a priority date rather than a strict deadline, meaning that students are encouraged to apply by that date in order to have the best chance of obtaining aid.

Athletics

Membership in one or more of the following athletic associations is indicated by their initials: National Collegiate Athletic Association (NCAA), National Association of Intercollegiate Athletics (NAIA), National Little College Athletic Association (NLCAA), and National Junior College Athletic Association (NJCAA).

Sports offered by the college are divided into two groups: *intercollegiate* (*M* and/or *W* following the name of each sport indicates that it is offered for men and/or women) and *intramural.* A roman numeral *I*, *II*, or *III* in parentheses following an M or W for an intercollegiate sport indicates that the college competes in NCAA Division I, II, or III in that men's or women's sport. (For men's football, Division I is subdivided into I-A and I-AA.) An *s* in parentheses following an M or W for an intercollegiate sport indicates that athletic scholarships (or grants-in-aid) are offered for men or women in that sport, and a *c* indicates a club team as opposed to a varsity team.

Majors

This section lists the major fields of study offered by the college. The degree level is indicated by an *A* for associate and/or a *B* for bachelor's. Following the phrase *majors with highest enrollment* are listed the most popular field or fields of study at the college during the 1984–85 academic year in terms of the number of undergraduate students enrolled in each program. The names of the major areas represent their most widely used designations. However, many institutions use different terms for the same or similar areas. Readers should refer to a college's catalog for its exact terminology. In addition, while the term "major" is used in this guide, some colleges may use other terms, such as concentration, program of study, or field.

LD PROGRAM INFORMATION

This portion of the profile presents specific data on services for LD students, divided into the following paragraphs.

Name of Program

The name of the specific program providing services for LD students or the office (such as handicapped or disabled student services) responsible for serving a broader group of students with special needs that includes those with learning disabilities is given. The term *not specified* indicates that there is no single such program or office, in which case LD students draw on services provided by two or more sources at the college, such as learning centers, reading labs, counseling offices, and special education programs.

Availability of Services

This paragraph lists the year that the college began offering LD services, the class levels (freshman through senior) eligible to receive these services, and the number of LD students served by the program during the 1984–85 academic year, with a breakdown by class level if available.

Fees

The costs given here are those that LD students must pay for services not covered by the regular tuition and fees listed in the Expenses paragraph of the profile. These costs may be expressed as a fixed amount per year covering a full LD program, a variable amount per year depending upon the type or level of services required by the individual, fixed one-time charges for specific services such as testing and evaluation, or hourly rates for services such as tutoring and remediation.

Staff

The number of staff members with full-time and part-time responsibility for administering or providing LD services is given, followed by the titles (e.g., director or coordinator) of the individuals with primary responsibility for overseeing the LD program. Also listed are the types of specialized personnel available to work with LD students, including remediation specialists, tutors, counselors, and diagnostic specialists.

Admissions

This paragraph lists the types of information and documentation that an LD student must submit for evaluation when applying for admission to the college. Items that are recommended or required for some applicants are also listed. These items may include a high school transcript and grade point average; scores on standard or untimed administrations of standardized college entrance examinations, most commonly the College Board's Scholastic Aptitude Test (SAT) or the American College Testing Program's ACT Assessment (ACT); a personal interview; an autobiographical statement; letters of recommendation; and a psychoeducational report, which may include documentation of the student's specific learning disability, a history of previous support services, an individual educational program (IEP) from high school, teacher evaluations, and results of previously administered assessment batteries and diagnostic tests such as the Wechsler Intelligence Scale for Children—Revised (WISC-R) and Wechsler Adult Intelligence Scale—Revised (WAIS-R). Other standardized tests that may be required include the College Board's Achievement Tests and English Composition Test, College-Level Examination Program tests (CLEP), the General Educational Development test (GED), the Preliminary Scholastic Aptitude Test (PSAT), and the Washington Pre-College Test (WPCT). A college may also state that it has an *open admissions policy*, indicating that virtually all applicants are accepted without regard to standardized test scores, grade average, or class rank.

Following the list of application requirements is information on what term or terms during the academic year newly admitted LD students may begin taking classes and how far in advance of their initial anticipated enrollment LD students should submit an application for admission. For a detailed discussion of the college admissions process for LD students, see the section entitled "How Learning-Disabled Students Are Admitted to College" in the essay on College Opportunities for Learning-Disabled Students above.

Orientation

If a college has a special orientation procedure for new LD students (whether in a group setting, on an individual basis, or incorporated into a general orientation program for all new students), this paragraph indicates whether the orientation is required, optional, or required for some students and whether it is offered before registration, during registration, or after classes begin.

Housing

This paragraph indicates whether or not college-owned or -operated housing is available to undergraduates, and, if it is, whether coeducational housing facilities are included. The college's housing policy for LD students is indicated as to whether they are housed with other LD students only, with other LD students and non-LD students, with non-LD students only, or randomly, and whether they are required to live on campus for a specified period.

Diagnostic Testing

Listed here are the types of diagnostic tests that may be administered to LD students as part of the services provided by the college. These may include tests of intelligence, reading, mathematics, spelling, handwriting, spoken language, written language, motor abilities, perceptual skills, work and study habits, personality, social skills, psychoneurology, speech, hearing, learning styles, and career interests.

For a detailed discussion of diagnostic testing, as well as the material covered in the following paragraphs on tutoring, basic skills remediation, academic advisement, special courses, auxiliary aids and services, and counseling services, see the section entitled "What Do Colleges with Programs for Learning-Disabled Students Provide?" in the essay on College Opportunities for Learning-Disabled Students above.

Tutoring

If subject-area tutoring is available to LD students, the following items will be covered: whether tutoring is offered on a one-to-one basis, in small groups, or in class-size groups; who provides the tutoring (professional teachers, undergraduate peer tutors, graduate students, or others); whether tutoring is available in all, most, or only some subject areas; and the number of courses in which a student may receive tutoring each term.

Basic Skills Remediation

If basic skills remediation is available, the following items are covered: whether remediation is offered on a one-to-one basis, in small groups, or in class-size groups; who provides the remediation (LD teachers, regular teachers, teacher trainees, peer teachers, graduate students, or others); and in what areas remediation is available, including reading, mathematics, spelling, handwriting, spoken language, written language, learning strategies, motor abilities, perceptual skills, work and study habits, social skills, and speech.

Academic Advisement

This paragraph specifies whether LD students are helped in planning their academic program by LD staff members, academic advisers, or both. Information on course load limits and requirements includes the maximum number of credits or courses that an LD student may take during any one term, the number of credits or courses that most LD students take during each term, and the minimum number of credits or courses per term required to maintain full-time status.

Special Courses

If special courses are available to LD students, the areas in which they are offered are listed. These may include college survival skills, reading, vocabulary development, communication skills, composition, language development, mathematics, typing, word processing, personal psychology, study skills, and career planning. Also indicated is what portion (none, some, most, or all) of these courses are offered for credit and what portion of the grades from these courses are averaged into the student's overall grade point average.

Auxiliary Aids and Services

The auxiliary aids available to LD students may include taped textbooks, tape recorders, calculators (sometimes including voice-synthesized "talking" calculators), typewriters, word processors, access to computer terminals or microcomputers (some also with voice synthesis), various specialized devices such as the Kurzweil reading machine and Visual Tech machine, special study rooms, and a variety of audiovisual aids. Auxiliary services may include alternative course examination arrangements, advocacy, notetakers, readers, transcribers, early registration, support groups, and research, editorial, typing, and proofreading assistance.

Counseling Services

The counseling services available to LD students may include individual and/or small-group counseling, rap sessions, career counseling, and peer counseling.

Contact

The name, title, mailing address, and telephone number of the person at the college to contact for further information about services for LD students are listed at the end of the profile.

CRITERIA FOR INCLUSION

This book covers 279 colleges and universities that responded positively to Peterson's Survey of Special Services for Learning-Disabled College Students, out of the 1,841 accredited institutions in the United States and U.S. territories that grant bachelor's degrees, to which questionnaires were sent. To be eligible for inclusion, a college must have full accreditation or candidacy (preaccreditation) status granted by an institutional or specialized accrediting body recognized by the U.S. Department of Education and/or the Council on Postsecondary

Accreditation. A substitute for standard accreditation is recognition under the "three-institutional-certification method" by the U.S. Department of Education. For a full explanation of the accrediting process and complete information on recognized accrediting bodies, the reader should refer to the *Education Directory: Colleges and Universities*, published by the National Center for Education Statistics of the U.S. Department of Education, and *Accredited Institutions of Postsecondary Education*, published by the American Council on Education for the Council on Postsecondary Accreditation.

The colleges selected for inclusion in the profiles are those whose responses to the questionnaire indicated that they provide special services for learning-disabled undergraduate students, in accordance with the federal government's definition of learning disabilities as contained in the Education of All Handicapped Children Act of 1975 (Public Law 94-142).

RESEARCH PROCEDURES

The data contained in the college profiles were collected between December 1984 and July 1985 through Peterson's Annual Survey of Undergraduate Institutions and the new Peterson's Survey of Special Services for Learning-Disabled College Students. All information was submitted by responsible officials at the colleges themselves, and, in addition, the great majority of institutions were contacted directly by Peterson's editorial staff to verify unusual figures, resolve discrepancies, and obtain additional data. The omission of any particular item from a profile listing signifies either that the item is not applicable to that institution or that data were not available.

Because of the comprehensive editorial review that takes place, and because all material comes directly from college officials, there is every reason to believe that the information presented in this guide is accurate. However, students should check with a specific college or university at the time of application to verify such figures as tuition and fees, which may have changed since the publication of this volume.

ADELPHI UNIVERSITY

Garden City, New York

Year Program Began	1979	Special Courses	✓
Special Fee	$2000 per year	Taped Textbooks	
Special Orientation	✓	Alternative Exam Arrangements	✓
Diagnostic Testing	✓	Notetakers	
Subject-Area Tutoring	✓	Staff	14 full-time
Basic Skills Remediation	✓	Number of Students Served	70

General Information Independent coed university. Founded 1896. Awards B, M, D. Institutionally accredited by regional association; programs accredited by NLN (nursing). Small-town setting, with easy access to New York City; 75-acre campus. Total enrollment: 10,717. Faculty: 835 (322 full-time, 513 part-time); 75% have doctoral degrees; graduate assistants teach a few undergraduate courses. Calendar: 4-1-4. Grading system: letters or numbers. Library holdings: 399,484 bound volumes, 448,363 titles on microform, 2,794 periodical subscriptions, 15,448 records/tapes.

Undergraduate Profile Fall 1984: 6,092 undergraduates (712 freshmen) from 28 states and territories and 50 foreign countries; 38% part-time; 84% state residents; 53% transfers; 85% financial aid recipients; 67% women; 13% blacks; 1% Native Americans; 4% Hispanics; 1% Asian Americans; 1% foreign nationals; 42 legally handicapped students.

Expenses (1985–86) Comprehensive fee of $9274 includes full-time tuition ($5950), mandatory fees ($420), and college room and board ($2904 minimum). College room only: $1700. Part-time tuition: $193 per credit.

Financial Aid Fall 1984 full-time freshmen: 70% applied for aid, 96% of those were judged to have need, 100% of those were aided; the average aided freshman received an aid package worth $5766 (63% scholarships/grants, 37% self-help) meeting 100% of need. College-administered aid for all 1984–85 undergraduates: 1,744 need-based scholarships (average $1150); 1,558 non-need scholarships (average $1700); College Work-Study; 320 part-time jobs. Supporting data: FAF, IRS, AFSA/SAR required; institutional form required for some. Priority application deadline: 7/1.

Athletics Member NCAA (Division II). Intercollegiate sports: baseball/softball M(II,s), W(I,s); basketball M(II,s), W(II,s); cross-country running M(II,s), W(II,s); golf M(II,s), W(II,s); lacrosse M(II,s); soccer M(I,s), W(II,s); swimming and diving M(II,s), W(II,s); tennis M(II,s), W(II,s); track and field M(II,s), W(II,s). Intramural sports: badminton, baseball/softball, basketball, equestrian sports, football, golf, racquetball, soccer, squash, swimming and diving, tennis, volleyball, weight lifting.

Majors Accounting B; adult and continuing education B; American studies B; anthropology B; art education B; art/fine arts B; art history B; biology/biological sciences B; business administration/commerce/management B; chemistry B; communication B; computer science B; dance B; (pre)dentistry sequence B; earth science B; economics B; education B; elementary education B; English B; finance/banking B; French B; German B; history B; Latin American studies B; (pre)law sequence B; mathematics B; medical technology B; (pre)medicine sequence B; music B; nursing B; philosophy B; physical education B; physics B; political science/government B; psychology B; religious studies B; social work B; sociology B; Spanish B; speech pathology and audiology B; speech/rhetoric/public address/debate B; speech therapy B; theater arts/drama B; (pre)veterinary medicine sequence B. Majors with highest enrollment: business administration/commerce/management, nursing, biology/biological sciences.

LD Program Information

Name of Program Learning Disabilities College Program.

Availability of Services Began offering services in 1979. Services provided to freshmen, sophomores, juniors, seniors. Program currently serves 70 LD students.

Fees $2000 per year.

Staff 14 full-time staff members, including director, associate directors. Services provided by tutors, counselors, educators, social workers.

Admissions LD applicants evaluated on the basis of high school transcript and grade point average, untimed SAT, personal interview, letters of recommendation, psychoeducational report, handwritten letter from student. LD students may begin taking classes in summer only. Application should be submitted 1 year in advance of initial anticipated enrollment.

Orientation Required orientation held before registration.

Housing College housing (including coed) available. LD students housed randomly. LD students not required to live on campus.

Diagnostic Testing Available in reading, math, handwriting, written language, work and study habits, personality, social skills.

Tutoring Offered one-to-one by professional teachers. Available in all subjects. LD students may receive tutoring in all courses each term.

Basic Skills Remediation Offered in small groups by regular teachers. Available in reading, handwriting, spoken language, written language, learning strategies, work and study habits.

Academic Advisement Help with program planning provided by LD staff members, academic advisers. LD students may take up to 15 credits each semester; most take 12 credits; 12 credits required to maintain full-time status.

Special Courses Offered in college survival skills, composition. All offered for credit; all enter into overall grade point average.

Auxiliary Aids and Services Services include alternative exam arrangements, advocacy.

Counseling Services Individual counseling, small-group counseling, rap sessions, career counseling available.

Contact Dr. Fred Barbaro, Director, Learning Disabilities College Program, Adelphi University, Box 701, Eddy Hall, Garden City, NY 11530, 516-663-1006.

ADRIAN COLLEGE

Adrian, Michigan

Year Program Began	1981	Special Courses	✓
Special Fee	None	Taped Textbooks	✓
Special Orientation	✓	Alternative Exam Arrangements	✓
Diagnostic Testing	✓	Notetakers	✓
Subject-Area Tutoring	✓	Staff	3 part-time
Basic Skills Remediation	✓	Number of Students Served	2

General Information 4-year coed college, affiliated with United Methodist Church. Founded 1859. Awards A (college transfer and terminal), B. Institutionally accredited by regional association; programs accredited by NCATE (teacher education). Small-town setting, with easy access to Detroit and Toledo; 100-acre barrier-free campus. Total enrollment: 1,220. Faculty: 102 (66 full-time, 36 part-time); 79% have doctoral degrees. Calendar: semesters. Grading system: letters or numbers. Library holdings: 125,000 bound volumes, 888 periodical subscriptions, 1,500 records/tapes.

Undergraduate Profile Fall 1984: 1,220 undergraduates (372 freshmen) from 12 states and territories and 11 foreign countries; 9% part-time; 80% state residents; 9% transfers; 87% financial aid recipients; 51% women; 5% blacks; 0% Native Americans; 3% Hispanics; 0% Asian Americans; 1% foreign nationals; 4% of undergraduates over 25 years of age; 4 legally handicapped students.

Expenses (1985–86) Comprehensive fee of $8220 includes full-time tuition ($5872), mandatory fees ($254), and college room and board ($2094). College room only: $836. Part-time tuition: $135 per credit hour.

Financial Aid Fall 1984 full-time freshmen: 91% applied for aid, 85% of those were judged to have need, 100% of those were aided; the average aided freshman received an aid package worth $6029 (67% scholarships/grants, 33% self-help) meeting 99% of need. College-administered aid for all 1984–85 undergraduates: 803 need-based scholarships (average $1797); 107 non-need scholarships (average $1768); short-term loans (average $50); low-interest long-term loans from external sources (average $1952); SEOG; College Work-Study; 193 part-time jobs. Supporting data: FAF, institutional form required; IRS, AFSA/SAR required for some; FFS acceptable. Priority application deadline: 6/1.

Athletics Member NCAA (Division III). Intercollegiate sports: baseball/softball M(III), W(III); basketball M(III), W(III); cross-country running M(III), W(III); field hockey W(III); football M(III); golf M(III), W(III); soccer M(III); swimming and diving M(III), W(III); tennis M(III), W(III); track and field M(III), W(III); volleyball W(III). Intramural sports: badminton, baseball/softball, basketball, bowling, football, golf, gymnastics, soccer, tennis, volleyball, water polo.

Majors Accounting B; anthropology B; art education B; art/fine arts B; biology/biological sciences B; broadcasting B; business administration/commerce/management B; chemistry B; child care/child and family studies A, B; child psychology/child development A; communication B; community services B; computer science B; consumer services B; (pre)dentistry sequence B; early childhood education B; earth science B; economics B; education B; elementary education B; (pre)engineering sequence A; English B; family services B; fashion merchandising B; food services management A; French B; German B; health education B; history B; home economics A, B; home economics education B; interior design B; international business B; journalism B; (pre)law sequence B; liberal arts/general studies B; marketing/retailing/merchandising B; mathematics B; medical technology B; (pre) medicine sequence B; modern languages B; music B; music education B; philosophy B; physical education B; physics B; political science/government B; psychology B; radio and television studies B; religious studies B; science B; science education B; secondary education B; social science B; social work B; sociology B; Spanish B; speech/rhetoric/public address/debate B; sports medicine A; telecommunications B; theater arts/drama B; (pre)veterinary medicine sequence B; voice B. Majors with highest enrollment: business administration/commerce/management, accounting, (pre)medicine sequence.

LD Program Information

Name of Program Learning Development.

Availability of Services Began offering services in 1981. Services provided to freshmen, sophomores, juniors, seniors. Program currently serves 2 LD students: 1 sophomore, 1 senior.

Staff 3 part-time staff members, including director. Services provided by remediation specialist, tutors, counselor, reading specialist.

Admissions LD applicants evaluated on the basis of high school transcript and grade point average, standard or untimed SAT or ACT, personal interview, letters of recommendation, psychoeducational report. LD students may begin taking classes in fall, winter, spring, or summer. Application should be submitted 6 months in advance of initial anticipated enrollment.

Orientation Optional orientation offered after classes begin.

Housing College housing (including coed) available. LD students housed randomly. LD freshmen required to live on campus except if living with relatives.

Diagnostic Testing Available in reading, math, spelling, written language, work and study habits, personality, speech.

Tutoring Offered one-to-one and in small groups by professional teachers, peer tutors. Available in all subjects. LD students may receive tutoring in all courses each term.

Basic Skills Remediation Offered one-to-one and in small groups by regular teachers. Available in reading, math, spelling, written language, learning strategies, perceptual skills, work and study habits, social skills, speech.

Academic Advisement Help with program planning provided by LD staff members, academic advisers. LD students may take up to 16 credit hours each semester; most take 12 to 14 credit hours; 12 credit hours required to maintain full-time status.

Special Courses Offered in college survival skills, reading, vocabulary development, communication skills, composition, math, study skills, career planning. All offered for credit; some enter into overall grade point average.

Auxiliary Aids and Services Aids include taped textbooks, tape recorders, calculators, word processors. Services include alternative exam arrangements, notetakers, advocacy.

Counseling Services Individual counseling, small-group counseling, career counseling available.

Contact Mrs. Gretchen Lovett, Director of Learning Development, Adrian College, Jones Hall, Adrian, MI 49221, 517-265-5161 Ext. 413.

ALLENTOWN COLLEGE OF ST FRANCIS DE SALES

Center Valley, Pennsylvania

Year Program Began	1979	Special Courses	✓
Special Fee	None	Taped Textbooks	
Special Orientation	✓	Alternative Exam Arrangements	✓
Diagnostic Testing	✓	Notetakers	
Subject-Area Tutoring	✓	Staff	3 part-time
Basic Skills Remediation		Number of Students Served	9

General Information Roman Catholic comprehensive coed institution. Founded 1962. Awards B, M. Institutionally accredited by regional association; programs accredited by NLN (nursing). Rural setting, with easy access to Philadelphia; 300-acre campus. Total enrollment: 800. Faculty: 75 (55 full-time, 20 part-time); 65% have doctoral degrees. Calendar: semesters. Grading system: letters or numbers. Library holdings: 135,000 bound volumes, 700 periodical subscriptions, 500 records/tapes.

Undergraduate Profile Fall 1984: 800 undergraduates (273 freshmen) from 7 states and territories and 3 foreign countries; 5% part-time; 70% state residents; 17% transfers; 80% financial aid recipients; 54% women; 2% blacks; 0% Native Americans; 2% Hispanics; 1% Asian Americans; 2% foreign nationals; 1% of undergraduates over 25 years of age; 4 legally handicapped students.

Expenses (1985–86) Comprehensive fee of $7930 includes full-time tuition ($4950), mandatory fees ($40), and college room and board ($2940). Part-time tuition: $185 per credit.

Financial Aid Fall 1984 full-time freshmen: 96% applied for aid, 83% of those were judged to have need, 100% of those were aided; the average aided freshman received an aid package worth $4637 (46% scholarships/grants, 54% self-help) meeting 100% of need. College-administered aid for all 1984–85 undergraduates: 305 need-based scholarships (average $1028); 136 non-need scholarships (average $1267); low-interest long-term loans from external sources (average $1800); SEOG; College Work-Study; part-time jobs. Supporting data: state form required for some. Application deadline: continuous to 5/1.

Athletics Member NCAA (Division III). Intercollegiate sports: baseball/softball M(III), W(III); basketball M(III), W(III); cross-country running M(III), W(III); soccer M(III); tennis M(III), W(III); volleyball W(III). Intramural sports: badminton, baseball/softball, basketball, field hockey, football, soccer, volleyball.

Majors Accounting B; biology/biological sciences B; business administration/commerce/management B; chemistry B; communication B; computer science B; criminal justice B; dance B; (pre)dentistry sequence B; English B; liberal arts/general studies B; marketing/retailing/merchandising B; mathematics B; modern languages B; nursing B; political science/government B; psychology B; safety and security technologies B; theater arts/drama B; theology B. Majors with highest enrollment: accounting, business administration/commerce/management, nursing.

LD Program Information

Name of Program Learning Center.

Availability of Services Began offering services in 1979. Services provided to freshmen, sophomores, juniors, seniors. Program currently serves 9 LD students: 6 freshmen, 1 sophomore, 1 junior, 1 senior.

Staff 3 part-time staff members, including director. Services provided by remediation specialist, tutors, tutorial coordinator, reading specialists.

Admissions LD applicants evaluated on the basis of high school transcript and grade point average, untimed SAT, personal interview, psychoeducational report. LD students may begin taking classes in fall or summer. Application should be submitted 3 months in advance of initial anticipated enrollment.

Orientation Required orientation held before registration.

Housing College housing available. LD students housed randomly. LD students not required to live on campus.

Diagnostic Testing Available in reading, spelling, handwriting, written language, work and study habits, personality.

Tutoring Offered one-to-one and in small groups by professional teachers, peer tutors. Available in all subjects. LD students may receive tutoring in all courses each term.

Academic Advisement Help with program planning provided by LD staff members, academic advisers. LD students may take up to 15 credits each semester; most take 12 credits; 12 credits required to maintain full-time status.

Special Courses Offered in reading, composition, study skills. All offered for credit; all enter into overall grade point average.

Auxiliary Aids and Services Services include alternative exam arrangements.

Counseling Services Individual counseling available.

Contact Mrs. Margaret I. Bilheimer, Director, Learning Center, Allentown College of St Francis de Sales, Center Valley, PA 18034, 215-282-3019.

AMERICAN INTERNATIONAL COLLEGE

Springfield, Massachusetts

Year Program Began	1977	Special Courses	✓
Special Fee	$1200 per year	Taped Textbooks	✓
Special Orientation		Alternative Exam Arrangements	✓
Diagnostic Testing	✓	Notetakers	
Subject-Area Tutoring	✓	Staff	15 full-time, 5 part-time
Basic Skills Remediation	✓	Number of Students Served	104

General Information Independent comprehensive coed institution. Founded 1885. Awards B, M, D. Institutionally accredited by regional association; programs accredited by NCATE (teacher education). City setting; 58-acre campus. Total enrollment: 2,280. Faculty: 123 (83 full-time, 40 part-time); 46% have doctoral degrees; graduate assistants teach no undergraduate courses. Calendar: semesters. Grading system: letters or numbers. Library holdings: 106,324 bound volumes, 12,759 titles on microform, 519 periodical subscriptions, 3,423 records/tapes.

Undergraduate Profile Fall 1984: 1,325 undergraduates (410 freshmen); 7% part-time; 64% state residents; 22% transfers; 70% financial aid recipients; 44% women; 5% blacks; 1% Native Americans; 1% Hispanics; 1% foreign nationals; 2% of undergraduates over 25 years of age; 7 legally handicapped students.

Expenses (1985–86) Comprehensive fee of $7911 includes full-time tuition ($4950), mandatory fees ($290), and college room and board ($2671). College room only: $1046. Part-time tuition: $165 per credit. Tuition prepayment plan available.

Financial Aid College-administered aid for all 1984–85 undergraduates: 980 need-based scholarships (average $2600); 245 non-need scholarships (average $1500); low-interest long-term loans from external sources; SEOG; College Work-Study; part-time jobs. Supporting data: FAF, IRS, institutional form, AFSA/SAR required; FFS acceptable. Priority application deadline: 4/1.

Athletics Member NCAA (Division II). Intercollegiate sports: baseball/softball M(II,s), W(II,s); basketball M(II,s), W(II,s); football M(II,s); golf M(II), W; ice hockey M(II,s); soccer M(II); tennis M(II); volleyball W(II,s). Intramural sports: baseball/softball, basketball, equestrian sports, field hockey, football, golf, gymnastics, skiing (cross-country), skiing (downhill), swimming and diving, tennis, volleyball.

Majors Accounting B; adult and continuing education B; American studies B; biochemistry B; biology/biological sciences B; business administration/commerce/management B; business education B; chemistry B; computer information systems B; criminal justice B; (pre)dentistry sequence B; economics B; education B; elementary education B; English B; finance/banking B; French B; history B; human services B; international business B; law enforcement/police sciences B; (pre)law sequence B; liberal arts/general studies B; marketing/retailing/merchandising B; mathematics B; medical technology B; (pre)medicine sequence B; nursing B; philosophy B; political science/government B; psychology B; public administration B; secondary education B; sociology B; Spanish B; special education B; (pre)veterinary medicine sequence B. Majors with highest enrollment: accounting, criminal justice, nursing.

LD Program Information

Name of Program Supportive Learning Services.

Availability of Services Began offering services in 1977. Services provided to freshmen, sophomores, juniors, seniors. Program currently serves 104 LD students: 41 freshmen, 24 sophomores, 17 juniors, 22 seniors.

Fees $1200 per year.

Staff 15 full-time, 5 part-time staff members, including coordinator. Services provided by remediation specialists, tutors, diagnostic specialists, testing staff.

Admissions LD applicants evaluated on the basis of high school transcript, standard or untimed SAT, personal interview, letters of recommendation, psychoeducational report, WAIS. LD students may begin taking classes in fall or spring. Application should be submitted 10 to 12 months in advance of initial anticipated enrollment.

Housing College housing (including coed) available. LD students housed randomly. LD students not required to live on campus.

Diagnostic Testing Available in intelligence, reading, math, spelling, spoken language, written language.

Tutoring Offered one-to-one by professional teachers, peer tutors. Available in all subjects. LD students may receive tutoring in all courses each term.

Basic Skills Remediation Offered one-to-one by LD teachers. Available in reading, math, spelling, handwriting, written language, learning strategies.

Academic Advisement Help with program planning provided by LD staff members, academic advisers. LD students may take up to 15 credits each semester; 12 credits required to maintain full-time status.

Special Courses Offered in vocabulary development, composition, study skills. None offered for credit; none enter into overall grade point average.

Auxiliary Aids and Services Aids include taped textbooks. Services include alternative exam arrangements.

Counseling Services Individual counseling, career counseling available.

Contact Ms. Mary M. Saltus, Coordinator of Supportive Learning Services and Professor of Special Education, American International College, 1000 State Street, Springfield, MA 01109, 413-737-7000 Ext. 430.

AMERICAN UNIVERSITY

Washington, District of Columbia

Year Program Began	1979	Special Courses	✓
Special Fee	$800 per year	Taped Textbooks	✓
Special Orientation	✓	Alternative Exam Arrangements	✓
Diagnostic Testing	✓	Notetakers	✓
Subject-Area Tutoring	✓	Staff	10 part-time
Basic Skills Remediation	✓	Number of Students Served	46

General Information Methodist coed university. Founded 1893. Awards A (college transfer and terminal), B, M, D. Institutionally accredited by regional association; programs accredited by AACSB (business), NASM (music), NLN (nursing), NCATE (teacher education). Metropolitan setting; 77-acre campus. Total enrollment: 9,129. Faculty: 1,069 (379 full-time, 690 part-time); 69% have doctoral degrees; graduate assistants teach a few undergraduate courses. Calendar: semesters. Grading system: letters or numbers. Library holdings: 440,881 bound volumes, 425,409 titles on microform, 2,576 periodical subscriptions, 10,093 records/tapes.

Undergraduate Profile Fall 1984: 4,943 undergraduates (922 freshmen) from 52 states and territories and 99 foreign countries; 16% part-time; 6% district residents; 12% transfers; 70% financial aid recipients; 57% women; 6% blacks; 0% Native Americans; 4% Hispanics; 2% Asian Americans; 13% foreign nationals; 12% of undergraduates over 25 years of age; 20 legally handicapped students.

Expenses (1985–86) Comprehensive fee of $12,198 includes full-time tuition ($8200), mandatory fees ($70), and college room and board ($3928). College room only: $2400. Part-time tuition: $274 per semester hour.

Financial Aid Fall 1984 full-time freshmen: 71% applied for aid, 81% of those were judged to have need, 100% of those were aided; the average aided freshman received an aid package worth $5705 (63% scholarships/grants, 37% self-help) meeting 100% of need. College-administered aid for all 1984–85 undergraduates: 540 need-based scholarships (average $5000); 260 non-need scholarships (average $3000); short-term loans (average $500); low-interest long-term loans from college funds (average $1100), from external sources (average $2500); SEOG; College Work-Study; part-time jobs. Supporting data: FAF required; IRS required for some; AFSA/SAR acceptable. Priority application deadline: 3/1.

Athletics Member NCAA (Division I). Intercollegiate sports: baseball/softball M(I,s); basketball M(I,s), W(I); cross-country running M(I), W(I); field hockey W(I,s); golf M(I); soccer M(I,s); swimming and diving M(I,s), W(I,s); tennis M(I), W(I,s); volleyball W(I,s); wrestling M(I,s). Intramural sports: badminton, baseball/softball, basketball, bowling, football, soccer, swimming and diving, tennis, track and field, volleyball.

Majors Accounting B; American studies B; anthropology B; applied art B; applied mathematics B; art education B; art/fine arts B; art history B; audio engineering B; biology/biological sciences B; broadcasting B; business administration/commerce/management B; chemistry B; communication B; computer science B; criminal justice A, B; dance B; early childhood education B; ecology/environmental studies B; economics B; education B; elementary education B; environmental sciences B; European studies B; film studies B; finance/banking B; French B; German B; Germanic languages and literature B; graphic arts B; history B; interdisciplinary studies B; international business B; international studies B; journalism B; Judaic studies B; labor and industrial relations B; Latin American studies B; legal studies B; liberal arts/general studies A, B; literature B; marketing/retailing/merchandising B; mathematics B; medical technology B; microbiology B; music B; music education B; nursing B; philosophy B; physical education B; physics B; political science/government B; psychology B; public administration B; public relations B; radio and television studies B; real estate B; Russian B; Russian and Slavic studies B; science B; secondary education B; social science A, B; sociology B; Spanish B; special education B; statistics B; studio art B; theater arts/drama B; urban studies B. Majors with highest enrollment: communication, political science/government, international studies.

LD Program Information

Name of Program Learning Services Program.

Availability of Services Began offering services in 1979. Services provided to freshmen, sophomores, juniors, seniors. Program currently serves 46 LD students: 15 freshmen, 11 sophomores, 10 juniors, 10 seniors.

Fees $800 per year for freshmen; sophomores, juniors, seniors pay $7 to $8 per hour for tutoring services.

Staff 10 part-time staff members, including director. Services provided by remediation specialists, tutors, diagnostic specialist, admissions officer, psychologist, assistant instructors.

Admissions LD applicants evaluated on the basis of high school transcript and grade point average, untimed SAT, autobiographical statement, letters of recommendation, psychoeducational report; personal interview required for some. LD students may begin taking classes in fall only. Application should be submitted 1 year in advance of initial anticipated enrollment.

Orientation Required orientation held before registration.

Housing College housing (including coed) available. LD students housed randomly. LD students not required to live on campus.

Diagnostic Testing Available in intelligence, reading, math, spelling, handwriting, spoken language, written language, perceptual skills, work and study habits, personality, social skills.

Tutoring Offered one-to-one by peer tutors. Available in all subjects. LD students may receive tutoring in all courses each term.

Basic Skills Remediation Offered one-to-one and in small groups by LD teachers, teacher trainees. Available in reading, math, spelling, handwriting, spoken language, written language, learning strategies, work and study habits, social skills.

Academic Advisement Help with program planning provided by LD staff members, academic advisers. LD students may take up to 17 semester hours each semester; most take 12 semester hours; 12 semester hours required to maintain full-time status.

Special Courses Offered in college survival skills, reading, vocabulary development, communication skills, composition, personal psychology, study skills. All offered for credit; all enter into overall grade point average.

Auxiliary Aids and Services Aids include taped textbooks. Services include alternative exam arrangements, notetakers, advocacy.

Counseling Services Individual counseling, small-group counseling, career counseling available.

Contact Ms. Faith Leonard, Director, Learning Services Program, Center for Psychological and Learning Services, American University, 201 Mary Graydon Center, 4400 Massachusetts Avenue, NW, Washington, DC 20016, 202-885-3360.

AMHERST COLLEGE
Amherst, Massachusetts

Year Program Began	1983	Special Courses	
Special Fee	None	Taped Textbooks	✓
Special Orientation		Alternative Exam Arrangements	✓
Diagnostic Testing		Notetakers	✓
Subject-Area Tutoring	✓	Staff	1 part-time
Basic Skills Remediation		Number of Students Served	3

General Information Independent 4-year coed college. Founded 1821. Awards B. Institutionally accredited by regional association. Small-town setting; 950-acre campus. Total enrollment: 1,543. Faculty: 169 (153 full-time, 16 part-time); 85% have doctoral degrees. Calendar: 4-1-4 (no credit for January term). Grading system: letters or numbers. Library holdings: 613,102 bound volumes, 181,718 titles on microform, 1,823 periodical subscriptions.

Undergraduate Profile Fall 1984: 1,543 undergraduates (425 freshmen) from 48 states and territories and 21 foreign countries; 0% part-time; 16% state residents; 1% transfers; 37% financial aid recipients; 43% women; 6% blacks; 0% Native Americans; 2% Hispanics; 4% Asian Americans; 2% foreign nationals; 1% of undergraduates over 25 years of age; 5 legally handicapped students.

Expenses (1985–86) Comprehensive fee of $13,511 includes full-time tuition ($10,150), mandatory fees ($111), and college room and board ($3250).

Financial Aid Fall 1984 full-time freshmen: 44% applied for aid, 83% of those were judged to have need, 100% of those were aided; the average aided freshman received an aid package worth $8030 (72% scholarships/grants, 28% self-help) meeting 100% of need. College-administered aid for all 1984–85 undergraduates: 560 need-based scholarships (average $5190); short-term loans (average $75); low-interest long-term loans from college funds (average $1625), from external sources (average $1950); SEOG; College Work-Study; 630 part-time jobs. Supporting data: FAF, IRS, institutional form, AFSA/SAR required. Priority application deadline: 1/15.

Athletics Member NCAA (Division III). Intercollegiate sports: baseball/softball M(III); basketball M(III), W(III); crew M, W; cross-country running M(III), W(III); field hockey W; football M(III); golf M(III), W(III); ice hockey M(III); lacrosse M(III), W(III); rugby M(c), W(c); sailing M(c), W(c); skiing (downhill) M(III), W(III); soccer M(III), W(III); squash M, W; swimming and diving M(III), W(III); tennis M(III), W(III); track and field M(III), W(III); volleyball M(c), W(c); water polo M(c), W(c); wrestling M. Intramural sports: baseball/softball, basketball, golf, ice hockey, racquetball, skiing (cross-country), soccer, squash, swimming and diving, tennis, track and field, volleyball.

Majors American studies B; anthropology B; art/fine arts B; Asian/Oriental studies B; astronomy B; biology/biological sciences B; black/Afro-American studies B; chemistry B; classics B; economics B; English B; European studies B; French B; geology B; German B; Greek B; history B; interdisciplinary studies B; Latin B; mathematics B; music B; neurosciences B; philosophy B; physics B; political science/government B; psychology B; religious studies B; Romance languages B; Russian B; sociology B; Spanish B; theater arts/drama B. Majors with highest enrollment: English, political science/government, economics.

LD Program Information

Name of Program Not specified.

Availability of Services Began offering services in 1983. Services provided to freshmen, sophomores, juniors, seniors. Program currently serves 3 LD students: 2 sophomores, 1 junior.

Staff 1 part-time staff member (assistant dean of students).

Admissions LD applicants evaluated on the basis of high school transcript, standard or untimed SAT or ACT, letters of recommendation, 3 Achievement Tests (untimed acceptable), talk with high school counselor and/or instructors; personal interview recommended. LD students may begin taking classes in fall only. Application should be submitted at least 8 to 10 months in advance of initial anticipated enrollment.

Housing College housing (including coed) available. LD students housed randomly. LD freshmen required to live on campus.

Tutoring Offered one-to-one. Available in all subjects. LD students may receive tutoring in 4 courses per term.

Academic Advisement Help with program planning provided by academic advisers. LD students may take up to 4 courses each semester; most take 4 courses; 4 courses required to maintain full-time status.

Auxiliary Aids and Services Aids include taped textbooks. Services include alternative exam arrangements, notetakers, transcribers.

Counseling Services Individual counseling, career counseling available.

Contact Ms. Kathleen A. Gentile, Assistant Dean of Students, Amherst College, 104 Converse Hall, PO Box 66, Amherst, MA 01002, 413-542-2296.

APPALACHIAN STATE UNIVERSITY

Boone, North Carolina

Year Program Began	1979	Special Courses	✓
Special Fee	None	Taped Textbooks	✓
Special Orientation		Alternative Exam Arrangements	✓
Diagnostic Testing	✓	Notetakers	✓
Subject-Area Tutoring	✓	Staff	1 full-time, 4 part-time
Basic Skills Remediation	✓	Number of Students Served	35

General Information State-supported comprehensive coed institution. Part of University of North Carolina System. Founded 1899. Awards B, M. Institutionally accredited by regional association; programs accredited by AACSB (business), NASM (music), NCATE (teacher education). Small-town setting; 255-acre campus. Total enrollment: 10,043. Faculty: 592 (535 full-time, 57 part-time); 80% have doctoral degrees; graduate assistants teach a few undergraduate courses. Calendar: semesters. Grading system: letters or numbers. Library holdings: 441,133 bound volumes, 686,577 titles on microform, 3,816 periodical subscriptions, 14,160 records/tapes.

Undergraduate Profile Fall 1984: 8,981 undergraduates (1,868 freshmen) from 47 states and territories and 26 foreign countries; 9% part-time; 90% state residents; 6% transfers; 60% financial aid recipients; 51% women; 4% blacks; 1% Native Americans; 1% Hispanics; 1% Asian Americans; 1% foreign nationals; 45 legally handicapped students.

Expenses (1985–86) State resident tuition: $771 full-time. Nonresident tuition: $3329 full-time. Part-time tuition and fees per semester (1 to 11 hours) range from $51 to $334 for state residents, $371 to $1293 for nonresidents. College room and board: $1640. College room only: $920.

Financial Aid Fall 1984 full-time freshmen: 75% applied for aid, 45% of those were judged to have need, 99% of those were aided; the average aided freshman received an aid package worth $2707 (40% scholarships/grants, 60% self-help) meeting 97% of need. College-administered aid for all 1984–85 undergraduates: need-based scholarships; 658 non-need scholarships (average $400); short-term loans (average $200); low-interest long-term loans from external sources (average $700); SEOG; College Work-Study; 1,550 part-time jobs. Supporting data: FAF, IRS, institutional form required; AFSA/SAR required for some; FFS acceptable. Priority application deadline: 3/15.

Athletics Member NCAA (Division I). Intercollegiate sports: baseball/softball M(I,s), W(I,s); basketball M(I,s), W(I,s); cross-country running M(I,s), W(I,s); field hockey W(I,s); football M(I-AA,s); golf M(I,s), W(I,s); soccer M(I,s); tennis M(I,s), W(I,s); track and field M(I,s), W(I); volleyball W(I,s); wrestling M(I,s). Intramural sports: baseball/softball, basketball, bowling, cross-country running, fencing, football, golf, gymnastics, skiing (cross-country), skiing (downhill), soccer, squash, swimming and diving, tennis, track and field, volleyball, wrestling.

Majors Accounting B; anthropology B; art education B; biology/biological sciences B; broadcasting B; business administration/commerce/management B; business education B; chemistry B; city, community, and regional planning B; commercial art B; communication B; computer information systems B; computer science B; criminal justice B; early childhood education B; economics B; education B; elementary education B; engineering sciences B; engineering technology B; English B; finance/banking B; French B; geography B; geology B; health education B; health services administration B; history B; home economics B; home economics education B; industrial arts B; industrial design B; insurance B; interior design B; liberal arts/general studies B; library science B; marketing/retailing/merchandising B; mathematics B; medical technology B; music B; music education B; music history B; natural sciences B; nutrition B; physical education B; physics B; piano/organ B; political science/government B; printing technologies B; psychology B; reading education B; real estate B; recreation and leisure services B; rehabilitation therapy B; religious studies B; sacred music B; science education B; secretarial studies/office management B; social science B; sociology B; Spanish B; special education B; speech pathology and audiology B; speech/rhetoric/public address/debate B; statistics B; textiles and clothing B; theater arts/drama B; voice B; wind and percussion instruments B. Majors with highest enrollment: marketing/retailing/merchandising, business administration/commerce/management, accounting.

LD Program Information

Name of Program Learning Disability Program.

Availability of Services Began offering services in 1979. Services provided to freshmen, sophomores, juniors, seniors. Program currently serves 35 LD students: 9 freshmen, 10 sophomores, 13 juniors, 3 seniors.

Staff 1 full-time, 4 part-time staff members, including coordinator. Services provided by tutors.

Admissions LD applicants evaluated on the basis of high school transcript and grade point average, untimed SAT. LD students may begin taking classes in fall or spring. Application should be submitted 10 to 12 months in advance of initial anticipated enrollment.

Housing College housing (including coed) available. LD students housed randomly. LD freshmen required to live on campus.

Diagnostic Testing Available in intelligence, reading, math, spelling, spoken language, written language, perceptual skills, personality, speech.

Tutoring Offered one-to-one by peer tutors, trained graduate assistants. Available in all subjects. LD students may receive tutoring in all courses each term.

Basic Skills Remediation Offered one-to-one and in small groups by regular teachers, teacher trainees. Available in reading, spoken language, written language.

Academic Advisement Help with program planning provided by LD staff members, academic advisers. LD students may take up to 15 semester hours each semester; 12 semester hours required to maintain full-time status.

Special Courses Offered in college survival skills, reading, vocabulary development, communication skills, composition, math, study skills, career planning. Some offered for credit; some enter into overall grade point average.

Auxiliary Aids and Services Aids include taped textbooks, tape recorders, word processors. Services include alternative exam arrangements, notetakers.

Counseling Services Individual counseling, small-group counseling, career counseling available.

Contact Ms. Arlene J. Lundquist, Coordinator, Learning Disability Program, Appalachian State University, Boone, NC 28608, 704-262-2291.

ARIZONA STATE UNIVERSITY

Tempe, Arizona

Year Program Began	1980	Special Courses	✓
Special Fee	None	Taped Textbooks	✓
Special Orientation	✓	Alternative Exam Arrangements	✓
Diagnostic Testing	✓	Notetakers	
Subject-Area Tutoring	✓	Staff	1 full-time, 2 part-time
Basic Skills Remediation		Number of Students Served	73

General Information State-supported coed university. Founded 1885. Awards B, M, D. Institutionally accredited by regional association; programs accredited by NAAB (architecture), AACSB (business), ABET (engineering and technology), FIDER (interior design), NASM (music), NLN (nursing), NCATE (teacher education). City setting, with easy access to Phoenix; 566-acre barrier-free campus. Total enrollment: 40,563. Faculty: 2,248 (1,659 full-time, 589 part-time); 80% have doctoral degrees; graduate assistants teach a few undergraduate courses. Calendar: semesters. Grading system: letters or numbers. Library holdings: 1.7 million bound volumes, 1.6 million titles on microform, 25,000 periodical subscriptions, 13,500 records/tapes.

Undergraduate Profile Fall 1984: 30,376 undergraduates (4,032 freshmen) from 54 states and territories and 87 foreign countries; 24% part-time; 73% state residents; 64% transfers; 40% financial aid recipients; 48% women; 2% blacks; 1% Native Americans; 6% Hispanics; 2% Asian Americans; 5% foreign nationals; 24% of undergraduates over 25 years of age; 450 legally handicapped students.

Expenses (1985–86) State resident tuition: $990 full-time, $51 per semester hour part-time. Nonresident tuition: $3844 full-time, $51 per semester hour part-time. College room and board: $2500.

Financial Aid Fall 1984 full-time freshmen: 48% applied for aid, 83% of those were judged to have need, 100% of those were aided; the average aided freshman received an aid package worth $3519 (38% scholarships/grants, 62% self-help) meeting 100% of need. College-administered aid for all 1984–85 undergraduates: 16,000 need-based scholarships (average $2000); 7,500 non-need scholarships (average $1267); short-term loans (average $150); low-interest long-term loans from college funds (average $1500), from external sources (average $2100); SEOG; College Work-Study; 6,500 part-time jobs. Supporting data: FFS, IRS required; FAF, AFSA/SAR acceptable. Priority application deadline: 3/1.

Athletics Member NCAA (Division I). Intercollegiate sports: archery M, W; badminton M, W; baseball/softball M(I,s), W(I,s); basketball M(I,s), W(I,s); cross-country running M(I,s), W(I,s); football M(I-A,s); golf M(s), W(s); gymnastics M(s), W(s); swimming and diving M(I,s), W(I,s); tennis M(I,s), W(I,s); track and field M(I,s), W(I,s); volleyball W(I,s); wrestling M(I,s). Intramural sports: baseball/softball, basketball, bowling, cross-country running, football, golf, gymnastics, ice hockey, lacrosse, martial arts, rugby, skiing (cross-country), skiing (downhill), soccer, swimming and diving, tennis, track and field, volleyball, wrestling.

Majors Accounting B; advertising B; aerospace engineering B; agricultural business B; agricultural engineering B; agricultural sciences B; anthropology B; architectural engineering B; architecture B; art education B; art/fine arts B; art history B; Asian/Oriental studies B; aviation administration B; aviation technology B; bilingual/bicultural education B; bioengineering B; biology/biological sciences B; biomedical engineering B; botany/plant sciences B; broadcasting B; business administration/commerce/management B; business economics B; business education B; ceramic art and design B; chemical engineering B; chemistry B; child care/child and family studies B; child psychology/child development B; Chinese B; city, community, and regional planning B; civil engineering B; commercial art B; communication B; computer engineering B; computer information systems B; computer science B; construction engineering B; criminal justice B; dance B; (pre)dentistry sequence B; early childhood education B; economics B; education B; electrical and electronics technologies B; electrical engineering B; electrical engineering technology B; elementary education B; engineering (general) B; engineering sciences B; engineering technology B; English B; fashion merchandising B; finance/banking B; flight training B; food marketing B; food services management B; food services technology B; French B; geography B; geology B; German B; graphic arts B; health science B; history B; home economics B; home economics education B; horticulture B; humanities B; industrial administration B; industrial arts B; industrial design B; industrial engineering B; industrial engineering technology B; insurance B; interdisciplinary studies B; interior design B; international business B; Italian B; Japanese B; jazz B; journalism B; landscape architecture/design B; land use management and reclamation B; Latin American studies B; (pre)law sequence B; liberal arts/general studies B; management information systems B; manufacturing technology B; marketing/retailing/merchandising B; materials sciences B; mathematics B; mechanical engineering B; mechanical engineering technology B; medical technology B; (pre)medicine sequence B; microbiology B; music B; music education B; music history B; music therapy B; natural resource management B; nuclear engineering B; nursing B; nutrition B; ornamental horticulture B; painting/drawing B; philosophy B; photography B; physical education B; physics B; political science/government B; psychology B; radio and television studies B; radiological technology B; range management B; real estate B; recreation and leisure services B; religious studies B; Russian B; science education B; sculpture B; secondary education B; secretarial studies/office management B; social work B; sociology B; solar technologies B; Spanish B; special education B; speech pathology and audiology B; speech/rhetoric/public address/debate B; speech therapy B; stringed instruments B; studio art B; systems engineering B; telecommunications B; textiles and clothing B; theater arts/drama B; transportation engineering B; urban studies B; (pre)veterinary medicine sequence B; vocational education B; voice B; welding technology B; wildlife biology B; wind and percussion instruments B; women's studies B; zoology B. Majors with highest enrollment: business administration/commerce/management, accounting, marketing/retailing/merchandising.

LD Program Information

Name of Program Learning Disabled Program.

Availability of Services Began offering services in 1980. Services provided to freshmen, sophomores, juniors, seniors. Program currently serves 73 LD students.

Staff 1 full-time, 2 part-time staff members, including director, supervisor of academic services. Services provided by tutors, instructional specialist for computers.

Admissions LD applicants evaluated on the basis of high school transcript and grade point average, standard or untimed SAT or ACT; letters of recommendation, psychoeducational report recommended. LD students may begin taking classes in fall, spring, or summer. Application should be submitted 6 months in advance of initial anticipated enrollment.

Orientation Required orientation held before registration.

Housing College housing (including coed) available. LD students housed randomly. LD students not required to live on campus.

Diagnostic Testing Available in intelligence, reading, math, spelling, written language, personality.

Tutoring Offered one-to-one and in small groups by peer tutors. Available in some subjects. LD students may receive tutoring in all courses each term (depending on availability of tutors, course level, and individual need).

Academic Advisement Help with program planning provided by LD staff members, academic advisers. Most LD students take 6 to 12 semester hours each semester; 12 semester hours required to maintain full-time status for financial aid eligibility, 7 semester hours for tuition purposes.

Special Courses Offered in college survival skills, career planning. All offered for credit; all enter into overall grade point average.

Auxiliary Aids and Services Aids include taped textbooks, tape recorders, calculators, typewriters, word processors, Kurzweil reading machine. Services include alternative exam arrangements, advocacy, readers, library research aides.

Counseling Services Individual counseling, rap sessions, career counseling available.

Contact Mrs. Sue Henderson, Supervisor of Academic Support Services, Arizona State University, Tempe, AZ 85287, 602-965-1234.

AUBURN UNIVERSITY

Auburn University, Alabama

Year Program Began	1984	Special Courses	✓
Special Fee	None	Taped Textbooks	✓
Special Orientation		Alternative Exam Arrangements	✓
Diagnostic Testing	✓	Notetakers	
Subject-Area Tutoring	✓	Staff	1 part-time
Basic Skills Remediation		Number of Students Served	8

General Information State-supported coed university. Founded 1856. Awards B, M, D. Institutionally accredited by regional association; programs accredited by NAAB (architecture), NASAD (art and design), AACSB (business), ABET (engineering and technology), FIDER (interior design), NASM (music), NLN (nursing), ACPE (pharmacy), NCATE (teacher education). Small-town setting; 1,871-acre campus. Total enrollment: 18,888. Faculty: 1,130 (1,053 full-time, 77 part-time); 75% have doctoral degrees; graduate assistants teach a few undergraduate courses. Calendar: quarters. Grading system: letters or numbers. Library holdings: 1.3 million bound volumes, 1.5 million titles on microform, 15,000 periodical subscriptions, 4,253 records/tapes.

Undergraduate Profile Fall 1984: 17,139 undergraduates (2,979 freshmen) from 50 states and territories and 40 foreign countries; 7% part-time; 64% state residents; 35% transfers; 25% financial aid recipients; 41% women; 3% blacks; 1% Native Americans; 1% Hispanics; 1% Asian Americans; 1% foreign nationals; 7% of undergraduates over 25 years of age; 50 legally handicapped students.

Expenses (1985–86) State resident tuition: $1095 full-time. Nonresident tuition: $2505 full-time. Part-time tuition and fees per quarter (1 to 9 quarter hours) range from $86 to $334 for state residents, $191 to $759 for nonresidents. College room only: $1000.

Financial Aid Fall 1984 full-time freshmen: 69% applied for aid, 75% of those were judged to have need, 83% of those were aided; the average aided freshman received an aid package worth $2631 (24% scholarships/grants, 76% self-help) meeting 85% of need. College-administered aid for all 1984–85 undergraduates: 247 need-based scholarships (average $975); 290 non-need scholarships (average $920); short-term loans (average $100); low-interest long-term loans from college funds (average $1000), from external sources (average $1200); SEOG; College Work-Study; 1,800 part-time jobs. Supporting data: FFS, IRS required. Priority application deadline: 3/15.

Athletics Member NCAA (Division I). Intercollegiate sports: baseball/softball M(I,s); basketball M(I,s), W(I,s); cross-country running M(I,s), W(I,s); football M(I-A,s); golf M(I,s), W(I); gymnastics W(I,s); swimming and diving M(I,s), W(I,s); tennis M(I,s), W(I,s); track and field M(I,s), W(I,s). Intramural sports: archery, badminton, baseball/softball, basketball, bowling, football, golf, gymnastics, racquetball, swimming and diving, tennis, track and field, volleyball, wrestling.

Majors Accounting B; adult and continuing education B; aerospace engineering B; agricultural business B; agricultural economics B; agricultural education B; agricultural engineering B; agricultural sciences B; agronomy/soil and crop sciences B; animal sciences B; anthropology B; applied art B; applied mathematics B; architecture B; art education B; art/fine arts B; aviation administration B; biochemistry B; biology/biological sciences B; botany/plant sciences B; broadcasting B; business administration/commerce/management B; business economics B; business education B; chemical engineering B; chemistry B; child care/child and family studies B; child psychology/child development B; civil engineering B; commercial art B; communication B; comparative literature B; computer engineering B; computer science B; construction management B; consumer services B; corrections B; criminal justice B; dairy sciences B; (pre)dentistry sequence B; dietetics B; early childhood education B; earth science B; East European and Soviet studies B; economics B; electrical engineering B; elementary education B; English B; entomology B; environmental design B; environmental health sciences B; family and consumer studies B; family services B; fashion merchandising B; finance/banking B; fish and game management B; food sciences B; food services management B; forest engineering B; forestry B; forest technology B; French B; geography B; geology B; German B; graphic arts B; health education B; health services administration B; history B; home economics B; home economics education B; horticulture B; illustration B; industrial administration B; industrial arts B; industrial design B; industrial engineering B; interior design B; international business B; journalism B; labor and industrial relations B; laboratory technologies B; landscape architecture/design B; Latin American studies B; law enforcement/police sciences B; (pre)law sequence B; marine biology B; marketing/retailing/merchandising B; materials engineering B; mathematics B; mechanical engineering B; medical laboratory technology B; medical technology B; (pre)medicine sequence B; microbiology B; music B; music education B; music history B; nursing B; nutrition B; ornamental horticulture B; painting/drawing B; pest control technology B; pharmacy/pharmaceutical sciences B; philosophy B; physical education B; physics B; piano/organ B; political science/government B; poultry sciences B; psychology B; public administration B; public relations B; radio and television studies B; recreation and leisure services B; rehabilitation therapy B; religious studies B; sacred music B; science education B; sculpture B; secondary education B; secretarial studies/office management B; social work B; sociology B; Spanish B; special education B; speech pathology and audiology B; speech/rhetoric/public address/debate B; speech therapy B; studio art B; textile arts B; textile engineering B; textiles and clothing B; theater arts/drama B; transportation technologies B; (pre)veterinary medicine sequence B; veterinary sciences B; vocational education B; voice B; wildlife management B; wood sciences B; zoology B. Majors with highest enrollment: electrical engineering, architecture, mechanical engineering.

LD Program Information

Name of Program Office of Special Programs.

Availability of Services Began offering services in 1984. Services provided to freshmen, sophomores, juniors, seniors. Program currently serves 8 LD students: 2 freshmen, 1 sophomore, 3 juniors, 2 seniors.

Staff 1 part-time staff member (coordinator).

Admissions LD applicants evaluated on the basis of high school transcript and grade point average, standard or untimed SAT or ACT. LD students may begin taking classes in fall, winter, spring, or summer. Application should be submitted 1 year in advance of initial anticipated enrollment.

Housing College housing available. LD students housed randomly. LD students not required to live on campus.

Diagnostic Testing Available in work and study habits.

Tutoring Offered one-to-one and in small groups by peer tutors. Available in some subjects. LD students may receive tutoring in all courses each term.

Academic Advisement Help with program planning provided by academic advisers. Most LD students take 12 to 15 quarter hours each quarter; 12 quarter hours required to maintain full-time status.

Special Courses Offered in college survival skills, reading, communication skills, study skills, career planning. None offered for credit; none enter into overall grade point average.

Auxiliary Aids and Services Aids include taped textbooks, tape recorders. Services include alternative exam arrangements, advocacy.

Counseling Services Individual counseling, small-group counseling, career counseling available.

Contact Ms. Debora Liddell, Coordinator, Office of Special Programs, Auburn University, 307 Martin Hall, Auburn University, AL 36849, 205-826-2353.

AUGSBURG COLLEGE

Minneapolis, Minnesota

Year Program Began	1982
Special Fee	$200 to $1000 per year
Special Orientation	✓
Diagnostic Testing	✓
Subject-Area Tutoring	✓
Basic Skills Remediation	✓
Special Courses	✓
Taped Textbooks	✓
Alternative Exam Arrangements	✓
Notetakers	
Staff	2 full-time, 3 part-time
Number of Students Served	16

General Information Lutheran 4-year coed college. Founded 1869. Awards B. Institutionally accredited by regional association; programs accredited by NLN (nursing), NCATE (teacher education). Metropolitan setting; 28-acre barrier-free campus. Total enrollment: 1,375. Faculty: 183; 45% have doctoral degrees. Calendar: 4-1-4. Grading system: letters or numbers. Library holdings: 163,590 bound volumes, 22,560 titles on microform, 13,221 periodical subscriptions, 1,500 records/tapes.

Undergraduate Profile Fall 1984: 1,375 undergraduates (285 freshmen); 3% part-time; 85% state residents; 15% transfers; 80% financial aid recipients; 52% women; 3% blacks; 1% Native Americans; 1% Hispanics; 1% Asian Americans; 2% foreign nationals; 11 legally handicapped students.

Expenses (1985–86) Comprehensive fee of $8690 includes full-time tuition ($6190) and college room and board ($2500). Part-time tuition: $800 per course.

Financial Aid College-administered aid for all 1984–85 undergraduates: 1,100 need-based scholarships (average $1356); non-need scholarships (average $5890); low-interest long-term loans from college funds (average $1325), from external sources (average $1880); SEOG; College Work-Study. Supporting data: FFS, IRS, AFSA/SAR required; state form required for some; FAF, institutional form acceptable. Priority application deadline: 4/23.

Athletics Member NCAA (Division III), NAIA. Intercollegiate sports: baseball/softball M(III), W(III); basketball M(III), W(III); cross-country running M(III), W(III); football M(III); golf M(III), W(III); ice hockey M(III); soccer M(III), W(III); tennis M(III), W(III); track and field M(III), W(III); volleyball W(III); wrestling M(III). Intramural sports: baseball/softball, basketball, football, martial arts, racquetball, skiing (cross-country), volleyball, weight lifting.

Majors Accounting B; art education B; art history B; biology/biological sciences B; business administration/commerce/management B; business economics B; chemistry B; Chinese B; communication B; computer science B; (pre)dentistry sequence B; early childhood education B; East Asian studies B; economics B; education B; elementary education B; engineering (general) B; English B; French B; German B; health education B; history B; humanities B; international business B; international studies B; Japanese B; (pre)law sequence B; liberal arts/general studies B; management information systems B; mathematics B; (pre)medicine sequence B; music B; music education B; music therapy B; natural sciences B; nursing B; philosophy B; physical education B; physics B; political science/government B; psychology B; religious studies B; Russian B; Russian and Slavic studies B; Scandinavian languages/studies B; science B; secondary education B; social science B; social work B; sociology B; Spanish B; speech/rhetoric/public address/debate B; studio art B; theater arts/drama B; theology B; urban studies B; (pre)veterinary medicine sequence B. Majors with highest enrollment: business administration/commerce/management, natural sciences, humanities.

LD Program Information

Name of Program Learning Disabilities Program.

Availability of Services Began offering services in 1982. Services provided to freshmen, sophomores, juniors, seniors. Program currently serves 16 LD students: 5 freshmen, 5 sophomores, 4 juniors, 2 seniors.

Fees Range from $200 to $1000 per year according to level of services required.

Staff 2 full-time, 3 part-time staff members, including director, assistant directors. Services provided by remediation specialist, tutors.

Admissions LD applicants evaluated on the basis of high school transcript, untimed SAT or ACT, personal interview, autobiographical statement, letters of recommendation; psychoeducational report, IEP recommended. LD students may begin taking classes in fall, winter, or spring. Application should be submitted 6 months in advance of initial anticipated enrollment.

Orientation Optional orientation offered before registration.

Housing College housing (including coed) available. LD students housed randomly. LD students not required to live on campus.

Diagnostic Testing Available in intelligence, reading, math, spelling, spoken language, written language, perceptual skills, work and study habits, personality.

Tutoring Offered one-to-one and in small groups by professional teachers, peer tutors. Available in all subjects. LD students may receive tutoring in all courses each term.

Basic Skills Remediation Offered one-to-one by LD teachers. Available in reading, math, spelling, spoken language, written language, learning strategies, work and study habits, social skills.

Academic Advisement Help with program planning provided by LD staff members, academic advisers. LD students may take up to 4 courses each semester; most take 3 courses (2 to 3 recommended for freshmen); 2.5 courses required to maintain full-time status.

Special Courses Offered in introduction to liberal arts. All offered for credit; all enter into overall grade point average.

Auxiliary Aids and Services Aids include taped textbooks, tape recorders, typewriters, word processors, color-coded textbooks, study guides, textbook guides, vocabulary guides. Services include alternative exam arrangements, advocacy, LD peer tours of campus, support group.

Counseling Services Individual counseling, small-group counseling, rap sessions, career counseling available.

Contact Miss Kathleen Heikkila, Learning Disabilities Specialist, Augsburg College, 731 21st Avenue South, Minneapolis, MN 55454, 612-330-1167.

AUGUSTA COLLEGE
Augusta, Georgia

Year Program Began	1980	Special Courses	
Special Fee	None	Taped Textbooks	✓
Special Orientation	✓	Alternative Exam Arrangements	✓
Diagnostic Testing	✓	Notetakers	
Subject-Area Tutoring		Staff	1 part-time
Basic Skills Remediation		Number of Students Served	28

General Information State-supported comprehensive coed institution. Part of University System of Georgia. Founded 1925. Awards A (college transfer), B, M. Institutionally accredited by regional association; programs accredited by NASM (music), NLN (nursing), NCATE (teacher education). City setting; 72-acre campus. Total enrollment: 4,091. Faculty: 172 (150 full-time, 22 part-time); 61% have doctoral degrees; graduate assistants teach no undergraduate courses. Calendar: quarters. Grading system: letters or numbers. Library holdings: 364,000 bound volumes, 698,000 titles on microform, 1,161 periodical subscriptions, 4,005 records/tapes.

Undergraduate Profile Fall 1984: 3,490 undergraduates (566 freshmen); 45% part-time; 92% state residents; 25% transfers; 24% financial aid recipients; 60% women; 15% blacks; 1% Native Americans; 1% Hispanics; 2% Asian Americans; 1% foreign nationals; 41% of undergraduates over 25 years of age; 21 legally handicapped students.

Expenses (1985–86) State resident tuition: $1095 full-time, $27 per quarter hour part-time. Nonresident tuition: $3015 full-time, $81 per quarter hour part-time. Mandatory fees: $135.

Financial Aid Fall 1984 full-time freshmen: 55% applied for aid, 100% of those were judged to have need, 100% of those were aided; the average aided freshman received an aid package worth $1341 (53% scholarships/grants, 47% self-help) meeting 52% of need. College-administered aid for all 1984–85 undergraduates: need-based scholarships; 60 non-need scholarships (average $456); short-term loans (average $100); low-interest long-term loans from external sources (average $1168); SEOG; College Work-Study; 166 part-time jobs. Supporting data: FAF, institutional form, AFSA/SAR required; state form required for some. Priority application deadline: 6/1.

Athletics Member NCAA (Division I), NAIA. Intercollegiate sports: baseball/softball M(I,s), W; basketball M(I,s), W(s); cross-country running M(I,s), W(II,s); golf M(I,s); riflery M(I), W(I); soccer M(I,s); swimming and diving M(I,s), W(I,s); tennis M(II,s). Intramural sports: baseball/softball, basketball, football, volleyball, weight lifting.

Majors Accounting A, B; art education B; art/fine arts B; biology/biological sciences B; business administration/commerce/management B; business education B; chemistry B; child care/child and family studies A; child psychology/child development A; communication B; computer science B; criminal justice A; data processing A; (pre)dentistry sequence B; drafting and design A; early childhood education B; economics B; education B; electrical and electronics technologies A; elementary education B; English B; fashion merchandising A; finance/banking B; history B; horticulture A; instrumentation technology A; liberal arts/general studies A; marketing/retailing/merchandising A, B; mathematics B; medical laboratory technology A, B; medical secretarial studies A; (pre)medicine sequence B; music B; music education B; nursing A; physical education B; physical sciences B; physics B; political science/government B; psychology B; public administration B; secretarial studies/office management A, B; sociology B; special education B; studio art B; (pre) veterinary medicine sequence B. Majors with highest enrollment: business administration/commerce/management, computer science, communication.

LD Program Information

Name of Program Not specified.

Availability of Services Began offering services in 1980. Services provided to freshmen, sophomores, juniors, seniors. Program currently serves 28 LD students: 8 freshmen, 12 sophomores, 4 juniors, 4 seniors.

Staff 1 part-time staff member (director).

Admissions LD applicants evaluated on the basis of high school transcript and grade point average, untimed SAT, personal interview, letters of recommendation, psychoeducational report. LD students may begin taking classes in fall only. Application should be submitted 3 months in advance of initial anticipated enrollment.

Orientation Optional orientation offered after classes begin.

Housing College housing not available.

Diagnostic Testing Available in reading, math, spelling, written language, work and study habits, personality, social skills.

Academic Advisement Help with program planning provided by LD staff member, academic advisers. LD students may take up to 12 quarter hours each quarter; most take 10 to 12 quarter hours; 12 quarter hours required to maintain full-time status.

Auxiliary Aids and Services Aids include taped textbooks, tape recorders, word processors. Services include alternative exam arrangements, advocacy.

Counseling Services Individual counseling, rap sessions available.

Contact Dr. Ronald Weber, Associate Professor of Education, Augusta College, Augusta, GA 30910, 404-737-1496.

BARAT COLLEGE
Lake Forest, Illinois

Year Program Began	1980	Special Courses	✓
Special Fee	$350 to $1000 per year	Taped Textbooks	✓
Special Orientation	✓	Alternative Exam Arrangements	✓
Diagnostic Testing	✓	Notetakers	✓
Subject-Area Tutoring	✓	Staff	3 full-time, 2 part-time
Basic Skills Remediation	✓	Number of Students Served	26

General Information Roman Catholic 4-year primarily women's college. Founded 1858. Awards B. Institutionally accredited by regional association. Small-town setting, with easy access to Chicago; 30-acre barrier-free campus. Total enrollment: 668. Faculty: 72 (40 full-time, 32 part-time); 62% have doctoral degrees. Calendar: semesters. Grading system: letters or numbers. Library holdings: 85,000 bound volumes, 624 periodical subscriptions, 1,000 records/tapes.

Undergraduate Profile Fall 1984: 668 undergraduates (66 freshmen) from 20 states and territories and 18 foreign countries; 58% part-time; 88% state residents; 53% transfers; 65% financial aid recipients; 84% women; 18% blacks; 1% Native Americans; 5% Hispanics; 3% Asian Americans; 15% foreign nationals; 53% of undergraduates over 25 years of age; 1 legally handicapped student.

Expenses (1985–86) Comprehensive fee of $8000 includes full-time tuition ($5245), mandatory fees ($55), and college room and board ($2700). Part-time tuition: $175 per semester hour.

Financial Aid Fall 1984 full-time freshmen: 76% applied for aid, 80% of those were aided; the average aided freshman received an aid package meeting 95% of need. College-administered aid for all 1984–85 undergraduates: need-based scholarships; 10 non-need scholarships (average $500); low-interest long-term loans from external sources (average $2400); SEOG; College Work-Study; 139 part-time jobs. Supporting data: FAF, IRS, institutional form, AFSA/SAR required; state form required for some; FFS acceptable. Priority application deadline: 8/15.

Majors Accounting B; art/fine arts B; art history B; arts administration B; art therapy B; behavioral sciences B; biology/biological sciences B; business administration/commerce/management B; business economics B; ceramic art and design B; chemistry B; child psychology/child development B; computer management B; computer science B; dance B; dance therapy B; early childhood education B; economics B; education B; elementary education B; English B; finance/banking B; health science B; history B; humanities B; human services B; interdisciplinary studies B; international business B; international studies B; (pre)law sequence B; liberal arts/general studies B; literature B; management information systems B; marketing/retailing/merchandising B; mathematics B; medical technology B; music B; nursing B; painting/drawing B; philosophy B; photography B; political science/government B; psychology B; public administration B; public affairs and policy studies B; religious studies B; science B; sculpture B; secondary education B; sociology B; special education B; studio art B; theater arts/drama B. Majors with highest enrollment: business administration/commerce/management, studio art, theater arts/drama.

LD Program Information

Name of Program Learning Opportunities Program.

Availability of Services Began offering services in 1980. Services provided to freshmen, sophomores, juniors, seniors. Program currently serves 26 LD students: 10 freshmen, 8 sophomores, 6 juniors, 2 seniors.

Fees Range from $350 to $1000 per year depending on length of weekly sessions with LD specialist.

Staff 3 full-time, 2 part-time staff members, including director, assistant director. Services provided by tutors, LD specialists.

Admissions LD applicants evaluated on the basis of high school transcript and grade point average, standard or untimed SAT or ACT, personal interview, autobiographical statement, letters of recommendation, psychoeducational report, hearing and vision screening. LD students may begin taking classes in fall or spring. Application should be submitted 6 months in advance of initial anticipated enrollment.

Orientation Required orientation held after classes begin.

Housing College housing available. LD students housed randomly. LD students not required to live on campus.

Diagnostic Testing Available in intelligence, reading, math, spelling, handwriting, spoken language, written language, motor abilities, perceptual skills, work and study habits.

Tutoring Offered one-to-one and in small groups by professional teachers, peer tutors. Available in all subjects. LD students may receive tutoring in 2 courses per term.

Basic Skills Remediation Offered one-to-one by LD teachers. Available in reading, math, spelling, handwriting, spoken language, written language, learning strategies, motor abilities, perceptual skills, work and study habits, social skills.

Academic Advisement Help with program planning provided by LD staff members, academic advisers. LD students may take up to 18 semester hours each semester; most take 12 semester hours; 12 semester hours required to maintain full-time status.

Special Courses Offered in college survival skills, reading, vocabulary development, communication skills, composition, language development, math, typing, personal psychology, study skills, career planning, proofreading, sentence combining. Some offered for credit; some enter into overall grade point average.

Auxiliary Aids and Services Aids include taped textbooks, tape recorders, typewriters, word processors. Services include alternative exam arrangements, notetakers, advocacy, study groups.

Counseling Services Individual counseling, career counseling available.

Contact Dr. Pamela B. Adelman, Acting Director, Learning Opportunities Program, Barat College, 700 Westleigh Road, Lake Forest, IL 60045, 312-234-3000 Ext. 331.

BETHEL COLLEGE

Mishawaka, Indiana

Year Program Began	1981	Special Courses	✓
Special Fee	None	Taped Textbooks	✓
Special Orientation		Alternative Exam Arrangements	✓
Diagnostic Testing	✓	Notetakers	✓
Subject-Area Tutoring	✓	Staff	2 part-time
Basic Skills Remediation	✓	Number of Students Served	2

General Information Comprehensive coed institution, affiliated with Missionary Church. Founded 1947. Awards A (college transfer and terminal), B, M. Institutionally accredited by regional association. City setting; 60-acre campus. Total enrollment: 550. Faculty: 45 (27 full-time, 18 part-time); 44% have doctoral degrees; graduate assistants teach no undergraduate courses. Calendar: semesters. Grading system: letters or numbers. Library holdings: 56,525 bound volumes, 404 periodical subscriptions, 2,000 records/tapes.

Undergraduate Profile Fall 1984: 539 undergraduates (182 freshmen) from 11 states and territories and 5 foreign countries; 39% part-time; 84% state residents; 8% transfers; 60% financial aid recipients; 66% women; 2% blacks; 0% Native Americans; 1% Hispanics; 4% foreign nationals; no legally handicapped students.

Expenses (1985–86) Comprehensive fee of $6955 includes full-time tuition ($4495), mandatory fees ($120), and college room and board ($2340). College room only: $940. Part-time tuition: $145 per semester hour.

Financial Aid Fall 1984 full-time freshmen: 85% applied for aid, 70% of those were judged to have need, 100% of those were aided; the average aided freshman received an aid package worth $3087 (52% scholarships/grants, 48% self-help) meeting 100% of need. College-administered aid for all 1984–85 undergraduates: need-based scholarships (average $500); non-need scholarships (average $500); low-interest long-term loans from college funds (average $1600), from external sources (average $1575); SEOG; College Work-Study; part-time jobs. Supporting data: FAF, institutional form, AFSA/SAR required; FFS acceptable. Priority application deadline: 3/1.

Athletics Member NAIA. Intercollegiate sports: baseball/softball M(s), W(s); basketball M(s), W(s); golf M(s); soccer M(s); tennis M(s), W(s); volleyball W(s). Intramural sports: baseball/softball, basketball, volleyball.

Majors Accounting B; art/fine arts B; biblical studies A; biology/biological sciences A, B; business administration/commerce/management A, B; business education B; chemistry A, B; commercial art A, B; communication B; computer science A, B; early childhood education A; education B; elementary education B; English B; gerontology A; history B; journalism A; liberal arts/general studies A, B; mathematics B; medical laboratory technology B; ministries B; music A, B; music education B; nursing B; physical education B; piano/organ A, B; psychology B; recreation and leisure services B; religious studies B; sacred music A, B; science B; science education B; secondary education B; secretarial studies/office management A; social science A, B; sociology B; voice B. Majors with highest enrollment: elementary education, business administration/commerce/management, accounting.

LD Program Information

Name of Program Teaching Learning Center.

Availability of Services Began offering services in 1981. Services provided to freshmen, sophomores. Program currently serves 2 LD students (both freshmen).

Staff 2 part-time staff members, including director. Services provided by remediation specialists, tutors.

Admissions LD applicants evaluated on the basis of high school transcript and grade point average, personal interview; standard or untimed SAT or ACT recommended. LD students may begin taking classes in fall or spring. Application should be submitted 6 months in advance of initial anticipated enrollment.

Housing College housing available. LD students housed randomly. LD freshmen and sophomores required to live on campus except if married, 21 or over, or living with relatives, or by special permission.

Diagnostic Testing Available in reading, work and study habits.

Tutoring Offered one-to-one and in small groups by professional teachers, peer tutors. Available in some subjects. LD students may receive tutoring in all courses each term.

Basic Skills Remediation Offered one-to-one and in small groups by LD teachers, regular teachers. Available in reading, math, written language, learning strategies, work and study habits.

Academic Advisement Help with program planning provided by LD staff members, academic advisers. Most LD students take 12 semester hours first semester, 12 to 15 thereafter; 12 semester hours required to maintain full-time status.

Special Courses Offered in college survival skills, reading, study skills. Most offered for credit; most enter into overall grade point average.

Auxiliary Aids and Services Aids include taped textbooks, tape recorders. Services include alternative exam arrangements, notetakers.

Counseling Services Individual counseling, career counseling available.

Contact Ms. Pauline Medhurst, Director of Teaching Learning Center, Bethel College, Mishawaka, IN 46545, 219-259-8511.

BETHEL COLLEGE

North Newton, Kansas

Year Program Began	1979
Special Fee	None
Special Orientation	
Diagnostic Testing	✓
Subject-Area Tutoring	✓
Basic Skills Remediation	✓
Special Courses	✓
Taped Textbooks	✓
Alternative Exam Arrangements	✓
Notetakers	✓
Staff	1 full-time, 16 part-time
Number of Students Served	21

General Information 4-year coed college, affiliated with General Conference Mennonite Church. Founded 1887. Awards A (terminal), B. Institutionally accredited by regional association; programs accredited by NLN (nursing). Small-town setting; 47-acre campus. Total enrollment: 641. Faculty: 65 (47 full-time, 18 part-time); 60% have doctoral degrees. Calendar: 4-1-4. Grading system: letters or numbers. Library holdings: 73,000 bound volumes, 2,300 titles on microform, 350 periodical subscriptions, 190 records/tapes.

Undergraduate Profile Fall 1984: 641 undergraduates (186 freshmen) from 31 states and territories and 13 foreign countries; 13% part-time; 61% state residents; 25% transfers; 91% financial aid recipients; 51% women; 7% blacks; 1% Native Americans; 1% Hispanics; 1% Asian Americans; 5% foreign nationals; 8% of undergraduates over 25 years of age; 15 legally handicapped students.

Expenses (1985–86) Comprehensive fee of $6896 includes full-time tuition ($4370), mandatory fees ($134), and college room and board ($2392). College room only: $996. Part-time tuition per credit hour: $78 for the first 5 credit hours, $156 for the next 6 credit hours.

Financial Aid Fall 1984 full-time freshmen: 98% applied for aid, 80% of those were judged to have need, 100% of those were aided; the average aided freshman received an aid package worth $5527 (57% scholarships/grants, 43% self-help) meeting 100% of need. College-administered aid for all 1984–85 undergraduates: 265 need-based scholarships (average $925); 454 non-need scholarships (average $805); low-interest long-term loans from external sources (average $1249); College Work-Study; 138 part-time jobs. Supporting data: FFS, FAF, IRS, institutional form, AFSA/SAR acceptable. Priority application deadline: 4/1.

Athletics Member NAIA. Intercollegiate sports: basketball M(s), W(s); cross-country running M(s); football M(s); soccer M, W; tennis M(s), W(s); track and field M(s), W(s); volleyball W(s). Intramural sports: baseball/softball, basketball, bowling, football, golf, tennis, track and field, volleyball, weight lifting.

Majors Accounting B; agricultural sciences A; art education B; art/fine arts B; biblical studies B; biology/biological sciences B; business administration/commerce/management B; business education B; ceramic art and design B; chemistry B; communication B; computer science B; (pre)dentistry sequence B; early childhood education B; economics B; education B; elementary education B; (pre)engineering sequence A; English B; environmental sciences B; fashion merchandising B; German B; health education B; history B; home economics B; home economics education B; human services B; industrial arts A, B; interdisciplinary studies B; interior design B; international studies B; (pre)law sequence B; liberal arts/general studies A, B; mathematics B; medical technology B; (pre)medicine sequence B; music B; music education B; natural sciences B; nursing B; painting/drawing B; peace studies B; philosophy B; physical education B; physics B; political science/government B; psychology B; science B; science education B; secondary education B; secretarial studies/office management A; social work A, B; sociology B; special education B; speech/rhetoric/public address/debate B; theater arts/drama B; theology B. Majors with highest enrollment: business administration/commerce/management, nursing, social work.

LD Program Information

Name of Program Learning Resource Center.

Availability of Services Began offering services in 1979. Services provided to freshmen, sophomores, juniors, seniors. Program currently serves 21 LD students: 15 freshmen, 2 sophomores, 3 juniors, 1 senior.

Staff 1 full-time, 16 part-time staff members, including director. Services provided by tutors, diagnostic specialist, readers.

Admissions LD applicants evaluated on the basis of high school transcript and grade point average, standard or untimed SAT or ACT, personal interview, autobiographical statement, letters of recommendation. LD students may begin taking classes in fall or spring. Application should be submitted at least 1 month in advance of initial anticipated enrollment.

Housing College housing (including coed) available. LD students housed randomly. LD freshmen, sophomores, juniors, and seniors required to live on campus except if 23 or over, married, or living with relatives.

Diagnostic Testing Available in intelligence, reading, math, spelling, written language, perceptual skills, work and study habits, speech, various other areas as appropriate.

Tutoring Offered one-to-one and in small groups by professional teachers, peer tutors, supplemental instructors. Available in most subjects. LD students may receive tutoring in 5 courses per term.

Basic Skills Remediation Offered one-to-one and in small groups by LD teachers, regular teachers. Available in reading, math, spoken language, written language, learning strategies, work and study habits, social skills.

Academic Advisement Help with program planning provided by LD staff member, academic advisers. LD students may take up to 16 credit hours each semester; most take 12 credit hours; 12 credit hours required to maintain full-time status.

Special Courses Offered in college survival skills, reading, vocabulary development, composition, typing, study skills, career planning. Most offered for credit; most enter into overall grade point average.

Auxiliary Aids and Services Aids include taped textbooks, tape recorders, calculators, typewriters, word processors. Services include alternative exam arrangements, notetakers, advocacy, readers.

Counseling Services Individual counseling, career counseling available.

Contact Ms. Sandra Zerger, Director, Learning Resource Center, Bethel College, North Newton, KS 67117, 316-283-2500 Ext. 334.

BLACK HILLS STATE COLLEGE

Spearfish, South Dakota

Year Program Began	1978	Special Courses	✓
Special Fee	None	Taped Textbooks	
Special Orientation		Alternative Exam Arrangements	✓
Diagnostic Testing	✓	Notetakers	
Subject-Area Tutoring	✓	Staff	3 part-time
Basic Skills Remediation	✓	Number of Students Served	6

General Information State-supported comprehensive coed institution. Founded 1883. Awards A (college transfer and terminal), B, M (M in summer session only). Institutionally accredited by regional association; programs accredited by NCATE (teacher education); candidate for program accreditation by NASM (music). Small-town setting; 123-acre campus. Total enrollment: 2,280. Faculty: 104 (96 full-time, 8 part-time); 37% have doctoral degrees. Calendar: semesters. Grading system: letters or numbers. Library holdings: 200,000 bound volumes, 30,000 titles on microform, 700 periodical subscriptions, 200 records/tapes.

Undergraduate Profile Fall 1984: 2,280 undergraduates (586 freshmen) from 41 states and territories and 10 foreign countries; 3% part-time; 91% state residents; 11% transfers; 80% financial aid recipients; 55% women; 1% blacks; 7% Native Americans; 1% foreign nationals; 12% of undergraduates over 25 years of age; 4 legally handicapped students.

Expenses (1985–86) State resident tuition: $1000 full-time, $44.15 per semester hour part-time. Nonresident tuition: $2112 full-time, $78.90 per semester hour part-time. Mandatory fees: $310. College room and board: $1620. College room only: $740.

Financial Aid Fall 1984 full-time freshmen: 80% applied for aid, 83% of those were judged to have need, 100% of those were aided; the average aided freshman received an aid package meeting 90% of need. College-administered aid for all 1984–85 undergraduates: need-based scholarships; 100 non-need scholarships (average $150); short-term loans (average $100); low-interest long-term loans from college funds (average $750), from external sources (average $2100); SEOG; College Work-Study; part-time jobs. Supporting data: FFS, IRS, institutional form, AFSA/SAR required; state form required for some; FAF acceptable. Priority application deadline: 5/1.

Athletics Member NAIA. Intercollegiate sports: basketball M(s), W(s); cross-country running M(s), W(s); football M(s); track and field M(s), W(s); volleyball W(s); wrestling M(s). Intramural sports: baseball/softball, basketball, bowling, equestrian sports, fencing, football, golf, gymnastics, martial arts, skiing (cross-country), skiing (downhill), soccer, swimming and diving, tennis, volleyball, wrestling.

Majors Accounting A, B; American studies B; art education B; art/fine arts A, B; biology/biological sciences B; broadcasting A, B; business administration/commerce/management B; carpentry B; chemistry B; commercial art A; communication A, B; computer programming A; computer science B; construction technologies B; (pre) dentistry sequence B; drafting and design A, B; early childhood education B; earth science B; education B; electrical and electronics technologies B; elementary education B; English B; finance/banking B; food services management A; history B; hotel and restaurant management A, B; industrial arts B; journalism B; (pre)law sequence B; legal secretarial studies A; library science A; mathematics B; medical secretarial studies A; (pre)medicine sequence B; military science B; music B; music education B; Native American studies B; photography B; physical education B; physical sciences B; physical therapy B; physics B; piano/organ B; political science/government B; radio and television studies A, B; science B; science education B; secondary education B; secretarial studies/office management A, B; social science B; social work B; sociology B; special education B; speech/rhetoric/public address/debate B; studio art B; theater arts/drama B; tourism and travel A, B; (pre) veterinary medicine sequence B; vocational education B. Majors with highest enrollment: accounting, business administration/commerce/management, biology/biological sciences.

LD Program Information

Name of Program Developmental Center.

Availability of Services Began offering services in 1978. Services provided to freshmen, sophomores, juniors, seniors. Program currently serves 6 LD students: 2 freshmen, 1 sophomore, 2 juniors, 1 senior.

Staff 3 part-time staff members, including director. Services provided by remediation specialists.

Admissions LD applicants evaluated on the basis of high school transcript, standard or untimed SAT or ACT, letters of recommendation, psychoeducational report. LD students may begin taking classes in fall, spring, or summer.

Housing College housing (including coed) available. LD students housed randomly. LD freshmen required to live on campus.

Diagnostic Testing Available in intelligence, reading, math, spelling, work and study habits, speech.

Tutoring Offered one-to-one and in small groups by peer tutors. Available in all subjects. LD students may receive tutoring in all courses each term.

Basic Skills Remediation Offered one-to-one and in small groups by teacher trainees. Available in reading, math.

Academic Advisement Help with program planning provided by LD staff members, academic advisers. LD students may take up to 17 semester hours each semester; most take 14 semester hours; 12 semester hours required to maintain full-time status.

Special Courses Offered in college survival skills, communication skills, composition, math, study skills. Some offered for credit; some enter into overall grade point average.

Auxiliary Aids and Services Aids include calculators, typewriters, word processors. Services include alternative exam arrangements, advocacy.

Counseling Services Individual counseling, career counseling available.

Contact Ms. Betty Anderson, Director, Developmental Center, Black Hills State College, Spearfish, SD 57783, 605-642-6259.

BOSTON COLLEGE
Chestnut Hill, Massachusetts

Year Program Began	1979
Special Fee	None
Special Orientation	
Diagnostic Testing	
Subject-Area Tutoring	✓
Basic Skills Remediation	
Special Courses	
Taped Textbooks	✓
Alternative Exam Arrangements	✓
Notetakers	✓
Staff	10 part-time
Number of Students Served	37

General Information Roman Catholic coed university. Founded 1863. Awards B, M, D. Institutionally accredited by regional association; programs accredited by AACSB (business), NLN (nursing), NCATE (teacher education). City setting, with easy access to Boston; 200-acre campus. Total enrollment: 14,210. Faculty: 704 (563 full-time, 141 part-time); 83% have doctoral degrees; graduate assistants teach a few undergraduate courses. Calendar: semesters. Grading system: letters or numbers. Library holdings: 943,639 bound volumes, 1.1 million titles on microform, 6,246 periodical subscriptions, 27,000 records/tapes.

Undergraduate Profile Fall 1984: 10,583 undergraduates (2,280 freshmen) from 48 states and territories and 66 foreign countries; 16% part-time; 49% state residents; 12% transfers; 76% financial aid recipients; 57% women; 2% blacks; 1% Native Americans; 3% Hispanics; 3% Asian Americans; 2% foreign nationals; 68 legally handicapped students.

Expenses (1985–86) Comprehensive fee of $12,443 includes full-time tuition ($8200), mandatory fees ($151), and college room and board ($4092). College room only: $2142. Part-time tuition: $155 per credit. Tuition prepayment plan available.

Financial Aid Fall 1984 full-time freshmen: 71% applied for aid, 71% of those were judged to have need, 99% of those were aided; the average aided freshman received an aid package worth $6883 (49% scholarships/grants, 51% self-help) meeting 89% of need. College-administered aid for all 1984–85 undergraduates: need-based scholarships; non-need scholarships; low-interest long-term loans from college funds, from external sources; SEOG; College Work-Study; part-time jobs. Supporting data: FAF, IRS, institutional form, AFSA/SAR required. Priority application deadline: 2/1.

Athletics Member NCAA (Division I). Intercollegiate sports: baseball/softball M(I); basketball M(I,s), W(I,s); cross-country running M(I,s), W(I,s); field hockey W(I,s); football M(I-A,s); golf M, W; ice hockey M(I,s); lacrosse M(I), W(I); skiing (downhill) M, W(s); soccer M(I), W(I,s); swimming and diving M, W(s); tennis M, W; track and field M(s), W(s); volleyball W; water polo M; wrestling M. Intramural sports: baseball/softball, basketball, cross-country running, equestrian sports, fencing, football, golf, ice hockey, martial arts, rugby, sailing, skiing (cross-country), skiing (downhill), swimming and diving, tennis, volleyball.

Majors Accounting B; American studies B; art history B; biology/biological sciences B; business administration/commerce/management B; chemistry B; classics B; communication B; computer science B; (pre)dentistry sequence B; early childhood education B; economics B; education B; elementary education B; English B; finance/banking B; French B; geology B; geophysics B; German B; Germanic languages and literature B; history B; human development B; human resources B; Italian B; (pre)law sequence B; linguistics B; marketing/retailing/merchandising B; mathematics B; (pre)medicine sequence B; nursing B; philosophy B; physics B; political science/government B; psychology B; Romance languages B; Russian B; Russian and Slavic studies B; secondary education B; Slavic languages B; sociology B; Spanish B; special education B; speech/rhetoric/public address/debate B; studio art B; theater arts/drama B; theology B. Majors with highest enrollment: English, economics, accounting.

LD Program Information

Name of Program Special Needs Assistance Program.

Availability of Services Began offering services in 1979. Services provided to freshmen, sophomores, juniors, seniors. Program currently serves 37 LD students: 18 freshmen, 11 sophomores, 4 juniors, 4 seniors.

Staff 10 part-time staff members, including associate director. Services provided by tutors, counselors.

Admissions LD applicants evaluated on the basis of high school transcript and grade point average, untimed SAT or ACT, autobiographical statement, letters of recommendation; personal interview, psychoeducational report recommended. LD students may begin taking classes in fall or spring. Application should be submitted 2 months in advance of initial anticipated enrollment.

Housing College housing (including coed) available. LD students housed randomly. LD students not required to live on campus.

Tutoring Offered one-to-one by professional teachers, peer tutors. Available in all subjects. LD students may receive tutoring in all courses each term.

Academic Advisement Help with program planning provided by LD staff members, academic advisers. LD students may take up to 16 credits each semester; most take 16 credits; 12 credits required to maintain full-time status.

Auxiliary Aids and Services Aids include taped textbooks, tape recorders, word processors. Services include alternative exam arrangements, notetakers, advocacy.

Counseling Services Individual counseling, career counseling available.

Contact Dr. David John Smith, Associate Director of Counseling Service, Boston College, Chestnut Hill, MA 02167, 617-552-3310.

BOSTON UNIVERSITY
Boston, Massachusetts

Year Program Began	1975	Special Courses	✓
Special Fee	None	Taped Textbooks	✓
Special Orientation	✓	Alternative Exam Arrangements	✓
Diagnostic Testing		Notetakers	✓
Subject-Area Tutoring	✓	Staff	3 part-time
Basic Skills Remediation	✓	Number of Students Served	*Not reported*

General Information Independent coed university. Founded 1839. Awards A (terminal), B, M, D. Institutionally accredited by regional association; programs accredited by AACSB (business), ABET (engineering and technology), NASM (music), NLN (nursing), NCATE (teacher education). Metropolitan setting; 68-acre campus. Total enrollment: 27,633. Faculty: 2,600 (1,475 full-time, 1,125 part-time); 72% have doctoral degrees; graduate assistants teach a few undergraduate courses. Calendar: semesters. Grading system: letters or numbers. Library holdings: 1.5 million bound volumes, 2.1 million titles on microform, 26,500 periodical subscriptions, 20,000 records/tapes.

Undergraduate Profile Fall 1984: 13,052 undergraduates (3,595 freshmen) from 55 states and territories and 116 foreign countries; 2% part-time; 31% state residents; 6% transfers; 77% financial aid recipients; 50% women; 4% blacks; 0% Native Americans; 2% Hispanics; 4% Asian Americans; 7% foreign nationals.

Expenses (1985–86) Comprehensive fee of $14,650 includes full-time tuition ($10,100), mandatory fees ($120), and college room and board ($4430). Part-time tuition: $316 per credit. Tuition prepayment plan available.

Financial Aid College-administered aid for all 1984–85 undergraduates: 4,984 need-based scholarships (average $4780); 894 non-need scholarships (average $7515); short-term loans; low-interest long-term loans from college funds, from external sources (average $1000); SEOG; College Work-Study; 229 part-time jobs. Supporting data: FAF, state form, institutional form, AFSA/SAR required; IRS required for some; FFS acceptable. Priority application deadline: 3/1.

Athletics Member NCAA (Division I). Intercollegiate sports: baseball/softball M(III); basketball M(I,s), W(I,s); crew M, W; cross-country running M(I), W(I); field hockey W(I,s); football M(I-AA,s); ice hockey M(I,s); lacrosse W; sailing M, W; soccer M(I,s); swimming and diving M(I,s), W(I,s); tennis M(I), W(I,s); track and field M(I,s), W(I,s); volleyball W; wrestling M(I,s). Intramural sports: badminton, baseball/softball, basketball, bowling, equestrian sports, field hockey, football, golf, gymnastics, ice hockey, lacrosse, martial arts, rugby, skiing (cross-country), skiing (downhill), soccer, volleyball, wrestling.

Majors Accounting B; advertising B; aerospace engineering B; African languages B; anatomy B; anthropology B; applied art A, B; applied mathematics B; archaeology B; art education B; art/fine arts B; art history B; astronomy B; astrophysics B; bilingual/bicultural education B; biology/biological sciences B; biomedical engineering B; black/Afro-American studies B; broadcasting B; business administration/commerce/management A, B; business economics B; business education B; ceramic art and design A, B; ceramic sciences A, B; chemistry B; child psychology/child development B; classics B; communication B; community services B; comparative literature B; computer engineering B; computer information systems B; computer science B; creative writing B; criminal justice A; data processing A; dental services A; (pre)dentistry sequence B; drafting and design B; early childhood education B; earth science B; East European and Soviet studies B; economics B; education B; electrical engineering B; elementary education B; engineering (general) B; engineering and applied sciences B; engineering sciences B; English B; European studies B; experimental psychology B; film studies B; finance/banking B; French B; geography B; geology B; German B; Germanic languages and literature B; graphic arts B; Greek B; health science B; Hispanic studies B; history B; hotel and restaurant management B; humanities B; human services B; industrial engineering B; information science B; interior design B; international business B; international economics B; Italian B; jewelry and metalsmithing A, B; journalism B; Judaic studies B; Latin B; (pre)law sequence B; liberal arts/general studies B; linguistics B; literature B; management engineering B; manufacturing engineering B; marine biology B; marine sciences B; marketing/retailing/merchandising B; mathematics B; mechanical engineering B; (pre)medicine sequence B; metallurgy A, B; modern languages B; music B; music education B; music history B; nursing B; occupational therapy B; operations research B; painting/drawing B; philosophy B; photography B; physical education B; physical sciences B; physical therapy B; physics B; physiology B; piano/organ B; political science/government B; psychology B; public relations B; radio and television studies B; recreation and leisure services B; rehabilitation therapy B; religious studies B; Romance languages B; Russian B; Russian and Slavic studies B; science B; science education B; sculpture B; secondary education B; social science B; sociology B; Spanish B; special education B; speech pathology and audiology B; speech therapy B; statistics B; stringed instruments B; studio art B; systems engineering B; systems science B; teaching English as a second language B; telecommunications B; textile arts A, B; textiles and clothing B; theater arts/drama B; urban studies B; vocational education B; wind and percussion instruments B; wood sciences A, B. Majors with highest enrollment: business administration/commerce/management, psychology, communication.

LD Program Information

Name of Program Disabled Student Services.

Availability of Services Began offering services in 1975. Services provided to freshmen, sophomores, juniors, seniors.

Staff 3 part-time staff members, including director, assistant director. Services provided by remediation specialist.

Admissions LD applicants evaluated on the basis of high school transcript and grade point average, standard or untimed SAT or ACT, personal interview, autobiographical statement, letters of recommendation, psychoeducational report. LD students may begin taking classes in fall or spring. Application should be submitted 6 months in advance of initial anticipated enrollment.

Orientation Optional orientation offered before registration.

Housing College housing (including coed) available. LD students housed randomly. LD freshmen required to live on campus except if living with relatives.

Tutoring Offered one-to-one by professional teachers, peer tutors. Available in some subjects. LD students may receive tutoring in 4 courses per term.

Basic Skills Remediation Offered one-to-one by LD teachers. Available in reading, math, spelling, handwriting, spoken language, written language, learning strategies, work and study habits, social skills, speech.

Academic Advisement Help with program planning provided by LD staff members, academic advisers. LD students may take up to 18 credits each semester; most take 12 credits; 12 credits required to maintain full-time status.

Special Courses Offered in college survival skills, study skills, career planning. None offered for credit; none enter into overall grade point average.

Auxiliary Aids and Services Aids include taped textbooks, tape recorders, Kurzweil reading machine, soundproof study rooms. Services include alternative exam arrangements, notetakers, advocacy, readers, taping of lectures.

Counseling Services Individual counseling, career counseling available.

Contact Mr. Kip Opperman, Assistant Director, Disabled Student Services, Boston University, 775 Commonwealth Avenue, Boston, MA 02215, 617-353-3658.

BOWLING GREEN STATE UNIVERSITY

Bowling Green, Ohio

Year Program Began	1980	Special Courses	
Special Fee	None	Taped Textbooks	
Special Orientation	✓	Alternative Exam Arrangements	✓
Diagnostic Testing	✓	Notetakers	✓
Subject-Area Tutoring	✓	Staff	1 full-time, 6 part-time
Basic Skills Remediation	✓	Number of Students Served	21

General Information State-supported coed university. Founded 1910. Awards A (terminal), B, M, D. Institutionally accredited by regional association; programs accredited by NASAD (art and design), AACSB (business), NASM (music), NLN (nursing), NCATE (teacher education). Small-town setting, with easy access to Toledo; 1,247-acre campus. Total enrollment: 16,690. Faculty: 839 (732 full-time, 107 part-time); 75% have doctoral degrees; graduate assistants teach about a quarter of the undergraduate courses. Calendar: semesters. Grading system: letters or numbers. Library holdings: 755,871 bound volumes, 1.3 million titles on microform, 8,454 periodical subscriptions, 61,660 records/tapes.

Undergraduate Profile Fall 1984: 14,777 undergraduates (2,990 freshmen) from 47 states and territories and 57 foreign countries; 5% part-time; 91% state residents; 4% transfers; 64% financial aid recipients; 57% women; 3% blacks; 0% Native Americans; 1% Hispanics; 1% Asian Americans; 1% foreign nationals; 5% of undergraduates over 25 years of age; 175 legally handicapped students.

Expenses (1985–86) State resident tuition: $1952 full-time, $96.50 per semester hour part-time. Nonresident tuition: $4260 full-time, $206.50 per semester hour part-time. College room and board: $1940 (minimum).

Financial Aid Fall 1984 full-time freshmen: 69% applied for aid, 82% of those were judged to have need, 81% of those were aided; the average aided freshman received an aid package worth $3305 (43% scholarships/grants, 57% self-help) meeting 76% of need. College-administered aid for all 1984–85 undergraduates: 2,200 need-based scholarships (average $346); 736 non-need scholarships (average $520); short-term loans (average $400); low-interest long-term loans from external sources (average $1750); SEOG; College Work-Study; 3,000 part-time jobs. Supporting data: institutional form required; FFS, FAF, AFSA/SAR acceptable. Priority application deadline: 2/1.

Athletics Member NCAA (Division I). Intercollegiate sports: baseball/softball M(I,s), W(I,s); basketball M(I,s), W(I,s); cross-country running M(I,s), W(I,s); football M(I-A,s); golf M(I,s), W(I,s); gymnastics W(I,s); ice hockey M(I,s); soccer M(I,s); swimming and diving M(I,s), W(I,s); tennis M(I,s), W(I,s); track and field M(I,s), W(I,s); volleyball W(I,s). Intramural sports: baseball/softball, basketball, bowling, cross-country running, fencing, football, golf, ice hockey, lacrosse, racquetball, riflery, rugby, sailing, skiing (downhill), soccer, squash, swimming and diving, tennis, track and field, volleyball, water polo, weight lifting, wrestling.

Majors Accounting B; advertising B; American studies B; art education B; art/fine arts B; art history B; art therapy B; Asian/Oriental studies B; aviation technology B; biology/biological sciences B; black/Afro-American studies B; broadcasting B; business administration/commerce/management B; business economics B; business education B; ceramic art and design B; chemistry B; child care/child and family studies B; child psychology/child development B; classics B; commercial art B; communication B; computer science B; construction technologies B; corrections B; creative writing B; criminal justice B; (pre)dentistry sequence B; dietetics B; early childhood education B; earth science B; ecology/environmental studies B; economics B; education B; educational media B; elementary education B; English B; environmental health sciences B; environmental sciences B; ethnic studies B; family services B; fashion merchandising B; film studies B; finance/banking B; food sciences B; food services management B; French B; geochemistry B; geography B; geology B; geophysics B; German B; gerontology B; health education B; health services administration B; history B; home economics B; home economics education B; hotel and restaurant management B; human resources B; insurance B; interior design B; international business B; jewelry and metalsmithing B; journalism B; labor and industrial relations B; Latin B; Latin American studies B; law enforcement/police sciences B; (pre)law sequence B; liberal arts/general studies B; library science B; management information systems B; manufacturing technology B; marketing/retailing/merchandising B; mathematics B; mechanical design technology B; medical records services B; medical technology B; (pre)medicine sequence B; microbiology B; music B; music education B; music history B; nursing B; operations research B; painting/drawing B; philosophy B; photography B; physical education B; physical therapy B; physics B; piano/organ B; political science/government B; printing technologies B; psychology B; public administration B; public relations B; radio and television studies B; recreation and leisure services B; Romance languages B; Russian B; sacred music B; science education B; sculpture B; secondary education B; secretarial studies/office management A, B; social work B; sociology B; Spanish B; special education B; speech pathology and audiology B; speech/rhetoric/public address/debate B; speech therapy B; statistics B; stringed instruments B; studio art B; technical writing B; textiles and clothing B; theater arts/drama B; voice B; wind and percussion instruments B; women's studies B. Majors with highest enrollment: accounting, elementary education, business administration/commerce/management.

LD Program Information

Name of Program Handicapped Services.

Availability of Services Began offering services in 1980. Services provided to freshmen, sophomores, juniors, seniors. Program currently serves 21 LD students: 8 freshmen, 4 sophomores, 8 juniors, 1 senior.

Staff 1 full-time, 6 part-time staff members, including director. Services provided by remediation specialists, diagnostic specialist, directors of writing lab and general studies/English.

Admissions LD applicants evaluated on the basis of high school transcript and grade point average, standard SAT or ACT, autobiographical statement. LD students may begin taking classes in fall, spring, or summer.

Orientation Optional orientation offered before registration.

Housing College housing (including coed) available. LD students housed randomly. LD freshmen and sophomores required to live on campus.

Diagnostic Testing Available in intelligence, reading, math, spelling, motor abilities, perceptual skills, psychoneurology.

Tutoring Offered one-to-one and in small groups by professional teachers, peer tutors. Available in some subjects. LD students may receive tutoring in 2 courses per term.

Basic Skills Remediation Offered one-to-one and in small groups by regular teachers. Available in reading, math, written language, learning strategies, work and study habits.

Academic Advisement Help with program planning provided by LD staff members, academic advisers. LD students may take up to 16 credit hours each semester; most take 12 credit hours; 12 credit hours required to maintain full-time status.

Auxiliary Aids and Services Aids include tape recorders. Services include alternative exam arrangements, notetakers, letters to professors explaining disability.

Counseling Services Individual counseling, career counseling available.

Contact Ms. Janet L. Scottbey, Director of Handicapped Services, Bowling Green State University, 705 Administration Building, Bowling Green, OH 43403, 419-372-0495.

BRADFORD COLLEGE
Bradford, Massachusetts

Year Program Began	1979	Special Courses	✓
Special Fee	$2300 per year	Taped Textbooks	✓
Special Orientation	✓	Alternative Exam Arrangements	✓
Diagnostic Testing	✓	Notetakers	
Subject-Area Tutoring	✓	Staff	2 full-time
Basic Skills Remediation	✓	Number of Students Served	28

General Information Independent 4-year coed college. Founded 1803. Awards A (college transfer), B. Institutionally accredited by regional association. Small-town setting, with easy access to Boston; 70-acre campus. Total enrollment: 400. Faculty: 44 (25 full-time, 19 part-time); 35% have doctoral degrees. Calendar: semesters. Grading system: letters or numbers. Library holdings: 55,000 bound volumes, 200 periodical subscriptions, 650 records/tapes.

Undergraduate Profile Fall 1984: 400 undergraduates (118 freshmen) from 20 states and territories and 9 foreign countries; 15% part-time; 30% state residents; 8% transfers; 40% financial aid recipients; 52% women; 5% blacks; 1% Native Americans; 3% Hispanics; 12% foreign nationals; 5% of undergraduates over 25 years of age; no legally handicapped students.

Expenses (1985–86) Comprehensive fee of $11,443 includes full-time tuition ($7495), mandatory fees ($100), and college room and board ($3848). Part-time tuition: $150 per credit.

Financial Aid Fall 1984 full-time freshmen: 83% applied for aid, 71% of those were judged to have need, 87% of those were aided; the average aided freshman received an aid package worth $8174 (63% scholarships/grants, 37% self-help) meeting 86% of need. College-administered aid for all 1984–85 undergraduates: 150 need-based scholarships (average $3000); low-interest long-term loans from external sources (average $2500); SEOG; College Work-Study; 33 part-time jobs. Supporting data: FAF, IRS, institutional form, AFSA/SAR required; FFS acceptable. Priority application deadline: 3/15.

Athletics Intramural sports: baseball/softball, basketball, field hockey, skiing (cross-country), soccer, swimming and diving, volleyball, water polo, wrestling.

Majors Accounting B; American studies B; art/fine arts B; business administration/commerce/management B; English B; finance/banking B; history B; humanities B; interdisciplinary studies B; international studies B; liberal arts/general studies A, B; literature B; music B; philosophy B; political science/government B; psychology B; social science B; sociology B; studio art B; theater arts/drama B. Majors with highest enrollment: business administration/commerce/management, liberal arts/general studies, art/fine arts.

LD Program Information

Name of Program College Learning Program.

Availability of Services Began offering services in 1979. Services provided to freshmen, sophomores. Program currently serves 28 LD students: 14 freshmen, 14 sophomores.

Fees $2300 per year.

Staff 2 full-time staff members, including director. Services provided by remediation specialist, tutors.

Admissions LD applicants evaluated on the basis of high school transcript and grade point average, personal interview, autobiographical statement, letters of recommendation, psychoeducational report; untimed SAT recommended. LD students may begin taking classes in fall only.

Orientation Orientation offered after classes begin.

Housing College housing (including coed) available. LD students housed randomly. LD freshmen, sophomores, juniors, and seniors required to live on campus except if living with relatives or by special permission.

Diagnostic Testing Available in work and study habits.

Tutoring Offered one-to-one and in small groups by professional teachers, peer tutors. Available in all subjects. LD students may receive tutoring in all courses each term.

Basic Skills Remediation Offered in small groups by LD teachers, regular teachers. Available in written language, learning strategies, work and study habits, social skills.

Academic Advisement Help with program planning provided by LD staff members, academic advisers. LD students may take up to 13 credits each semester; most take 13 credits; 12 credits required to maintain full-time status.

Special Courses Offered in college survival skills, study skills. None offered for credit.

Auxiliary Aids and Services Aids include taped textbooks, tape recorders, word processors. Services include alternative exam arrangements.

Counseling Services Individual counseling, small-group counseling, rap sessions, career counseling available.

Contact Ms. Diane Waldron, Director, College Learning Program, Bradford College, South Main Street, Bradford, MA 01830, 617-372-7161 Ext. 318.

BRENAU WOMEN'S COLLEGE
Gainesville, Georgia

Year Program Began	1983	Special Courses	✓
Special Fee	$0 to $3000 per year	Taped Textbooks	✓
Special Orientation	✓	Alternative Exam Arrangements	✓
Diagnostic Testing	✓	Notetakers	
Subject-Area Tutoring	✓	Staff	3 part-time
Basic Skills Remediation	✓	Number of Students Served	21

General Information Independent 4-year women's college. Administratively affiliated with Brenau Professional College. Founded 1878. Awards B. Institutionally accredited by regional association. Small-town setting, with easy access to Atlanta; 37-acre campus. Total enrollment: 642. Faculty: 86 (71 full-time, 15 part-time); 49% have doctoral degrees. Calendar: quarters. Grading system: letters or numbers. Library holdings: 54,000 bound volumes, 200 titles on microform, 360 periodical subscriptions, 800 records/tapes.

Undergraduate Profile Fall 1984: 642 undergraduates (203 freshmen) from 20 states and territories and 2 foreign countries; 14% part-time; 70% state residents; 10% transfers; 67% financial aid recipients; 100% women; 3% blacks; 2% foreign nationals; 2 legally handicapped students.

Expenses (1985–86) Comprehensive fee of $7900 includes full-time tuition ($4100) and college room and board ($3800). Part-time tuition: $91 per quarter hour.

Financial Aid Fall 1984 full-time freshmen: 61% applied for aid, 83% of those were judged to have need, 100% of those were aided; the average aided freshman received an aid package worth $3039 (49% scholarships/grants, 51% self-help) meeting 90% of need. College-administered aid for all 1984–85 undergraduates: 100 need-based scholarships (average $4600); 75 non-need scholarships (average $1000); low-interest long-term loans; SEOG; College Work-Study; part-time jobs. Supporting data: FAF, IRS, institutional form required; state form required for some; FFS, AFSA/SAR acceptable. Priority application deadline: 5/1.

Athletics Member NAIA. Intercollegiate sports: swimming and diving (s); tennis (s). Intramural sports: badminton, baseball/softball, basketball, bowling, soccer, tennis, volleyball.

Majors Accounting B; art education B; art/fine arts B; arts administration B; biology/biological sciences B; broadcasting B; business administration/commerce/management B; commercial art B; communication B; computer information systems B; criminal justice B; dance B; early childhood education B; education B; elementary education B; English B; equestrian studies B; fashion merchandising B; history B; human resources B; human services B; interior design B; journalism B; (pre)law sequence B; liberal arts/general studies B; medical technology B; (pre)medicine sequence B; music B; music education B; nursing B; physical education B; piano/organ B; political science/government B; psychology B; public administration B; public relations B; secondary education B; special education B; studio art B; theater arts/drama B; voice B. Majors with highest enrollment: nursing, business administration/commerce/management, education.

LD Program Information

Name of Program LD Program.

Availability of Services Began offering services in 1983. Services provided to freshmen, sophomores, juniors, seniors. Program currently serves 21 LD students: 14 freshmen, 6 sophomores, 1 senior.

Fees Range from $0 to $3000 per year according to level of services required.

Staff 3 part-time staff members, including director, assistant director. Services provided by remediation specialist, tutors, diagnostic specialist.

Admissions LD applicants evaluated on the basis of high school transcript, standard or untimed SAT, personal interview, letters of recommendation, psychoeducational report. LD students may begin taking classes in fall, winter, or spring. Application should be submitted at least 1 month in advance of initial anticipated enrollment.

Orientation Required orientation held before registration.

Housing College housing available. LD students housed randomly. LD freshmen, sophomores, juniors, and seniors required to live on campus except if 22 or over, married, or living with relatives within 50-mile radius.

Diagnostic Testing Available in spoken language, written language.

Tutoring Offered one-to-one by professional teachers. Available in all subjects. LD students may receive tutoring in 2 courses per term.

Basic Skills Remediation Offered one-to-one by LD teachers. Available in reading, math, written language, learning strategies, perceptual skills, work and study habits, social skills.

Academic Advisement Help with program planning provided by LD staff members. LD students may take up to 17 quarter hours each quarter; most take 12 to 17 quarter hours (12 quarter hours recommended for first quarter); 12 quarter hours required to maintain full-time status.

Special Courses Offered in reading, vocabulary development, communication skills, composition, language development, math, typing, personal psychology, study skills, career planning. Most offered for credit; most enter into overall grade point average.

Auxiliary Aids and Services Aids include taped textbooks, tape recorders, typewriters, word processors. Services include alternative exam arrangements, advocacy.

Counseling Services Individual counseling, career counseling available.

Contact Ms. Karen Pfunder, Director of LD Program and Assistant Professor of Education and Behavioral Sciences, Brenau Women's College, Gainesville, GA 30501, 404-534-6227.

BRESCIA COLLEGE
Owensboro, Kentucky

Year Program Began	1981	Special Courses	✓
Special Fee	None	Taped Textbooks	
Special Orientation	✓	Alternative Exam Arrangements	✓
Diagnostic Testing	✓	Notetakers	✓
Subject-Area Tutoring	✓	Staff	9 part-time
Basic Skills Remediation	✓	Number of Students Served	2

General Information Roman Catholic 4-year coed college. Founded 1950. Awards A (terminal), B. Institutionally accredited by regional association. City setting; 6-acre campus. Total enrollment: 815. Faculty: 78 (47 full-time, 31 part-time); 37% have doctoral degrees. Calendar: semesters. Grading system: letters or numbers. Library holdings: 116,000 bound volumes, 500 periodical subscriptions, 500 records/tapes.

Undergraduate Profile Fall 1984: 815 undergraduates (147 freshmen); 41% part-time; 95% state residents; 88% financial aid recipients; 42% women; 2% blacks; 5% foreign nationals.

Expenses (1985–86) Comprehensive fee of $5695 includes full-time tuition ($3700) and college room and board ($1995). College room only: $550. Part-time tuition: $103 per credit hour.

Financial Aid Fall 1984 full-time freshmen: 80% applied for aid, 75% of those were judged to have need, 70% of those were aided; the average aided freshman received an aid package meeting 60% of need. College-administered aid for all 1984–85 undergraduates: need-based scholarships (average $3000); non-need scholarships (average $500); short-term loans; low-interest long-term loans from external sources (average $700); SEOG; College Work-Study; part-time jobs. Supporting data: FAF, institutional form, AFSA/SAR required. Priority application deadline: 3/31.

Athletics Member NLCAA. Intercollegiate sports: basketball M(s); soccer M(s); volleyball W(s). Intramural sports: basketball, volleyball.

Majors Accounting A, B; applied mathematics B; art education B; art/fine arts B; biology/biological sciences B; business administration/commerce/management A, B; business education B; chemical engineering technology A; computer science A, B; (pre)dentistry sequence B; electrical engineering technology A; elementary education B; engineering (general) A; (pre)engineering sequence A; engineering technology A; English B; history B; human development A; (pre)law sequence B; liberal arts/general studies B; mathematics B; medical technology B; (pre)medicine sequence B; photography A; psychology B; secondary education B; secretarial studies/office management A; social science B; sociology B; speech pathology and audiology B; speech therapy B; teacher aide studies A; (pre)veterinary medicine sequence B. Majors with highest enrollment: business administration/commerce/management, accounting, elementary education.

LD Program Information

Name of Program Special Services.

Availability of Services Began offering services in 1981. Services provided to freshmen, sophomores, juniors, seniors. Program currently serves 2 LD students (both freshmen).

Staff 9 part-time staff members, including director. Services provided by remediation specialists, tutors, counselors.

Admissions LD applicants evaluated on the basis of high school transcript and grade point average, untimed SAT or ACT, letters of recommendation, psychoeducational report. LD students may begin taking classes in fall, spring, or summer. Application should be submitted 2 to 3 months in advance of initial anticipated enrollment.

Orientation Optional orientation offered during registration.

Housing College housing available. LD students housed randomly. LD students not required to live on campus.

Diagnostic Testing Available in reading, math, written language, work and study habits, personality.

Tutoring Offered one-to-one by professional teachers, peer tutors. Available in some subjects. LD students may receive tutoring in 5 courses per term.

Basic Skills Remediation Offered in small groups by reading specialist. Available in reading, math, spelling, written language, learning strategies, work and study habits, social skills.

Academic Advisement Help with program planning provided by LD staff members, academic advisers. LD students may take up to 18 credit hours each semester; most take 12 credit hours; 12 credit hours required to maintain full-time status.

Special Courses Offered in college survival skills, reading, composition, math, study skills, career planning. All offered for credit; all enter into overall grade point average.

Auxiliary Aids and Services Aids include tape recorders. Services include alternative exam arrangements, notetakers, readers.

Counseling Services Individual counseling, small-group counseling, career counseling available.

Contact Dr. Ellen Dugan-Barrette, Director of Special Services, Brescia College, 120 West Seventh Street, Owensboro, KY 42301, 502-685-3131 Ext. 259.

BRIGHAM YOUNG UNIVERSITY
Provo, Utah

Year Program Began	1982	Special Courses	✓
Special Fee	None	Taped Textbooks	✓
Special Orientation	✓	Alternative Exam Arrangements	✓
Diagnostic Testing	✓	Notetakers	✓
Subject-Area Tutoring	✓	Staff	1 full-time, 8 part-time
Basic Skills Remediation	✓	Number of Students Served	47

General Information Coed university, affiliated with Church of Jesus Christ of Latter-day Saints. Founded 1875. Awards A (college transfer and terminal), B, M, D. Institutionally accredited by regional association; programs accredited by AACSB (business), ABET (engineering and technology), NASM (music), NLN (nursing), NCATE (teacher education). City setting; 630-acre barrier-free campus. Total enrollment: 26,963. Faculty: 1,536 (1,237 full-time, 299 part-time); 75% have doctoral degrees; graduate assistants teach a few undergraduate courses. Calendar: 4-4-2-2. Grading system: letters or numbers.

Undergraduate Profile Fall 1984: 24,619 undergraduates (4,356 freshmen) from 52 states and territories and 77 foreign countries; 18% part-time; 27% state residents; 46% transfers; 15% financial aid recipients; 44% women; 1% blacks; 2% Native Americans; 1% Hispanics; 1% Asian Americans; 3% foreign nationals; 17% of undergraduates over 25 years of age; 300 legally handicapped students.

Expenses (1985–86) Comprehensive fee of $3790 includes full-time tuition ($1480) and college room and board ($2310). Part-time tuition: $80 per credit. Tuition for non–church members: $2220 full-time, $115 per credit part-time.

Financial Aid College-administered aid for all 1984–85 undergraduates: 150 need-based scholarships (average $670); 4,150 non-need scholarships (average $861); short-term loans (average $526); low-interest long-term loans from college funds (average $636), from external sources (average $1500); 5,000 part-time jobs. Supporting data: IRS, institutional form required for some; FFS, FAF, AFSA/SAR acceptable. Application deadline: continuous to 4/30.

Athletics Member NCAA (Division I). Intercollegiate sports: baseball/softball M(I,s); basketball M(I,s), W(I,s); cross-country running M(I,s), W(I,s); field hockey W; football M(I-A,s); golf M(I,s), W(I,s); gymnastics M(I,s), W(I,s); soccer M(I,s); swimming and diving M(I,s), W(I,s); tennis M(I,s), W(I,s); track and field M(I,s), W(I,s); volleyball M, W(I,s); wrestling M(I,s). Intramural sports: baseball/softball, bowling, fencing, ice hockey, lacrosse, rugby, skiing (cross-country), skiing (downhill).

Majors Accounting B; advertising B; agricultural business A, B; agricultural economics A, B; agricultural sciences B; agronomy/soil and crop sciences A, B; American studies B; animal sciences B; anthropology B; archaeology B; art education B; art/fine arts B; art history B; Asian/Oriental studies B; astronomy B; bacteriology B; biblical languages B; biology/biological sciences B; botany/plant sciences B; broadcasting B; business administration/commerce/management B; business education B; Canadian studies B; carpentry B; cartography A, B; ceramic art and design B; chemical engineering B; chemistry B; child care/child and family studies A, B; child psychology/child development A, B; Chinese B; civil engineering B; classics B; commercial art B; communication B; comparative literature B; computer programming B; computer science B; construction technologies B; criminal justice A, B; dance B; (pre)dentistry sequence B; drafting and design A, B; early childhood education B; earth science B; East Asian studies B; economics B; education B; electrical and electronics technologies A, B; electrical engineering B; elementary education B; engineering (general) B; engineering technology B; English A, B; environmental health sciences A; European studies B; family and consumer studies B; family services B; farm and ranch management B; fashion design and technology B; fashion merchandising B; finance/banking B; food marketing B; food sciences B; food services management B; French B; geography B; geology B; German B; Greek B; health education B; health science B; history A, B; home economics B; home economics education B; horticulture B; human development B; humanities B; industrial arts B; information science B; interior design B; Italian B; Japanese B; journalism B; Latin B; Latin American studies B; law enforcement/police sciences B; (pre)law sequence B; library science A; literature B; manufacturing technology B; marketing/retailing/merchandising B; mathematics B; mechanical engineering B; medical technology B; (pre)medicine sequence B; Mexican-American/Chicano studies B; microbiology B; music B; music education B; music history B; Native American studies B; Near and Middle Eastern studies B; nursing A, B; nutrition B; philosophy B; physical education B; physics B; political science/government B; Portuguese B; psychology B; public affairs and policy studies B; public health A; public relations B; range management B; recreation and leisure services B; retail management B; Russian B; secondary education B; social work B; sociology B; Spanish A, B; special education B; sports administration B; statistics B; textile arts B; textiles and clothing B; theater arts/drama B; tourism and travel A, B; zoology B.

LD Program Information

Name of Program Handicapped Student Services.

Availability of Services Began offering services in 1982. Services provided to freshmen, sophomores, juniors, seniors. Program currently serves 47 LD students: 7 freshmen, 12 sophomores, 15 juniors, 13 seniors.

Staff 1 full-time, 8 part-time staff members, including director, assistant directors. Services provided by tutors, counselors, diagnostic specialists, readers.

Admissions LD applicants evaluated on the basis of high school transcript and grade point average, standard or untimed ACT, autobiographical statement, letters of recommendation. LD students may begin taking classes in fall, winter, spring, or summer. Application should be submitted 7 months in advance of initial anticipated enrollment.

Orientation Optional orientation offered during registration.

Housing College housing available. LD students housed randomly. LD students not required to live on campus.

Diagnostic Testing Available in intelligence, reading, math, spelling, handwriting, spoken language, written language, motor abilities, perceptual skills, work and study habits, personality, social skills, psychoneurology, speech.

Tutoring Offered one-to-one by peer tutors. Available in all subjects. LD students may receive tutoring in all courses each term.

Basic Skills Remediation Offered one-to-one and in small groups by regular teachers. Available in reading, math, spelling, handwriting, spoken language, written language, learning strategies, motor abilities, perceptual skills, work and study habits, social skills, speech.

Academic Advisement Help with program planning provided by LD staff members, academic advisers. Most LD students take 10 to 12 credits each semester; 8.5 credits required to maintain full-time status.

Special Courses Offered in college survival skills, reading, vocabulary development, communication skills, composition, language development, math, typing, personal psychology, study skills, career planning. Some offered for credit; some enter into overall grade point average.

Auxiliary Aids and Services Aids include taped textbooks, tape recorders, calculators, typewriters, word processors. Services include alternative exam arrangements, notetakers, advocacy.

Counseling Services Individual counseling, small-group counseling, career counseling available.

Contact Mr. Norman L. Roberts, Director, Handicapped Student Services, Brigham Young University, 390 Spencer W. Kimball Tower, Provo, UT 84602, 801-378-2767.

BRYANT COLLEGE

Smithfield, Rhode Island

Year Program Began	1984	Special Courses	
Special Fee	None	Taped Textbooks	✓
Special Orientation		Alternative Exam Arrangements	✓
Diagnostic Testing		Notetakers	
Subject-Area Tutoring	✓	Staff	1 part-time
Basic Skills Remediation		Number of Students Served	*Not reported*

General Information Independent comprehensive specialized coed institution. Founded 1863. Awards B, M. Institutionally accredited by regional association. Small-town setting, with easy access to Boston; 290-acre barrier-free campus. Total enrollment: 6,780. Faculty: 233 (136 full-time, 97 part-time); 54% have doctoral degrees; graduate assistants teach no undergraduate courses. Calendar: semesters. Grading system: letters or numbers. Library holdings: 104,000 bound volumes, 189 titles on microform, 820 periodical subscriptions, 745 records/tapes.

Undergraduate Profile Fall 1984: 3,018 undergraduates (759 freshmen) from 31 states and territories and 17 foreign countries; 1% part-time; 24% state residents; 18% transfers; 70% financial aid recipients; 44% women; 2% blacks; 0% Native Americans; 1% Hispanics; 1% foreign nationals; 7 legally handicapped students.

Expenses (1985–86) Comprehensive fee of $8800 includes full-time tuition ($5100) and college room and board ($3700). College room only: $2145. Part-time tuition: $189 per course.

Financial Aid Fall 1984 full-time freshmen: 88% applied for aid, 86% of those were judged to have need, 89% of those were aided; the average aided freshman received an aid package worth $4239 (40% scholarships/grants, 60% self-help) meeting 91% of need. College-administered aid for all 1984–85 undergraduates: 1,449 need-based scholarships (average $983); 191 non-need scholarships (average $1784); low-interest long-term loans from external sources (average $2260); SEOG; College Work-Study; 205 part-time jobs. Supporting data: FAF, IRS, state form, AFSA/SAR required; institutional form required for some. Application deadline: 2/15.

Athletics Member NCAA (Division II). Intercollegiate sports: baseball/softball M(II), W(II); basketball M(II,s), W(II,s); bowling M, W; cross-country running M(II), W(II); golf M(II), W(II); soccer M(II), W(II); tennis M(II), W(II); track and field M(II), W(II); volleyball M(II), W(II). Intramural sports: baseball/softball, basketball, bowling, football, lacrosse, martial arts, racquetball, soccer, swimming and diving, tennis, volleyball.

Majors Accounting B; actuarial science B; business administration/commerce/management B; business economics B; communication B; computer information systems B; finance/banking B; hotel and restaurant management B; marketing/retailing/merchandising B. Majors with highest enrollment: accounting, business administration/commerce/management, computer information systems.

LD Program Information

Name of Program Not specified.

Availability of Services Began offering services in 1984. Services provided to freshmen, sophomores, juniors, seniors.

Staff 1 part-time staff member (adviser).

Admissions LD applicants evaluated on the basis of high school transcript and grade point average, standard or untimed SAT or ACT, personal interview, autobiographical statement, letters of recommendation; psychoeducational report recommended. LD students may begin taking classes in fall or spring. Application should be submitted 9 months in advance of initial anticipated enrollment.

Housing College housing (including coed) available. LD students housed randomly. LD students not required to live on campus.

Tutoring Offered one-to-one and in small groups by peer tutors. Available in all subjects. LD students may receive tutoring in all courses each term.

Academic Advisement Help with program planning provided by academic advisers. LD students may take up to 18 credits each semester; most take 12 credits; 12 credits required to maintain full-time status.

Auxiliary Aids and Services Aids include taped textbooks, tape recorders, typewriters, word processors. Services include alternative exam arrangements.

Counseling Services Individual counseling, career counseling available.

Contact Ms. Noreen Mattis, Health Educator/Handicapped Student Adviser, Bryant College, Box 33, Smithfield, RI 02917, 401-232-6045.

CALIFORNIA POLYTECHNIC STATE UNIVERSITY, SAN LUIS OBISPO

San Luis Obispo, California

Year Program Began	1979	Special Courses	✓
Special Fee	None	Taped Textbooks	✓
Special Orientation	✓	Alternative Exam Arrangements	✓
Diagnostic Testing	✓	Notetakers	✓
Subject-Area Tutoring	✓	Staff	2 full-time, 2 part-time
Basic Skills Remediation	✓	Number of Students Served	45

General Information State-supported comprehensive coed institution. Part of California State University System. Founded 1901. Awards A (terminal), B, M. Institutionally accredited by regional association; programs accredited by NAAB (architecture), AACSB (business), ABET (engineering and technology). Small-town setting; 5,000-acre barrier-free campus. Total enrollment: 15,967. Faculty: 1,062 (850 full-time, 212 part-time); 62% have doctoral degrees; graduate assistants teach a few undergraduate courses. Calendar: quarters. Grading system: letters or numbers. Library holdings: 629,344 bound volumes, 1.3 million titles on microform, 3,900 periodical subscriptions.

Undergraduate Profile Fall 1984: 15,006 undergraduates (1,940 freshmen) from 8 states and territories and 75 foreign countries; 15% part-time; 99% state residents; 53% transfers; 44% financial aid recipients; 44% women; 1% blacks; 1% Native Americans; 5% Hispanics; 6% Asian Americans; 1% foreign nationals; 270 legally handicapped students.

Expenses (1985–86) State resident tuition: $0 full-time. Nonresident tuition: $4554 full-time. Part-time tuition and fees per quarter (1 to 11 units) range from $150 to $230 for state residents, $234 to $1154 for nonresidents. Mandatory fees: $690. College room and board: $3108. College room only: $1512.

Financial Aid Fall 1984 full-time freshmen: the average aided freshman received an aid package meeting 70% of need. College-administered aid for all 1984–85 undergraduates: 1,215 need-based scholarships (average $2379); 107 non-need scholarships (average $500); short-term loans (average $200); low-interest long-term loans from college funds (average $750), from external sources (average $2500); SEOG; College Work-Study; 2,400 part-time jobs. Supporting data: IRS, state form, AFSA/SAR required. Priority application deadline: 3/1.

Athletics Member NCAA (Division II). Intercollegiate sports: baseball/softball M(II,s), W(II,s); basketball M(II,s), W(II,s); cross-country running M(II,s), W(II,s); equestrian sports M, W; football M(II,s); gymnastics W(II,s); soccer M; swimming and diving M(II), W(II); tennis M(II), W(II); track and field M(II,s), W(II,s); volleyball W(I,s); wrestling M(I,s). Intramural sports: baseball/softball, basketball, bowling, crew, fencing, football, gymnastics, lacrosse, martial arts, racquetball, rugby, skiing (cross-country), skiing (downhill), soccer, volleyball.

Majors Aerospace engineering B; agricultural business B; agricultural engineering B; agricultural sciences B; agronomy/soil and crop sciences A, B; animal sciences A, B; applied art B; architectural engineering B; architecture B; biochemistry B; biology/biological sciences B; business administration/commerce/management B; chemistry B; child psychology/child development B; city, community, and regional planning B; civil engineering B; computer science B; construction management B; dairy sciences A, B; dietetics B; early childhood education B; economics B; electrical engineering B; electronics engineering B; engineering sciences B; engineering technology B; English B; environmental biology B; environmental engineering B; farm and ranch management B; food sciences A, B; history B; home economics B; horticulture B; industrial engineering B; journalism B; landscape architecture/design B; liberal arts/general studies B; mathematics B; mechanical engineering B; metallurgical engineering B; microbiology B; natural resource management B; ornamental horticulture A, B; physical education B; physical sciences B; physics B; political science/government B; poultry sciences A, B; printing technologies B; recreation and leisure services B; social science B; speech/rhetoric/public address/debate B; statistics B; (pre)veterinary medicine sequence B; vocational education B.

Majors with highest enrollment: business administration/commerce/management, agricultural business, architecture.

LD Program Information

Name of Program Disabled Student Services.

Availability of Services Began offering services in 1979. Services provided to freshmen, sophomores, juniors, seniors. Program currently serves 45 LD students.

Staff 2 full-time, 2 part-time staff members, including coordinator, assistant coordinator. Services provided by LD specialist.

Admissions LD applicants evaluated on the basis of high school transcript and grade point average, untimed SAT or ACT, personal interview, letters of recommendation; psychoeducational report recommended. LD students may begin taking classes in fall, winter, spring, or summer. Application should be submitted 8 months in advance of initial anticipated enrollment.

Orientation Optional orientation offered after classes begin.

Housing College housing (including coed) available. LD students housed randomly. LD students not required to live on campus.

Diagnostic Testing Available in intelligence, reading, math, spelling, written language, perceptual skills, work and study habits, personality.

Tutoring Offered one-to-one and in small groups by professional teachers, peer tutors. Available in all subjects. LD students may receive tutoring in all courses each term.

Basic Skills Remediation Offered one-to-one by LD teachers.

Academic Advisement Help with program planning provided by LD staff members, academic advisers. Most LD students take 12 units each quarter; 12 units required to maintain full-time status.

Special Courses Offered in college survival skills, reading, vocabulary development, communication skills, composition, language development, math, study skills, career planning. Some offered for credit; some enter into overall grade point average.

Auxiliary Aids and Services Aids include taped textbooks, tape recorders, calculators, typewriters, word processors, voice-synthesized computer. Services include alternative exam arrangements, notetakers, advocacy, readers, registration priority.

Counseling Services Individual counseling, small-group counseling, career counseling available.

Contact Ms. Harriet Clendenen, Coordinator, Disabled Student Services, California Polytechnic State University, San Luis Obispo, Room 119A, Julian A. McPhee University Union, San Luis Obispo, CA 93407, 805-546-1395.

CALIFORNIA STATE POLYTECHNIC UNIVERSITY, POMONA

Pomona, California

Year Program Began	1980	Special Courses	
Special Fee	None	Taped Textbooks	✓
Special Orientation		Alternative Exam Arrangements	✓
Diagnostic Testing		Notetakers	✓
Subject-Area Tutoring	✓	Staff	3 part-time
Basic Skills Remediation		Number of Students Served	41

General Information State-supported comprehensive coed institution. Part of California State University System. Founded 1938. Awards B, M. Institutionally accredited by regional association; programs accredited by NAAB (architecture), ABET (engineering and technology). City setting, with easy access to Los Angeles; 1,211-acre barrier-free campus. Total enrollment: 17,024. Faculty: 992 (619 full-time, 373 part-time); 46% have doctoral degrees; graduate assistants teach no undergraduate courses. Calendar: quarters. Grading system: letters or numbers. Library holdings: 409,247 bound volumes, 1.2 million titles on microform, 3,144 periodical subscriptions, 3,188 records/tapes.

Undergraduate Profile Fall 1984: 15,567 undergraduates (1,878 freshmen); 25% part-time; 87% state residents; 51% transfers; 25% financial aid recipients; 40% women; 4% blacks; 1% Native Americans; 13% Hispanics; 11% Asian Americans; 2% foreign nationals; 25% of undergraduates over 25 years of age; 214 legally handicapped students.

Expenses (1985–86) State resident tuition: $0 full-time, $420 per year part-time. Nonresident tuition: $3780 full-time. State residents taking 6 or more units are charged the full-time rate for tuition and fees. Nonresident part-time tuition per quarter (1 to 11 units) ranges from $224 to $1139. Mandatory fees: $645. College room and board: $3048.

Financial Aid Fall 1984 full-time freshmen: 25% applied for aid, 100% of those were judged to have need, 100% of those were aided; the average aided freshman received an aid package meeting 100% of need. College-administered aid for all 1984–85 undergraduates: need-based scholarships; 143 non-need scholarships (average $1041); short-term loans (average $234); low-interest long-term loans from external sources (average $1462); SEOG; College Work-Study; 1,500 part-time jobs. Supporting data: FAF, IRS, AFSA/SAR required; institutional form required for some. Priority application deadline: 3/1.

Athletics Member NCAA (Division II). Intercollegiate sports: baseball/softball M(II,s), W(I,s); basketball M(II,s), W(II,s); cross-country running M(II,s), W(II); gymnastics W(II,s); soccer M(II,s), W(II,s); tennis M(II,s), W(II,s); track and field M(II,s), W(II,s); volleyball W(II,s). Intramural sports: archery, badminton, baseball/softball, basketball, fencing, golf, skiing (downhill), soccer, swimming and diving, tennis, track and field, volleyball, wrestling.

Majors Accounting B; aerospace engineering B; agricultural business B; agricultural education B; agricultural engineering B; agricultural sciences B; agronomy/soil and crop sciences B; American studies B; animal sciences B; anthropology B; applied mathematics B; architecture B; art/fine arts B; behavioral sciences B; bilingual/bicultural education B; biology/biological sciences B; botany/plant sciences B; business administration/commerce/management B; cartography B; chemical engineering B; chemistry B; city, community, and regional planning B; civil engineering B; clinical psychology B; communication B; computer information systems B; computer science B; construction technologies B; dairy sciences B; data processing B; dietetics B; earth science B; economics B; electrical engineering B; electrical engineering technology B; electronics engineering B; engineering technology B; English B; ethnic studies B; farm and ranch management B; finance/banking B; geography B; geology B; guidance and counseling B; history B; home economics B; horticulture B; hotel and restaurant management B; humanities B; human resources B; industrial engineering B; industrial engineering technology B; information science B; insurance B; journalism B; landscape architecture/design B; liberal arts/general studies B; manufacturing engineering B; marketing/retailing/merchandising B; materials engineering B; mathematics B; mechanical engineering B; mechanical engineering technology B; microbiology B; music B; nutrition B; ornamental horticulture B; parks management B; philosophy B; physical education B; physics B; political science/government B; poultry sciences B; psychology B; public administration B; public relations B; real estate B; recreation and leisure services B; social science B; social work B; statistics B; telecommunications B; theater arts/drama B; urban studies B; women's studies B; zoology B. Majors with highest enrollment: business administration/commerce/management, electrical engineering, engineering technology.

LD Program Information

Name of Program Disabled Student Services.

Availability of Services Began offering services in 1980. Services provided to freshmen, sophomores, juniors, seniors. Program currently serves 41 LD students: 15 freshmen, 9 sophomores, 8 juniors, 9 seniors.

Staff 3 part-time staff members, including director, assistant director. Services provided by diagnostic specialist.

Admissions LD applicants evaluated on the basis of high school transcript and grade point average, untimed SAT, personal interview. LD students may begin taking classes in fall, winter, spring, or summer. Application should be submitted 3 to 9 months in advance of initial anticipated enrollment.

Housing College housing (including coed) available. LD students housed randomly. LD students not required to live on campus.

Tutoring Offered one-to-one. Available in all subjects. LD students may receive tutoring in all courses each term.

Academic Advisement Help with program planning provided by academic advisers. LD students may take up to 20 units each quarter; most take 12 to 16 units; 12 units required to maintain full-time status.

Auxiliary Aids and Services Aids include taped textbooks, tape recorders, typewriters, word processors. Services include alternative exam arrangements, notetakers, advocacy, readers.

Counseling Services Individual counseling, small-group counseling, rap sessions, career counseling available.

Contact Ms. Carol A. Goldstein, Director, Disabled Student Services, California State Polytechnic University, Pomona, 3801 West Temple Avenue, Pomona, CA 91768, 714-598-4810.

CALIFORNIA STATE UNIVERSITY, CHICO

Chico, California

Year Program Began	1980	Special Courses	
Special Fee	None	Taped Textbooks	✓
Special Orientation		Alternative Exam Arrangements	✓
Diagnostic Testing	✓	Notetakers	✓
Subject-Area Tutoring		Staff	1 full-time
Basic Skills Remediation		Number of Students Served	64

General Information State-supported comprehensive coed institution. Part of California State University System. Founded 1887. Awards B, M. Institutionally accredited by regional association; programs accredited by NASAD (art and design), AACSB (business), ABET (engineering and technology), NASM (music), NLN (nursing), NCATE (teacher education). Small-town setting; 240-acre barrier-free campus. Total enrollment: 14,196. Faculty: 877 (656 full-time, 221 part-time); 70% have doctoral degrees; graduate assistants teach a few undergraduate courses. Calendar: semesters. Grading system: letters or numbers. Library holdings: 575,000 bound volumes, 4,025 periodical subscriptions, 9,200 records/tapes.

Undergraduate Profile Fall 1984: 12,700 undergraduates (1,170 freshmen) from 37 states and territories and 78 foreign countries; 11% part-time; 94% state residents; 62% transfers; 46% financial aid recipients; 49% women; 2% blacks; 1% Native Americans; 4% Hispanics; 4% Asian Americans; 5% foreign nationals; 16% of undergraduates over 25 years of age; 192 legally handicapped students.

Expenses (1985–86) State resident tuition: $0 full-time, $447 per year part-time. Nonresident tuition: $3780 full-time. State residents taking 6 or more units are charged the full-time rate for tuition and fees. Nonresident part-time tuition and fees per semester (1 to 11 units) range from $350.50 to $1730.50. Mandatory fees: $689. College room and board: $2640.

Financial Aid Fall 1984 full-time freshmen: 88% applied for aid, 65% of those were judged to have need, 74% of those were aided; the average aided freshman received an aid package worth $2985 (54% scholarships/grants, 46% self-help) meeting 90% of need. College-administered aid for all 1984–85 undergraduates: 2,200 need-based scholarships (average $1000); 19 non-need scholarships (average $550); short-term loans (average $100); low-interest long-term loans from external sources (average $2200); SEOG; College Work-Study; 1,300 part-time jobs. Supporting data: IRS, state form required; AFSA/SAR acceptable. Priority application deadline: 3/1.

Athletics Member NCAA (Division II). Intercollegiate sports: baseball/softball M(II), W(II); basketball M(II), W(II); cross-country running M(II), W(II); field hockey W(II); football M(II); gymnastics M(II), W(II); soccer M(II), W(II); swimming and diving M(II), W(II); tennis W(II); track and field M(II), W(II); volleyball W(II); wrestling M(II). Intramural sports: badminton, baseball/softball, basketball, cross-country running, football, gymnastics, martial arts, racquetball, rugby, skiing (cross-country), skiing (downhill), soccer, tennis, volleyball, water polo, wrestling.

Majors Accounting B; agricultural business B; agricultural education B; agricultural technologies B; agronomy/soil and crop sciences B; American studies B; animal sciences B; anthropology B; applied mathematics B; art education B; art/fine arts B; art history B; biochemistry B; biology/biological sciences B; broadcasting B; business administration/commerce/management B; business education B; chemistry B; child psychology/child development B; civil engineering B; communication B; community services B; computer engineering B; computer information systems B; computer science B; computer technologies B; construction management B; criminal justice B; (pre)dentistry sequence B; dietetics B; early childhood education B; earth science B; economics B; educational media B; electrical engineering B; electronics engineering B; elementary education B; English B; ethnic studies B; fashion merchandising B; finance/banking B; French B; geography B; geology B; German B; gerontology B; health education B; health science B; health services administration B; history B; home economics B; horticulture B; humanities B; industrial arts B; industrial engineering technology B; interdisciplinary studies B; interior design B; international business B; international studies B; labor and industrial relations B; Latin American studies B; (pre)law sequence B; liberal arts/general studies B; manufacturing technology B; marketing/retailing/merchandising B; mathematics B; mechanical engineering B; medical technology B; (pre)medicine sequence B; microbiology B; music B; music education B; natural resource management B; nursing B; nutrition B; operations research B; ornamental horticulture B; philosophy B; physical education B; physical fitness/human movement B; physical sciences B; physics B; political science/government B; polymer science B; psychology B; public administration B; radio and television studies B; range management B; recreation and leisure services B; religious studies B; science education B; secondary education B; secretarial studies/office management B; social science B; social work B; sociology B; Spanish B; special education B; speech pathology and audiology B; speech/rhetoric/public address/debate B; statistics B; studio art B; telecommunications B; textiles and clothing B; theater arts/drama B; (pre)veterinary medicine sequence B; vocational education B; women's studies B. Majors with highest enrollment: business administration/commerce/management, computer science, elementary education.

LD Program Information

Name of Program Disabled Student Services.

Availability of Services Began offering services in 1980. Services provided to freshmen, sophomores, juniors, seniors. Program currently serves 64 LD students: 4 freshmen, 11 sophomores, 8 juniors, 41 seniors.

Staff 1 full-time staff member (LD specialist).

Admissions LD applicants evaluated on the basis of high school transcript and grade point average, untimed SAT or ACT, personal interview, letters of recommendation, psychoeducational report. LD students may begin taking classes in fall, winter, spring, or summer. Application should be submitted 8 to 9 months in advance of initial anticipated enrollment.

Housing College housing (including coed) available. LD students housed with other LD students only. LD students not required to live on campus.

Diagnostic Testing Available in intelligence, reading, math, spelling, spoken language, written language, perceptual skills, psychoneurology.

Academic Advisement Help with program planning provided by LD staff members, academic advisers. LD students may take up to 19 units each semester; most take 12 to 15 units; 12 units required to maintain full-time status.

Auxiliary Aids and Services Aids include taped textbooks, tape recorders, word processors, computer software. Services include alternative exam arrangements, notetakers, advocacy, readers.

Counseling Services Individual counseling, rap sessions, career counseling available.

Contact Ms. Patricia G. Stewart, Learning Disabilities Specialist, California State University, Chico, Disabled Student Services, Sutter Hall, Chico, CA 95929, 916-895-5959.

CALIFORNIA STATE UNIVERSITY, DOMINGUEZ HILLS

Carson, California

Year Program Began	1979	Special Courses	
Special Fee	None	Taped Textbooks	✓
Special Orientation		Alternative Exam Arrangements	✓
Diagnostic Testing		Notetakers	✓
Subject-Area Tutoring	✓	Staff	4 part-time
Basic Skills Remediation	✓	Number of Students Served	10

General Information State-supported comprehensive coed institution. Part of California State University System. Founded 1960. Awards B, M. Institutionally accredited by regional association; programs accredited by NASAD (art and design), NASM (music), NCATE (teacher education). City setting, with easy access to Los Angeles; 350-acre barrier-free campus. Total enrollment: 7,927. Faculty: 489 (287 full-time, 202 part-time); 80% have doctoral degrees; graduate assistants teach no undergraduate courses. Calendar: quarters. Grading system: letters or numbers. Library holdings: 313,000 bound volumes, 417,000 titles on microform, 2,200 periodical subscriptions, 12,750 records/tapes.

Undergraduate Profile Fall 1984: 6,647 undergraduates (397 freshmen) from 25 states and territories and 60 foreign countries; 36% part-time; 95% state residents; 60% transfers; 30% financial aid recipients; 57% women; 34% blacks; 2% Native Americans; 7% Hispanics; 9% Asian Americans; 4% foreign nationals; 188 legally handicapped students.

Expenses (1985–86) State resident tuition: $0 full-time, $392 per year part-time. Nonresident tuition: $3690 full-time. State residents taking 6 or more units are charged the full-time rate for tuition. Nonresident part-time tuition per quarter (1 to 11 units) ranges from $213 to $1113. Mandatory fees: $632. College room only: $1430.

Financial Aid Fall 1984 full-time freshmen: 51% applied for aid, 36% of those were judged to have need, 100% of those were aided; the average aided freshman received an aid package worth $2130 (96% scholarships/grants, 4% self-help) meeting 100% of need. College-administered aid for all 1984–85 undergraduates: 640 need-based scholarships (average $982); 25 non-need scholarships (average $200); short-term loans (average $189); low-interest long-term loans from college funds (average $1497), from external sources (average $2920); SEOG; College Work-Study; 319 part-time jobs. Supporting data: IRS, state form required; AFSA/SAR acceptable. Priority application deadline: 4/15.

Athletics Member NCAA (Division II). Intercollegiate sports: badminton M(c), W(c); baseball/softball M(II,s), W(II,s); basketball M(II,s), W(II,s); cross-country running M(II,s), W(II,s); golf M(II,s); soccer M(II,s), W(II,s); track and field M(II,s), W(II,s); volleyball W(II,s).

Majors Accounting B; anthropology B; applied art B; art/fine arts B; art history B; behavioral sciences B; biochemistry B; biology/biological sciences B; black/Afro-American studies B; business administration/commerce/management B; chemistry B; communication B; computer information systems B; computer science B; (pre) dentistry sequence B; earth science B; economics B; English B; finance/banking B; French B; geography B; geology B; gerontology B; graphic arts B; health science B; history B; humanities B; human services B; interdisciplinary studies B; international business B; journalism B; labor studies B; (pre)law sequence B; liberal arts/general studies B; linguistics B; literature B; marketing/retailing/merchandising B; mathematics B; medical technology B; (pre)medicine sequence B; Mexican-American/Chicano studies B; microbiology B; music B; nuclear medical technology B; philosophy B; physical education B; physician's assistant studies B; physics B; political science/government B; psychology B; public administration B; public relations B; recreation and leisure services B; sociology B; Spanish B; studio art B; theater arts/drama B; (pre)veterinary medicine sequence B. Majors with highest enrollment: business administration/commerce/management, accounting, computer science.

LD Program Information

Name of Program Disabled Student Services.

Availability of Services Began offering services in 1979. Services provided to freshmen, sophomores, juniors, seniors. Program currently serves 10 LD students: 1 sophomore, 4 juniors, 5 seniors.

Staff 4 part-time staff members, including director. Services provided by counselor, auxiliary services supervisors.

Admissions LD applicants evaluated on the basis of high school transcript and grade point average, untimed SAT or ACT. LD students may begin taking classes in fall, winter, or spring. Application should be submitted 2 months in advance of initial anticipated enrollment.

Housing College housing available. LD students housed randomly. LD students not required to live on campus.

Tutoring Offered one-to-one and in small groups by peer tutors. Available in some subjects. LD students may receive tutoring in all courses each term.

Basic Skills Remediation Offered one-to-one and in small groups by regular teachers. Available in reading, math, spelling, written language, learning strategies, work and study habits.

Academic Advisement Help with program planning provided by LD staff members, academic advisers. Most LD students take 12 units each quarter; 12 units required to maintain full-time status.

Auxiliary Aids and Services Aids include taped textbooks, tape recorders. Services include alternative exam arrangements, notetakers, advocacy, readers, transcribers.

Counseling Services Individual counseling, small-group counseling, career counseling available.

Contact Mr. Mark Matsui, Coordinator, Disabled Student Services, California State University, Dominguez Hills, 1000 East Victoria Street, Carson, CA 90747, 213-516-3660.

CALIFORNIA STATE UNIVERSITY, FRESNO

Fresno, California

Year Program Began	1980	Special Courses	
Special Fee	None	Taped Textbooks	✓
Special Orientation	✓	Alternative Exam Arrangements	✓
Diagnostic Testing	✓	Notetakers	✓
Subject-Area Tutoring	✓	Staff	6 part-time
Basic Skills Remediation	✓	Number of Students Served	*Not reported*

General Information State-supported comprehensive coed institution. Part of California State University System. Founded 1911. Awards B, M. Institutionally accredited by regional association; programs accredited by AACSB (business), ABET (engineering and technology), NASM (music), NLN (nursing), NCATE (teacher education). City setting; 1,410-acre barrier-free campus. Total enrollment: 16,454. Faculty: 1,083 (769 full-time, 314 part-time); 62% have doctoral degrees; graduate assistants teach a few undergraduate courses. Calendar: semesters. Grading system: letters or numbers. Library holdings: 666,870 bound volumes, 783,758 titles on microform, 4,000 periodical subscriptions, 44,488 records/tapes.

Undergraduate Profile Fall 1984: 13,854 undergraduates (1,394 freshmen); 17% part-time; 89% state residents; 17% transfers; 33% financial aid recipients; 50% women; 3% blacks; 1% Native Americans; 13% Hispanics; 5% Asian Americans; 6% foreign nationals; 32% of undergraduates over 25 years of age; 225 legally handicapped students.

Expenses (1985–86) State resident tuition: $0 full-time. Nonresident tuition: $3510 full-time. Part-time tuition and fees per semester (1 to 11 units) range from $233 to $353 for state residents, $350 to $1640 for nonresidents. Mandatory fees: $707. College room and board: $2625.

Financial Aid Fall 1984 full-time freshmen: 61% applied for aid, 71% of those were judged to have need, 85% of those were aided; the average aided freshman received an aid package worth $2738 (65% scholarships/grants, 35% self-help) meeting 71% of need. College-administered aid for all 1984–85 undergraduates: need-based scholarships; 500 non-need scholarships (average $250); short-term loans (average $100); low-interest long-term loans from external sources (average $1900); SEOG; College Work-Study; part-time jobs. Supporting data: IRS, state form, AFSA/SAR, Financial Aid Transcript (for transfers) required; FAF acceptable. Priority application deadline: 3/1.

Athletics Member NCAA (Division I). Intercollegiate sports: badminton M, W; baseball/softball M(I,s), W(I,s); basketball M(I,s), W(I,s); cross-country running M(I,s), W(I); football M(I-A,s); golf M(I,s); gymnastics W(I,s); soccer M(I,s); swimming and diving M(I,s), W(I,s); tennis M(I,s), W(I,s); track and field M(I,s), W(I); volleyball W(I,s); water polo M(I); wrestling M(I,s). Intramural sports: baseball/softball, basketball, bowling, equestrian sports, football, racquetball, soccer, swimming and diving, tennis, track and field, volleyball, water polo.

Majors Accounting B; advertising B; agricultural business B; agricultural economics B; agricultural education B; agricultural sciences B; agronomy/soil and crop sciences B; animal sciences B; anthropology B; art education B; art/fine arts B; art history B; automotive technologies B; biology/biological sciences B; botany/plant sciences B; business administration/commerce/management B; business economics B; business education B; cell biology B; chemistry B; child care/child and family studies B; child psychology/child development B; civil engineering B; commercial art B; communication B; computer science B; construction technologies B; corrections B; creative writing B; criminal justice B; dairy sciences B; dance B; (pre)dentistry sequence B; dietetics B; early childhood education B; economics B; electrical engineering B; English B; environmental biology B; environmental health sciences B; farm and ranch management B; fashion design and technology B; fashion merchandising B; finance/banking B; food sciences B; French B; geography B; geology B; German B; health science B; health services administration B; history B; home economics B; home economics education B; horticulture B; industrial arts B; industrial engineering B; insurance B; interior design B; journalism B; labor and industrial relations B; law enforcement/police sciences B; (pre)law sequence B; liberal arts/general studies B; linguistics B; marine sciences B; marketing/retailing/merchandising B; mathematics B; mechanical engineering B; medical laboratory technology B; (pre)medicine sequence B; microbiology B; music B; music education B; music history B; nursing B; nutrition B; occupational safety and health B; ornamental horticulture B; philosophy B; photography B; physical education B; physical therapy B; physics B; political science/government B; poultry sciences B; psychology B; public administration B; public relations B; radio and television studies B; range management B; real estate B; recreation and leisure services B; recreation therapy B; religious studies B; Russian B; secretarial studies/office management B; social science B; social work B; sociology B; Spanish B; speech pathology and audiology B; speech/rhetoric/public address/debate B; surveying engineering B; surveying technology B; textiles and clothing B; theater arts/drama B; (pre)veterinary medicine sequence B; vocational education B; zoology B. Majors with highest enrollment: business administration/commerce/management, civil engineering, agricultural sciences.

LD Program Information

Name of Program Disabled Student Services.

Availability of Services Began offering services in 1980. Services provided to freshmen, sophomores, juniors, seniors.

Staff 6 part-time staff members, including director. Services provided by tutors, diagnostic specialists.

Admissions LD applicants evaluated on the basis of high school transcript and grade point average, untimed SAT or ACT, personal interview, autobiographical statement, psychoeducational report. LD students may begin taking classes in fall, spring, or summer. Application should be submitted 3 months in advance of initial anticipated enrollment.

Orientation Required orientation held before registration.

Housing College housing (including coed) available. LD students housed randomly. LD students not required to live on campus.

Diagnostic Testing Available in intelligence, reading, math, spelling, handwriting, spoken language, written language, perceptual skills, work and study habits.

Tutoring Offered one-to-one and in small groups by peer tutors, graduate students in special education. Available in all subjects. LD students may receive tutoring in all courses each term.

Basic Skills Remediation Offered one-to-one and in small groups by graduate students in special education. Available in learning strategies.

Academic Advisement Help with program planning provided by LD staff members, academic advisers. LD students may take up to 18 units each semester; most take 9 to 12 units; 12 units required to maintain full-time status for financial aid.

Auxiliary Aids and Services Aids include taped textbooks, word processors. Services include alternative exam arrangements, notetakers, advocacy.

Counseling Services Individual counseling, small-group counseling, rap sessions, career counseling available.

Contact Mr. Weldon Percy, Coordinator, Disabled Student Services, California State University, Fresno, Fresno, CA 93740-0001, 209-294-2562.

CALIFORNIA STATE UNIVERSITY, LONG BEACH

Long Beach, California

Year Program Began	1979	Special Courses	✓
Special Fee	None	Taped Textbooks	✓
Special Orientation	✓	Alternative Exam Arrangements	✓
Diagnostic Testing	✓	Notetakers	✓
Subject-Area Tutoring	✓	Staff	4 full-time, 12 part-time
Basic Skills Remediation	✓	Number of Students Served	43

General Information State-supported comprehensive coed institution. Part of California State University System. Founded 1949. Awards B, M. Institutionally accredited by regional association; programs accredited by NASAD (art and design), AACSB (business), ABET (engineering and technology), FIDER (interior design), NASM (music), NLN (nursing). City setting, with easy access to Los Angeles; 320-acre barrier-free campus. Total enrollment: 31,124. Faculty: 1,739 (857 full-time, 882 part-time); 75% have doctoral degrees; graduate assistants teach a few undergraduate courses. Calendar: semesters. Grading system: letters or numbers. Library holdings: 868,164 bound volumes, 832,862 titles on microform, 5,702 periodical subscriptions, 22,637 records/tapes.

Undergraduate Profile Fall 1984: 25,625 undergraduates (2,196 freshmen); 33% part-time; 90% state residents; 13% transfers; 43% financial aid recipients; 52% women; 7% blacks; 1% Native Americans; 8% Hispanics; 12% Asian Americans; 3% foreign nationals; 386 legally handicapped students.

Expenses (1985–86) State resident tuition: $0 full-time, $414 per year part-time. Nonresident tuition: $4234 full-time. State residents taking 6 or more units are charged the full-time rate for tuition. Nonresident part-time tuition (1 to 11 units) ranges from $334 to $1714. Mandatory fees: $656. College room and board: $3500.

Financial Aid Fall 1984 full-time freshmen: the average aided freshman received an aid package meeting 75% of need. College-administered aid for all 1984–85 undergraduates: need-based scholarships; non-need scholarships; College Work-Study. Supporting data: FFS, IRS, institutional form required. Priority application deadline: 3/15.

Athletics Member NCAA (Division I). Intercollegiate sports: baseball/softball M(I,s), W(I,s); basketball M(I,s), W(I,s); cross-country running M(I,s), W(I,s); fencing M(s), W(s); field hockey W(s); football M(I-A,s); golf M(I,s), W(I,s); gymnastics M(s), W(I,s); soccer M(s); swimming and diving M(I,s), W(I,s); tennis M(I,s), W(I,s); track and field M(I,s), W(I,s); volleyball M(I,s), W(I,s); water polo M(I,s); wrestling M(s). Intramural sports: archery, baseball/softball, basketball, crew, cross-country running, football, golf, soccer, swimming and diving, tennis, track and field, volleyball, wrestling.

Majors Accounting B; American studies B; anthropology B; applied mathematics B; art education B; art/fine arts B; art history B; Asian/Oriental studies B; behavioral sciences B; biology/biological sciences B; biomedical engineering B; black/Afro-American studies B; botany/plant sciences B; broadcasting B; business administration/commerce/management B; ceramic art and design B; chemical engineering B; chemistry B; civil engineering B; communication B; comparative literature B; computer engineering B; computer science B; creative writing B; criminal justice B; dance B; dietetics B; earth science B; economics B; education B; electrical engineering B; English B; entomology B; finance/banking B; French B; geography B; geology B; German B; health science B; history B; home economics B; human development B; illustration B; industrial arts B; industrial design B; industrial engineering B; interior design B; jewelry and metalsmithing B; journalism B; liberal arts/general studies B; linguistics B; literature B; marine biology B; marine engineering B; marketing/retailing/merchandising B; materials engineering B; mathematics B; mechanical engineering B; Mexican-American/Chicano studies B; microbiology B; music B; music history B; nursing B; nutrition B; ocean engineering B; painting/drawing B; philosophy B; photography B; physical education B; physical therapy B; physics B; physiology B; political science/government B; psychology B; public administration B; public relations B; quality control technology B; radio and television studies B; recreation and leisure services B; religious studies B; Russian B; sculpture B; social work B; sociology B; Spanish B; speech pathology and audiology B; speech/rhetoric/public address/debate B; statistics B; textile arts B; theater arts/drama B; vocational education B; zoology B. Majors with highest enrollment: electrical engineering, accounting, marketing/retailing/merchandising.

LD Program Information

Name of Program Adult Learning Disabled Program.

Availability of Services Began offering services in 1979. Services provided to freshmen, sophomores, juniors, seniors. Program currently serves 43 LD students: 6 freshmen, 7 sophomores, 12 juniors, 18 seniors.

Staff 4 full-time, 12 part-time staff members, including director, coordinator. Services provided by remediation specialist, counselors.

Admissions LD applicants evaluated on the basis of high school transcript and grade point average, untimed SAT or ACT, personal interview, autobiographical statement, letters of recommendation. LD students may begin taking classes in fall or spring. Application should be submitted 2 months in advance of initial anticipated enrollment.

Orientation Optional orientation offered before registration.

Housing College housing (including coed) available. LD students housed randomly. LD students not required to live on campus.

Diagnostic Testing Available in intelligence, reading, math, spelling, handwriting, spoken language, written language, motor abilities, perceptual skills, work and study habits, personality, social skills, psychoneurology, speech, Irlen Differential Tests.

Tutoring Offered one-to-one and in small groups by professional teachers, peer tutors. Available in all subjects. LD students may receive tutoring in all courses each term.

Basic Skills Remediation Offered one-to-one and in small groups by regular teachers. Available in reading, spelling, spoken language, written language, learning strategies, perceptual skills, work and study habits, social skills, speech, computer usage.

Academic Advisement Help with program planning provided by LD staff members, academic advisers. LD students may take up to 12 units each semester; 9 units required to maintain full-time status.

Special Courses Offered in college survival skills, typing, personal psychology, career planning, word processing. Most offered for credit; most enter into overall grade point average.

Auxiliary Aids and Services Aids include taped textbooks, tape recorders, calculators, typewriters, word processors, Phonic Ears, special lenses. Services include alternative exam arrangements, notetakers, advocacy, readers, support group.

Counseling Services Individual counseling, small-group counseling, rap sessions, career counseling available.

Contact Mr. David Sanfilippo, Director, Disabled Student Services, California State University, Long Beach, 1250 Bellflower Boulevard, Long Beach, CA 90840, 213-498-5401.

CALIFORNIA STATE UNIVERSITY, LOS ANGELES

Los Angeles, California

Year Program Began	*Not reported*	Special Courses	
Special Fee	None	Taped Textbooks	✓
Special Orientation		Alternative Exam Arrangements	✓
Diagnostic Testing	✓	Notetakers	✓
Subject-Area Tutoring	✓	Staff	1 part-time
Basic Skills Remediation		Number of Students Served	50 to 100

General Information State-supported comprehensive coed institution. Part of California State University System. Founded 1947. Awards B, M, D. Institutionally accredited by regional association; programs accredited by NASAD (art and design), AACSB (business), ABET (engineering and technology), NASM (music), NLN (nursing), NCATE (teacher education). Metropolitan setting; 100-acre barrier-free campus. Total enrollment: 21,000. Faculty: 1,150 (750 full-time, 400 part-time); 80% have doctoral degrees; graduate assistants teach no undergraduate courses. Calendar: quarters. Grading system: letters or numbers. Library holdings: 825,000 bound volumes, 5,000 periodical subscriptions.

Undergraduate Profile Fall 1984: 15,000 undergraduates (1,135 freshmen) from 40 states and territories and 120 foreign countries; 44% part-time; 93% state residents; 75% transfers; 45% financial aid recipients; 56% women; 12% blacks; 1% Native Americans; 25% Hispanics; 25% Asian Americans; 5% foreign nationals; 40% of undergraduates over 25 years of age; 300 legally handicapped students.

Expenses (1985–86) State resident tuition: $0 full-time. Nonresident tuition: $3780 full-time. Part-time tuition and fees per quarter (1 to 14 units) range from $140 to $230 for state residents, $222 to $1378 for nonresidents. Mandatory fees: $650. College room only: $1800.

Financial Aid Fall 1984 full-time freshmen: 48% applied for aid, 90% of those were judged to have need, 100% of those were aided; the average aided freshman received an aid package worth $1537 (77% scholarships/grants, 23% self-help) meeting 100% of need. College-administered aid for all 1984–85 undergraduates: need-based scholarships; non-need scholarships (average $300); short-term loans; low-interest long-term loans; SEOG; College Work-Study; part-time jobs. Supporting data: IRS, state form, institutional form, AFSA/SAR required. Priority application deadline: 4/15.

Athletics Member NCAA (Division II). Intercollegiate sports: baseball/softball M(II,s); basketball M(II,s), W(II,s); cross-country running M(II,s), W(II,s); soccer M(I,s); swimming and diving M(s), W(s); tennis M(s), W(s); track and field M(II,s), W(I,s); volleyball W; water polo M(s). Intramural sports: baseball/softball, basketball, football, soccer, tennis, volleyball.

Majors Accounting B; advertising B; anthropology B; applied art B; art/fine arts B; art history B; aviation administration B; biochemistry B; biology/biological sciences B; biophysics B; black/Afro-American studies B; broadcasting B; business administration/commerce/management B; business education B; chemistry B; child care/child and family studies B; child psychology/child development B; civil engineering B; communication B; computer information systems B; computer science B; criminal justice B; dietetics B; economics B; electrical engineering B; engineering (general) B; English B; environmental biology B; fashion design and technology B; fashion merchandising B; finance/banking B; fire protection engineering B; fire science B; French B; geography B; geology B; health science B; history B; home economics B; industrial arts B; interior design B; international business B; international economics B; Japanese B; journalism B; labor studies B; Latin American studies B; law enforcement/police sciences B; liberal arts/general studies B; marketing/retailing/merchandising B; mathematics B; mechanical engineering B; medical laboratory technology B; Mexican-American/Chicano studies B; microbiology B; music B; nursing B; philosophy B; physical education B; physics B; political science/government B; printing technologies B; psychology B; public administration B; radio and television studies B; real estate B; rehabilitation therapy B; retail management B; social science B; social work B; sociology B; Spanish B; speech pathology and audiology B; speech/rhetoric/public address/debate B; statistics B; telecommunications B; theater arts/drama B; transportation technologies B; urban studies B; vocational education B. Majors with highest enrollment: business administration/commerce/management, engineering (general), nursing.

LD Program Information

Name of Program Disabled Student Services.

Availability of Services Services provided to freshmen, sophomores, juniors, seniors. Program currently serves 50 to 100 LD students.

Staff 1 part-time staff member (director). Services provided by tutors, readers, notetakers.

Admissions LD applicants evaluated on the basis of high school transcript and grade point average, standard or untimed SAT or ACT, personal interview. Students should apply through EOP office. LD students may begin taking classes in fall, winter, spring, or summer. Application should be submitted 6 months in advance of initial anticipated enrollment.

Housing College housing (including coed) available. LD students housed with other LD students and non-LD students. LD students not required to live on campus.

Diagnostic Testing Available in reading, math, spelling.

Tutoring Offered one-to-one by peer tutors. Available in all subjects. LD students may receive tutoring in 1 course per term.

Academic Advisement Help with program planning provided by academic advisers. Most LD students take 12 to 16 units each quarter; 12 units required to maintain full-time status.

Auxiliary Aids and Services Aids include taped textbooks, tape recorders, calculators, typewriters, word processors. Services include alternative exam arrangements, notetakers, readers.

Counseling Services Individual counseling available.

Contact Mr. George Umezawa, Director, Disabled Student Services, California State University, Los Angeles, 5151 State University Drive, Los Angeles, CA 90032, 213-224-3382.

CALIFORNIA STATE UNIVERSITY, NORTHRIDGE

Northridge, California

Year Program Began	1979	Special Courses	
Special Fee	None	Taped Textbooks	✓
Special Orientation		Alternative Exam Arrangements	✓
Diagnostic Testing	✓	Notetakers	✓
Subject-Area Tutoring	✓	Staff	*Not reported*
Basic Skills Remediation	✓	Number of Students Served	56

General Information State-supported comprehensive coed institution. Part of California State University System. Founded 1958. Awards B, M. Institutionally accredited by regional association; programs accredited by AACSB (business), ABET (engineering and technology), NASM (music). Metropolitan setting; 350-acre campus. Total enrollment: 28,068. Faculty: 1,554 (956 full-time, 598 part-time); 78% have doctoral degrees; graduate assistants teach a few undergraduate courses. Calendar: semesters. Grading system: letters or numbers. Library holdings: 600,000 bound volumes, 1.5 million titles on microform, 4,500 periodical subscriptions, 16,000 records/tapes.

Undergraduate Profile Fall 1984: 23,106 undergraduates (3,021 freshmen) from 52 states and territories and 58 foreign countries; 32% part-time; 98% state residents; 65% transfers; 26% financial aid recipients; 53% women; 6% blacks; 1% Native Americans; 8% Hispanics; 9% Asian Americans; 2% foreign nationals; 650 legally handicapped students.

Expenses (1984–85) State resident tuition: $0 full-time, $450 per year part-time. Nonresident tuition: $3510 full-time, $117 per unit part-time. State residents taking 6 or more units are charged the full-time rate for tuition. Mandatory fees: $700. College room and board: $3920.

Financial Aid Fall 1984 full-time freshmen: the average aided freshman received an aid package meeting 40% of need. College-administered aid for all 1984–85 undergraduates: 2,150 need-based scholarships (average $1747); 77 non-need scholarships (average $200); short-term loans (average $150); low-interest long-term loans from external sources (average $2500); SEOG; College Work-Study; 644 part-time jobs. Supporting data: state form, AFSA/SAR required; IRS required for some; FAF acceptable. Priority application deadline: 3/1.

Athletics Member NCAA (Division II). Intercollegiate sports: baseball/softball M(II,s), W(II,s); basketball M(II,s), W(II,s); cross-country running M(II,s), W(II,s); fencing M(II,s), W(II,s); football M(II,s); golf M(II,s); gymnastics W(II,s); swimming and diving M(II,s), W(II,s); tennis M(II,s), W(II,s); track and field M(II,s), W(II,s); volleyball M(II,s), W(II,s). Intramural sports: baseball/softball, basketball, cross-country running, football, golf, ice hockey, rugby, soccer, swimming and diving, tennis, track and field, volleyball.

Majors Accounting B; aerospace engineering B; African studies B; anthropology B; applied art B; applied mathematics B; art education B; art/fine arts B; art history B; bacteriology B; biology/biological sciences B; black/Afro-American studies B; broadcasting B; business administration/commerce/management B; business education B; cartography B; cell biology B; ceramic art and design B; chemical engineering B; chemistry B; child psychology/child development B; civil engineering B; commercial art B; computer engineering B; computer information systems B; computer science B; creative writing B; (pre)dentistry sequence B; dietetics B; earth science B; economics B; electrical engineering B; elementary education B; engineering (general) B; engineering physics B; English B; environmental biology B; environmental engineering B; environmental health sciences B; experimental psychology B; family and consumer studies B; fashion merchandising B; film studies B; finance/banking B; food services management B; French B; geography B; geology B; geophysics B; German B; graphic arts B; health education B; health science B; health services administration B; history B; home economics B; home economics education B; humanities B; industrial design B; industrial engineering B; interior design B; jazz B; journalism B; (pre)law sequence B; liberal arts/general studies B; linguistics B; literature B; marketing/retailing/merchandising B; materials engineering B; mathematics B; mechanical engineering B; medical laboratory technology B; medical technology B; (pre)medicine sequence B; Mexican-American/Chicano studies B; microbiology B; molecular biology B; music B; music education B; nuclear engineering B; nutrition B; occupational safety and health B; operations research B; painting/drawing B; philosophy B; physical education B; physical sciences B; physical therapy B; physics B; piano/organ B; political science/government B; psychology B; radio and television studies B; radiological technology B; real estate B; recreation and leisure services B; recreation therapy B; religious studies B; retail management B; sculpture B; secretarial studies/office management B; social work B; sociology B; Spanish B; speech pathology and audiology B; speech/rhetoric/public address/debate B; statistics B; stringed instruments B; studio art B; systems engineering B; textile arts B; textiles and clothing B; theater arts/drama B; urban studies B; (pre)veterinary medicine sequence B; voice B; wind and percussion instruments B. Majors with highest enrollment: accounting, psychology, engineering (general).

LD Program Information

Name of Program Office of Disabled Student Services.

Availability of Services Began offering services in 1979. Services provided to freshmen, sophomores, juniors, seniors. Program currently serves 56 LD students.

Staff Includes coordinator. Services provided by remediation specialists, tutors, counselors, diagnostic specialist.

Admissions LD applicants evaluated on the basis of high school transcript and grade point average, standard or untimed SAT or ACT, personal interview, autobiographical statement, letters of recommendation, psychoeducational report. LD students may begin taking classes in fall or spring. Application should be submitted 6 months in advance of initial anticipated enrollment.

Housing College housing (including coed) available. LD students housed with non-LD students only. LD students not required to live on campus.

Diagnostic Testing Available in intelligence, reading, math, spelling, spoken language, written language, motor abilities, perceptual skills, work and study habits, personality, social skills, speech.

Tutoring Offered one-to-one and in small groups by peer tutors. Available in all subjects. LD students may receive tutoring in all courses each term.

Basic Skills Remediation Offered one-to-one and in small groups by regular teachers, teacher trainees. Available in reading, math, spelling, handwriting, spoken language, written language, learning strategies, motor abilities, perceptual skills, work and study habits, social skills, speech.

Academic Advisement Help with program planning provided by academic advisers. LD students may take up to 18 units each semester; most take 10 to 12 units; 12 units required to maintain full-time status.

Auxiliary Aids and Services Aids include taped textbooks, tape recorders, calculators, typewriters. Services include alternative exam arrangements, notetakers, readers.

Counseling Services Individual counseling, small-group counseling, rap sessions available.

Contact Dr. Harry J. Murphy, Coordinator, Office of Disabled Student Services, California State University, Northridge, 18111 Nordhoff Street, Northridge, CA 91330, 818-885-2578.

CALIFORNIA STATE UNIVERSITY, SACRAMENTO

Sacramento, California

Year Program Began	1980	Special Courses	✓
Special Fee	None	Taped Textbooks	✓
Special Orientation		Alternative Exam Arrangements	✓
Diagnostic Testing	✓	Notetakers	✓
Subject-Area Tutoring	✓	Staff	2 part-time
Basic Skills Remediation	✓	Number of Students Served	50

General Information State-supported comprehensive coed institution. Part of California State University System. Founded 1947. Awards B, M. Institutionally accredited by regional association; programs accredited by NASAD (art and design), AACSB (business), ABET (engineering and technology), NASM (music), NLN (nursing), NCATE (teacher education). Metropolitan setting; 288-acre barrier-free campus. Total enrollment: 22,483. Faculty: 1,163 (850 full-time, 313 part-time); 70% have doctoral degrees; graduate assistants teach no undergraduate courses. Calendar: semesters. Grading system: letters or numbers. Library holdings: 780,000 bound volumes, 872,005 titles on microform, 51,000 periodical subscriptions, 3,868 records/tapes.

Undergraduate Profile Fall 1984: 18,197 undergraduates (1,380 freshmen); 23% part-time; 95% state residents; 18% transfers; 40% financial aid recipients; 52% women; 6% blacks; 1% Native Americans; 7% Hispanics; 8% Asian Americans; 2% foreign nationals; 60% of undergraduates over 25 years of age; 400 legally handicapped students.

Expenses (1985–86) State resident tuition: $0 full-time. Nonresident tuition: $4431 full-time. Part-time tuition and fees per semester (1 to 11 units) range from $205.50 to $325.50 for state residents,$331.50 to $1711.50 for nonresidents. Mandatory fees: $651. College room and board: $2600.

Financial Aid Fall 1984 full-time freshmen: 79% applied for aid, 86% of those were judged to have need, 100% of those were aided; the average aided freshman received an aid package meeting 80% of need. College-administered aid for all 1984–85 undergraduates: 1,200 need-based scholarships (average $300); 10 non-need scholarships (average $500); short-term loans; low-interest long-term loans from external sources; SEOG; College Work-Study; part-time jobs. Supporting data: IRS, state form, AFSA/SAR required; FAF required for some; FFS acceptable. Priority application deadline: 3/1.

Athletics Member NCAA (Division II). Intercollegiate sports: baseball/softball M(II), W(II); basketball M(II), W(II); cross-country running M(II), W(II); football M(II); golf M(II), W(II); gymnastics W(II); soccer M(II); swimming and diving M(II), W(II); track and field M(II), W(II); volleyball W(II). Intramural sports: baseball/softball, basketball, bowling, crew, cross-country running, fencing, football, golf, gymnastics, lacrosse, racquetball, rugby, soccer, swimming and diving, track and field, volleyball.

Majors Accounting B; anthropology B; art/fine arts B; Asian/Oriental studies B; biology/biological sciences B; biomedical engineering B; black/Afro-American studies B; broadcasting B; business administration/commerce/management B; business education B; chemistry B; civil engineering B; civil engineering technology B; communication B; computer engineering B; computer science B; construction technologies B; criminal justice B; early childhood education B; ecology/environmental studies B; economics B; electrical engineering B; electronics engineering B; engineering (general) B; engineering and applied sciences B; engineering technology B; English B; ethnic studies B; finance/banking B; forensic sciences B; French B; geography B; geology B; German B; health science B; history B; home economics B; humanities B; human resources B; information science B; insurance B; international studies B; journalism B; laboratory technologies B; (pre) law sequence B; liberal arts/general studies B; marine sciences B; marketing/retailing/merchandising B; mathematics B; mechanical engineering B; mechanical engineering technology B; medical laboratory technology B; Mexican-American/Chicano studies B; music B; Native American studies B; nursing B; parks management B; philosophy B; physical education B; physical sciences B; physics B; piano/organ B; political science/government B; psychology B; public administration B; real estate B; recreation and leisure services B; secretarial studies/office management B; social science B; social work B; sociology B; Spanish B; speech pathology and audiology B; statistics B; theater arts/drama B; (pre)veterinary medicine sequence B; voice B; wildlife biology B; women's studies B.

LD Program Information

Name of Program Learning Disabilities Program.

Availability of Services Began offering services in 1980. Services provided to freshmen, sophomores, juniors, seniors. Program currently serves 50 LD students.

Staff 2 part-time staff members, including coordinator. Services provided by remediation specialist, tutors, counselor, diagnostic specialist.

Admissions LD applicants evaluated on the basis of high school transcript and grade point average, standard or untimed SAT or ACT, personal interview, letters of recommendation, psychoeducational report. LD students may begin taking classes in fall or spring. Application should be submitted 1 month in advance of initial anticipated enrollment.

Housing College housing (including coed) available. LD students housed randomly. LD students not required to live on campus.

Diagnostic Testing Available in reading, math, spelling, handwriting, written language, motor abilities, perceptual skills, work and study habits. Hearing and auditory tests available through Speech and Hearing Clinic.

Tutoring Offered one-to-one by peer tutors. Available in all subjects. LD students may receive tutoring in 3 courses per term.

Basic Skills Remediation Offered one-to-one and in small groups by peer teachers. Available in reading, math, spelling, handwriting, written language, learning strategies, perceptual skills, work and study habits.

Academic Advisement Help with program planning provided by LD staff members, academic advisers. LD students may take up to 12 units, plus as many more as individual can handle, each semester; most take 12 units; 12 units required to maintain full-time status.

Special Courses Offered in college survival skills, reading, vocabulary development, composition, math, study skills, career planning. Most offered for credit; some enter into overall grade point average.

Auxiliary Aids and Services Aids include taped textbooks, tape recorders, calculators, word processors. Services include alternative exam arrangements, notetakers, advocacy, readers for tests.

Counseling Services Individual counseling, small-group counseling, rap sessions, career counseling available.

Contact Ms. Susan Eiland, Learning Disabilities Specialist, California State University, Sacramento, 6000 J Street, Sacramento, CA 95819, 916-454-6740.

CALIFORNIA UNIVERSITY OF PENNSYLVANIA

California, Pennsylvania

Year Program Began	1980	Special Courses	✓
Special Fee	None	Taped Textbooks	✓
Special Orientation	✓	Alternative Exam Arrangements	✓
Diagnostic Testing	✓	Notetakers	✓
Subject-Area Tutoring	✓	Staff	6 part-time
Basic Skills Remediation	✓	Number of Students Served	7

General Information State-supported comprehensive coed institution. Part of State System of Higher Education. Founded 1852. Awards A (college transfer and terminal), B, M. Institutionally accredited by regional association; programs accredited by NCATE (teacher education). Small-town setting, with easy access to Pittsburgh; 148-acre campus. Total enrollment: 4,882. Faculty: 305 (285 full-time, 20 part-time); 52% have doctoral degrees; graduate assistants teach no undergraduate courses. Calendar: semesters. Grading system: letters or numbers. Library holdings: 231,025 bound volumes, 910,343 titles on microform, 1,200 periodical subscriptions, 25,000 records/tapes.

Undergraduate Profile Fall 1984: 4,542 undergraduates (1,302 freshmen) from 20 states and territories and 21 foreign countries; 20% part-time; 94% state residents; 20% transfers; 81% financial aid recipients; 47% women; 8% blacks; 1% Native Americans; 1% Hispanics; 1% Asian Americans; 3% foreign nationals; 8% of undergraduates over 25 years of age; 27 legally handicapped students.

Expenses (1984–85) State resident tuition: $1570 full-time, $66 per credit part-time. Nonresident tuition: $2748 full-time, $115 per credit part-time. Mandatory fees: $244. College room and board: $1800. College room only: $1000.

Financial Aid Fall 1984 full-time freshmen: 83% applied for aid, 87% of those were judged to have need, 96% of those were aided; the average aided freshman received an aid package worth $3290 (38% scholarships/grants, 62% self-help) meeting 90% of need. College-administered aid for all 1984–85 undergraduates: need-based scholarships; 27 non-need scholarships (average $563); short-term loans; low-interest long-term loans from external sources; SEOG; College Work-Study; part-time jobs. Supporting data: state form, institutional form, AFSA/SAR required. Priority application deadline: 4/15.

Athletics Member NCAA (Division II), NAIA. Intercollegiate sports: baseball/softball M(II), W(II); basketball M(II,s), W(II,s); cross-country running M(II), W(III); fencing M(II), W(II); football M(II,s); rugby M, W; soccer M(II,s); tennis W(II); track and field M(II), W(II); volleyball M(II), W(II,s); wrestling M(II,s). Intramural sports: baseball/softball, basketball, cross-country running, fencing, football, martial arts, rugby, skiing (cross-country), skiing (downhill), soccer, swimming and diving, tennis, track and field, volleyball, wrestling.

Majors Accounting A, B; adult and continuing education B; American studies B; anesthesiology B; anthropology B; art/fine arts B; art history B; arts administration B; biology/biological sciences B; broadcasting B; business administration/commerce/management A, B; business economics B; chemistry B; child care/child and family studies A; city, community, and regional planning B; commercial art B; communication B; communication equipment technology B; community services A, B; computer programming A; computer science A, B; conservation B; creative writing B; (pre)dentistry sequence B; drafting and design A; early childhood education A, B; earth science B; East European and Soviet studies B; ecology/environmental studies B; economics B; education B; electrical and electronics technologies B; elementary education B; emergency medical technology A; engineering technology A, B; English B; environmental biology B; environmental health sciences B; environmental sciences B; French B; geography B; geology B; German B; gerontology A, B; graphic arts B; history B; history of philosophy B; humanities B; human resources B; industrial administration B; industrial arts B; industrial engineering technology B; instrumentation technology B; interdisciplinary studies B; journalism B; (pre)law sequence B; liberal arts/general studies B; literature B; manufacturing technology B; marketing/retailing/merchandising B; mathematics B; medical laboratory technology B; medical technology B; (pre)medicine sequence B; military science B; modern languages B; natural resource management B; natural sciences B; nursing B; parks management B; petroleum technology B; philosophy B; physical sciences B; physics B; political science/government B; printing technologies A, B; psychology B; public affairs and policy studies B; radio and television studies B; recreation therapy B; robotics A; Russian and Slavic studies B; science B; science education B; secondary education B; social science B; social work B; sociology B; soil conservation B; Spanish B; special education B; speech pathology and audiology B; speech/rhetoric/public address/debate B; sports medicine B; technical writing B; theater arts/drama B; urban studies B; (pre)veterinary medicine sequence B; water resources B. Majors with highest enrollment: business administration/commerce/management, computer science, industrial arts.

LD Program Information

Name of Program Not specified.

Availability of Services Began offering services in 1980. Services provided to freshmen, sophomores, juniors, seniors. Program currently serves 7 LD students: 3 freshmen, 2 sophomores, 1 junior, 1 senior.

Staff 6 part-time staff members, including coordinator.

Admissions LD applicants evaluated on the basis of high school transcript and grade point average, untimed SAT, personal interview, autobiographical statement, letters of recommendation, psychoeducational report. LD students may begin taking classes in fall, winter, or summer. Application should be submitted at least 4 months in advance of initial anticipated enrollment.

Orientation Required orientation held before registration.

Housing College housing available. LD students housed randomly. LD students not required to live on campus.

Diagnostic Testing Available in reading, math, spelling, written language, various other areas as appropriate.

Tutoring Offered one-to-one and in small groups by professional teachers, peer tutors. Available in all subjects. LD students may receive tutoring in all courses each term.

Basic Skills Remediation Offered one-to-one and in small groups by teacher trainees. Available in reading, math, spelling, handwriting, written language, learning strategies, work and study habits.

Academic Advisement Help with program planning provided by LD staff member, academic advisers. LD students may take up to 15 credits each semester; 12 credits required to maintain full-time status.

Special Courses Offered in reading, vocabulary development, communication skills, composition, math, study skills. Most offered for credit; most enter into overall grade point average.

Auxiliary Aids and Services Aids include taped textbooks. Services include alternative exam arrangements, notetakers, advocacy.

Counseling Services Individual counseling, small-group counseling, career counseling available.

Contact Mr. Arthur Bakewell, Handicapped Student Coordinator, California University of Pennsylvania, California, PA 15419, 412-938-4076.

CALVIN COLLEGE
Grand Rapids, Michigan

Year Program Began	1983
Special Fee	None
Special Orientation	
Diagnostic Testing	✓
Subject-Area Tutoring	✓
Basic Skills Remediation	
Special Courses	✓
Taped Textbooks	
Alternative Exam Arrangements	✓
Notetakers	
Staff	2 part-time
Number of Students Served	8

General Information Comprehensive coed institution, affiliated with Christian Reformed Church. Founded 1876. Awards B, M. Institutionally accredited by regional association; programs accredited by NCATE (teacher education). City setting; 200-acre barrier-free campus. Total enrollment: 3,971. Faculty: 255 (215 full-time, 40 part-time); 70% have doctoral degrees; graduate assistants teach no undergraduate courses. Calendar: 4-1-4. Grading system: letters or numbers. Library holdings: 455,000 bound volumes, 30,000 titles on microform, 2,325 periodical subscriptions, 12,100 records/tapes.

Undergraduate Profile Fall 1984: 3,784 undergraduates (963 freshmen) from 42 states and territories and 26 foreign countries; 8% part-time; 57% state residents; 15% transfers; 99% financial aid recipients; 52% women; 1% blacks; 1% Native Americans; 1% Hispanics; 1% Asian Americans; 10% foreign nationals; 3% of undergraduates over 25 years of age; 13 legally handicapped students.

Expenses (1985–86) Comprehensive fee of $7200 includes full-time tuition ($4980) and college room and board ($2220). Part-time tuition: $660 per course. Tuition prepayment plan available.

Financial Aid Fall 1984 full-time freshmen: 73% applied for aid, 89% of those were judged to have need, 100% of those were aided; the average aided freshman received an aid package worth $4166 (61% scholarships/grants, 39% self-help) meeting 89% of need. College-administered aid for all 1984–85 undergraduates: 1,455 need-based scholarships (average $809); 3,761 non-need scholarships (average $567); short-term loans (average $70); low-interest long-term loans from college funds (average $1538), from external sources (average $1690); SEOG; College Work-Study; 500 part-time jobs. Supporting data: FAF required; FFS acceptable. Priority application deadline: 2/15.

Athletics Member NCAA (Division III). Intercollegiate sports: baseball/softball M, W; basketball M, W; cross-country running M, W; field hockey W; golf M; ice hockey M; soccer M; swimming and diving M, W; tennis M, W; track and field M, W; volleyball M, W. Intramural sports: baseball/softball, basketball, field hockey, football, golf, ice hockey, racquetball, soccer, swimming and diving, tennis, track and field, volleyball.

Majors Accounting B; art education B; art/fine arts B; biology/biological sciences B; business administration/commerce/management B; business economics B; chemistry B; civil engineering B; classics B; communication B; computer science B; criminal justice B; (pre)dentistry sequence B; ecology/environmental studies B; economics B; education B; electrical engineering B; elementary education B; engineering (general) B; English B; environmental sciences B; European studies B; French B; geology B; German B; Germanic languages and literature B; Greek B; history B; humanities B; Latin B; (pre)law sequence B; liberal arts/general studies B; literature B; mathematics B; mechanical engineering B; medical technology B; (pre) medicine sequence B; music B; music education B; nursing B; philosophy B; physical education B; physical sciences B; physics B; political science/government B; psychology B; recreation and leisure services B; religious education B; religious studies B; sacred music B; science B; science education B; secondary education B; social science B; social work B; sociology B; Spanish B; special education B; speech/rhetoric/public address/debate B; telecommunications B; theology B; (pre)veterinary medicine sequence B; voice B. Majors with highest enrollment: economics, education, engineering (general).

LD Program Information

Name of Program Academic Support Program.

Availability of Services Began offering services in 1983. Services provided to freshmen, sophomores. Program currently serves 8 LD students: 6 freshmen, 2 sophomores.

Staff 2 part-time staff members, including director. Services provided by tutors, LD specialist.

Admissions LD applicants evaluated on the basis of high school transcript and grade point average, standard or untimed SAT or ACT, personal interview, letters of recommendation. LD students may begin taking classes in fall only. Application should be submitted 6 months in advance of initial anticipated enrollment.

Housing College housing available. LD students housed randomly. LD freshmen and sophomores required to live on campus except if living with relatives or by special permission.

Diagnostic Testing Available in intelligence, reading, math, written language, perceptual skills.

Tutoring Offered one-to-one by peer tutors. Available in all subjects. LD students may receive tutoring in all courses each term.

Academic Advisement Help with program planning provided by LD staff members, academic advisers. LD students may take up to 4 courses each semester; 3 courses required to maintain full-time status.

Special Courses Offered in college survival skills, composition, math, study skills. None offered for credit; none enter into overall grade point average.

Auxiliary Aids and Services Aids include word processors. Services include alternative exam arrangements.

Counseling Services Individual counseling, career counseling available.

Contact Ms. Evelyn Diephouse, Director, Academic Support Program, Calvin College, 3201 Burton, SE, Grand Rapids, MI 49506, 616-957-6122.

CASTLETON STATE COLLEGE
Castleton, Vermont

Year Program Began	1980	Special Courses	
Special Fee	None	Taped Textbooks	✓
Special Orientation	✓	Alternative Exam Arrangements	✓
Diagnostic Testing	✓	Notetakers	✓
Subject-Area Tutoring	✓	Staff	2 part-time
Basic Skills Remediation	✓	Number of Students Served	11

General Information State-supported comprehensive coed institution. Part of Vermont State Colleges System. Founded 1787. Awards A (college transfer and terminal), B, M. Institutionally accredited by regional association; programs accredited by NLN (nursing). Rural setting; 130-acre campus. Total enrollment: 2,200. Faculty: 114 (78 full-time, 36 part-time); 61% have doctoral degrees; graduate assistants teach no undergraduate courses. Calendar: semesters. Grading system: letters or numbers. Library holdings: 100,000 bound volumes, 33,500 titles on microform, 222 periodical subscriptions, 15,000 records/tapes.

Undergraduate Profile Fall 1984: 1,770 undergraduates (348 freshmen) from 28 states and territories and 3 foreign countries; 30% part-time; 60% state residents; 26% transfers; 75% financial aid recipients; 55% women; 1% blacks; 1% Native Americans; 1% Hispanics; 1% foreign nationals; 20% of undergraduates over 25 years of age; 4 legally handicapped students.

Expenses (1985–86) State resident tuition: $1802 full-time, $75 per credit part-time. Nonresident tuition: $4150 full-time, $172 per credit part-time. Mandatory fees: $377. College room and board: $3042.

Financial Aid Fall 1984 full-time freshmen: 80% applied for aid, 63% of those were judged to have need, 100% of those were aided; the average aided freshman received an aid package worth $3675 (38% scholarships/grants, 62% self-help) meeting 80% of need. College-administered aid for all 1984–85 undergraduates: need-based scholarships (average $350); 36 non-need scholarships (average $500); SEOG; College Work-Study; part-time jobs. Supporting data: FFS required; FAF acceptable. Priority application deadline: 3/15.

Athletics Member NCAA (Division III), NAIA. Intercollegiate sports: baseball/softball M(III), W(III); basketball M(III), W(III); cross-country running M(III), W(III); field hockey W(III); lacrosse M(III), W(III); skiing (cross-country) M(III), W(III); skiing (downhill) M(III), W(III); soccer M(III), W(III); tennis M(III), W(III). Intramural sports: baseball/softball, basketball, equestrian sports, football, golf, ice hockey, martial arts, racquetball, soccer, tennis, volleyball, weight lifting.

Majors Accounting B; applied art B; art education B; art/fine arts B; behavioral sciences B; biology/biological sciences B; business administration/commerce/management B; business education B; communication A, B; computer information systems B; computer programming A; computer science B; criminal justice A, B; early childhood education B; education B; elementary education B; English B; French B; geology B; graphic arts B; history B; journalism B; law enforcement/police sciences A, B; (pre)law sequence B; legal secretarial studies A; liberal arts/general studies A; literature B; marketing/retailing/merchandising B; mathematics B; medical secretarial studies A; (pre)medicine sequence B; modern languages B; music B; music education B; natural sciences B; nursing A, B; physical education B; political science/government B; psychology B; reading education B; science B; science education B; secondary education B; secretarial studies/office management A, B; social science B; social work B; sociology B; Spanish B; special education B; sports medicine B; theater arts/drama B; (pre)veterinary medicine sequence B. Majors with highest enrollment: business administration/commerce/management, education, nursing.

LD Program Information

Name of Program Success Through Educational Program (STEP).

Availability of Services Began offering services in 1980. Services provided to freshmen, sophomores, juniors, seniors. Program currently serves 11 LD students: 4 freshmen, 4 sophomores, 3 juniors.

Staff 2 part-time staff members, including coordinator. Services provided by tutors, counselor.

Admissions LD applicants evaluated on the basis of high school transcript and grade point average, standard or untimed SAT or ACT, personal interview, letters of recommendation, psychoeducational report. LD students may begin taking classes in fall or spring.

Orientation Optional orientation offered before registration.

Housing College housing (including coed) available. LD students housed with non-LD students only. LD freshmen required to live on campus except if living with relatives or by special permission.

Diagnostic Testing Available in reading, math, written language.

Tutoring Offered one-to-one and in small groups by peer tutors. Available in all subjects. LD students may receive tutoring in all courses each term.

Basic Skills Remediation Offered in small groups by regular teachers. Available in reading, math, written language, learning strategies, work and study habits.

Academic Advisement Help with program planning provided by LD staff members, academic advisers. LD students may take up to 18 credits each semester; most take 12 to 15 credits; 12 credits required to maintain full-time status.

Auxiliary Aids and Services Aids include taped textbooks, tape recorders, calculators, typewriters, word processors. Services include alternative exam arrangements, notetakers, advocacy.

Counseling Services Individual counseling, small-group counseling, rap sessions, career counseling available.

Contact Mr. Robert Rummel, Coordinator, STEP Program, Castleton State College, Castleton, VT 05735, 802-468-5611.

CATHEDRAL COLLEGE OF THE IMMACULATE CONCEPTION
Douglaston, New York

Year Program Began	1983	Special Courses	✓
Special Fee	None	Taped Textbooks	
Special Orientation		Alternative Exam Arrangements	✓
Diagnostic Testing	✓	Notetakers	
Subject-Area Tutoring	✓	Staff	4 part-time
Basic Skills Remediation	✓	Number of Students Served	2

General Information Roman Catholic 4-year men's college. Founded 1914. Awards B. Institutionally accredited by regional association. Metropolitan setting; 27-acre barrier-free campus. Total enrollment: 91. Faculty: 29 (16 full-time, 13 part-time); 56% have doctoral degrees. Calendar: semesters. Grading system: letters or numbers. Library holdings: 75,000 bound volumes, 96 titles on microform, 375 periodical subscriptions, 1,170 records/tapes.

Undergraduate Profile Fall 1984: 91 undergraduates (22 freshmen) from 3 states and territories and 2 foreign countries; 0% part-time; 97% state residents; 2% transfers; 75% financial aid recipients; 0% women; 9% blacks; 0% Native Americans; 11% Hispanics; 2% Asian Americans; 2% foreign nationals; 2% of undergraduates over 25 years of age; no legally handicapped students.

Expenses (1985–86) Comprehensive fee of $5800 includes full-time tuition ($3600), mandatory fees ($200), and college room and board ($2000). College room only: $1000.

Financial Aid Fall 1984 full-time freshmen: 95% applied for aid, 85% of those were judged to have need, 100% of those were aided; the average aided freshman received an aid package worth $5433 (90% scholarships/grants, 10% self-help) meeting 100% of need. College-administered aid for all 1984–85 undergraduates: need-based scholarships; non-need scholarships; low-interest long-term loans from external sources (average $2122); SEOG; 50 part-time jobs. Supporting data: FAF required; FFS, AFSA/SAR acceptable. Priority application deadline: 8/15.

Athletics Member NAIA. Intercollegiate sport: basketball. Intramural sports: baseball/softball, basketball, football, skiing (cross-country), skiing (downhill), tennis, volleyball.

Majors English B; history B; philosophy B; psychology B. Majors with highest enrollment: psychology, English.

LD Program Information

Name of Program Not specified.

Availability of Services Began offering services in 1983. Services provided to freshmen, sophomores. Program currently serves 2 LD students (both sophomores).

Staff 4 part-time staff members, including director. Services provided by counselors, director of library.

Admissions LD applicants evaluated on the basis of high school transcript and grade point average, personal interview, letters of recommendation, psychoeducational report. LD students may begin taking classes in fall or spring. Application should be submitted 2 months in advance of initial anticipated enrollment.

Housing College housing available. LD students housed with non-LD students only. LD freshmen, sophomores, juniors, and seniors required to live on campus.

Diagnostic Testing Available in intelligence, reading, spelling, handwriting, spoken language, written language, motor abilities, perceptual skills, work and study habits, personality, social skills, speech.

Tutoring Offered one-to-one and in small groups by professional teachers, peer tutors. Available in all subjects. LD students may receive tutoring in all courses each term.

Basic Skills Remediation Offered one-to-one by LD teachers. Available in reading, spelling, handwriting, written language, work and study habits.

Academic Advisement Help with program planning provided by LD staff members, academic advisers. LD students may take up to 18 credits each semester; most take 12 to 15 credits; 12 credits required to maintain full-time status.

Special Courses Offered in college survival skills, reading, vocabulary development, communication skills, composition, typing, personal psychology, study skills, career planning. Some offered for credit; some enter into overall grade point average.

Auxiliary Aids and Services Aids include tape recorders, word processors. Services include alternative exam arrangements.

Counseling Services Individual counseling, career counseling available.

Contact Rev. Martin T. Geraghty, Academic Dean, Cathedral College of the Immaculate Conception, Douglaston, NY 11362, 718-631-4600.

CATHOLIC UNIVERSITY OF PUERTO RICO

Ponce, Puerto Rico

Year Program Began	1973	Special Courses	✓
Special Fee	None	Taped Textbooks	
Special Orientation	✓	Alternative Exam Arrangements	✓
Diagnostic Testing	✓	Notetakers	✓
Subject-Area Tutoring	✓	Staff	6 full-time, 22 part-time
Basic Skills Remediation	✓	Number of Students Served	41

General Information Roman Catholic comprehensive coed institution. Founded 1948. Awards A (college transfer and terminal), B, M. Institutionally accredited by regional association; programs registered by New York State Board of Regents; programs accredited by NLN (nursing). City setting, with easy access to San Juan; 120-acre barrier-free campus. Total enrollment: 9,930. Faculty: 403 (295 full-time, 108 part-time); 13% have doctoral degrees; graduate assistants teach no undergraduate courses. Calendar: semesters. Grading system: letters or numbers. Library holdings: 315,395 bound volumes, 65,920 titles on microform, 1,836 periodical subscriptions, 7,950 records/tapes.

Undergraduate Profile Fall 1984: 9,249 undergraduates (3,377 freshmen); 23% part-time; 99% commonwealth residents; 9% transfers; 91% financial aid recipients; 65% women; 99% Hispanics; 1% foreign nationals.

Expenses (1985–86) Comprehensive fee of $4108 includes full-time tuition ($1760), mandatory fees ($148), and college room and board ($2200). College room only: $650. Part-time tuition: $55 per credit.

Financial Aid Fall 1984 full-time freshmen: 84% applied for aid, 100% of those were judged to have need, 100% of those were aided; the average aided freshman received an aid package worth $2622 (80% scholarships/grants, 20% self-help) meeting 50% of need. College-administered aid for all 1984–85 undergraduates: need-based scholarships; non-need scholarships; short-term loans (average $500); low-interest long-term loans from external sources (average $1000); SEOG; College Work-Study; 700 part-time jobs. Supporting data: institutional form, AFSA/SAR required; IRS required for some. Application deadline: 4/30.

Athletics Intercollegiate sports: baseball/softball M, W; basketball M; cross-country running M, W; martial arts M; soccer M; swimming and diving M; tennis M, W; track and field M(s), W(s); volleyball M, W; water polo M. Intramural sports: archery, baseball/softball, basketball, martial arts, soccer, swimming and diving, tennis, track and field, volleyball.

Majors Accounting B; art/fine arts A, B; biology/biological sciences B; business administration/commerce/management B; chemistry B; computer programming A, B; criminal justice B; early childhood education B; education A, B; elementary education B; English B; finance/banking B; French B; gerontology A; history B; home economics B; human development B; marketing/retailing/merchandising B; mathematics B; medical technology B; nursing B; physical education B; radio and television studies A; real estate A; recreation and leisure services A; secretarial studies/office management A; social science B; social work B; Spanish B; special education B.

LD Program Information

Name of Program Special Services Program.

Availability of Services Began offering services in 1973. Services provided to freshmen. Program currently serves 41 LD students (all freshmen).

Staff 6 full-time, 22 part-time staff members, including director. Services provided by remediation specialists, tutors, counselors, diagnostic specialists.

Admissions LD applicants evaluated on the basis of high school transcript and grade point average, personal interview, autobiographical statement, psychoeducational report. LD students may begin taking classes in fall only. Application should be submitted 1 to 2 months in advance of initial anticipated enrollment.

Orientation Orientation offered after classes begin.

Housing College housing available. LD students housed randomly. LD students not required to live on campus.

Diagnostic Testing Available in intelligence, reading, math, handwriting, spoken language, written language, motor abilities, perceptual skills, work and study habits, personality, social skills, psychoneurology, speech.

Tutoring Offered one-to-one and in small groups by peer tutors. Available in all subjects. LD students may receive tutoring in all courses each term.

Basic Skills Remediation Offered one-to-one and in small groups by regular teachers, study skills professor. Available in reading, math, spelling, spoken language, written language, learning strategies, perceptual skills, work and study habits, social skills.

Academic Advisement Help with program planning provided by academic advisers. LD students may take up to 12.5 credits each semester; 12.5 credits required to maintain full-time status.

Special Courses Offered in college survival skills, communication skills, composition, math, personal psychology, study skills, career planning. All offered for credit; all enter into overall grade point average.

Auxiliary Aids and Services Services include alternative exam arrangements, notetakers, advocacy, readers.

Counseling Services Individual counseling, small-group counseling, career counseling available.

Contact Miss Ana María Torres, Director, Special Services Program, Catholic University of Puerto Rico, Box 599 Station 6, Ponce, PR 00732, 809-844-4150 Ext. 140.

CENTER FOR CREATIVE STUDIES–COLLEGE OF ART AND DESIGN
Detroit, Michigan

Year Program Began	*Not reported*	Special Courses	✓
Special Fee	None	Taped Textbooks	
Special Orientation	✓	Alternative Exam Arrangements	✓
Diagnostic Testing	✓	Notetakers	
Subject-Area Tutoring	✓	Staff	1 full-time, 2 part-time
Basic Skills Remediation	✓	Number of Students Served	39

General Information Independent 4-year specialized coed college. Founded 1926. Awards B. Institutionally accredited by regional association; programs accredited by NASAD (art and design). Metropolitan setting; 8-acre barrier-free campus. Total enrollment: 954. Faculty: 182 (48 full-time, 134 part-time). Calendar: semesters. Grading system: letters or numbers. Library holdings: 15,000 bound volumes, 100 periodical subscriptions.

Undergraduate Profile Fall 1984: 954 undergraduates (137 freshmen) from 21 states and territories and 8 foreign countries; 35% part-time; 90% state residents; 50% transfers; 75% financial aid recipients; 50% women; 14% blacks; 1% Native Americans; 1% Hispanics; 1% Asian Americans; 5% foreign nationals; 6 legally handicapped students.

Expenses (1985–86) Tuition: $5460 full-time, $195 per semester hour part-time. Mandatory fees: $36. College room only: $1725 (minimum).

Financial Aid Fall 1984 full-time freshmen: 72% applied for aid, 85% of those were judged to have need, 100% of those were aided; the average aided freshman received an aid package worth $2105 (70% scholarships/grants, 30% self-help) meeting 50% of need. College-administered aid for all 1984–85 undergraduates: 250 need-based scholarships (average $1000); 100 non-need scholarships (average $500); short-term loans (average $50); low-interest long-term loans from external sources (average $2000); SEOG; College Work-Study; 10 part-time jobs. Supporting data: IRS, institutional form, Financial Aid Transcript (for transfers) required; state form, AFSA/SAR required for some; FFS, FAF acceptable. Priority application deadline: 3/1.

Athletics Intramural sports: baseball/softball, volleyball.

Majors Applied art B; art/fine arts B; art therapy B; ceramic art and design B; commercial art B; environmental design B; graphic arts B; illustration B; industrial design B; interior design B; jewelry and metalsmithing B; painting/drawing B; photography B; sculpture B; studio art B; textile arts B.

LD Program Information

Name of Program Reading and Study Skills.

Availability of Services Services provided to freshmen, sophomores, juniors, seniors. Program currently serves 39 LD students: 15 freshmen, 10 sophomores, 8 juniors, 6 seniors.

Staff 1 full-time, 2 part-time staff members, including director. Services provided by remediation specialists, counselors, diagnostic specialists.

Admissions LD applicants evaluated on the basis of high school transcript and grade point average, standard SAT or ACT, personal interview, letters of recommendation. LD students may begin taking classes in fall, winter, or summer. Application should be submitted 2 to 5 months in advance of initial anticipated enrollment.

Orientation Optional orientation offered before registration.

Housing College housing available. LD students housed with other LD students and non-LD students. LD students not required to live on campus.

Diagnostic Testing Available in intelligence, reading, math, spelling, spoken language, written language, work and study habits.

Tutoring Offered one-to-one. Available in all subjects. LD students may receive tutoring in 6 courses per term.

Basic Skills Remediation Offered one-to-one by LD teachers. Available in reading, math, spelling, handwriting, spoken language, written language, learning strategies, motor abilities, perceptual skills, work and study habits, social skills, speech.

Academic Advisement Help with program planning provided by LD staff members, academic advisers. LD students may take up to 15 semester hours each semester; most take 6 semester hours; 5 semester hours required to maintain full-time status.

Special Courses Offered in college survival skills, reading, vocabulary development, communication skills, composition, language development, personal psychology. All offered for credit; all enter into overall grade point average.

Auxiliary Aids and Services Aids include tape recorders. Services include alternative exam arrangements.

Counseling Services Individual counseling, career counseling available.

Contact Ms. Susan Jager, Reading Specialist, Center for Creative Studies–College of Art and Design, 245 East Kirby, Detroit, MI 48202, 313-872-3118.

CENTRAL CONNECTICUT STATE UNIVERSITY

New Britain, Connecticut

Year Program Began	1977	Special Courses	
Special Fee	None	Taped Textbooks	✓
Special Orientation	✓	Alternative Exam Arrangements	✓
Diagnostic Testing	✓	Notetakers	✓
Subject-Area Tutoring	✓	Staff	1 full-time
Basic Skills Remediation	✓	Number of Students Served	85

General Information State-supported comprehensive coed institution. Part of Connecticut State University System. Founded 1849. Awards B, M. Institutionally accredited by regional association; programs accredited by NCATE (teacher education). City setting, with easy access to Hartford; 142-acre campus. Total enrollment: 13,333. Faculty: 641 (392 full-time, 249 part-time); 43% have doctoral degrees; graduate assistants teach a few undergraduate courses. Calendar: semesters. Grading system: letters or numbers. Library holdings: 381,604 bound volumes, 81,046 titles on microform, 1,620 periodical subscriptions, 6,969 records/tapes.

Undergraduate Profile Fall 1984: 10,953 undergraduates (1,179 freshmen) from 19 states and territories and 39 foreign countries; 38% part-time; 96% state residents; 28% transfers; 48% financial aid recipients; 48% women; 3% blacks; 0% Native Americans; 2% Hispanics; 1% Asian Americans; 1% foreign nationals; 30% of undergraduates over 25 years of age; 135 legally handicapped students.

Expenses (1985–86) State resident tuition: $1174 full-time, $60 per credit hour part-time. Nonresident tuition: $2994 full-time, $60 per credit hour part-time. College room and board: $2601. College room only: $1376.

Financial Aid Fall 1984 full-time freshmen: the average aided freshman received an aid package meeting 76% of need. College-administered aid for all 1984–85 undergraduates: need-based scholarships; 50 non-need scholarships (average $1000); low-interest long-term loans from external sources (average $1700); SEOG; College Work-Study; 500 part-time jobs. Supporting data: FAF, IRS, institutional form, AFSA/SAR, Student Emancipation Form required. Priority application deadline: 3/15.

Athletics Member NCAA (Division II). Intercollegiate sports: baseball/softball M(II), W(II); basketball M(II), W(II); cross-country running M(II), W(II); field hockey W(II); football M(II); golf M(II); soccer M(II); swimming and diving M(II), W(II); tennis M(II), W(II); track and field M(II), W(II); volleyball W(II); wrestling M(II). Intramural sports: badminton, baseball/softball, basketball, bowling, football, golf, skiing (cross-country), skiing (downhill), swimming and diving, volleyball, wrestling.

Majors Accounting B; actuarial science B; anthropology B; art education B; biology/biological sciences B; business administration/commerce/management B; business education B; chemistry B; communication B; computer science B; early childhood education B; earth science B; East Asian studies B; ecology/environmental studies B; economics B; education B; elementary education B; engineering technology B; English B; finance/banking B; French B; geography B; German B; history B; industrial arts B; industrial engineering technology B; Italian B; (pre)law sequence B; management information systems B; marketing/retailing/merchandising B; mathematics B; medical technology B; (pre)medicine sequence B; music education B; nursing B; philosophy B; physical education B; physics B; political science/government B; psychology B; public administration B; science B; secondary education B; secretarial studies/office management B; social science B; social work B; sociology B; Spanish B; special education B; statistics B; theater arts/drama B; vocational education B. Majors with highest enrollment: accounting, business administration/commerce/management, marketing/retailing/merchandising.

LD Program Information

Name of Program Office of Special Student Services.

Availability of Services Began offering services in 1977. Services provided to freshmen, sophomores, juniors, seniors. Program currently serves 85 LD students: 30 freshmen, 27 sophomores, 16 juniors, 12 seniors.

Staff 1 full-time staff member (coordinator). Services provided by tutors.

Admissions LD applicants evaluated on the basis of high school transcript and grade point average, untimed SAT, personal interview, autobiographical statement, letters of recommendation, psychoeducational report. LD students may begin taking classes in fall or spring. Application should be submitted 8 months in advance of initial anticipated enrollment.

Orientation Optional orientation offered before registration.

Housing College housing (including coed) available. LD students housed randomly. LD students not required to live on campus.

Diagnostic Testing Available in reading, math, spelling, spoken language, written language.

Tutoring Offered one-to-one by peer tutors. Available in all subjects. LD students may receive tutoring in all courses each term.

Basic Skills Remediation Offered one-to-one by regular teachers. Available in reading, math, spelling, written language.

Academic Advisement Help with program planning provided by LD staff members. Most LD students take 9 credit hours first semester, 12 thereafter; 12 credit hours required to maintain full-time status.

Auxiliary Aids and Services Aids include taped textbooks, tape recorders, calculators, word processors. Services include alternative exam arrangements, notetakers, advocacy, readers.

Counseling Services Individual counseling, career counseling available.

Contact Mr. George R. Tenney, Coordinator of Special Student Services, Central Connecticut State University, Administration Building 101, 1615 Stanley Street, New Britain, CT 06050, 203-827-7475.

CENTRAL UNIVERSITY OF IOWA

Pella, Iowa

Year Program Began	1973
Special Fee	None
Special Orientation	✓
Diagnostic Testing	✓
Subject-Area Tutoring	✓
Basic Skills Remediation	✓
Special Courses	✓
Taped Textbooks	✓
Alternative Exam Arrangements	✓
Notetakers	✓
Staff	3 part-time
Number of Students Served	5

General Information 4-year coed college, affiliated with Reformed Church in America. Founded 1853. Awards B. Institutionally accredited by regional association; programs accredited by NCATE (teacher education); candidate for program accreditation by NASM (music). Small-town setting; 77-acre campus. Total enrollment: 1,548. Faculty: 93 (72 full-time, 21 part-time); 60% have doctoral degrees. Calendar: 3-3. Grading system: letters or numbers. Library holdings: 124,000 bound volumes, 500 titles on microform, 800 periodical subscriptions, 2,624 records/tapes.

Undergraduate Profile Fall 1984: 1,548 undergraduates (424 freshmen) from 41 states and territories and 23 foreign countries; 6% part-time; 68% state residents; 4% transfers; 89% financial aid recipients; 54% women; 4% blacks; 1% Native Americans; 1% Hispanics; 3% foreign nationals; 3 legally handicapped students.

Expenses (1985–86) Comprehensive fee of $8327 includes full-time tuition ($5885), mandatory fees ($77), and college room and board ($2365). College room only: $1050. Part-time tuition: $585 per course.

Financial Aid Fall 1984 full-time freshmen: 93% applied for aid, 85% of those were judged to have need, 100% of those were aided; the average aided freshman received an aid package worth $6975 (64% scholarships/grants, 36% self-help) meeting 100% of need. College-administered aid for all 1984–85 undergraduates: 845 need-based scholarships (average $1000); 245 non-need scholarships (average $1000); low-interest long-term loans from external sources (average $2072); SEOG; College Work-Study; 100 part-time jobs. Supporting data: FAF required; FFS, AFSA/SAR acceptable. Priority application deadline: 4/1.

Athletics Member NCAA (Division III). Intercollegiate sports: baseball/softball M(III), W(III); basketball M(III), W(III); cross-country running M(III), W(III); football M(III); golf M(III), W(III); tennis M(III), W(III); track and field M(III), W(III); volleyball W(III); wrestling M(III). Intramural sports: baseball/softball, basketball, football, racquetball, rugby, soccer, tennis, track and field, volleyball, weight lifting, wrestling.

Majors Accounting B; art/fine arts B; behavioral sciences B; biology/biological sciences B; business administration/commerce/management B; chemistry B; communication B; computer science B; (pre)dentistry sequence B; economics B; education B; elementary education B; English B; French B; geography B; German B; history B; Latin American studies B; (pre)law sequence B; liberal arts/general studies B; linguistics B; mathematics B; (pre)medicine sequence B; music B; music education B; philosophy B; physical education B; physics B; political science/government B; psychology B; recreation and leisure services B; religious studies B; secondary education B; sociology B; Spanish B; special education B; systems science B; theater arts/drama B. Majors with highest enrollment: business administration/commerce/management, education, computer science.

LD Program Information

Name of Program Special Services.

Availability of Services Began offering services in 1973. Services provided to freshmen, sophomores, juniors, seniors. Program currently serves 5 LD students: 2 freshmen, 2 sophomores, 1 junior.

Staff 3 part-time staff members, including assistant director. Services provided by remediation specialists, tutors, counselors, diagnostic specialist.

Admissions LD applicants evaluated on the basis of high school transcript and grade point average, standard or untimed SAT or ACT, letters of recommendation; personal interview, psychoeducational report required for some. LD students may begin taking classes in fall, winter, or spring. Application should be submitted 1 to 2 months in advance of initial anticipated enrollment.

Orientation Optional orientation offered after classes begin.

Housing College housing available. LD students housed randomly. LD freshmen, sophomores, juniors, and seniors required to live on campus.

Diagnostic Testing Available in intelligence, reading, math, spelling, handwriting, written language, motor abilities, perceptual skills, work and study habits, social skills, psychoneurology.

Tutoring Offered one-to-one by peer tutors. Available in all subjects. LD students may receive tutoring in all courses each term.

Basic Skills Remediation Offered one-to-one and in small groups by regular teachers, peer teachers. Available in reading, math, spelling, handwriting, written language, learning strategies, work and study habits.

Academic Advisement Help with program planning provided by academic advisers. LD students may take up to 17 credits each quarter; most take 15 credits; 14 credits required to maintain full-time status.

Special Courses Offered in college survival skills, reading, vocabulary development, composition, math, personal psychology, study skills. Some offered for credit; some enter into overall grade point average.

Auxiliary Aids and Services Aids include taped textbooks, tape recorders, typewriters, word processors. Services include alternative exam arrangements, notetakers.

Counseling Services Individual counseling, small-group counseling, career counseling available.

Contact Ms. Meredyth L. Goodwin, Assistant Director of Special Services, Central University of Iowa, 812 University, Pella, IA 50219, 515-628-5247.

CENTRAL WASHINGTON UNIVERSITY
Ellensburg, Washington

Year Program Began	1980	Special Courses	✓
Special Fee	None	Taped Textbooks	✓
Special Orientation	✓	Alternative Exam Arrangements	✓
Diagnostic Testing	✓	Notetakers	✓
Subject-Area Tutoring	✓	Staff	2 part-time
Basic Skills Remediation	✓	Number of Students Served	98

General Information State-supported comprehensive coed institution. Founded 1891. Awards B, M. Institutionally accredited by regional association; programs accredited by NASM (music), NCATE (teacher education). Small-town setting; 350-acre campus. Total enrollment: 7,377. Faculty: 317 (287 full-time, 30 part-time); 74% have doctoral degrees; graduate assistants teach a few undergraduate courses. Calendar: quarters. Grading system: letters or numbers. Library holdings: 374,043 bound volumes, 110,330 titles on microform, 1,911 periodical subscriptions, 18,164 records/tapes.

Undergraduate Profile Fall 1984: 6,264 undergraduates (946 freshmen); 18% part-time; 96% state residents; 18% transfers; 25% financial aid recipients; 51% women; 2% blacks; 1% Native Americans; 2% Hispanics; 2% Asian Americans; 2% foreign nationals; 26% of undergraduates over 25 years of age; 90 legally handicapped students.

Expenses (1985–86) State resident tuition: $1212 full-time, $40.38 per credit part-time. Nonresident tuition: $4206 full-time, $140.38 per credit part-time. Part-time tuition and fees per quarter (1 to 9 credits) range from $83.50 to $363.50 for state residents, $283.50 to $1263.50 for nonresidents. Mandatory fees: $36. College room and board: $2565.

Financial Aid Fall 1984 full-time freshmen: 60% applied for aid, 60% of those were judged to have need, 100% of those were aided; the average aided freshman received an aid package worth $3805 (36% scholarships/grants, 64% self-help) meeting 85% of need. College-administered aid for all 1984–85 undergraduates: 561 need-based scholarships (average $578); 148 non-need scholarships (average $563); short-term loans (average $505); low-interest long-term loans from external sources (average $1625); SEOG; College Work-Study; 1,400 part-time jobs. Supporting data: FAF, AFSA/SAR required; IRS required for some. Priority application deadline: 4/1.

Athletics Member NCAA (Division II), NAIA. Intercollegiate sports: baseball/softball M(II); basketball M(II,s), W(II,s); cross-country running M(II), W(II); football M(II,s); golf M(II); swimming and diving M(II,s), W(II); tennis M(II), W(II); track and field M(II), W(II); volleyball W(II); wrestling M(II,s). Intramural sports: baseball/softball, basketball, fencing, soccer, swimming and diving, tennis, track and field, volleyball.

Majors Accounting B; anthropology B; art education B; art/fine arts B; aviation technology B; bilingual/bicultural education B; biology/biological sciences B; black/Afro-American studies B; botany/plant sciences B; business administration/commerce/management B; business economics B; business education B; chemistry B; communication B; computer information systems B; computer science B; construction management B; construction technologies B; corrections B; criminal justice B; (pre) dentistry sequence B; early childhood education B; earth science B; economics B; education B; electrical and electronics technologies B; electrical engineering technology B; elementary education B; emergency medical technology B; English B; environmental health sciences B; ethnic studies B; family and consumer studies B; fashion merchandising B; finance/banking B; food sciences B; French B; geography B; geology B; German B; gerontology B; graphic arts B; health education B; health science B; history B; home economics B; home economics education B; industrial administration B; industrial arts B; industrial engineering technology B; interdisciplinary studies B; international business B; journalism B; law enforcement/police sciences B; (pre)law sequence B; liberal arts/general studies B; manufacturing technology B; marketing/retailing/merchandising B; mathematics B; medical records services B; medical technology B; (pre)medicine sequence B; Mexican-American/Chicano studies B; military science B; music B; music education B; Native American studies B; nutrition B; occupational safety and health B; operations research B; paralegal studies B; philosophy B; physical education B; physical fitness/human movement B; physical sciences B; physics B; piano/organ B; political science/government B; psychology B; public relations B; real estate B; recreation and leisure services B; religious studies B; respiratory therapy B; retail management B; science education B; secondary education B; secretarial studies/office management B; social science B; social work B; sociology B; Spanish B; special education B; speech/rhetoric/public address/debate B; stringed instruments B; theater arts/drama B; (pre) veterinary medicine sequence B; vocational education B; voice B; zoology B. Majors with highest enrollment: education, business administration/commerce/management, social science.

LD Program Information

Name of Program Handicapped Student Service.

Availability of Services Began offering services in 1980. Services provided to freshmen, sophomores, juniors, seniors. Program currently serves 98 LD students: 28 freshmen, 27 sophomores, 23 juniors, 20 seniors.

Staff 2 part-time staff members, including coordinator. Services provided by remediation specialists, tutors, readers, transcribers.

Admissions LD applicants evaluated on the basis of high school transcript and grade point average, personal interview, psychoeducational report; standard SAT or ACT recommended. LD students may begin taking classes in fall, winter, spring, or summer. Application should be submitted 1 quarter in advance of initial anticipated enrollment.

Orientation Optional orientation offered before registration.

Housing College housing (including coed) available. LD students housed randomly. LD freshmen and sophomores required to live on campus except if 21 or over.

Diagnostic Testing Available in reading, math, spelling, handwriting, spoken language, written language, perceptual skills, personality, speech.

Tutoring Offered one-to-one and in small groups by peer tutors. Available in some subjects. LD students may receive tutoring in 2 courses per term.

Basic Skills Remediation Offered one-to-one and in small groups by regular teachers. Available in reading, math, spelling, handwriting, spoken language, written language, learning strategies, work and study habits.

Academic Advisement Help with program planning provided by LD staff members, academic advisers. Most LD students take 12 to 17 credits each quarter; 12 credits required to maintain full-time status.

Special Courses Offered in college survival skills, reading, vocabulary development, communication skills, composition, language development, math, typing, personal psychology, study skills, career planning. Some offered for credit; some enter into overall grade point average.

Auxiliary Aids and Services Aids include taped textbooks, typewriters, word processors. Services include alternative exam arrangements, notetakers, advocacy.

Counseling Services Individual counseling, career counseling available.

Contact Ms. Ann Thompson, Coordinator, Handicapped Student Service, Central Washington University, Ellensburg, WA 98926, 509-963-2171.

CENTRAL WESLEYAN COLLEGE

Central, South Carolina

Year Program Began	*Not reported*	Special Courses	✓
Special Fee	None	Taped Textbooks	✓
Special Orientation		Alternative Exam Arrangements	✓
Diagnostic Testing	✓	Notetakers	
Subject-Area Tutoring	✓	Staff	2 part-time
Basic Skills Remediation	✓	Number of Students Served	6

General Information 4-year coed college, affiliated with Wesleyan Church. Founded 1906. Awards B. Institutionally accredited by regional association. Small-town setting; 190-acre barrier-free campus. Total enrollment: 398. Faculty: 44 (26 full-time, 18 part-time); 60% have doctoral degrees. Calendar: semesters. Grading system: letters or numbers. Library holdings: 58,500 bound volumes, 325 titles on microform, 360 periodical subscriptions, 1,500 records/tapes.

Undergraduate Profile Fall 1984: 398 undergraduates (159 freshmen) from 15 states and territories and 7 foreign countries; 15% part-time; 67% state residents; 18% transfers; 85% financial aid recipients; 50% women; 12% blacks; 0% Native Americans; 0% Hispanics; 3% foreign nationals; 3 legally handicapped students.

Expenses (1985–86) Comprehensive fee of $6590 includes full-time tuition ($4400), mandatory fees ($60), and college room and board ($2130). College room only: $670. Part-time tuition: $150 per hour.

Financial Aid Fall 1984 full-time freshmen: 90% applied for aid, 100% of those were judged to have need, 100% of those were aided; the average aided freshman received an aid package worth $2935 (72% scholarships/grants, 28% self-help) meeting 85% of need. College-administered aid for all 1984–85 undergraduates: need-based scholarships; non-need scholarships; low-interest long-term loans from external sources (average $1500); SEOG; College Work-Study; 5 part-time jobs. Supporting data: FAF, IRS, institutional form required; state form, AFSA/SAR required for some. Priority application deadline: 5/1.

Athletics Member NAIA. Intercollegiate sports: baseball/softball M(s), W(s); basketball M(s), W(s); golf M; soccer M(s); volleyball W(s). Intramural sports: baseball/softball, basketball, soccer, tennis, volleyball.

Majors Accounting B; adult and continuing education B; biology/biological sciences B; business administration/commerce/management B; business education B; chemistry B; criminal justice B; early childhood education B; education B; English B; history B; mathematics B; medical technology B; music education B; physical education B; psychology B; religious studies B; sacred music B; social science B; special education B; theology B.

LD Program Information

Name of Program Learning Assistance Center.

Availability of Services Services provided to freshmen, sophomores, juniors, seniors. Program currently serves 6 LD students: 5 freshmen, 1 junior.

Staff 2 part-time staff members, including director. Services provided by remediation specialists, tutors, counselors, diagnostic specialists, professor of special education.

Admissions LD applicants evaluated on the basis of high school transcript, standard SAT or ACT, personal interview, letters of recommendation, psychoeducational report. LD students may begin taking classes in fall, spring, or summer. Application should be submitted 1 month in advance of initial anticipated enrollment.

Housing College housing available. LD students housed randomly. LD freshmen required to live on campus except if 21 or over or living with relatives.

Diagnostic Testing Available in reading, math, written language.

Tutoring Offered one-to-one by professional teachers, peer tutors. Available in all subjects. LD students may receive tutoring in all courses each term.

Basic Skills Remediation Offered one-to-one and in small groups by director of Learning Assistance Center. Available in reading, math, spelling, written language, work and study habits.

Academic Advisement Help with program planning provided by academic advisers. LD students may take up to 15 hours each semester; most take 9 to 12 hours; 12 hours required to maintain full-time status.

Special Courses Offered in college survival skills, reading, composition, math, study skills. Some offered for credit; some enter into overall grade point average.

Auxiliary Aids and Services Aids include taped textbooks, tape recorders, calculators. Services include alternative exam arrangements, advocacy.

Counseling Services Individual counseling, career counseling available.

Contact Ms. Sally S. Wood, Director, Learning Assistance Center, Central Wesleyan College, Box 485, Central, SC 29630, 803-639-2453 Ext. 364.

THE CITADEL

Charleston, South Carolina

Year Program Began	1979	Special Courses	
Special Fee	None	Taped Textbooks	
Special Orientation		Alternative Exam Arrangements	
Diagnostic Testing	✓	Notetakers	
Subject-Area Tutoring		Staff	1 part-time
Basic Skills Remediation		Number of Students Served	20

General Information State-supported comprehensive men's institution. Founded 1842. Awards B, M. Institutionally accredited by regional association; programs accredited by ABET (engineering and technology), NCATE (teacher education). City setting; 130-acre barrier-free campus. Total enrollment: 3,001. Faculty: 150 (all full-time); 73% have doctoral degrees; graduate assistants teach no undergraduate courses. Calendar: semesters. Grading system: letters or numbers. Library holdings: 204,000 bound volumes, 440,000 titles on microform, 1,450 periodical subscriptions.

Undergraduate Profile Fall 1984: 2,308 undergraduates (523 freshmen) from 34 states and territories and 6 foreign countries; 0% part-time; 51% state residents; 4% transfers; 67% financial aid recipients; 0% women; 6% blacks; 0% Native Americans; 1% Hispanics; 0% Asian Americans; 1% foreign nationals; 0% of undergraduates over 25 years of age; no legally handicapped students.

Expenses (1985–86) State resident tuition: $65 per semester hour part-time. Nonresident tuition: $65 per semester hour part-time. Full-time tuition ranges from $2709 to $4454 for South Carolina residents, $4807 to $6652 for nonresidents. College room and board: $1702. College room only: $557.

Financial Aid Fall 1984 full-time freshmen: 72% applied for aid, 93% of those were judged to have need, 97% of those were aided; the average aided freshman received an aid package worth $1198 (30% scholarships/grants, 70% self-help) meeting 85% of need. College-administered aid for all 1984–85 undergraduates: 325 need-based scholarships (average $1394); 294 non-need scholarships (average $1758); low-interest long-term loans from college funds (average $1800), from external sources (average $2000); 132 part-time jobs. Supporting data: FAF, institutional form, AFSA/SAR required; IRS required for some. Application deadline: 3/1.

Athletics Member NCAA (Division I). Intercollegiate sports: baseball/softball (I,s); basketball (I,s); bowling (c); crew (c); cross-country running (I,s); fencing (c); football (I-AA,s); golf (I,s); lacrosse (c); riflery (I); rugby (c); sailing (c); soccer (I,s); tennis (I,s); track and field (I,s); wrestling (I,s). Intramural sports: badminton, baseball/softball, basketball, bowling, cross-country running, football, gymnastics, martial arts, racquetball, swimming and diving, tennis, track and field, volleyball, water polo, weight lifting, wrestling.

Majors Biology/biological sciences B; business administration/commerce/management B; chemistry B; civil engineering B; computer science B; education B; electrical engineering B; English B; history B; mathematics B; modern languages B; physical education B; physics B; political science/government B; psychology B. Majors with highest enrollment: business administration/commerce/management, electrical engineering, civil engineering.

LD Program Information

Name of Program Not specified.

Availability of Services Began offering services in 1979. Services provided to freshmen, sophomores, juniors, seniors. Program currently serves 20 LD students: 3 freshmen, 5 sophomores, 6 juniors, 6 seniors.

Staff 1 part-time staff member (coordinator).

Admissions LD applicants evaluated on the basis of high school transcript and grade point average, standard or untimed SAT or ACT, letters of recommendation; Achievement Tests required for some. LD students may begin taking classes in fall only. Application should be submitted 8 months in advance of initial anticipated enrollment.

Housing College housing available. LD students housed randomly. LD freshmen, sophomores, juniors, and seniors required to live on campus.

Diagnostic Testing Available in intelligence, reading, math, spelling, handwriting, written language, career interest inventories.

Academic Advisement Help with program planning provided by LD staff member, academic advisers. LD students may take up to 21 semester hours each semester; most take 15 semester hours; 12 semester hours required to maintain full-time status.

Counseling Services Individual counseling available.

Contact Dr. Gordon A. Wallace, Associate Professor of Education and Coordinator for LD Students, The Citadel, Department of Education, Charleston, SC 29409, 803-792-2064.

CITY UNIVERSITY OF NEW YORK, HUNTER COLLEGE

New York, New York

Year Program Began	1978	Special Courses	✓
Special Fee	None	Taped Textbooks	✓
Special Orientation	✓	Alternative Exam Arrangements	✓
Diagnostic Testing		Notetakers	✓
Subject-Area Tutoring	✓	Staff	1 part-time
Basic Skills Remediation	✓	Number of Students Served	40

General Information State and locally supported comprehensive coed institution. Part of City University of New York System. Founded 1870. Awards B, M. Institutionally accredited by regional association; programs accredited by NLN (nursing), NCATE (teacher education). Metropolitan setting. Total enrollment: 17,944. Faculty: 1,122 (641 full-time, 481 part-time); 75% have doctoral degrees; graduate assistants teach no undergraduate courses. Calendar: semesters. Grading system: letters or numbers. Library holdings: 512,710 bound volumes, 4,000 periodical subscriptions, 3,500 records/tapes.

Undergraduate Profile Fall 1984: 14,462 undergraduates (1,569 freshmen) from 25 states and territories and 10 foreign countries; 32% part-time; 93% state residents; 10% transfers; 80% financial aid recipients; 73% women; 22% blacks; 1% Native Americans; 15% Hispanics; 5% Asian Americans; 2% foreign nationals; 37% of undergraduates over 25 years of age; 224 legally handicapped students.

Expenses (1985–86) State resident tuition: $1250 full-time, $47 per credit part-time. Nonresident tuition: $2550 full-time, $96 per credit part-time. College room only: $1350.

Financial Aid Fall 1984 full-time freshmen: 75% applied for aid, 70% of those were judged to have need, 100% of those were aided; the average aided freshman received an aid package worth $968 (76% scholarships/grants, 24% self-help) meeting 90% of need. College-administered aid for all 1984–85 undergraduates: need-based scholarships; 150 non-need scholarships (average $800); short-term loans (average $100); low-interest long-term loans from college funds (average $250), from external sources (average $750); SEOG; College Work-Study. Supporting data: FAF, state form, institutional form, AFSA/SAR required. Priority application deadline: 5/20.

Athletics Member NCAA (Division III). Intercollegiate sports: baseball/softball M(III), W(III); basketball M(III), W(III); cross-country running M(III), W(III); fencing M(III), W(III); field hockey W(III); gymnastics W(III); rugby M(III), W; soccer M(III); swimming and diving W(III); tennis M(III), W(III); track and field M(III), W(III); volleyball W(III); wrestling M(III). Intramural sports: baseball/softball, basketball, bowling, cross-country running, gymnastics, soccer, swimming and diving, tennis, volleyball.

Majors Accounting B; anthropology B; archaeology B; art education B; art/fine arts B; art history B; Asian/Oriental studies B; astronomy B; biology/biological sciences B; black/Afro-American studies B; chemistry B; Chinese B; classics B; communication B; comparative literature B; computer science B; dance B; early childhood education B; economics B; education B; elementary education B; energy management technologies B; English B; environmental health sciences B; film studies B; French B; geography B; geology B; German B; Greek B; health education B; Hebrew B; Hispanic studies B; history B; home economics B; Italian B; Judaic studies B; Latin B; literature B; mathematics B; medical laboratory technology B; (pre)medicine sequence B; music B; music education B; music history B; nursing B; philosophy B; physical education B; physical fitness/human movement B; physical therapy B; physics B; political science/government B; psychology B; public health B; religious studies B; Romance languages B; Russian B; sociology B; Spanish B; speech pathology and audiology B; statistics B; studio art B; technology and public affairs B; theater arts/drama B; urban studies B; women's studies B. Majors with highest enrollment: psychology, communication, sociology.

LD Program Information

Name of Program Student Services.

Availability of Services Began offering services in 1978. Services provided to freshmen, sophomores, juniors, seniors. Program currently serves 40 LD students.

Staff 1 part-time staff member (coordinator). Services provided by counselors.

Admissions LD applicants evaluated on the basis of high school transcript and grade point average; personal interview recommended. LD students may begin taking classes in fall, spring, or summer. Application should be submitted at least 9 months in advance of initial anticipated enrollment.

Orientation Optional orientation offered individually by special arrangement.

Housing College housing (including coed) available. LD students housed with other LD students and non-LD students. LD students not required to live on campus.

Tutoring Offered one-to-one and in small groups by peer tutors. Available in some subjects. LD students may receive tutoring in all courses each term.

Basic Skills Remediation Offered one-to-one and in class-size groups by regular teachers. Available in reading, math, work and study habits.

Academic Advisement Help with program planning provided by academic advisers. Most LD students take 12 credits each semester; 12 credits required to maintain full-time status.

Special Courses Offered in reading, composition, math, study skills, career planning. All offered for credit; all enter into overall grade point average.

Auxiliary Aids and Services Aids include taped textbooks, calculators, typewriters. Services include alternative exam arrangements, notetakers, advocacy, readers, early registration, LD support group.

Counseling Services Individual counseling, small-group counseling, rap sessions available.

Contact Ms. Sandra LaPorta, Coordinator for Disabled Students, City University of New York, Hunter College, 695 Park Avenue, New York, NY 10021, 212-772-4888.

CITY UNIVERSITY OF NEW YORK, QUEENS COLLEGE

Flushing, New York

Year Program Began	1979	Special Courses	
Special Fee	None	Taped Textbooks	
Special Orientation	✓	Alternative Exam Arrangements	✓
Diagnostic Testing		Notetakers	
Subject-Area Tutoring	✓	Staff	2 full-time
Basic Skills Remediation	✓	Number of Students Served	12

General Information State and locally supported comprehensive coed institution. Part of City University of New York System. Founded 1937. Awards B, M. Institutionally accredited by regional association. Metropolitan setting; 76-acre campus. Total enrollment: 16,369. Faculty: 1,435 (842 full-time, 593 part-time); 95% have doctoral degrees; graduate assistants teach a few undergraduate courses. Calendar: semesters. Grading system: letters or numbers. Library holdings: 600,000 bound volumes, 3,000 periodical subscriptions, 2,000 records/tapes.

Undergraduate Profile Fall 1984: 13,308 undergraduates (1,949 freshmen); 33% part-time; 94% state residents; 6% transfers; 60% financial aid recipients; 58% women; 12% blacks; 1% Native Americans; 10% Hispanics; 9% Asian Americans; 5% foreign nationals; 3% of undergraduates over 25 years of age; 23 legally handicapped students.

Expenses (1985–86) State resident tuition: $1250 full-time, $47 per credit part-time. Nonresident tuition: $2550 full-time, $96 per credit part-time. Mandatory fees: $132.

Financial Aid College-administered aid for all 1984–85 undergraduates: need-based scholarships; 95 non-need scholarships (average $1225); short-term loans; low-interest long-term loans from external sources (average $1820); SEOG; College Work-Study; part-time jobs. Supporting data: IRS, state form, institutional form required. Priority application deadline: 8/15.

Athletics Member NCAA (Division II). Intercollegiate sports: baseball/softball M(II,s), W(II,s); basketball M(II,s), W(I,s); bowling M, W; cross-country running M(II), W(II); gymnastics M(II), W(II); lacrosse M(II); soccer M(II,s); swimming and diving M(II,s), W(II,s); tennis M(II,s), W(II,s); track and field M(II), W(II); volleyball M(II), W(II); water polo M(II). Intramural sports: badminton, baseball/softball, basketball, cross-country running, football, racquetball, soccer, swimming and diving, tennis, track and field, volleyball.

Majors Accounting B; adult and continuing education B; African studies B; American studies B; anthropology B; art education B; art/fine arts B; art history B; Asian/Oriental studies B; biblical studies B; biochemistry B; biology/biological sciences B; chemistry B; child psychology/child development B; Chinese B; classics B; communication B; communication equipment technology B; comparative literature B; computer science B; creative writing B; dance B; (pre)dentistry sequence B; dietetics B; early childhood education B; earth science B; East Asian studies B; ecology/environmental studies B; economics B; education B; educational media B; elementary education B; English B; environmental education B; ethnic studies B; experimental psychology B; film studies B; French B; geography B; geology B; German B; Germanic languages and literature B; Greek B; health education B; Hebrew B; history B; history of philosophy B; home economics B; home economics education B; humanities B; interdisciplinary studies B; Italian B; Judaic studies B; Latin B; Latin American studies B; (pre)law sequence B; liberal arts/general studies B; linguistics B; literature B; mathematics B; (pre)medicine sequence B; modern languages B; music B; music education B; music history B; Near and Middle Eastern studies B; painting/drawing B; philosophy B; physical education B; physics B; piano/organ B; political science/government B; Portuguese B; psychology B; radio and television studies B; religious studies B; Romance languages B; Russian B; science B; science education B; secondary education B; Slavic languages B; social science B; sociology B; Spanish B; speech pathology and audiology B; speech therapy B; statistics B; stringed instruments B; studio art B; telecommunications B; theater arts/drama B; urban studies B; (pre)veterinary medicine sequence B; voice B; wind and percussion instruments B. Majors with highest enrollment: accounting, computer science, education.

LD Program Information

Name of Program Special Services.

Availability of Services Began offering services in 1979. Services provided to freshmen, sophomores, juniors, seniors. Program currently serves 12 LD students.

Staff 2 full-time staff members, including director. Services provided by counselor.

Admissions LD applicants evaluated on the basis of high school transcript and grade point average. LD students may begin taking classes in fall, spring, or summer. Application should be submitted 6 months in advance of initial anticipated enrollment.

Orientation Optional orientation offered before registration.

Housing College housing not available.

Tutoring Offered by professional teachers, peer tutors, professional tutors. Available in some subjects.

Basic Skills Remediation Offered one-to-one and in small groups by professional tutors. Available in reading, math, written language.

Academic Advisement Help with program planning provided by LD staff members, academic advisers. LD students may take up to 18 credits each semester; most take 12 credits; 12 credits required to maintain full-time status.

Auxiliary Aids and Services Aids include tape recorders, typewriters. Services include alternative exam arrangements.

Counseling Services Individual counseling, small-group counseling, career counseling, peer counseling available.

Contact Ms. Gail Uellendahl, Director of Special Services, City University of New York, Queens College, Flushing, NY 11367, 718-520-7636.

CLARION UNIVERSITY OF PENNSYLVANIA

Clarion, Pennsylvania

Year Program Began	1982	Special Courses	✓
Special Fee	None	Taped Textbooks	✓
Special Orientation		Alternative Exam Arrangements	✓
Diagnostic Testing	✓	Notetakers	
Subject-Area Tutoring	✓	Staff	3 part-time
Basic Skills Remediation	✓	Number of Students Served	11

General Information State-supported comprehensive coed institution. Part of State System of Higher Education. Founded 1867. Awards A (terminal), B, M. Institutionally accredited by regional association; programs accredited by NLN (nursing), NCATE (teacher education). Small-town setting; 100-acre barrier-free campus. Total enrollment: 5,888. Faculty: 320 (300 full-time, 20 part-time); 60% have doctoral degrees; graduate assistants teach a few undergraduate courses. Calendar: semesters. Grading system: letters or numbers. Library holdings: 350,000 bound volumes, 1,446 periodical subscriptions, 2,667 records/tapes.

Undergraduate Profile Fall 1984: 4,875 undergraduates (1,300 freshmen) from 34 states and territories and 38 foreign countries; 5% part-time; 85% state residents; 6% transfers; 65% financial aid recipients; 54% women; 5% blacks; 1% Native Americans; 1% Hispanics; 1% Asian Americans; 2% foreign nationals; 5% of undergraduates over 25 years of age.

Expenses (1985–86) State resident tuition: $1480 full-time, $66 per credit part-time. Nonresident tuition: $2670 full-time, $80 per credit part-time. Mandatory fees: $170. College room and board: $2010.

Financial Aid Fall 1984 full-time freshmen: 80% applied for aid, 80% of those were judged to have need, 83% of those were aided; the average aided freshman received an aid package worth $3100 (34% scholarships/grants, 66% self-help) meeting 75% of need. College-administered aid for all 1984–85 undergraduates: need-based scholarships; non-need scholarships; low-interest long-term loans; College Work-Study; part-time jobs. Supporting data: state form, AFSA/SAR required; FFS, FAF, institutional form acceptable. Priority application deadline: 5/1.

Athletics Member NCAA (Division II), NAIA. Intercollegiate sports: baseball/softball M(II,s), W(II); basketball M(II,s), W(II,s); cross-country running M(II,s), W(II,s); football M(II,s); golf M(II,s); gymnastics W(I,s); riflery M(II), W(II); swimming and diving M(II,s), W(II,s); tennis W(II,s); track and field M(II,s), W(II,s); volleyball W(II,s); wrestling M(I,s). Intramural sports: badminton, baseball/softball, basketball, bowling, football, golf, racquetball, soccer, swimming and diving, tennis, track and field, volleyball, water polo, weight lifting, wrestling.

Majors Accounting B; anthropology B; art/fine arts B; biology/biological sciences B; business administration/commerce/management A, B; business economics B; chemistry B; communication B; computer information systems B; computer science A, B; (pre)dentistry sequence B; early childhood education B; earth science B; economics B; education B; elementary education B; English B; finance/banking B; French B; geography B; German B; history B; humanities B; labor and industrial relations B; (pre)law sequence B; liberal arts/general studies B; library science B; marketing/retailing/merchandising B; mathematics B; medical technology B; (pre) medicine sequence B; modern languages B; music B; music education B; natural sciences B; nursing A, B; philosophy B; physics B; political science/government B; psychology B; real estate B; rehabilitation therapy A, B; Russian B; science education B; secondary education B; social science B; sociology B; Spanish B; special education B; speech pathology and audiology B; speech/rhetoric/public address/debate B; theater arts/drama B; (pre)veterinary medicine sequence B. Majors with highest enrollment: business administration/commerce/management, communication, liberal arts/general studies.

LD Program Information

Name of Program Special Services Program.

Availability of Services Began offering services in 1982. Services provided to freshmen, sophomores, juniors, seniors. Program currently serves 11 LD students: 8 freshmen, 1 sophomore, 1 junior, 1 senior.

Staff 3 part-time staff members, including director. Services provided by counselor, learning skills specialist.

Admissions LD applicants evaluated on the basis of high school transcript and grade point average, untimed SAT, letters of recommendation, psychoeducational report; personal interview recommended. LD students may begin taking classes in fall, spring, or summer. Application should be submitted 3 months in advance of initial anticipated enrollment.

Housing College housing (including coed) available. LD students housed randomly. LD students not required to live on campus.

Diagnostic Testing Available in reading, spelling, written language, work and study habits, personality, career interest inventories.

Tutoring Offered one-to-one and in small groups by peer tutors, learning skills specialists. Available in some subjects. LD students may receive tutoring in all courses each term.

Basic Skills Remediation Offered one-to-one and in small groups by learning skills specialists. Available in learning strategies, work and study habits.

Academic Advisement Help with program planning provided by academic advisers. Most LD students take 12 to 15 credits each semester; 12 credits required to maintain full-time status.

Special Courses Offered in college survival skills, reading, study skills. All offered for credit; all enter into overall grade point average.

Auxiliary Aids and Services Aids include taped textbooks. Services include alternative exam arrangements, advocacy, registration priority.

Counseling Services Individual counseling, small-group counseling, disabled students organization available.

Contact Mr. Gregory K. Clary, Director, Special Services Program, Clarion University of Pennsylvania, 130 Davis Hall, Clarion, PA 16214, 814-226-2347.

CLARK UNIVERSITY
Worcester, Massachusetts

Year Program Began	*Not reported*	Special Courses	
Special Fee	None	Taped Textbooks	✓
Special Orientation		Alternative Exam Arrangements	✓
Diagnostic Testing	✓	Notetakers	
Subject-Area Tutoring		Staff	1 full-time
Basic Skills Remediation		Number of Students Served	32

General Information Independent coed university. Founded 1887. Awards B, M, D. Institutionally accredited by regional association. City setting, with easy access to Boston; 40-acre campus. Total enrollment: 2,636. Faculty: 256 (156 full-time, 100 part-time); 98% have doctoral degrees; graduate assistants teach a few undergraduate courses. Calendar: semesters. Grading system: letters or numbers (with pass/no record option). Library holdings: 480,000 bound volumes, 2,300 periodical subscriptions.

Undergraduate Profile Fall 1984: 2,083 undergraduates (560 freshmen) from 26 states and territories and 71 foreign countries; 2% part-time; 25% state residents; 12% transfers; 48% financial aid recipients; 52% women; 4% blacks; 3% Hispanics; 1% Asian Americans; 6% foreign nationals.

Expenses (1985–86) Comprehensive fee of $12,450 includes full-time tuition ($9200), mandatory fees ($230), and college room and board ($3020). College room only: $1450. Part-time tuition: $1150 per course. Tuition prepayment plan available.

Financial Aid Fall 1984 full-time freshmen: 50% applied for aid, 99% of those were judged to have need, 100% of those were aided; the average aided freshman received an aid package worth $7120 (67% scholarships/grants, 33% self-help) meeting 95% of need. College-administered aid for all 1984–85 undergraduates: 959 need-based scholarships (average $5200); low-interest long-term loans from college funds (average $1000), from external sources (average $500); SEOG; College Work-Study; part-time jobs. Supporting data: FAF, IRS, AFSA/SAR, Financial Aid Transcript (for transfers) required; FFS acceptable. Application deadline: 2/15.

Athletics Member NCAA (Division III). Intercollegiate sports: baseball/softball M(III), W(III); basketball M(III), W(III); bowling M(c), W(c); crew M, W; cross-country running M(III), W(III); field hockey W(III); golf M(III); ice hockey M(c); lacrosse M(c); martial arts M(c), W(c); soccer M(III); swimming and diving M(III), W(III); tennis M(III), W(III); track and field M(III), W(III); volleyball W(III). Intramural sports: baseball/softball, basketball, bowling, equestrian sports, ice hockey, lacrosse, martial arts, racquetball, soccer, volleyball.

Majors Adult and continuing education B; anthropology B; art/fine arts B; art history B; biochemistry B; biology/biological sciences B; business administration/commerce/management B; chemistry B; communication B; comparative literature B; computer science B; (pre)dentistry sequence B; ecology/environmental studies B; economics B; education B; English B; environmental sciences B; film studies B; French B; geography B; German B; history B; international studies B; Judaic studies B; (pre)law sequence B; mathematics B; (pre)medicine sequence B; music B; philosophy B; physics B; political science/government B; psychology B; Romance languages B; sociology B; Spanish B; studio art B; technology and public affairs B; theater arts/drama B; (pre)veterinary medicine sequence B. Majors with highest enrollment: psychology, business administration/commerce/management, biology/biological sciences.

LD Program Information

Name of Program Not specified.

Availability of Services Services provided to freshmen, sophomores, juniors, seniors. Program currently serves 32 LD students: 15 freshmen, 12 sophomores, 3 juniors, 2 seniors.

Staff 1 full-time staff member (coordinator). Services provided by remediation specialists, counselors, diagnostic specialists.

Admissions LD applicants evaluated on the basis of high school transcript and grade point average, standard or untimed SAT, letters of recommendation; personal interview, psychoeducational report recommended. LD students may begin taking classes in fall only. Application should be submitted 7 months in advance of initial anticipated enrollment.

Housing College housing (including coed) available. LD students housed randomly. LD freshmen required to live on campus.

Diagnostic Testing Available in intelligence, reading, math, spelling, handwriting, spoken language, written language, perceptual skills, work and study habits, personality, social skills.

Academic Advisement Help with program planning provided by LD staff members, academic advisers. LD students may take up to 4 courses each semester; most take 4 courses; 3 courses required to maintain full-time status.

Auxiliary Aids and Services Aids include taped textbooks, word processors. Services include alternative exam arrangements.

Counseling Services Individual counseling, small-group counseling, rap sessions available.

Contact Dr. Renee L. Goldberg, Coordinator of Services for Learning Disabled Students, Clark University, Worcester, MA 01610, 617-793-7214.

CLEVELAND STATE UNIVERSITY

Cleveland, Ohio

Year Program Began	1969	Special Courses	✓
Special Fee	None	Taped Textbooks	✓
Special Orientation	✓	Alternative Exam Arrangements	✓
Diagnostic Testing	✓	Notetakers	✓
Subject-Area Tutoring	✓	Staff	1 full-time, 1 part-time
Basic Skills Remediation	✓	Number of Students Served	11

General Information State-supported coed university. Founded 1964. Awards B, M, D. Institutionally accredited by regional association; programs accredited by AACSB (business), ABET (engineering and technology), NASM (music), NLN (nursing), NCATE (teacher education). Metropolitan setting; 50-acre barrier-free campus. Total enrollment: 18,033. Faculty: 763 (515 full-time, 248 part-time); 95% have doctoral degrees; graduate assistants teach a few undergraduate courses. Calendar: quarters. Grading system: letters or numbers. Library holdings: 640,000 bound volumes, 360,000 titles on microform, 4,000 periodical subscriptions, 6,000 records/tapes.

Undergraduate Profile Fall 1984: 13,426 undergraduates (1,781 freshmen) from 33 states and territories and 50 foreign countries; 37% part-time; 98% state residents; 44% transfers; 25% financial aid recipients; 45% women; 12% blacks; 0% Native Americans; 1% Hispanics; 1% Asian Americans; 1% foreign nationals; 29% of undergraduates over 25 years of age; 70 legally handicapped students.

Expenses (1985–86) State resident tuition: $1833 full-time, $51 per quarter hour part-time. Nonresident tuition: $3666 full-time, $102 per quarter hour part-time. College room only: $810.

Financial Aid Fall 1984 full-time freshmen: 89% applied for aid, 92% of those were judged to have need, 73% of those were aided; the average aided freshman received an aid package worth $1852 (73% scholarships/grants, 27% self-help) meeting 72% of need. College-administered aid for all 1984–85 undergraduates: 6,000 need-based scholarships (average $650); 250 non-need scholarships (average $1665); short-term loans (average $230); low-interest long-term loans from college funds (average $340), from external sources (average $1940); SEOG; College Work-Study; 435 part-time jobs. Supporting data: FAF, state form required; IRS required for some; FFS, AFSA/SAR acceptable. Priority application deadline: 5/15.

Athletics Member NCAA (Division I). Intercollegiate sports: baseball/softball M(I,s), W(I,s); basketball M(I,s), W(I,s); cross-country running M(I,s), W(I,s); fencing M(I,s), W(I,s); golf M(I,s); soccer M(I,s); swimming and diving M(I,s), W(I,s); tennis M(I,s), W(I,s); track and field M(I,s), W(I,s); volleyball W(I,s); wrestling M(I,s). Intramural sports: badminton, baseball/softball, basketball, bowling, cross-country running, fencing, field hockey, football, golf, martial arts, racquetball, sailing, soccer, swimming and diving, tennis, track and field, volleyball, water polo, weight lifting, wrestling.

Majors Accounting B; anthropology B; art education B; art/fine arts B; art history B; Asian/Oriental studies B; biology/biological sciences B; business administration/commerce/management B; business education B; chemical engineering B; chemistry B; civil engineering B; communication B; computer science B; construction technologies B; corrections B; deaf interpreter training B; (pre)dentistry sequence B; early childhood education B; economics B; electrical and electronics technologies B; electrical engineering B; elementary education B; English B; finance/banking B; French B; geology B; German B; history B; industrial engineering B; labor and industrial relations B; (pre)law sequence B; linguistics B; manufacturing technology B; marketing/retailing/merchandising B; mathematics B; mechanical engineering B; medical technology B; (pre)medicine sequence B; medieval studies B; music B; music education B; music history B; music therapy B; nursing B; occupational therapy B; philosophy B; physical education B; physical therapy B; physics B; political science/government B; psychology B; religious studies B; social science B; social work B; sociology B; Spanish B; special education B; speech pathology and audiology B; theater arts/drama B; urban studies B; (pre)veterinary medicine sequence B. Majors with highest enrollment: accounting, marketing/retailing/merchandising, computer science.

LD Program Information

Name of Program Handicapped Services.

Availability of Services Began offering services in 1969. Services provided to freshmen, sophomores, juniors, seniors. Program currently serves 11 LD students: 7 freshmen, 2 sophomores, 2 juniors.

Staff 1 full-time, 1 part-time staff members, including coordinator. Services provided by remediation specialist.

Admissions LD applicants evaluated on the basis of high school transcript and grade point average, standard or untimed SAT or ACT, psychoeducational report, including high school LD specialist's report. LD students may begin taking classes in fall only. Application should be submitted 2 months in advance of initial anticipated enrollment.

Orientation Optional orientation offered before registration.

Housing College housing (including coed) available. LD students housed randomly. LD students not required to live on campus.

Diagnostic Testing Available in reading, math, written language.

Tutoring Offered one-to-one by peer tutors. Available in all subjects. LD students may receive tutoring in all courses each term.

Basic Skills Remediation Offered in small groups by regular teachers. Available in reading, math, spelling, written language, work and study habits.

Academic Advisement Help with program planning provided by LD staff members. LD students may take up to 16 quarter hours each quarter; most take 12 quarter hours; 12 quarter hours required to maintain full-time status.

Special Courses Offered in college survival skills, reading, vocabulary development, composition, math, study skills, career planning. Some offered for credit; some enter into overall grade point average.

Auxiliary Aids and Services Aids include taped textbooks, tape recorders, calculators, typewriters. Services include alternative exam arrangements, notetakers, advocacy.

Counseling Services Individual counseling, rap sessions, career counseling available.

Contact Mr. Michael J. Zuccaro, Coordinator of Handicapped Services, Cleveland State University, East 24th and Euclid Avenue, Cleveland, OH 44115, 216-687-2015.

COLLEGE MISERICORDIA

Dallas, Pennsylvania

Year Program Began	1979	Special Courses	✓
Special Fee	$500 per year	Taped Textbooks	✓
Special Orientation	✓	Alternative Exam Arrangements	✓
Diagnostic Testing	✓	Notetakers	✓
Subject-Area Tutoring	✓	Staff	7 part-time
Basic Skills Remediation	✓	Number of Students Served	12

General Information Roman Catholic comprehensive coed institution. Founded 1924. Awards A (terminal), B, M. Institutionally accredited by regional association; programs accredited by NASM (music), NLN (nursing). Small-town setting; 100-acre barrier-free campus. Total enrollment: 1,292. Faculty: 128 (79 full-time, 49 part-time); 23% have doctoral degrees; graduate assistants teach a few undergraduate courses. Calendar: semesters. Grading system: letters or numbers. Library holdings: 73,043 bound volumes, 356 titles on microform, 763 periodical subscriptions, 11,445 records/tapes.

Undergraduate Profile Fall 1984: 1,181 undergraduates (240 freshmen) from 15 states and territories and 4 foreign countries; 25% part-time; 80% state residents; 5% transfers; 85% financial aid recipients; 80% women; 1% blacks; 0% Native Americans; 1% Hispanics; 1% foreign nationals; 20% of undergraduates over 25 years of age; 3 legally handicapped students.

Expenses (1985–86) Comprehensive fee of $7070 includes full-time tuition ($4350 minimum), mandatory fees ($120), and college room and board ($2600). Full-time tuition is $4750 for some programs. Part-time tuition per credit ranges from $110 to $120 according to program.

Financial Aid Fall 1984 full-time freshmen: 84% applied for aid, 93% of those were judged to have need, 100% of those were aided; the average aided freshman received an aid package worth $4001 (44% scholarships/grants, 56% self-help) meeting 86% of need. College-administered aid for all 1984–85 undergraduates: 507 need-based scholarships (average $390); 231 non-need scholarships (average $981); low-interest long-term loans from external sources (average $607); SEOG; College Work-Study; 104 part-time jobs. Supporting data: state form, institutional form required; IRS required for some; FAF, AFSA/SAR acceptable. Priority application deadline: 4/1.

Athletics Member NAIA. Intercollegiate sports: baseball/softball M(s), W(s); basketball M(s), W(s); cross-country running M(c), W(c); field hockey W(s); golf M(c), W(c); martial arts M(c), W(c); racquetball M(c), W(c); soccer M(s), W(s); tennis M(c), W(c); volleyball W(s). Intramural sports: baseball/softball, basketball, cross-country running, football, tennis.

Majors Biology/biological sciences B; business administration/commerce/management B; computer information systems B; computer science B; (pre)dentistry sequence B; early childhood education B; elementary education B; English B; history B; (pre)law sequence B; liberal arts/general studies B; marketing/retailing/merchandising B; mathematics B; medical technology B; (pre)medicine sequence B; music B; music education B; music therapy B; nursing B; occupational therapy B; paralegal studies B; radiological technology A, B; social work B; special education B; (pre)veterinary medicine sequence B. Majors with highest enrollment: nursing, occupational therapy, business administration/commerce/management.

LD Program Information

Name of Program Alternative Learners Project (ALP).

Availability of Services Began offering services in 1979. Services provided to freshmen, sophomores, juniors, seniors. Program currently serves 12 LD students: 6 freshmen, 2 sophomores, 1 junior, 3 seniors.

Fees $500 per year.

Staff 7 part-time staff members, including coordinator, assistant coordinator. Services provided by remediation specialists, counselor, diagnostic specialist.

Admissions LD applicants evaluated on the basis of high school transcript and grade point average, untimed SAT, personal interview, autobiographical statement, letters of recommendation, psychoeducational report. LD students may begin taking classes in fall only. Application should be submitted 4 or 5 months in advance of initial anticipated enrollment.

Orientation Required orientation held before registration.

Housing College housing available. LD students housed with other LD students and non-LD students. LD students not required to live on campus.

Diagnostic Testing Available in reading, math, spelling, written language, perceptual skills, work and study habits, personality.

Tutoring Offered one-to-one and in small groups by peer tutors. Available in all subjects. LD students may receive tutoring in all courses each term.

Basic Skills Remediation Offered one-to-one and in class-size groups by LD teachers, regular teachers. Available in reading, math, spelling, written language, learning strategies, work and study habits, social skills.

Academic Advisement Help with program planning provided by LD staff members, academic advisers. LD students may take up to 18 credits each semester; most take 12 to 15 credits; 12 credits required to maintain full-time status.

Special Courses Offered in college survival skills, reading, vocabulary development, communication skills, composition, math. Some offered for credit; none enter into overall grade point average.

Auxiliary Aids and Services Aids include taped textbooks, tape recorders, calculators, typewriters. Services include alternative exam arrangements, notetakers, advocacy.

Counseling Services Individual counseling, rap sessions, career counseling available.

Contact Dr. Joseph Rogan, Coordinator, Alternative Learners Project, College Misericordia, Dallas, PA 18612, 717-675-2181.

COLLEGE OF CHARLESTON
Charleston, South Carolina

Year Program Began	1981	Special Courses	
Special Fee	None	Taped Textbooks	✓
Special Orientation		Alternative Exam Arrangements	✓
Diagnostic Testing		Notetakers	
Subject-Area Tutoring	✓	Staff	1 part-time
Basic Skills Remediation	✓	Number of Students Served	40

General Information State-supported comprehensive coed institution. Founded 1770. Awards B, M. Institutionally accredited by regional association; programs accredited by AACSB (business). City setting; 8-acre barrier-free campus. Total enrollment: 5,395. Faculty: 326 (222 full-time, 104 part-time); 86% have doctoral degrees; graduate assistants teach no undergraduate courses. Calendar: semesters. Grading system: letters or numbers. Library holdings: 226,000 bound volumes, 2,000 periodical subscriptions, 2,300 records/tapes.

Undergraduate Profile Fall 1984: 5,166 undergraduates (912 freshmen) from 35 states and territories and 18 foreign countries; 25% part-time; 88% state residents; 27% transfers; 47% financial aid recipients; 61% women; 7% blacks; 0% Native Americans; 0% Hispanics; 1% Asian Americans; 2% foreign nationals; 17% of undergraduates over 25 years of age; 32 legally handicapped students.

Expenses (1985–86) State resident tuition: $1470 full-time, $65 per semester hour part-time. Nonresident tuition: $2670 full-time, $65 per semester hour part-time. College room and board: $2460. College room only: $1580.

Financial Aid Fall 1984 full-time freshmen: 61% applied for aid, 75% of those were judged to have need, 100% of those were aided; the average aided freshman received an aid package worth $2308 (27% scholarships/grants, 73% self-help) meeting 84% of need. College-administered aid for all 1984–85 undergraduates: 91 need-based scholarships (average $1280); 265 non-need scholarships (average $583); short-term loans (average $198); low-interest long-term loans from external sources (average $1661); SEOG; College Work-Study; 660 part-time jobs. Supporting data: FAF, institutional form, AFSA/SAR, Financial Aid Transcript (for transfers) required; IRS required for some; FFS acceptable. Priority application deadline: 4/1.

Athletics Member NAIA. Intercollegiate sports: basketball M(s), W(s); sailing M(s), W(s); soccer M(s); swimming and diving M(s), W(s); tennis M(s), W(s); volleyball W(s). Intramural sports: badminton, baseball/softball, basketball, bowling, equestrian sports, football, golf, racquetball, swimming and diving, tennis, track and field, volleyball, water polo.

Majors Art/fine arts B; biology/biological sciences B; business administration/commerce/management B; chemistry B; classics B; computer science B; (pre)dentistry sequence B; early childhood education B; economics B; education B; elementary education B; English B; French B; geology B; German B; Greek B; history B; Latin B; (pre)law sequence B; marine biology B; mathematics B; (pre)medicine sequence B; philosophy B; physical education B; physics B; political science/government B; psychology B; secondary education B; sociology B; Spanish B; special education B; urban studies B; (pre)veterinary medicine sequence B. Majors with highest enrollment: business administration/commerce/management, biology/biological sciences, education.

LD Program Information

Name of Program Learning Disability Services.

Availability of Services Began offering services in 1981. Services provided to freshmen, sophomores, juniors, seniors. Program currently serves 40 LD students: 6 freshmen, 16 sophomores, 8 juniors, 10 seniors.

Staff 1 part-time staff member (coordinator).

Admissions LD applicants evaluated on the basis of high school transcript, standard or untimed SAT; personal interview, letters of recommendation recommended. LD students may begin taking classes in fall, spring, or summer. Application should be submitted 3 to 4 months in advance of initial anticipated enrollment.

Housing College housing (including coed) available. LD students housed randomly. LD students not required to live on campus.

Tutoring Offered one-to-one and in small groups by College Skills Lab tutors. Available in all subjects. LD students may receive tutoring in all courses each term.

Basic Skills Remediation Offered one-to-one and in small groups by College Skills Lab staff. Available in reading, math, work and study habits.

Academic Advisement Help with program planning provided by LD staff member. LD students may take up to 15 semester hours each semester; most take 9 to 12 semester hours; 12 semester hours required to maintain full-time status.

Auxiliary Aids and Services Aids include taped textbooks. Services include alternative exam arrangements.

Counseling Services Individual counseling, small-group counseling, career counseling available.

Contact Dr. Susan J. Schenck, Associate Professor of Education and Coordinator of Learning Disability Services, College of Charleston, 9 College Way, Charleston, SC 29424, 803-792-5613.

COLLEGE OF MOUNT ST JOSEPH ON THE OHIO

Mount St Joseph, Ohio

Year Program Began	1982	Special Courses	✓
Special Fee	$800 to $1500 per year	Taped Textbooks	✓
Special Orientation	✓	Alternative Exam Arrangements	✓
Diagnostic Testing	✓	Notetakers	✓
Subject-Area Tutoring	✓	Staff	1 full-time, 4 part-time
Basic Skills Remediation		Number of Students Served	13

General Information Roman Catholic comprehensive coed institution. Founded 1920. Awards A (terminal), B, M. Institutionally accredited by regional association; programs accredited by NLN (nursing); candidate for program accreditation by NASM (music). Metropolitan setting; 75-acre barrier-free campus. Total enrollment: 2,135. Faculty: 183 (63 full-time, 120 part-time); 41% have doctoral degrees; graduate assistants teach no undergraduate courses. Calendar: semesters. Grading system: letters or numbers. Library holdings: 87,000 bound volumes, 75 titles on microform, 525 periodical subscriptions, 2,100 records/tapes.

Undergraduate Profile Fall 1984: 2,035 undergraduates (207 freshmen) from 10 states and territories and 11 foreign countries; 58% part-time; 98% state residents; 12% transfers; 56% financial aid recipients; 88% women; 4% blacks; 0% Native Americans; 1% Hispanics; 2% foreign nationals; 55% of undergraduates over 25 years of age.

Expenses (1985–86) Comprehensive fee of $7734 includes full-time tuition ($4800), mandatory fees ($170), and college room and board ($2764). Part-time tuition: $150 per credit hour.

Financial Aid Fall 1984 full-time freshmen: 65% applied for aid, 84% of those were judged to have need, 100% of those were aided; the average aided freshman received an aid package worth $5460 (64% scholarships/grants, 36% self-help) meeting 97% of need. College-administered aid for all 1984–85 undergraduates: 408 need-based scholarships (average $1315); 222 non-need scholarships (average $1130); low-interest long-term loans from college funds (average $1215), from external sources; SEOG; College Work-Study. Supporting data: FAF, institutional form required; IRS, state form required for some. Priority application deadline: 4/15.

Athletics Member NCAA (Division II). Intercollegiate sports: baseball/softball W(II); basketball W(III); soccer W(II); volleyball W(II,s). Intramural sports: badminton, basketball, football, tennis, volleyball.

Majors Accounting B; adult and continuing education B; art education B; art/fine arts A, B; art therapy B; biology/biological sciences B; business administration/commerce/management B; ceramic art and design B; chemistry B; communication A, B; criminal justice B; data processing B; (pre)dentistry sequence B; dietetics B; early childhood education A, B; education B; elementary education B; English B; food services management A; graphic arts B; health education B; history B; home economics B; home economics education B; human services A, B; interior design B; (pre)law sequence B; liberal arts/general studies B; marketing/retailing/merchandising B; medical laboratory technology A; medical technology B; (pre) medicine sequence B; music B; music business B; music education B; music therapy B; natural sciences B; nursing B; painting/drawing B; paralegal studies A, B; pastoral studies B; photography B; physical education B; physical fitness/human movement B; religious education B; religious studies B; respiratory therapy A; sculpture B; secondary education B; social work B; sociology B; special education B; sports administration B; textile arts B. Majors with highest enrollment: nursing, business administration/commerce/management, education.

LD Program Information

Name of Program Project EXCEL.

Availability of Services Began offering services in 1982. Services provided to freshmen, sophomores, juniors, seniors. Program currently serves 13 LD students: 5 freshmen, 3 sophomores, 1 junior, 4 seniors.

Fees Range from $800 to $1500 per year according to level of services.

Staff 1 full-time, 4 part-time staff members, including director, project committee members. Services provided by tutors, counselors, diagnostic specialists.

Admissions LD applicants evaluated on the basis of high school transcript and grade point average, untimed SAT or ACT, personal interview, psychoeducational report, vision and hearing examination, Project EXCEL testing. LD students may begin taking classes in fall or spring. Application should be submitted 6 months in advance of initial anticipated enrollment.

Orientation Required orientation held before registration.

Housing College housing available. LD students housed randomly. LD freshmen, sophomores, juniors, and seniors required to live on campus except by special permission.

Diagnostic Testing Available in intelligence, reading, math, spelling, spoken language, written language, work and study habits, personality.

Tutoring Offered one-to-one and in small groups by professional teachers, peer tutors. Available in all subjects. LD students may receive tutoring in all courses each term.

Academic Advisement Help with program planning provided by LD staff members. LD students may take up to 12 credit hours each semester; most take 9 to 12 credit hours; 8 credit hours required to maintain full-time status.

Special Courses Offered in reading, vocabulary development, composition, study skills, career planning. All offered for credit; all enter into overall grade point average.

Auxiliary Aids and Services Aids include taped textbooks, tape recorders, calculators, typewriters. Services include alternative exam arrangements, notetakers, advocacy, typing services.

Counseling Services Individual counseling, small-group counseling, rap sessions, career counseling available.

Contact Dr. Clifford L. Ramig, Director, Project EXCEL, College of Mount St Joseph on the Ohio, Education Department, Mount St Joseph, OH 45051, 513-244-4859.

COLLEGE OF ST CATHERINE
St Paul, Minnesota

Year Program Began	1982	Special Courses	✓
Special Fee	None	Taped Textbooks	✓
Special Orientation		Alternative Exam Arrangements	✓
Diagnostic Testing	✓	Notetakers	✓
Subject-Area Tutoring	✓	Staff	16 part-time
Basic Skills Remediation	✓	Number of Students Served	18

General Information Roman Catholic comprehensive women's institution. Founded 1905. Awards B, M. Institutionally accredited by regional association; programs accredited by NLN (nursing), NCATE (teacher education); candidate for program accreditation by NASM (music). Metropolitan setting; 110-acre campus. Total enrollment: 2,458. Faculty: 213 (145 full-time, 68 part-time); 37% have doctoral degrees; graduate assistants teach no undergraduate courses. Calendar: 4-1-4. Grading system: letters or numbers. Library holdings: 224,666 bound volumes, 4,503 titles on microform, 1,036 periodical subscriptions, 7,600 records/tapes.

Undergraduate Profile Fall 1984: 2,442 undergraduates (329 freshmen) from 35 states and territories and 27 foreign countries; 41% part-time; 97% state residents; 21% transfers; 60% financial aid recipients; 100% women; 1% blacks; 1% Native Americans; 1% Hispanics; 1% Asian Americans; 3% foreign nationals; 25% of undergraduates over 25 years of age.

Expenses (1985–86) Comprehensive fee of $8425 includes full-time tuition ($5880), mandatory fees ($65), and college room and board ($2480). College room only: $1300. Part-time tuition: $735 per course.

Financial Aid Fall 1984 full-time freshmen: 79% applied for aid, 92% of those were judged to have need, 100% of those were aided; the average aided freshman received an aid package worth $5481 (53% scholarships/grants, 47% self-help) meeting 97% of need. College-administered aid for all 1984–85 undergraduates: 950 need-based scholarships (average $1100); 18 non-need scholarships (average $1400); low-interest long-term loans from external sources (average $2000); SEOG; College Work-Study; 400 part-time jobs. Supporting data: FFS, IRS, institutional form, AFSA/SAR required; FAF acceptable. Priority application deadline: 4/1.

Athletics Member NCAA (Division III). Intercollegiate sports: baseball/softball (III); basketball (III); cross-country running (III); swimming and diving (III); tennis (III); track and field (III); volleyball (III). Intramural sports: baseball/softball, football, rugby, soccer, tennis, volleyball.

Majors Accounting B; American studies B; anthropology B; art education B; art/fine arts B; art history B; biochemistry B; biology/biological sciences B; business administration/commerce/management B; chemistry B; classics B; communication B; computer science B; criminal justice B; (pre)dentistry sequence B; dietetics B; early childhood education B; East Asian studies B; ecology/environmental studies B; economics B; education B; elementary education B; English B; finance/banking B; French B; geography B; geology B; German B; health education B; history B; home economics B; home economics education B; information science B; international studies B; journalism B; Latin B; Latin American studies B; (pre)law sequence B; liberal arts/general studies B; linguistics B; literature B; marketing/retailing/merchandising B; mathematics B; medical technology B; (pre)medicine sequence B; music B; music education B; nursing B; nutrition B; occupational therapy B; philosophy B; physical education B; physics B; political science/government B; psychology B; Russian B; Russian and Slavic studies B; Scandinavian languages/studies B; secondary education B; social science B; social work B; sociology B; Spanish B; studio art B; telecommunications B; textiles and clothing B; theater arts/drama B; theology B; urban studies B; (pre)veterinary medicine sequence B. Majors with highest enrollment: business administration/commerce/management, nursing, education.

LD Program Information

Name of Program Learning Center.

Availability of Services Began offering services in 1982. Services provided to freshmen, sophomores, juniors, seniors. Program currently serves 18 LD students.

Staff 16 part-time staff members, including director, associate directors. Services provided by remediation specialist, tutors, counselor, diagnostic specialist.

Admissions LD applicants evaluated on the basis of high school transcript and grade point average, standard or untimed SAT or ACT. LD students may begin taking classes in fall or spring. Application should be submitted 3 to 6 months in advance of initial anticipated enrollment.

Housing College housing available. LD students housed randomly. LD students not required to live on campus.

Diagnostic Testing Available in reading, math, spelling, handwriting, written language, perceptual skills, work and study habits, personality.

Tutoring Offered one-to-one and in small groups by professional teachers, peer tutors. Available in some subjects. LD students may receive tutoring in all courses each term.

Basic Skills Remediation Offered one-to-one and in small groups by LD teachers. Available in reading, math, written language, learning strategies, work and study habits.

Academic Advisement Help with program planning provided by LD staff members, academic advisers. LD students may take up to 4 courses each semester; most take 3 courses; 3 courses required to maintain full-time status.

Special Courses Offered in college survival skills, reading, vocabulary development, composition, math, study skills. Some offered for credit; some enter into overall grade point average.

Auxiliary Aids and Services Aids include taped textbooks, tape recorders, typewriters, word processors. Services include alternative exam arrangements, notetakers, advocacy, term paper assistance.

Counseling Services Individual counseling, small-group counseling available.

Contact Ms. Mary Lundeberg, Director, Whitby Learning Centers, College of St Catherine, 2004 Randolph Avenue, St Paul, MN 55105, 612-690-6718.

COLLEGE OF SANTA FE

Santa Fe, New Mexico

Year Program Began	1976	Special Courses	✓
Special Fee	None	Taped Textbooks	
Special Orientation		Alternative Exam Arrangements	
Diagnostic Testing	✓	Notetakers	
Subject-Area Tutoring	✓	Staff	5 part-time
Basic Skills Remediation	✓	Number of Students Served	4

General Information Roman Catholic comprehensive coed institution. Founded 1947. Awards A (college transfer and terminal), B, M. Institutionally accredited by regional association; programs accredited by NLN (nursing). City setting; 118-acre campus. Total enrollment: 910. Faculty: 90 (60 full-time, 30 part-time); 65% have doctoral degrees; graduate assistants teach no undergraduate courses. Calendar: semesters. Grading system: letters or numbers. Library holdings: 87,000 bound volumes, 300 periodical subscriptions, 1,000 records/tapes.

Undergraduate Profile Fall 1984: 857 undergraduates (320 freshmen); 33% part-time; 72% state residents; 45% transfers; 73% financial aid recipients; 59% women; 4% blacks; 9% Native Americans; 38% Hispanics; 1% Asian Americans; 3% foreign nationals; 3 legally handicapped students.

Expenses (1985–86) Comprehensive fee of $6018 includes full-time tuition ($3500), mandatory fees ($88), and college room and board ($2430). College room only: $1100. Part-time tuition: $125 per semester hour.

Financial Aid Fall 1984 full-time freshmen: 62% applied for aid, 96% of those were judged to have need, 100% of those were aided; the average aided freshman received an aid package worth $4195 (54% scholarships/grants, 46% self-help) meeting 73% of need. College-administered aid for all 1984–85 undergraduates: need-based scholarships; 30 non-need scholarships (average $750); low-interest long-term loans from external sources (average $2000); SEOG; College Work-Study; 10 part-time jobs. Supporting data: FAF, IRS, state form required; FFS, AFSA/SAR acceptable. Priority application deadline: 3/1.

Athletics Member NAIA. Intercollegiate sports: basketball M(s); tennis M(s), W(s); volleyball W(s). Intramural sports: badminton, baseball/softball, basketball, bowling, football, golf, gymnastics, racquetball, skiing (cross-country), skiing (downhill), swimming and diving, tennis, track and field, volleyball, weight lifting.

Majors Accounting B; art education B; art/fine arts B; arts administration B; biology/biological sciences B; business administration/commerce/management A, B; business education B; chemistry B; computer science A, B; (pre)dentistry sequence B; education B; elementary education B; (pre)engineering sequence A; English A, B; history B; humanities B; human services B; (pre)law sequence B; liberal arts/general studies B; literature B; management information systems B; mathematics A, B; medical technology B; (pre)medicine sequence B; nursing A, B; physical sciences B; political science/government B; psychology B; public administration A, B; religious studies B; science B; science education B; secondary education B; secretarial studies/office management A; social science A, B; studio art B; theater arts/drama A, B; (pre)veterinary medicine sequence B. Majors with highest enrollment: business administration/commerce/management, theater arts/drama, nursing.

LD Program Information

Name of Program Special Services for Disadvantaged Students.

Availability of Services Began offering services in 1976. Services provided to freshmen, sophomores, juniors, seniors. Program currently serves 4 LD students (all freshmen).

Staff 5 part-time staff members, including director. Services provided by remediation specialists, counselors.

Admissions LD applicants evaluated on the basis of high school transcript, standard ACT. LD students may begin taking classes in fall or winter. Application should be submitted 2 months in advance of initial anticipated enrollment.

Housing College housing (including coed) available. LD students housed randomly. LD freshmen required to live on campus except if living with relatives.

Diagnostic Testing Available in reading, math, written language.

Tutoring Offered one-to-one and in small groups by professional teachers, peer tutors. Available in all subjects. LD students may receive tutoring in all courses each term.

Basic Skills Remediation Offered one-to-one and in small groups by regular teachers. Available in reading, math, written language, learning strategies, work and study habits, social skills.

Academic Advisement Help with program planning provided by LD staff members, academic advisers. LD students may take up to 17 semester hours each semester; most take 12 to 14 semester hours; 12 semester hours required to maintain full-time status.

Special Courses Offered in reading, composition, math. All offered for credit; all enter into overall grade point average.

Auxiliary Aids and Services Aids include tape recorders, calculators, typewriters, word processors.

Counseling Services Individual counseling, small-group counseling, career counseling available.

Contact Dr. Marylou Butler, Director of Special Services for Disadvantaged Students, College of Santa Fe, Santa Fe, NM 87501, 505-473-6447.

COLLEGE OF THE OZARKS

Clarksville, Arkansas

Year Program Began	1973	Special Courses	✓
Special Fee	$1100 to $4600 per year	Taped Textbooks	✓
Special Orientation	✓	Alternative Exam Arrangements	✓
Diagnostic Testing	✓	Notetakers	✓
Subject-Area Tutoring	✓	Staff	15 full-time
Basic Skills Remediation	✓	Number of Students Served	52

General Information Presbyterian 4-year coed college. Founded 1834. Awards A (terminal), B. Institutionally accredited by regional association; programs accredited by NCATE (teacher education). Small-town setting; 40-acre campus. Total enrollment: 723. Faculty: 40 (29 full-time, 11 part-time); 33% have doctoral degrees. Calendar: 4-1-4. Grading system: letters or numbers. Library holdings: 15,129 bound volumes, 3,056 titles on microform, 450 periodical subscriptions, 1,876 records/tapes.

Undergraduate Profile Fall 1984: 723 undergraduates (220 freshmen); 1% part-time; 60% state residents; 21% transfers; 85% financial aid recipients; 52% women; 7% blacks; 1% Native Americans; 1% Hispanics; 13% foreign nationals; 2 legally handicapped students.

Expenses (1985–86) Comprehensive fee of $3480 includes full-time tuition ($1760), mandatory fees ($110), and college room and board ($1610). College room only: $660. Part-time tuition: $75 per semester hour.

Financial Aid Fall 1984 full-time freshmen: 57% applied for aid, 76% of those were judged to have need, 100% of those were aided; the average aided freshman received an aid package worth $3474 (78% scholarships/grants, 22% self-help) meeting 90% of need. College-administered aid for all 1984–85 undergraduates: need-based scholarships (average $400); 132 non-need scholarships (average $400); low-interest long-term loans; part-time jobs. Supporting data: FFS, institutional form, AFSA/SAR required. Priority application deadline: 7/1.

Athletics Member NAIA. Intercollegiate sports: baseball/softball M(s); basketball M(s), W(s); cross-country running M(s); soccer M; tennis M(s), W(s); track and field M(s). Intramural sports: badminton, baseball/softball, basketball, football, golf, soccer, tennis, track and field, volleyball, weight lifting.

Majors Accounting B; applied art B; art education B; art/fine arts B; biblical studies B; biology/biological sciences B; broadcasting B; business administration/commerce/management B; business economics B; business education B; chemistry B; communication B; (pre)dentistry sequence B; economics B; education B; elementary education B; (pre)engineering sequence A; English B; history B; journalism B; (pre) law sequence B; liberal arts/general studies B; marketing/retailing/merchandising B; mathematics B; (pre)medicine sequence B; ministries B; music B; music education B; pharmacy/pharmaceutical sciences B; philosophy B; physical education B; political science/government B; psychology B; public administration B; radio and television studies B; radiological technology B; religious education B; religious studies B; science B; science education B; secondary education B; secretarial studies/office management A; social science B; sociology B; theater arts/drama B; theology B; (pre) veterinary medicine sequence B. Majors with highest enrollment: business administration/commerce/management, education, science.

LD Program Information

Name of Program Special Learning Center.

Availability of Services Began offering services in 1973. Services provided to freshmen, sophomores, juniors, seniors. Program currently serves 52 LD students: 17 freshmen, 12 sophomores, 12 juniors, 11 seniors.

Fees Range from $1100 to $4600 per year according to phase of program.

Staff 15 full-time staff members, including director. Services provided by diagnostic specialists, coordinators, coordinator assistant, reading remediation specialist, developmental writing specialist, tape librarian.

Admissions LD applicants evaluated on the basis of high school transcript, untimed ACT, personal interview, autobiographical statement, psychoeducational report, including personality appraisals. LD students may begin taking classes in fall or spring. Application should be submitted 1 to 2 years in advance of initial anticipated enrollment.

Orientation Required orientation held before registration.

Housing College housing (including coed) available. LD students housed randomly. LD freshmen, sophomores, juniors, and seniors required to live on campus except if 21 or over or living with relatives.

Diagnostic Testing Available in intelligence, reading, math, spelling, spoken language, written language, motor abilities, perceptual skills, personality, social skills.

Tutoring Offered one-to-one by peer tutors, coordinators, coordinator assistant. Available in all subjects. LD students may receive tutoring in all courses each term in first phase of program (decreasing number in later phases).

Basic Skills Remediation Offered one-to-one by regular teachers. Available in reading, spelling, handwriting, spoken language, written language, learning strategies, work and study habits.

Academic Advisement Help with program planning provided by LD staff members, academic advisers. Most LD students take 12 to 15 semester hours each semester.

Special Courses Offered in college survival skills, reading, vocabulary development, study skills, career planning, developmental writing. Some offered for credit; none enter into overall grade point average.

Auxiliary Aids and Services Aids include taped textbooks, tape recorders, computers. Services include alternative exam arrangements, notetakers, advocacy, typing services.

Counseling Services Individual counseling available.

Contact Ms. Betty Robinson, Director of Special Learning Center, College of the Ozarks, 415 College Avenue, Clarksville, AR 72830, 501-754-3839.

COLLEGE OF WOOSTER

Wooster, Ohio

Year Program Began	1979	Special Courses	
Special Fee	None	Taped Textbooks	✓
Special Orientation		Alternative Exam Arrangements	✓
Diagnostic Testing	✓	Notetakers	
Subject-Area Tutoring	✓	Staff	4 part-time
Basic Skills Remediation	✓	Number of Students Served	49

General Information Presbyterian 4-year coed college. Founded 1866. Awards B. Institutionally accredited by regional association; programs accredited by NASAD (art and design), NASM (music). Small-town setting, with easy access to Cleveland; 320-acre campus. Total enrollment: 1,691. Faculty: 138 (124 full-time, 14 part-time); 77% have doctoral degrees. Calendar: semesters. Grading system: letters or numbers. Library holdings: 306,000 bound volumes, 137,350 titles on microform, 1,250 periodical subscriptions, 4,725 records/tapes.

Undergraduate Profile Fall 1984: 1,691 undergraduates (555 freshmen) from 42 states and territories and 50 foreign countries; 41% state residents; 7% transfers; 55% financial aid recipients; 47% women; 5% blacks; 0% Native Americans; 0% Hispanics; 1% Asian Americans; 9% foreign nationals.

Expenses (1985–86) Comprehensive fee: $11,245.

Financial Aid Fall 1984 full-time freshmen: 68% applied for aid, 89% of those were judged to have need, 100% of those were aided; the average aided freshman received an aid package worth $6651 (62% scholarships/grants, 38% self-help) meeting 100% of need. College-administered aid for all 1984–85 undergraduates: 835 need-based scholarships (average $3200); 450 non-need scholarships (average $1500); low-interest long-term loans from college funds (average $1100), from external sources (average $1500); SEOG; College Work-Study; 500 part-time jobs. Supporting data: FAF, IRS required; state form, AFSA/SAR required for some; FFS acceptable. Priority application deadline: 3/1.

Athletics Member NCAA (Division III). Intercollegiate sports: baseball/softball M(III), W(III); basketball M(III), W(III); cross-country running M(III), W(III); field hockey W(III); football M(III); golf M(III); lacrosse M(III), W(III); rugby M(c); soccer M(III), W(III); swimming and diving M(III), W(III); tennis M(III), W(III); track and field M(III), W(III); volleyball M(c), W(III); wrestling M(c). Intramural sports: baseball/softball, basketball, bowling, football, golf, tennis, track and field, volleyball.

Majors African studies B; art/fine arts B; art history B; Asian/Oriental studies B; biology/biological sciences B; black/Afro-American studies B; business economics B; chemistry B; classics B; communication B; comparative literature B; computer science B; (pre)dentistry sequence B; economics B; English B; European studies B; French B; geology B; German B; Greek B; history B; international studies B; Latin B; Latin American studies B; (pre)law sequence B; mathematics B; (pre)medicine sequence B; music B; music education B; music history B; music therapy B; Near and Middle Eastern studies B; philosophy B; physics B; political science/government B; psychology B; religious studies B; Russian and Slavic studies B; sociology B; South Asian studies B; Spanish B; speech pathology and audiology B; speech/rhetoric/public address/debate B; studio art B; theater arts/drama B; urban studies B; (pre)veterinary medicine sequence B; voice B. Majors with highest enrollment: history, chemistry, economics.

LD Program Information

Name of Program Program for Learning Disabled Students.

Availability of Services Began offering services in 1979. Services provided to freshmen, sophomores, juniors, seniors. Program currently serves 49 LD students: 23 freshmen, 13 sophomores, 9 juniors, 4 seniors.

Staff 4 part-time staff members, including coordinator. Services provided by tutors.

Admissions LD applicants evaluated on the basis of high school transcript and grade point average, standard or untimed SAT or ACT, personal interview, autobiographical statement, letters of recommendation; psychoeducational report recommended. LD students may begin taking classes in fall only. Application should be submitted 4 months in advance of initial anticipated enrollment.

Housing College housing (including coed) available. LD students housed randomly. LD freshmen, sophomores, juniors, and seniors required to live on campus except by special permission.

Diagnostic Testing Available in learning styles assessment.

Tutoring Offered one-to-one by professional teachers, peer tutors. Available in all subjects. LD students may receive tutoring in all courses each term.

Basic Skills Remediation Offered one-to-one by LD teachers. Available in reading, math, spelling, spoken language, written language, learning strategies, work and study habits, social skills.

Academic Advisement Help with program planning provided by LD staff members, academic advisers. LD students may take up to 4 courses each semester; 3 courses required to maintain full-time status.

Auxiliary Aids and Services Aids include taped textbooks. Services include alternative exam arrangements.

Counseling Services Individual counseling, career counseling available.

Contact Ms. Patricia Hilton, Coordinator, Program for Learning Disabled Students, College of Wooster, Wooster, OH 44691, 216-263-2420.

COLORADO STATE UNIVERSITY

Fort Collins, Colorado

Year Program Began	1979	Special Courses	✓
Special Fee	None	Taped Textbooks	✓
Special Orientation		Alternative Exam Arrangements	✓
Diagnostic Testing	✓	Notetakers	✓
Subject-Area Tutoring	✓	Staff	2 part-time
Basic Skills Remediation	✓	Number of Students Served	10

General Information State-supported coed university. Founded 1870. Awards B, M, D. Institutionally accredited by regional association; programs accredited by AACSB (business), ABET (engineering and technology), NASM (music), NCATE (teacher education). City setting, with easy access to Denver; 833-acre campus. Total enrollment: 18,094. Faculty: 1,158 (905 full-time, 253 part-time); 79% have doctoral degrees; graduate assistants teach a few undergraduate courses. Calendar: semesters. Grading system: letters or numbers. Library holdings: 1.2 million bound volumes, 16,900 periodical subscriptions, 8,300 records/tapes.

Undergraduate Profile Fall 1984: 15,182 undergraduates (2,668 freshmen) from 54 states and territories and 34 foreign countries; 9% part-time; 85% state residents; 9% transfers; 37% financial aid recipients; 49% women; 1% blacks; 1% Native Americans; 3% Hispanics; 2% Asian Americans; 1% foreign nationals; 10% of undergraduates over 25 years of age; 140 legally handicapped students.

Expenses (1984–85) State resident tuition: $1159 full-time, $48 per credit part-time. Nonresident tuition: $4411 full-time, $184 per credit part-time. Mandatory fees: $287. College room and board: $2600.

Financial Aid Fall 1984 full-time freshmen: 42% applied for aid, 63% of those were judged to have need, 73% of those were aided; the average aided freshman received an aid package worth $2825 (59% scholarships/grants, 41% self-help) meeting 75% of need. College-administered aid for all 1984–85 undergraduates: 2,154 need-based scholarships (average $658); 2,092 non-need scholarships (average $876); short-term loans (average $300); low-interest long-term loans from external sources (average $638); SEOG; College Work-Study; 3,322 part-time jobs. Supporting data: FFS, IRS required; institutional form required for some; FAF, AFSA/SAR acceptable. Application deadline: 4/1.

Athletics Member NCAA (Division I), NAIA. Intercollegiate sports: baseball/softball M(I,s), W(I,s); basketball M(I,s), W(I,s); cross-country running M(I,s), W(I,s); football M(I-A,s); golf W(I); swimming and diving W(I,s); tennis M(I), W(I); track and field M(I,s), W(I,s); volleyball W(I,s); wrestling M(I,s). Intramural sports: baseball/softball, basketball, golf, lacrosse, martial arts, racquetball, skiing (cross-country), skiing (downhill), soccer, tennis, volleyball, wrestling.

Majors Accounting B; agricultural business B; agricultural economics B; agricultural education B; agricultural engineering B; agricultural sciences B; agronomy/soil and crop sciences B; animal sciences B; anthropology B; applied mathematics B; art education B; art/fine arts B; art history B; biochemistry B; biology/biological sciences B; botany/plant sciences B; business administration/commerce/management B; business education B; cell biology B; chemical engineering B; chemistry B; child care/child and family studies B; civil engineering B; computer information systems B; computer science B; construction management B; consumer services B; creative writing B; dance B; (pre)dentistry sequence B; dietetics B; economics B; electrical engineering B; engineering (general) B; engineering sciences B; English B; entomology B; environmental health sciences B; family and consumer studies B; farm and ranch management B; fashion merchandising B; finance/banking B; fish and game management B; food sciences B; forestry B; French B; geology B; German B; history B; home economics B; home economics education B; horticulture B; human development B; humanities B; industrial arts B; industrial design B; information science B; interior design B; journalism B; labor and industrial relations B; landscape architecture/design B; (pre)law sequence B; liberal arts/general studies B; manufacturing technology B; marketing/retailing/merchandising B; mathematics B; mechanical engineering B; medical technology B; (pre)medicine sequence B; microbiology B; music B; music education B; music therapy B; natural resource management B; nutrition B; occupational therapy B; parks management B; philosophy B; physical education B; physical sciences B; physics B; political science/government B; psychology B; range management B; real estate B; secondary education B; social science B; social work B; sociology B; Spanish B; speech pathology and audiology B; speech/rhetoric/public address/debate B; statistics B; textiles and clothing B; theater arts/drama B; (pre)veterinary medicine sequence B; veterinary sciences B; vocational education B; wildlife biology B; wood sciences B; zoology B. Majors with highest enrollment: mathematics, electrical engineering, accounting.

LD Program Information

Name of Program Resources for Disabled Students.

Availability of Services Began offering services in 1979. Services provided to freshmen, sophomores, juniors, seniors. Program currently serves 10 LD students: 2 freshmen, 1 sophomore, 4 juniors, 3 seniors.

Staff 2 part-time staff members, including director. Services provided by program assistant, peer counselors.

Admissions LD applicants evaluated on the basis of high school transcript and grade point average, standard or untimed SAT or ACT, personal interview. LD students may begin taking classes in fall, spring, or summer. Application should be submitted at least 6 months in advance of initial anticipated enrollment.

Housing College housing (including coed) available. LD students housed randomly. LD freshmen required to live on campus.

Diagnostic Testing Available in intelligence, reading, math, spelling, handwriting, spoken language, written language, motor abilities, perceptual skills, work and study habits, personality, social skills, speech.

Tutoring Offered one-to-one and in small groups by professional teachers, peer tutors. Available in some subjects. LD students may receive tutoring in all courses each term.

Basic Skills Remediation Offered one-to-one and in small groups by regular teachers, teacher trainees. Available in reading, spoken language, written language, learning strategies, work and study habits, speech.

Academic Advisement Help with program planning provided by LD staff member, academic advisers. LD students may take up to 18 credits each semester; most take 9 to 16 credits; 12 credits required to maintain full-time status.

Special Courses Offered in reading, math, study skills. Some offered for credit; some enter into overall grade point average.

Auxiliary Aids and Services Aids include taped textbooks, tape recorders, calculators. Services include alternative exam arrangements, notetakers, advocacy.

Counseling Services Individual counseling, small-group counseling available.

Contact Ms. Rosemary Kreston, Director, Resources for Disabled Students, Colorado State University, 112 Student Services, Fort Collins, CO 80523, 303-491-6385.

CONCEPTION SEMINARY COLLEGE

Conception, Missouri

Year Program Began	1982	Special Courses	✓
Special Fee	None	Taped Textbooks	
Special Orientation		Alternative Exam Arrangements	
Diagnostic Testing	✓	Notetakers	
Subject-Area Tutoring	✓	Staff	1 part-time
Basic Skills Remediation		Number of Students Served	1

General Information Roman Catholic 4-year men's college. Founded 1886. Awards B. Institutionally accredited by regional association. Rural setting; 30-acre campus. Total enrollment: 105. Faculty: 27; 43% have doctoral degrees. Calendar: semesters. Grading system: letters or numbers. Library holdings: 94,501 bound volumes, 304 periodical subscriptions, 3,300 records/tapes.

Undergraduate Profile Fall 1984: 105 undergraduates (20 freshmen) from 15 states and territories and 1 foreign country; 15% part-time; 35% state residents; 11% transfers; 87% financial aid recipients; 0% women; 1% blacks; 4% Hispanics; 3% Asian Americans; 1% foreign nationals; 20% of undergraduates over 25 years of age; 1 legally handicapped student.

Expenses (1985–86) Comprehensive fee of $5130 includes full-time tuition ($2520), mandatory fees ($90), and college room and board ($2520). College room only: $860. Part-time tuition: $60 per semester hour.

Financial Aid Fall 1984 full-time freshmen: 100% applied for aid, 100% of those were judged to have need, 100% of those were aided; the average aided freshman received an aid package worth $3327 (59% scholarships/grants, 41% self-help) meeting 100% of need. College-administered aid for all 1984–85 undergraduates: 37 need-based scholarships (average $435); 12 non-need scholarships (average $300); low-interest long-term loans from external sources; SEOG; College Work-Study; 32 part-time jobs. Supporting data: FFS, AFSA/SAR required for some. Application deadline: continuous.

Athletics Intramural sports: baseball/softball, basketball, bowling, cross-country running, football, gymnastics, racquetball, soccer, swimming and diving, tennis, volleyball, weight lifting.

Majors Philosophy B; religious studies B; social science B. Major with highest enrollment: religious studies.

LD Program Information

Name of Program Learning Resources Center.

Availability of Services Began offering services in 1982. Services provided to freshmen, sophomores, juniors, seniors. Program currently serves 1 LD freshman.

Staff 1 part-time staff member (director).

Admissions LD applicants evaluated on the basis of high school transcript and grade point average, standard ACT, letters of recommendation. LD students may begin taking classes in fall or spring. Application should be submitted 3 months in advance of initial anticipated enrollment.

Housing College housing available. LD students housed with other LD students and non-LD students. LD freshmen, sophomores, juniors, and seniors required to live on campus.

Diagnostic Testing Available in intelligence, reading, math, spelling, handwriting, spoken language, perceptual skills, work and study habits, personality.

Tutoring Offered one-to-one and in small groups by professional teachers, peer tutors. Available in some subjects. LD students may receive tutoring in 2 courses per term.

Academic Advisement Help with program planning provided by LD staff member, academic advisers. LD students may take up to 12 semester hours each semester; 12 semester hours required to maintain full-time status.

Special Courses Offered in college survival skills, reading, composition, math, personal psychology, study skills, career planning. None offered for credit; none enter into overall grade point average.

Auxiliary Aids and Services Aids include tape recorders.

Counseling Services Individual counseling, small-group counseling, career counseling available.

Contact Ms. Deborah A. Bailey, Director of Learning Resources Center, Conception Seminary College, Conception, MO 64433, 816-944-2218.

CONCORDIA COLLEGE
Moorhead, Minnesota

Year Program Began	1973	Special Courses	✓
Special Fee	None	Taped Textbooks	✓
Special Orientation		Alternative Exam Arrangements	✓
Diagnostic Testing	✓	Notetakers	✓
Subject-Area Tutoring	✓	Staff	3 part-time
Basic Skills Remediation	✓	Number of Students Served	3

General Information 4-year coed college, affiliated with Lutheran Church. Founded 1891. Awards B. Institutionally accredited by regional association; programs accredited by NASM (music), NCATE (teacher education). City setting; 120-acre barrier-free campus. Total enrollment: 2,467. Faculty: 194 (148 full-time, 46 part-time); 56% have doctoral degrees. Calendar: semesters. Grading system: letters or numbers. Library holdings: 260,000 bound volumes, 28,823 titles on microform, 1,350 periodical subscriptions, 7,230 records/tapes.

Undergraduate Profile Fall 1984: 2,467 undergraduates (723 freshmen) from 40 states and territories and 15 foreign countries; 2% part-time; 63% state residents; 4% transfers; 82% financial aid recipients; 58% women; 1% blacks; 1% Native Americans; 0% Hispanics; 2% foreign nationals; 2% of undergraduates over 25 years of age; 10 legally handicapped students.

Expenses (1985–86) Comprehensive fee of $8000 includes full-time tuition ($5950), mandatory fees ($50), and college room and board ($2000). College room only: $890. Part-time tuition: $925 per course.

Financial Aid Fall 1984 full-time freshmen: 90% applied for aid, 85% of those were judged to have need, 100% of those were aided; the average aided freshman received an aid package worth $6038 (63% scholarships/grants, 37% self-help) meeting 100% of need. College-administered aid for all 1984–85 undergraduates: 1,525 need-based scholarships (average $2030); 96 non-need scholarships (average $2275); short-term loans (average $50); low-interest long-term loans from external sources (average $2188); SEOG; College Work-Study; 800 part-time jobs. Supporting data: FFS, FAF, institutional form required. Priority application deadline: 8/1.

Athletics Member NCAA (Division III), NAIA. Intercollegiate sports: baseball/softball M(III); basketball M(III), W(III); cross-country running M(III), W(III); football M(III); golf M(III), W(III); gymnastics W(III); ice hockey M(III); martial arts M(c), W(c); soccer M(c), W(III); tennis M(III), W(III); track and field M(III), W(III); volleyball W(III); wrestling M(III). Intramural sports: badminton, baseball/softball, basketball, bowling, cross-country running, football, golf, ice hockey, skiing (cross-country), soccer, swimming and diving, tennis, track and field, volleyball, water polo, weight lifting.

Majors Accounting B; art education B; art/fine arts B; art history B; biology/biological sciences B; business administration/commerce/management B; business education B; chemistry B; classics B; communication B; computer science B; (pre) dentistry sequence B; economics B; education B; elementary education B; English B; French B; German B; health education B; health services administration B; history B; home economics B; home economics education B; humanities B; international studies B; Latin B; (pre)law sequence B; mathematics B; medical technology B; (pre) medicine sequence B; music B; music education B; nursing B; nutrition B; philosophy B; physical education B; physics B; physiology B; piano/organ B; political science/government B; psychology B; recreation and leisure services B; religious studies B; science education B; secondary education B; secretarial studies/office management B; social work B; sociology B; Spanish B; speech/rhetoric/public address/debate B; studio art B; theater arts/drama B; voice B; wind and percussion instruments B. Majors with highest enrollment: business administration/commerce/management, biology/biological sciences, elementary education.

LD Program Information

Name of Program Not specified.

Availability of Services Began offering services in 1973. Services provided to freshmen, sophomores, juniors, seniors. Program currently serves 3 LD students: 1 freshman, 1 sophomore, 1 senior.

Staff 3 part-time staff members, including co-coordinators. Services provided by remediation specialists, counselors, diagnostic specialists.

Admissions LD applicants evaluated on the basis of high school transcript and grade point average, standard or untimed SAT or ACT, personal interview, psychoeducational report. LD students may begin taking classes in fall only. Application should be submitted 5 to 6 months in advance of initial anticipated enrollment.

Housing College housing available. LD students housed randomly. LD freshmen and sophomores required to live on campus.

Diagnostic Testing Available in intelligence, reading, written language, personality.

Tutoring Offered one-to-one and in small groups by peer tutors. Available in some subjects. LD students may receive tutoring in 3 courses per term.

Basic Skills Remediation Offered one-to-one and in small groups by regular teachers, counselors. Available in reading, written language, learning strategies, work and study habits, social skills.

Academic Advisement Help with program planning provided by LD staff members, academic advisers. LD students may take up to 16 semester hours each semester; 12 semester hours required to maintain full-time status.

Special Courses Offered in reading, communication skills, composition, study skills. Some offered for credit; some enter into overall grade point average.

Auxiliary Aids and Services Aids include taped textbooks, tape recorders. Services include alternative exam arrangements, notetakers, advocacy, early registration.

Counseling Services Individual counseling, career counseling available.

Contact Mr. Donald Dale, Registrar, Concordia College, Moorhead, MN 56560, 218-299-3949.

CONCORDIA COLLEGE
Portland, Oregon

Year Program Began	1982	Special Courses	✓
Special Fee	None	Taped Textbooks	
Special Orientation	✓	Alternative Exam Arrangements	✓
Diagnostic Testing	✓	Notetakers	✓
Subject-Area Tutoring	✓	Staff	1 part-time
Basic Skills Remediation	✓	Number of Students Served	2

General Information 4-year coed college, affiliated with Lutheran Church–Missouri Synod. Founded 1905. Awards A (college transfer), B. Institutionally accredited by regional association. Metropolitan setting; 10-acre campus. Total enrollment: 445. Faculty: 44 (30 full-time, 14 part-time); 32% have doctoral degrees. Calendar: quarters. Grading system: letters or numbers. Library holdings: 40,000 bound volumes, 565 periodical subscriptions, 5,400 records/tapes.

Undergraduate Profile Fall 1984: 445 undergraduates (105 freshmen) from 14 states and territories and 8 foreign countries; 13% part-time; 40% state residents; 15% transfers; 88% financial aid recipients; 53% women; 3% blacks; 1% Native Americans; 0% Hispanics; 1% Asian Americans; 5% foreign nationals; 4% of undergraduates over 25 years of age; 2 legally handicapped students.

Expenses (1985–86) Comprehensive fee of $8260 includes full-time tuition ($4800), mandatory fees ($340), and college room and board ($3120). College room only: $1200. Part-time tuition: $115 per quarter hour.

Financial Aid Fall 1984 full-time freshmen: 58% applied for aid, 93% of those were judged to have need, 100% of those were aided; the average aided freshman received an aid package worth $5700 (64% scholarships/grants, 36% self-help) meeting 100% of need. College-administered aid for all 1984–85 undergraduates: 233 need-based scholarships (average $2500); 27 non-need scholarships (average $1400); low-interest long-term loans from external sources (average $900); SEOG; College Work-Study; 191 part-time jobs. Supporting data: FAF, IRS, institutional form, AFSA/SAR required; FFS acceptable. Priority application deadline: 5/1.

Athletics Member NAIA. Intercollegiate sports: baseball/softball M(s), W(s); basketball M(s), W(s); soccer M(s); volleyball W(s). Intramural sports: badminton, baseball/softball, basketball, football, golf, skiing (cross-country), skiing (downhill), tennis, volleyball.

Majors Accounting B; behavioral sciences B; biology/biological sciences B; business administration/commerce/management B; (pre)dentistry sequence B; early childhood education B; education B; elementary education B; English B; history B; (pre)law sequence B; liberal arts/general studies A, B; (pre)medicine sequence B; music B; natural sciences B; nursing A; physical sciences B; religious education B; religious studies B; secondary education B; social work B; special education B; theology B; (pre)veterinary medicine sequence B. Majors with highest enrollment: elementary education, business administration/commerce/management, liberal arts/general studies.

LD Program Information

Name of Program Not specified.

Availability of Services Began offering services in 1982. Services provided to freshmen, sophomores, juniors, seniors. Program currently serves 2 LD students: 1 freshman, 1 junior.

Staff 1 part-time staff member (director).

Admissions LD applicants evaluated on the basis of high school transcript, standard SAT or ACT, personal interview, letters of recommendation, psychoeducational report. LD students may begin taking classes in fall, winter, or spring. Application should be submitted 6 months in advance of initial anticipated enrollment.

Orientation Required orientation held before registration.

Housing College housing (including coed) available. LD students housed randomly. LD freshmen required to live on campus.

Diagnostic Testing Available in reading, math, spelling.

Tutoring Offered one-to-one by professional teachers, peer tutors. Available in all subjects. LD students may receive tutoring in all courses each term.

Basic Skills Remediation Offered one-to-one and in small groups by peer teachers. Available in reading, math, spelling, written language, learning strategies, work and study habits.

Academic Advisement Help with program planning provided by academic advisers. LD students may take up to 18 quarter hours each quarter; most take 15 to 16 quarter hours; 12 quarter hours required to maintain full-time status.

Special Courses Offered in college survival skills, reading, vocabulary development, composition, math. None offered for credit; none enter into overall grade point average.

Auxiliary Aids and Services Aids include word processors. Services include alternative exam arrangements, notetakers.

Counseling Services Individual counseling, career counseling available.

Contact Dr. Fred Kramer, Academic Dean, Concordia College, 2811 Northeast Holman, Portland, OR 97211, 503-288-9371.

CONVERSE COLLEGE
Spartanburg, South Carolina

Year Program Began	1978
Special Fee	None
Special Orientation	
Diagnostic Testing	
Subject-Area Tutoring	✓
Basic Skills Remediation	
Special Courses	
Taped Textbooks	
Alternative Exam Arrangements	✓
Notetakers	✓
Staff	6 part-time
Number of Students Served	1

General Information Independent comprehensive women's institution. Founded 1889. Awards B, M. Institutionally accredited by regional association; programs accredited by NASM (music). City setting; 70-acre campus. Total enrollment: 1,037. Faculty: 85 (65 full-time, 20 part-time); 75% have doctoral degrees; graduate assistants teach no undergraduate courses. Calendar: 4-2-4. Grading system: letters or numbers. Library holdings: 115,000 bound volumes, 520 periodical subscriptions, 7,800 records/tapes.

Undergraduate Profile Fall 1984: 715 undergraduates (199 freshmen) from 22 states and territories and 1 foreign country; 10% part-time; 50% state residents; 3% transfers; 63% financial aid recipients; 100% women; 3% blacks; 0% Native Americans; 0% Hispanics; 0% Asian Americans; 18% of undergraduates over 25 years of age; 4 legally handicapped students.

Expenses (1985–86) Comprehensive fee of $8650 includes full-time tuition ($5575), mandatory fees ($75), and college room and board ($3000). Part-time tuition: $150 per credit hour.

Financial Aid Fall 1984 full-time freshmen: 71% applied for aid, 69% of those were judged to have need, 100% of those were aided; the average aided freshman received an aid package worth $5143 (88% scholarships/grants, 12% self-help) meeting 100% of need. College-administered aid for all 1984–85 undergraduates: 202 need-based scholarships (average $2000); 237 non-need scholarships (average $2300); short-term loans (average $1500); low-interest long-term loans from external sources (average $1500); SEOG; College Work-Study; 60 part-time jobs. Supporting data: FAF, IRS, institutional form required; state form, AFSA/SAR required for some. Priority application deadline: 2/15.

Athletics Intercollegiate sports: basketball (s); tennis (s); volleyball (s). Intramural sports: basketball, golf, swimming and diving, tennis, volleyball.

Majors Accounting B; applied art B; art/fine arts B; art history B; biology/biological sciences B; business administration/commerce/management B; chemistry B; classics B; computer science B; (pre)dentistry sequence B; early childhood education B; economics B; education B; elementary education B; English B; French B; history B; humanities B; interior design B; (pre)law sequence B; mathematics B; medical technology B; (pre)medicine sequence B; modern languages B; music B; music education B; music history B; philosophy B; physics B; piano/organ B; political science/government B; psychology B; religious studies B; science B; sociology B; Spanish B; special education B; stringed instruments B; studio art B; theater arts/drama B; (pre)veterinary medicine sequence B; voice B. Majors with highest enrollment: music, education, business administration/commerce/management.

LD Program Information

Name of Program Committee on Academic Program Accessibility (CAPA).

Availability of Services Began offering services in 1978. Services provided to freshmen, sophomores, juniors, seniors. Program currently serves 1 LD senior.

Staff 6 part-time staff members, including chairman, faculty committee members.

Admissions LD applicants evaluated on the basis of high school transcript and grade point average, standard or untimed SAT or ACT; psychoeducational report recommended. LD students may begin taking classes in fall only. Application should be submitted 8 to 9 months in advance of initial anticipated enrollment.

Housing College housing available. LD students housed randomly. LD freshmen, sophomores, juniors, and seniors required to live on campus except if living with relatives.

Tutoring Offered one-to-one by peer tutors. Available in all subjects. LD students may receive tutoring in all courses each term.

Academic Advisement Help with program planning provided by academic advisers. LD students may take up to 15 credit hours each semester; most take 12 credit hours; 9 credit hours required to maintain full-time status.

Auxiliary Aids and Services Services include alternative exam arrangements, notetakers.

Counseling Services Individual counseling available.

Contact Dr. Robert E. Muzzy, Chairman of Committee on Academic Program Accessibility, Converse College, Spartanburg, SC 29301, 803-596-9097.

CORNELL UNIVERSITY

Ithaca, New York

Year Program Began	1976	Special Courses	
Special Fee	Varies	Taped Textbooks	✓
Special Orientation		Alternative Exam Arrangements	✓
Diagnostic Testing		Notetakers	✓
Subject-Area Tutoring	✓	Staff	1 part-time
Basic Skills Remediation		Number of Students Served	25

General Information Independent coed university. Founded 1865. Awards B, M, D. Institutionally accredited by regional association; programs accredited by NAAB (architecture), AACSB (business), ABET (engineering and technology). Small-town setting, with easy access to Syracuse; 740-acre campus. Total enrollment: 17,540. Faculty: 1,534; 90% have doctoral degrees; graduate assistants teach a few undergraduate courses. Calendar: semesters. Grading system: letters or numbers. Library holdings: 5 million bound volumes, 57,000 periodical subscriptions.

Undergraduate Profile Fall 1984: 12,388 undergraduates (2,945 freshmen) from 50 states and territories; 0% part-time; 50% state residents; 5% transfers; 55% financial aid recipients; 46% women; 5% blacks; 1% Native Americans; 4% Hispanics; 8% Asian Americans; 72 legally handicapped students.

Expenses (1985–86) Comprehensive fee of $14,100 includes full-time tuition ($10,500) and college room and board ($3600). Tuition for state-supported programs: $4360 full-time for state residents; $7420 full-time for nonresidents. Tuition prepayment plan available.

Financial Aid Fall 1984 full-time freshmen: 70% applied for aid, 67% of those were judged to have need, 100% of those were aided; the average aided freshman received an aid package worth $7635 (66% scholarships/grants, 34% self-help) meeting 100% of need. College-administered aid for all 1984–85 undergraduates: 3,888 need-based scholarships (average $4175); short-term loans (average $350); low-interest long-term loans from college funds (average $1350), from external sources (average $2380); SEOG; College Work-Study; 3,500 part-time jobs. Supporting data: FAF, IRS, institutional form required. Priority application deadline: 1/1.

Athletics Member NCAA (Division I). Intercollegiate sports: baseball/softball M(I), W(c); basketball M(I), W(I); crew M, W; cross-country running M(I), W(I); equestrian sports M(c), W(c); fencing M(I), W(I); field hockey W(I); football M(I-AA); golf M(I); gymnastics M(I), W(I); ice hockey M(I), W(c); lacrosse M(I), W(I); martial arts M(c), W(c); riflery M(c), W(c); rugby M(c), W(c); sailing M(c), W(c); skiing (cross-country) M(c), W(c); skiing (downhill) M(c), W(c); soccer M(I), W(I); squash M(c), W(c); swimming and diving M(I), W(I); tennis M(I), W(I); track and field M(I), W(I); volleyball M(c), W(I); water polo M(c); wrestling M(I). Intramural sports: archery, badminton, baseball/softball, basketball, bowling, cross-country running, equestrian sports, fencing, field hockey, football, golf, ice hockey, lacrosse, martial arts, racquetball, sailing, skiing (cross-country), skiing (downhill), soccer, squash, swimming and diving, tennis, track and field, volleyball, water polo, weight lifting, wrestling.

Majors African studies B; agricultural business B; agricultural economics B; agricultural education B; agricultural engineering B; agricultural sciences B; agronomy/soil and crop sciences B; American studies B; anatomy B; animal sciences B; anthropology B; archaeology B; architecture B; art/fine arts B; art history B; Asian/Oriental studies B; astronomy B; atmospheric sciences B; biochemistry B; biology/biological sciences B; biometrics B; biophysics B; black/Afro-American studies B; botany/plant sciences B; cell biology B; chemical engineering B; chemistry B; child care/child and family studies B; child psychology/child development B; Chinese B; city, community, and regional planning B; civil engineering B; classics B; communication B; community services B; comparative literature B; computer science B; consumer services B; dairy sciences B; dance B; East Asian studies B; East European and Soviet studies B; ecology/environmental studies B; economics B; education B; electrical engineering B; engineering (general) B; engineering physics B; English B; entomology B; environmental design B; environmental engineering B; environmental sciences B; European studies B; family and consumer studies B; family services B; farm and ranch management B; fish and game management B; food sciences B; forest technology B; French B; genetics B; geography B; geology B; German B; Greek B; history B; home economics B; home economics education B; horticulture B; hotel and restaurant management B; human development B; human services B; industrial engineering B; interdisciplinary studies B; Italian B; labor and industrial relations B; labor studies B; landscape architecture/design B; Latin B; liberal arts/general studies B; linguistics B; materials engineering B; mathematics B; mechanical engineering B; medieval studies B; meteorology B; microbiology B; modern languages B; molecular biology B; music B; natural resource management B; Near and Middle Eastern studies B; neurosciences B; nutrition B; ornamental horticulture B; painting/drawing B; philosophy B; photography B; physics B; physiology B; political science/government B; poultry sciences B; psychology B; Russian B; Russian and Slavic studies B; social science B; sociobiology B; sociology B; Spanish B; theater arts/drama B; urban studies B; wildlife management B; women's studies B.

LD Program Information

Name of Program Not specified.

Availability of Services Began offering services in 1976. Services provided to freshmen, sophomores, juniors, seniors. Program currently serves 25 LD students.

Fees $1 to $5 per hour for tutoring by work-study peer tutors.

Staff 1 part-time staff member (coordinator).

Admissions LD applicants evaluated on the basis of high school transcript and grade point average, standard or untimed SAT or ACT, autobiographical statement, letters of recommendation, psychoeducational report; personal interview recommended; 2 Achievement Tests, English Composition Test required for some. LD students may begin taking classes in fall only. Application should be submitted 9 to 12 months in advance of initial anticipated enrollment.

Housing College housing (including coed) available. LD students housed randomly. LD students not required to live on campus.

Tutoring Offered one-to-one by peer tutors, graduate teaching assistants. Available in all subjects. LD students may receive tutoring in all courses each term.

Academic Advisement Help with program planning provided by LD staff member, academic advisers. LD students may take up to 18 credits each semester; 12 credits required to maintain full-time status.

Auxiliary Aids and Services Aids include taped textbooks, tape recorders, word processors. Services include alternative exam arrangements, notetakers.

Counseling Services Individual counseling, small-group counseling, rap sessions, career counseling available.

Contact Ms. Kathleen Donovan, Coordinator for the Disabled and Vietnam Veterans, Cornell University, 234 Day Hall, Ithaca, NY 14853, 607-256-5298.

CURRY COLLEGE
Milton, Massachusetts

Year Program Began	1970	Special Courses	✓
Special Fee	$2200 per year	Taped Textbooks	✓
Special Orientation	✓	Alternative Exam Arrangements	✓
Diagnostic Testing	✓	Notetakers	
Subject-Area Tutoring	✓	Staff	8 full-time, 5 part-time
Basic Skills Remediation	✓	Number of Students Served	213

General Information Independent comprehensive coed institution. Founded 1879. Awards B, M. Institutionally accredited by regional association; programs accredited by NLN (nursing). Small-town setting, with easy access to Boston; 120-acre campus. Total enrollment: 1,396. Faculty: 112 (60 full-time, 52 part-time); 50% have doctoral degrees; graduate assistants teach no undergraduate courses. Calendar: semesters. Grading system: letters or numbers. Library holdings: 90,000 bound volumes, 10,000 titles on microform, 620 periodical subscriptions.

Undergraduate Profile Fall 1984: 1,381 undergraduates (334 freshmen) from 38 states and territories and 5 foreign countries; 30% part-time; 52% state residents; 5% transfers; 70% financial aid recipients; 46% women; 4% blacks; 1% Native Americans; 1% Hispanics; 1% Asian Americans; 2% foreign nationals; 9% of undergraduates over 25 years of age.

Expenses (1985–86) Comprehensive fee of $11,610 includes full-time tuition ($7450), mandatory fees ($235), and college room and board ($3925). Part-time tuition: $248 per credit hour.

Financial Aid Fall 1984 full-time freshmen: 49% applied for aid, 94% of those were judged to have need, 100% of those were aided; the average aided freshman received an aid package worth $5065 (61% scholarships/grants, 39% self-help) meeting 85% of need. College-administered aid for all 1984–85 undergraduates: 315 need-based scholarships (average $2800); low-interest long-term loans from external sources (average $2200); SEOG; College Work-Study; 75 part-time jobs. Supporting data: FAF, IRS, institutional form, AFSA/SAR required; FFS, state form acceptable. Application deadline: continuous.

Athletics Member NCAA (Division III). Intercollegiate sports: baseball/softball M(III), W(III); basketball M(III), W(III); football M(III); ice hockey M(III); lacrosse M(c); soccer M(III), W(III); tennis M(III). Intramural sports: baseball/softball, basketball, tennis, volleyball.

Majors Art/fine arts B; biology/biological sciences B; broadcasting B; business administration/commerce/management B; chemistry B; communication B; (pre) dentistry sequence B; early childhood education B; education B; elementary education B; English B; history B; human services B; journalism B; (pre)law sequence B; (pre) medicine sequence B; music B; nursing B; philosophy B; photography B; physics B; political science/government B; psychology B; radio and television studies B; social work B; sociology B; special education B. Majors with highest enrollment: business administration/commerce/management, nursing, communication.

LD Program Information

Name of Program Program for Advancement of Learning (PAL).

Availability of Services Began offering services in 1970. Services provided to freshmen, sophomores, juniors, seniors (initial phase of program is full-time, followed by half-time consulting program after completion of initial phase). Program currently serves 213 LD students.

Fees $2200 per year for full-time program, $1000 for half-time program.

Staff 8 full-time, 5 part-time staff members, including director, assistant director. Services provided by remediation specialists, counselors, diagnostic specialists, librarian.

Admissions LD applicants evaluated on the basis of high school transcript and grade point average, standard or untimed SAT or ACT, personal interview, autobiographical statement, letters of recommendation, psychoeducational report, including PAL language and readiness assessment. LD students may begin taking classes in fall or spring. Application should be submitted 9 to 12 months in advance of initial anticipated enrollment.

Orientation Required orientation held during registration (program held during summer prior to enrollment is required for some).

Housing College housing (including coed) available. LD students housed randomly. LD freshmen required to live on campus except if living with relatives within 20-mile radius or by special permission.

Diagnostic Testing Available in various areas as appropriate.

Tutoring Offered one-to-one and in small groups by professional teachers, peer tutors. Available in all subjects. LD students may receive tutoring in all courses each term.

Basic Skills Remediation Offered one-to-one and in small groups by LD teachers. Available in reading, math, spelling, handwriting, spoken language, written language, learning strategies, motor abilities, perceptual skills, work and study habits, social skills.

Academic Advisement Help with program planning provided by LD staff members, academic advisers. LD students may take up to 18 credit hours each semester; most take 13.5 credit hours first semester, 16.5 thereafter; 12 credit hours required to maintain full-time status.

Special Courses Offered according to individual needs through PAL program. All offered for credit; none enter into overall grade point average.

Auxiliary Aids and Services Aids include taped textbooks, tape recorders, calculators, typewriters, word processors. Services include alternative exam arrangements.

Counseling Services Individual counseling, small-group counseling, rap sessions, career counseling available.

Contact Dr. Gertrude M. Webb, Director of the Learning Center, Curry College, Milton, MA 02186, 617-333-0500 Ext. 250.

EARLHAM COLLEGE

Richmond, Indiana

Year Program Began	1982	Special Courses	
Special Fee	None	Taped Textbooks	✓
Special Orientation		Alternative Exam Arrangements	✓
Diagnostic Testing	✓	Notetakers	✓
Subject-Area Tutoring	✓	Staff	3 part-time
Basic Skills Remediation	✓	Number of Students Served	5

General Information Comprehensive coed institution, affiliated with Society of Friends. Founded 1847. Awards B, M. Institutionally accredited by regional association. Small-town setting, with easy access to Cincinnati, Indianapolis and Dayton; 800-acre campus. Total enrollment: 1,050. Faculty: 104 (91 full-time, 13 part-time); 75% have doctoral degrees; graduate assistants teach no undergraduate courses. Calendar: three 10-week terms. Grading system: letters or numbers. Library holdings: 300,000 bound volumes, 7,000 titles on microform, 1,300 periodical subscriptions, 1,900 records/tapes.

Undergraduate Profile Fall 1984: 980 undergraduates (241 freshmen) from 46 states and territories and 21 foreign countries; 1% part-time; 21% state residents; 10% transfers; 65% financial aid recipients; 54% women; 8% blacks; 1% Hispanics; 1% Asian Americans; 4% foreign nationals.

Expenses (1985–86) Comprehensive fee of $10,581 includes full-time tuition ($7670), mandatory fees ($211), and college room and board ($2700). College room only: $1110. Part-time tuition: $800 per course.

Financial Aid Fall 1984 full-time freshmen: 71% applied for aid, 87% of those were judged to have need, 100% of those were aided; the average aided freshman received an aid package worth $7526 (63% scholarships/grants, 37% self-help) meeting 100% of need. College-administered aid for all 1984–85 undergraduates: 743 need-based scholarships (average $2169); 119 non-need scholarships (average $1882); short-term loans (average $50); low-interest long-term loans from college funds (average $1000), from external sources (average $1850); SEOG; College Work-Study; 80 part-time jobs. Supporting data: FAF, AFSA/SAR required; IRS, institutional form required for some; FFS acceptable. Priority application deadline: 3/1.

Athletics Member NCAA (Division III), NAIA. Intercollegiate sports: baseball/softball M(III), W(III); basketball M(III), W(III); cross-country running M(III), W(III); field hockey W(III); football M(III); golf M(III), W(III); lacrosse W(III); soccer M(III); tennis M(III), W(III); track and field M(III), W(III); volleyball M(III), W(III). Intramural sports: baseball/softball, basketball, equestrian sports, football, martial arts, racquetball, rugby, sailing, skiing (cross-country), skiing (downhill), soccer, squash, swimming and diving, tennis, volleyball.

Majors African studies B; anthropology B; art/fine arts B; astronomy B; biology/biological sciences B; black/Afro-American studies B; business administration/commerce/management B; chemistry B; classics B; computer science B; East Asian studies B; ecology/environmental studies B; economics B; education B; elementary education B; English B; environmental sciences B; French B; geology B; German B; history B; human development B; international studies B; Japanese B; (pre)law sequence B; liberal arts/general studies B; literature B; mathematics B; (pre)medicine sequence B; museum studies B; music B; peace studies B; philosophy B; physical education B; physics B; political science/government B; psychology B; religious studies B; secondary education B; sociology B; Spanish B; (pre)veterinary medicine sequence B; women's studies B. Majors with highest enrollment: biology/biological sciences, psychology, English.

LD Program Information

Name of Program Supportive Services.

Availability of Services Began offering services in 1982. Services provided to freshmen, sophomores, juniors, seniors. Program currently serves 5 LD students: 1 freshman, 3 sophomores, 1 junior.

Staff 3 part-time staff members, including director, assistant director. Services provided by tutors.

Admissions LD applicants evaluated on the basis of high school transcript and grade point average, untimed SAT or ACT, personal interview, autobiographical statement, letters of recommendation, psychoeducational report. LD students may begin taking classes in fall or winter. Application should be submitted 10 weeks in advance of initial anticipated enrollment.

Housing College housing (including coed) available. LD students housed randomly. LD freshmen, sophomores, juniors, and seniors required to live on campus except for veterans, or if 23 or over, married, or living with relatives.

Diagnostic Testing Available in intelligence, reading, spelling, spoken language, written language, motor abilities, perceptual skills.

Tutoring Offered one-to-one by professional teachers, peer tutors. Available in all subjects. LD students may receive tutoring in all courses each term.

Basic Skills Remediation Offered one-to-one by director of Supportive Services, LD specialist. Available in spelling, learning strategies, work and study habits.

Academic Advisement Help with program planning provided by LD staff members, academic advisers. LD students may take up to 3 courses each term; most take 2 to 3 courses; 3 courses required to maintain full-time status (except by special permission).

Auxiliary Aids and Services Aids include taped textbooks, tape recorders, typewriters, word processors. Services include alternative exam arrangements, notetakers, advocacy.

Counseling Services Individual counseling available.

Contact Ms. Stacey A. Elder, Director, Supportive Services, Earlham College, Box E15, Richmond, IN 47374, 317-962-6561 Ext. 501.

EAST CAROLINA UNIVERSITY

Greenville, North Carolina

Year Program Began	1983	Special Courses	✓
Special Fee	None	Taped Textbooks	✓
Special Orientation	✓	Alternative Exam Arrangements	✓
Diagnostic Testing	✓	Notetakers	✓
Subject-Area Tutoring	✓	Staff	4 full-time, 12 part-time
Basic Skills Remediation	✓	Number of Students Served	25

General Information State-supported coed university. Part of University of North Carolina System. Founded 1907. Awards B, M, D. Institutionally accredited by regional association; programs accredited by NASAD (art and design), AACSB (business), NASM (music), NLN (nursing), NCATE (teacher education). Small-town setting; 411-acre campus. Total enrollment: 13,826. Faculty: 902 (889 full-time, 13 part-time); 65% have doctoral degrees; graduate assistants teach a few undergraduate courses. Calendar: semesters. Grading system: letters or numbers. Library holdings: 506,653 bound volumes, 1.2 million titles on microform, 4,853 periodical subscriptions, 8,200 records/tapes.

Undergraduate Profile Fall 1984: 11,688 undergraduates (2,683 freshmen) from 45 states and territories and 43 foreign countries; 9% part-time; 80% state residents; 7% transfers; 52% financial aid recipients; 55% women; 11% blacks; 1% Native Americans; 1% Hispanics; 1% Asian Americans; 1% foreign nationals; 9% of undergraduates over 25 years of age; 125 legally handicapped students.

Expenses (1984–85) State resident tuition: $410 full-time. Nonresident tuition: $2968 full-time. Part-time tuition per semester (1 to 11 semester hours) ranges from $51 to $154 for state residents, $371 to $1113 for nonresidents. Mandatory fees: $336. College room and board: $2010. College room only: $890.

Financial Aid College-administered aid for all 1984–85 undergraduates: 1,371 need-based scholarships (average $342); 146 non-need scholarships (average $526); short-term loans (average $250); low-interest long-term loans from college funds (average $500), from external sources (average $725); SEOG; College Work-Study; 1,260 part-time jobs. Supporting data: FFS, FAF, AFSA/SAR required; IRS required for some. Priority application deadline: 3/1.

Athletics Member NCAA (Division I). Intercollegiate sports: baseball/softball M(I,s), W(I,s); basketball M(I,s), W(I,s); cross-country running M(I); football M(I-A,s); golf M(I,s); soccer M(I,s); swimming and diving M(I,s), W(II,s); tennis M(I,s), W(I,s); track and field M(I,s), W(I,s); volleyball W(I,s). Intramural sports: archery, badminton, baseball/softball, basketball, bowling, cross-country running, equestrian sports, fencing, football, gymnastics, ice hockey, lacrosse, martial arts, racquetball, rugby, skiing (downhill), soccer, swimming and diving, tennis, track and field, volleyball, water polo, weight lifting, wrestling.

Majors Accounting B; anthropology B; art education B; art/fine arts B; art history B; arts administration B; biochemistry B; biology/biological sciences B; broadcasting B; business administration/commerce/management B; business education B; ceramic art and design B; chemistry B; child care/child and family studies B; child psychology/child development B; city, community, and regional planning B; commercial art B; computer science B; conservation B; corrections B; creative writing B; dance B; (pre)dentistry sequence B; dietetics B; early childhood education B; economics B; education B; educational administration B; elementary education B; English B; environmental health sciences B; environmental sciences B; finance/banking B; food services management B; French B; geography B; geology B; German B; graphic arts B; health education B; history B; home economics B; home economics education B; industrial arts B; interior design B; jewelry and metalsmithing B; law enforcement/police sciences B; (pre)law sequence B; marine sciences B; marketing/retailing/merchandising B; mathematics B; medical records services B; medical technology B; (pre)medicine sequence B; music B; music education B; music therapy B; nursing B; nutrition B; occupational therapy B; operations research B; painting/drawing B; parks management B; philosophy B; physical education B; physical therapy B; physics B; piano/organ B; political science/government B; psychology B; public health B; reading education B; real estate B; recreation and leisure services B; recreation therapy B; sacred music B; science education B; sculpture B; secondary education B; secretarial studies/office management B; social work B; sociology B; Spanish B; special education B; speech pathology and audiology B; textiles and clothing B; theater arts/drama B; urban studies B; voice B. Majors with highest enrollment: education, business administration/commerce/management, nursing.

LD Program Information

Name of Program Handicapped Student Services.

Availability of Services Began offering services in 1983. Services provided to freshmen, sophomores, juniors, seniors. Program currently serves 25 LD students: 12 freshmen, 7 sophomores, 4 juniors, 2 seniors.

Staff 4 full-time, 12 part-time staff members, including coordinator. Services provided by tutors, counselors, diagnostic specialists.

Admissions LD applicants evaluated on the basis of high school transcript and grade point average, untimed SAT or ACT, psychoeducational report. LD students may begin taking classes in fall, spring, or summer. Application should be submitted 3 months in advance of initial anticipated enrollment.

Orientation Optional orientation offered before registration.

Housing College housing (including coed) available. LD students housed randomly. LD students not required to live on campus.

Diagnostic Testing Available in intelligence, reading, math, spelling, handwriting, written language, perceptual skills, work and study habits, personality, speech.

Tutoring Offered one-to-one and in small groups by professional teachers, peer tutors. Available in all subjects. LD students may receive tutoring in all courses each term.

Basic Skills Remediation Offered one-to-one and in small groups by LD teachers, teacher trainees. Available in reading, math, spelling, handwriting, written language, learning strategies, motor abilities, perceptual skills, work and study habits, social skills, speech.

Academic Advisement Help with program planning provided by academic advisers. LD students may take up to 15 semester hours each semester; most take 12 semester hours; 12 semester hours required to maintain full-time status.

Special Courses Offered in reading, vocabulary development, communication skills, composition, language development, math, study skills, career planning. None offered for credit; none enter into overall grade point average.

Auxiliary Aids and Services Aids include taped textbooks, tape recorders, calculators, typewriters, word processors. Services include alternative exam arrangements, notetakers, advocacy.

Counseling Services Individual counseling, small-group counseling, rap sessions, career counseling available.

Contact C. C. Rowe, Coordinator, Handicapped Student Services, East Carolina University, 212 Whichard Building, Greenville, NC 27834, 919-757-6799.

EAST CENTRAL OKLAHOMA STATE UNIVERSITY

Ada, Oklahoma

Year Program Began	1980	Special Courses	✓
Special Fee	None	Taped Textbooks	✓
Special Orientation	✓	Alternative Exam Arrangements	✓
Diagnostic Testing	✓	Notetakers	✓
Subject-Area Tutoring	✓	Staff	4 part-time
Basic Skills Remediation		Number of Students Served	*Not reported*

General Information State-supported comprehensive coed institution. Founded 1909. Awards B, M. Institutionally accredited by regional association; programs accredited by NLN (nursing), NCATE (teacher education). Small-town setting, with easy access to Oklahoma City; 140-acre barrier-free campus. Total enrollment: 4,144. Faculty: 178 (157 full-time, 21 part-time); 50% have doctoral degrees; graduate assistants teach a few undergraduate courses. Calendar: semesters. Grading system: letters or numbers. Library holdings: 203,301 bound volumes, 293,094 titles on microform, 1,300 periodical subscriptions, 5,131 records/tapes.

Undergraduate Profile Fall 1984: 3,120 undergraduates (701 freshmen) from 21 states and territories and 7 foreign countries; 12% part-time; 97% state residents; 14% transfers; 60% financial aid recipients; 59% women; 5% blacks; 6% Native Americans; 1% Hispanics; 1% Asian Americans; 1% foreign nationals; 20 legally handicapped students.

Expenses (1984–85) State resident tuition: $564 full-time. Nonresident tuition: $1545 full-time. Part-time tuition per semester hour ranges from $18.80 to $20.15 for state residents, $51.50 to $56.25 for nonresidents, according to course level. College room and board: $2612. College room only: $636.

Financial Aid Fall 1984 full-time freshmen: the average aided freshman received an aid package meeting 100% of need. College-administered aid for all 1984–85 undergraduates: 282 need-based scholarships (average $244); 402 non-need scholarships (average $240); short-term loans (average $75); low-interest long-term loans from external sources (average $985); SEOG; College Work-Study; 296 part-time jobs. Supporting data: FFS, IRS, state form, institutional form, AFSA/SAR required. Priority application deadline: 7/1.

Athletics Member NAIA. Intercollegiate sports: baseball/softball M; basketball M(s), W(s); football M(s); golf M; tennis M; track and field M. Intramural sports: baseball/softball, basketball, football, volleyball.

Majors Accounting B; art education B; art/fine arts B; biology/biological sciences B; business administration/commerce/management B; business education B; cartography B; chemistry B; communication B; computer information systems B; computer science B; criminal justice B; (pre)dentistry sequence B; drafting and design B; economics B; education B; elementary education B; English B; environmental sciences B; health services administration B; history B; home economics B; human resources B; industrial arts B; (pre)law sequence B; mathematics B; medical laboratory technology B; medical records services B; (pre)medicine sequence B; music B; music education B; nursing B; nutrition B; physical education B; physics B; political science/government B; psychology B; radiological technology B; secretarial studies/office management B; social work B; sociology B; special education B; speech/rhetoric/public address/debate B; (pre)veterinary medicine sequence B.

Majors with highest enrollment: business administration/commerce/management, elementary education, accounting.

LD Program Information

Name of Program Learning Resource and Counseling Center.

Availability of Services Began offering services in 1980. Services provided to freshmen, sophomores, juniors, seniors.

Staff 4 part-time staff members, including director. Services provided by tutors, counselors.

Admissions LD applicants evaluated on the basis of high school transcript and grade point average, standard or untimed ACT, psychoeducational report. LD students may begin taking classes in fall, spring, or summer. Application should be submitted 6 months in advance of initial anticipated enrollment.

Orientation Required orientation held before registration.

Housing College housing (including coed) available. LD students housed randomly. LD freshmen required to live on campus.

Diagnostic Testing Available in reading, math, spelling, written language, work and study habits.

Tutoring Offered one-to-one and in small groups by peer tutors. Available in all subjects. LD students may receive tutoring in 2 courses per term.

Academic Advisement Help with program planning provided by LD staff members, academic advisers. LD students may take up to 12 semester hours, plus as many more as individual can handle, each semester; most take 9 to 12 semester hours; 12 semester hours required to maintain full-time status.

Special Courses Offered in reading, study skills, career planning. Most offered for credit; most enter into overall grade point average.

Auxiliary Aids and Services Aids include taped textbooks. Services include alternative exam arrangements, notetakers.

Counseling Services Individual counseling, career counseling available.

Contact Dr. Jim Caruthers, Director, Learning Resource and Counseling Center, East Central Oklahoma State University, Ada, OK 74820, 405-332-8000 Ext. 292.

EASTERN COLLEGE
St Davids, Pennsylvania

Year Program Began	1975	Special Courses	✓
Special Fee	None	Taped Textbooks	✓
Special Orientation		Alternative Exam Arrangements	✓
Diagnostic Testing	✓	Notetakers	
Subject-Area Tutoring	✓	Staff	13 part-time
Basic Skills Remediation	✓	Number of Students Served	8

General Information American Baptist comprehensive coed institution. Founded 1932. Awards B, M. Institutionally accredited by regional association. Small-town setting, with easy access to Philadelphia; 92-acre barrier-free campus. Total enrollment: 937. Faculty: 96 (45 full-time, 51 part-time); 38% have doctoral degrees; graduate assistants teach a few undergraduate courses. Calendar: semesters. Grading system: letters or numbers. Library holdings: 80,458 bound volumes, 14,906 titles on microform, 530 periodical subscriptions, 2,271 records/tapes.

Undergraduate Profile Fall 1984: 836 undergraduates (158 freshmen) from 23 states and territories and 12 foreign countries; 30% part-time; 69% state residents; 42% transfers; 64% financial aid recipients; 70% women; 8% blacks; 1% Native Americans; 1% Hispanics; 2% Asian Americans; 3% foreign nationals; 1 legally handicapped student.

Expenses (1985–86) Comprehensive fee of $8290 includes full-time tuition ($5590), mandatory fees ($400), and college room and board ($2300). Part-time tuition: $165 per credit.

Financial Aid Fall 1984 full-time freshmen: 86% applied for aid, 96% of those were judged to have need, 100% of those were aided; the average aided freshman received an aid package worth $4000 (45% scholarships/grants, 55% self-help) meeting 95% of need. College-administered aid for all 1984–85 undergraduates: 481 need-based scholarships (average $898); 68 non-need scholarships (average $1329); short-term loans (average $600); low-interest long-term loans from external sources (average $672); SEOG; College Work-Study; 51 part-time jobs. Supporting data: IRS, state form, institutional form required; FFS, FAF, AFSA/SAR acceptable. Priority application deadline: 5/1.

Athletics Member NAIA. Intercollegiate sports: baseball/softball M(s), W(s); basketball M(s), W(s); cross-country running M(s), W(s); field hockey W(s); soccer M(s); tennis M, W; volleyball M, W; wrestling M(s). Intramural sports: baseball/softball, basketball, football, soccer, tennis, volleyball, wrestling.

Majors Accounting B; American studies B; art history B; biblical studies B; bilingual/bicultural education B; biology/biological sciences B; business administration/commerce/management B; chemistry B; computer science B; creative writing B; economics B; elementary education B; French B; health science B; health services administration B; history B; (pre)law sequence B; literature B; mathematics B; medical technology B; (pre)medicine sequence B; ministries B; nursing B; philosophy B; physical education B; psychology B; religious studies B; secondary education B; social work B; sociology B; Spanish B; studio art B. Majors with highest enrollment: nursing, business administration/commerce/management, psychology.

LD Program Information

Name of Program Center for Counseling and Academic Support.

Availability of Services Began offering services in 1975. Services provided to freshmen, sophomores, juniors, seniors. Program currently serves 8 LD students: 4 freshmen, 2 sophomores, 1 junior, 1 senior.

Staff 13 part-time staff members, including director. Services provided by remediation specialist, tutors, counselors, diagnostic specialist.

Admissions LD applicants evaluated on the basis of high school transcript and grade point average, standard or untimed SAT or ACT, personal interview, autobiographical statement, letters of recommendation, psychoeducational report. LD students may begin taking classes in fall, spring, or summer. Application should be submitted at least 3 months in advance of initial anticipated enrollment.

Housing College housing (including coed) available. LD students housed randomly. LD freshmen, sophomores, juniors, and seniors required to live on campus except for veterans, or if 25 or over, married, or living with relatives, or by special permission.

Diagnostic Testing Available in intelligence, reading, math, spelling, motor abilities, perceptual skills, work and study habits, personality, social skills.

Tutoring Offered one-to-one and in small groups by professional teachers, peer tutors. Available in all subjects. LD students may receive tutoring in all courses each term.

Basic Skills Remediation Offered one-to-one and in small groups by regular teachers, peer teachers. Available in reading, math, spelling, written language, learning strategies, work and study habits.

Academic Advisement Help with program planning provided by LD staff members, academic advisers. LD students may take up to 18 credits each semester; 12 credits per semester required to maintain full-time status in freshman year, 13 in sophomore year, 14 in junior year, 15 in senior year.

Special Courses Offered in college survival skills, reading, vocabulary development, communication skills, composition, math, personal psychology, study skills, career planning. Some offered for credit; some enter into overall grade point average.

Auxiliary Aids and Services Aids include taped textbooks, tape recorders. Services include alternative exam arrangements.

Counseling Services Individual counseling, small-group counseling, career counseling available.

Contact Ms. Dolores McCabe, Director of Center for Counseling and Academic Support, Eastern College, St Davids, PA 19087, 215-341-5838.

EASTERN NEW MEXICO UNIVERSITY

Portales, New Mexico

Year Program Began	1979	Special Courses	✓
Special Fee	None	Taped Textbooks	✓
Special Orientation		Alternative Exam Arrangements	✓
Diagnostic Testing	✓	Notetakers	✓
Subject-Area Tutoring	✓	Staff	1 full-time, 6 part-time
Basic Skills Remediation	✓	Number of Students Served	9

General Information State-supported comprehensive coed institution. Part of Eastern New Mexico University System. Founded 1934. Awards A (college transfer and terminal), B, M. Institutionally accredited by regional association; programs accredited by NASM (music), NCATE (teacher education). Small-town setting; 240-acre barrier-free campus. Total enrollment: 3,549. Faculty: 200 (141 full-time, 59 part-time); 60% have doctoral degrees; graduate assistants teach a few undergraduate courses. Calendar: semesters. Grading system: letters or numbers. Library holdings: 368,000 bound volumes, 67,230 titles on microform, 1,328 periodical subscriptions, 31,081 records/tapes.

Undergraduate Profile Fall 1984: 3,081 undergraduates (637 freshmen) from 50 states and territories and 22 foreign countries; 10% part-time; 86% state residents; 10% transfers; 75% financial aid recipients; 43% women; 4% blacks; 2% Native Americans; 15% Hispanics; 1% Asian Americans; 3% foreign nationals; 28% of undergraduates over 25 years of age; 45 legally handicapped students.

Expenses (1985–86) State resident tuition: $786 full-time, $32.75 per credit hour part-time. Nonresident tuition: $2490 full-time, $103.75 per credit hour part-time. College room and board: $1796. College room only: $810.

Financial Aid Fall 1984 full-time freshmen: 80% were aided; the average aided freshman received an aid package meeting 75% of need. College-administered aid for all 1984–85 undergraduates: need-based scholarships; 300 non-need scholarships (average $400); short-term loans (average $250); low-interest long-term loans from college funds (average $250), from external sources (average $500); SEOG; College Work-Study. Supporting data: FAF, institutional form required; FFS, state form, AFSA/SAR acceptable. Priority application deadline: 3/1.

Athletics Member NAIA. Intercollegiate sports: basketball M(s), W(s); cross-country running M(s), W(s); football M(s); golf M(s), W(s); riflery M(s), W(s); track and field M(s), W(s); volleyball W(s). Intramural sports: baseball/softball, basketball, bowling, cross-country running, football, golf, riflery, rugby, soccer, swimming and diving, tennis, track and field, volleyball, wrestling.

Majors Accounting A, B; agricultural business B; American studies B; anthropology B; art education B; art/fine arts A; biology/biological sciences B; business administration/commerce/management A, B; business education B; chemistry B; civil engineering technology A; commercial art B; communication B; computer information systems B; computer science B; criminal justice A; (pre)dentistry sequence B; drafting and design A; early childhood education B; earth science B; ecology/environmental studies B; economics B; education A; electrical and electronics technologies A; electrical engineering technology A; elementary education B; English B; environmental health sciences B; ethnic studies B; finance/banking B; geology B; graphic arts B; history B; home economics B; industrial arts B; information science B; journalism B; Latin American studies B; (pre)law sequence B; legal secretarial studies A; liberal arts/general studies A; marketing/retailing/merchandising B; mathematics B; medical secretarial studies A; medical technology B; (pre)medicine sequence B; music B; music education B; music history B; music therapy B; physical education B; physics B; piano/organ B; political science/government B; psychology A, B; radio and television studies B; reading education B; real estate A, B; religious studies B; sculpture B; secondary education B; secretarial studies/office management A, B; social science B; sociology B; Spanish B; special education B; speech pathology and audiology B; speech/rhetoric/public address/debate B; speech therapy B; statistics B; stringed instruments B; teaching English as a second language B; theater arts/drama B; (pre)veterinary medicine sequence B; vocational education B; voice B; wildlife management B; wind and percussion instruments B. Majors with highest enrollment: business administration/commerce/management, elementary education, physical education.

LD Program Information

Name of Program Handicapped Services.

Availability of Services Began offering services in 1979. Services provided to freshmen, sophomores, juniors, seniors. Program currently serves 9 LD students: 2 freshmen, 4 sophomores, 1 junior, 2 seniors.

Staff 1 full-time, 6 part-time staff members, including director. Services provided by tutors, readers, proctors, interpreters.

Admissions LD applicants evaluated on the basis of high school transcript, standard or untimed SAT or ACT, autobiographical statement, letters of recommendation. LD students may begin taking classes in fall, spring, or summer. Application should be submitted 6 weeks in advance of initial anticipated enrollment.

Housing College housing (including coed) available. LD students housed randomly. LD students not required to live on campus.

Diagnostic Testing Available in intelligence, reading, math, motor abilities, work and study habits, personality, social skills.

Tutoring Offered one-to-one by professional teachers, peer tutors. Available in all subjects. LD students may receive tutoring in all courses each term.

Basic Skills Remediation Offered in small groups by regular teachers. Available in reading, math, learning strategies, motor abilities, work and study habits, social skills.

Academic Advisement Help with program planning provided by academic advisers. LD students may take up to 18 credits each semester; most take 13 to 15 credits; 12 credits required to maintain full-time status.

Special Courses Offered in college survival skills, reading, vocabulary development, communication skills, composition, language development, math, typing, personal psychology, study skills, career planning. All offered for credit; most enter into overall grade point average.

Auxiliary Aids and Services Aids include taped textbooks, tape recorders, calculators, typewriters, word processors. Services include alternative exam arrangements, notetakers, advocacy.

Counseling Services Individual counseling, small-group counseling, rap sessions, career counseling available.

Contact Mr. Rick Cox, Director of Handicapped Services, Eastern New Mexico University, Station 34, Portales, NM 88130, 505-562-2472.

EAST TEXAS STATE UNIVERSITY
Commerce, Texas

Year Program Began	1974	Special Courses	✓
Special Fee	None	Taped Textbooks	✓
Special Orientation	✓	Alternative Exam Arrangements	✓
Diagnostic Testing	✓	Notetakers	✓
Subject-Area Tutoring	✓	Staff	2 full-time, 15 part-time
Basic Skills Remediation	✓	Number of Students Served	210

General Information State-supported coed university. Founded 1889. Awards B, M, D. Institutionally accredited by regional association; programs accredited by AACSB (business), NASM (music), NCATE (teacher education). Small-town setting, with easy access to Dallas–Fort Worth; 140-acre campus. Total enrollment: 7,135. Faculty: 363 (311 full-time, 52 part-time); 69% have doctoral degrees; graduate assistants teach a few undergraduate courses. Calendar: semesters. Grading system: letters or numbers. Library holdings: 939,095 bound volumes, 296,742 titles on microform, 2,622 periodical subscriptions, 1,773 records/tapes.

Undergraduate Profile Fall 1984: 4,319 undergraduates (671 freshmen) from 40 states and territories and 32 foreign countries; 22% part-time; 95% state residents; 29% transfers; 35% financial aid recipients; 52% women; 11% blacks; 1% Native Americans; 3% Hispanics; 1% Asian Americans; 4% foreign nationals.

Expenses (1984–85) State resident tuition: $510 full-time. Nonresident tuition: $1590 full-time, $54.75 per semester hour part-time. State resident part-time tuition per semester (1 to 11 semester hours) ranges from $64.75 to $212.25. College room and board: $2255.

Financial Aid Fall 1984 full-time freshmen: 55% applied for aid. College-administered aid for all 1984–85 undergraduates: need-based scholarships; non-need scholarships; SEOG; College Work-Study; part-time jobs. Supporting data: IRS, institutional form, AFSA/SAR required; FFS, FAF acceptable. Priority application deadline: 6/1.

Athletics Member NCAA (Division II), NAIA. Intercollegiate sports: basketball M(II,s), W(II,s); cross-country running M(II), W; football M(II,s); golf M(II); tennis M(II,s), W(II,s); track and field M(II), W(II); volleyball W(II). Intramural sports: basketball, football, racquetball, tennis, volleyball.

Majors Accounting B; agricultural business B; agricultural economics B; agricultural sciences B; animal sciences B; anthropology B; art education B; art/fine arts B; biology/biological sciences B; botany/plant sciences B; broadcasting B; business administration/commerce/management B; business education B; chemistry B; commercial art B; computer science B; construction technologies B; dietetics B; early childhood education B; earth science B; economics B; education B; elementary education B; English B; fashion merchandising B; finance/banking B; French B; geography B; German B; guidance and counseling B; health education B; health services administration B; history B; home economics B; home economics education B; industrial arts B; interior design B; journalism B; law enforcement/police sciences B; liberal arts/general studies B; marketing/retailing/merchandising B; mathematics B; music B; music education B; painting/drawing B; photography B; physical education B; physics B; piano/organ B; political science/government B; printing technologies B; psychology B; radio and television studies B; science education B; sculpture B; secondary education B; secretarial studies/office management B; social science B; social work B; sociology B; Spanish B; special education B; speech pathology and audiology B; speech/rhetoric/public address/debate B; speech therapy B; theater arts/drama B; vocational education B; voice B; zoology B. Majors with highest enrollment: computer science, accounting, photography.

LD Program Information

Name of Program LD Student Program.

Availability of Services Began offering services in 1974. Services provided to freshmen, sophomores, juniors, seniors. Program currently serves 210 LD students: 80 freshmen, 66 sophomores, 40 juniors, 24 seniors.

Staff 2 full-time, 15 part-time staff members, including director, program chairman, committee members. Services provided by remediation specialists, tutors, counselors.

Admissions LD applicants evaluated on the basis of high school transcript, untimed SAT or ACT, psychoeducational report, untimed GED (for students who did not complete high school). LD students may begin taking classes in fall, spring, or summer. Application should be submitted 2 months in advance of initial anticipated enrollment.

Orientation Required orientation held after classes begin.

Housing College housing available. LD students housed randomly. LD freshmen required to live on campus.

Diagnostic Testing Available in reading, math, handwriting.

Tutoring Offered one-to-one by professional teachers, peer tutors. Available in all subjects. LD students may receive tutoring in all courses each term.

Basic Skills Remediation Offered one-to-one by LD teachers, regular teachers. Available in reading, math, spelling, handwriting, written language, learning strategies, work and study habits.

Academic Advisement Help with program planning provided by LD staff members, academic advisers. LD students may take up to 15 semester hours each semester; most take 12 semester hours; 12 semester hours required to maintain full-time status.

Special Courses Offered in college survival skills, reading, vocabulary development, communication skills, composition, language development, math, personal psychology, study skills, career planning. Some offered for credit; some enter into overall grade point average.

Auxiliary Aids and Services Aids include taped textbooks, tape recorders, typewriters, word processors. Services include alternative exam arrangements, notetakers, advocacy, LAUNCH (LD student group).

Counseling Services Individual counseling, small-group counseling, career counseling available.

Contact Dr. John Moss, Professor of Special Education and Chairman, Committee for Students with Learning Disabilities, East Texas State University, Department of Special Education, Commerce, TX 75428, 214-886-5932.

EDINBORO UNIVERSITY OF PENNSYLVANIA

Edinboro, Pennsylvania

Year Program Began	1981	Special Courses	✓
Special Fee	None	Taped Textbooks	✓
Special Orientation		Alternative Exam Arrangements	✓
Diagnostic Testing	✓	Notetakers	✓
Subject-Area Tutoring	✓	Staff	1 part-time
Basic Skills Remediation	✓	Number of Students Served	33 to 50

General Information State-supported comprehensive coed institution. Part of State System of Higher Education. Founded 1857. Awards A (college transfer and terminal), B, M. Institutionally accredited by regional association; programs accredited by NCATE (teacher education); candidate for program accreditation by NASM (music). Small-town setting; 600-acre barrier-free campus. Total enrollment: 6,053. Faculty: 348 (336 full-time, 12 part-time); 48% have doctoral degrees; graduate assistants teach no undergraduate courses. Calendar: semesters. Grading system: letters or numbers. Library holdings: 360,077 bound volumes, 1.3 million titles on microform, 1,639 periodical subscriptions, 22,006 records/tapes.

Undergraduate Profile Fall 1984: 5,498 undergraduates (1,370 freshmen) from 35 states and territories and 25 foreign countries; 14% part-time; 88% state residents; 5% transfers; 73% financial aid recipients; 51% women; 4% blacks; 1% Native Americans; 1% Hispanics; 1% Asian Americans; 1% foreign nationals; 200 legally handicapped students.

Expenses (1984–85) State resident tuition: $1480 full-time, $62 per credit part-time. Nonresident tuition: $2590 full-time, $108 per credit part-time. Mandatory fees: $188. College room and board: $1790. College room only: $970.

Financial Aid Fall 1984 full-time freshmen: 70% applied for aid, 83% of those were judged to have need, 98% of those were aided; the average aided freshman received an aid package worth $3120 (42% scholarships/grants, 58% self-help) meeting 92% of need. College-administered aid for all 1984–85 undergraduates: need-based scholarships (average $300); non-need scholarships (average $500); short-term loans (average $25); low-interest long-term loans from college funds (average $500); SEOG; College Work-Study; part-time jobs. Supporting data: state form, institutional form required; FFS, FAF, AFSA/SAR acceptable. Priority application deadline: 5/1.

Athletics Member NCAA (Division II). Intercollegiate sports: baseball/softball M(II), W(II,s); basketball M(II,s), W(II,s); cross-country running M(II,s), W(II,s); football M(II,s); soccer M(II,s); swimming and diving M(II,s), W(II,s); tennis M(II,s), W(II,s); track and field M(II,s), W(II,s); volleyball M(II,s), W(II,s); wrestling M(II,s). Intramural sports: badminton, baseball/softball, basketball, bowling, football, ice hockey, racquetball, swimming and diving, tennis, volleyball.

Majors Accounting B; anesthesiology B; anthropology B; applied art B; art education B; art/fine arts B; art history B; behavioral sciences B; biology/biological sciences B; biomedical technologies A; black/Afro-American studies B; business administration/commerce/management A, B; ceramic art and design B; chemistry B; child care/child and family studies A; commercial art B; communication B; computer science B; computer technologies A; criminal justice A, B; dental services A; (pre) dentistry sequence B; dietetics B; early childhood education B; earth science B; ecology/environmental studies B; economics B; education B; elementary education B; English B; environmental biology B; environmental sciences B; French B; geography B; geology B; German B; graphic arts B; health education B; health science B; history B; humanities B; human services A, B; industrial administration B; interdisciplinary studies B; jewelry and metalsmithing B; journalism B; law enforcement/police sciences A, B; (pre)law sequence B; liberal arts/general studies A, B; mathematics B; medical technology B; (pre)medicine sequence B; modern languages B; music B; music education B; natural sciences B; nuclear medical technology B; nursing B; nutrition B; painting/drawing B; philosophy B; photography B; physical education B; physical sciences B; physics B; political science/government B; psychology B; public relations B; radio and television studies B; Russian B; science B; science education B; sculpture B; secondary education B; secretarial studies/office management A; social science B; social work B; sociology B; Spanish B; special education B; speech pathology and audiology B; speech/rhetoric/public address/debate B; speech therapy B; studio art B; teacher aide studies A; textile arts B; theater arts/drama B; urban studies B; (pre)veterinary medicine sequence B; wildlife biology B. Majors with highest enrollment: business administration/commerce/management, computer science, art/fine arts.

LD Program Information

Name of Program Academic Development Center.

Availability of Services Began offering services in 1981. Services provided to freshmen, sophomores, juniors, seniors. Program currently serves 33 to 50 LD students: 15 to 20 freshmen, 10 to 15 sophomores, 5 to 10 juniors, 3 to 5 seniors.

Staff 1 part-time staff member (coordinator).

Admissions LD applicants evaluated on the basis of high school transcript and grade point average, standard SAT or ACT, personal interview, letters of recommendation. LD students may begin taking classes in fall, spring, or summer. Application should be submitted 6 months in advance of initial anticipated enrollment.

Housing College housing (including coed) available. LD students housed randomly. LD freshmen required to live on campus.

Diagnostic Testing Available in intelligence, reading, math, spelling, handwriting, spoken language, written language, motor abilities, perceptual skills, work and study habits.

Tutoring Offered one-to-one and in small groups by peer tutors. Available in all subjects. LD students may receive tutoring in all courses each term.

Basic Skills Remediation Offered in small groups by regular teachers, graduate students. Available in reading, math, spelling, spoken language, written language, learning strategies, work and study habits, social skills, speech.

Academic Advisement Help with program planning provided by academic advisers. LD students may take up to 15 credits each semester; 12 credits required to maintain full-time status.

Special Courses Offered in college survival skills, study skills. None offered for credit; none enter into overall grade point average.

Auxiliary Aids and Services Aids include taped textbooks, tape recorders, Kurzweil reading machine. Services include alternative exam arrangements, notetakers.

Counseling Services Individual counseling, small-group counseling, rap sessions, career counseling available.

Contact Mr. Ronald K. Swift, Assistant to the Provost/Vice President for Academic Affairs, Edinboro University of Pennsylvania, Edinboro, PA 16444, 814-732-2218.

EMERSON COLLEGE
Boston, Massachusetts

Year Program Began	1977	Special Courses	✓
Special Fee	None	Taped Textbooks	
Special Orientation		Alternative Exam Arrangements	✓
Diagnostic Testing	✓	Notetakers	✓
Subject-Area Tutoring	✓	Staff	1 full-time, 4 part-time
Basic Skills Remediation	✓	Number of Students Served	*Not reported*

General Information Independent comprehensive coed institution. Founded 1880. Awards B, M. Institutionally accredited by regional association. Metropolitan setting. Total enrollment: 2,287. Faculty: 167 (83 full-time, 84 part-time); 52% have doctoral degrees; graduate assistants teach a few undergraduate courses. Calendar: semesters. Grading system: letters or numbers. Library holdings: 85,000 bound volumes, 11,000 titles on microform, 500 periodical subscriptions, 4,000 records/tapes.

Undergraduate Profile Fall 1984: 1,737 undergraduates (455 freshmen); 6% part-time; 44% state residents; 13% transfers; 80% financial aid recipients; 58% women; 6% blacks; 0% Native Americans; 2% Hispanics; 0% Asian Americans; 3% foreign nationals; 3% of undergraduates over 25 years of age.

Expenses (1985–86) Comprehensive fee of $12,865 includes full-time tuition ($7620), mandatory fees ($365), and college room and board ($4880). College room only: $3220. Part-time tuition: $145 per credit.

Financial Aid Fall 1984 full-time freshmen: 80% applied for aid, 80% of those were judged to have need, 100% of those were aided; the average aided freshman received an aid package worth $5205 (41% scholarships/grants, 59% self-help) meeting 60% of need. College-administered aid for all 1984–85 undergraduates: need-based scholarships; non-need scholarships; low-interest long-term loans from external sources; SEOG; College Work-Study; part-time jobs. Supporting data: FAF, IRS, AFSA/SAR required; FFS acceptable. Priority application deadline: 4/1.

Athletics Member NCAA (Division III). Intercollegiate sports: baseball/softball M(III), W; basketball M(III), W(III); ice hockey M; sailing M, W; soccer M(III); wrestling M(III). Intramural sports: baseball/softball, basketball, cross-country running, fencing, football, martial arts, sailing, tennis.

Majors Advertising B; broadcasting B; business administration/commerce/management B; communication B; creative writing B; dance B; film studies B; interdisciplinary studies B; journalism B; (pre)law sequence B; literature B; music B; public relations B; publishing B; radio and television studies B; speech pathology and audiology B; speech/rhetoric/public address/debate B; speech therapy B; technical writing B; theater arts/drama B. Majors with highest enrollment: communication, theater arts/drama, speech/rhetoric/public address/debate.

LD Program Information

Name of Program Reading and Study Skills Center.

Availability of Services Began offering services in 1977. Services provided to freshmen, sophomores, juniors, seniors.

Staff 1 full-time, 4 part-time staff members, including director. Services provided by remediation specialists, tutors, diagnostic specialists.

Admissions LD applicants evaluated on the basis of high school transcript and grade point average, untimed SAT, autobiographical statement, letters of recommendation; personal interview, psychoeducational report recommended. LD students may begin taking classes in fall, spring, or summer. Application should be submitted 6 to 9 months in advance of initial anticipated enrollment.

Housing College housing (including coed) available. LD students housed randomly. LD freshmen required to live on campus except if living with relatives.

Diagnostic Testing Available in intelligence, reading, math, spelling, spoken language, work and study habits, personality, speech.

Tutoring Offered one-to-one and in small groups by professional teachers, peer tutors. Available in all subjects. LD students may receive tutoring in all courses each term.

Basic Skills Remediation Offered one-to-one and in small groups by LD teachers, regular teachers. Available in reading, math, spelling, spoken language, written language, learning strategies, work and study habits, speech.

Academic Advisement Help with program planning provided by LD staff members, academic advisers. LD students may take up to 16 credits each semester; most take 16 credits; 12 credits required to maintain full-time status.

Special Courses Offered in college survival skills, reading, vocabulary development, study skills, grammar, punctuation, spelling. None offered for credit; none enter into overall grade point average.

Auxiliary Aids and Services Services include alternative exam arrangements, notetakers, advocacy.

Counseling Services Individual counseling available.

Contact Dr. John Colligan, Director, Reading and Study Skills Center, Emerson College, 100 Beacon Street, Boston, MA 02116, 617-578-8583.

EMORY UNIVERSITY

Atlanta, Georgia

Year Program Began	1979	Special Courses	✓
Special Fee	None	Taped Textbooks	✓
Special Orientation	✓	Alternative Exam Arrangements	✓
Diagnostic Testing	✓	Notetakers	✓
Subject-Area Tutoring	✓	Staff	2 part-time
Basic Skills Remediation	✓	Number of Students Served	*Not reported*

General Information Methodist coed university. Founded 1836. Awards B, M, D. Institutionally accredited by regional association; programs accredited by AACSB (business), NLN (nursing). Metropolitan setting; 550-acre barrier-free campus. Total enrollment: 8,533. Faculty: 1,397 (1,158 full-time, 239 part-time); 98% have doctoral degrees; graduate assistants teach a few undergraduate courses. Calendar: semesters. Grading system: letters or numbers. Library holdings: 1.7 million bound volumes, 975,000 titles on microform, 15,000 periodical subscriptions, 2,600 records/tapes.

Undergraduate Profile Fall 1984: 3,728 undergraduates (948 freshmen) from 40 states and territories and 30 foreign countries; 1% part-time; 20% state residents; 5% transfers; 56% financial aid recipients; 51% women; 7% blacks; 0% Native Americans; 2% Hispanics; 2% Asian Americans; 3% foreign nationals; 6 legally handicapped students.

Expenses (1985–86) Comprehensive fee of $11,805 includes full-time tuition ($8400), mandatory fees ($80), and college room and board ($3325). College room only: $1775. Part-time tuition: $350 per semester hour.

Financial Aid Fall 1984 full-time freshmen: 53% applied for aid, 90% of those were judged to have need, 100% of those were aided; the average aided freshman received an aid package worth $7400 (70% scholarships/grants, 30% self-help) meeting 90% of need. College-administered aid for all 1984–85 undergraduates: 1,126 need-based scholarships (average $4140); 241 non-need scholarships (average $4595); low-interest long-term loans from external sources (average $1500); SEOG; College Work-Study; part-time jobs. Supporting data: FAF, institutional form required. Application deadline: continuous to 4/1.

Athletics Member NCAA (Division III). Intercollegiate sports: crew M; cross-country running M(III), W(III); soccer M(III); swimming and diving M(III), W(III); tennis M(III), W(III); track and field M(III), W(III). Intramural sports: baseball/softball, basketball, football, golf, racquetball, rugby, soccer, swimming and diving, tennis, track and field, volleyball, water polo, wrestling.

Majors Accounting B; anthropology B; art history B; biology/biological sciences B; black/Afro-American studies B; business administration/commerce/management B; chemistry B; classics B; computer science B; economics B; education B; English B; finance/banking B; French B; geology B; German B; Greek B; history B; humanities B; international studies B; Judaic studies B; Latin B; Latin American studies B; liberal arts/general studies B; mathematics B; music B; nursing B; philosophy B; physics B; political science/government B; psychology B; radiological technology B; respiratory therapy B; Russian B; sociology B; Spanish B. Majors with highest enrollment: psychology, chemistry, political science/government.

LD Program Information

Name of Program Handicapped Student Services.

Availability of Services Began offering services in 1979. Services provided to freshmen, sophomores, juniors, seniors.

Staff 2 part-time staff members, including director. Services provided by remediation specialist, tutors.

Admissions LD applicants evaluated on the basis of high school transcript and grade point average, untimed SAT or ACT, personal interview, autobiographical statement, letters of recommendation, psychoeducational report. LD students may begin taking classes in fall, spring, or summer. Application should be submitted 8 months in advance of initial anticipated enrollment.

Orientation Optional orientation offered before registration.

Housing College housing (including coed) available. LD students housed randomly. LD freshmen required to live on campus.

Diagnostic Testing Available in intelligence, reading, math, spelling, work and study habits, personality, social skills.

Tutoring Offered one-to-one by peer tutors. Available in all subjects. LD students may receive tutoring in all courses each term.

Basic Skills Remediation Offered one-to-one by director of Reading Center. Available in reading, math, written language, learning strategies, work and study habits, social skills.

Academic Advisement Help with program planning provided by LD staff members, academic advisers. LD students may take up to 18 semester hours each semester; 12 semester hours required to maintain full-time status.

Special Courses Offered in college survival skills, study skills, career planning. None offered for credit; none enter into overall grade point average.

Auxiliary Aids and Services Aids include taped textbooks, tape recorders. Services include alternative exam arrangements, notetakers.

Counseling Services Individual counseling, career counseling available.

Contact Ms. Lelia Crawford, Assistant Dean for Campus Life, Emory University, Drawer VV, Atlanta, GA 30322, 404-329-6202.

FLORIDA AGRICULTURAL AND MECHANICAL UNIVERSITY

Tallahassee, Florida

Year Program Began	1982
Special Fee	None
Special Orientation	
Diagnostic Testing	✓
Subject-Area Tutoring	✓
Basic Skills Remediation	✓
Special Courses	✓
Taped Textbooks	✓
Alternative Exam Arrangements	✓
Notetakers	✓
Staff	1 full-time, 1 part-time
Number of Students Served	24

General Information State-supported comprehensive coed institution. Part of State University System of Florida. Founded 1887. Awards A (college transfer), B, M, D. Institutionally accredited by regional association; programs accredited by NAAB (architecture), ABET (engineering and technology), NLN (nursing), ACPE (pharmacy), NCATE (teacher education). City setting; 419-acre campus. Total enrollment: 5,269. Faculty: 327 (308 full-time, 19 part-time); 54% have doctoral degrees; graduate assistants teach a few undergraduate courses. Calendar: semesters. Grading system: letters or numbers. Library holdings: 411,000 bound volumes, 37,322 titles on microform, 2,255 periodical subscriptions, 62,610 records/tapes.

Undergraduate Profile Fall 1984: 4,981 undergraduates (822 freshmen) from 36 states and territories and 48 foreign countries; 4% part-time; 70% state residents; 20% transfers; 75% financial aid recipients; 53% women; 87% blacks; 3% Hispanics; 2% Asian Americans; 8% foreign nationals; 9% of undergraduates over 25 years of age; 32 legally handicapped students.

Expenses (1985–86) State resident tuition ranges from $879 to $1021 full-time, $29.30 to $34.05 per semester hour part-time, according to class level. Nonresident tuition ranges from $2503 to $3510 full-time, $83.45 to $117 per semester hour part-time, according to class level. Mandatory fees: $60. College room and board: $2080.

Financial Aid Fall 1984 full-time freshmen: 86% applied for aid, 92% of those were judged to have need, 100% of those were aided; the average aided freshman received an aid package worth $3298 (69% scholarships/grants, 31% self-help) meeting 50% of need. College-administered aid for all 1984–85 undergraduates: need-based scholarships (average $500); 484 non-need scholarships (average $1530); short-term loans (average $100); low-interest long-term loans from external sources (average $1014); SEOG; College Work-Study; 420 part-time jobs. Supporting data: IRS, institutional form, AFSA/SAR required; FFS, FAF acceptable. Priority application deadline: 4/1.

Athletics Member NCAA (Division I). Intercollegiate sports: baseball/softball M(I,s), W(I,s); basketball M(I,s), W(I,s); cross-country running M(I,s), W(I,s); football M(I-AA,s); golf M(I,s), W(I,s); swimming and diving M(I,s), W(I,s); tennis M(I,s), W(I,s); track and field M(I,s), W(I,s); volleyball W(I,s). Intramural sports: baseball/softball, basketball, cross-country running, football, tennis, volleyball.

Majors Accounting B; agricultural business B; animal sciences B; architectural technologies B; architecture B; art education B; art/fine arts B; biology/biological sciences B; black/Afro-American studies B; business administration/commerce/management B; business economics B; business education B; chemical engineering B; chemistry B; civil engineering B; civil engineering technology B; communication B; computer science B; construction technologies B; corrections B; criminal justice B; data processing B; (pre)dentistry sequence B; early childhood education B; economics B; education B; electrical and electronics technologies B; electrical engineering B; electrical engineering technology B; electronics engineering B; elementary education B; engineering technology B; English B; entomology B; finance/banking B; graphic arts B; health services administration B; history B; industrial arts B; journalism B; landscape architecture/design B; liberal arts/general studies A; mathematics B; mechanical engineering B; medical records services B; music B; music education B; nursing B; ornamental horticulture B; pharmacy/pharmaceutical sciences B; philosophy B; physical education B; physical therapy B; physics B; political science/government B; printing technologies B; psychology B; public relations B; religious education B; respiratory therapy B; secondary education B; secretarial studies/office management B; social work B; sociology B; theater arts/drama B; (pre)veterinary medicine sequence B; vocational education B. Majors with highest enrollment: computer science, accounting, pharmacy/pharmaceutical sciences.

LD Program Information

Name of Program Learning Disabilities Laboratory.

Availability of Services Began offering services in 1982. Services provided to freshmen, sophomores, juniors, seniors. Program currently serves 24 LD students: 10 freshmen, 5 sophomores, 5 juniors, 4 seniors.

Staff 1 full-time, 1 part-time staff members, including director. Services provided by remediation specialists, LD specialist, readers.

Admissions LD applicants evaluated on the basis of high school transcript and grade point average, untimed SAT or ACT, personal interview, letters of recommendation, psychoeducational report. LD students may begin taking classes in fall, spring, or summer. Application should be submitted 6 months in advance of initial anticipated enrollment.

Housing College housing available. LD students housed randomly. LD freshmen required to live on campus.

Diagnostic Testing Available in intelligence, reading, math, perceptual skills.

Tutoring Offered one-to-one by professional teachers, peer tutors. Available in all subjects. LD students may receive tutoring in all courses each term.

Basic Skills Remediation Offered one-to-one and in small groups by LD teachers. Available in reading, math, spelling, handwriting, spoken language, written language, learning strategies, work and study habits, social skills.

Academic Advisement Help with program planning provided by LD staff members, academic advisers. LD students may take up to 12 semester hours each semester; 12 semester hours required to maintain full-time status.

Special Courses Offered in college survival skills, reading, vocabulary development, communication skills, composition, language development, math, typing, personal psychology, study skills, career planning. Some offered for credit; some enter into overall grade point average.

Auxiliary Aids and Services Aids include taped textbooks, tape recorders, calculators, typewriters, computers, slides and filmstrips (to enhance course syllabus). Services include alternative exam arrangements, notetakers, advocacy.

Counseling Services Individual counseling, small-group counseling, rap sessions, career counseling available.

Contact Dr. Sharon Wooten, Director, Learning Disabilities Laboratory, Florida Agricultural and Mechanical University, Gore Educational Complex A200, Tallahassee, FL 32307, 904-599-3259.

FLORIDA ATLANTIC UNIVERSITY

Boca Raton, Florida

Year Program Began	1981	Special Courses	
Special Fee	None	Taped Textbooks	
Special Orientation		Alternative Exam Arrangements	✓
Diagnostic Testing		Notetakers	✓
Subject-Area Tutoring	✓	Staff	1 part-time
Basic Skills Remediation		Number of Students Served	4

General Information State-supported coed university. Part of State University System of Florida. Founded 1961. Awards B, M, D. Institutionally accredited by regional association; programs accredited by AACSB (business), ABET (engineering and technology), NASM (music), NCATE (teacher education). City setting, with easy access to Miami; 1,000-acre barrier-free campus. Total enrollment: 8,150. Faculty: 593 (384 full-time, 209 part-time); 80% have doctoral degrees; graduate assistants teach a few undergraduate courses. Calendar: semesters. Grading system: letters or numbers. Library holdings: 410,000 bound volumes, 640,000 titles on microform, 5,000 periodical subscriptions, 14,000 records/tapes.

Undergraduate Profile Fall 1984: 6,887 undergraduates (257 freshmen); 52% part-time; 94% state residents; 96% transfers; 42% financial aid recipients; 51% women; 4% blacks; 1% Native Americans; 4% Hispanics; 1% Asian Americans; 5% foreign nationals; 37 legally handicapped students.

Expenses (1984–85) State resident tuition ranges from $865 to $983 full-time, $28.84 to $32.77 per semester hour part-time, according to class level. Nonresident tuition ranges from $2395 to $3353 full-time, $79.84 to $111.77 per semester hour part-time, according to class level. College room and board: $2650. College room only: $1000.

Financial Aid Fall 1984 full-time freshmen: 67% applied for aid, 74% of those were judged to have need, 100% of those were aided; the average aided freshman received an aid package meeting 95% of need. College-administered aid for all 1984–85 undergraduates: need-based scholarships; non-need scholarships (average $750); short-term loans; low-interest long-term loans; SEOG; College Work-Study; part-time jobs. Supporting data: FAF, institutional form, AFSA/SAR, Financial Aid Transcript (for transfers) required; FFS acceptable. Priority application deadline: 3/1.

Athletics Member NCAA (Division II). Intercollegiate sports: baseball/softball M(II,s); basketball W(II,s); cross-country running M(II), W(II); fencing M(II), W(II); golf M(II,s), W(II,s); soccer M(II,s); swimming and diving W(II,s); tennis M(II,s), W(II,s). Intramural sports: baseball/softball, bowling, football, martial arts, swimming and diving, tennis, volleyball, weight lifting.

Majors Accounting B; anthropology B; art education B; art/fine arts B; biology/biological sciences B; botany/plant sciences B; business administration/commerce/management B; ceramic art and design B; chemistry B; communication B; computer information systems B; computer science B; criminal justice B; (pre)dentistry sequence B; early childhood education B; economics B; education B; electrical engineering B; elementary education B; English B; experimental psychology B; finance/banking B; French B; geography B; geology B; German B; health services administration B; history B; humanities B; human resources B; international business B; journalism B; law enforcement/police sciences B; (pre)law sequence B; linguistics B; marine biology B; marketing/retailing/merchandising B; mathematics B; mechanical engineering B; medical technology B; (pre)medicine sequence B; microbiology B; music B; music education B; nursing B; ocean engineering B; philosophy B; physical education B; physics B; political science/government B; psychology B; public affairs and policy studies B; radio and television studies B; real estate B; science B; science education B; secondary education B; social science B; social work B; sociology B; Spanish B; special education B; speech/rhetoric/public address/debate B; studio art B; theater arts/drama B; urban studies B; (pre) veterinary medicine sequence B; zoology B. Majors with highest enrollment: business administration/commerce/management, accounting, computer information systems.

LD Program Information

Name of Program Handicapped Student Services.

Availability of Services Began offering services in 1981. Services provided to freshmen, sophomores, juniors, seniors. Program currently serves 4 LD students: 3 juniors, 1 senior.

Staff 1 part-time staff member (director).

Admissions LD applicants evaluated on the basis of high school transcript and grade point average, standard or untimed SAT or ACT, personal interview, autobiographical statement, letters of recommendation. LD students may begin taking classes in fall, spring, or summer. Application should be submitted 6 to 8 months in advance of initial anticipated enrollment.

Housing College housing available. LD students housed randomly. LD students not required to live on campus.

Tutoring Offered one-to-one by peer tutors. Available in some subjects. LD students may receive tutoring in all courses each term.

Academic Advisement Help with program planning provided by academic advisers. LD students may take up to 20 semester hours each semester; most take 9 to 12 semester hours; 12 semester hours required to maintain full-time status.

Auxiliary Aids and Services Aids include tape recorders, calculators. Services include alternative exam arrangements, notetakers.

Counseling Services Individual counseling, career counseling available.

Contact Ms. Phebe H. Kerr, Associate Dean for Student Affairs, Florida Atlantic University, 500 Northwest 20th Street, Boca Raton, FL 33431, 305-393-3546.

FLORIDA STATE UNIVERSITY

Tallahassee, Florida

Year Program Began	1979	Special Courses	✓
Special Fee	None	Taped Textbooks	✓
Special Orientation	✓	Alternative Exam Arrangements	✓
Diagnostic Testing	✓	Notetakers	✓
Subject-Area Tutoring	✓	Staff	1 full-time
Basic Skills Remediation	✓	Number of Students Served	8

General Information State-supported coed university. Part of State University System of Florida. Founded 1857. Awards A (college transfer), B, M, D. Institutionally accredited by regional association; programs accredited by AACSB (business), FIDER (interior design), NASM (music), NLN (nursing), NCATE (teacher education). City setting; 343-acre campus. Total enrollment: 19,904. Faculty: 1,489; 85% have doctoral degrees; graduate assistants teach a few undergraduate courses. Calendar: semesters. Grading system: letters or numbers. Library holdings: 1.3 million bound volumes, 13,543 periodical subscriptions.

Undergraduate Profile Fall 1984: 16,071 undergraduates (2,222 freshmen) from 52 states and territories and 80 foreign countries; 14% part-time; 90% state residents; 56% financial aid recipients; 53% women; 8% blacks; 1% Native Americans; 1% Hispanics; 3% foreign nationals.

Expenses (1985–86) State resident tuition ranges from $834 to $958 full-time, $27.80 to $31.93 per credit hour part-time, according to class level. Nonresident tuition ranges from $2440 to $3446 full-time, 81.35 to $114.88 per credit hour part-time, according to class level. Mandatory fees: $78. College room and board: $2554. College room only: $1154.

Financial Aid Fall 1984 full-time freshmen: 46% applied for aid, 87% of those were judged to have need, 86% of those were aided; the average aided freshman received an aid package worth $2806 (50% scholarships/grants, 50% self-help) meeting 100% of need. College-administered aid for all 1984–85 undergraduates: need-based scholarships; non-need scholarships; short-term loans; low-interest long-term loans; SEOG; College Work-Study; part-time jobs. Supporting data: FFS, AFSA/SAR required; FAF acceptable. Priority application deadline: 3/15.

Athletics Member NCAA (Division I). Intercollegiate sports: baseball/softball M(I,s), W(I,s); basketball M(I,s), W(I,s); cross-country running M(I,s), W(I); football M(I-A,s); golf M(I,s), W(I,s); swimming and diving M(I,s), W(I,s); tennis M(I,s), W(I,s); track and field M(I,s), W(I,s); volleyball W(I,s). Intramural sports: baseball/softball, basketball, fencing, golf, gymnastics, martial arts, rugby, sailing, soccer, swimming and diving, tennis, volleyball, wrestling.

Majors Accounting B; advertising B; American studies B; anthropology B; applied art B; archaeology B; art education B; art/fine arts B; art history B; Asian/Oriental studies B; biochemistry B; biology/biological sciences B; business administration/commerce/management B; chemical engineering B; chemistry B; child psychology/child development B; city, community, and regional planning B; civil engineering B; classics B; communication B; comparative literature B; computer engineering B; computer science B; creative writing B; criminal justice B; dance B; (pre)dentistry sequence B; dietetics B; early childhood education B; East Asian studies B; economics B; education B; electrical engineering B; electronics engineering B; elementary education B; English B; experimental psychology B; family services B; fashion design and technology B; fashion merchandising B; finance/banking B; French B; geography B; geology B; German B; Greek B; health education B; history B; home economics B; home economics education B; hotel and restaurant management B; humanities B; insurance B; interior design B; international business B; international studies B; Italian B; Latin B; law enforcement/police sciences B; (pre)law sequence B; liberal arts/general studies A; linguistics B; literature B; marketing/retailing/merchandising B; mathematics B; mechanical engineering B; medical technology B; (pre)medicine sequence B; meteorology B; music B; music education B; music history B; music therapy B; nursing B; nutrition B; philosophy B; physical education B; physics B; piano/organ B; political science/government B; psychology B; public relations B; radio and television studies B; real estate B; recreation and leisure services B; religious studies B; Russian B; science education B; secondary education B; social science B; social work B; sociology B; Spanish B; special education B; speech pathology and audiology B; statistics B; stringed instruments B; studio art B; textiles and clothing B; theater arts/drama B; (pre) veterinary medicine sequence B; voice B.

LD Program Information

Name of Program Disabled Student Services.

Availability of Services Began offering services in 1979. Services provided to freshmen, sophomores, juniors, seniors. Program currently serves 8 LD students: 4 sophomores, 2 juniors, 2 seniors.

Staff 1 full-time staff member (director). Services provided by tutors.

Admissions LD applicants evaluated on the basis of high school transcript and grade point average, standard or untimed SAT or ACT, personal interview, letters of recommendation, psychoeducational report. LD students may begin taking classes in fall, spring, or summer. Application should be submitted at least 1 month in advance of initial anticipated enrollment.

Orientation Optional orientation offered before registration.

Housing College housing (including coed) available. LD students housed randomly. LD students not required to live on campus.

Diagnostic Testing Available in intelligence, reading, math, spelling, written language, motor abilities, perceptual skills, personality.

Tutoring Offered one-to-one by peer tutors. Available in all subjects. LD students may receive tutoring in all courses each term.

Basic Skills Remediation Offered in small groups by regular teachers. Available in reading, math, spelling, written language.

Academic Advisement Help with program planning provided by academic advisers. LD students may take up to 18 credit hours each semester; most take 12 to 15 credit hours; 12 credit hours required to maintain full-time status.

Special Courses Offered in reading, language development, math, study skills, career planning. Some offered for credit; some enter into overall grade point average.

Auxiliary Aids and Services Aids include taped textbooks, tape recorders, word processors. Services include alternative exam arrangements, notetakers, advocacy.

Counseling Services Individual counseling, career counseling available.

Contact Mr. Halie Nabi, Director, Disabled Student Services, Florida State University, 303 Bryan Hall, Tallahassee, FL 32306, 904-644-1741.

FORT LEWIS COLLEGE

Durango, Colorado

Year Program Began	1981	Special Courses	✓
Special Fee	None	Taped Textbooks	
Special Orientation		Alternative Exam Arrangements	✓
Diagnostic Testing	✓	Notetakers	✓
Subject-Area Tutoring	✓	Staff	4 part-time
Basic Skills Remediation	✓	Number of Students Served	10

General Information State-supported 4-year coed college. Founded 1911. Awards A (terminal), B. Institutionally accredited by regional association; programs accredited by AACSB (business), NCATE (teacher education); candidate for program accreditation by NASM (music). Small-town setting; 300-acre campus. Total enrollment: 3,708. Faculty: 158 (150 full-time, 8 part-time); 74% have doctoral degrees. Calendar: modified trimesters. Grading system: letters or numbers. Library holdings: 150,000 bound volumes, 48,000 titles on microform, 950 periodical subscriptions, 3,600 records/tapes.

Undergraduate Profile Fall 1984: 3,708 undergraduates (1,050 freshmen) from 46 states and territories and 16 foreign countries; 6% part-time; 70% state residents; 25% transfers; 30% financial aid recipients; 43% women; 1% blacks; 7% Native Americans; 1% Hispanics; 1% foreign nationals.

Expenses (1985–86) State resident tuition: $786 full-time, $46 per credit hour part-time. Nonresident tuition: $3226 full-time, $194 per credit hour part-time. Mandatory fees: $170. College room and board: $2234. College room only: $730.

Financial Aid College-administered aid for all 1984–85 undergraduates: need-based scholarships; non-need scholarships; SEOG; College Work-Study. Supporting data: FFS required. Priority application deadline: 5/1.

Athletics Member NCAA (Division II), NAIA. Intercollegiate sports: baseball/softball W(s); basketball M(s), W(s); cross-country running M(s), W(s); football M(II,s); golf M(s); tennis M(s), W(s); volleyball W(s); wrestling M(s). Intramural sports: archery, badminton, baseball/softball, basketball, bowling, cross-country running, fencing, field hockey, football, golf, gymnastics, lacrosse, martial arts, racquetball, rugby, skiing (cross-country), skiing (downhill), soccer, swimming and diving, tennis, track and field, volleyball, water polo, weight lifting, wrestling.

Majors Accounting B; agricultural sciences A; anthropology B; art education B; art/fine arts B; Asian/Oriental studies B; biology/biological sciences B; business administration/commerce/management B; chemistry B; communication B; computer science B; economics B; elementary education B; (pre)engineering sequence A; English B; environmental biology B; ethnic studies B; European studies B; geology B; history B; Latin American studies B; mathematics B; medical technology B; music B; music education B; physical education B; physics B; political science/government B; psychology B; public relations B; secretarial studies/office management A; sociology B; Spanish B; studio art B; theater arts/drama B. Majors with highest enrollment: business administration/commerce/management, geology.

LD Program Information

Name of Program Learning Assistance Center.

Availability of Services Began offering services in 1981. Services provided to freshmen, sophomores, juniors, seniors. Program currently serves 10 LD students: 5 freshmen, 2 sophomores, 3 juniors.

Staff 4 part-time staff members, including director. Services provided by writing specialist, math specialists.

Admissions LD applicants evaluated on the basis of high school transcript and grade point average, standard or untimed SAT or ACT, personal interview, letters of recommendation. LD students may begin taking classes in fall, winter, or summer. Application should be submitted 9 months in advance of initial anticipated enrollment.

Housing College housing (including coed) available. LD students housed randomly. LD students not required to live on campus.

Diagnostic Testing Available in reading, math, written language, perceptual skills, work and study habits.

Tutoring Offered one-to-one and in small groups by professional teachers, peer tutors. Available in most subjects. LD students may receive tutoring in all courses each term.

Basic Skills Remediation Offered one-to-one and in small groups by Learning Assistance Center staff. Available in reading, math, spelling, spoken language, written language, learning strategies, perceptual skills, work and study habits, speech.

Academic Advisement Help with program planning provided by LD staff members, academic advisers. LD students may take up to 18 credit hours each trimester; most take 12 to 14 credit hours; 9 credit hours required to maintain full-time status (12 credit hours for financial aid, dormitory eligibility).

Special Courses Offered in college survival skills, reading, communication skills, composition, math, study skills, career planning. Some offered for credit; some enter into overall grade point average.

Auxiliary Aids and Services Aids include tape recorders, typewriters, word processors. Services include alternative exam arrangements, notetakers, advocacy.

Counseling Services Individual counseling, career counseling available.

Contact Mr. Robert P. Lundquist, Director, Learning Assistance Center, Fort Lewis College, Durango, CO 81301, 303-247-7383.

FRAMINGHAM STATE COLLEGE

Framingham, Massachusetts

Year Program Began	1979	Special Courses	✓
Special Fee	None	Taped Textbooks	✓
Special Orientation		Alternative Exam Arrangements	✓
Diagnostic Testing	✓	Notetakers	✓
Subject-Area Tutoring	✓	Staff	1 full-time, 2 part-time
Basic Skills Remediation	✓	Number of Students Served	*Not reported*

General Information State-supported comprehensive coed institution. Founded 1839. Awards B, M. Institutionally accredited by regional association. City setting, with easy access to Boston; 73-acre barrier-free campus. Total enrollment: 3,782. Faculty: 214; 72% have doctoral degrees; graduate assistants teach no undergraduate courses. Calendar: semesters. Grading system: letters or numbers. Library holdings: 144,319 bound volumes, 365,961 titles on microform, 1,403 periodical subscriptions.

Undergraduate Profile Fall 1984: 3,238 undergraduates (793 freshmen) from 12 states and territories and 12 foreign countries; 7% part-time; 95% state residents; 31% transfers; 47% financial aid recipients; 60% women; 2% blacks; 1% Native Americans; 1% Hispanics; 1% Asian Americans; 1% foreign nationals; 12% of undergraduates over 25 years of age; 8 legally handicapped students.

Expenses (1985–86) State resident tuition: $936 full-time, $156 per course part-time. Nonresident tuition: $3132 full-time, $474 per course part-time. Mandatory fees: $378. College room and board: $1870 (minimum). College room only: $1100 (minimum).

Financial Aid Fall 1984 full-time freshmen: 31% applied for aid, 80% of those were judged to have need, 100% of those were aided; the average aided freshman received an aid package worth $2283 (38% scholarships/grants, 62% self-help) meeting 80% of need. College-administered aid for all 1984–85 undergraduates: 557 need-based scholarships (average $350); 30 non-need scholarships (average $300); short-term loans (average $50); low-interest long-term loans from external sources (average $1000); SEOG; College Work-Study; part-time jobs. Supporting data: FAF, IRS, institutional form required; FFS, AFSA/SAR acceptable. Priority application deadline: 4/15.

Athletics Member NCAA (Division III). Intercollegiate sports: baseball/softball M(III), W(III); basketball M(III), W(III); cross-country running M(III), W(III); equestrian sports W; field hockey W(III); football M(III); ice hockey M(III); soccer M(III), W(III); tennis M(III), W(III); volleyball W(III). Intramural sports: baseball/softball, basketball, equestrian sports, football, golf, racquetball.

Majors Art education B; art/fine arts B; art history B; biology/biological sciences B; chemistry B; communication B; computer science B; consumer services B; dietetics B; early childhood education B; earth science B; economics B; elementary education B; English B; family and consumer studies B; fashion merchandising B; food sciences B; French B; geography B; history B; home economics B; home economics education B; mathematics B; medical technology B; nursing B; nutrition B; philosophy B; political science/government B; psychology B; sociology B; Spanish B; textiles and clothing B. Majors with highest enrollment: economics, psychology, computer science.

LD Program Information

Name of Program Skills Center.

Availability of Services Began offering services in 1979. Services provided to freshmen, sophomores, juniors, seniors.

Staff 1 full-time, 2 part-time staff members, including director. Services provided by remediation specialists, tutors, diagnostic specialists.

Admissions LD applicants evaluated on the basis of high school transcript and grade point average, standard or untimed SAT or ACT, personal interview, autobiographical statement, letters of recommendation, psychoeducational report, Stanford Reading Test, writing sample. LD students may begin taking classes in fall or spring. Application should be submitted 6 months in advance of initial anticipated enrollment.

Housing College housing (including coed) available. LD students housed randomly. LD students not required to live on campus.

Diagnostic Testing Available in reading, math, spelling, written language, work and study habits.

Tutoring Offered one-to-one and in small groups by professional teachers, peer tutors. Available in some subjects. LD students may receive tutoring in all courses each term.

Basic Skills Remediation Offered one-to-one and in small groups by LD teachers, regular teachers, peer teachers. Available in reading, math, spelling, learning strategies, work and study habits.

Academic Advisement Help with program planning provided by LD staff members, academic advisers. LD students may take up to 4 courses each semester; most take 3 courses (recommended in freshman year); 3 courses required to maintain full-time status.

Special Courses Offered in reading, vocabulary development, composition, study skills, career planning. Some offered for credit; some enter into overall grade point average.

Auxiliary Aids and Services Aids include taped textbooks, tape recorders, calculators, typewriters, word processors. Services include alternative exam arrangements, notetakers, advocacy.

Counseling Services Individual counseling, rap sessions, career counseling available.

Contact Ms. Nancy Nyhan, Director of Skills Center, Framingham State College, 100 State Street, Framingham, MA 01701, 617-620-1220 Ext. 445.

FRANKLIN UNIVERSITY
Columbus, Ohio

Year Program Began	1982	Special Courses	✓
Special Fee	None	Taped Textbooks	✓
Special Orientation		Alternative Exam Arrangements	✓
Diagnostic Testing	✓	Notetakers	✓
Subject-Area Tutoring	✓	Staff	1 full-time
Basic Skills Remediation	✓	Number of Students Served	11

General Information Independent 4-year coed college. Founded 1902. Awards A (college transfer and terminal), B. Institutionally accredited by regional association; programs accredited by ABET (engineering and technology). Metropolitan setting; 12-acre barrier-free campus. Total enrollment: 4,621. Faculty: 221 (59 full-time, 162 part-time); 19% have doctoral degrees. Calendar: trimesters. Grading system: letters or numbers. Library holdings: 64,087 bound volumes, 81,753 titles on microform, 1,200 periodical subscriptions, 639 records/tapes.

Undergraduate Profile Fall 1984: 4,621 undergraduates (419 freshmen); 70% part-time; 100% state residents; 67% transfers; 22% financial aid recipients; 53% women; 13% blacks; 1% Native Americans; 1% Hispanics; 1% Asian Americans; 2% foreign nationals; 55% of undergraduates over 25 years of age; 55 legally handicapped students.

Expenses (1985–86) Tuition: $2848 full-time, $89 per credit hour part-time. Mandatory fees: $15.

Financial Aid Fall 1984 full-time freshmen: 95% applied for aid, 76% of those were judged to have need, 88% of those were aided; the average aided freshman received an aid package worth $4600 (24% scholarships/grants, 76% self-help) meeting 75% of need. College-administered aid for all 1984–85 undergraduates: 272 need-based scholarships (average $849); 112 non-need scholarships (average $973); low-interest long-term loans from external sources (average $2500); SEOG; College Work-Study; part-time jobs. Supporting data: IRS, state form, institutional form, AFSA/SAR required; FAF, CFS acceptable. Priority application deadline: 7/2.

Athletics Member NAIA. Intercollegiate sports: basketball M, W; soccer M. Intramural sports: baseball/softball, golf, skiing (cross-country), skiing (downhill), soccer, tennis, volleyball.

Majors Accounting A, B; behavioral sciences B; business administration/commerce/management A, B; communication B; computer management B; computer science B; computer technologies A; drafting and design A; electronics engineering technology A, B; engineering technology A, B; finance/banking B; human resources A, B; marketing/retailing/merchandising B; mechanical engineering technology A, B; nursing B; operations research A, B; public administration A, B; real estate A, B. Majors with highest enrollment: business administration/commerce/management, accounting, computer management.

LD Program Information

Name of Program Disability Services.

Availability of Services Began offering services in 1982. Services provided to freshmen, sophomores, juniors, seniors. Program currently serves 11 LD students: 3 freshmen, 4 sophomores, 2 juniors, 2 seniors.

Staff 1 full-time staff member (director).

Admissions LD applicants evaluated on the basis of high school transcript, personal interview, letters of recommendation, psychoeducational report, IEP, assessments by LD specialists. LD students may begin taking classes in fall, winter, spring, or summer. Application should be submitted 3 months in advance of initial anticipated enrollment.

Housing College housing not available.

Diagnostic Testing Available in reading, math, written language.

Tutoring Offered one-to-one and in small groups by professional teachers, peer tutors. Available in most subjects. LD students may receive tutoring in all courses each term.

Basic Skills Remediation Offered in small groups by regular teachers. Available in reading, math, spelling, spoken language, written language, work and study habits.

Academic Advisement Help with program planning provided by LD staff member. LD students may take up to 16 credit hours each trimester; most take 12 credit hours; 12 credit hours required to maintain full-time status.

Special Courses Offered in personal psychology, study skills. None offered for credit.

Auxiliary Aids and Services Aids include taped textbooks, tape recorders, calculators, typewriters, word processors. Services include alternative exam arrangements, notetakers, advocacy.

Counseling Services Individual counseling, small-group counseling, rap sessions, career counseling available.

Contact Ms. Jennifer King, Coordinator of Disability Services, Franklin University, 201 South Grant Avenue, Columbus, OH 43215, 614-224-6237.

FROSTBURG STATE COLLEGE
Frostburg, Maryland

Year Program Began	*Not reported*	Special Courses	✓
Special Fee	None	Taped Textbooks	✓
Special Orientation	✓	Alternative Exam Arrangements	✓
Diagnostic Testing	✓	Notetakers	✓
Subject-Area Tutoring	✓	Staff	5 part-time
Basic Skills Remediation	✓	Number of Students Served	36

General Information State-supported comprehensive coed institution. Founded 1898. Awards B, M. Institutionally accredited by regional association; programs accredited by NCATE (teacher education). Small-town setting; 220-acre campus. Total enrollment: 3,400. Faculty: 185 (150 full-time, 35 part-time); 60% have doctoral degrees; graduate assistants teach no undergraduate courses. Calendar: semesters. Grading system: letters or numbers. Library holdings: 339,500 bound volumes, 875 periodical subscriptions, 41,535 records/tapes.

Undergraduate Profile Fall 1984: 2,900 undergraduates (700 freshmen) from 17 states and territories and 3 foreign countries; 7% part-time; 87% state residents; 10% transfers; 35% financial aid recipients; 53% women; 8% blacks; 25 legally handicapped students.

Expenses (1985–86) State resident tuition: $1166 full-time, $50 per credit hour part-time. Nonresident tuition: $2422 full-time, $50 per credit hour part-time. Mandatory fees: $306. College room and board: $2720. College room only: $1370.

Financial Aid Fall 1984 full-time freshmen: 86% applied for aid, 79% of those were judged to have need, 100% of those were aided; the average aided freshman received an aid package worth $3000 (20% scholarships/grants, 80% self-help) meeting 65% of need. College-administered aid for all 1984–85 undergraduates: need-based scholarships (average $1200); non-need scholarships (average $700); low-interest long-term loans; College Work-Study; part-time jobs. Supporting data: FAF, institutional form, AFSA/SAR required. Application deadline: 5/1.

Athletics Member NCAA (Division III). Intercollegiate sports: baseball/softball M(III,s); basketball M(III), W(III); cross-country running M(III); field hockey W(III); football M(III); lacrosse W(III); soccer M(III); swimming and diving M(III), W(III); tennis M(III), W(III); track and field M(III), W(III). Intramural sports: baseball/softball, basketball, cross-country running, football, martial arts, rugby, soccer, swimming and diving, volleyball.

Majors Accounting B; art education B; art/fine arts B; biology/biological sciences B; business administration/commerce/management B; cartography B; chemistry B; computer science B; early childhood education B; economics B; education B; English B; French B; geography B; German B; history B; land use management and reclamation B; mathematics B; music B; music education B; philosophy B; physical education B; physics B; political science/government B; psychology B; recreation and leisure services B; secondary education B; social science B; sociology B; Spanish B; speech/rhetoric/public address/debate B; theater arts/drama B; wildlife management B. Majors with highest enrollment: business administration/commerce/management, education.

LD Program Information

Name of Program Student Special Services.

Availability of Services Services provided to freshmen, sophomores, juniors, seniors. Program currently serves 36 LD students: 23 freshmen, 6 sophomores, 7 juniors.

Staff 5 part-time staff members, including director, assistant director, coordinator. Services provided by remediation specialist, counselor.

Admissions LD applicants evaluated on the basis of high school transcript and grade point average, untimed SAT, autobiographical statement, letters of recommendation; personal interview recommended. LD students may begin taking classes in fall, spring, or summer.

Orientation Optional orientation offered before registration.

Housing College housing (including coed) available. LD students housed randomly. LD students not required to live on campus.

Diagnostic Testing Available in intelligence, reading, math, spelling, written language, motor abilities, perceptual skills, work and study habits.

Tutoring Offered one-to-one and in small groups by professional teachers, peer tutors. Available in all subjects. LD students may receive tutoring in all courses each term.

Basic Skills Remediation Offered one-to-one and in small groups by regular teachers, peer teachers. Available in reading, math, spelling, written language, work and study habits, social skills.

Academic Advisement Help with program planning provided by LD staff members, academic advisers. LD students may take up to 18 credit hours each semester; most take 12 credit hours; 12 credit hours required to maintain full-time status.

Special Courses Offered in college survival skills, reading, vocabulary development, study skills, career planning. None offered for credit; none enter into overall grade point average.

Auxiliary Aids and Services Aids include taped textbooks, tape recorders, calculators, word processors. Services include alternative exam arrangements, notetakers, advocacy, peer support group.

Counseling Services Individual counseling, career counseling available.

Contact Dr. Todd S. Hutton, Director, Student Special Services, Frostburg State College, Frostburg, MD 21532, 301-689-4481.

GEORGE WASHINGTON UNIVERSITY

Washington, District of Columbia

Year Program Began	1979	Special Courses	
Special Fee	None	Taped Textbooks	✓
Special Orientation		Alternative Exam Arrangements	✓
Diagnostic Testing	✓	Notetakers	✓
Subject-Area Tutoring	✓	Staff	2 part-time
Basic Skills Remediation	✓	Number of Students Served	*Not reported*

General Information Independent coed university. Founded 1821. Awards A (terminal), B, M, D. Institutionally accredited by regional association; programs accredited by AACSB (business), ABET (engineering and technology), NCATE (teacher education); candidate for program accreditation by NASM (music). Metropolitan setting; 36-acre barrier-free campus. Total enrollment: 14,832. Faculty: 1,679 (1,104 full-time, 575 part-time); 76% have doctoral degrees; graduate assistants teach a few undergraduate courses. Calendar: semesters. Grading system: letters or numbers. Library holdings: 1.3 million bound volumes, 1.1 million titles on microform, 15,300 periodical subscriptions, 3,500 records/tapes.

Undergraduate Profile Fall 1984: 6,031 undergraduates (1,263 freshmen) from 52 states and territories and 106 foreign countries; 15% part-time; 7% district residents; 47% transfers; 40% financial aid recipients; 49% women; 6% blacks; 2% Hispanics; 4% Asian Americans; 15% foreign nationals; 16% of undergraduates over 25 years of age; 69 legally handicapped students.

Expenses (1985–86) Comprehensive fee of $11,900 includes full-time tuition ($7350), mandatory fees ($250), and college room and board ($4300). Part-time tuition: $275 per semester hour. Tuition prepayment plan available.

Financial Aid Fall 1984 full-time freshmen: 50% applied for aid, 87% of those were judged to have need, 92% of those were aided; the average aided freshman received an aid package worth $5600 (36% scholarships/grants, 64% self-help) meeting 91% of need. College-administered aid for all 1984–85 undergraduates: 811 need-based scholarships (average $4224); 128 non-need scholarships (average $2949); short-term loans (average $200); low-interest long-term loans from external sources (average $1500); SEOG; College Work-Study; part-time jobs. Supporting data: FAF, IRS, institutional form required. Application deadline: continuous to 3/1.

Athletics Member NCAA (Division I). Intercollegiate sports: badminton W(s); baseball/softball M(I,s); basketball M(I,s), W(I,s); crew M, W; golf M(I,s); gymnastics W(I,s); soccer M(I,s), W(I,s); swimming and diving M(I,s), W(I,s); tennis M(I,s), W(I,s); volleyball W(I,s); water polo M(I,s); wrestling M(I,s). Intramural sports: badminton, baseball/softball, basketball, football, martial arts, racquetball, soccer, squash, swimming and diving, tennis, volleyball, water polo, wrestling.

Majors Accounting B; American studies B; anthropology B; applied mathematics B; archaeology B; art education B; art/fine arts B; art history B; Asian/Oriental studies B; biology/biological sciences B; botany/plant sciences B; broadcasting B; business administration/commerce/management B; business economics B; cartography A, B; chemistry B; Chinese B; civil engineering B; classics B; communication B; computer engineering B; computer information systems B; computer science B; criminal justice B; dance B; dance therapy B; (pre)dentistry sequence B; early childhood education B; East Asian studies B; East European and Soviet studies B; ecology/environmental studies B; economics B; education B; electrical engineering B; elementary education B; engineering and applied sciences B; English B; environmental sciences B; European studies B; finance/banking B; French B; geodetic sciences B; geography B; geology B; German B; Germanic languages and literature B; history B; human services B; interdisciplinary studies B; international business B; international studies B; journalism B; Judaic studies B; Latin American studies B; (pre)law sequence B; liberal arts/general studies B; literature B; marketing/retailing/merchandising B; mathematics B; mechanical engineering B; medical assistant technologies A, B; medical records services B; medical technology A, B; (pre)medicine sequence B; music B; music education B; Near and Middle Eastern studies B; nuclear medical technology A, B; operations research B; philosophy B; physical education B; physician's assistant studies B; physics B; political science/government B; psychology B; public affairs and policy studies B; radio and television studies B; radiological technology A, B; recreation and leisure services B; religious studies B; Russian and Slavic studies B; science education B; secondary education B; Slavic languages B; sociology B; Spanish B; special education B; speech pathology and audiology B; speech/rhetoric/public address/debate B; statistics B; studio art B; theater arts/drama B; tourism and travel B; urban studies B; zoology B. Majors with highest enrollment: electrical engineering, international studies, political science/government.

LD Program Information

Name of Program Disabled Student Services.

Availability of Services Began offering services in 1979. Services provided to freshmen, sophomores, juniors, seniors.

Staff 2 part-time staff members, including director, assistant director. Services provided by counselors, diagnostic specialists.

Admissions LD applicants evaluated on the basis of high school transcript and grade point average, standard or untimed SAT or ACT. LD students may begin taking classes in fall, spring, or summer. Application should be submitted 6 months in advance of initial anticipated enrollment.

Housing College housing (including coed) available. LD students housed randomly. LD students not required to live on campus.

Diagnostic Testing Available in intelligence, reading, math, spelling, written language, perceptual skills, work and study habits, personality.

Tutoring Offered one-to-one by professional teachers, peer tutors. Available in all subjects. LD students may receive tutoring in all courses each term.

Basic Skills Remediation Offered one-to-one by staff of Disabled Student Services. Available in work and study habits.

Academic Advisement Help with program planning provided by LD staff members, academic advisers. LD students may take up to 17 semester hours each semester; most take 9 to 12 semester hours; 12 semester hours required to maintain full-time status.

Auxiliary Aids and Services Aids include taped textbooks, tape recorders, word processors, special study carrels. Services include alternative exam arrangements, notetakers, advocacy, lab assistance, scribes.

Counseling Services Individual counseling, rap sessions, career counseling available.

Contact Ms. Linda Donnels, Assistant Dean, Educational Services, George Washington University, Washington, DC 20052, 202-676-8250.

GEORGIA COLLEGE
Milledgeville, Georgia

Year Program Began	1984	Special Courses	
Special Fee	None	Taped Textbooks	✓
Special Orientation		Alternative Exam Arrangements	✓
Diagnostic Testing		Notetakers	
Subject-Area Tutoring	✓	Staff	1 part-time
Basic Skills Remediation	✓	Number of Students Served	2

General Information State-supported comprehensive coed institution. Part of University System of Georgia. Founded 1889. Awards A (terminal), B, M. Institutionally accredited by regional association; programs accredited by NASM (music), NLN (nursing), NCATE (teacher education). Small-town setting; 42-acre barrier-free campus. Total enrollment: 3,779. Faculty: 179 (153 full-time, 26 part-time); 70% have doctoral degrees; graduate assistants teach no undergraduate courses. Calendar: quarters. Grading system: letters or numbers. Library holdings: 140,409 bound volumes, 1,346 periodical subscriptions, 13,199 records/tapes.

Undergraduate Profile Fall 1984: 3,037 undergraduates (625 freshmen) from 15 states and territories and 12 foreign countries; 20% part-time; 95% state residents; 20% transfers; 52% financial aid recipients; 60% women; 18% blacks; 0% Native Americans; 2% Hispanics; 1% foreign nationals; 7 legally handicapped students.

Expenses (1985–86) State resident tuition: $960 full-time, $27 per quarter hour part-time. Nonresident tuition: $2712 full-time, $81 per quarter hour part-time. Mandatory fees: $168. College room and board: $1596. College room only: $630.

Financial Aid Fall 1984 full-time freshmen: 76% applied for aid, 87% of those were judged to have need, 94% of those were aided; the average aided freshman received an aid package worth $1585 (67% scholarships/grants, 33% self-help) meeting 73% of need. College-administered aid for all 1984–85 undergraduates: need-based scholarships; non-need scholarships; short-term loans; low-interest long-term loans from college funds; College Work-Study; part-time jobs. Supporting data: FAF required; IRS, AFSA/SAR acceptable. Application deadline: continuous to 3/15.

Athletics Member NAIA. Intercollegiate sports: baseball/softball M(s), W(s); basketball M(s), W(s); golf M(s); gymnastics W(s); soccer M(s); tennis M(s), W(s). Intramural sports: badminton, baseball/softball, basketball, football, golf, soccer, tennis, volleyball.

Majors Accounting B; art/fine arts B; biology/biological sciences B; business administration/commerce/management B; business education A, B; chemistry B; computer programming B; computer science B; criminal justice B; (pre)dentistry sequence B; dietetics B; early childhood education B; economics B; education B; educational administration B; elementary education B; English B; fashion merchandising B; French B; health education B; history B; home economics B; home economics education B; journalism B; marketing/retailing/merchandising B; mathematics B; medical technology B; (pre)medicine sequence B; music B; music education B; music therapy B; nursing B; nutrition B; physical education B; piano/organ B; political science/government B; psychology B; public administration B; recreation and leisure services B; retail management B; secondary education B; secretarial studies/office management A, B; sociology B; Spanish B; special education B; (pre)veterinary medicine sequence B; voice B. Majors with highest enrollment: business administration/commerce/management, education, biology/biological sciences.

LD Program Information

Name of Program Student Support Services.

Availability of Services Began offering services in 1984. Services provided to freshmen, sophomores, juniors, seniors. Program currently serves 2 LD students: 1 freshman, 1 sophomore.

Staff 1 part-time staff member (director). Services provided by tutors, counselors.

Admissions LD applicants evaluated on the basis of high school transcript and grade point average, untimed SAT, personal interview, autobiographical statement, letters of recommendation, psychoeducational report, medical history. LD students may begin taking classes in fall, winter, spring, or summer. Application should be submitted 20 days in advance of initial anticipated enrollment.

Housing College housing available. LD students housed randomly. LD students not required to live on campus.

Tutoring Offered one-to-one by professional teachers, peer tutors. Available in some subjects. LD students may receive tutoring in all courses each term.

Basic Skills Remediation Offered in small groups by regular teachers. Available in reading, math, spelling, spoken language, written language.

Academic Advisement Help with program planning provided by academic advisers. LD students may take up to 25 quarter hours each quarter; most take 15 quarter hours; 12 quarter hours required to maintain full-time status.

Auxiliary Aids and Services Aids include taped textbooks, tape recorders, typewriters. Services include alternative exam arrangements, advocacy.

Counseling Services Individual counseling, career counseling available.

Contact Dr. Helen T. Hill, Director of Student Support Services, Georgia College, CPO Box 483, Milledgeville, GA 31061, 912-453-5160.

GEORGIA SOUTHERN COLLEGE

Statesboro, Georgia

Year Program Began	1970
Special Fee	None
Special Orientation	
Diagnostic Testing	✓
Subject-Area Tutoring	✓
Basic Skills Remediation	✓
Special Courses	✓
Taped Textbooks	
Alternative Exam Arrangements	✓
Notetakers	
Staff	5 part-time
Number of Students Served	16

General Information State-supported comprehensive coed institution. Part of University System of Georgia. Founded 1906. Awards A (college transfer and terminal), B, M. Institutionally accredited by regional association; programs accredited by AACSB (business), ABET (engineering and technology), NASM (music), NCATE (teacher education). Small-town setting; 457-acre campus. Total enrollment: 6,526. Faculty: 400 (364 full-time, 36 part-time); 54% have doctoral degrees; graduate assistants teach a few undergraduate courses. Calendar: quarters. Grading system: letters or numbers. Library holdings: 337,511 bound volumes, 584,653 titles on microform, 2,450 periodical subscriptions, 19,008 records/tapes.

Undergraduate Profile Fall 1984: 5,738 undergraduates (1,308 freshmen) from 36 states and territories and 39 foreign countries; 7% part-time; 91% state residents; 13% transfers; 46% financial aid recipients; 54% women; 12% blacks; 1% Native Americans; 1% Hispanics; 1% Asian Americans; 1% foreign nationals; 5% of undergraduates over 25 years of age; 11 legally handicapped students.

Expenses (1985–86) State resident tuition: $960 full-time, $27 per quarter hour part-time. Nonresident tuition: $2880 full-time, $81 per quarter hour part-time. Mandatory fees: $282. College room and board: $1890. College room only: $840.

Financial Aid Fall 1984 full-time freshmen: 91% applied for aid, 83% of those were judged to have need, 100% of those were aided; the average aided freshman received an aid package worth $1424 (44% scholarships/grants, 56% self-help) meeting 85% of need. College-administered aid for all 1984–85 undergraduates: 1,580 need-based scholarships (average $990); 158 non-need scholarships (average $1071); short-term loans (average $75); low-interest long-term loans from college funds (average $600), from external sources (average $1875); SEOG; College Work-Study; 560 part-time jobs. Supporting data: IRS, institutional form, AFSA/SAR required; FFS, FAF acceptable. Priority application deadline: 4/15.

Athletics Member NCAA (Division I). Intercollegiate sports: baseball/softball M(I,s), W(s); basketball M(I,s), W(I,s); cross-country running M(I,s), W(I,s); football M(I-AA,s); golf M(I,s); soccer M(I); swimming and diving M(I,s); tennis M(I,s), W(I,s); water polo M(c), W(c). Intramural sports: badminton, baseball/softball, basketball, bowling, fencing, football, golf, racquetball, rugby, soccer, swimming and diving, tennis, volleyball.

Majors Accounting B; agricultural business B; anthropology B; art education B; art/fine arts B; biology/biological sciences B; broadcasting B; business administration/commerce/management B; business economics B; business education B; business machine technologies B; chemistry B; child care/child and family studies B; civil engineering technology B; communication B; computer science B; construction engineering B; construction technologies B; criminal justice A, B; data processing B; (pre)dentistry sequence B; early childhood education B; economics B; education A, B; electrical engineering technology B; elementary education B; English B; family and consumer studies B; family services B; fashion merchandising B; finance/banking B; food services management B; French B; geology B; German B; health education B; history B; home economics B; home economics education B; humanities B; industrial arts B; industrial design B; industrial engineering technology B; interior design B; journalism B; law enforcement/police sciences B; (pre)law sequence B; manufacturing technology B; marketing/retailing/merchandising B; mathematics B; mechanical engineering technology B; medical technology B; (pre) medicine sequence B; music B; music education B; nursing B; nutrition B; physical education B; physics B; piano/organ B; political science/government B; printing technologies B; psychology B; reading education B; recreation and leisure services B; retail management B; science education B; secondary education B; secretarial studies/ office management A, B; social science B; social work B; sociology B; Spanish B; special education B; speech/rhetoric/public address/debate B; teacher aide studies A; textiles and clothing B; theater arts/drama B; (pre)veterinary medicine sequence B; voice B; wind and percussion instruments B. Majors with highest enrollment: business administration/commerce/management, education, elementary education.

LD Program Information

Name of Program Learning Analysis Center.

Availability of Services Began offering services in 1970. Services provided to freshmen, sophomores, juniors, seniors. Program currently serves 16 LD students: 10 freshmen, 5 sophomores, 1 junior.

Staff 5 part-time staff members, including director, coordinator. Services provided by remediation specialists, diagnostic specialists.

Admissions LD applicants evaluated on the basis of high school transcript and grade point average, standard SAT. LD students may begin taking classes in fall, winter, spring, or summer. Application should be submitted 3 months in advance of initial anticipated enrollment.

Housing College housing (including coed) available. LD students housed randomly. LD freshmen and sophomores required to live on campus.

Diagnostic Testing Available in intelligence, reading, math, spelling, handwriting, written language, motor abilities, perceptual skills, work and study habits, personality, psychoneurology.

Tutoring Offered one-to-one by peer tutors, Learning Resource Center computers. Available in some subjects. LD students may receive tutoring in 2 courses per term.

Basic Skills Remediation Offered in small groups by regular teachers. Available in reading, math, spelling, written language.

Academic Advisement Help with program planning provided by academic advisers. Most LD students take 12 quarter hours each quarter; 6 quarter hours required to maintain full-time status.

Special Courses Offered in college survival skills, study skills, career planning. Most offered for credit; most enter into overall grade point average.

Auxiliary Aids and Services Services include alternative exam arrangements.

Counseling Services Individual counseling, small-group counseling, career counseling available.

Contact Mr. William Tucker Anderson, Coordinator, Learning Analysis Center, Georgia Southern College, Landrum Box 8131, Statesboro, GA 30458, 912-681-5302.

GEORGIA STATE UNIVERSITY

Atlanta, Georgia

Year Program Began	1973	Special Courses	✓
Special Fee	None	Taped Textbooks	✓
Special Orientation		Alternative Exam Arrangements	✓
Diagnostic Testing	✓	Notetakers	✓
Subject-Area Tutoring	✓	Staff	6 part-time
Basic Skills Remediation	✓	Number of Students Served	13

General Information State-supported coed university. Part of University System of Georgia. Founded 1913. Awards A (college transfer and terminal), B, M, D. Institutionally accredited by regional association; programs accredited by NASAD (art and design), AACSB (business), NASM (music), NLN (nursing), NCATE (teacher education). Metropolitan setting; 24-acre barrier-free campus. Total enrollment: 21,366. Faculty: 996 (755 full-time, 241 part-time); 80% have doctoral degrees; graduate assistants teach a few undergraduate courses. Calendar: quarters. Grading system: letters or numbers. Library holdings: 912,875 bound volumes, 1.2 million titles on microform, 5,046 periodical subscriptions, 1,225 records/tapes.

Undergraduate Profile Fall 1984: 14,560 undergraduates (1,247 freshmen) from 46 states and territories and 92 foreign countries; 56% part-time; 92% state residents; 20% financial aid recipients; 56% women; 19% blacks; 0% Native Americans; 1% Hispanics; 2% Asian Americans; 3% foreign nationals; 450 legally handicapped students.

Expenses (1985–86) State resident tuition: $1260 full-time, $28 per quarter hour part-time. Nonresident tuition: $4320 full-time, $96 per quarter hour part-time. Mandatory fees: $60.

Financial Aid College-administered aid for all 1984–85 undergraduates: 200 need-based scholarships (average $825); 500 non-need scholarships (average $1120); short-term loans (average $197); low-interest long-term loans from external sources (average $1450); SEOG; College Work-Study; 2,425 part-time jobs. Supporting data: FAF, institutional form required; IRS, state form, AFSA/SAR required for some; FFS acceptable. Priority application deadline: 6/1.

Athletics Member NCAA (Division I). Intercollegiate sports: baseball/softball M(I,s), W(I,s); basketball M(I,s), W(I,s); cross-country running M(I,s), W(I,s); golf M(I,s), W(I,s); soccer M(I,s); swimming and diving M(I,s), W(I,s); tennis M(I,s), W(I,s); track and field M(I,s), W(I,s). Intramural sports: archery, badminton, baseball/softball, basketball, bowling, cross-country running, fencing, field hockey, football, golf, ice hockey, martial arts, sailing, soccer, swimming and diving, tennis, track and field, volleyball, water polo, weight lifting, wrestling.

Majors Accounting B; actuarial science B; anthropology B; applied art B; archaeology B; art education B; art/fine arts B; art history B; arts administration B; astronomy B; audio engineering A, B; aviation administration A; biochemistry B; biology/biological sciences B; business administration/commerce/management B; business economics B; business education B; ceramic art and design B; chemistry B; classics B; communication B; computer information systems B; computer science B; creative writing B; criminal justice A, B; data processing A; (pre)dentistry sequence B; dietetics B; early childhood education A, B; economics B; education B; elementary education B; English B; finance/banking B; French B; geography B; geology B; German B; graphic arts B; health education B; health services administration B; history B; hotel and restaurant management A, B; human resources B; illustration B; insurance B; interdisciplinary studies B; interior design B; jazz B; jewelry and metalsmithing B; journalism B; labor studies A; (pre)law sequence B; liberal arts/general studies A; literature B; marketing/retailing/merchandising B; mathematics B; medical secretarial studies A; medical technology B; (pre)medicine sequence B; mental health/rehabilitation counseling B; music B; music education B; music history B; nursing B; nutrition B; painting/drawing B; philosophy B; photography B; physical education B; physical fitness/human movement B; physical therapy B; physics B; piano/organ B; political science/government B; psychology B; reading education B; real estate B; recreation and leisure services B; respiratory therapy B; science education B; sculpture B; secondary education B; secretarial studies/office management A, B; social work B; sociology B; Spanish B; special education B; speech/rhetoric/public address/debate B; stringed instruments B; studio art B; teacher aide studies A; textile arts B; theater arts/drama B; tourism and travel A, B; urban studies A, B; (pre)veterinary medicine sequence B; vocational education B; voice B; wind and percussion instruments B. Majors with highest enrollment: accounting, business administration/commerce/management, nursing.

LD Program Information

Name of Program Services for the Handicapped.

Availability of Services Began offering services in 1973. Services provided to freshmen, sophomores, juniors, seniors. Program currently serves 13 LD students.

Staff 6 part-time staff members, including director, university coordinator. Services provided by remediation specialist, tutors, counselors, diagnostic specialist.

Admissions LD applicants evaluated on the basis of high school transcript and grade point average, standard SAT or ACT, autobiographical statement, letters of recommendation. LD students may begin taking classes in fall, winter, spring, or summer. Application should be submitted 7 months in advance of initial anticipated enrollment.

Housing College housing not available.

Diagnostic Testing Available in intelligence, reading, math, spelling, handwriting, spoken language, written language, motor abilities, perceptual skills, personality, social skills, psychoneurology, speech.

Tutoring Offered one-to-one and in small groups by professional teachers, peer tutors. Available in some subjects. LD students may receive tutoring in all courses each term.

Basic Skills Remediation Offered one-to-one and in small groups by regular teachers. Available in reading, math, spelling, written language, learning strategies, work and study habits, social skills.

Academic Advisement Help with program planning provided by LD staff members, academic advisers. LD students may take up to 15 quarter hours each quarter; most take 10 quarter hours; 10 quarter hours required to maintain full-time status.

Special Courses Offered in college survival skills, reading, vocabulary development, communication skills, composition, math, typing, personal psychology, study skills, career planning. Some offered for credit; some enter into overall grade point average.

Auxiliary Aids and Services Aids include taped textbooks, word processors. Services include alternative exam arrangements, notetakers, advocacy.

Counseling Services Individual counseling, small-group counseling, career counseling available.

Contact Ms. Carole Pearson, Assistant Dean of Student Development and University Coordinator for Services to the Handicapped, Georgia State University, 402 Student Center, University Plaza, Atlanta, GA 30303, 404-658-2206.

GREEN MOUNTAIN COLLEGE

Poultney, Vermont

Year Program Began	*Not reported*	Special Courses	
Special Fee	$400 to $1300 per year	Taped Textbooks	✓
Special Orientation	✓	Alternative Exam Arrangements	✓
Diagnostic Testing	✓	Notetakers	✓
Subject-Area Tutoring	✓	Staff	2 full-time
Basic Skills Remediation	✓	Number of Students Served	37

General Information Independent 4-year coed college. Founded 1834. Awards A (college transfer and terminal), B. Institutionally accredited by regional association. Small-town setting; 155-acre campus. Total enrollment: 395. Faculty: 45 (25 full-time, 20 part-time); 25% have doctoral degrees. Calendar: semesters. Grading system: letters or numbers. Library holdings: 64,200 bound volumes, 30,000 titles on microform, 155 periodical subscriptions, 1,420 records/tapes.

Undergraduate Profile Fall 1984: 395 undergraduates (195 freshmen) from 18 states and territories and 6 foreign countries; 10% part-time; 10% state residents; 10% transfers; 52% financial aid recipients; 55% women; 1% blacks; 0% Native Americans; 1% Hispanics; 1% Asian Americans; 3% foreign nationals; 3 legally handicapped students.

Expenses (1985–86) Comprehensive fee of $9019 includes full-time tuition ($5516), mandatory fees ($225), and college room and board ($3278). College room only: $1847. Part-time tuition: $167.50 per credit.

Financial Aid Fall 1984 full-time freshmen: 60% applied for aid, 92% of those were judged to have need, 100% of those were aided; the average aided freshman received an aid package worth $7346 (18% scholarships/grants, 82% self-help) meeting 100% of need. College-administered aid for all 1984–85 undergraduates: 94 need-based scholarships (average $800); 20 non-need scholarships; low-interest long-term loans from external sources (average $2500); SEOG; College Work-Study; 144 part-time jobs. Supporting data: AFSA/SAR required; FFS, FAF, IRS acceptable. Priority application deadline: 4/1.

Athletics Member NAIA. Intercollegiate sports: baseball/softball W; basketball M(s), W(s); golf M, W; skiing (downhill) M, W; soccer M(s), W(s); swimming and diving W; tennis M, W; volleyball W. Intramural sports: badminton, baseball/softball, basketball, football, ice hockey, lacrosse, martial arts, sailing, skiing (cross-country), skiing (downhill), soccer, swimming and diving, tennis, volleyball, water polo, weight lifting.

Majors Accounting B; applied art A; art education B; art/fine arts A; art therapy B; behavioral sciences B; business administration/commerce/management A, B; commercial art A; education B; elementary education B; fashion merchandising A, B; gerontology B; liberal arts/general studies A; marketing/retailing/merchandising A, B; painting/drawing A; psychology B; recreation and leisure services A, B; recreation therapy B; retail management A, B; social science B; sociology B; special education B; studio art A. Majors with highest enrollment: business administration/commerce/management, retail management, recreation and leisure services.

LD Program Information

Name of Program Developmental Skills Program.

Availability of Services Services provided to freshmen, sophomores, juniors, seniors. Program currently serves 37 LD students: 34 freshmen, 3 sophomores.

Fees Range from $400 to $1300 per year according to level of services.

Staff 2 full-time staff members, including director, assistant director. Services provided by remediation specialists.

Admissions LD applicants evaluated on the basis of high school transcript and grade point average, standard or untimed SAT or ACT, personal interview, autobiographical statement, letters of recommendation, psychoeducational report. LD students may begin taking classes in fall or spring. Application should be submitted 3 months in advance of initial anticipated enrollment.

Orientation Optional orientation offered before registration.

Housing College housing (including coed) available. LD students housed randomly. LD freshmen and sophomores required to live on campus except if 21 or over.

Diagnostic Testing Available in reading, math.

Tutoring Offered one-to-one and in small groups by professional teachers, peer tutors. Available in all subjects. LD students may receive tutoring in all courses each term.

Basic Skills Remediation Offered one-to-one and in small groups by LD teachers. Available in reading, math, spelling, written language, learning strategies, work and study habits, social skills.

Academic Advisement Help with program planning provided by LD staff members, academic advisers. LD students may take up to 12 credits each semester; 9 credits required to maintain full-time status.

Auxiliary Aids and Services Aids include taped textbooks, tape recorders, typewriters. Services include alternative exam arrangements, notetakers.

Counseling Services Individual counseling, small-group counseling, career counseling available.

Contact Ms. Nancy Klump, Director of Developmental Skills Program, Green Mountain College, Poultney, VT 05764, 802-287-9313.

GRINNELL COLLEGE

Grinnell, Iowa

Year Program Began	1978
Special Fee	None
Special Orientation	✓
Diagnostic Testing	✓
Subject-Area Tutoring	✓
Basic Skills Remediation	✓
Special Courses	✓
Taped Textbooks	✓
Alternative Exam Arrangements	✓
Notetakers	✓
Staff	3 part-time
Number of Students Served	10

General Information Independent 4-year coed college. Founded 1846. Awards B. Institutionally accredited by regional association; programs accredited by NCATE (teacher education). Small-town setting; 90-acre barrier-free campus. Total enrollment: 1,207. Faculty: 115 (105 full-time, 10 part-time); 81% have doctoral degrees. Calendar: semesters. Grading system: letters or numbers. Library holdings: 274,000 bound volumes, 6,983 titles on microform, 1,400 periodical subscriptions, 7,400 records/tapes.

Undergraduate Profile Fall 1984: 1,207 undergraduates (377 freshmen) from 48 states and territories and 27 foreign countries; 1% part-time; 14% state residents; 11% transfers; 67% financial aid recipients; 50% women; 4% blacks; 0% Native Americans; 1% Hispanics; 3% Asian Americans; 6% foreign nationals; 1% of undergraduates over 25 years of age; 2 legally handicapped students.

Expenses (1985–86) Comprehensive fee of $10,980 includes full-time tuition ($8210), mandatory fees ($226), and college room and board ($2544). College room only: $1048. Part-time tuition: $270 per credit. Tuition prepayment plan available.

Financial Aid Fall 1984 full-time freshmen: 74% applied for aid, 95% of those were judged to have need, 100% of those were aided; the average aided freshman received an aid package worth $5626 (88% scholarships/grants, 12% self-help) meeting 100% of need. College-administered aid for all 1984–85 undergraduates: 803 need-based scholarships (average $4875); 110 non-need scholarships (average $2183); short-term loans (average $100); low-interest long-term loans from college funds (average $1202), from external sources (average $1347); SEOG; College Work-Study; 442 part-time jobs. Supporting data: FAF required; IRS required for some. Priority application deadline: 2/15.

Athletics Member NCAA (Division III). Intercollegiate sports: baseball/softball M(III), W(III); basketball M(III), W(III); cross-country running M(III), W(III); field hockey W(III); football M(III); golf M(III); soccer M(III); swimming and diving M(III), W(III); tennis M(III), W(III); track and field M(III), W(III); volleyball W(III); water polo M. Intramural sports: archery, badminton, baseball/softball, basketball, bowling, cross-country running, fencing, football, ice hockey, martial arts, racquetball, rugby, sailing, skiing (cross-country), soccer, squash, swimming and diving, tennis, volleyball, water polo, weight lifting.

Majors American studies B; anthropology B; art/fine arts B; biology/biological sciences B; chemistry B; classics B; computer science B; (pre)dentistry sequence B; early childhood education B; East European and Soviet studies B; ecology/environmental studies B; economics B; education B; elementary education B; English B; environmental sciences B; European studies B; French B; German B; Greek B; history B; interdisciplinary studies B; Latin B; Latin American studies B; (pre)law sequence B; liberal arts/general studies B; mathematics B; (pre)medicine sequence B; music B; philosophy B; physical sciences B; physics B; political science/government B; psychology B; religious studies B; Romance languages B; Russian B; Russian and Slavic studies B; science B; science education B; secondary education B; sociology B; Spanish B; theater arts/drama B; (pre)veterinary medicine sequence B; zoology B. Majors with highest enrollment: history, English, biology/biological sciences.

LD Program Information

Name of Program Not specified.

Availability of Services Began offering services in 1978. Services provided to freshmen, sophomores, juniors, seniors. Program currently serves 10 LD students: 4 freshmen, 2 sophomores, 3 juniors, 1 senior.

Staff 3 part-time staff members, including director. Services provided by remediation specialists, tutors.

Admissions LD applicants evaluated on the basis of high school transcript and grade point average, standard or untimed SAT or ACT, personal interview, autobiographical statement, letters of recommendation, psychoeducational report. LD students may begin taking classes in fall or spring. Application should be submitted 6 months in advance of initial anticipated enrollment.

Orientation Optional orientation offered before registration.

Housing College housing (including coed) available. LD students housed randomly. LD freshmen and sophomores required to live on campus except by special permission.

Diagnostic Testing Available in reading, math, spelling, work and study habits.

Tutoring Offered one-to-one by professional teachers, peer tutors. Available in all subjects. LD students may receive tutoring in 4 courses per term.

Basic Skills Remediation Offered one-to-one by LD teachers. Available in reading, math, spelling, learning strategies, work and study habits.

Academic Advisement Help with program planning provided by LD staff members, academic advisers. LD students may take up to 16 credits each semester; most take 12 to 14 credits; 12 credits required to maintain full-time status.

Special Courses Offered in reading, vocabulary development, communication skills, composition, math, study skills, career planning. Some offered for credit; none enter into overall grade point average.

Auxiliary Aids and Services Aids include taped textbooks, tape recorders, calculators, word processors. Services include alternative exam arrangements, notetakers.

Counseling Services Individual counseling, career counseling available.

Contact Mr. Ray Obermiller, Director of Academic Advising, Grinnell College, Grinnell, IA 50112, 515-236-2190.

HARDING UNIVERSITY

Searcy, Arkansas

Year Program Began	1975	Special Courses	✓
Special Fee	None	Taped Textbooks	
Special Orientation	✓	Alternative Exam Arrangements	
Diagnostic Testing	✓	Notetakers	
Subject-Area Tutoring	✓	Staff	6 part-time
Basic Skills Remediation	✓	Number of Students Served	2

General Information Comprehensive coed institution, affiliated with Church of Christ. Founded 1924. Awards A (terminal), B, M. Institutionally accredited by regional association; programs accredited by NLN (nursing), NCATE (teacher education). Small-town setting; 200-acre campus. Total enrollment: 2,828. Faculty: 168 (111 full-time, 57 part-time); 46% have doctoral degrees; graduate assistants teach a few undergraduate courses. Calendar: semesters. Grading system: letters or numbers. Library holdings: 161,022 bound volumes, 450,920 titles on microform, 1,473 periodical subscriptions, 3,424 records/tapes.

Undergraduate Profile Fall 1984: 2,705 undergraduates (811 freshmen) from 49 states and territories and 20 foreign countries; 8% part-time; 30% state residents; 4% transfers; 87% financial aid recipients; 51% women; 2% blacks; 2% foreign nationals; 2% of undergraduates over 25 years of age; 6 legally handicapped students.

Expenses (1985–86) Comprehensive fee of $5514 includes full-time tuition ($3045), mandatory fees ($203), and college room and board ($2266). College room only: $966. Part-time tuition: $101.50 per semester hour.

Financial Aid Fall 1984 full-time freshmen: 87% applied for aid, 59% of those were judged to have need, 97% of those were aided; the average aided freshman received an aid package worth $4535 (32% scholarships/grants, 68% self-help) meeting 70% of need. College-administered aid for all 1984–85 undergraduates: need-based scholarships (average $650); non-need scholarships (average $400); low-interest long-term loans; part-time jobs. Supporting data: FFS required. Priority application deadline: 5/1.

Athletics Member NAIA. Intercollegiate sports: baseball/softball M, W; basketball M(s); cross-country running M, W; football M(s); golf M; swimming and diving M; tennis M; track and field M. Intramural sports: baseball/softball, basketball, bowling, cross-country running, football, golf, gymnastics, soccer, swimming and diving, tennis, track and field, volleyball.

Majors Accounting B; advertising B; American studies B; art education B; art/fine arts B; biblical languages B; biblical studies B; biochemistry B; biology/biological sciences B; business administration/commerce/management B; business education B; chemistry B; communication B; computer programming B; dietetics B; economics B; education B; elementary education B; English B; fashion merchandising B; French B; history B; home economics B; home economics education B; journalism B; (pre)law sequence B; marketing/retailing/merchandising B; mathematics B; (pre)medicine sequence B; modern languages B; music B; music education B; nursing B; physical education B; physics B; piano/organ B; political science/government B; psychology B; public administration B; religious studies B; science B; science education B; secondary education B; secretarial studies/office management A; social science B; social work B; sociology B; Spanish B; special education B; speech/rhetoric/public address/debate B; stringed instruments B; systems science B; (pre)veterinary medicine sequence B; voice B. Majors with highest enrollment: accounting, nursing, elementary education.

LD Program Information

Name of Program Not specified.

Availability of Services Began offering services in 1975. Services provided to freshmen, sophomores, juniors, seniors. Program currently serves 2 LD students (both freshmen).

Staff 6 part-time staff members. Services provided by remediation specialists, counselors, speech-language pathologist.

Admissions LD applicants evaluated on the basis of high school transcript and grade point average, standard SAT, personal interview, letters of recommendation, psychoeducational report. LD students may begin taking classes in fall, spring, or summer. Application should be submitted 9 months in advance of initial anticipated enrollment.

Orientation Optional orientation offered before registration.

Housing College housing available. LD students housed randomly. LD freshmen, sophomores, juniors, and seniors required to live on campus except for veterans, or if married, 23 or over, or living with relatives, or by special permission.

Diagnostic Testing Available in intelligence, reading, math, spelling, handwriting, spoken language, written language, motor abilities, perceptual skills, work and study habits, personality, social skills, speech, hearing.

Tutoring Offered one-to-one by professional teachers, peer tutors. Available in all subjects. LD students may receive tutoring in all courses each term.

Basic Skills Remediation Offered in small groups by regular teachers. Available in reading, math, handwriting, spoken language, written language, speech.

Academic Advisement Help with program planning provided by LD staff members, academic advisers. LD students may take up to 15 semester hours each semester; most take 12 semester hours; 12 semester hours required to maintain full-time status.

Special Courses Offered in communication skills, composition, typing, career planning. Most offered for credit; most enter into overall grade point average.

Auxiliary Aids and Services Aids include tape recorders, typewriters.

Counseling Services Individual counseling, career counseling available.

Contact Dr. Evan Ulrey, Chairman, Department of Communications, Harding University, Box 771, Searcy, AR 72143, 501-268-6161 Ext. 445.

HOFSTRA UNIVERSITY
Hempstead, New York

Year Program Began	1979	Special Courses	
Special Fee	$2000 per year	Taped Textbooks	✓
Special Orientation		Alternative Exam Arrangements	✓
Diagnostic Testing	✓	Notetakers	✓
Subject-Area Tutoring	✓	Staff	6 part-time
Basic Skills Remediation	✓	Number of Students Served	71

General Information Independent coed university. Founded 1935. Awards B, M, D. Institutionally accredited by regional association; programs accredited by AACSB (business), ABET (engineering and technology), NCATE (teacher education). City setting, with easy access to New York City; 238-acre barrier-free campus. Total enrollment: 11,298. Faculty: 731 (397 full-time, 334 part-time); 82% have doctoral degrees; graduate assistants teach no undergraduate courses. Calendar: 4-1-4. Grading system: letters or numbers. Library holdings: 1 million bound volumes, 993,000 titles on microform, 6,000 periodical subscriptions.

Undergraduate Profile Fall 1984: 7,863 undergraduates (1,424 freshmen) from 30 states and territories and 53 foreign countries; 17% part-time; 75% state residents; 37% transfers; 80% financial aid recipients; 49% women; 6% blacks; 0% Native Americans; 2% Hispanics; 1% foreign nationals; 12% of undergraduates over 25 years of age; 150 legally handicapped students.

Expenses (1985–86) Comprehensive fee of $9556 includes full-time tuition ($5950), mandatory fees ($370), and college room and board ($3236). College room only: $1570. Part-time tuition: $192 per credit.

Financial Aid Fall 1984 full-time freshmen: 100% applied for aid, 85% of those were judged to have need, 80% of those were aided; the average aided freshman received an aid package worth $5011 (30% scholarships/grants, 70% self-help) meeting 65% of need. College-administered aid for all 1984–85 undergraduates: 1,601 need-based scholarships (average $1179); 1,402 non-need scholarships (average $1486); low-interest long-term loans from college funds (average $500), from external sources (average $2000); College Work-Study; 700 part-time jobs. Supporting data: FFS, FAF required; IRS required for some; AFSA/SAR acceptable. Priority application deadline: 2/15.

Athletics Member NCAA (Division I). Intercollegiate sports: baseball/softball M(I,s), W(I,s); basketball M(I,s), W(I,s); cross-country running M(I), W(I); field hockey W(I,s); football M(III); golf M; gymnastics W(II,s); lacrosse M(I,s), W(I,s); rugby M; soccer M(I); tennis M(I,s), W(I,s); volleyball W(I,s); wrestling M(I,s). Intramural sports: badminton, baseball/softball, basketball, bowling, cross-country running, football, gymnastics, martial arts, riflery, soccer, swimming and diving, tennis, volleyball, wrestling.

Majors Accounting B; aerospace engineering B; African studies B; American studies B; anthropology B; art education B; art/fine arts B; art history B; Asian/Oriental studies B; biochemistry B; biology/biological sciences B; biomedical engineering B; broadcasting B; business administration/commerce/management B; business education B; ceramic art and design B; chemistry B; civil engineering B; classics B; communication B; computer engineering B; computer information systems B; computer science B; creative writing B; dance B; (pre)dentistry sequence B; earth science B; ecology/environmental studies B; economics B; education B; electrical engineering B; elementary education B; engineering (general) B; engineering sciences B; English B; environmental engineering B; environmental sciences B; finance/banking B; French B; geography B; geology B; German B; Greek B; Hebrew B; history B; humanities B; industrial engineering B; interdisciplinary studies B; international business B; Italian B; jewelry and metalsmithing B; journalism B; Judaic studies B; Latin B; (pre)law sequence B; liberal arts/general studies B; marketing/retailing/merchandising B; mathematics B; mechanical engineering B; (pre)medicine sequence B; music B; music education B; music history B; natural sciences B; painting/drawing B; philosophy B; photography B; physical education B; physics B; political science/government B; psychology B; Russian B; sculpture B; secondary education B; social science B; sociology B; Spanish B; speech pathology and audiology B; speech/rhetoric/public address/debate B; speech therapy B; studio art B; technology and public affairs B; theater arts/drama B; (pre)veterinary medicine sequence B. Majors with highest enrollment: accounting, computer science, communication.

LD Program Information

Name of Program Program for Academic Learning Skills (PALS).

Availability of Services Began offering services in 1979. Services provided to freshmen, sophomores, juniors, seniors. Program currently serves 71 LD students: 11 freshmen, 20 sophomores, 20 juniors, 20 seniors.

Fees $2000 per year for freshmen.

Staff 6 part-time staff members, including director. Services provided by remediation specialists, diagnostic specialist.

Admissions LD applicants evaluated on the basis of high school transcript and grade point average, standard or untimed SAT or ACT, personal interview, autobiographical statement, letters of recommendation, psychoeducational report, WAIS. LD students may begin taking classes in fall only. Application should be submitted 10 months in advance of initial anticipated enrollment.

Housing College housing (including coed) available. LD students housed randomly. LD students not required to live on campus.

Diagnostic Testing Available in intelligence, reading, spelling, spoken language, written language, motor abilities, perceptual skills, work and study habits, personality.

Tutoring Offered one-to-one and in small groups by professional teachers, peer tutors. Available in all subjects. LD students may receive tutoring in all courses each term.

Basic Skills Remediation Offered one-to-one and in small groups by LD teachers. Available in reading, spelling, written language, learning strategies, perceptual skills, work and study habits, social skills.

Academic Advisement Help with program planning provided by LD staff members, academic advisers. LD students may take up to 18 credits each semester; most take 16 to 18 credits; 12 credits required to maintain full-time status.

Auxiliary Aids and Services Aids include taped textbooks, tape recorders, calculators, typewriters, word processors. Services include alternative exam arrangements, notetakers, advocacy.

Counseling Services Individual counseling, small-group counseling, career counseling available.

Contact Dr. Ignacio L. Götz, Director, Division of Special Studies and Director, Program for Academic Learning Skills, Hofstra University, 107 Barnard Hall, Hempstead, NY 11550, 516-560-5841.

HUMBOLDT STATE UNIVERSITY

Arcata, California

Year Program Began	1976	Special Courses	
Special Fee	None	Taped Textbooks	✓
Special Orientation	✓	Alternative Exam Arrangements	✓
Diagnostic Testing	✓	Notetakers	✓
Subject-Area Tutoring	✓	Staff	1 full-time, 1 part-time
Basic Skills Remediation	✓	Number of Students Served	20

General Information State-supported comprehensive coed institution. Part of California State University System. Founded 1913. Awards B, M. Institutionally accredited by regional association; programs accredited by NASAD (art and design), ABET (engineering and technology), NLN (nursing); candidate for program accreditation by NASM (music). Rural setting; 142-acre campus. Total enrollment: 6,113. Faculty: 488 (358 full-time, 130 part-time); 75% have doctoral degrees; graduate assistants teach no undergraduate courses. Calendar: quarters. Grading system: letters or numbers. Library holdings: 324,000 bound volumes, 410,000 titles on microform, 2,100 periodical subscriptions, 10,300 records/tapes.

Undergraduate Profile Fall 1984: 5,016 undergraduates (564 freshmen) from 50 states and territories and 20 foreign countries; 28% part-time; 98% state residents; 60% transfers; 50% financial aid recipients; 47% women; 1% blacks; 3% Native Americans; 2% Hispanics; 1% Asian Americans; 1% foreign nationals; 32% of undergraduates over 25 years of age; 67 legally handicapped students.

Expenses (1985–86) State resident tuition: $0 full-time, $150 per quarter hour part-time. Nonresident tuition: $4147 full-time. Nonresident part-time tuition and fees per quarter (1 to 5 quarter hours) range from $235 to $1165. Mandatory fees: $681. College room and board: $2827.

Financial Aid Fall 1984 full-time freshmen: 41% applied for aid, 90% of those were judged to have need, 100% of those were aided; the average aided freshman received an aid package worth $2496 (52% scholarships/grants, 48% self-help) meeting 90% of need. College-administered aid for all 1984–85 undergraduates: need-based scholarships; non-need scholarships; short-term loans; low-interest long-term loans; SEOG; College Work-Study; part-time jobs. Supporting data: IRS, state form required. Priority application deadline: 3/1.

Athletics Member NCAA (Division II). Intercollegiate sports: basketball M(II), W(II); crew M(c), W(c); cross-country running M(II), W(II); football M(II); lacrosse M(c); rugby M(c); soccer M(II); swimming and diving W(II); tennis W(II); track and field M(II), W(II); volleyball W(II); wrestling M(II). Intramural sports: badminton, baseball/softball, basketball, cross-country running, fencing, football, golf, gymnastics, martial arts, racquetball, sailing, skiing (cross-country), skiing (downhill), soccer, swimming and diving, tennis, track and field, volleyball, water polo, wrestling.

Majors Accounting B; anthropology B; art/fine arts B; biology/biological sciences B; botany/plant sciences B; business administration/commerce/management B; cell biology B; chemistry B; child psychology/child development B; computer information systems B; conservation B; (pre)dentistry sequence B; early childhood education B; economics B; English B; environmental biology B; environmental engineering B; finance/banking B; fish and game management B; forestry B; French B; geography B; geology B; German B; history B; home economics B; industrial arts B; journalism B; (pre)law sequence B; linguistics B; marine biology B; marketing/retailing/merchandising B; mathematics B; medical technology B; (pre)medicine sequence B; microbiology B; molecular biology B; music B; natural resource management B; natural sciences B; nursing B; oceanography B; philosophy B; physical education B; physical sciences B; physics B; political science/government B; psychology B; range management B; recreation and leisure services B; social work B; sociology B; Spanish B; speech pathology and audiology B; speech/rhetoric/public address/debate B; textile arts B; theater arts/drama B; (pre)veterinary medicine sequence B; wildlife management B; zoology B. Majors with highest enrollment: natural resource management, business administration/commerce/management, biology/biological sciences.

LD Program Information

Name of Program Disabled Student Services.

Availability of Services Began offering services in 1976. Services provided to freshmen, sophomores, juniors, seniors. Program currently serves 20 LD students.

Staff 1 full-time, 1 part-time staff members, including coordinator. Services provided by diagnostic specialist.

Admissions LD applicants evaluated on the basis of high school transcript and grade point average, standard or untimed SAT, personal interview, autobiographical statement, letters of recommendation, psychoeducational report. LD students may begin taking classes in fall, winter, spring, or summer. Application should be submitted 10 months in advance of initial anticipated enrollment.

Orientation Optional orientation offered before registration.

Housing College housing (including coed) available. LD students housed randomly. LD students not required to live on campus.

Diagnostic Testing Available in reading, math, spelling, written language, perceptual skills, psychoneurology, speech.

Tutoring Offered one-to-one and in small groups by peer tutors. Available in all subjects. LD students may receive tutoring in all courses each term.

Basic Skills Remediation Offered one-to-one and in small groups by LD teachers. Available in reading, math, spelling, learning strategies, motor abilities, perceptual skills, work and study habits.

Academic Advisement Help with program planning provided by LD staff members, academic advisers. Most LD students take 12 quarter hours each quarter; 12 quarter hours required to maintain full-time status.

Auxiliary Aids and Services Aids include taped textbooks, tape recorders. Services include alternative exam arrangements, notetakers.

Counseling Services Individual counseling available.

Contact Ms. Theresa A. Jordan, Coordinator, Disabled Student Services, Humboldt State University, Arcata, CA 95521, 707-826-4678.

HUSSON COLLEGE
Bangor, Maine

Year Program Began	1978	Special Courses	
Special Fee	None	Taped Textbooks	✓
Special Orientation		Alternative Exam Arrangements	✓
Diagnostic Testing	✓	Notetakers	✓
Subject-Area Tutoring	✓	Staff	2 full-time, 3 part-time
Basic Skills Remediation	✓	Number of Students Served	11

General Information Independent comprehensive coed institution. Founded 1898. Awards A (college transfer and terminal), B, M. Institutionally accredited by regional association. Small-town setting; 250-acre barrier-free campus. Total enrollment: 1,611. Faculty: 100 (35 full-time, 65 part-time); 33% have doctoral degrees; graduate assistants teach no undergraduate courses. Calendar: semesters. Grading system: letters or numbers. Library holdings: 33,000 bound volumes, 460 periodical subscriptions.

Undergraduate Profile Fall 1984: 1,499 undergraduates (324 freshmen) from 12 states and territories and 14 foreign countries; 45% part-time; 70% state residents; 7% transfers; 70% financial aid recipients; 63% women; 1% blacks; 1% Native Americans; 1% Hispanics; 3% foreign nationals; 49 legally handicapped students.

Expenses (1985–86) Comprehensive fee of $8525 includes full-time tuition ($5550), mandatory fees ($75), and college room and board ($2900). Part-time tuition: $185 per semester hour. Tuition prepayment plan available.

Financial Aid Fall 1984 full-time freshmen: 95% applied for aid, 98% of those were judged to have need, 100% of those were aided; the average aided freshman received an aid package worth $5472 (47% scholarships/grants, 53% self-help) meeting 80% of need. College-administered aid for all 1984–85 undergraduates: need-based scholarships; non-need scholarships; low-interest long-term loans from external sources (average $1500); SEOG; College Work-Study. Supporting data: FAF, AFSA/SAR required; IRS required for some; FFS acceptable. Priority application deadline: 4/15.

Athletics Member NCAA (Division III), NAIA. Intercollegiate sports: baseball/softball M(III), W; basketball M(III), W(III); golf M; soccer M; volleyball W. Intramural sports: baseball/softball, basketball, cross-country running, martial arts, racquetball, riflery, soccer, swimming and diving, volleyball, water polo.

Majors Accounting A, B; business administration/commerce/management A, B; business education B; computer information systems A, B; court reporting A, B; finance/banking B; insurance A, B; legal secretarial studies A; marketing/retailing/merchandising B; medical assistant technologies A; medical secretarial studies A; nursing B; recreation and leisure services B; retail management A; secretarial studies/office management A, B. Majors with highest enrollment: business administration/commerce/management, accounting, secretarial studies/office management.

LD Program Information

Name of Program Special Services.

Availability of Services Began offering services in 1978. Services provided to freshmen, sophomores, juniors, seniors. Program currently serves 11 LD students: 6 freshmen, 3 sophomores, 1 junior, 1 senior.

Staff 2 full-time, 3 part-time staff members, including director. Services provided by remediation specialist, tutors, counselor.

Admissions LD applicants evaluated on the basis of high school transcript and grade point average, standard or untimed SAT or ACT, personal interview, autobiographical statement, letters of recommendation, psychoeducational report; WAIS recommended. LD students may begin taking classes in fall or spring. Application should be submitted at least 3 months in advance of initial anticipated enrollment.

Housing College housing available. LD students housed with other LD students and non-LD students. LD freshmen, sophomores, juniors, and seniors required to live on campus except if 23 or over or living with relatives.

Diagnostic Testing Available in intelligence, reading, math, spelling, written language, motor abilities, perceptual skills, work and study habits, personality, social skills.

Tutoring Offered one-to-one and in small groups by professional teachers, peer tutors. Available in some subjects. LD students may receive tutoring in all courses each term.

Basic Skills Remediation Offered one-to-one and in small groups by LD teachers. Available in reading, math, spelling, written language, learning strategies, work and study habits, social skills.

Academic Advisement Help with program planning provided by LD staff members, academic advisers. LD students may take up to 15 semester hours each semester; most take 12 semester hours; 12 semester hours required to maintain full-time status.

Auxiliary Aids and Services Aids include taped textbooks, tape recorders, calculators, typewriters, word processors. Services include alternative exam arrangements, notetakers, advocacy.

Counseling Services Individual counseling, career counseling available.

Contact Ms. Suzanne M. Comins, Director, Special Services/ACHIEVE Program, Husson College, Bangor, ME 04401, 207-947-1121.

Note The College also offers an ACHIEVE Program for nonmatriculated LD students to prepare them for college-level work.

IDAHO STATE UNIVERSITY
Pocatello, Idaho

Year Program Began	*Not reported*	Special Courses	✓
Special Fee	None	Taped Textbooks	✓
Special Orientation		Alternative Exam Arrangements	
Diagnostic Testing		Notetakers	✓
Subject-Area Tutoring	✓	Staff	2 full-time
Basic Skills Remediation		Number of Students Served	2

General Information State-supported coed university. Founded 1901. Awards A (college transfer and terminal), B, M, D. Institutionally accredited by regional association; programs accredited by AACSB (business), NASM (music), NLN (nursing), ACPE (pharmacy), NCATE (teacher education). Small-town setting; 274-acre campus. Total enrollment: 6,068. Faculty: 505 (415 full-time, 90 part-time); 67% have doctoral degrees; graduate assistants teach a few undergraduate courses. Calendar: semesters. Grading system: letters or numbers. Library holdings: 306,038 bound volumes, 1 million titles on microform, 44,667 periodical subscriptions, 3,148 records/tapes.

Undergraduate Profile Fall 1984: 5,124 undergraduates (931 freshmen) from 43 states and territories and 30 foreign countries; 42% part-time; 89% state residents; 14% transfers; 78% financial aid recipients; 52% women; 1% blacks; 2% Native Americans; 2% Hispanics; 3% Asian Americans; 4% foreign nationals; 51% of undergraduates over 25 years of age; 200 legally handicapped students.

Expenses (1985–86) State resident tuition: $1040 full-time, $50.25 per credit part-time. Nonresident tuition: $2940 full-time, $50.25 per credit part-time. College room and board: $1892.

Financial Aid Fall 1984 full-time freshmen: 88% applied for aid, 82% of those were judged to have need, 100% of those were aided; the average aided freshman received an aid package worth $1166 (31% scholarships/grants, 69% self-help) meeting 67% of need. College-administered aid for all 1984–85 undergraduates: need-based scholarships; non-need scholarships; short-term loans (average $365); low-interest long-term loans from external sources (average $1930); SEOG; College Work-Study; part-time jobs. Supporting data: FAF, IRS, institutional form, AFSA/SAR required; FFS acceptable. Priority application deadline: 2/15.

Athletics Member NCAA (Division I). Intercollegiate sports: basketball M(I,s), W(I,s); cross-country running M(I,s), W(I,s); football M(I-AA,s); golf M(s), W; skiing (downhill) M(I), W(I); tennis M(I,s), W(II,s); track and field M(I,s), W(I,s); volleyball W(I,s); wrestling M(I,s). Intramural sports: archery, badminton, baseball/softball, basketball, bowling, cross-country running, field hockey, football, riflery, skiing (cross-country), skiing (downhill), soccer, swimming and diving, tennis, track and field, volleyball, water polo, wrestling.

Majors Accounting B; aircraft and missile maintenance A; American studies B; anthropology B; art education B; art/fine arts B; automotive technologies A; biochemistry B; biology/biological sciences B; botany/plant sciences B; business administration/commerce/management A, B; business education B; business machine technologies A; chemistry B; civil engineering technology A; computer information systems B; conservation B; cosmetology A; criminal justice A; data processing A; dental services B; (pre)dentistry sequence B; dietetics B; drafting and design A; early childhood education B; ecology/environmental studies B; economics B; education B; electrical and electronics technologies A; electrical engineering technology A; elementary education B; engineering (general) B; English B; fashion merchandising A; finance/banking B; food services technology A; French B; geology B; German B; graphic arts A; guidance and counseling B; health education B; health services administration B; history B; home economics B; home economics education B; journalism B; law enforcement/police sciences A; (pre)law sequence B; liberal arts/general studies A; machine and tool technologies A; marketing/retailing/merchandising B; mathematics B; medical technology B; (pre)medicine sequence B; microbiology B; music B; music education B; nursing B; pharmacy/pharmaceutical sciences B; philosophy B; physical education B; physics B; political science/government B; practical nursing A; psychology B; radiological technology A, B; science education B; secondary education B; secretarial studies/office management A; social work B; sociology B; Spanish B; special education B; speech pathology and audiology B; speech/rhetoric/public address/debate B; telecommunications A; theater arts/drama B; (pre)veterinary medicine sequence B; vocational education B; welding technology A; zoology B.

LD Program Information

Name of Program Special Services.

Availability of Services Services provided to freshmen, sophomores, juniors, seniors. Program currently serves 2 LD students (both sophomores).

Staff 2 full-time staff members, including director. Services provided by tutors, counselor.

Admissions LD applicants evaluated on the basis of high school transcript, standard ACT. LD students may begin taking classes in fall, spring, or summer. Application should be submitted 2 to 3 months in advance of initial anticipated enrollment.

Housing College housing available. LD students housed randomly. LD students not required to live on campus.

Tutoring Offered one-to-one and in small groups by peer tutors. Available in all subjects. LD students may receive tutoring in 3 courses per term.

Academic Advisement Help with program planning provided by academic advisers. LD students may take up to 18 credits each semester; most take 12 credits; 12 credits required to maintain full-time status.

Special Courses Offered in study skills, career planning. All offered for credit; all enter into overall grade point average.

Auxiliary Aids and Services Aids include taped textbooks, tape recorders. Services include notetakers.

Counseling Services Individual counseling, career counseling available.

Contact Mr. James Yizar, Counselor/Learning Specialist, Idaho State University, Box 8345, Pocatello, ID 83209, 208-236-3242.

ILLINOIS STATE UNIVERSITY

Normal, Illinois

Year Program Began	1978	Special Courses	
Special Fee	None	Taped Textbooks	✓
Special Orientation		Alternative Exam Arrangements	
Diagnostic Testing		Notetakers	✓
Subject-Area Tutoring	✓	Staff	1 part-time
Basic Skills Remediation		Number of Students Served	*Not reported*

General Information State-supported coed university. Founded 1857. Awards B, M, D. Institutionally accredited by regional association; programs accredited by NASAD (art and design), AACSB (business), NASM (music), NCATE (teacher education). City setting; 850-acre campus. Total enrollment: 20,134. Faculty: 1,064 (848 full-time, 216 part-time); 60% have doctoral degrees; graduate assistants teach a few undergraduate courses. Calendar: semesters. Grading system: letters or numbers. Library holdings: 975,734 bound volumes, 5,305 periodical subscriptions, 20,444 records/tapes.

Undergraduate Profile Fall 1984: 18,050 undergraduates (4,126 freshmen); 9% part-time; 99% state residents; 30% transfers; 53% women; 6% blacks; 1% Native Americans; 1% Hispanics; 2% Asian Americans; 1% foreign nationals; 7% of undergraduates over 25 years of age; 101 legally handicapped students.

Expenses (1985–86) State resident tuition: $1050 full-time, $43.75 per credit hour part-time. Nonresident tuition: $3150 full-time, $131.25 per credit hour part-time. Mandatory fees: $441. College room and board: $2289. College room only: $996.

Financial Aid College-administered aid for all 1984–85 undergraduates: 6,621 need-based scholarships (average $902); 4,211 non-need scholarships (average $772); low-interest long-term loans from external sources (average $1829); SEOG; College Work-Study; 5,420 part-time jobs. Supporting data: IRS, institutional form required; FFS, FAF, AFSA/SAR acceptable. Priority application deadline: 3/1.

Athletics Member NCAA (Division I). Intercollegiate sports: baseball/softball M(I,s), W(I,s); basketball M(I,s), W(I,s); cross-country running M(I,s), W(I,s); football M(I-AA,s); golf M(I,s), W(I,s); gymnastics W(I,s); soccer M(I,s); swimming and diving W(I,s); tennis M(I,s), W(I,s); track and field M(I,s), W(I,s); volleyball W(I,s); wrestling M(I,s). Intramural sports: badminton, baseball/softball, basketball, football, golf, soccer, swimming and diving, tennis, volleyball, water polo, wrestling.

Majors Accounting B; agricultural business B; agricultural sciences B; anthropology B; art education B; art/fine arts B; biology/biological sciences B; business administration/commerce/management B; business education B; chemistry B; communication B; computer science B; criminal justice B; dance B; early childhood education B; economics B; elementary education B; English B; environmental health sciences B; finance/banking B; French B; geography B; geology B; German B; health education B; history B; home economics B; home economics education B; industrial arts B; industrial engineering technology B; liberal arts/general studies B; library science B; marketing/retailing/merchandising B; mathematics B; medical records services B; medical technology B; music B; music education B; parks management B; philosophy B; physical education B; physics B; political science/government B; psychology B; recreation and leisure services B; Russian and Slavic studies B; safety and security technologies B; secretarial studies/office management B; social science B; social work B; sociology B; Spanish B; special education B; speech pathology and audiology B; speech/rhetoric/public address/debate B; theater arts/drama B. Majors with highest enrollment: special education, elementary education, computer science.

LD Program Information

Name of Program Services for the Handicapped.

Availability of Services Began offering services in 1978. Services provided to freshmen, sophomores, juniors, seniors.

Staff 1 part-time staff member (coordinator).

Admissions LD applicants evaluated on the basis of high school transcript and grade point average, standard ACT, psychoeducational report. LD students may begin taking classes in fall, spring, or summer. Application should be submitted 1 year in advance of initial anticipated enrollment.

Housing College housing (including coed) available. LD students housed randomly. LD freshmen and sophomores required to live on campus.

Tutoring Offered one-to-one by peer tutors. Available in all subjects. LD students may receive tutoring in all courses each term.

Academic Advisement Help with program planning provided by LD staff member, academic advisers. Most LD students take 12 to 15 credit hours each semester; 12 credit hours required to maintain full-time status.

Auxiliary Aids and Services Aids include taped textbooks, tape recorders, calculators. Services include notetakers.

Counseling Services Individual counseling available.

Contact Dr. Judith Smithson, Coordinator of Services for the Handicapped, Illinois State University, Hovey Hall, Room 207, Normal, IL 61761, 309-438-5853.

INDIANA CENTRAL UNIVERSITY

Indianapolis, Indiana

Year Program Began	1983	Special Courses	
Special Fee	Varies	Taped Textbooks	✓
Special Orientation		Alternative Exam Arrangements	✓
Diagnostic Testing	✓	Notetakers	✓
Subject-Area Tutoring	✓	Staff	2 part-time
Basic Skills Remediation	✓	Number of Students Served	8

General Information Comprehensive coed institution, affiliated with United Methodist Church. Founded 1902. Awards A (college transfer and terminal), B, M. Institutionally accredited by regional association; programs accredited by AACSB (business), NLN (nursing), NCATE (teacher education); candidate for program accreditation by NASM (music). Metropolitan setting; 60-acre barrier-free campus. Total enrollment: 3,042. Faculty: 212 (101 full-time, 111 part-time); 32% have doctoral degrees; graduate assistants teach no undergraduate courses. Calendar: 4-4-1. Grading system: letters or numbers. Library holdings: 134,000 bound volumes, 268 titles on microform, 721 periodical subscriptions, 1,188 records/tapes.

Undergraduate Profile Fall 1984: 2,681 undergraduates (333 freshmen) from 8 states and territories and 15 foreign countries; 63% part-time; 95% state residents; 4% transfers; 85% financial aid recipients; 70% women; 5% blacks; 1% foreign nationals; 4 legally handicapped students.

Expenses (1985–86) Comprehensive fee of $7850 includes full-time tuition ($5490) and college room and board ($2360). Part-time tuition: $216 per semester hour.

Financial Aid Fall 1984 full-time freshmen: 80% applied for aid, 70% of those were judged to have need, 100% of those were aided; the average aided freshman received an aid package worth $4804 (60% scholarships/grants, 40% self-help) meeting 75% of need. College-administered aid for all 1984–85 undergraduates: need-based scholarships; non-need scholarships; low-interest long-term loans; SEOG; College Work-Study; part-time jobs. Supporting data: FAF, institutional form, AFSA/SAR required. Application deadline: continuous to 3/1.

Athletics Member NCAA (Division II). Intercollegiate sports: baseball/softball M(II,s), W(II,s); basketball M(II,s), W(II,s); cross-country running M(II,s), W(II,s); football M(II,s); golf M(II,s); soccer M(II,s); swimming and diving M(II,s), W(II,s); tennis M(II,s), W(II,s); track and field M(II,s), W(II,s); volleyball W(II,s); wrestling M(II,s). Intramural sports: badminton, basketball, football, racquetball, volleyball.

Majors Accounting B; art education B; art/fine arts B; art therapy B; behavioral sciences B; biology/biological sciences B; business administration/commerce/management A, B; business economics A, B; business education B; chemistry A, B; communication B; community services A; computer information systems A, B; computer technologies A; corrections A, B; criminal justice B; data processing A; (pre)dentistry sequence B; earth science B; economics B; education B; elementary education B; English B; finance/banking A; French B; funeral service B; German B; history B; human services B; international business B; journalism B; law enforcement/police sciences A, B; (pre)law sequence B; legal secretarial studies A; liberal arts/general studies A; marketing/retailing/merchandising B; mathematics B; medical technology B; (pre)medicine sequence B; music B; music education B; nursing A, B; paralegal studies A; philosophy B; physical education B; physical sciences B; physics B; political science/government B; psychology B; radio and television studies B; religious studies B; science B; science education B; secondary education B; secretarial studies/office management A; social work B; sociology B; Spanish B; speech/rhetoric/public address/debate B; telecommunications B; theater arts/drama B; theology B; (pre)veterinary medicine sequence B. Majors with highest enrollment: accounting, nursing, business administration/commerce/management.

LD Program Information

Name of Program Not specified.

Availability of Services Began offering services in 1983. Services provided to freshmen, sophomores, juniors, seniors. Program currently serves 8 LD students: 5 freshmen, 3 sophomores.

Fees $5 to $10 per hour for tutoring.

Staff 2 part-time staff members, including codirectors. Services provided by tutors.

Admissions LD applicants evaluated on the basis of high school transcript and grade point average, standard or untimed SAT or ACT, personal interview, autobiographical statement, letters of recommendation, psychoeducational report, including evaluations from admissions officers or high school personnel. LD students may begin taking classes in fall, winter, spring, or summer. Application should be submitted 3 to 4 months in advance of initial anticipated enrollment.

Housing College housing (including coed) available. LD students housed with other LD students and non-LD students. LD students not required to live on campus.

Diagnostic Testing Available in intelligence, reading, math, spelling, handwriting, spoken language, written language, motor abilities, perceptual skills.

Tutoring Offered one-to-one and in small groups by professional teachers, peer tutors. Available in all subjects. LD students may receive tutoring in 4 courses per term.

Basic Skills Remediation Offered one-to-one by teacher trainees, staff of Diagnostic Center. Available in reading, math, spelling, handwriting, written language, learning strategies, motor abilities, perceptual skills, work and study habits.

Academic Advisement Help with program planning provided by LD staff members, academic advisers. LD students may take up to 15 semester hours each semester; most take 9 to 12 semester hours; 9 semester hours required to maintain full-time status.

Auxiliary Aids and Services Aids include taped textbooks, tape recorders, calculators, typewriters, word processors. Aids are provided by individual arrangement. Services include alternative exam arrangements, notetakers, advocacy.

Counseling Services Individual counseling, career counseling available.

Contact Dr. Patricia Cook, Associate Professor of Special Education and Codirector of Miriam Bender Diagnostic Center, Indiana Central University, 1400 East Hanna Avenue, Indianapolis, IN 46227, 317-788-3285.

INDIANA STATE UNIVERSITY

Terre Haute, Indiana

Year Program Began	1978	Special Courses	✓
Special Fee	None	Taped Textbooks	
Special Orientation	✓	Alternative Exam Arrangements	✓
Diagnostic Testing	✓	Notetakers	
Subject-Area Tutoring	✓	Staff	4 part-time
Basic Skills Remediation	✓	Number of Students Served	*Not reported*

General Information State-supported coed university. Founded 1865. Awards A (college transfer and terminal), B, M, D. Institutionally accredited by regional association; programs accredited by AACSB (business), FIDER (interior design), NASM (music), NLN (nursing), NCATE (teacher education). City setting, with easy access to Indianapolis; 91-acre barrier-free campus. Total enrollment: 11,638. Faculty: 713 (659 full-time, 54 part-time); 62% have doctoral degrees; graduate assistants teach a few undergraduate courses. Calendar: semesters. Grading system: letters or numbers. Library holdings: 936,294 bound volumes, 528,699 titles on microform, 4,862 periodical subscriptions, 48,049 records/tapes.

Undergraduate Profile Fall 1984: 9,964 undergraduates (3,220 freshmen); 15% part-time; 81% state residents; 5% transfers; 52% financial aid recipients; 49% women; 9% blacks; 1% Native Americans; 1% Hispanics; 1% Asian Americans; 7% foreign nationals; 13% of undergraduates over 25 years of age; 51 legally handicapped students.

Expenses (1985–86) State resident tuition: $1542 full-time, $53 per credit hour part-time. Nonresident tuition: $3622 full-time, $123 per credit hour part-time. College room and board: $2176.

Financial Aid Fall 1984 full-time freshmen: 39% applied for aid, 70% of those were judged to have need, 90% of those were aided; the average aided freshman received an aid package worth $2955 (59% scholarships/grants, 41% self-help) meeting 78% of need. College-administered aid for all 1984–85 undergraduates: 1,726 need-based scholarships (average $754); 2,382 non-need scholarships (average $1040); short-term loans (average $1000); low-interest long-term loans from college funds (average $577), from external sources (average $2070); College Work-Study; part-time jobs. Supporting data: FAF, institutional form, AFSA/SAR required. Priority application deadline: 3/1.

Athletics Member NCAA (Division I). Intercollegiate sports: baseball/softball M(I,s), W(I,s); basketball M(I,s), W(I,s); bowling W(s); cross-country running M(I,s), W(I,s); football M(I-AA,s); gymnastics M(I,s), W(I,s); tennis M(I,s), W(I,s); track and field M(I,s), W(I,s); volleyball W(I,s); wrestling M(I,s). Intramural sports: archery, badminton, baseball/softball, basketball, bowling, cross-country running, swimming and diving, tennis, track and field, volleyball, weight lifting, wrestling.

Majors Accounting B; American studies B; anthropology B; art education B; art/fine arts B; art history B; automotive technologies B; aviation technology A, B; biology/biological sciences B; black/Afro-American studies B; broadcasting B; business administration/commerce/management A, B; business education B; chemistry B; child care/child and family studies A; child psychology/child development B; commercial art B; communication B; computer engineering B; computer programming B; computer science B; construction technologies B; criminal justice A, B; dental services B; (pre)dentistry sequence B; dietetics B; drafting and design A, B; early childhood education B; economics B; educational media B; electrical and electronics technologies A, B; elementary education B; engineering sciences B; English B; environmental health sciences B; environmental sciences B; family and consumer studies B; finance/banking B; French B; geography B; geology B; German B; graphic arts B; Greek B; health education B; history B; home economics B; home economics education B; hotel and restaurant management B; humanities B; industrial arts B; industrial engineering technology B; interdisciplinary studies B; interior design B; international studies B; journalism B; Latin B; Latin American studies B; law enforcement/police sciences A, B; (pre)law sequence B; liberal arts/general studies A; manufacturing technology B; marketing/retailing/merchandising B; mathematics B; medical technology A, B; (pre)medicine sequence B; music B; Near and Middle Eastern studies B; nursing A, B; nutrition B; occupational safety and health B; philosophy B; physical education B; physical sciences B; physics B; political science/government B; psychology B; public health B; radio and television studies B; real estate A; recreation and leisure services B; religious studies B; Russian B; science education B; secretarial studies/office management A, B; social work B; sociology B; Spanish B; special education B; speech pathology and audiology B; speech/rhetoric/public address/debate B; studio art B; textiles and clothing B; theater arts/drama B; urban studies B; (pre)veterinary medicine sequence B. Majors with highest enrollment: finance/banking, accounting, elementary education.

LD Program Information

Name of Program Special Services.

Availability of Services Began offering services in 1978. Services provided to freshmen, sophomores, juniors, seniors.

Staff 4 part-time staff members, including directors of Special Services, Reading Lab, and Learning Skills Center. Services provided by remediation specialists, tutors, counselors, diagnostic specialists.

Admissions LD applicants evaluated on the basis of high school transcript and grade point average, untimed SAT, personal interview, letters of recommendation; psychoeducational report recommended. LD students may begin taking classes in fall, spring, or summer. Application should be submitted at least 3 or 4 months in advance of initial anticipated enrollment.

Orientation Required orientation held before registration.

Housing College housing (including coed) available. LD students housed randomly. LD freshmen required to live on campus except if 20 or over.

Diagnostic Testing Available in intelligence, reading, spelling, handwriting, spoken language, written language, perceptual skills, speech.

Tutoring Offered one-to-one and in small groups by peer tutors. Available in some subjects. LD students may receive tutoring in all courses each term.

Basic Skills Remediation Offered one-to-one and in small groups by LD teachers, Special Services staff. Available in reading, written language, speech.

Academic Advisement Help with program planning provided by LD staff members, academic advisers. LD students may take up to 17 credit hours each semester; most take 10 to 12 credit hours; 12 credit hours required to maintain full-time status.

Special Courses Offered in study skills. None offered for credit; none enter into overall grade point average.

Auxiliary Aids and Services Services include alternative exam arrangements, advocacy.

Counseling Services Individual counseling, small-group counseling, rap sessions, career counseling available.

Contact Dr. Catherine A. Baker, Reading Specialist, Indiana State University, Learning Resource Center 7, 526 North Sixth Street, Terre Haute, IN 47809, 812-237-4135.

INDIANA UNIVERSITY AT SOUTH BEND

South Bend, Indiana

Year Program Began	1983	Special Courses	✓
Special Fee	None	Taped Textbooks	✓
Special Orientation	✓	Alternative Exam Arrangements	✓
Diagnostic Testing		Notetakers	✓
Subject-Area Tutoring	✓	Staff	1 part-time
Basic Skills Remediation		Number of Students Served	6

General Information State-supported comprehensive coed institution. Part of Indiana University System. Founded 1922. Awards A (college transfer and terminal), B, M. Institutionally accredited by regional association; programs accredited by NCATE (teacher education). City setting, with easy access to Chicago; barrier-free campus. Total enrollment: 5,442. Faculty: 294 (142 full-time, 152 part-time); 83% have doctoral degrees; graduate assistants teach no undergraduate courses. Calendar: semesters. Grading system: letters or numbers. Library holdings: 202,000 bound volumes, 169,000 titles on microform, 1,770 periodical subscriptions, 116,000 records/tapes.

Undergraduate Profile Fall 1984: 4,185 undergraduates (1,071 freshmen); 64% part-time; 96% state residents; 13% transfers; 35% financial aid recipients; 57% women; 4% blacks; 1% Native Americans; 1% Hispanics; 1% Asian Americans; 1% foreign nationals; 77 legally handicapped students.

Expenses (1985–86) State resident tuition: $1350 full-time, $45 per credit hour part-time. Nonresident tuition: $3315 full-time, $110.50 per credit hour part-time. Mandatory fees: $18.

Financial Aid College-administered aid for all 1984–85 undergraduates: 102 need-based scholarships (average $564); 109 non-need scholarships (average $214); short-term loans (average $100); low-interest long-term loans from external sources (average $878); SEOG; College Work-Study. Supporting data: FAF, IRS, institutional form required; AFSA/SAR required for some. Priority application deadline: 3/1.

Athletics Intramural sports: baseball/softball, basketball, volleyball.

Majors Accounting B; advertising B; art/fine arts B; biology/biological sciences B; business administration/commerce/management B; chemistry B; communication B; computer science B; criminal justice A, B; dental services A; (pre)dentistry sequence B; early childhood education A; economics B; education B; elementary education B; English B; finance/banking A; French B; German B; history B; jazz A; labor and industrial relations B; labor studies A, B; (pre)law sequence B; marketing/retailing/merchandising B; mathematics B; (pre)medicine sequence B; music A, B; music education B; nursing B; philosophy B; physics B; political science/government B; psychology B; public affairs and policy studies A, B; secondary education B; secretarial studies/office management A; sociology B; Spanish B; special education B; speech/rhetoric/public address/debate B; studio art B; theater arts/drama B.

LD Program Information

Name of Program Disabled Student Services.

Availability of Services Began offering services in 1983. Services provided to freshmen, sophomores, juniors, seniors. Program currently serves 6 LD students: 1 freshman, 3 sophomores, 2 juniors.

Staff 1 part-time staff member (coordinator).

Admissions LD applicants evaluated on the basis of high school transcript, personal interview, autobiographical statement, psychoeducational report. LD students may begin taking classes in fall, spring, or summer. Application should be submitted 2 months in advance of initial anticipated enrollment.

Orientation Required orientation held before registration.

Housing College housing not available.

Tutoring Offered one-to-one and in small groups. Available in all subjects. LD students may receive tutoring in all courses each term.

Academic Advisement Help with program planning provided by LD staff member, academic advisers. LD students may take up to 18 credit hours each semester; most take 6 to 9 credit hours; 12 credit hours required to maintain full-time status.

Special Courses Offered in college survival skills, reading, composition, math, study skills, career planning. All offered for credit; some enter into overall grade point average.

Auxiliary Aids and Services Aids include taped textbooks, tape recorders. Services include alternative exam arrangements, notetakers, advocacy.

Counseling Services Individual counseling, career counseling available.

Contact Ms. Karen Goepfrich, Coordinator, Disabled Student Services, Indiana University at South Bend, 1700 Mishawaka Avenue, PO Box 7111, South Bend, IN 46634, 219-237-4479.

INDIANA UNIVERSITY BLOOMINGTON

Bloomington, Indiana

Year Program Began	1982	Special Courses	
Special Fee	None	Taped Textbooks	✓
Special Orientation		Alternative Exam Arrangements	✓
Diagnostic Testing	✓	Notetakers	
Subject-Area Tutoring	✓	Staff	11 part-time
Basic Skills Remediation		Number of Students Served	29

General Information State-supported coed university. Part of Indiana University System. Founded 1820. Awards A (college transfer and terminal), B, M, D. Institutionally accredited by regional association; programs accredited by AACSB (business), NASM (music), NLN (nursing), COE (optometry), NCATE (teacher education). City setting, with easy access to Indianapolis; 1,900-acre barrier-free campus. Total enrollment: 32,715. Faculty: 1,581 (1,353 full-time, 228 part-time); 88% have doctoral degrees; graduate assistants teach a few undergraduate courses. Calendar: semesters. Grading system: letters or numbers. Library holdings: 4.4 million bound volumes, 1.5 million titles on microform, 29,000 periodical subscriptions, 207,000 records/tapes.

Undergraduate Profile Fall 1984: 24,608 undergraduates (5,665 freshmen) from 53 states and territories and 119 foreign countries; 7% part-time; 72% state residents; 4% transfers; 67% financial aid recipients; 53% women; 6% blacks; 1% Native Americans; 1% Hispanics; 1% Asian Americans; 3% foreign nationals; 6% of undergraduates over 25 years of age; 110 legally handicapped students.

Expenses (1985–86) State resident tuition: $1600 full-time, $53.25 per credit hour part-time. Nonresident tuition: $4500 full-time, $142.50 per credit hour part-time. College room and board: $2350.

Financial Aid Fall 1984 full-time freshmen: 56% applied for aid, 62% of those were judged to have need, 98% of those were aided; the average aided freshman received an aid package worth $3592 (55% scholarships/grants, 45% self-help) meeting 100% of need. College-administered aid for all 1984–85 undergraduates: need-based scholarships; 1,500 non-need scholarships (average $585); short-term loans (average $120); low-interest long-term loans from college funds (average $857), from external sources (average $902); SEOG; College Work-Study; 6,900 part-time jobs. Supporting data: institutional form required; FAF, IRS, AFSA/SAR required for some. Priority application deadline: 3/1.

Athletics Member NCAA (Division I). Intercollegiate sports: baseball/softball M(I,s), W(I,s); basketball M(I,s), W(I,s); cross-country running M(I,s), W(I,s); football M(I-A,s); golf M(I,s), W(I,s); gymnastics W(I,s); soccer M(I,s), W; swimming and diving M(I,s), W(I,s); tennis M(I,s), W(I,s); track and field M(I,s), W(I,s); volleyball W(I,s); wrestling M(I,s). Intramural sports: badminton, baseball/softball, basketball, bowling, cross-country running, fencing, field hockey, football, golf, gymnastics, ice hockey, lacrosse, martial arts, racquetball, riflery, rugby, sailing, skiing (downhill), squash, swimming and diving, tennis, track and field, volleyball, water polo, weight lifting, wrestling.

Majors Accounting B; adult and continuing education B; African studies B; anthropology B; applied art B; applied mathematics B; Arabic B; art education B; art/fine arts B; art history B; Asian/Oriental studies B; astronomy B; audio engineering A; bilingual/bicultural education B; biochemistry B; biology/biological sciences B; botany/plant sciences B; broadcasting B; business administration/commerce/management B; business economics B; ceramic art and design B; chemistry B; child care/child and family studies B; Chinese B; city, community, and regional planning B; classics B; communication B; comparative literature B; computer science B; creative writing B; criminal justice B; dance B; dental services A; (pre)dentistry sequence B; dietetics B; early childhood education B; East Asian studies B; East European and Soviet studies B; ecology/environmental studies B; economics B; education B; educational media A; elementary education B; English B; environmental design B; family and consumer studies B; fashion design and technology A, B; fashion merchandising B; finance/banking B; folklore B; forensic sciences B; French B; geography B; geology B; German B; Germanic languages and literature B; graphic arts B; Greek B; health science B; health services administration B; Hebrew B; history B; history of science B; human development B; insurance B; interior design B; Islamic studies B; Italian B; Japanese B; jazz B; jewelry and metalsmithing B; journalism B; labor and industrial relations B; labor studies A, B; Latin B; law enforcement/police sciences B; (pre)law sequence B; liberal arts/general studies A, B; linguistics B; literature B; management information systems B; marketing/retailing/merchandising B; mathematics B; (pre)medicine sequence B; microbiology B; music B; musical instrument technology A; music education B; music history B; Near and Middle Eastern studies B; nursing B; nutrition B; occupational safety and health B; operations research B; optical technologies A; optometric/ophthalmic technologies A; optometry B; painting/drawing B; parks management B; philosophy B; photography B; physical education B; physics B; piano/organ B; political science/government B; Portuguese B; psychology B; public administration B; public affairs and policy studies A, B; public health B; radio and television studies B; recreation and leisure services B; recreation therapy B; religious studies B; Russian B; Russian and Slavic studies B; science education B; sculpture B; secondary education B; Slavic languages B; sociology B; Spanish B; special education B; speech pathology and audiology B; speech/rhetoric/public address/debate B; speech therapy B; sports administration B; sports medicine B; stringed instruments A; studio art B; telecommunications B; textiles and clothing A, B; theater arts/drama A, B; transportation technologies B; urban studies B; (pre)veterinary medicine sequence B; voice B; wind and percussion instruments B; zoology B. Majors with highest enrollment: business administration/commerce/management, mathematics, education.

LD Program Information

Name of Program Disabled Student Services.

Availability of Services Began offering services in 1982. Services provided to freshmen, sophomores, juniors, seniors. Program currently serves 29 LD students: 6 freshmen, 10 sophomores, 7 juniors, 6 seniors.

Staff 11 part-time staff members, including coordinator. Services provided by tutors.

Admissions LD applicants evaluated on the basis of high school transcript and grade point average, standard or untimed SAT or ACT. LD students may begin taking classes in fall, spring, or summer. Application should be submitted 6 months in advance of initial anticipated enrollment.

Housing College housing (including coed) available. LD students housed randomly. LD students not required to live on campus.

Diagnostic Testing Available in intelligence, reading, math, spelling, handwriting, written language, work and study habits, personality.

Tutoring Offered one-to-one by peer tutors. Available in all subjects. LD students may receive tutoring in all courses each term (but limited to 1 hour of tutoring per week for each credit hour of course load).

Academic Advisement Help with program planning provided by LD staff member, academic advisers. Most LD students take 12 to 15 credit hours each semester (12 credit hours recommended in first semester).

Auxiliary Aids and Services Aids include taped textbooks, tape recorders, calculators, typewriters. Services include alternative exam arrangements, advocacy.

Counseling Services Individual counseling, career counseling available.

Contact Mr. Sam Goodin, Coordinator, Disabled Student Services, Indiana University Bloomington, Student Services 096, Bloomington, IN 47405, 812-335-5043.

INDIANA UNIVERSITY–PURDUE UNIVERSITY AT FORT WAYNE

Fort Wayne, Indiana

Year Program Began	1978	Special Courses	✓
Special Fee	None	Taped Textbooks	✓
Special Orientation		Alternative Exam Arrangements	✓
Diagnostic Testing		Notetakers	
Subject-Area Tutoring	✓	Staff	1 full-time
Basic Skills Remediation	✓	Number of Students Served	15

General Information State-supported comprehensive coed institution. Part of Indiana and Purdue University Systems. Founded 1917. Awards A (college transfer and terminal), B, M. Institutionally accredited by regional association; programs accredited by ABET (engineering and technology), NASM (music), NLN (nursing), NCATE (teacher education). City setting; 412-acre barrier-free campus. Total enrollment: 10,185. Faculty: 594 (301 full-time, 293 part-time); 65% have doctoral degrees; graduate assistants teach no undergraduate courses. Calendar: semesters. Grading system: letters or numbers. Library holdings: 312,154 bound volumes, 159,844 titles on microform, 1,700 periodical subscriptions, 2,700 records/tapes.

Undergraduate Profile Fall 1984: 9,301 undergraduates (1,353 freshmen) from 40 states and territories and 43 foreign countries; 63% part-time; 95% state residents; 25% transfers; 40% financial aid recipients; 54% women; 4% blacks; 1% Hispanics; 44% of undergraduates over 25 years of age; 95 legally handicapped students.

Expenses (1985–86) State resident tuition: $1395 full-time, $45 per semester hour part-time. Nonresident tuition: $3464 full-time, $111.75 per semester hour part-time. Mandatory fees: $40.

Financial Aid Fall 1984 full-time freshmen: the average aided freshman received an aid package meeting 70% of need. College-administered aid for all 1984–85 undergraduates: need-based scholarships (average $515); non-need scholarships (average $100); low-interest long-term loans; SEOG; College Work-Study; part-time jobs. Supporting data: FAF, institutional form, AFSA/SAR required; IRS acceptable. Priority application deadline: 3/1.

Athletics Member NCAA (Division II). Intercollegiate sports: baseball/softball M(II,s), W(II); basketball M(II,s), W(II); cross-country running M(II,s), W(II,s); golf M(II,s), W(II,s); soccer M(II,s); tennis M(II,s), W(II,s); volleyball M(II,s), W(II,s). Intramural sports: baseball/softball, basketball, football, golf, martial arts, racquetball, tennis, volleyball.

Majors Accounting A, B; anthropology B; architectural technologies A; art/fine arts B; biology/biological sciences B; business administration/commerce/management A, B; chemistry B; civil engineering technology A; commercial art A; communication B; computer technologies A, B; construction technologies B; criminal justice A, B; dental services A, B; (pre)dentistry sequence B; drafting and design A; early childhood education A; earth science B; economics B; education B; electrical and electronics technologies B; electrical engineering technology A, B; elementary education B; engineering (general) B; (pre)engineering sequence A; engineering technology A, B; English B; finance/banking B; food services management A; French B; geology B; German B; health science A; history B; industrial design A; industrial engineering technology A, B; interior design A; labor studies A, B; liberal arts/general studies A, B; manufacturing technology B; marketing/retailing/merchandising A, B; mathematics B; mechanical design technology A; mechanical engineering technology A, B; medical technology B; (pre)medicine sequence B; mental health/rehabilitation counseling A; music B; music education B; music therapy B; nursing A, B; philosophy B; physics B; piano/organ B; political science/government B; psychology B; public administration A, B; public affairs and policy studies A, B; radio and television studies B; robotics A, B; science B; science education B; secondary education B; secretarial studies/office management A; social science B; sociology B; Spanish B; speech/rhetoric/public address/debate B; stringed instruments B; studio art B; theater arts/drama B; voice B; wind and percussion instruments B. Majors with highest enrollment: business administration/commerce/management, engineering technology, education.

LD Program Information

Name of Program Disabled Student Services.

Availability of Services Began offering services in 1978. Services provided to freshmen, sophomores, juniors, seniors. Program currently serves 15 LD students.

Staff 1 full-time staff member (counselor). Services provided by remediation specialist.

Admissions LD applicants evaluated on the basis of high school transcript and grade point average, standard or untimed SAT or ACT. LD students may begin taking classes in fall or spring. Application should be submitted 2 months in advance of initial anticipated enrollment.

Housing College housing not available.

Tutoring Offered one-to-one by peer tutors. Available in most subjects. LD students may receive tutoring in all courses each term (but limited to 2 hours of tutoring per week for each course; provided to full-time students only).

Basic Skills Remediation Offered one-to-one and in small groups by regular teachers. Available in reading, math, spelling, written language, work and study habits.

Academic Advisement Help with program planning provided by LD staff member, academic advisers. LD students may take up to 15 semester hours each semester; most take 9 semester hours; 12 semester hours required to maintain full-time status.

Special Courses Offered in reading, vocabulary development, communication skills, composition, math, study skills, career planning. All offered for credit; all enter into overall grade point average.

Auxiliary Aids and Services Aids include taped textbooks, tape recorders, calculators, typewriters, word processors. Services include alternative exam arrangements, advocacy.

Counseling Services Individual counseling, rap sessions, career counseling available.

Contact Disabled Student Counselor, Indiana University–Purdue University at Fort Wayne, 2101 Coliseum Boulevard East, Fort Wayne, IN 46805, 219-482-5580.

INDIANA UNIVERSITY–PURDUE UNIVERSITY AT INDIANAPOLIS

Indianapolis, Indiana

Year Program Began	1980	Special Courses	✓
Special Fee	None	Taped Textbooks	✓
Special Orientation	✓	Alternative Exam Arrangements	✓
Diagnostic Testing		Notetakers	✓
Subject-Area Tutoring	✓	Staff	1 full-time, 8 part-time
Basic Skills Remediation	✓	Number of Students Served	18

General Information State-supported coed university. Part of Indiana and Purdue University Systems. Founded 1969. Awards A (college transfer and terminal), B, M, D. Institutionally accredited by regional association; programs accredited by NASAD (art and design), ABET (engineering and technology), NLN (nursing). Metropolitan setting; 300-acre barrier-free campus. Total enrollment: 23,546. Faculty: 1,922 (1,206 full-time, 716 part-time); 80% have doctoral degrees; graduate assistants teach a few undergraduate courses. Calendar: semesters. Grading system: letters or numbers. Library holdings: 652,743 bound volumes, 436,255 titles on microform, 10,429 periodical subscriptions.

Undergraduate Profile Fall 1984: 16,990 undergraduates (2,259 freshmen); 57% part-time; 87% state residents; 33% transfers; 60% financial aid recipients; 55% women; 8% blacks; 1% Native Americans; 1% Hispanics; 2% Asian Americans; 1% foreign nationals; 49% of undergraduates over 25 years of age.

Expenses (1985–86) State resident tuition: $1500 full-time, $50 per semester hour part-time. Nonresident tuition: $3990 full-time, $133 per semester hour part-time. College room only: $1100.

Financial Aid Fall 1984 full-time freshmen: 73% applied for aid, 97% of those were judged to have need, 98% of those were aided; the average aided freshman received an aid package worth $1127 (53% scholarships/grants, 47% self-help) meeting 90% of need. College-administered aid for all 1984–85 undergraduates: need-based scholarships (average $500); non-need scholarships (average $1500); short-term loans (average $50); low-interest long-term loans from external sources; SEOG; College Work-Study; part-time jobs. Supporting data: FAF, IRS, state form, institutional form, AFSA/SAR required; FFS acceptable. Priority application deadline: 3/1.

Athletics Member NAIA. Intercollegiate sports: baseball/softball M(s), W(s); basketball M(s), W(s); golf M; tennis M; volleyball W(s). Intramural sports: badminton, baseball/softball, basketball, cross-country running, football, golf, martial arts, soccer, swimming and diving, tennis, track and field, volleyball, water polo.

Majors Accounting B; anthropology B; applied art B; architectural technologies A; art education B; art/fine arts B; art history B; biology/biological sciences B; biomedical technologies A; business administration/commerce/management A, B; chemistry B; civil engineering technology A; commercial art B; communication B; computer science B; computer technologies A, B; construction technologies B; criminal justice A, B; cytotechnology B; dental services A, B; (pre)dentistry sequence B; drafting and design A; early childhood education B; economics B; education B; electrical engineering B; electrical engineering technology A, B; elementary education B; engineering (general) B; English B; finance/banking B; food services management A; food services technology A; French B; geography B; geology B; German B; health education B; health services administration B; history B; hotel and restaurant management A; humanities A; industrial engineering technology A, B; journalism B; labor and industrial relations B; labor studies A, B; (pre)law sequence B; liberal arts/general studies A; marketing/retailing/merchandising B; mathematics B; mechanical design technology A; mechanical engineering B; mechanical engineering technology A, B; medical records services B; medical technology B; (pre)medicine sequence B; nursing A, B; occupational therapy A, B; painting/drawing B; philosophy B; physical education B; physical therapy B; physics B; political science/government B; psychology B; public administration B; public affairs and policy studies A, B; public health B; radiological sciences B; radiological technology A; religious studies B; respiratory therapy A; science education B; sculpture B; secondary education B; secretarial studies/office management A; social science A; social work B; sociology B; Spanish B; speech/rhetoric/public address/debate B; telecommunications B; theater arts/drama B; urban studies B; (pre)veterinary medicine sequence B; vocational education B.

LD Program Information

Name of Program Disabled Student Services.

Availability of Services Began offering services in 1980. Services provided to freshmen, sophomores, juniors, seniors. Program currently serves 18 LD students: 8 freshmen, 4 sophomores, 2 juniors, 4 seniors.

Staff 1 full-time, 8 part-time staff members, including director, assistant director. Services provided by tutors, notetakers.

Admissions LD applicants evaluated on the basis of high school transcript and grade point average, standard SAT or ACT, personal interview, psychoeducational report. LD students may begin taking classes in fall, spring, or summer. Application should be submitted 3 months in advance of initial anticipated enrollment.

Orientation Optional orientation offered before registration.

Housing College housing (including coed) available. LD students housed with other LD students and non-LD students. LD students not required to live on campus.

Tutoring Offered one-to-one by peer tutors. Available in some subjects. LD students may receive tutoring in all courses each term.

Basic Skills Remediation Offered in small groups by regular teachers. Available in math, spelling, written language, work and study habits.

Academic Advisement Help with program planning provided by academic advisers. LD students may take up to 12 semester hours each semester; most take 9 semester hours; 12 semester hours required to maintain full-time status.

Special Courses Offered in study skills. None offered for credit; none enter into overall grade point average.

Auxiliary Aids and Services Aids include taped textbooks, tape recorders, typewriters. Services include alternative exam arrangements, notetakers, advocacy.

Counseling Services Individual counseling available.

Contact Dr. Donald P. Wakefield, Director, Disabled Student Services, Indiana University–Purdue University at Indianapolis, 419 North Blackford Street, Indianapolis, IN 46202, 317-264-2548.

JOHNS HOPKINS UNIVERSITY
Baltimore, Maryland

Year Program Began	*Not reported*	Special Courses	
Special Fee	None	Taped Textbooks	
Special Orientation	✓	Alternative Exam Arrangements	✓
Diagnostic Testing		Notetakers	
Subject-Area Tutoring	✓	Staff	*Not reported*
Basic Skills Remediation		Number of Students Served	*Not reported*

General Information Independent coed university. Founded 1876. Awards B, M, D. Institutionally accredited by regional association; programs accredited by ABET (engineering and technology). Metropolitan setting; 140-acre barrier-free campus. Total enrollment: 3,397. Faculty: 398 (323 full-time, 75 part-time); 95% have doctoral degrees; graduate assistants teach a few undergraduate courses. Calendar: 4-1-4. Grading system: letters or numbers. Library holdings: 1.9 million bound volumes, 1.2 million titles on microform, 10,699 periodical subscriptions, 6,655 records/tapes.

Undergraduate Profile Fall 1984: 2,374 undergraduates (635 freshmen) from 52 states and territories; 0% part-time; 23% state residents; 5% transfers; 70% financial aid recipients; 35% women; 4% blacks; 0% Native Americans; 2% Hispanics; 10% Asian Americans; 7% foreign nationals; 0% of undergraduates over 25 years of age; 5 legally handicapped students.

Expenses (1985–86) Comprehensive fee of $13,300 includes full-time tuition ($9400) and college room and board ($3900). Tuition prepayment plan available.

Financial Aid Fall 1984 full-time freshmen: 74% applied for aid, 94% of those were judged to have need, 100% of those were aided; the average aided freshman received an aid package worth $4669 (64% scholarships/grants, 36% self-help) meeting 100% of need. College-administered aid for all 1984–85 undergraduates: 1,100 need-based scholarships (average $3800); 100 non-need scholarships (average $4000); short-term loans (average $300); low-interest long-term loans from college funds (average $1500), from external sources (average $1250); SEOG; College Work-Study; 900 part-time jobs. Supporting data: FAF, IRS, state form, institutional form, AFSA/SAR required. Application deadline: 2/1.

Athletics Member NCAA (Division III). Intercollegiate sports: baseball/softball M(III); basketball M(III), W(III); crew M(c), W(c); cross-country running M(III), W(III); fencing M(III), W(III); field hockey W(III); football M(III); golf M(III), W(III); lacrosse M(I), W(III); soccer M(III); squash W; swimming and diving M(III), W(III); tennis M(III), W(III); track and field M(III), W(III); water polo M(III); wrestling M(III). Intramural sports: baseball/softball, basketball, cross-country running, football, lacrosse, martial arts, riflery, sailing, soccer, squash, swimming and diving, tennis, track and field, volleyball.

Majors Anthropology B; art history B; astrophysics B; behavioral sciences B; biology/biological sciences B; biomedical engineering B; biophysics B; chemical engineering B; chemistry B; civil engineering B; classics B; computer science B; creative writing B; earth science B; economics B; electrical engineering B; engineering mechanics B; English B; environmental engineering B; French B; geography B; German B; history B; history of science B; humanities B; international studies B; Italian B; materials engineering B; materials sciences B; mathematics B; mechanical engineering B; Near and Middle Eastern studies B; philosophy B; physics B; planetary and space sciences B; political science/government B; psychology B; sociology B; Spanish B. Majors with highest enrollment: biology/biological sciences, chemistry, political science/government.

LD Program Information

Name of Program Not specified.

Availability of Services Services provided to freshmen, sophomores, juniors, seniors.

Admissions LD applicants evaluated on the basis of high school transcript and grade point average, standard or untimed SAT or ACT, letters of recommendation, 3 Achievement Tests, essay; autobiographical statement recommended. LD students may begin taking classes in fall only. Application should be submitted 1 year in advance of initial anticipated enrollment.

Orientation Optional orientation offered before registration.

Housing College housing (including coed) available. LD students housed randomly. LD freshmen required to live on campus.

Tutoring Offered one-to-one by peer tutors. Available in all subjects. LD students may receive tutoring in all courses each term.

Academic Advisement Help with program planning provided by academic advisers. LD students may take up to 12 credits, plus as many more as individual can handle, each semester; 12 credits required to maintain full-time status.

Auxiliary Aids and Services Aids include Kurzweil reading machine. Services include alternative exam arrangements.

Counseling Services Individual counseling, career counseling available.

Contact Mrs. Martha Roseman, Assistant Dean for Academic Studies, Johns Hopkins University, 122 Merryman Hall, Baltimore, MD 21218, 301-335-8216.

JOHNSON STATE COLLEGE
Johnson, Vermont

Year Program Began	*Not reported*	Special Courses	✓
Special Fee	None	Taped Textbooks	✓
Special Orientation	✓	Alternative Exam Arrangements	✓
Diagnostic Testing	✓	Notetakers	✓
Subject-Area Tutoring	✓	Staff	3 full-time, 2 part-time
Basic Skills Remediation	✓	Number of Students Served	36

General Information State-supported comprehensive coed institution. Part of Vermont State Colleges System. Founded 1828. Awards A (college transfer and terminal), B, M. Institutionally accredited by regional association. Rural setting, with easy access to Montreal; 500-acre campus. Total enrollment: 1,349. Faculty: 101 (74 full-time, 27 part-time); 82% have doctoral degrees; graduate assistants teach a few undergraduate courses. Calendar: semesters. Grading system: letters or numbers. Library holdings: 96,000 bound volumes, 6,750 titles on microform, 600 periodical subscriptions, 1,468 records/tapes.

Undergraduate Profile Fall 1984: 970 undergraduates (308 freshmen) from 24 states and territories and 10 foreign countries; 16% part-time; 65% state residents; 38% transfers; 87% financial aid recipients; 50% women; 1% blacks; 1% Native Americans; 1% Hispanics; 1% Asian Americans; 1% foreign nationals; 4% of undergraduates over 25 years of age; 11 legally handicapped students.

Expenses (1985–86) State resident tuition: $1802 full-time, $75 per credit part-time. Nonresident tuition: $4114 full-time, $171 per credit part-time. Tuition for nonresidents who are eligible for the New England Board of Higher Education Program: $2252 full-time, $94 per credit part-time. Mandatory fees: $335. College room and board: $3042. College room only: $1622.

Financial Aid Fall 1984 full-time freshmen: 76% applied for aid, 71% of those were judged to have need, 80% of those were aided; the average aided freshman received an aid package worth $2711 (29% scholarships/grants, 71% self-help) meeting 41% of need. College-administered aid for all 1984–85 undergraduates: need-based scholarships; 60 non-need scholarships (average $200); low-interest long-term loans from external sources; SEOG; College Work-Study; part-time jobs. Supporting data: FFS, AFSA/SAR required; IRS, institutional form required for some; FAF acceptable. Priority application deadline: 4/1.

Athletics Member NCAA (Division III), NAIA. Intercollegiate sports: baseball/softball W(III); basketball M(III), W(III); cross-country running M(III), W(III); field hockey W(III); lacrosse M(c); rugby M(c), W(c); skiing (cross-country) M(II), W(II); skiing (downhill) M(II), W(II); soccer M(III), W(III); tennis M(III). Intramural sports: badminton, baseball/softball, basketball, cross-country running, golf, skiing (cross-country), skiing (downhill), tennis, volleyball.

Majors Accounting A; anthropology B; art education B; art/fine arts B; business administration/commerce/management A, B; community services B; computer information systems A, B; computer technologies A, B; creative writing B; early childhood education B; ecology/environmental studies B; education B; elementary education B; environmental sciences B; health education B; health science B; hospitality services B; hotel and restaurant management B; humanities A; human services B; management information systems B; mathematics B; music B; music education B; physical education B; political science/government B; psychology B; reading education B; recreation and leisure services B; secondary education B; sociology B; special education B; studio art B; theater arts/drama B. Majors with highest enrollment: hotel and restaurant management, business administration/commerce/management, education.

LD Program Information

Name of Program Special Services for Disadvantaged Students (PROVE).

Availability of Services Services provided to freshmen, sophomores, juniors, seniors. Program currently serves 36 LD students: 19 freshmen, 9 sophomores, 3 juniors, 5 seniors.

Staff 3 full-time, 2 part-time staff members, including director, student development coordinator, learning resource coordinator. Services provided by tutors, counselor, diagnostic specialist.

Admissions LD applicants evaluated on the basis of high school transcript and grade point average, untimed SAT or ACT, personal interview, letters of recommendation. LD students may begin taking classes in fall, spring, or summer (5-week summer program required for LD students who self-identify). Application should be submitted at least 1 month in advance of initial anticipated enrollment.

Orientation Optional orientation offered during registration.

Housing College housing (including coed) available. LD students housed randomly. LD freshmen and sophomores required to live on campus.

Diagnostic Testing Available in intelligence, reading, math, written language, perceptual skills, work and study habits.

Tutoring Offered one-to-one and in small groups by professional teachers, peer tutors. Available in all subjects. LD students may receive tutoring in all courses each term.

Basic Skills Remediation Offered one-to-one and in small groups by regular teachers, Special Services staff. Available in reading, math, spelling, written language, learning strategies, work and study habits.

Academic Advisement Help with program planning provided by LD staff members, academic advisers. LD students may take up to 17 credits each semester; most take 12 to 15 credits; 12 credits required to maintain full-time status.

Special Courses Offered in college survival skills, reading, vocabulary development, composition, math, study skills, career planning. Some offered for credit; some enter into overall grade point average.

Auxiliary Aids and Services Aids include taped textbooks, tape recorders, typewriters, word processors. Services include alternative exam arrangements, notetakers, advocacy.

Counseling Services Individual counseling, small-group counseling, career counseling available.

Contact Ms. Susan Davidson, Director of Special Services, Johnson State College, Johnson, VT 05656, 802-635-2356 Ext. 342.

KANSAS CITY ART INSTITUTE
Kansas City, Missouri

Year Program Began	1983	Special Courses	✓
Special Fee	Varies	Taped Textbooks	✓
Special Orientation		Alternative Exam Arrangements	✓
Diagnostic Testing	✓	Notetakers	
Subject-Area Tutoring	✓	Staff	2 part-time
Basic Skills Remediation	✓	Number of Students Served	10

General Information Independent 4-year specialized coed college. Founded 1885. Awards B. Institutionally accredited by regional association; programs accredited by NASAD (art and design). Metropolitan setting; 15-acre campus. Total enrollment: 474. Faculty: 48 (41 full-time, 7 part-time). Calendar: semesters. Grading system: letters or numbers. Library holdings: 32,000 bound volumes, 115 periodical subscriptions.

Undergraduate Profile Fall 1984: 474 undergraduates (168 freshmen) from 38 states and territories and 3 foreign countries; 8% part-time; 32% state residents; 50% transfers; 60% financial aid recipients; 49% women; 4% blacks; 1% Native Americans; 2% Hispanics; 1% Asian Americans; 1% foreign nationals; 22% of undergraduates over 25 years of age; 4 legally handicapped students.

Expenses (1985–86) Tuition: $7210 full-time, $280 per semester hour part-time. College room only: $1400.

Financial Aid Fall 1984 full-time freshmen: 74% applied for aid, 87% of those were judged to have need, 100% of those were aided; the average aided freshman received an aid package worth $8276 (47% scholarships/grants, 53% self-help) meeting 85% of need. College-administered aid for all 1984–85 undergraduates: 220 need-based scholarships (average $1674); 24 non-need scholarships (average $2000); short-term loans (average $100); low-interest long-term loans from college funds (average $1000), from external sources (average $2500); SEOG; College Work-Study; 20 part-time jobs. Supporting data: FAF, IRS, institutional form required. Priority application deadline: 2/15.

Majors Applied art B; art/fine arts B; ceramic art and design B; commercial art B; drafting and design B; environmental design B; graphic arts B; illustration B; industrial design B; painting/drawing B; photography B; sculpture B; studio art B; textile arts B.

LD Program Information

Name of Program Not specified.

Availability of Services Began offering services in 1983. Services provided to freshmen, sophomores, juniors, seniors. Program currently serves 10 LD students: 5 freshmen, 4 juniors, 1 senior.

Fees $12 to $20 per hour for tutoring.

Staff 2 part-time staff members, including dean of students. Services provided by tutors.

Admissions LD applicants evaluated on the basis of high school transcript and grade point average, standard SAT, autobiographical statement, portfolio of art work; personal interview recommended. LD students may begin taking classes in fall or spring. Application should be submitted 6 to 8 months in advance of initial anticipated enrollment.

Housing College housing (including coed) available. LD students not required to live on campus.

Diagnostic Testing Available in reading, spelling, written language, perceptual skills.

Tutoring Offered one-to-one by professional teachers, peer tutors. Available in all subjects. LD students may receive tutoring in all courses each term.

Basic Skills Remediation Offered in small groups by regular teachers. Available in spelling, written language, learning strategies, work and study habits.

Academic Advisement Help with program planning provided by academic advisers. LD students may take up to 18 semester hours each semester; most take 12 to 15 semester hours; 12 semester hours required to maintain full-time status.

Special Courses Offered in college survival skills, study skills, career planning. Some offered for credit; some enter into overall grade point average.

Auxiliary Aids and Services Aids include taped textbooks, tape recorders. Services include alternative exam arrangements, taping of lectures.

Counseling Services Individual counseling, career counseling available.

Contact Ms. Pamela A. Hoelzel, Dean of Students, Kansas City Art Institute, 4415 Warwick Boulevard, Kansas City, MO 64111, 816-561-4852.

KANSAS STATE UNIVERSITY
Manhattan, Kansas

Year Program Began	1978	Special Courses	✓
Special Fee	None	Taped Textbooks	✓
Special Orientation		Alternative Exam Arrangements	✓
Diagnostic Testing	✓	Notetakers	✓
Subject-Area Tutoring	✓	Staff	3 part-time
Basic Skills Remediation	✓	Number of Students Served	15

General Information State-supported coed university. Founded 1863. Awards A (college transfer), B, M, D. Institutionally accredited by regional association; programs accredited by NAAB (architecture), AACSB (business), ABET (engineering and technology), FIDER (interior design), NASM (music), NCATE (teacher education). Small-town setting; 668-acre campus. Total enrollment: 18,089. Faculty: 1,544 (all full-time); 75% have doctoral degrees; graduate assistants teach a few undergraduate courses. Calendar: semesters. Grading system: letters or numbers and pass/fail. Library holdings: 1.5 million bound volumes, 12,000 periodical subscriptions.

Undergraduate Profile Fall 1984: 14,076 undergraduates (3,898 freshmen) from 52 states and territories and 72 foreign countries; 5% part-time; 85% state residents; 33% transfers; 60% financial aid recipients; 45% women; 3% blacks; 1% Native Americans; 2% Hispanics; 1% Asian Americans; 4% foreign nationals; 17% of undergraduates over 25 years of age; 50 legally handicapped students.

Expenses (1985–86) State resident tuition: $1251 full-time. Nonresident tuition: $3055 full-time. Part-time tuition and fees per semester (1 to 6 semester hours) range from $68.50 to $233.50 for state residents, $128.50 to $593 for nonresidents. College room and board: $1980.

Financial Aid Fall 1984 full-time freshmen: the average aided freshman received an aid package meeting 70% of need. College-administered aid for all 1984–85 undergraduates: 1,000 need-based scholarships (average $1500); 2,000 non-need scholarships (average $1000); short-term loans; low-interest long-term loans from external sources (average $1500); SEOG; College Work-Study; part-time jobs. Supporting data: FFS, institutional form, AFSA/SAR required; IRS, state form required for some; FAF acceptable. Priority application deadline: 3/15.

Athletics Member NCAA (Division I). Intercollegiate sports: baseball/softball M(I,s), W(I,s); basketball M(I,s), W(I,s); cross-country running M(I,s), W(I,s); football M(I-A,s); golf M(I,s), W(I,s); tennis M(I,s), W(I,s); track and field M(I,s), W(I,s); volleyball W(I,s). Intramural sports: baseball/softball, basketball, bowling, crew, cross-country running, equestrian sports, football, golf, martial arts, racquetball, riflery, rugby, soccer, swimming and diving, tennis, track and field, volleyball, water polo, wrestling.

Majors Accounting B; adult and continuing education B; advertising B; agricultural business B; agricultural economics B; agricultural education B; agricultural engineering B; agricultural sciences B; agronomy/soil and crop sciences B; animal sciences B; anthropology B; applied art B; architectural engineering B; architecture B; art education B; art/fine arts B; Asian/Oriental studies B; biochemistry B; biology/biological sciences B; botany/plant sciences B; broadcasting B; business administration/commerce/management A, B; business education B; ceramic art and design B; chemical engineering B; chemical engineering technology B; chemistry B; child care/child and family studies B; child psychology/child development B; civil engineering B; civil engineering technology B; commercial art B; communication B; community services B; computer engineering B; computer information systems B; computer programming B; computer science B; computer technologies B; conservation B; construction engineering B; construction management B; dairy sciences B; dance B; (pre)dentistry sequence B; dietetics B; early childhood education B; earth science B; economics B; education B; electrical engineering B; electrical engineering technology B; electronics engineering B; elementary education B; engineering (general) B; engineering technology B; English B; environmental engineering technology B; family and consumer studies B; farm and ranch management B; fashion merchandising B; finance/banking B; fish and game management B; food sciences B; food services management B; food services technology B; French B; geography B; geology B; geophysics B; German B; Germanic languages and literature B; health education B; health science B; history B; home economics B; home economics education B; horticulture B; hotel and restaurant management B; humanities A; industrial engineering B; industrial engineering technology B; interior design B; journalism B; landscape architecture/design B; (pre)law sequence B; liberal arts/general studies A, B; literature B; marketing/retailing/merchandising B; mathematics B; mechanical engineering B; mechanical engineering technology B; medical technology B; (pre)medicine sequence B; microbiology B; modern languages B; music B; music education B; natural resource management B; nuclear engineering B; nutrition B; painting/drawing B; parks management B; philosophy B; physical education B; physical sciences A; physical therapy B; physics B; physiology B; political science/government B; poultry sciences B; psychology B; public relations B; radio and television studies B; range management B; recreation and leisure services B; rehabilitation therapy B; science B; science education B; secondary education B; social science B; social work B; sociology B; Southeast Asian studies B; Spanish B; special education B; speech pathology and audiology B; speech/rhetoric/public address/debate B; speech therapy B; statistics B; studio art B; technical writing B; textiles and clothing B; theater arts/drama B; (pre)veterinary medicine sequence B; veterinary sciences B; vocational education B; wildlife biology B; women's studies B. Majors with highest enrollment: business administration/commerce/management, accounting, electrical engineering.

LD Program Information

Name of Program Services for Students with Physical Limitations.

Availability of Services Began offering services in 1978. Services provided to freshmen, sophomores, juniors, seniors. Program currently serves 15 LD students.

Staff 3 part-time staff members, including coordinator. Services provided by tutors, mathematics coordinator, supervisor of tutorial program.

Admissions LD applicants evaluated on the basis of high school transcript and grade point average; personal interview, autobiographical statement, letters of recommendation, psychoeducational report recommended; standard or untimed SAT or ACT required for some. Open admissions for state residents. LD students may begin taking classes in fall, spring, or summer. Application should be submitted 2 to 3 months in advance of initial anticipated enrollment.

Housing College housing (including coed) available. LD students housed randomly. LD students not required to live on campus.

Diagnostic Testing Available in intelligence, reading, math, work and study habits, personality, special administrations of ACT.

Tutoring Offered one-to-one and in small groups by peer tutors. Available in all subjects. LD students may receive tutoring in all courses each term.

Basic Skills Remediation Offered one-to-one and in small groups by regular teachers, teacher trainees. Available in reading, math, written language, learning strategies, work and study habits, speech.

Academic Advisement Help with program planning provided by LD staff members, academic advisers. LD students may take up to 12 semester hours, plus as many more as individual can handle, each semester; most take 12 to 15 semester hours; 12 semester hours required to maintain full-time status.

Special Courses Offered in college survival skills, reading, vocabulary development, composition, math, study skills, career planning. Some offered for credit; some enter into overall grade point average.

Auxiliary Aids and Services Aids include taped textbooks, tape recorders, calculators, word processors, Kurzweil reading machine. Services include alternative exam arrangements, notetakers, advocacy, typing services.

Counseling Services Individual counseling, rap sessions, career counseling available.

Contact Ms. Gretchen Holden, Coordinator, Services for Students with Physical Limitations, Kansas State University, Holton Hall, Room 101, Manhattan, KS 66506, 913-532-6441.

KENT STATE UNIVERSITY

Kent, Ohio

Year Program Began	1964	Special Courses	✓
Special Fee	Varies	Taped Textbooks	✓
Special Orientation	✓	Alternative Exam Arrangements	✓
Diagnostic Testing	✓	Notetakers	✓
Subject-Area Tutoring	✓	Staff	2 part-time
Basic Skills Remediation	✓	Number of Students Served	20 to 25

General Information State-supported coed university. Part of Kent State University System. Founded 1910. Awards B, M, D. Institutionally accredited by regional association; programs accredited by NAAB (architecture), NASAD (art and design), AACSB (business), ABET (engineering and technology), NASM (music), NLN (nursing), NCATE (teacher education). Small-town setting, with easy access to Cleveland; 1,200-acre barrier-free campus. Total enrollment: 20,066. Faculty: 1,035 (739 full-time, 296 part-time); 70% have doctoral degrees; graduate assistants teach a few undergraduate courses. Calendar: semesters. Grading system: letters or numbers. Library holdings: 1.5 million bound volumes, 900,000 titles on microform, 8,700 periodical subscriptions.

Undergraduate Profile Fall 1984: 16,165 undergraduates (3,253 freshmen) from 39 states and territories and 67 foreign countries; 17% part-time; 92% state residents; 35% transfers; 62% financial aid recipients; 55% women; 6% blacks; 1% Hispanics; 1% Asian Americans; 3% foreign nationals; 8% of undergraduates over 25 years of age.

Expenses (1985–86) State resident tuition: $2104 full-time. Nonresident tuition: $3704 full-time. Part-time tuition and fees per semester (1 to 11 semester hours) range from $102 to $972 for state residents, $172 to $1742 for nonresidents. College room and board: $2396. College room only: $1432. Tuition prepayment plan available.

Financial Aid Fall 1984 full-time freshmen: 80% applied for aid, 94% of those were judged to have need, 94% of those were aided; the average aided freshman received an aid package worth $2048 (33% scholarships/grants, 67% self-help) meeting 85% of need. College-administered aid for all 1984–85 undergraduates: 1,181 need-based scholarships (average $447); 1,640 non-need scholarships (average $915); short-term loans (average $200); low-interest long-term loans from external sources (average $2000); SEOG; College Work-Study; 1,800 part-time jobs. Supporting data: state form, institutional form, AFSA/SAR required; IRS required for some; FFS, FAF, CFS acceptable. Application deadline: continuous to 5/1.

Athletics Member NCAA (Division I). Intercollegiate sports: baseball/softball M(I,s), W(I,s); basketball M(I,s), W(I,s); field hockey W(I,s); football M(I-A,s); golf M(I,s); gymnastics M(I,s), W(I,s); ice hockey M(I,s); swimming and diving M(I,s), W(I,s); track and field M(I,s), W(I,s); volleyball W(I,s); wrestling M(I,s). Intramural sports: archery, badminton, baseball/softball, basketball, bowling, fencing, football, golf, gymnastics, ice hockey, lacrosse, martial arts, racquetball, rugby, sailing, skiing (cross-country), skiing (downhill), soccer, swimming and diving, tennis, track and field, volleyball, water polo, weight lifting, wrestling.

Majors Accounting B; advertising B; aerospace sciences B; American studies B; anthropology B; applied art B; applied mathematics B; architecture B; art education B; art/fine arts B; art history B; aviation administration B; aviation technology B; biology/biological sciences B; black/Afro-American studies B; botany/plant sciences B; broadcasting B; business administration/commerce/management B; business economics B; business education B; ceramic art and design B; chemistry B; child care/child and family studies B; classics B; commercial art B; communication B; computer programming B; computer science B; computer technologies B; conservation B; consumer services B; corrections B; criminal justice B; dance B; (pre) dentistry sequence B; dietetics B; early childhood education B; earth science B; East European and Soviet studies B; economics B; education B; electrical and electronics technologies B; elementary education B; engineering technology B; English B; ethnic studies B; family services B; fashion design and technology B; fashion merchandising B; finance/banking B; flight training B; food services management B; French B; geography B; geology B; German B; gerontology B; graphic arts B; health education B; history B; home economics B; home economics education B; humanities B; human resources B; illustration B; industrial administration B; industrial arts B; industrial design B; industrial engineering technology B; interdisciplinary studies B; interior design B; journalism B; labor and industrial relations B; Latin B; Latin American studies B; law enforcement/police sciences B; (pre)law sequence B; liberal arts/general studies B; manufacturing technology B; marketing/retailing/merchandising B; mathematics B; medical technology B; (pre)medicine sequence B; music B; music education B; music history B; natural resource management B; nursing B; nutrition B; peace studies B; philosophy B; photography B; physical education B; physics B; political science/government B; printing technologies B; psychology B; public relations B; real estate B; recreation and leisure services B; Russian B; science B; science education B; secondary education B; secretarial studies/office management B; sociology B; Spanish B; special education B; speech pathology and audiology B; speech/rhetoric/public address/debate B; speech therapy B; studio art B; telecommunications B; theater arts/drama B; transportation engineering B; (pre) veterinary medicine sequence B; vocational education B; voice B; wildlife management B; wind and percussion instruments B; zoology B. Majors with highest enrollment: nursing, mathematics, psychology.

LD Program Information

Name of Program Disabled Student Services.

Availability of Services Began offering services in 1964. Services provided to freshmen, sophomores, juniors, seniors. Program currently serves 20 to 25 LD students.

Fees Rates for individually arranged tutoring negotiated by students themselves.

Staff 2 part-time staff members, including coordinator. Services provided by counselors.

Admissions LD applicants evaluated on the basis of high school transcript, standard or untimed SAT or ACT; psychoeducational report, medical certification recommended. LD students may begin taking classes in fall, spring, or summer. Application should be submitted 6 months in advance of initial anticipated enrollment.

Orientation Optional orientation offered before registration.

Housing College housing (including coed) available. LD students housed randomly. LD freshmen and sophomores required to live on campus except for veterans, or if 21 or over, living with relatives, married, or living in a sorority or fraternity.

Diagnostic Testing Available in intelligence, reading, math, spelling, written language, work and study habits, personality.

Tutoring Offered one-to-one by professional teachers, peer tutors. Available in most subjects. LD students may receive tutoring in all courses each term.

Basic Skills Remediation Offered one-to-one and in small groups by regular teachers. Available in reading, math, written language.

Academic Advisement Help with program planning provided by LD staff members, academic advisers. LD students may take up to 18 semester hours each semester; 12 semester hours required to maintain full-time status.

Special Courses Offered in college survival skills, communication skills, composition, math, study skills, career planning. Some offered for credit; some enter into overall grade point average.

Auxiliary Aids and Services Aids include taped textbooks, tape recorders. Services include alternative exam arrangements, notetakers, advocacy.

Counseling Services Individual counseling, small-group counseling, rap sessions, career counseling available.

Contact Ms. Joanna M. Gartner, Coordinator, Disabled Student Services, Kent State University, Kent, OH 44242, 216-672-3391.

LEE COLLEGE
Cleveland, Tennessee

Year Program Began	1979	Special Courses	✓
Special Fee	None	Taped Textbooks	✓
Special Orientation	✓	Alternative Exam Arrangements	✓
Diagnostic Testing	✓	Notetakers	
Subject-Area Tutoring	✓	Staff	5 full-time, 1 part-time
Basic Skills Remediation	✓	Number of Students Served	*Not reported*

General Information 4-year coed college, affiliated with Church of God. Founded 1918. Awards B. Institutionally accredited by regional association. Small-town setting; 22-acre campus. Total enrollment: 1,154. Faculty: 70 (60 full-time, 10 part-time); 75% have doctoral degrees; graduate assistants teach a few undergraduate courses. Calendar: semesters. Grading system: letters or numbers.

Undergraduate Profile Fall 1984: 1,154 undergraduates (467 freshmen) from 40 states and territories; 6% part-time; 16% state residents; 24% transfers; 80% financial aid recipients; 50% women; 7% blacks; 6% Hispanics; 4% foreign nationals; 10% of undergraduates over 25 years of age; 3 legally handicapped students.

Expenses (1985–86) Comprehensive fee of $5654 includes full-time tuition ($3520), mandatory fees ($300), and college room and board ($1834). College room only: $754. Part-time tuition: $110 per semester hour.

Financial Aid Fall 1984 full-time freshmen: 70% applied for aid, 86% of those were judged to have need, 70% of those were aided; the average aided freshman received an aid package worth $3494 (34% scholarships/grants, 66% self-help) meeting 71% of need. College-administered aid for all 1984–85 undergraduates: need-based scholarships (average $200); non-need scholarships (average $1800); low-interest long-term loans; part-time jobs. Supporting data: FAF, institutional form required; AFSA/SAR acceptable. Priority application deadline: 4/1.

Athletics Intercollegiate sports: baseball/softball M(s), W(s); basketball M(s), W(s); golf M(s); tennis M(s), W(s). Intramural sports: baseball/softball, basketball, golf, soccer, tennis.

Majors Accounting B; biblical studies B; biology/biological sciences B; business administration/commerce/management B; business education B; chemistry B; communication B; education B; elementary education B; English B; French B; health education B; history B; mathematics B; medical technology B; music B; music education B; natural sciences B; physical education B; piano/organ B; psychology B; religious education B; social science B; social work B; sociology B; Spanish B; special education B; voice B. Majors with highest enrollment: business administration/commerce/management, biblical studies, education.

LD Program Information

Name of Program Special Services Center.

Availability of Services Began offering services in 1979. Services provided to freshmen, sophomores, juniors, seniors.

Staff 5 full-time, 1 part-time staff members, including director, assistant director. Services provided by tutors, counselors, reading specialist, math specialist, tutoring coordinator.

Admissions LD applicants evaluated on the basis of high school transcript and grade point average, standard or untimed SAT or ACT, personal interview, letters of recommendation. LD students may begin taking classes in fall, spring, or summer. Application should be submitted at least 5 months in advance of initial anticipated enrollment.

Orientation Optional orientation offered before registration.

Housing College housing available. LD students housed with other LD students and non-LD students. LD freshmen, sophomores, and juniors required to live on campus except for veterans, or if married, living with relatives, or by special permission.

Diagnostic Testing Available in intelligence, reading, math, spelling, work and study habits, personality, speech.

Tutoring Offered one-to-one and in small groups by professional teachers, peer tutors. Available in all subjects. LD students may receive tutoring in all courses each term.

Basic Skills Remediation Offered one-to-one and in small groups by LD teachers. Available in reading, math, work and study habits, speech.

Academic Advisement Help with program planning provided by LD staff members, academic advisers. LD students may take up to 17 semester hours each semester; most take 9 to 12 semester hours; 12 semester hours required to maintain full-time status.

Special Courses Offered in college survival skills, reading, vocabulary development, communication skills, language development, math, study skills, career planning. Most offered for credit; most enter into overall grade point average.

Auxiliary Aids and Services Aids include taped textbooks, tape recorders, specialized taped programs, filmstrips, computers. Services include alternative exam arrangements, readers.

Counseling Services Individual counseling, small-group counseling, rap sessions, career counseling available.

Contact Ms. Lucille Walker, Director, Special Services Center, Lee College, 1489 Church Street, Cleveland, TN 37311, 615-472-2111 Ext. 375.

LOCK HAVEN UNIVERSITY OF PENNSYLVANIA

Lock Haven, Pennsylvania

Year Program Began	1981	Special Courses	✓
Special Fee	None	Taped Textbooks	✓
Special Orientation		Alternative Exam Arrangements	✓
Diagnostic Testing	✓	Notetakers	✓
Subject-Area Tutoring	✓	Staff	5 part-time
Basic Skills Remediation	✓	Number of Students Served	4

General Information State-supported 4-year coed college. Part of State System of Higher Education. Founded 1870. Awards B. Institutionally accredited by regional association; programs accredited by NCATE (teacher education). Small-town setting; 135-acre barrier-free campus. Total enrollment: 2,624. Faculty: 170 (166 full-time, 4 part-time); 47% have doctoral degrees. Calendar: semesters. Grading system: letters or numbers. Library holdings: 304,000 bound volumes, 12,306 titles on microform, 1,238 periodical subscriptions, 2,824 records/tapes.

Undergraduate Profile Fall 1984: 2,624 undergraduates (596 freshmen) from 20 states and territories and 34 foreign countries; 4% part-time; 81% state residents; 21% transfers; 80% financial aid recipients; 51% women; 3% blacks; 1% Native Americans; 1% Hispanics; 1% Asian Americans; 2% foreign nationals; 6% of undergraduates over 25 years of age; 50 legally handicapped students.

Expenses (1984–85) State resident tuition: $1570 full-time, $66 per credit part-time. Nonresident tuition: $2748 full-time, $115 per credit part-time. Mandatory fees: $105. College room and board: $1726.

Financial Aid Fall 1984 full-time freshmen: 92% applied for aid, 87% of those were judged to have need, 100% of those were aided; the average aided freshman received an aid package worth $2267 (42% scholarships/grants, 58% self-help) meeting 90% of need. College-administered aid for all 1984–85 undergraduates: 1,000 need-based scholarships (average $900); 100 non-need scholarships (average $200); low-interest long-term loans from external sources (average $1500); SEOG; College Work-Study; 325 part-time jobs. Supporting data: state form, institutional form required; FAF, AFSA/SAR required for some. Priority application deadline: 4/15.

Athletics Member NCAA (Division II). Intercollegiate sports: baseball/softball M(II), W(II); basketball M(II,s), W(II,s); cross-country running M(II), W(II); field hockey W(I,s); football M(II,s); golf M(II); gymnastics W(II); lacrosse W(II); soccer M(II); swimming and diving W(II); tennis M(II), W(II); track and field M(II), W(II); wrestling M(I,s). Intramural sports: badminton, baseball/softball, basketball, cross-country running, field hockey, football, golf, ice hockey, lacrosse, martial arts, racquetball, skiing (cross-country), skiing (downhill), soccer, tennis, track and field, volleyball, weight lifting, wrestling.

Majors Anthropology B; art/fine arts B; biochemistry B; biology/biological sciences B; chemistry B; communication B; computer science B; (pre)dentistry sequence B; early childhood education B; earth science B; economics B; elementary education B; English B; environmental biology B; French B; geography B; German B; health education B; history B; humanities B; international studies B; journalism B; Latin American studies B; (pre)law sequence B; liberal arts/general studies B; library science B; mathematics B; medical technology B; (pre)medicine sequence B; music B; natural sciences B; operations research B; philosophy B; physical education B; physics B; political science/government B; psychology B; radio and television studies B; secondary education B; social science B; social work B; sociology B; Spanish B; special education B; speech/rhetoric/public address/debate B; theater arts/drama B; (pre)veterinary medicine sequence B. Majors with highest enrollment: physical education, computer science, elementary education.

LD Program Information

Name of Program Office for Students with Disabling Conditions.

Availability of Services Began offering services in 1981. Services provided to freshmen, sophomores, juniors, seniors. Program currently serves 4 LD students: 1 freshman, 1 sophomore, 1 junior, 1 senior.

Staff 5 part-time staff members, including director. Services provided by math specialist, writing specialist, tutorial coordinator, counseling psychologist.

Admissions LD applicants evaluated on the basis of high school transcript and grade point average, standard or untimed SAT or ACT, personal interview, autobiographical statement, letters of recommendation. LD students may begin taking classes in fall, spring, or summer. Application should be submitted 3 months in advance of initial anticipated enrollment.

Housing College housing (including coed) available. LD students housed randomly. LD students not required to live on campus.

Diagnostic Testing Available in intelligence, reading, math, written language, work and study habits, personality.

Tutoring Offered one-to-one and in small groups by professional teachers, peer tutors. Available in all subjects. LD students may receive tutoring in all courses each term.

Basic Skills Remediation Offered one-to-one and in small groups by regular teachers, peer teachers. Available in reading, math, written language, learning strategies, work and study habits, speech.

Academic Advisement Help with program planning provided by LD staff members, academic advisers. LD students may take up to 18 credits each semester; most take 12 to 15 credits; 12 credits required to maintain full-time status.

Special Courses Offered in reading, composition, math. All offered for credit; all enter into overall grade point average.

Auxiliary Aids and Services Aids include taped textbooks, tape recorders. Requests for other aids are reviewed on an individual basis. Services include alternative exam arrangements, notetakers, advocacy.

Counseling Services Individual counseling, career counseling, peer counseling available.

Contact Mr. Bruce D. Skolnick, Director, Office for Students with Disabling Conditions, Lock Haven University of Pennsylvania, G-6, Smith Hall, Lock Haven, PA 17745, 717-893-2324.

LONG ISLAND UNIVERSITY, BROOKLYN CAMPUS

Brooklyn, New York

Year Program Began	1975	Special Courses	✓
Special Fee	None	Taped Textbooks	✓
Special Orientation	✓	Alternative Exam Arrangements	✓
Diagnostic Testing	✓	Notetakers	✓
Subject-Area Tutoring	✓	Staff	9 part-time
Basic Skills Remediation	✓	Number of Students Served	11

General Information Independent coed university. Part of Long Island University. Founded 1926. Awards A (college transfer), B, M, D. Institutionally accredited by regional association; programs accredited by ACPE (pharmacy). Metropolitan setting; 23-acre campus. Total enrollment: 5,795. Faculty: 406; 90% have doctoral degrees; graduate assistants teach a few undergraduate courses. Calendar: semesters. Grading system: letters or numbers. Library holdings: 341,000 bound volumes, 1,300 periodical subscriptions.

Undergraduate Profile Fall 1984: 4,003 undergraduates (1,066 freshmen); 21% part-time; 90% state residents; 3% transfers; 55% women; 0% Native Americans; 7% foreign nationals; 36 legally handicapped students.

Expenses (1985–86) Comprehensive fee of $8500 includes full-time tuition ($5400), mandatory fees ($100), and college room and board ($3000 minimum). College room only: $1600 (minimum). Part-time tuition: $180 per credit hour.

Financial Aid Fall 1984 full-time freshmen: 92% applied for aid, 82% of those were judged to have need, 100% of those were aided; the average aided freshman received an aid package worth $5349 (78% scholarships/grants, 22% self-help) meeting 86% of need. College-administered aid for all 1984–85 undergraduates: need-based scholarships; non-need scholarships; low-interest long-term loans from external sources; SEOG; College Work-Study; part-time jobs. Supporting data: FFS, FAF, IRS, institutional form required; AFSA/SAR acceptable. Priority application deadline: 5/15.

Athletics Member NCAA (Division I). Intercollegiate sports: baseball/softball M(I,s), W(II,s); basketball M(I,s), W(I,s); cross-country running M(I), W(I,s); golf M(I,s); gymnastics M(I,s), W(I,s); soccer M(I,s); tennis M(I,s); track and field W(I,s). Intramural sports: baseball/softball, football, martial arts, tennis, track and field, volleyball, wrestling.

Majors Accounting B; anthropology B; art/fine arts B; biology/biological sciences B; business administration/commerce/management B; business education B; chemistry B; clinical psychology B; communication B; computer information systems B; computer science B; criminal justice B; cytotechnology B; early childhood education B; economics B; education B; educational administration B; elementary education B; English B; finance/banking B; health science B; history B; humanities B; information science B; jazz B; journalism B; (pre)law sequence B; liberal arts/general studies A, B; marketing/retailing/merchandising B; mathematics B; medical technology B; (pre)medicine sequence B; molecular biology B; music B; nuclear medical technology B; nursing B; pharmacy/pharmaceutical sciences B; philosophy B; photography B; physical education B; physical therapy B; physician's assistant studies B; political science/government B; psychology B; radio and television studies B; respiratory therapy B; secondary education B; social science B; sociology B; special education B; speech/rhetoric/public address/debate B; theater arts/drama B. Majors with highest enrollment: health science, business administration/commerce/management.

LD Program Information

Name of Program Special Educational Services.

Availability of Services Began offering services in 1975. Services provided to freshmen, sophomores, juniors, seniors. Program currently serves 11 LD students: 3 freshmen, 4 sophomores, 4 juniors.

Staff 9 part-time staff members, including director, associate director. Services provided by remediation specialists, tutors, counselors, social workers.

Admissions LD applicants evaluated on the basis of high school transcript and grade point average, untimed SAT, personal interview, letters of recommendation, psychoeducational report. LD students may begin taking classes in fall, spring, or summer. Application should be submitted at least 6 months in advance of initial anticipated enrollment.

Orientation Optional orientation offered before registration.

Housing College housing available. LD students housed randomly. LD students not required to live on campus.

Diagnostic Testing Available in reading, math, written language.

Tutoring Offered one-to-one and in small groups by professional teachers, peer tutors. Available in all subjects. LD students may receive tutoring in all courses each term.

Basic Skills Remediation Offered in small groups by regular teachers. Available in reading, math, spelling, written language, learning strategies, work and study habits, social skills.

Academic Advisement Help with program planning provided by LD staff members, academic advisers. LD students may take up to 15 credit hours each semester; most take 6 to 12 credit hours; 12 credit hours required to maintain full-time status.

Special Courses Offered in college survival skills, reading, vocabulary development, composition, language development, math, study skills, career planning. Some offered for credit; some enter into overall grade point average.

Auxiliary Aids and Services Aids include taped textbooks, tape recorders, typewriters. Services include alternative exam arrangements, notetakers, advocacy.

Counseling Services Individual counseling, small-group counseling, rap sessions, career counseling available.

Contact Mr. Robert Nathanson, Director, Special Educational Services, Long Island University, Brooklyn Campus, University Plaza, Brooklyn, NY 11201, 718-403-1044.

LONG ISLAND UNIVERSITY, C W POST CAMPUS

Greenvale, New York

Year Program Began	Not reported
Special Fee	None
Special Orientation	
Diagnostic Testing	✓
Subject-Area Tutoring	✓
Basic Skills Remediation	
Special Courses	✓
Taped Textbooks	✓
Alternative Exam Arrangements	✓
Notetakers	✓
Staff	3 full-time, 1 part-time
Number of Students Served	45

General Information Independent comprehensive coed institution. Part of Long Island University. Founded 1954. Awards A (college transfer), B, M. Institutionally accredited by regional association; programs registered by New York State Board of Regents. Small-town setting, with easy access to New York City; 350-acre campus. Total enrollment: 12,460. Faculty: 705 (360 full-time, 345 part-time); 69% have doctoral degrees; graduate assistants teach a few undergraduate courses. Calendar: semesters. Grading system: letters or numbers. Library holdings: 960,000 bound volumes, 241,694 titles on microform, 4,636 periodical subscriptions, 18,847 records/tapes.

Undergraduate Profile Fall 1984: 7,705 undergraduates (1,323 freshmen) from 20 states and territories and 5 foreign countries; 32% part-time; 87% state residents; 50% transfers; 75% financial aid recipients; 52% women; 11% blacks; 1% Native Americans; 3% Hispanics; 2% Asian Americans; 1% foreign nationals; 13% of undergraduates over 25 years of age; 50 legally handicapped students.

Expenses (1985–86) Comprehensive fee of $9484 includes full-time tuition ($6020), mandatory fees ($390), and college room and board ($3074). College room only: $1700. Part-time tuition: $184 per credit.

Financial Aid Fall 1984 full-time freshmen: 82% applied for aid, 80% of those were judged to have need, 100% of those were aided; the average aided freshman received an aid package worth $2914 (54% scholarships/grants, 46% self-help) meeting 85% of need. College-administered aid for all 1984–85 undergraduates: 1,200 need-based scholarships (average $1333); non-need scholarships (average $1400); low-interest long-term loans from external sources; SEOG; College Work-Study; part-time jobs. Supporting data: FAF, IRS, institutional form required; state form required for some. Priority application deadline: 3/1.

Athletics Member NCAA (Division II), NAIA. Intercollegiate sports: baseball/softball M(II,s), W(II,s); basketball M(II,s), W(II,s); cross-country running M(II,s), W(II); field hockey M(II), W(II,s); football M(II); golf M(II,s); lacrosse M(I,s); soccer M(II,s); tennis M(II,s), W(II,s); track and field M(II,s); volleyball W(II,s); wrestling M(II,s). Intramural sports: baseball/softball, basketball, bowling, cross-country running, equestrian sports, field hockey, football, golf, gymnastics, ice hockey, lacrosse, soccer, tennis, track and field, volleyball, wrestling.

Majors Accounting B; American studies B; applied art B; art education B; art/fine arts B; art history B; arts administration B; art therapy B; biology/biological sciences B; broadcasting B; business administration/commerce/management B; business education B; chemistry B; communication B; computer science B; criminal justice B; (pre)dentistry sequence B; early childhood education B; earth science B; economics B; education B; elementary education B; English B; film studies B; finance/banking B; French B; geography B; geology B; German B; health education B; history B; international studies B; Italian B; journalism B; Judaic studies B; Latin American studies B; (pre)law sequence B; liberal arts/general studies A; marketing/retailing/merchandising B; mathematics B; medical technology B; (pre)medicine sequence B; music B; music education B; music therapy B; nuclear medical technology B; nursing B; pharmacy/pharmaceutical sciences B; philosophy B; photography B; physical education B; physics B; political science/government B; psychology B; public administration B; radiological technology B; Russian and Slavic studies B; secondary education B; sociology B; Spanish B; special education B; studio art B; theater arts/drama B; (pre)veterinary medicine sequence B. Majors with highest enrollment: business administration/commerce/management, accounting, elementary education.

LD Program Information

Name of Program Special Services.

Availability of Services Services provided to freshmen, sophomores, juniors, seniors. Program currently serves 45 LD students: 16 freshmen, 16 sophomores, 8 juniors, 5 seniors.

Staff 3 full-time, 1 part-time staff members, including director, assistant director. Services provided by tutors, graduate assistant coordinator for readers and notetakers, language arts specialist.

Admissions LD applicants evaluated on the basis of high school transcript and grade point average, standard or untimed SAT or ACT, personal interview, autobiographical statement, letters of recommendation, psychoeducational report. LD students may begin taking classes in fall or spring. Application should be submitted 10 months in advance of initial anticipated enrollment.

Housing College housing (including coed) available. LD students housed randomly. LD students not required to live on campus.

Diagnostic Testing Available in various areas as appropriate.

Tutoring Offered one-to-one and in small groups by professional teachers, peer tutors, language arts specialist. Available in all subjects. LD students may receive tutoring in all courses each term.

Academic Advisement Help with program planning provided by LD staff members, academic advisers. LD students may take up to 15 credits, plus as many more as individual can handle, each semester; most take 12 to 15 credits (some freshmen limited to 12); 12 credits required to maintain full-time status.

Special Courses Offered in reading, vocabulary development, math, study skills. All offered for credit; all enter into overall grade point average.

Auxiliary Aids and Services Aids include taped textbooks, tape recorders, typewriters, word processors. Services include alternative exam arrangements, notetakers, advocacy, readers.

Counseling Services Individual counseling, career counseling available.

Contact Mr. James E. Boatwright, Director of Special Services, Long Island University, C W Post Campus, Lower Level, Post Hall, Greenvale, NY 11548, 516-299-2241.

LOUISIANA STATE UNIVERSITY AND AGRICULTURAL AND MECHANICAL COLLEGE

Baton Rouge, Louisiana

Year Program Began	1982	Special Courses	✓
Spécial Fee	None	Taped Textbooks	✓
Special Orientation	✓	Alternative Exam Arrangements	✓
Diagnostic Testing	✓	Notetakers	✓
Subject-Area Tutoring	✓	Staff	4 part-time
Basic Skills Remediation	✓	Number of Students Served	9

General Information State-supported coed university. Part of Louisiana State University System. Founded 1860. Awards B, M, D. Institutionally accredited by regional association; programs accredited by NAAB (architecture), NASAD (art and design), AACSB (business), ABET (engineering and technology), FIDER (interior design), NASM (music), NCATE (teacher education). City setting, with easy access to New Orleans; 1,944-acre campus. Total enrollment: 29,497. Faculty: 1,282 (1,154 full-time, 128 part-time); 64% have doctoral degrees; graduate assistants teach a few undergraduate courses. Calendar: semesters. Grading system: letters or numbers. Library holdings: 2 million bound volumes, 1.5 million titles on microform, 23,193 periodical subscriptions, 9,575 records/tapes.

Undergraduate Profile Fall 1984: 24,186 undergraduates (4,762 freshmen) from 52 states and territories and 116 foreign countries; 20% part-time; 82% state residents; 9% transfers; 52% financial aid recipients; 48% women; 7% blacks; 0% Native Americans; 1% Hispanics; 0% Asian Americans; 9% foreign nationals; 22% of undergraduates over 25 years of age; 77 legally handicapped students.

Expenses (1984–85) State resident tuition: $977 full-time. Nonresident tuition: $2477 full-time. Part-time tuition per semester (1 to 11 semester hours) ranges from $135 to $367 for state residents, $195 to $975 for nonresidents. College room and board: $2350. College room only: $1200.

Financial Aid Fall 1984 full-time freshmen: 74% applied for aid, 87% of those were judged to have need, 100% of those were aided; the average aided freshman received an aid package worth $1673 (47% scholarships/grants, 53% self-help) meeting 100% of need. College-administered aid for all 1984–85 undergraduates: need-based scholarships; non-need scholarships (average $950); low-interest long-term loans; SEOG; College Work-Study; part-time jobs. Supporting data: institutional form required; FFS, FAF acceptable. Priority application deadline: 4/1.

Athletics Member NCAA (Division I). Intercollegiate sports: baseball/softball M(I,s), W(I); basketball M(I,s), W(I,s); cross-country running M(I,s); football M(I-A,s); golf M(I,s), W(I); gymnastics M(I,s), W(I,s); swimming and diving M(I,s), W(I,s); tennis M(I,s), W(I,s); track and field M(I,s), W(I,s); volleyball W(I,s); wrestling M(I,s). Intramural sports: archery, baseball/softball, basketball, fencing, football, golf, lacrosse, martial arts, rugby, soccer, swimming and diving, tennis, track and field, volleyball, water polo, wrestling.

Majors Accounting B; adult and continuing education B; advertising B; agricultural business B; agricultural economics B; agricultural engineering B; agricultural sciences B; agricultural technologies B; agronomy/soil and crop sciences B; animal sciences B; anthropology B; applied art B; architecture B; art education B; art/fine arts B; art history B; astronomy B; biochemistry B; botany/plant sciences B; broadcasting B; business administration/commerce/management B; business economics B; ceramic art and design B; chemical engineering B; chemistry B; child care/child and family studies B; civil engineering B; classics B; commercial art B; communication B; computer science B; construction technologies B; criminal justice B; cytotechnology B; dairy sciences B; dance B; dietetics B; economics B; education B; electrical engineering B; elementary education B; engineering (general) B; engineering sciences B; English B; entomology B; environmental health sciences B; fashion merchandising B; finance/banking B; fish and game management B; food sciences B; forestry B; forest technology B; French B; geography B; geology B; German B; graphic arts B; history B; home economics B; home economics education B; horticulture B; industrial arts B; industrial engineering B; industrial engineering technology B; insurance B; interior design B; international economics B; Italian B; jewelry and metalsmithing B; journalism B; labor and industrial relations B; labor studies B; landscape architecture/design B; Latin B; Latin American studies B; liberal arts/general studies B; marketing/retailing/merchandising B; mathematics B; mechanical engineering B; medical technology B; microbiology B; music B; music education B; music history B; nutrition B; painting/drawing B; parks management B; petroleum/natural gas engineering B; philosophy B; physical education B; physics B; piano/organ B; political science/government B; poultry sciences B; psychology B; public administration B; radio and television studies B; reading education B; real estate B; religious studies B; Russian B; Russian and Slavic studies B; sacred music B; science education B; sculpture B; secondary education B; secretarial studies/office management B; social work B; sociology B; Spanish B; speech pathology and audiology B; speech/rhetoric/public address/debate B; stringed instruments B; studio art B; textiles and clothing B; transportation technologies B; veterinary sciences B; vocational education B; voice B; wildlife management B; wind and percussion instruments B; wood sciences B; zoology B. Majors with highest enrollment: accounting, liberal arts/general studies, business administration/commerce/management.

LD Program Information

Name of Program Special Services.

Availability of Services Began offering services in 1982. Services provided to freshmen, sophomores. Program currently serves 9 LD students: 7 freshmen, 2 sophomores.

Staff 4 part-time staff members, including director. Services provided by remediation specialist, counselors.

Admissions Open admissions for state residents; psychoeducational report recommended; high school transcript, standard or untimed ACT required for some. LD students may begin taking classes in fall, spring, or summer. Application should be submitted 2 months in advance of initial anticipated enrollment.

Orientation Optional orientation offered during registration.

Housing College housing available. LD students housed randomly. LD students not required to live on campus.

Diagnostic Testing Available in reading, math, written language.

Tutoring Offered one-to-one and in small groups by professional teachers, peer tutors. Available in all subjects. LD students may receive tutoring in all courses each term.

Basic Skills Remediation Offered in small groups by regular teachers. Available in reading, math, spelling, written language, learning strategies, perceptual skills, work and study habits, social skills.

Academic Advisement Help with program planning provided by LD staff members, academic advisers. LD students may take up to 19 semester hours each semester; most take 12 semester hours; 12 semester hours required to maintain full-time status.

Special Courses Offered in college survival skills, reading, career planning. Most offered for credit; none enter into overall grade point average.

Auxiliary Aids and Services Aids include taped textbooks, tape recorders. Services include alternative exam arrangements, notetakers, advocacy.

Counseling Services Individual counseling, small-group counseling, career counseling available.

Contact Dr. Kaylene A. Long, Associate Director of Developmental Education and Director of Special Services, Louisiana State University and Agricultural and Mechanical College, 136 Allen Hall, Baton Rouge, LA 70803, 504-388-2873.

LYCOMING COLLEGE
Williamsport, Pennsylvania

Year Program Began	1980	Special Courses	✓
Special Fee	Varies	Taped Textbooks	✓
Special Orientation	✓	Alternative Exam Arrangements	✓
Diagnostic Testing	✓	Notetakers	
Subject-Area Tutoring	✓	Staff	1 part-time
Basic Skills Remediation	✓	Number of Students Served	5

General Information United Methodist 4-year coed college. Founded 1812. Awards B. Institutionally accredited by regional association. Small-town setting; 32-acre campus. Total enrollment: 1,286. Faculty: 75 (71 full-time, 4 part-time); 70% have doctoral degrees. Calendar: 4-4-1. Grading system: letters or numbers. Library holdings: 145,000 bound volumes, 900 periodical subscriptions, 1,400 records/tapes.

Undergraduate Profile Fall 1984: 1,286 undergraduates (396 freshmen) from 15 states and territories and 2 foreign countries; 1% part-time; 60% state residents; 15% transfers; 80% financial aid recipients; 48% women; 1% blacks; 0% Native Americans; 0% Hispanics; 0% Asian Americans; 1% foreign nationals; no legally handicapped students.

Expenses (1985–86) Comprehensive fee of $9470 includes full-time tuition ($6800) and college room and board ($2670). College room only: $1320. Part-time tuition: $850 per course.

Financial Aid Fall 1984 full-time freshmen: 54% applied for aid, 90% of those were judged to have need, 100% of those were aided; the average aided freshman received an aid package worth $6212 (56% scholarships/grants, 44% self-help) meeting 86% of need. College-administered aid for all 1984–85 undergraduates: 625 need-based scholarships (average $1760); 79 non-need scholarships (average $1309); low-interest long-term loans from external sources (average $1145); SEOG; College Work-Study; 600 part-time jobs. Supporting data: FAF, IRS, institutional form, AFSA/SAR required; state form required for some; FFS acceptable. Priority application deadline: 4/1.

Athletics Member NCAA (Division III). Intercollegiate sports: basketball M(III), W(III); cross-country running M(III), W(III); field hockey W(III); football M(III); golf M(III), W(III); soccer M(III), W(III); swimming and diving M(III), W(III); tennis M(III), W(III); track and field M(III), W(III); wrestling M(III). Intramural sports: baseball/softball, basketball, field hockey, football, gymnastics, skiing (cross-country), skiing (downhill), soccer, volleyball, wrestling.

Majors Accounting B; American studies B; anthropology B; art/fine arts B; biochemistry B; biology/biological sciences B; business administration/commerce/management B; chemistry B; communication B; computer science B; criminal justice B; (pre)dentistry sequence B; economics B; education B; elementary education B; English B; French B; German B; history B; (pre)law sequence B; mathematics B; medical technology B; (pre)medicine sequence B; music B; nursing B; philosophy B; physics B; political science/government B; psychology B; sculpture B; secondary education B; sociology B; Spanish B; theater arts/drama B; (pre)veterinary medicine sequence B. Majors with highest enrollment: business administration/commerce/management, accounting, biology/biological sciences.

LD Program Information

Name of Program Not specified.

Availability of Services Began offering services in 1980. Services provided to freshmen, sophomores, juniors, seniors. Program currently serves 5 LD students: 3 freshmen, 1 sophomore, 1 junior.

Fees $5 per hour recommended for peer tutoring.

Staff 1 part-time staff member (dean of student services).

Admissions LD applicants evaluated on the basis of high school transcript and grade point average, untimed SAT or ACT, personal interview, letters of recommendation. LD students may begin taking classes in fall, spring, or summer. Application should be submitted 8 months in advance of initial anticipated enrollment.

Orientation Orientation offered during summer prior to enrollment.

Housing College housing (including coed) available. LD students housed randomly. LD freshmen, sophomores, juniors, and seniors required to live on campus except if living with relatives.

Diagnostic Testing Available in reading, written language.

Tutoring Offered one-to-one by professional teachers, peer tutors. Available in all subjects. LD students may receive tutoring in all courses each term.

Basic Skills Remediation Offered in class-size groups by regular teachers. Available in reading, math, written language, work and study habits.

Academic Advisement Help with program planning provided by academic advisers. LD students may take up to 16 semester hours each semester; most take 16 semester hours; 12 semester hours required to maintain full-time status.

Special Courses Offered in communication skills, composition, math. All offered for credit; all enter into overall grade point average.

Auxiliary Aids and Services Aids include taped textbooks, tape recorders. Services include alternative exam arrangements, advocacy.

Counseling Services Individual counseling, career counseling available.

Contact Mr. Jack C. Buckle, Dean of Student Services, Lycoming College, Williamsport, PA 17701, 717-326-1951 Ext. 236.

MANHATTANVILLE COLLEGE

Purchase, New York

Year Program Began	1983	Special Courses	
Special Fee	$2000 per year	Taped Textbooks	✓
Special Orientation	✓	Alternative Exam Arrangements	✓
Diagnostic Testing	✓	Notetakers	
Subject-Area Tutoring	✓	Staff	1 part-time
Basic Skills Remediation	✓	Number of Students Served	2

General Information Independent comprehensive coed institution. Founded 1841. Awards B, M. Institutionally accredited by regional association; programs accredited by NASM (music). Small-town setting, with easy access to New York City; 125-acre barrier-free campus. Total enrollment: 1,300. Faculty: 170 (80 full-time, 90 part-time); 80% have doctoral degrees; graduate assistants teach no undergraduate courses. Calendar: semesters. Grading system: letters or numbers. Library holdings: 250,000 bound volumes, 3,000 titles on microform, 1,600 periodical subscriptions.

Undergraduate Profile Fall 1984: 950 undergraduates (247 freshmen) from 35 states and territories and 39 foreign countries; 7% part-time; 40% state residents; 12% transfers; 60% financial aid recipients; 65% women; 6% blacks; 1% Native Americans; 4% Hispanics; 17% foreign nationals; 9 legally handicapped students.

Expenses (1985–86) Comprehensive fee of $11,990 includes full-time tuition ($8000) and college room and board ($3990). Part-time tuition: $138 per credit.

Financial Aid Fall 1984 full-time freshmen: 62% applied for aid, 95% of those were judged to have need, 100% of those were aided; the average aided freshman received an aid package worth $9421 (71% scholarships/grants, 29% self-help) meeting 90% of need. College-administered aid for all 1984–85 undergraduates: 525 need-based scholarships (average $3900); 59 non-need scholarships (average $1865); low-interest long-term loans from external sources (average $2000); SEOG; College Work-Study; part-time jobs. Supporting data: FAF, IRS, state form, institutional form, AFSA/SAR required; FFS acceptable. Priority application deadline: 4/1.

Athletics Member NCAA (Division III). Intercollegiate sports: baseball/softball M(III), W(III); basketball M(III), W(III); cross-country running M(III), W(III); field hockey W(III); lacrosse M(III); soccer M(III), W(III); swimming and diving W(III); tennis M(III), W(III); volleyball W(III). Intramural sports: baseball/softball, basketball, golf, martial arts, rugby, skiing (downhill), volleyball, water polo.

Majors American studies B; art/fine arts B; art history B; Asian/Oriental studies B; biochemistry B; biology/biological sciences B; business administration/commerce/management B; chemistry B; classics B; computer science B; ecology/environmental studies B; economics B; English B; French B; history B; interdisciplinary studies B; international studies B; (pre)law sequence B; mathematics B; (pre)medicine sequence B; music B; music business B; music education B; philosophy B; physics B; political science/government B; psychology B; religious studies B; Romance languages B; Russian and Slavic studies B; sociology B; Spanish B; women's studies B. Majors with highest enrollment: psychology, political science/government, business administration/commerce/management.

LD Program Information

Name of Program Learning Disabled College Student Program.

Availability of Services Began offering services in 1983. Services provided to freshmen. Program currently serves 2 LD students (both freshmen).

Fees $2000 per year.

Staff 1 part-time staff member. Services provided by remediation specialist, tutors.

Admissions LD applicants evaluated on the basis of high school transcript, untimed SAT, personal interview, autobiographical statement, letters of recommendation, psychoeducational report. LD students may begin taking classes in fall only. Application should be submitted 6 months in advance of initial anticipated enrollment.

Orientation Required orientation held before registration.

Housing College housing (including coed) available. LD students housed randomly. LD students not required to live on campus.

Diagnostic Testing Available in reading, math, spelling, written language, work and study habits.

Tutoring Offered one-to-one and in small groups by professional teachers, peer tutors. Available in all subjects. LD students may receive tutoring in all courses each term.

Basic Skills Remediation Offered one-to-one and in small groups by LD teachers. Available in reading, spelling, handwriting, written language, learning strategies, work and study habits.

Academic Advisement Help with program planning provided by LD staff member, academic advisers. LD students may take up to 15 credits each semester; most take 12 credits in freshman year, 15 thereafter; 12 credits required to maintain full-time status.

Auxiliary Aids and Services Aids include taped textbooks, tape recorders, calculators, typewriters, word processors. Services include alternative exam arrangements, advocacy.

Counseling Services Individual counseling available.

Contact Ms. Arlene Jellnick, Reading Skills Specialist, Manhattanville College, Academic Resource Center, Purchase, NY 10577, 914-694-2200 Ext. 283.

MANKATO STATE UNIVERSITY

Mankato, Minnesota

Year Program Began	1980	Special Courses	✓
Special Fee	None	Taped Textbooks	✓
Special Orientation	✓	Alternative Exam Arrangements	✓
Diagnostic Testing		Notetakers	✓
Subject-Area Tutoring	✓	Staff	4 part-time
Basic Skills Remediation	✓	Number of Students Served	36

General Information State-supported comprehensive coed institution. Part of Minnesota State University System. Founded 1867. Awards A (college transfer and terminal), B, M. Institutionally accredited by regional association; programs accredited by NASAD (art and design), NASM (music), NLN (nursing), NCATE (teacher education). Small-town setting, with easy access to Minneapolis–St. Paul; 400-acre barrier-free campus. Total enrollment: 12,367. Faculty: 620 (565 full-time, 55 part-time); 50% have doctoral degrees; graduate assistants teach a few undergraduate courses. Calendar: quarters. Grading system: letters or numbers. Library holdings: 538,378 bound volumes, 510,272 titles on microform, 2,323 periodical subscriptions, 14,117 records/tapes.

Undergraduate Profile Fall 1984: 10,881 undergraduates (1,958 freshmen); 13% part-time; 88% state residents; 38% transfers; 50% financial aid recipients; 52% women; 1% blacks; 1% Native Americans; 1% Hispanics; 2% foreign nationals; 38% of undergraduates over 25 years of age.

Expenses (1985–86) State resident tuition: $1608 full-time, $33.50 per quarter hour part-time. Nonresident tuition: $2782 full-time, $57.95 per quarter hour part-time. College room and board: $1712. College room only: $1107.

Financial Aid Fall 1984 full-time freshmen: 55% applied for aid, 73% of those were judged to have need, 99% of those were aided; the average aided freshman received an aid package worth $2876 (55% scholarships/grants, 45% self-help) meeting 100% of need. College-administered aid for all 1984–85 undergraduates: 735 need-based scholarships (average $540); 230 non-need scholarships (average $300); short-term loans (average $170); low-interest long-term loans from college funds (average $585), from external sources (average $2050); SEOG; College Work-Study; 1,000 part-time jobs. Supporting data: FFS, IRS, institutional form, AFSA/SAR required. Priority application deadline: 4/22.

Athletics Member NCAA (Division II), NAIA. Intercollegiate sports: baseball/softball M(II,s), W(II,s); basketball M(II,s), W(II,s); cross-country running M(II,s), W(II,s); football M(II,s); golf M(II,s), W(II,s); ice hockey M(II,s); swimming and diving M(II,s), W(II,s); tennis M(II,s), W(II,s); track and field M(II,s), W(II,s); volleyball W(II,s); wrestling M(II,s). Intramural sports: baseball/softball, basketball, bowling, cross-country running, fencing, football, golf, ice hockey, martial arts, racquetball, rugby, skiing (cross-country), skiing (downhill), soccer, swimming and diving, tennis, track and field, volleyball, weight lifting, wrestling.

Majors Accounting B; advertising B; agricultural economics B; American studies B; anthropology B; applied art B; art education B; art/fine arts B; astronomy B; automotive technologies B; aviation administration B; behavioral sciences B; biochemistry B; biology/biological sciences B; biotechnology B; business administration/commerce/management B; business education B; chemistry B; child care/child and family studies B; child psychology/child development B; city, community, and regional planning B; clinical psychology B; communication B; computer information systems B; computer programming B; computer science B; construction management B; corrections B; data processing B; dental services A; (pre)dentistry sequence B; dietetics B; early childhood education B; earth science B; ecology/environmental studies B; economics B; education B; electrical engineering B; electrical engineering technology B; elementary education B; emergency medical technology A; (pre)engineering sequence A; English B; environmental sciences B; ethnic studies B; family services B; fashion merchandising B; finance/banking B; French B; geography B; German B; health education B; health science B; history B; home economics B; home economics education B; humanities B; industrial arts B; industrial engineering technology B; insurance B; interior design B; international business B; international studies B; journalism B; labor and industrial relations B; law enforcement/police sciences A, B; (pre)law sequence B; liberal arts/general studies A, B; linguistics B; manufacturing technology B; marketing/retailing/merchandising B; mathematics B; medical laboratory technology A; medical technology B; (pre) medicine sequence B; military science B; music B; music education B; natural sciences B; nursing B; nutrition B; parks management B; philosophy B; physical education B; physical sciences B; physical therapy B; physics B; piano/organ B; political science/government B; psychology B; public administration B; public health B; public relations B; real estate B; recreation and leisure services B; recreation therapy B; religious studies B; Russian B; Scandinavian languages/studies B; science B; science education B; secondary education B; secretarial studies/office management B; social science B; social work B; sociology B; Spanish B; special education B; speech pathology and audiology B; speech/rhetoric/public address/debate B; sports medicine B; statistics B; technical writing B; textiles and clothing B; theater arts/drama B; urban studies B; (pre)veterinary medicine sequence B; voice B; wind and percussion instruments B; women's studies B. Majors with highest enrollment: business administration/commerce/management, accounting, elementary education.

LD Program Information

Name of Program Handicapped Student Services.

Availability of Services Began offering services in 1980. Services provided to freshmen, sophomores, juniors, seniors. Program currently serves 36 LD students: 10 freshmen, 9 sophomores, 8 juniors, 9 seniors.

Staff 4 part-time staff members, including coordinator, director of Learning Skills Center. Services provided by remediation specialists, tutors, counselors.

Admissions LD applicants evaluated on the basis of high school transcript and grade point average, standard or untimed SAT or ACT, personal interview, letters of recommendation, untimed PSAT (in lieu of SAT or ACT). LD students may begin taking classes in fall, winter, spring, or summer. Application should be submitted 3 months in advance of initial anticipated enrollment.

Orientation Optional orientation offered during registration.

Housing College housing (including coed) available. LD students housed randomly. LD students not required to live on campus.

Tutoring Offered one-to-one by peer tutors. Available in some subjects. LD students may receive tutoring in all courses each term.

Basic Skills Remediation Offered one-to-one by regular teachers, graduate students. Available in reading, math, spelling, handwriting, spoken language, written language, learning strategies.

Academic Advisement Help with program planning provided by LD staff members, academic advisers. LD students may take up to 20 quarter hours each quarter; most take 12 to 14 quarter hours; 12 quarter hours required to maintain full-time status.

Special Courses Offered in language development, math. Some offered for credit; some enter into overall grade point average.

Auxiliary Aids and Services Aids include taped textbooks, word processors. Services include alternative exam arrangements, notetakers, advocacy.

Counseling Services Individual counseling available.

Contact Dr. J. Daniel Beebe, Coordinator, Handicapped Student Services, Mankato State University, Mankato, MN 56001, 507-389-2825.

MARION COLLEGE

Marion, Indiana

Year Program Began	1978	Special Courses	✓
Special Fee	$50 per year	Taped Textbooks	
Special Orientation		Alternative Exam Arrangements	✓
Diagnostic Testing	✓	Notetakers	✓
Subject-Area Tutoring	✓	Staff	3 part-time
Basic Skills Remediation	✓	Number of Students Served	*Not reported*

General Information Wesleyan comprehensive coed institution. Founded 1920. Awards A (college transfer and terminal), B, M. Institutionally accredited by regional association; programs accredited by NLN (nursing). Small-town setting, with easy access to Indianapolis; 50-acre campus. Total enrollment: 1,083. Faculty: 88 (65 full-time, 23 part-time); 35% have doctoral degrees; graduate assistants teach no undergraduate courses. Calendar: 4-1-4. Grading system: letters or numbers. Library holdings: 104,650 bound volumes, 6,819 titles on microform, 390 periodical subscriptions, 6,741 records/tapes.

Undergraduate Profile Fall 1984: 1,058 undergraduates (216 freshmen) from 30 states and territories and 4 foreign countries; 24% part-time; 75% state residents; 6% transfers; 85% financial aid recipients; 59% women; 4% blacks; 0% Native Americans; 0% Hispanics; 0% Asian Americans; 1% foreign nationals; 2 legally handicapped students.

Expenses (1985–86) Comprehensive fee of $7280 includes full-time tuition ($4800), mandatory fees ($164), and college room and board ($2316). Part-time tuition and fees per semester (1 to 11 semester hours) range from $77 to $2227.

Financial Aid Fall 1984 full-time freshmen: 93% applied for aid, 72% of those were judged to have need, 100% of those were aided; the average aided freshman received an aid package worth $6718 (52% scholarships/grants, 48% self-help) meeting 95% of need. College-administered aid for all 1984–85 undergraduates: need-based scholarships; non-need scholarships; low-interest long-term loans from external sources (average $2200); SEOG; College Work-Study; 100 part-time jobs. Supporting data: FAF, institutional form, AFSA/SAR required; IRS required for some; FFS acceptable. Priority application deadline: 4/15.

Athletics Member NAIA. Intercollegiate sports: baseball/softball M(s); basketball M(s), W(s); cross-country running M(s); field hockey W(s); golf M(s); soccer M(s); tennis M(s); track and field M(s), W(s); volleyball W(s). Intramural sports: badminton, baseball/softball, basketball, bowling, golf, racquetball, soccer, tennis, volleyball.

Majors Accounting A, B; art education B; art/fine arts A, B; biblical studies A, B; biology/biological sciences B; business administration/commerce/management A, B; chemistry B; communication B; computer science A, B; criminal justice A, B; data processing A, B; (pre)dentistry sequence B; economics B; elementary education B; English A, B; history B; information science A; law enforcement/police sciences A; (pre)law sequence B; liberal arts/general studies A, B; mathematics B; medical laboratory technology A; medical technology B; (pre)medicine sequence B; ministries A, B; music A, B; music education B; nursing B; philosophy B; physical education B; political science/government B; psychology B; recreation and leisure services A; religious education A, B; religious studies B; sacred music B; science A, B; science education B; secretarial studies/office management A; social science A, B; social work B; sociology B; Spanish B; theology B; (pre)veterinary medicine sequence B. Majors with highest enrollment: nursing, religious studies, business administration/commerce/management.

LD Program Information

Name of Program Learning Center.

Availability of Services Began offering services in 1978. Services provided to freshmen, sophomores, juniors, seniors.

Fees $50 per year.

Staff 3 part-time staff members, including director. Services provided by remediation specialists, tutors.

Admissions LD applicants evaluated on the basis of high school transcript and grade point average, standard or untimed SAT or ACT, personal interview, letters of recommendation. LD students may begin taking classes in fall, winter, or spring.

Housing College housing available. LD students housed with other LD students and non-LD students. LD freshmen, sophomores, and juniors required to live on campus except if living with relatives.

Diagnostic Testing Available in reading, written language.

Tutoring Offered one-to-one and in small groups by peer tutors. Available in some subjects. LD students may receive tutoring in all courses each term (depending on availability of tutors).

Basic Skills Remediation Offered one-to-one and in small groups by Learning Center staff. Available in reading, math, spelling, written language, work and study habits.

Academic Advisement Help with program planning provided by LD staff members, academic advisers. Most LD students take 12 to 13 semester hours each semester; 12 semester hours required to maintain full-time status.

Special Courses Offered in reading, composition, language development. All offered for credit; all enter into overall grade point average.

Auxiliary Aids and Services Aids include word processors. Services include alternative exam arrangements, notetakers.

Counseling Services Individual counseling, career counseling available.

Contact Ms. Nancy Swauger, Director of Learning Center, Marion College, 4201 South Washington Street, Marion, IN 46953, 317-674-6901 Ext. 189.

MARIST COLLEGE

Poughkeepsie, New York

Year Program Began	1979	Special Courses	✓
Special Fee	$700 per year	Taped Textbooks	✓
Special Orientation		Alternative Exam Arrangements	✓
Diagnostic Testing	✓	Notetakers	✓
Subject-Area Tutoring	✓	Staff	2 full-time, 2 part-time
Basic Skills Remediation	✓	Number of Students Served	23

General Information Independent comprehensive coed institution. Founded 1949. Awards B, M. Institutionally accredited by regional association. Small-town setting; 120-acre barrier-free campus. Total enrollment: 3,427. Faculty: 120 (80 full-time, 40 part-time); 80% have doctoral degrees; graduate assistants teach no undergraduate courses. Calendar: semesters. Grading system: letters or numbers. Library holdings: 90,000 bound volumes, 1,000 periodical subscriptions, 2,600 records/tapes.

Undergraduate Profile Fall 1984: 3,017 undergraduates (721 freshmen) from 18 states and territories and 12 foreign countries; 10% part-time; 75% state residents; 10% transfers; 82% financial aid recipients; 43% women; 7% blacks; 1% Native Americans; 4% Hispanics; 1% foreign nationals; 85 legally handicapped students.

Expenses (1985–86) Comprehensive fee of $9462 includes full-time tuition ($5790), mandatory fees ($112), and college room and board ($3560). Part-time tuition: $155 per credit.

Financial Aid Fall 1984 full-time freshmen: 76% applied for aid, 90% of those were judged to have need, 100% of those were aided; the average aided freshman received an aid package worth $4982 (45% scholarships/grants, 55% self-help) meeting 85% of need. College-administered aid for all 1984–85 undergraduates: need-based scholarships (average $1000); 40 non-need scholarships (average $1150); low-interest long-term loans from college funds (average $1000), from external sources (average $2306); SEOG; College Work-Study; 484 part-time jobs. Supporting data: FAF, IRS, AFSA/SAR required; FFS acceptable. Priority application deadline: 3/1.

Athletics Member NCAA (Division I), NAIA. Intercollegiate sports: basketball M(I,s), W(I,s); crew M, W; cross-country running M(I), W; football M(III); ice hockey M; lacrosse M(I); skiing (downhill) M, W; soccer M(I); swimming and diving M(I), W(I); tennis M(I), W(I); track and field M(I), W; volleyball W(I). Intramural sports: baseball/softball, basketball, bowling, football, golf, ice hockey, lacrosse, martial arts, racquetball, skiing (downhill), soccer, swimming and diving, tennis, volleyball.

Majors Accounting B; American studies B; art/fine arts B; biology/biological sciences B; business administration/commerce/management B; chemistry B; communication B; computer science B; criminal justice B; economics B; English B; environmental sciences B; fashion design and technology B; fashion merchandising B; French B; history B; mathematics B; medical technology B; nursing B; political science/government B; psychology B; Russian B; secondary education B; social work B; Spanish B. Majors with highest enrollment: business administration/commerce/management, communication, computer science.

LD Program Information

Name of Program Special Services.

Availability of Services Began offering services in 1979. Services provided to freshmen, sophomores, juniors, seniors. Program currently serves 23 LD students: 9 freshmen, 8 sophomores, 5 juniors, 1 senior.

Fees $700 per year.

Staff 2 full-time, 2 part-time staff members, including director. Services provided by counselor, educational consultant, LD specialist.

Admissions LD applicants evaluated on the basis of high school transcript and grade point average, untimed SAT, personal interview, autobiographical statement, letters of recommendation, psychoeducational report. LD students may begin taking classes in fall or spring. Application should be submitted 8 to 9 months in advance of initial anticipated enrollment.

Housing College housing (including coed) available. LD students housed randomly. LD freshmen required to live on campus.

Diagnostic Testing Available in intelligence, reading, math, written language, work and study habits, personality.

Tutoring Offered one-to-one and in small groups by professional teachers, peer tutors. Available in all subjects. LD students may receive tutoring in 3 courses per term.

Basic Skills Remediation Offered one-to-one and in small groups by LD teachers. Available in written language.

Academic Advisement Help with program planning provided by LD staff members, academic advisers. LD students may take up to 15 credits each semester; most take 12 credits; 12 credits required to maintain full-time status.

Special Courses Offered in college survival skills, composition, language development, career planning. None offered for credit; none enter into overall grade point average.

Auxiliary Aids and Services Aids include taped textbooks, tape recorders, word processors. Services include alternative exam arrangements, notetakers, advocacy.

Counseling Services Individual counseling, small-group counseling, career counseling available.

Contact Ms. Diane C. Perreira, Director of Special Services, Marist College, Poughkeepsie, NY 12601, 914-471-3240 Ext. 274.

MARSHALL UNIVERSITY
Huntington, West Virginia

Year Program Began	1980	Special Courses	✓
Special Fee	None	Taped Textbooks	✓
Special Orientation	✓	Alternative Exam Arrangements	✓
Diagnostic Testing	✓	Notetakers	✓
Subject-Area Tutoring	✓	Staff	1 full-time
Basic Skills Remediation	✓	Number of Students Served	33

General Information State-supported coed university. Founded 1837. Awards A (college transfer and terminal), B, M, D. Institutionally accredited by regional association; programs accredited by NLN (nursing), NCATE (teacher education); candidate for program accreditation by NASM (music). City setting; 50-acre barrier-free campus. Total enrollment: 11,323. Faculty: 514 (361 full-time, 153 part-time); 57% have doctoral degrees; graduate assistants teach a few undergraduate courses. Calendar: semesters. Grading system: letters or numbers and pass/fail. Library holdings: 334,780 bound volumes, 2,760 periodical subscriptions, 10,092 records/tapes.

Undergraduate Profile Fall 1984: 8,500 undergraduates (2,255 freshmen) from 18 states and territories and 7 foreign countries; 39% part-time; 84% state residents; 15% transfers; 40% financial aid recipients; 54% women; 5% blacks; 3% foreign nationals; 47% of undergraduates over 25 years of age; 220 legally handicapped students.

Expenses (1985–86) State resident tuition: $960 full-time. Nonresident tuition: $2600 full-time. Part-time tuition per semester (1 to 11 semester hours) ranges from $31 to $440.50 for state residents, $100 to $1203.50 for nonresidents. College room and board: $2578.

Financial Aid College-administered aid for all 1984–85 undergraduates: need-based scholarships (average $1500); non-need scholarships (average $450); short-term loans (average $80); low-interest long-term loans; SEOG; College Work-Study; 200 part-time jobs. Supporting data: FAF required. Priority application deadline: 3/1.

Athletics Member NCAA (Division I). Intercollegiate sports: baseball/softball M(I), W(I); basketball M(I,s), W(I,s); bowling M, W; cross-country running M(I,s), W(I,s); football M(I-AA,s); golf M(I), W(I); riflery M(I), W(I); soccer M(I); swimming and diving M(I,s); tennis M(I,s), W(II,s); track and field M(I,s), W(I,s); volleyball M(I,s), W(I,s). Intramural sports: badminton, baseball/softball, basketball, bowling, cross-country running, fencing, field hockey, football, golf, martial arts, racquetball, riflery, skiing (cross-country), skiing (downhill), soccer, swimming and diving, tennis, track and field, volleyball, weight lifting.

Majors Accounting A, B; advertising B; anthropology B; applied art B; art education B; art/fine arts B; biology/biological sciences B; botany/plant sciences B; broadcasting B; business administration/commerce/management A, B; business economics B; business education B; chemistry B; classics B; commercial art B; communication B; computer information systems B; computer science B; corrections A, B; criminal justice A, B; cytotechnology A, B; (pre)dentistry sequence B; dietetics B; early childhood education B; economics B; education B; educational media B; elementary education B; (pre)engineering sequence A; English B; finance/banking A, B; fire science A; French B; geography B; geology B; German B; graphic arts B; health education B; health services administration B; history B; home economics B; home economics education B; humanities B; industrial administration A; insurance B; international studies B; journalism B; laboratory technologies A, B; Latin B; law enforcement/police sciences A, B; (pre)law sequence B; legal secretarial studies A; library science A, B; marketing/retailing/merchandising B; mathematics B; medical laboratory technology A; medical records services A; medical secretarial studies A; medical technology B; (pre)medicine sequence B; modern languages B; music B; music education B; music history B; nursing A, B; occupational safety and health A; painting/drawing B; paralegal studies A; philosophy B; physical education B; physics B; piano/organ B; political science/government B; psychology B; public health B; public relations B; radio and television studies B; real estate A; recreation and leisure services B; rehabilitation therapy B; retail management B; science education B; sculpture B; secondary education B; secretarial studies/office management A; social science B; social work B; sociology B; Spanish B; special education B; speech pathology and audiology B; speech/rhetoric/public address/debate B; theater arts/drama B; voice B; wind and percussion instruments B; zoology B. Majors with highest enrollment: secretarial studies/office management, elementary education, accounting.

LD Program Information

Name of Program Disabled Student Services.

Availability of Services Began offering services in 1980. Services provided to freshmen, sophomores, juniors, seniors. Program currently serves 33 LD students.

Staff 1 full-time staff member (assistant director). Services provided by peer helpers.

Admissions LD applicants evaluated on the basis of high school transcript and grade point average, standard or untimed ACT, psychoeducational report. LD students may begin taking classes in fall, spring, or summer. Application should be submitted 6 months in advance of initial anticipated enrollment.

Orientation Optional orientation offered before registration.

Housing College housing (including coed) available. LD students housed randomly. LD freshmen and sophomores required to live on campus except if living with relatives.

Diagnostic Testing Available in intelligence, reading, math, spelling, handwriting, spoken language, written language, motor abilities, perceptual skills, work and study habits, personality, social skills, psychoneurology, speech.

Tutoring Offered one-to-one and in small groups by peer tutors. Available in some subjects. LD students may receive tutoring in all courses each term.

Basic Skills Remediation Offered one-to-one and in small groups by LD teachers, regular teachers, teacher trainees. Available in reading, math, spelling, written language, learning strategies, perceptual skills, work and study habits, speech.

Academic Advisement Help with program planning provided by LD staff members, academic advisers. LD students may take up to 17 semester hours each semester; most take 10 to 12 semester hours; 12 semester hours required to maintain full-time status.

Special Courses Offered in college survival skills, reading, vocabulary development, communication skills, math, study skills, career planning. Some offered for credit; some enter into overall grade point average.

Auxiliary Aids and Services Aids include taped textbooks, tape recorders, calculators. Services include alternative exam arrangements, notetakers.

Counseling Services Individual counseling, small-group counseling, career counseling available.

Contact Mr. Stephen Hensley, Assistant Dean of Student Development and Director of Disabled Student Services, Marshall University, Huntington, WV 25701, 304-696-3164.

MCNEESE STATE UNIVERSITY

Lake Charles, Louisiana

Year Program Began	*Not reported*	Special Courses	✓
Special Fee	None	Taped Textbooks	✓
Special Orientation		Alternative Exam Arrangements	
Diagnostic Testing	✓	Notetakers	✓
Subject-Area Tutoring	✓	Staff	16 part-time
Basic Skills Remediation	✓	Number of Students Served	290

General Information State-supported comprehensive coed institution. Founded 1939. Awards A (terminal), B, M. Institutionally accredited by regional association; programs accredited by ABET (engineering and technology), ABFSE (funeral service), NASM (music), NLN (nursing), NCATE (teacher education). City setting; 165-acre barrier-free campus. Total enrollment: 7,981. Faculty: 331 (248 full-time, 83 part-time); 51% have doctoral degrees; graduate assistants teach a few undergraduate courses. Calendar: semesters. Grading system: letters or numbers. Library holdings: 202,870 bound volumes, 52 titles on microform, 1,369 periodical subscriptions, 2,876 records/tapes.

Undergraduate Profile Fall 1984: 6,645 undergraduates (1,540 freshmen) from 39 states and territories and 40 foreign countries; 17% part-time; 94% state residents; 6% transfers; 33% financial aid recipients; 54% women; 17% blacks; 0% Native Americans; 0% Hispanics; 0% Asian Americans; 1% foreign nationals; 20% of undergraduates over 25 years of age; 200 legally handicapped students.

Expenses (1984–85) State resident tuition: $781 full-time. Nonresident tuition: $1461 full-time. Part-time tuition per semester (1 to 11 credit hours) ranges from $123.50 to $371.50 for state residents, $123.50 to $683.50 for nonresidents. College room and board: $1584.

Financial Aid Fall 1984 full-time freshmen: 62% applied for aid, 66% of those were judged to have need, 83% of those were aided; the average aided freshman received an aid package worth $1810 (60% scholarships/grants, 40% self-help) meeting 80% of need. College-administered aid for all 1984–85 undergraduates: need-based scholarships; 2,708 non-need scholarships (average $500); short-term loans; low-interest long-term loans; SEOG; College Work-Study; part-time jobs. Supporting data: FFS, IRS, state form, AFSA/SAR required; FAF acceptable. Application deadline: continuous to 5/1.

Athletics Member NCAA (Division I). Intercollegiate sports: baseball/softball M(I,s), W(I,s); basketball M(I,s), W(I,s); cross-country running M(I,s); football M(I-AA,s); golf M(I,s); riflery M, W; tennis M(I,s), W(I,s); track and field M(I,s); volleyball W(I,s); weight lifting M(c), W(c). Intramural sports: archery, badminton, baseball/softball, basketball, bowling, cross-country running, football, golf, racquetball, swimming and diving, tennis, track and field, volleyball, weight lifting.

Majors Accounting B; agricultural business B; agricultural sciences B; agronomy/soil and crop sciences B; animal sciences B; architectural technologies A; art education B; botany/plant sciences B; business administration/commerce/management B; business economics B; business education B; chemical engineering B; chemistry B; child care/child and family studies B; civil engineering B; computer science B; criminal justice B; (pre)dentistry sequence B; early childhood education B; economics B; education B; electrical and electronics technologies A, B; electrical engineering B; elementary education B; engineering (general) B; English B; environmental sciences B; fashion merchandising B; finance/banking B; forestry B; forest technology A; French B; funeral service A; geology A, B; graphic arts B; history B; home economics B; home economics education B; horticulture B; instrumentation technology A; interior design B; (pre)law sequence B; liberal arts/general studies A, B; marketing/retailing/merchandising B; mathematics B; mechanical engineering B; medical technology B; (pre)medicine sequence B; microbiology B; music B; music education B; nursing B; nutrition B; painting/drawing B; paralegal studies A; petroleum technology A; photography B; physical education B; physics B; piano/organ B; political science/government B; psychology B; radio and television studies B; radiological technology B; sacred music B; science education B; sculpture B; secondary education B; secretarial studies/office management A, B; sociology B; Spanish B; special education B; speech/rhetoric/public address/debate B; statistics B; theater arts/drama B; veterinary sciences A; voice B; wildlife management B; zoology B. Majors with highest enrollment: business administration/commerce/management, liberal arts/general studies, accounting.

LD Program Information

Name of Program 504-Plus Program.

Availability of Services Services provided to freshmen, sophomores, juniors, seniors. Program currently serves 290 LD students.

Staff 16 part-time staff members, including director. Services provided by tutors, counselor.

Admissions LD applicants evaluated on the basis of high school transcript and grade point average, standard or untimed ACT; psychoeducational report recommended. LD students may begin taking classes in fall, spring, or summer. Application should be submitted 1 to 3 months in advance of initial anticipated enrollment.

Housing College housing available. LD students housed randomly. LD freshmen, sophomores, juniors, and seniors required to live on campus except by special permission.

Diagnostic Testing Available in various areas as appropriate.

Tutoring Offered one-to-one and in small groups by professional teachers, peer tutors. Available in all subjects. LD students may receive tutoring in all courses each term.

Basic Skills Remediation Offered in small groups by regular teachers, teacher trainees. Available in reading, math, spelling, written language.

Academic Advisement Help with program planning provided by academic advisers. Most LD students take 12 to 16 credit hours each semester; 12 credit hours required to maintain full-time status.

Special Courses Offered in reading, vocabulary development, communication skills, composition, language development, math. All offered for credit; all enter into overall grade point average.

Auxiliary Aids and Services Aids include taped textbooks, tape recorders, typewriters. Services include notetakers, advocacy.

Counseling Services Individual counseling, career counseling available.

Contact Ms. Brenda M. Ball, Director of Special Projects, 504-Plus Program, McNeese State University, PO Box 312, Lake Charles, LA 70609, 318-474-9127.

MEMPHIS STATE UNIVERSITY

Memphis, Tennessee

Year Program Began	1978	Special Courses	✓
Special Fee	None	Taped Textbooks	✓
Special Orientation	✓	Alternative Exam Arrangements	✓
Diagnostic Testing	✓	Notetakers	✓
Subject-Area Tutoring	✓	Staff	10 part-time
Basic Skills Remediation	✓	Number of Students Served	31

General Information State-supported coed university. Part of State University and Community College System of Tennessee. Founded 1912. Awards B, M, D. Institutionally accredited by regional association; programs accredited by NASAD (art and design), AACSB (business), ABET (engineering and technology), NASM (music), NCATE (teacher education). Metropolitan setting; 173-acre barrier-free campus. Total enrollment: 21,295. Faculty: 922 (709 full-time, 213 part-time); 71% have doctoral degrees; graduate assistants teach a few undergraduate courses. Calendar: semesters. Grading system: letters or numbers. Library holdings: 827,557 bound volumes, 594,437 titles on microform, 6,900 periodical subscriptions, 45,137 records/tapes.

Undergraduate Profile Fall 1984: 16,516 undergraduates (1,855 freshmen) from 50 states and territories and 73 foreign countries; 42% part-time; 91% state residents; 7% transfers; 25% financial aid recipients; 53% women; 19% blacks; 1% Native Americans; 1% Hispanics; 2% Asian Americans; 25% of undergraduates over 25 years of age; 285 legally handicapped students.

Expenses (1985–86) State resident tuition: $1006 full-time, $43 per semester hour part-time. Nonresident tuition: $3154 full-time, $137 per semester hour part-time. Mandatory fees: $60. College room only: $1400.

Financial Aid Fall 1984 full-time freshmen: 90% applied for aid, 72% of those were judged to have need, 92% of those were aided; the average aided freshman received an aid package worth $2197 (42% scholarships/grants, 58% self-help) meeting 58% of need. College-administered aid for all 1984–85 undergraduates: need-based scholarships; 200 non-need scholarships (average $1000); short-term loans; SEOG; College Work-Study; part-time jobs. Supporting data: FFS, AFSA/SAR required. Application deadline: continuous to 4/1.

Athletics Member NCAA (Division I). Intercollegiate sports: baseball/softball M(I,s); basketball M(I,s), W(I,s); football M(I-A,s); golf M(I,s), W(I,s); racquetball M(c), W(c); soccer M(I,s); swimming and diving M(c), W(c); tennis M(I,s), W(I,s); track and field M(I,s); volleyball W(I,s). Intramural sports: badminton, baseball/softball, basketball, bowling, cross-country running, football, golf, martial arts, rugby, soccer, swimming and diving, tennis, track and field, volleyball, water polo, wrestling.

Majors Accounting B; advertising B; anthropology B; architectural engineering B; art/fine arts B; art history B; biology/biological sciences B; business administration/commerce/management B; business economics B; chemistry B; civil engineering B; communication B; computer science B; computer technologies B; construction technologies B; criminal justice B; (pre)dentistry sequence B; early childhood education B; economics B; education B; electrical and electronics technologies B; electrical engineering B; elementary education B; English B; finance/banking B; geography B; geology B; health education B; history B; home economics B; insurance B; interdisciplinary studies B; international business B; international studies B; journalism B; Latin American studies B; (pre)law sequence B; management information systems B; manufacturing technology B; marketing/retailing/merchandising B; mathematics B; mechanical engineering B; medical technology B; (pre)medicine sequence B; modern languages B; music B; nursing B; philosophy B; physical education B; physical sciences B; physics B; political science/government B; psychology B; real estate B; recreation and leisure services B; rehabilitation therapy B; secondary education B; secretarial studies/office management B; social work B; sociology B; special education B; theater arts/drama B; urban studies B; (pre)veterinary medicine sequence B; vocational education B. Majors with highest enrollment: accounting, business administration/commerce/management, marketing/retailing/merchandising.

LD Program Information

Name of Program Handicapped Student Services.

Availability of Services Began offering services in 1978. Services provided to freshmen, sophomores, juniors, seniors. Program currently serves 31 LD students.

Staff 10 part-time staff members, including director, assistant director. Services provided by tutors, counselor, project technician.

Admissions LD applicants evaluated on the basis of high school transcript and grade point average, untimed ACT, autobiographical statement, letters of recommendation, psychoeducational report. LD students may begin taking classes in fall or spring. Application should be submitted 3 months in advance of initial anticipated enrollment.

Orientation Optional orientation offered during registration.

Housing College housing available. LD students housed randomly. LD students not required to live on campus.

Diagnostic Testing Available in intelligence, reading, math, spelling, written language, work and study habits, personality, speech, hearing.

Tutoring Offered one-to-one and in small groups by professional teachers, peer tutors. Available in some subjects. LD students may receive tutoring in all courses each term.

Basic Skills Remediation Offered one-to-one and in small groups by regular teachers, teacher trainees, peer teachers. Available in reading, math, spelling, written language, learning strategies, work and study habits, speech.

Academic Advisement Help with program planning provided by academic advisers. LD students may take up to 19 semester hours each semester; most take 12 semester hours; 12 semester hours required to maintain full-time status.

Special Courses Offered in college survival skills, reading, communication skills, composition, language development, math, study skills. Some offered for credit; none enter into overall grade point average.

Auxiliary Aids and Services Aids include taped textbooks, tape recorders. Services include alternative exam arrangements, notetakers, advocacy.

Counseling Services Individual counseling, small-group counseling, rap sessions available.

Contact Ms. Dona S. Sparger, Director, Handicapped Student Services, Memphis State University, 215 Scates Hall, Memphis, TN 38152, 901-454-2880.

MERCER UNIVERSITY

Macon, Georgia

Year Program Began	*Not reported*	Special Courses	✓
Special Fee	Varies	Taped Textbooks	✓
Special Orientation	✓	Alternative Exam Arrangements	✓
Diagnostic Testing	✓	Notetakers	✓
Subject-Area Tutoring	✓	Staff	1 full-time
Basic Skills Remediation	✓	Number of Students Served	20

General Information Baptist coed university. Founded 1833. Awards B, M, D. Institutionally accredited by regional association; programs accredited by NCATE (teacher education); candidate for program accreditation by NASM (music). City setting, with easy access to Atlanta; 130-acre barrier-free campus. Total enrollment: 2,219. Faculty: 128 (105 full-time, 23 part-time); 77% have doctoral degrees; graduate assistants teach no undergraduate courses. Calendar: quarters. Grading system: letters or numbers. Library holdings: 308,098 bound volumes, 3,581 titles on microform, 2,705 periodical subscriptions, 6,000 records/tapes.

Undergraduate Profile Fall 1984: 1,997 undergraduates (494 freshmen); 11% part-time; 73% state residents; 8% transfers; 62% financial aid recipients; 51% women; 15% blacks; 0% Native Americans; 1% Hispanics; 1% foreign nationals; 13% of undergraduates over 25 years of age; 40 legally handicapped students.

Expenses (1985–86) Comprehensive fee of $7899 includes full-time tuition ($5286) and college room and board ($2613). College room only: $1167. Part-time tuition: $597 per course. Tuition for residents of Bibb County and the six adjacent counties, graduates of Macon Junior College, and anyone 30 or over: $4107 full-time, $511 per course part-time.

Financial Aid Fall 1984 full-time freshmen: 83% applied for aid, 91% of those were judged to have need, 100% of those were aided; the average aided freshman received an aid package worth $4023 (56% scholarships/grants, 44% self-help) meeting 85% of need. College-administered aid for all 1984–85 undergraduates: 1,175 need-based scholarships (average $800); 544 non-need scholarships (average $2150); short-term loans (average $50); low-interest long-term loans from external sources (average $1300); SEOG; College Work-Study; 600 part-time jobs. Supporting data: FAF, institutional form required; IRS, state form, AFSA/SAR required for some. Priority application deadline: 5/1.

Athletics Member NCAA (Division I). Intercollegiate sports: baseball/softball M(I,s); basketball M(I,s), W(II,s); cross-country running M(I); golf M(I); riflery M(I), W(I); soccer M(I); tennis M(I), W(I); volleyball M(I). Intramural sports: baseball/softball, basketball, football, racquetball, swimming and diving, tennis, volleyball.

Majors Accounting B; art/fine arts B; biology/biological sciences B; black/Afro-American studies B; business administration/commerce/management B; chemistry B; communication B; computer science B; (pre)dentistry sequence B; early childhood education B; earth science B; economics B; education B; elementary education B; English B; finance/banking B; French B; German B; Greek B; health education B; history B; human services B; Latin B; (pre)law sequence B; liberal arts/general studies B; marketing/retailing/merchandising B; mathematics B; medical technology B; (pre)medicine sequence B; music B; music education B; natural sciences B; philosophy B; physical education B; physics B; piano/organ B; political science/government B; psychology B; religious studies B; secondary education B; social science B; social work B; sociology B; Spanish B; special education B; speech/rhetoric/public address/debate B; theater arts/drama B; voice B; wind and percussion instruments B. Majors with highest enrollment: communication, psychology, English.

LD Program Information

Name of Program Special Services.

Availability of Services Services provided to freshmen, sophomores, juniors, seniors. Program currently serves 20 LD students.

Fees $50 to $100 for diagnostic testing.

Staff 1 full-time staff member (coordinator).

Admissions LD applicants evaluated on the basis of high school transcript and grade point average, untimed SAT, personal interview, autobiographical statement, letters of recommendation. LD students may begin taking classes in fall, winter, spring, or summer. Application should be submitted 3 to 4 months in advance of initial anticipated enrollment.

Orientation Optional orientation offered before registration.

Housing College housing available. LD students housed randomly. LD freshmen and sophomores required to live on campus.

Diagnostic Testing Available in personality, interest inventories, various other areas as appropriate.

Tutoring Offered one-to-one and in small groups by peer tutors. Available in all subjects. LD students may receive tutoring in 2 courses per term.

Basic Skills Remediation Offered one-to-one and in class-size groups by regular teachers. Available in reading, math, written language, learning strategies, work and study habits.

Academic Advisement Help with program planning provided by LD staff member. LD students may take up to 3 courses each quarter; most take 2 to 3 courses (2 in first quarter); 2 courses required to maintain full-time status.

Special Courses Offered in reading, math, typing, career planning. Some offered for credit; some enter into overall grade point average.

Auxiliary Aids and Services Aids include taped textbooks, tape recorders, carbonless notepaper. Services include alternative exam arrangements, notetakers.

Counseling Services Individual counseling, rap sessions, career counseling available.

Contact Mr. Sam Hart, Director, Special Services, Mercer University, Macon, GA 31207, 912-744-2686.

MICHIGAN STATE UNIVERSITY

East Lansing, Michigan

Year Program Began	*Not reported*
Special Fee	None
Special Orientation	✓
Diagnostic Testing	✓
Subject-Area Tutoring	✓
Basic Skills Remediation	✓
Special Courses	
Taped Textbooks	✓
Alternative Exam Arrangements	✓
Notetakers	✓
Staff	5 part-time
Number of Students Served	20

General Information State-supported coed university. Founded 1855. Awards B, M, D. Institutionally accredited by regional association; programs accredited by AACSB (business), ABET (engineering and technology), FIDER (interior design), NASM (music), NLN (nursing), NCATE (teacher education). Small-town setting; 2,000-acre campus. Total enrollment: 40,272. Faculty: 2,494 (2,420 full-time, 74 part-time); 83% have doctoral degrees; graduate assistants teach a few undergraduate courses. Calendar: quarters. Grading system: letters or numbers. Library holdings: 3 million bound volumes, 1.9 million titles on microform, 19,980 periodical subscriptions, 17,700 records/tapes.

Undergraduate Profile Fall 1984: 32,539 undergraduates (6,531 freshmen) from 52 states and territories and 109 foreign countries; 10% part-time; 92% state residents; 7% transfers; 60% financial aid recipients; 50% women; 7% blacks; 1% Native Americans; 1% Hispanics; 1% Asian Americans; 1% foreign nationals; 17% of undergraduates over 25 years of age; 225 legally handicapped students.

Expenses (1984–85) State resident tuition ranges from $1845 to $2087 full-time, $41 to $46 per quarter hour part-time, according to course level. Nonresident tuition ranges from $4455 to $4635 full-time, $99 to $103 per quarter hour part-time, according to course level. Mandatory fees: $39. College room and board: $2412.

Financial Aid Fall 1984 full-time freshmen: 78% applied for aid, 76% of those were judged to have need, 100% of those were aided; the average aided freshman received an aid package worth $2716 (52% scholarships/grants, 48% self-help) meeting 95% of need. College-administered aid for all 1984–85 undergraduates: 18,390 need-based scholarships (average $728); 3,139 non-need scholarships (average $593); short-term loans (average $575); low-interest long-term loans from external sources (average $495); SEOG; College Work-Study; 11,848 part-time jobs. Supporting data: AFSA/SAR required; IRS, institutional form required for some; FFS, FAF acceptable. Priority application deadline: 3/1.

Athletics Member NCAA (Division I). Intercollegiate sports: baseball/softball M(I,s), W(I,s); basketball M(I,s), W(I,s); cross-country running M(I,s), W(I,s); fencing M(I); field hockey W(I,s); football M(I-A,s); golf M(I,s), W(I,s); gymnastics M(I,s), W(I,s); ice hockey M(I,s); lacrosse M(I); soccer M(I,s); swimming and diving M(I,s), W(I,s); tennis M(I,s), W(I,s); track and field M(I,s), W(I,s); volleyball W(I,s); wrestling M(I,s). Intramural sports: baseball/softball, basketball, crew, cross-country running, fencing, football, golf, gymnastics, ice hockey, martial arts, racquetball, rugby, sailing, skiing (cross-country), skiing (downhill), soccer, squash, swimming and diving, tennis, track and field, volleyball, weight lifting, wrestling.

Majors Accounting B; advertising B; agricultural business B; agricultural economics B; agricultural education B; agricultural engineering B; agricultural sciences B; agronomy/soil and crop sciences B; American studies B; animal sciences B; anthropology B; art history B; biochemistry B; biology/biological sciences B; botany/plant sciences B; business administration/commerce/management B; business education B; chemical engineering B; chemistry B; child psychology/child development B; Chinese B; civil engineering B; communication B; community services B; computer science B; construction technologies B; criminal justice B; dairy sciences B; dietetics B; early childhood education B; earth science B; economics B; electrical engineering B; elementary education B; engineering mechanics B; engineering sciences B; English B; entomology B; ethnic studies B; family services B; finance/banking B; fish and game management B; food sciences B; forestry B; French B; geography B; geology B; German B; health education B; history B; home economics education B; horticulture B; hotel and restaurant management B; humanities B; industrial arts B; insurance B; interior design B; international studies B; journalism B; landscape architecture/design B; Latin B; (pre)law sequence B; liberal arts/general studies B; linguistics B; marketing/retailing/merchandising B; materials sciences B; mathematics B; mechanical engineering B; medical technology B; metallurgical engineering B; microbiology B; music B; music education B; music therapy B; natural resource management B; nursing B; nutrition B; parks management B; philosophy B; physical education B; physical sciences B; physics B; physiology B; political science/government B; poultry sciences B; psychology B; public administration B; recreation and leisure services B; religious studies B; Russian B; science B; secretarial studies/office management B; social science B; social work B; sociology B; Spanish B; special education B; speech pathology and audiology B; statistics B; studio art B; systems science B; telecommunications B; textiles and clothing B; theater arts/drama B; tourism and travel B; transportation technologies B; urban studies B; (pre)veterinary medicine sequence B; veterinary sciences B; wildlife management B; zoology B. Majors with highest enrollment: accounting, business administration/commerce/management, psychology.

LD Program Information

Name of Program Office of Programs for Handicapper Students.

Availability of Services Services provided to freshmen, sophomores, juniors, seniors. Program currently serves 20 LD students: 6 freshmen, 5 sophomores, 4 juniors, 5 seniors.

Staff 5 part-time staff members, including director. Services provided by specialists (responsibilities include counseling, administrative duties, needs assessment, and service coordination).

Admissions LD applicants evaluated on the basis of high school transcript, standard or untimed SAT or ACT, history of supportive services. LD students may begin taking classes in fall, winter, spring, or summer. Application should be submitted at least 6 months in advance of initial anticipated enrollment.

Orientation Optional orientation offered before registration.

Housing College housing (including coed) available. LD students housed randomly. LD freshmen required to live on campus.

Diagnostic Testing Needs assessment based on interview with student who provides history of support services in previous school and documentation of diagnosis.

Tutoring Offered in small groups by peer tutors. Available in some subjects. LD students may receive tutoring in all courses each term.

Basic Skills Remediation Offered one-to-one and in small groups by LD teachers, regular teachers. Available in learning strategies, work and study habits.

Academic Advisement Help with program planning provided by LD staff members, academic advisers. LD students may take up to 15 quarter hours each quarter; 12 quarter hours required to maintain full-time status.

Auxiliary Aids and Services Aids include taped textbooks, word processors. Services include alternative exam arrangements, notetakers, advocacy, readers, support group.

Counseling Services Individual counseling, rap sessions, career counseling available.

Contact Ms. Judy K. Gentile, Director, Office of Programs for Handicapper Students, Michigan State University, 477 Communication Arts Building, East Lansing, MI 48824, 517-353-9642.

MILLIGAN COLLEGE

Milligan College, Tennessee

Year Program Began	1972	Special Courses	
Special Fee	None	Taped Textbooks	
Special Orientation		Alternative Exam Arrangements	✓
Diagnostic Testing	✓	Notetakers	
Subject-Area Tutoring	✓	Staff	3 part-time
Basic Skills Remediation	✓	Number of Students Served	4

General Information Christian 4-year coed college. Founded 1866. Awards A (terminal), B. Institutionally accredited by regional association; programs accredited by NCATE (teacher education). Rural setting; 135-acre campus. Total enrollment: 640. Faculty: 71 (42 full-time, 29 part-time); 50% have doctoral degrees. Calendar: semesters. Grading system: letters or numbers. Library holdings: 115,000 bound volumes, 400 periodical subscriptions.

Undergraduate Profile Fall 1984: 640 undergraduates (160 freshmen) from 36 states and territories and 9 foreign countries; 6% part-time; 30% state residents; 7% transfers; 75% financial aid recipients; 55% women; 2% blacks; 1% foreign nationals; 7% of undergraduates over 25 years of age; 4 legally handicapped students.

Expenses (1985–86) Comprehensive fee of $6290 includes full-time tuition ($3998) and college room and board ($2292). Part-time tuition: $125 per credit hour.

Financial Aid Fall 1984 full-time freshmen: 69% applied for aid, 91% of those were judged to have need, 100% of those were aided; the average aided freshman received an aid package worth $4140 (43% scholarships/grants, 57% self-help) meeting 80% of need. College-administered aid for all 1984–85 undergraduates: 160 need-based scholarships (average $1000); 95 non-need scholarships (average $800); short-term loans (average $750); low-interest long-term loans from external sources (average $2100); SEOG; College Work-Study; 150 part-time jobs. Supporting data: institutional form required; FFS, FAF, AFSA/SAR acceptable. Priority application deadline: 5/1.

Athletics Member NAIA. Intercollegiate sports: baseball/softball M(s), W(s); basketball M(s), W(s); soccer M; swimming and diving M, W; tennis M, W; track and field M, W; volleyball W(s). Intramural sports: baseball/softball, basketball, field hockey, football, tennis, volleyball.

Majors Accounting B; biblical studies B; biology/biological sciences B; business administration/commerce/management B; chemistry B; computer science B; (pre) dentistry sequence B; early childhood education B; elementary education B; English B; health education B; history B; humanities B; human services B; mathematics B; medical technology B; (pre)medicine sequence B; ministries B; music B; music education B; physical education B; political science/government B; psychology B; religious education B; sacred music B; secondary education B; secretarial studies/ office management A, B; social work B; sociology B; special education B; (pre) veterinary medicine sequence B. Majors with highest enrollment: business administration/commerce/management, human services.

LD Program Information

Name of Program Learning Center.

Availability of Services Began offering services in 1972. Services provided to freshmen, sophomores. Program currently serves 4 LD students: 2 freshmen, 2 sophomores.

Staff 3 part-time staff members, including director. Services provided by remediation specialist, tutors, diagnostic specialist.

Admissions LD applicants evaluated on the basis of high school transcript, standard or untimed SAT or ACT, letters of recommendation, psychoeducational report. LD students may begin taking classes in fall or winter. Application should be submitted at least 2 months in advance of initial anticipated enrollment.

Housing College housing available. LD students housed randomly. LD freshmen, sophomores, juniors, and seniors required to live on campus except if 25 or over, married, or living with relatives.

Diagnostic Testing Available in intelligence, reading, math, spelling, written language, motor abilities, perceptual skills, work and study habits, personality.

Tutoring Offered one-to-one by professional teachers, peer tutors. Available in all subjects. LD students may receive tutoring in all courses each term.

Basic Skills Remediation Offered in small groups by regular teachers. Available in reading, math, spoken language, written language, learning strategies, motor abilities, perceptual skills, work and study habits.

Academic Advisement Help with program planning provided by academic advisers. Most LD students take 12 credit hours each semester; 12 credit hours required to maintain full-time status.

Auxiliary Aids and Services Aids include tape recorders, calculators, typewriters, word processors. Services include alternative exam arrangements, advocacy.

Counseling Services Individual counseling, career counseling available.

Contact Dr. Paul Clark, Chairman of Professional Studies–Education and Director of Learning Center, Milligan College, Milligan College, TN 37682, 615-929-0116 Ext. 145.

MILWAUKEE INSTITUTE OF ART AND DESIGN

Milwaukee, Wisconsin

Year Program Began	1983	Special Courses	
Special Fee	None	Taped Textbooks	
Special Orientation		Alternative Exam Arrangements	✓
Diagnostic Testing		Notetakers	✓
Subject-Area Tutoring	✓	Staff	1 part-time
Basic Skills Remediation		Number of Students Served	4

General Information Independent 4-year specialized coed college. Founded 1974. Awards B. Programs accredited by NASAD (art and design). Metropolitan setting. Total enrollment: 363. Faculty: 48 (17 full-time, 31 part-time); 6% have doctoral degrees. Calendar: semesters. Grading system: letters or numbers. Library holdings: 14,000 bound volumes, 55 periodical subscriptions.

Undergraduate Profile Fall 1984: 363 undergraduates (101 freshmen) from 7 states and territories and 3 foreign countries; 19% part-time; 87% state residents; 34% transfers; 69% financial aid recipients; 52% women; 2% blacks; 1% Native Americans; 1% Hispanics; 1% Asian Americans; 1% foreign nationals; 2 legally handicapped students.

Expenses (1985–86) Comprehensive fee of $6490 includes full-time tuition ($3700), mandatory fees ($100), and college room and board ($2690). College room only: $1440. Part-time tuition: $120 per credit.

Financial Aid Fall 1984 full-time freshmen: 90% applied for aid, 90% of those were judged to have need, 100% of those were aided; the average aided freshman received an aid package worth $3010 (41% scholarships/grants, 59% self-help) meeting 68% of need. College-administered aid for all 1984–85 undergraduates: need-based scholarships; 20 non-need scholarships (average $1000); low-interest long-term loans from external sources (average $2200); SEOG; College Work-Study; part-time jobs. Supporting data: FAF, IRS, institutional form required; FFS, AFSA/SAR acceptable. Priority application deadline: 4/1.

Majors Art/fine arts B; graphic arts B; illustration B; industrial design B; interior design B; painting/drawing B; photography B; sculpture B. Majors with highest enrollment: art/fine arts, illustration, industrial design.

LD Program Information

Name of Program Individual Services.

Availability of Services Began offering services in 1983. Services provided to freshmen, sophomores, juniors, seniors. Program currently serves 4 LD students: 3 freshmen, 1 sophomore.

Staff 1 part-time staff member (director).

Admissions LD applicants evaluated on the basis of high school transcript, personal interview. LD students may begin taking classes in fall or spring. Application should be submitted at least 4 months in advance of initial anticipated enrollment.

Housing College housing (including coed) available.

Tutoring Offered one-to-one by peer tutors. Available in some subjects. LD students may receive tutoring in all courses each term.

Academic Advisement Help with program planning provided by LD staff member, academic advisers. LD students may take up to 15 credits each semester; most take 12 credits; 12 credits required to maintain full-time status.

Auxiliary Aids and Services Aids include tape recorders, typewriters. Services include alternative exam arrangements, notetakers.

Counseling Services Individual counseling available.

Contact Ms. Judy Luebke, Director of Student Services, Milwaukee Institute of Art and Design, 342 North Water Street, Milwaukee, WI 53202, 414-276-7889.

MINNEAPOLIS COLLEGE OF ART AND DESIGN

Minneapolis, Minnesota

Year Program Began	1971	Special Courses	✓
Special Fee	None	Taped Textbooks	
Special Orientation		Alternative Exam Arrangements	✓
Diagnostic Testing	✓	Notetakers	
Subject-Area Tutoring		Staff	3 part-time
Basic Skills Remediation		Number of Students Served	3

General Information Independent 4-year specialized coed college. Founded 1886. Awards B. Institutionally accredited by regional association; programs accredited by NASAD (art and design). Metropolitan setting; 7-acre campus. Total enrollment: 513. Faculty: 70 (40 full-time, 30 part-time); 5% have doctoral degrees. Calendar: semesters. Grading system: letters or numbers. Library holdings: 50,000 bound volumes, 175 periodical subscriptions, 720 records/tapes.

Undergraduate Profile Fall 1984: 513 undergraduates (111 freshmen) from 25 states and territories and 12 foreign countries; 8% part-time; 73% state residents; 14% transfers; 85% financial aid recipients; 48% women; 2% blacks; 1% Native Americans; 1% Hispanics; 2% Asian Americans; 4% foreign nationals; 25% of undergraduates over 25 years of age; 26 legally handicapped students.

Expenses (1985–86) Tuition: $6100 full-time, $255 per credit part-time. Mandatory fees: $20. College room only: $1550 (minimum).

Financial Aid Fall 1984 full-time freshmen: 77% applied for aid, 94% of those were judged to have need, 99% of those were aided; the average aided freshman received an aid package worth $6178 (54% scholarships/grants, 46% self-help) meeting 60% of need. College-administered aid for all 1984–85 undergraduates: 310 need-based scholarships (average $2008); 27 non-need scholarships (average $2000); short-term loans (average $100); low-interest long-term loans from external sources (average $850); SEOG; College Work-Study; part-time jobs. Supporting data: FFS, IRS required; state form, AFSA/SAR required for some; FAF acceptable. Priority application deadline: 3/1.

Majors Applied art B; art/fine arts B; commercial art B; environmental design B; film studies B; graphic arts B; industrial design B; interdisciplinary studies B; photography B; studio art B. Majors with highest enrollment: commercial art, art/fine arts, environmental design.

LD Program Information

Name of Program Language Center.

Availability of Services Began offering services in 1971. Services provided to freshmen. Program currently serves 3 LD students (all freshmen).

Staff 3 part-time staff members, including coordinator. Services provided by remediation specialist, counselor.

Admissions LD applicants evaluated on the basis of high school transcript, personal interview, autobiographical statement, letters of recommendation, psychoeducational report. LD students may begin taking classes in fall only. Application should be submitted 6 months in advance of initial anticipated enrollment.

Housing College housing (including coed) available. LD students housed randomly. LD students not required to live on campus.

Diagnostic Testing Available in written language.

Academic Advisement Help with program planning provided by LD staff members, academic advisers. LD students may take up to 15 credits each semester; most take 15 credits; 12 credits required to maintain full-time status.

Special Courses Offered in composition. All offered for credit; all enter into overall grade point average.

Auxiliary Aids and Services Services include alternative exam arrangements.

Counseling Services Individual counseling available.

Contact Mr. Richard Shaw, Coordinator of Language Center, Minneapolis College of Art and Design, 133 East 25th Street, Minneapolis, MN 55404, 612-870-3201.

MINOT STATE COLLEGE

Minot, North Dakota

Year Program Began	1974	Special Courses	
Special Fee	None	Taped Textbooks	✓
Special Orientation		Alternative Exam Arrangements	✓
Diagnostic Testing	✓	Notetakers	✓
Subject-Area Tutoring	✓	Staff	10 part-time
Basic Skills Remediation	✓	Number of Students Served	4

General Information State-supported comprehensive coed institution. Founded 1913. Awards A (college transfer and terminal), B, M. Institutionally accredited by regional association; programs accredited by NASM (music), NLN (nursing), NCATE (teacher education). Small-town setting; 160-acre campus. Total enrollment: 3,117. Faculty: 170 (132 full-time, 38 part-time); 60% have doctoral degrees; graduate assistants teach a few undergraduate courses. Calendar: quarters. Grading system: letters or numbers. Library holdings: 91,800 bound volumes, 800 periodical subscriptions, 2,000 records/tapes.

Undergraduate Profile Fall 1984: 3,045 undergraduates (744 freshmen) from 32 states and territories and 11 foreign countries; 13% part-time; 92% state residents; 5% transfers; 75% financial aid recipients; 60% women; 3% blacks; 2% Native Americans; 1% Hispanics; 3% foreign nationals; 26% of undergraduates over 25 years of age; 11 legally handicapped students.

Expenses (1985–86) State resident tuition: $1008 full-time, $24.75 per quarter hour part-time. Nonresident tuition: $1896 full-time, $44.67 per quarter hour part-time. College room and board: $1851. College room only: $555.

Financial Aid Fall 1984 full-time freshmen: 55% applied for aid, 51% of those were judged to have need, 100% of those were aided; the average aided freshman received an aid package worth $3300 (47% scholarships/grants, 53% self-help) meeting 77% of need. College-administered aid for all 1984–85 undergraduates: need-based scholarships (average $500); non-need scholarships (average $300); short-term loans (average $300); low-interest long-term loans from external sources (average $800); College Work-Study; 200 part-time jobs. Supporting data: FFS required; FAF acceptable. Application deadline: continuous.

Athletics Member NAIA. Intercollegiate sports: baseball/softball M(s), W; basketball M(s), W(s); cross-country running M(s), W(s); football M(s); golf M(s), W(s); gymnastics M(s), W(s); tennis M, W; track and field M(s), W(s); volleyball M, W(s); wrestling M(s). Intramural sports: archery, badminton, baseball/softball, basketball, bowling, field hockey, football, golf, gymnastics, ice hockey, martial arts, racquetball, rugby, skiing (cross-country), skiing (downhill), soccer, swimming and diving, tennis, track and field, volleyball, weight lifting, wrestling.

Majors Accounting B; art education B; art/fine arts B; biology/biological sciences B; broadcasting A, B; business administration/commerce/management B; chemistry A, B; computer programming B; computer science B; criminal justice A, B; earth science A, B; ecology/environmental studies A; economics B; education B; elementary education B; flight training A; German B; gerontology B; history B; home economics A; law enforcement/police sciences A, B; legal secretarial studies A; library science A; literature B; marketing/retailing/merchandising A; mathematics B; medical laboratory technology B; medical secretarial studies A, B; medical technology B; music B; music education B; Native American studies A; nursing B; physical education A, B; physical sciences A, B; physics B; piano/organ B; political science/government A; psychology A, B; radiological technology B; reading education B; real estate A; recreation and leisure services B; science B; science education B; secondary education B; secretarial studies/office management A; social science B; social work B; sociology B; special education B; speech pathology and audiology B; telecommunications B; theater arts/drama B; voice B; wildlife management A. Majors with highest enrollment: accounting, elementary education, business administration/commerce/management.

LD Program Information

Name of Program Graduate Program for Learning Disabilities Education.

Availability of Services Began offering services in 1974. Services provided to freshmen, sophomores, juniors, seniors. Program currently serves 4 LD students.

Staff 10 part-time staff members, including coordinator. Services provided by diagnostic specialists, LD teachers, graduate students.

Admissions LD applicants evaluated on the basis of high school transcript, standard ACT. Open admissions policy. LD students may begin taking classes in fall, winter, spring, or summer. Application should be submitted 1 quarter in advance of initial anticipated enrollment.

Housing College housing available. LD students housed randomly. LD students not required to live on campus.

Diagnostic Testing Available in intelligence, reading, math, spelling, handwriting, spoken language, written language, motor abilities, perceptual skills, speech.

Tutoring Offered one-to-one by professional teachers. Available in some subjects. LD students may receive tutoring in all courses each term (depending on course level and individual need).

Basic Skills Remediation Offered one-to-one by LD teachers, teacher trainees. Available in reading, math, spelling, handwriting, spoken language, written language, learning strategies, motor abilities, perceptual skills, work and study habits, speech.

Academic Advisement Help with program planning provided by academic advisers. LD students may take up to 18 quarter hours each quarter; 12 quarter hours required to maintain full-time status.

Auxiliary Aids and Services Aids include taped textbooks, tape recorders, typewriters, word processors. Services include alternative exam arrangements, notetakers, advocacy.

Counseling Services Individual counseling, career counseling available.

Contact Dr. Daryl Wilcox, Program Director, Learning Disabilities Education, Minot State College, Minot, ND 58701, 701-857-3020.

MONMOUTH COLLEGE

West Long Branch, New Jersey

Year Program Began	1982	Special Courses	✓
Special Fee	None	Taped Textbooks	✓
Special Orientation	✓	Alternative Exam Arrangements	✓
Diagnostic Testing	✓	Notetakers	✓
Subject-Area Tutoring	✓	Staff	6 part-time
Basic Skills Remediation	✓	Number of Students Served	13

General Information Independent comprehensive coed institution. Founded 1933. Awards A (college transfer), B, M. Institutionally accredited by regional association; programs accredited by ABET (engineering and technology). Small-town setting, with easy access to New York City; 125-acre barrier-free campus. Total enrollment: 4,225. Faculty: 279 (160 full-time, 119 part-time); 57% have doctoral degrees; graduate assistants teach no undergraduate courses. Calendar: semesters. Grading system: letters or numbers. Library holdings: 215,000 bound volumes, 1,800 periodical subscriptions.

Undergraduate Profile Fall 1984: 3,222 undergraduates (458 freshmen) from 16 states and territories and 10 foreign countries; 41% part-time; 90% state residents; 23% transfers; 60% financial aid recipients; 52% women; 5% blacks; 3% foreign nationals; 34% of undergraduates over 25 years of age; 9 legally handicapped students.

Expenses (1985–86) Comprehensive fee of $9082 includes full-time tuition ($6112), mandatory fees ($220), and college room and board ($2750). College room only: $1310. Part-time tuition: $184 per credit.

Financial Aid Fall 1984 full-time freshmen: 65% applied for aid, 90% of those were judged to have need, 99% of those were aided; the average aided freshman received an aid package worth $3293 (84% scholarships/grants, 16% self-help) meeting 31% of need. College-administered aid for all 1984–85 undergraduates: need-based scholarships (average $2600); non-need scholarships (average $1000); short-term loans; low-interest long-term loans; SEOG; College Work-Study; part-time jobs. Supporting data: FAF, institutional form, AFSA/SAR required; IRS required for some. Priority application deadline: 3/1.

Athletics Member NCAA (Division I). Intercollegiate sports: baseball/softball M(I,s); basketball M(I,s), W(I,s); cross-country running M(I,s); golf M(I), W(I); soccer M(I,s), W(I); swimming and diving M(I,s), W(I,s); tennis M(I,s), W(I,s); track and field W(I); volleyball W(I); water polo M(I,s). Intramural sports: baseball/softball, basketball, equestrian sports, fencing, football, gymnastics, martial arts, sailing, skiing (cross-country), skiing (downhill), swimming and diving, tennis, volleyball.

Majors Accounting B; art education B; art/fine arts B; biology/biological sciences B; business administration/commerce/management A, B; business economics B; chemistry B; communication B; computer programming B; computer science B; creative writing B; criminal justice B; early childhood education B; ecology/environmental studies B; economics B; education B; electrical engineering B; electronics engineering B; elementary education B; environmental sciences B; finance/banking B; French B; history B; liberal arts/general studies A; marketing/retailing/merchandising B; mathematics B; medical technology B; music B; music education B; nursing B; physical sciences B; physics B; psychology B; science education B; secondary education B; social work B; sociology B; special education B; speech/rhetoric/public address/debate B; studio art B; theater arts/drama B. Majors with highest enrollment: business administration/commerce/management, computer science, electrical engineering.

LD Program Information

Name of Program Special Program for Students with Learning Disabilities.

Availability of Services Began offering services in 1982. Services provided to freshmen, sophomores, juniors, seniors. Program currently serves 13 LD students: 4 freshmen, 4 sophomores, 3 juniors, 2 seniors.

Staff 6 part-time staff members, including director. Services provided by remediation specialists, tutors, counselor, adviser.

Admissions LD applicants evaluated on the basis of high school transcript and grade point average, untimed SAT, personal interview, letters of recommendation. LD students may begin taking classes in fall or summer. Application should be submitted 9 to 12 months in advance of initial anticipated enrollment.

Orientation Required orientation held before registration.

Housing College housing (including coed) available. LD students housed randomly. LD students not required to live on campus.

Diagnostic Testing Available in reading, math, handwriting, written language.

Tutoring Offered one-to-one by peer tutors. Available in all subjects. LD students may receive tutoring in all courses each term.

Basic Skills Remediation Offered one-to-one and in small groups by remediation specialists. Available in reading, math, written language, learning strategies, work and study habits.

Academic Advisement Help with program planning provided by LD staff members, academic advisers. Most LD students take 14 credits each semester; 12 credits required to maintain full-time status.

Special Courses Offered in college survival skills, composition, math, career planning. All offered for credit; most enter into overall grade point average.

Auxiliary Aids and Services Aids include taped textbooks, tape recorders. Services include alternative exam arrangements, notetakers, advocacy.

Counseling Services Individual counseling, rap sessions, career counseling available.

Contact Dr. Carol Giroud, Coordinator of Handicapped Student Affairs, Monmouth College, West Long Branch, NJ 07764, 201-222-6600 Ext. 373.

MONTANA STATE UNIVERSITY

Bozeman, Montana

Year Program Began	1978	Special Courses	✓
Special Fee	None	Taped Textbooks	✓
Special Orientation	✓	Alternative Exam Arrangements	✓
Diagnostic Testing	✓	Notetakers	✓
Subject-Area Tutoring	✓	Staff	6 part-time
Basic Skills Remediation	✓	Number of Students Served	73

General Information State-supported coed university. Founded 1893. Awards B, M, D. Institutionally accredited by regional association; programs accredited by NAAB (architecture), NASAD (art and design), AACSB (business), ABET (engineering and technology), NLN (nursing), NCATE (teacher education); candidate for program accreditation by NASM (music). Small-town setting; 1,170-acre campus. Total enrollment: 11,035. Faculty: 661 (541 full-time, 120 part-time); 70% have doctoral degrees; graduate assistants teach a few undergraduate courses. Calendar: quarters. Grading system: letters or numbers. Library holdings: 500,000 bound volumes, 300,000 titles on microform, 4,953 periodical subscriptions, 4,000 records/tapes.

Undergraduate Profile Fall 1984: 9,734 undergraduates (1,737 freshmen) from 49 states and territories and 37 foreign countries; 8% part-time; 85% state residents; 7% transfers; 65% financial aid recipients; 43% women; 2% Native Americans; 3% foreign nationals; 350 legally handicapped students.

Expenses (1985–86) State resident tuition: $1127 full-time. Nonresident tuition: $2876 full-time. Part-time tuition and fees per quarter (1 to 11 credits) range from $37.60 to $348.10 for state residents, $86.60 to $887.50 for nonresidents. College room and board: $2570. College room only: $984.

Financial Aid Fall 1984 full-time freshmen: 68% applied for aid, 95% of those were judged to have need, 100% of those were aided; the average aided freshman received an aid package worth $2746 (40% scholarships/grants, 60% self-help) meeting 90% of need. College-administered aid for all 1984–85 undergraduates: need-based scholarships; non-need scholarships; low-interest long-term loans from external sources; SEOG; College Work-Study; part-time jobs. Supporting data: institutional form, AFSA/SAR required; FAF required for some; FFS, IRS acceptable. Priority application deadline: 3/1.

Athletics Member NCAA (Division I). Intercollegiate sports: basketball M(I,s), W(I,s); cross-country running M(I,s), W(I,s); football M(I-AA,s); gymnastics W(I,s); skiing (cross-country) M(I,s), W(I,s); skiing (downhill) M(I,s), W(I,s); tennis M(I,s), W(II,s); track and field M(I,s), W(I,s); volleyball W(I,s); wrestling M(I,s). Intramural sports: archery, badminton, baseball/softball, basketball, bowling, cross-country running, fencing, football, golf, martial arts, racquetball, skiing (cross-country), skiing (downhill), soccer, swimming and diving, tennis, track and field, volleyball, water polo, weight lifting, wrestling.

Majors Accounting B; agricultural business B; agricultural economics B; agricultural engineering B; agricultural sciences B; agronomy/soil and crop sciences B; animal sciences B; applied art B; applied mathematics B; architecture B; art education B; art/fine arts B; biology/biological sciences B; biomedical sciences B; botany/plant sciences B; business administration/commerce/management B; business education B; chemical engineering B; chemistry B; child care/child and family studies B; child psychology/child development B; civil engineering B; civil engineering technology B; communication B; computer engineering B; computer science B; construction technologies B; criminal justice B; early childhood education B; earth science B; economics B; education B; electrical and electronics technologies B; electrical engineering B; electrical engineering technology B; elementary education B; engineering sciences B; English B; entomology B; environmental health sciences B; farm and ranch management B; film studies B; finance/banking B; fish and game management B; French B; geography B; geology B; geophysics B; German B; gerontology B; graphic arts B; health education B; Hispanic studies B; history B; home economics B; home economics education B; horticulture B; industrial arts B; industrial engineering B; interdisciplinary studies B; interior design B; landscape architecture/design B; land use management and reclamation B; (pre)law sequence B; management engineering B; marketing/retailing/merchandising B; mathematics B; mechanical engineering B; mechanical engineering technology B; medical technology B; microbiology B; modern languages B; music education B; natural resource management B; nursing B; nutrition B; philosophy B; photography B; physical education B; physics B; political science/government B; psychology B; public administration B; radio and television studies B; range management B; recreation and leisure services B; religious studies B; science education B; secondary education B; social work B; sociology B; Spanish B; speech pathology and audiology B; speech/rhetoric/public address/debate B; statistics B; theater arts/drama B; (pre)veterinary medicine sequence B; wildlife management B; zoology B. Majors with highest enrollment: business administration/commerce/management, nursing, electrical engineering.

LD Program Information

Name of Program Disabled Student Services.

Availability of Services Began offering services in 1978. Services provided to freshmen, sophomores, juniors, seniors. Program currently serves 73 LD students: 24 freshmen, 21 sophomores, 14 juniors, 14 seniors.

Staff 6 part-time staff members, including director. Services provided by remediation specialists, tutors, counselors, diagnostic specialist, director of tutoring and remediation center.

Admissions LD applicants evaluated on the basis of high school transcript and grade point average, untimed SAT or ACT, letters of recommendation. LD students may begin taking classes in fall, winter, spring, or summer. Application should be submitted at least 60 days in advance of initial anticipated enrollment.

Orientation Optional orientation offered before registration.

Housing College housing (including coed) available. LD students housed randomly. LD students not required to live on campus.

Diagnostic Testing Available in intelligence, reading, math, spelling, handwriting, written language, perceptual skills, work and study habits, speech.

Tutoring Offered one-to-one and in small groups by peer tutors. Available in most subjects. LD students may receive tutoring in all courses each term.

Basic Skills Remediation Offered in small groups by regular teachers. Available in reading, math, spelling, handwriting, written language, work and study habits.

Academic Advisement Help with program planning provided by LD staff members, academic advisers. LD students may take up to 18 credits each quarter; most take 12 to 15 credits; 12 credits required to maintain full-time status.

Special Courses Offered in college survival skills, reading, communication skills, composition, math, study skills, career planning. Most offered for credit; none enter into overall grade point average.

Auxiliary Aids and Services Aids include taped textbooks, tape recorders, calculators, typewriters, word processors. Services include alternative exam arrangements, notetakers, advocacy.

Counseling Services Individual counseling, small-group counseling available.

Contact Mr. Robert Frazier, Director, Disabled Student Services, Montana State University, 155 Strand Union, Bozeman, MT 59717, 406-994-2824.

MOORE COLLEGE OF ART

Philadelphia, Pennsylvania

Year Program Began	1982	Special Courses	✓
Special Fee	None	Taped Textbooks	
Special Orientation		Alternative Exam Arrangements	✓
Diagnostic Testing	✓	Notetakers	
Subject-Area Tutoring	✓	Staff	1 part-time
Basic Skills Remediation	✓	Number of Students Served	20

General Information Independent 4-year specialized women's college. Founded 1844. Awards B. Institutionally accredited by regional association; programs accredited by NASAD (art and design). Metropolitan setting; 3-acre barrier-free campus. Total enrollment: 548. Faculty: 84 (33 full-time, 51 part-time); 5% have doctoral degrees. Calendar: semesters. Grading system: letters or numbers. Library holdings: 33,000 bound volumes, 4 titles on microform, 340 periodical subscriptions, 1,500 records/tapes.

Undergraduate Profile Fall 1984: 548 undergraduates (141 freshmen) from 54 states and territories and 11 foreign countries; 15% part-time; 62% state residents; 22% transfers; 70% financial aid recipients; 100% women; 6% blacks; 1% Hispanics; 4% Asian Americans; 2% foreign nationals; 2% of undergraduates over 25 years of age; 3 legally handicapped students.

Expenses (1985–86) Comprehensive fee of $9960 includes full-time tuition ($6300), mandatory fees ($200), and college room and board ($3460). Part-time tuition: $270 per credit.

Financial Aid Fall 1984 full-time freshmen: 89% applied for aid, 100% of those were judged to have need, 100% of those were aided; the average aided freshman received an aid package worth $4825 (47% scholarships/grants, 53% self-help) meeting 70% of need. College-administered aid for all 1984–85 undergraduates: 375 need-based scholarships (average $837); 25 non-need scholarships (average $931); low-interest long-term loans from external sources (average $2500); SEOG; College Work-Study; 40 part-time jobs. Supporting data: FAF, IRS, institutional form, AFSA/SAR required; state form required for some; FFS acceptable. Priority application deadline: 4/1.

Majors Art education B; art/fine arts B; ceramic art and design B; commercial art B; fashion design and technology B; graphic arts B; illustration B; interior design B; jewelry and metalsmithing B; painting/drawing B; photography B; sculpture B; textile arts B. Majors with highest enrollment: fashion design and technology, commercial art, illustration.

LD Program Information

Name of Program Learning Skills Center.

Availability of Services Began offering services in 1982. Services provided to freshmen, sophomores, juniors, seniors. Program currently serves 20 LD students.

Staff 1 part-time staff member (director).

Admissions LD applicants evaluated on the basis of high school transcript, standard or untimed SAT, letters of recommendation, portfolio. LD students may begin taking classes in fall or spring. Application should be submitted 6 months in advance of initial anticipated enrollment.

Housing College housing available. LD students housed randomly. LD students not required to live on campus.

Diagnostic Testing Available in reading, math, spelling, handwriting, spoken language, written language, motor abilities, perceptual skills.

Tutoring Offered one-to-one by professional teachers, peer tutors. Available in all subjects. LD students may receive tutoring in all courses each term.

Basic Skills Remediation Offered one-to-one and in small groups by regular teachers. Available in spelling, written language, work and study habits.

Academic Advisement Help with program planning provided by academic advisers. LD students may take up to 17 credits each semester; most take 15.5 credits; 12 credits required to maintain full-time status (except by special permission).

Special Courses Offered in composition. All offered for credit; all enter into overall grade point average.

Auxiliary Aids and Services Aids include word processors. Services include alternative exam arrangements.

Counseling Services Individual counseling available.

Contact Dr. Noel Mawer, Director, Learning Skills Center, Moore College of Art, 20th and Race Streets, Philadelphia, PA 19103, 215-568-4515 Ext. 1503.

MUSKINGUM COLLEGE

New Concord, Ohio

Year Program Began	1983	Special Courses	
Special Fee	$1000 per year	Taped Textbooks	✓
Special Orientation	✓	Alternative Exam Arrangements	✓
Diagnostic Testing		Notetakers	✓
Subject-Area Tutoring	✓	Staff	2 full-time, 6 part-time
Basic Skills Remediation		Number of Students Served	41

General Information 4-year coed college, affiliated with Presbyterian Church (U.S.A.) Founded 1837. Awards B. Institutionally accredited by regional association; programs accredited by NASM (music). Rural setting, with easy access to Columbus; 215-acre campus. Total enrollment: 1,036. Faculty: 88 (70 full-time, 18 part-time); 70% have doctoral degrees. Calendar: semesters. Grading system: letters or numbers. Library holdings: 202,771 bound volumes, 56,712 titles on microform, 800 periodical subscriptions, 3,700 records/tapes.

Undergraduate Profile Fall 1984: 1,036 undergraduates (289 freshmen) from 21 states and territories and 10 foreign countries; 5% part-time; 80% state residents; 4% transfers; 83% financial aid recipients; 47% women; 2% blacks; 0% Native Americans; 0% Hispanics; 1% Asian Americans; 2% foreign nationals; 1% of undergraduates over 25 years of age; 5 legally handicapped students.

Expenses (1985–86) Comprehensive fee of $10,010 includes full-time tuition ($7360), mandatory fees ($100), and college room and board ($2550). College room only: $900. Part-time tuition: $230 per credit hour.

Financial Aid Fall 1984 full-time freshmen: 74% applied for aid, 93% of those were judged to have need, 100% of those were aided; the average aided freshman received an aid package worth $6222 (71% scholarships/grants, 29% self-help) meeting 100% of need. College-administered aid for all 1984–85 undergraduates: 680 need-based scholarships (average $2090); 360 non-need scholarships (average $1250); low-interest long-term loans from external sources (average $2100); SEOG; College Work-Study; 75 part-time jobs. Supporting data: FAF, IRS required; state form, AFSA/SAR required for some. Priority application deadline: 3/1.

Athletics Member NCAA (Division III). Intercollegiate sports: baseball/softball M(III), W(III); basketball M(III), W(III); cross-country running M(III), W(III); field hockey W(III); football M(III); golf M(III); soccer M(III); tennis M(III), W(III); track and field M(III), W(III); volleyball W(III); wrestling M(III). Intramural sports: badminton, baseball/softball, basketball, cross-country running, football, golf, soccer, swimming and diving, tennis, track and field, volleyball, wrestling.

Majors Accounting B; American studies B; applied art B; art education B; art/fine arts B; art history B; biology/biological sciences B; business administration/commerce/management B; business education B; chemistry B; communication B; computer programming B; computer science B; (pre)dentistry sequence B; early childhood education B; earth science B; ecology/environmental studies B; economics B; education B; elementary education B; English B; environmental sciences B; French B; geography B; geology B; German B; health education B; history B; humanities B; interdisciplinary studies B; international business B; international studies B; (pre)law sequence B; mathematics B; medical laboratory technology B; medical technology B; (pre)medicine sequence B; music B; music education B; philosophy B; physical education B; physics B; political science/government B; psychology B; public affairs and policy studies B; public relations B; religious studies B; Russian B; science education B; secondary education B; social science B; sociology B; Spanish B; special education B; theater arts/drama B; (pre)veterinary medicine sequence B. Majors with highest enrollment: business administration/commerce/management, computer science, education.

LD Program Information

Name of Program PLUS Learning Disabilities Program.

Availability of Services Began offering services in 1983. Services provided to freshmen, sophomores, juniors, seniors. Program currently serves 41 LD students: 29 freshmen, 8 sophomores, 4 juniors.

Fees $1000 per year.

Staff 2 full-time, 6 part-time staff members, including director, assistant director. Services provided by tutors.

Admissions LD applicants evaluated on the basis of high school transcript and grade point average, standard or untimed SAT or ACT, personal interview, letters of recommendation, psychoeducational report. LD students may begin taking classes in fall or spring. Application should be submitted 1 to 2 years in advance of initial anticipated enrollment.

Orientation Required orientation held before registration.

Housing College housing available. LD students housed randomly. LD freshmen, sophomores, juniors, and seniors required to live on campus except if living with relatives or by special permission.

Tutoring Offered one-to-one and in small groups by professional teachers, peer tutors. Available in all subjects. LD students may receive tutoring in all courses each term.

Academic Advisement Help with program planning provided by LD staff members, academic advisers. LD students may take up to 18 credit hours each semester; most take 12 to 14 credit hours; 12 credit hours required to maintain full-time status (or as arranged on an individual basis).

Auxiliary Aids and Services Aids include taped textbooks, tape recorders, calculators, typewriters, word processors. Services include alternative exam arrangements, notetakers, advocacy.

Counseling Services Individual counseling, career counseling available.

Contact Dr. Paul Naour, Director of PLUS Learning Disabilities Program and Assistant Professor of Education, Muskingum College, Montgomery Hall, New Concord, OH 43762, 614-826-8249.

NEW COLLEGE OF CALIFORNIA

San Francisco, California

Year Program Began	1980	Special Courses	✓
Special Fee	None	Taped Textbooks	
Special Orientation	✓	Alternative Exam Arrangements	
Diagnostic Testing	✓	Notetakers	
Subject-Area Tutoring	✓	Staff	1 full-time, 4 part-time
Basic Skills Remediation	✓	Number of Students Served	37

General Information Independent comprehensive coed institution. Founded 1971. Awards A (college transfer), B, M. Institutionally accredited by regional association. Metropolitan setting. Total enrollment: 800. Faculty: 35 (11 full-time, 24 part-time); 40% have doctoral degrees; graduate assistants teach a few undergraduate courses. Calendar: semesters. Grading system: letters or numbers (by request), pass/fail, and faculty reports. Library holdings: 12,000 bound volumes, 1 title on microform, 100 periodical subscriptions, 30 records/tapes.

Undergraduate Profile Fall 1984: 500 undergraduates (82 freshmen); 34% part-time; 90% state residents; 60% transfers; 90% financial aid recipients; 60% women; 18% blacks; 0% Native Americans; 9% Hispanics; 1% Asian Americans; 2% foreign nationals; 75% of undergraduates over 25 years of age.

Expenses (1985–86) Tuition: $3200 full-time, $135 per credit part-time. Mandatory fees: $40.

Financial Aid Fall 1984 full-time freshmen: 88% applied for aid, 81% of those were judged to have need, 100% of those were aided; the average aided freshman received an aid package worth $5916 (45% scholarships/grants, 55% self-help) meeting 58% of need. College-administered aid for all 1984–85 undergraduates: need-based scholarships; low-interest long-term loans from external sources (average $2500); SEOG; College Work-Study; 25 part-time jobs. Supporting data: FAF, IRS, institutional form, AFSA/SAR required; FFS acceptable. Priority application deadline: 5/31.

Major Humanities A, B.

LD Program Information

Name of Program Developmental Studies.

Availability of Services Began offering services in 1980. Services provided to freshmen and nonmatriculated students in postsecondary precollege program. Program currently serves 37 LD students.

Staff 1 full-time, 4 part-time staff members, including director. Services provided by instructors.

Admissions LD applicants evaluated on the basis of high school transcript, personal interview, placement testing. LD students may begin taking classes in fall or spring. Application should be submitted 1 month in advance of initial anticipated enrollment.

Orientation Optional orientation offered during registration.

Housing College housing not available.

Diagnostic Testing Available in math, written language.

Tutoring Offered one-to-one and in small groups by professional teachers. Available in all subjects. LD students may receive tutoring in all courses each term.

Basic Skills Remediation Offered one-to-one and in small groups by LD teachers. Available in reading, math, spelling, spoken language, written language, learning strategies, work and study habits, speech.

Academic Advisement Help with program planning provided by LD staff members, academic advisers. LD students may take up to 12 credits each semester; 12 credits required to maintain full-time status.

Special Courses Offered in reading, vocabulary development, communication skills, composition, language development, math. All offered for credit.

Auxiliary Aids and Services Aids include word processors, computer software.

Counseling Services Individual counseling, career counseling available.

Contact Ms. Beth Roy, Director, Developmental Studies, New College of California, 777 Valencia Street, San Francisco, CA 94110, 415-626-1694.

NEW ENGLAND COLLEGE
Henniker, New Hampshire

Year Program Began	1981	Special Courses	✓
Special Fee	None	Taped Textbooks	✓
Special Orientation		Alternative Exam Arrangements	✓
Diagnostic Testing	✓	Notetakers	✓
Subject-Area Tutoring	✓	Staff	3 full-time, 4 part-time
Basic Skills Remediation	✓	Number of Students Served	43

General Information Independent comprehensive coed institution. Founded 1946. Awards B, M. Institutionally accredited by regional association; programs accredited by ABET (engineering and technology). Rural setting, with easy access to Boston; 212-acre barrier-free campus. Total enrollment: 1,082. Faculty: 83 (75 full-time, 8 part-time); 37% have doctoral degrees; graduate assistants teach no undergraduate courses. Calendar: semesters. Grading system: letters or numbers. Library holdings: 80,000 bound volumes, 550 periodical subscriptions, 2,300 records/tapes.

Undergraduate Profile Fall 1984: 1,044 undergraduates (290 freshmen) from 25 states and territories and 30 foreign countries; 5% part-time; 11% state residents; 19% transfers; 60% financial aid recipients; 38% women; 1% blacks; 0% Native Americans; 0% Hispanics; 0% Asian Americans; 11% foreign nationals; 1% of undergraduates over 25 years of age; 5 legally handicapped students.

Expenses (1985–86) Comprehensive fee of $10,250 includes full-time tuition ($7110) and college room and board ($3140). College room only: $1560. Part-time tuition: $230 per credit.

Financial Aid Fall 1984 full-time freshmen: 63% applied for aid, 91% of those were judged to have need, 100% of those were aided; the average aided freshman received an aid package worth $5896 (51% scholarships/grants, 49% self-help) meeting 90% of need. College-administered aid for all 1984–85 undergraduates: 420 need-based scholarships (average $2200); low-interest long-term loans from external sources (average $1100); SEOG; College Work-Study; 40 part-time jobs. Supporting data: FAF, state form required; IRS required for some; FFS, AFSA/SAR acceptable. Priority application deadline: 4/1.

Athletics Member NCAA (Division III), NAIA. Intercollegiate sports: baseball/softball M(III), W(III); basketball M(III), W(III); cross-country running M(III), W(III); equestrian sports M, W; field hockey W(III); golf M(III), W(III); ice hockey M(III); lacrosse M, W; skiing (cross-country) M(I), W(I); skiing (downhill) M(I), W(I); soccer M(III); tennis M(III), W(III). Intramural sports: badminton, baseball/softball, basketball, cross-country running, football, golf, rugby, skiing (cross-country), skiing (downhill), soccer, tennis, volleyball.

Majors Accounting B; art/fine arts B; biology/biological sciences B; business administration/commerce/management B; business economics B; civil engineering B; communication B; computer science B; ecology/environmental studies B; economics B; education B; engineering management B; English B; environmental sciences B; history B; international business B; management engineering B; marketing/retailing/merchandising B; mathematics B; natural sciences B; painting/drawing B; philosophy B; photography B; physical education B; political science/government B; psychology B; public administration B; public relations B; radio and television studies B; secondary education B; sociology B; telecommunications B; theater arts/drama B. Majors with highest enrollment: business administration/commerce/management, communication, engineering management.

LD Program Information

Name of Program College Skills Center.

Availability of Services Began offering services in 1981. Services provided to freshmen, sophomores, juniors, seniors. Program currently serves 43 LD students: 20 freshmen, 15 sophomores, 5 juniors, 3 seniors.

Staff 3 full-time, 4 part-time staff members, including director, associate director. Services provided by remediation specialists, tutors, counselor, diagnostic specialist.

Admissions LD applicants evaluated on the basis of high school transcript, untimed SAT, personal interview, autobiographical statement, letters of recommendation. LD students may begin taking classes in fall only. Application should be submitted 4 months in advance of initial anticipated enrollment.

Housing College housing (including coed) available. LD students housed randomly. LD freshmen and sophomores required to live on campus except if married or 21 or over.

Diagnostic Testing Available in intelligence, reading, math, spelling, spoken language, written language, work and study habits, speech.

Tutoring Offered one-to-one and in small groups by professional teachers, peer tutors. Available in all subjects. LD students may receive tutoring in all courses each term.

Basic Skills Remediation Offered one-to-one by LD teachers, regular teachers. Available in reading, math, spelling, spoken language, learning strategies, work and study habits, speech.

Academic Advisement Help with program planning provided by LD staff members, academic advisers. LD students may take up to 17 credits each semester; most take 12 to 14 credits; 12 credits required to maintain full-time status.

Special Courses Offered in college survival skills, reading, communication skills, math, typing, computer and word processing skills. Some offered for credit; some enter into overall grade point average.

Auxiliary Aids and Services Aids include taped textbooks, tape recorders, calculators, typewriters, word processors. Services include alternative exam arrangements, notetakers, advocacy.

Counseling Services Individual counseling, career counseling available.

Contact Dr. Lyman Gilmore, Director, College Skills Center, New England College, Henniker, NH 03242, 603-428-2218.

NEW MEXICO STATE UNIVERSITY

Las Cruces, New Mexico

Year Program Began	*Not reported*	Special Courses	✓
Special Fee	Varies	Taped Textbooks	✓
Special Orientation		Alternative Exam Arrangements	✓
Diagnostic Testing	✓	Notetakers	✓
Subject-Area Tutoring	✓	Staff	4 part-time
Basic Skills Remediation	✓	Number of Students Served	*Not reported*

General Information State-supported coed university. Part of New Mexico State University System. Founded 1888. Awards A (college transfer and terminal), B, M, D. Institutionally accredited by regional association; programs accredited by AACSB (business), ABET (engineering and technology), NASM (music), NCATE (teacher education). City setting, with easy access to El Paso (TX); 6,000-acre barrier-free campus. Total enrollment: 12,786. Faculty: 712 (597 full-time, 115 part-time); 80% have doctoral degrees; graduate assistants teach a few undergraduate courses. Calendar: semesters. Grading system: letters or numbers. Library holdings: 700,000 bound volumes, 530,000 titles on microform, 275,000 periodical subscriptions, 369 records/tapes.

Undergraduate Profile Fall 1984: 11,197 undergraduates (1,765 freshmen) from 50 states and territories; 19% part-time; 89% state residents; 8% transfers; 75% financial aid recipients; 46% women; 1% blacks; 3% Native Americans; 26% Hispanics.

Expenses (1985–86) State resident tuition: $920 full-time, $38.25 per semester hour part-time. Nonresident tuition: $3066 full-time, $127.75 per semester hour part-time. College room and board: $1970. College room only: $1040.

Financial Aid Fall 1984 full-time freshmen: 68% applied for aid, 78% of those were judged to have need, 100% of those were aided; the average aided freshman received an aid package worth $1913 (49% scholarships/grants, 51% self-help) meeting 80% of need. College-administered aid for all 1984–85 undergraduates: need-based scholarships (average $650); non-need scholarships (average $650); short-term loans (average $75); low-interest long-term loans from college funds (average $75), from external sources (average $650); SEOG; College Work-Study; part-time jobs. Supporting data: FAF, institutional form, AFSA/SAR required; IRS required for some; FFS acceptable. Priority application deadline: 3/1.

Athletics Member NCAA (Division I). Intercollegiate sports: baseball/softball M(I,s), W(I,s); basketball M(I,s), W(I,s); cross-country running M(I,s), W(I,s); football M(I-A,s); golf M(I,s), W(I,s); swimming and diving M(I,s), W(I,s); tennis M(I,s), W(I,s); track and field M(I,s), W(I); volleyball W(I,s). Intramural sports: archery, badminton, baseball/softball, basketball, football, golf, gymnastics, martial arts, racquetball, riflery, rugby, soccer, swimming and diving, tennis, track and field, volleyball, wrestling.

Majors Accounting B; advertising B; agricultural business B; agricultural economics B; agricultural education B; agricultural engineering B; agricultural sciences B; agricultural technologies A; agronomy/soil and crop sciences B; animal sciences B; anthropology B; applied art B; architectural technologies A; art education B; art/fine arts B; art history B; bilingual/bicultural education B; biology/biological sciences B; botany/plant sciences B; broadcasting B; business administration/commerce/management B; business economics B; business education B; chemical engineering B; chemistry B; child care/child and family studies B; city, community, and regional planning B; civil engineering B; civil engineering technology A, B; communication B; computer engineering B; computer information systems B; computer science B; criminal justice A, B; dairy sciences B; (pre)dentistry sequence B; dietetics B; drafting and design A; early childhood education B; earth science B; economics B; education A, B; electrical and electronics technologies A, B; electrical engineering B; electrical engineering technology A, B; electromechanical technology A; elementary education B; engineering technology A, B; English B; family and consumer studies B; farm and ranch management B; fashion merchandising B; finance/banking B; fish and game management B; food sciences B; French B; geography B; geological engineering B; geology B; German B; health education B; health science B; history B; home economics B; home economics education B; horticulture B; industrial engineering B; industrial engineering technology A; international business B; journalism B; law enforcement/police sciences B; (pre)law sequence B; marketing/retailing/merchandising B; mathematics B; mechanical engineering B; mechanical engineering technology A, B; medical laboratory technology B; (pre)medicine sequence B; music B; music education B; nursing A, B; nutrition B; pest control technology B; philosophy B; physical education B; physics B; political science/government B; practical nursing A; psychology B; public health B; public relations B; radio and television studies B; radiological technology A; range management B; real estate B; recreation and leisure services B; retail management A; Russian B; science education B; secondary education B; secretarial studies/office management A; social work B; sociology B; Spanish B; special education B; speech pathology and audiology B; speech/rhetoric/public address/debate B; sports medicine B; textiles and clothing B; theater arts/drama B; (pre)veterinary medicine sequence B; wildlife biology B; wildlife management B. Majors with highest enrollment: electrical engineering, engineering technology, mechanical engineering.

LD Program Information

Name of Program Handicapped Services.

Availability of Services Services provided to freshmen, sophomores, juniors, seniors.

Fees $75 for testing, $10 to $15 per remediation tutorial session.

Staff 4 part-time staff members, including coordinator. Services provided by remediation specialists, counselor, diagnostic specialists.

Admissions LD applicants evaluated on the basis of high school transcript and grade point average, standard or untimed ACT; personal interview recommended. LD students may begin taking classes in fall, spring, or summer. Application should be submitted 2 to 3 months in advance of initial anticipated enrollment.

Housing College housing available. LD students housed randomly. LD students not required to live on campus.

Diagnostic Testing Available in intelligence, reading, math, spelling, handwriting, written language, motor abilities, perceptual skills, work and study habits, personality, psychoneurology, speech, cognitive learning styles.

Tutoring Offered one-to-one and in small groups by professional teachers, peer tutors. Available in most subjects. LD students may receive tutoring in all courses each term.

Basic Skills Remediation Offered by regular teachers, teacher trainees, graduate students. Available in reading, math, spelling, written language, learning strategies, work and study habits, speech.

Academic Advisement Help with program planning provided by academic advisers. LD students may take up to 18 semester hours each semester; most take 14 to 15 semester hours; 12 semester hours required to maintain full-time status.

Special Courses Offered in college survival skills, reading, vocabulary development, communication skills, composition, math, study skills, career planning. Most offered for credit; some enter into overall grade point average.

Auxiliary Aids and Services Aids include taped textbooks, tape recorders, typewriters, word processors. Services include alternative exam arrangements, notetakers, advocacy, typing services.

Counseling Services Individual counseling, career counseling available.

Contact Ms. Patricia C. McCoy, Counselor and Coordinator of Handicapped Services, New Mexico State University, Box 3575, Las Cruces, NM 88003, 505-646-2731.

NORFOLK STATE UNIVERSITY

Norfolk, Virginia

Year Program Began	1984	Special Courses	✓
Special Fee	None	Taped Textbooks	
Special Orientation		Alternative Exam Arrangements	
Diagnostic Testing		Notetakers	
Subject-Area Tutoring	✓	Staff	2 full-time, 6 part-time
Basic Skills Remediation	✓	Number of Students Served	*Not reported*

General Information State-supported comprehensive coed institution. Founded 1935. Awards A (college transfer and terminal), B, M. Institutionally accredited by regional association; programs accredited by NASM (music), NLN (nursing), NCATE (teacher education). City setting; 110-acre barrier-free campus. Total enrollment: 7,300. Faculty: 410 (345 full-time, 65 part-time); 53% have doctoral degrees; graduate assistants teach no undergraduate courses. Calendar: semesters. Grading system: letters or numbers. Library holdings: 200,000 bound volumes, 1,000 titles on microform, 2,300 periodical subscriptions.

Undergraduate Profile Fall 1984: 6,675 undergraduates (1,464 freshmen); 10% part-time; 80% state residents; 5% transfers; 90% financial aid recipients; 55% women; 86% blacks; 5% foreign nationals.

Expenses (1985–86) State resident tuition: $1090 full-time, $55 per semester hour part-time. Nonresident tuition: $1910 full-time, $96 per semester hour part-time. College room and board: $2190.

Financial Aid Fall 1984 full-time freshmen: 95% applied for aid, 90% of those were judged to have need, 95% of those were aided; the average aided freshman received an aid package worth $2321 (71% scholarships/grants, 29% self-help) meeting 87% of need. College-administered aid for all 1984–85 undergraduates: need-based scholarships; non-need scholarships; low-interest long-term loans; SEOG; College Work-Study; part-time jobs. Supporting data: FAF, AFSA/SAR required. Priority application deadline: 4/15.

Athletics Member NCAA (Division II). Intercollegiate sports: baseball/softball M(II), W(II); basketball M(II,s), W(II,s); cross-country running M(II,s); football M(II,s); track and field M(II), W(II); volleyball W(II); wrestling M(II). Intramural sports: baseball/softball, basketball, bowling, cross-country running, football, riflery, soccer, swimming and diving, tennis, track and field, volleyball.

Majors Accounting B; art education B; art/fine arts B; biology/biological sciences B; business administration/commerce/management B; business education B; chemistry B; communication B; computer science B; construction technologies A, B; consumer services B; drafting and design B; early childhood education B; electrical engineering technology A; electronics engineering B; elementary education B; English B; geography A, B; graphic arts B; health education B; health services administration B; history B; home economics B; home economics education B; industrial arts B; industrial engineering B; interdisciplinary studies B; journalism B; library science A; mathematics B; medical records services B; medical technology B; music B; music education B; nursing A, B; nutrition B; occupational safety and health B; physical education B; physics B; political science/government B; psychology B; recreation and leisure services B; secretarial studies/office management A; social work B; sociology B; special education B; speech pathology and audiology B; urban studies B. Majors with highest enrollment: business administration/commerce/management, communication, computer science.

LD Program Information

Name of Program Learning Disabled Program.

Availability of Services Began offering services in 1984. Services provided to freshmen, sophomores, juniors, seniors.

Staff 2 full-time, 6 part-time staff members, including director. Services provided by remediation specialists, tutors, counselors.

Admissions LD applicants evaluated on the basis of high school transcript and grade point average, standard or untimed SAT or ACT. LD students may begin taking classes in fall, spring, or summer. Application should be submitted 6 weeks in advance of initial anticipated enrollment.

Housing College housing available. LD students housed randomly. LD students not required to live on campus.

Tutoring Offered one-to-one and in small groups by professional teachers, peer tutors. LD students may receive tutoring in all courses each term.

Basic Skills Remediation Offered one-to-one and in small groups by LD teachers, teacher trainees. Available in reading, math, spoken language, written language.

Academic Advisement Help with program planning provided by academic advisers. LD students may take up to 18 semester hours each semester; 12 semester hours required to maintain full-time status.

Special Courses Offered in reading, study skills, career planning. None offered for credit; none enter into overall grade point average.

Auxiliary Aids and Services Services include advocacy.

Counseling Services Individual counseling, small-group counseling available.

Contact Dr. Sarah D. Lang, Director of Learning Disabled Program and Chairman of Department of Special Education, Norfolk State University, 2401 Corprew Avenue, Norfolk, VA 23504, 804-623-8714.

NORTH CAROLINA CENTRAL UNIVERSITY

Durham, North Carolina

Year Program Began	1985	Special Courses	
Special Fee	None	Taped Textbooks	✓
Special Orientation	✓	Alternative Exam Arrangements	
Diagnostic Testing	✓	Notetakers	
Subject-Area Tutoring	✓	Staff	8 part-time
Basic Skills Remediation	✓	Number of Students Served	3

General Information State-supported comprehensive coed institution. Part of University of North Carolina System. Founded 1910. Awards B, M. Institutionally accredited by regional association; programs accredited by NLN (nursing), NCATE (teacher education). City setting; 109-acre campus. Total enrollment: 5,002. Faculty: 379 (315 full-time, 64 part-time); 52% have doctoral degrees; graduate assistants teach no undergraduate courses. Calendar: semesters. Grading system: letters or numbers. Library holdings: 600,000 bound volumes, 274 periodical subscriptions.

Undergraduate Profile Fall 1984: 4,268 undergraduates (850 freshmen) from 41 states and territories and 7 foreign countries; 22% part-time; 86% state residents; 7% transfers; 92% financial aid recipients; 62% women; 88% blacks; 18% of undergraduates over 25 years of age; 2 legally handicapped students.

Expenses (1984–85) State resident tuition: $410 full-time. Nonresident tuition: $2722 full-time. Part-time tuition and fees per semester (1 to 11 semester hours) range from $70 to $211 for state residents, $359 to $1078 for nonresidents. Mandatory fees: $358. College room and board: $1866. College room only: $892.

Financial Aid Fall 1984 full-time freshmen: 90% applied for aid, 90% of those were judged to have need, 89% of those were aided; the average aided freshman received an aid package worth $3600 (62% scholarships/grants, 38% self-help) meeting 85% of need. College-administered aid for all 1984–85 undergraduates: need-based scholarships; non-need scholarships; low-interest long-term loans from external sources; SEOG; College Work-Study; part-time jobs. Supporting data: institutional form, AFSA/SAR required; state form required for some; FFS, FAF acceptable. Priority application deadline: 4/1.

Athletics Member NCAA (Division II), NAIA. Intercollegiate sports: baseball/softball W; basketball M(II,s), W(II,s); bowling M, W; cross-country running M; football M(II,s); tennis M(II); track and field M(II), W(II); volleyball W. Intramural sports: baseball/softball, basketball, golf, gymnastics, tennis, volleyball.

Majors Accounting B; art/fine arts B; biology/biological sciences B; black/Afro-American studies B; botany/plant sciences B; business administration/commerce/management B; business economics B; business education B; chemistry B; computer information systems B; computer programming B; computer science B; criminal justice B; data processing B; (pre)dentistry sequence B; early childhood education B; economics B; education B; elementary education B; English B; fashion design and technology B; French B; geography B; German B; health education B; history B; home economics B; home economics education B; jazz B; law enforcement/police sciences B; (pre)law sequence B; mathematics B; modern languages B; music B; music education B; nursing B; nutrition B; philosophy B; physical education B; physics B; political science/government B; psychology B; public administration B; sacred music B; science B; science education B; social science B; sociology B; Spanish B; studio art B; theater arts/drama B; (pre)veterinary medicine sequence B; voice B. Majors with highest enrollment: business administration/commerce/management, computer programming, nursing.

LD Program Information

Name of Program Learning Activity Center.

Availability of Services Began offering services in 1985. Services provided to freshmen, sophomores, juniors, seniors. Program currently serves 3 LD students (all sophomores).

Staff 8 part-time staff members, including director, assistant director, coordinator. Services provided by tutors, professors.

Admissions LD applicants evaluated on the basis of high school transcript and grade point average, standard or untimed SAT or ACT; psychoeducational report recommended. LD students may begin taking classes in fall or spring. Application should be submitted 1 year in advance of initial anticipated enrollment.

Orientation Required orientation held after classes begin.

Housing College housing available. LD students housed randomly. LD students not required to live on campus.

Diagnostic Testing Available in reading, math, spelling.

Tutoring Offered one-to-one by graduate students. Available in some subjects.

Basic Skills Remediation Offered one-to-one by teacher trainees. Available in reading, math, spelling, handwriting, learning strategies, work and study habits.

Academic Advisement Help with program planning provided by academic advisers. Most LD students take 15 to 16 semester hours each semester.

Auxiliary Aids and Services Aids include taped textbooks, tape recorders, calculators, typewriters, word processors, microcomputers. Services include advocacy.

Counseling Services Individual counseling, career counseling available.

Contact Dr. Cecelia Steppe-Jones, Director of Learning Activity Center, North Carolina Central University, PO Box 19746, Durham, NC 27701, 919-683-6478.

NORTH DAKOTA STATE UNIVERSITY

Fargo, North Dakota

Year Program Began	1981	Special Courses	✓
Special Fee	None	Taped Textbooks	✓
Special Orientation	✓	Alternative Exam Arrangements	✓
Diagnostic Testing	✓	Notetakers	✓
Subject-Area Tutoring	✓	Staff	1 part-time
Basic Skills Remediation	✓	Number of Students Served	*Not reported*

General Information State-supported coed university. Founded 1890. Awards A (college transfer and terminal), B, M, D. Institutionally accredited by regional association; programs accredited by NAAB (architecture), ABET (engineering and technology), NASM (music), NLN (nursing), ACPE (pharmacy), NCATE (teacher education). City setting; 2,100-acre barrier-free campus. Total enrollment: 9,453. Faculty: 510 (474 full-time, 36 part-time); 69% have doctoral degrees; graduate assistants teach a few undergraduate courses. Calendar: quarters. Grading system: letters or numbers. Library holdings: 367,537 bound volumes, 63,500 titles on microform, 2,845 periodical subscriptions, 1,220 records/tapes.

Undergraduate Profile Fall 1984: 8,519 undergraduates (1,589 freshmen); 5% part-time; 65% state residents; 17% transfers; 39% financial aid recipients; 43% women; 1% blacks; 1% Native Americans; 2% foreign nationals; 3% of undergraduates over 25 years of age; 58 legally handicapped students.

Expenses (1985–86) State resident tuition: $1095 full-time, $33 per credit part-time. Nonresident tuition: $2088 full-time, $66 per credit part-time. Tuition for Minnesota residents: $1302 full-time, $36 per credit part-time. College room and board: $1623. College room only: $650.

Financial Aid Fall 1984 full-time freshmen: 78% applied for aid, 76% of those were judged to have need, 95% of those were aided; the average aided freshman received an aid package worth $2923 (34% scholarships/grants, 66% self-help) meeting 98% of need. College-administered aid for all 1984–85 undergraduates: need-based scholarships; non-need scholarships; low-interest long-term loans from external sources; SEOG; College Work-Study; part-time jobs. Supporting data: FFS, FAF, IRS, institutional form required. Application deadline: 4/15.

Athletics Member NCAA (Division II). Intercollegiate sports: baseball/softball M(II), W(II); basketball M(II,s), W(II,s); bowling M(c), W(c); cross-country running M(II,s), W(II,s); equestrian sports M(c), W(c); football M(II,s); golf M(II), W(II); ice hockey M(c); riflery M(c), W(c); rugby M(c), W(c); soccer M(c), W(c); swimming and diving M(II), W(II); tennis M(II), W(II); track and field M(II,s), W(II,s); volleyball W(II,s); wrestling M(II,s). Intramural sports: archery, baseball/softball, basketball, cross-country running, football, golf, gymnastics, ice hockey, martial arts, racquetball, riflery, rugby, skiing (cross-country), skiing (downhill), soccer, swimming and diving, tennis, track and field, volleyball, water polo, wrestling.

Majors Accounting B; agricultural business A, B; agricultural economics A, B; agricultural education B; agricultural engineering B; agronomy/soil and crop sciences A, B; animal hospital technology A; animal sciences A, B; anthropology B; architecture B; art education B; art/fine arts B; art history B; arts administration B; bacteriology B; biochemistry B; bioengineering B; biology/biological sciences B; biomedical engineering B; botany/plant sciences B; business administration/commerce/management B; business education B; chemistry B; child care/child and family studies A, B; child psychology/child development B; civil engineering B; communication B; computer engineering B; computer science B; construction engineering B; construction management B; criminal justice B; (pre)dentistry sequence B; dietetics B; early childhood education B; economics B; education B; electrical engineering B; electronics engineering B; engineering physics B; English B; entomology B; family and consumer studies B; fashion design and technology A, B; fashion merchandising A, B; food sciences B; food services management B; French B; geology B; German B; history B; home economics A, B; home economics education B; horticulture A, B; hotel and restaurant management B; industrial engineering B; interior design A, B; liberal arts/general studies B; mathematics B; mechanical engineering B; medical technology B; music B; music education B; nursing B; nutrition B; parks management B; petroleum technology B; pharmacy/pharmaceutical sciences B; physical education B; physics B; political science/government B; polymer science B; psychology B; range management B; recreation and leisure services B; science B; secondary education B; social science B; sociology B; soil conservation B; Spanish B; speech pathology and audiology B; speech therapy B; sports medicine B; statistics B; textiles and clothing B; theater arts/drama B; transportation engineering B; (pre)veterinary medicine sequence B; veterinary sciences B; wildlife biology B; wildlife management B; zoology B. Majors with highest enrollment: electrical engineering, business administration/commerce/management, mechanical engineering.

LD Program Information

Name of Program Disabled Student Services.

Availability of Services Began offering services in 1981. Services provided to freshmen, sophomores, juniors, seniors.

Staff 1 part-time staff member (LD specialist). Services provided by tutors.

Admissions LD applicants evaluated on the basis of high school transcript, untimed ACT, personal interview, autobiographical statement, letters of recommendation, psychoeducational report, IEP. LD students may begin taking classes in fall, winter, spring, or summer. Application should be submitted at least 4 months in advance of initial anticipated enrollment.

Orientation Optional orientation offered during registration.

Housing College housing (including coed) available. LD students housed randomly. LD freshmen required to live on campus.

Diagnostic Testing Available in reading, math, spelling, handwriting, written language, perceptual skills, work and study habits, personality, social skills, speech.

Tutoring Offered one-to-one and in small groups by peer tutors, graduate students. Available in all subjects. LD students may receive tutoring in all courses each term.

Basic Skills Remediation Offered one-to-one by LD teachers, speech clinicians. Available in reading, spelling, written language, learning strategies, work and study habits, social skills, speech.

Academic Advisement Help with program planning provided by LD staff member, academic advisers. LD students may take up to 12 credits each quarter; 12 credits required to maintain full-time status.

Special Courses Offered in reading, study skills, career planning. All offered for credit; none enter into overall grade point average.

Auxiliary Aids and Services Aids include taped textbooks, tape recorders, typewriters, word processors. Services include alternative exam arrangements, notetakers, advocacy, support group.

Counseling Services Individual counseling, career counseling available.

Contact Ms. Liz Sepe, LD Specialist, North Dakota State University, 201 Old Main, Counseling Center, Fargo, ND 58105, 701-237-7671.

NORTHEASTERN UNIVERSITY

Boston, Massachusetts

Year Program Began	1980	Special Courses	✓
Special Fee	None	Taped Textbooks	✓
Special Orientation	✓	Alternative Exam Arrangements	✓
Diagnostic Testing	✓	Notetakers	✓
Subject-Area Tutoring	✓	Staff	4 part-time
Basic Skills Remediation	✓	Number of Students Served	82

General Information Independent coed university. Founded 1898. Awards A (terminal), B, M, D. Institutionally accredited by regional association; programs accredited by AACSB (business), ABET (engineering and technology), NLN (nursing), ACPE (pharmacy), NCATE (teacher education). Metropolitan setting; 55-acre campus. Total enrollment: 36,219. Faculty: 2,785 (782 full-time, 2,003 part-time); 78% have doctoral degrees; graduate assistants teach a few undergraduate courses. Calendar: quarters. Grading system: letters or numbers. Library holdings: 520,797 bound volumes, 590,611 titles on microform, 3,880 periodical subscriptions, 14,840 records/tapes.

Undergraduate Profile Fall 1984: 31,178 undergraduates (4,589 freshmen) from 50 states and territories and 105 foreign countries; 47% part-time; 18% transfers; 70% financial aid recipients; 43% women; 3% blacks; 0% Native Americans; 1% Hispanics; 2% Asian Americans; 3% foreign nationals; 250 legally handicapped students.

Expenses (1985–86) Comprehensive fee of $10,605 includes full-time tuition ($6450 minimum), mandatory fees ($300), and college room and board ($3855). College room only: $2055. Part-time tuition: $75 per credit. Full-time tuition ranges up to $7050, according to program.

Financial Aid Fall 1984 full-time freshmen: 80% applied for aid, 91% of those were judged to have need, 96% of those were aided; the average aided freshman received an aid package worth $4240 (54% scholarships/grants, 46% self-help) meeting 80% of need. College-administered aid for all 1984–85 undergraduates: need-based scholarships; 400 non-need scholarships (average $6000); low-interest long-term loans from external sources (average $1200); SEOG; College Work-Study. Supporting data: FAF, state form required; IRS, institutional form required for some; FFS acceptable. Priority application deadline: 2/15.

Athletics Member NCAA (Division I). Intercollegiate sports: baseball/softball M(I,s); basketball M(I,s), W(I,s); crew M(s), W(s); cross-country running M(I), W(I,s); field hockey W(I,s); football M(I-AA,s); gymnastics W(I,s); ice hockey M(I,s), W(s); lacrosse W(I,s); swimming and diving M(I,s), W(I,s); tennis W(I,s); track and field M(I,s), W(I,s); volleyball W(II,s). Intramural sports: archery, badminton, baseball/softball, basketball, football, golf, racquetball, sailing, skiing (downhill), soccer, swimming and diving, tennis, volleyball, wrestling.

Majors Accounting A, B; African studies B; anthropology B; architectural technologies A; art/fine arts B; aviation technology A; biology/biological sciences B; biomedical engineering B; black/Afro-American studies B; business administration/commerce/management A, B; chemical engineering B; chemical engineering technology B; chemistry B; civil engineering B; civil engineering technology B; communication B; computer engineering B; computer information systems B; computer science B; computer technologies A, B; corrections A, B; criminal justice B; cytotechnology A; data processing A; dental services A; early childhood education B; economics B; education B; electrical engineering B; electrical engineering technology A, B; elementary education B; engineering (general) B; engineering technology B; English B; environmental engineering technology A; finance/banking A, B; French B; geology B; German B; health education B; health science B; history B; hotel and restaurant management A, B; human resources A, B; human services B; industrial engineering B; insurance B; international business B; Italian B; journalism B; laboratory technologies A, B; law enforcement/police sciences A, B; (pre)law sequence B; liberal arts/general studies B; linguistics B; management information systems A; marketing/retailing/merchandising A, B; mathematics B; mechanical engineering B; mechanical engineering technology A, B; medical laboratory technology A, B; medical records services B; modern languages B; music B; music history B; nursing B; pharmacy/pharmaceutical sciences B; philosophy B; physical education B; physical therapy B; physics B; political science/government B; psychology B; public administration B; radiological technology A; reading education B; real estate A; recreation and leisure services B; recreation therapy A; respiratory therapy A, B; Russian B; science education B; secondary education B; sociology B; Spanish B; special education B; speech pathology and audiology B; surveying technology A; telecommunications A; theater arts/drama B; toxicology B; transportation technologies B. Majors with highest enrollment: electrical engineering, criminal justice, nursing.

LD Program Information

Name of Program Services for the Handicapped.

Availability of Services Began offering services in 1980. Services provided to freshmen, sophomores, juniors, seniors. Program currently serves 82 LD students.

Staff 4 part-time staff members, including director, assistant directors. Services provided by remediation specialists, tutors, counselors.

Admissions LD applicants evaluated on the basis of high school transcript and grade point average, standard or untimed SAT or ACT, 3 Achievement Tests, English Composition Test; letters of recommendation, psychoeducational report recommended. LD students may begin taking classes in fall, winter, spring, or summer. Application should be submitted at least 3 months in advance of initial anticipated enrollment.

Orientation Optional orientation offered during registration.

Housing College housing (including coed) available. LD students housed randomly. LD students not required to live on campus.

Diagnostic Testing Available in reading, math, written language.

Tutoring Offered one-to-one and in small groups by professional teachers, peer tutors. Available in some subjects. LD students may receive tutoring in all courses each term.

Basic Skills Remediation Offered one-to-one and in small groups by LD teachers. Available in reading, math, written language, work and study habits, speech.

Academic Advisement Help with program planning provided by LD staff members, academic advisers. LD students may take up to 16 credits each quarter; most take 12 credits; 12 credits required to maintain full-time status.

Special Courses Offered in college survival skills, reading, study skills, career planning. Some offered for credit; some enter into overall grade point average.

Auxiliary Aids and Services Aids include taped textbooks, tape recorders, calculators. Services include alternative exam arrangements, notetakers, advocacy.

Counseling Services Individual counseling, small-group counseling, career counseling available.

Contact Ms. G. Ruth Kukiela Bork, Dean of Student Affairs and Director of Services for the Handicapped, Northeastern University, 360 Huntington Avenue, Boston, MA 02115, 617-437-2675.

NORTHERN ARIZONA UNIVERSITY

Flagstaff, Arizona

Year Program Began	1981	Special Courses	✓
Special Fee	None	Taped Textbooks	✓
Special Orientation	✓	Alternative Exam Arrangements	✓
Diagnostic Testing	✓	Notetakers	✓
Subject-Area Tutoring	✓	Staff	2 part-time
Basic Skills Remediation	✓	Number of Students Served	13

General Information State-supported coed university. Founded 1899. Awards B, M, D. Institutionally accredited by regional association; programs accredited by AACSB (business), ABET (engineering and technology), NASM (music), NCATE (teacher education). Small-town setting; 689-acre barrier-free campus. Total enrollment: 11,826. Faculty: 489 (442 full-time, 47 part-time); 75% have doctoral degrees; graduate assistants teach a few undergraduate courses. Calendar: semesters. Grading system: letters or numbers. Library holdings: 710,703 bound volumes, 917,378 titles on microform, 4,917 periodical subscriptions, 21,878 records/tapes.

Undergraduate Profile Fall 1984: 9,503 undergraduates (1,574 freshmen) from 50 states and territories and 54 foreign countries; 16% part-time; 80% state residents; 40% transfers; 65% financial aid recipients; 49% women; 1% blacks; 6% Native Americans; 6% Hispanics; 1% Asian Americans; 3% foreign nationals; 75 legally handicapped students.

Expenses (1985–86) State resident tuition: $990 full-time, $53 per semester hour part-time. Nonresident tuition: $3244 full-time, $53 per semester hour part-time. College room and board: $1940. College room only: $900.

Financial Aid Fall 1984 full-time freshmen: 71% applied for aid, 80% of those were judged to have need, 91% of those were aided; the average aided freshman received an aid package worth $1458 (55% scholarships/grants, 45% self-help) meeting 95% of need. College-administered aid for all 1984–85 undergraduates: need-based scholarships; 1,285 non-need scholarships (average $1000); short-term loans (average $200); low-interest long-term loans from external sources (average $1500); SEOG; College Work-Study; 900 part-time jobs. Supporting data: FFS, IRS, institutional form, AFSA/SAR, proof of Selective Service registration (for men) required; FAF acceptable. Priority application deadline: 4/15.

Athletics Member NCAA (Division I). Intercollegiate sports: baseball/softball W(I,s); basketball M(I,s), W(I,s); cross-country running M(I,s), W(I,s); football M(I-AA,s); ice hockey M(I,s); swimming and diving W(I); tennis M(I,s), W(I,s); track and field M(I,s), W(I,s); volleyball W(I,s); wrestling M(I,s). Intramural sports: archery, badminton, baseball/softball, basketball, bowling, cross-country running, football, golf, ice hockey, racquetball, soccer, swimming and diving, tennis, track and field, volleyball, water polo, weight lifting, wrestling.

Majors Accounting B; advertising B; American studies B; anthropology B; applied mathematics B; art education B; art/fine arts B; art history B; arts administration B; astronomy B; atmospheric sciences B; biology/biological sciences B; botany/plant sciences B; broadcasting B; business administration/commerce/management B; business economics B; cartography B; ceramic art and design B; chemistry B; city, community, and regional planning B; civil engineering B; civil engineering technology B; commercial art B; communication B; comparative literature B; computer engineering B; computer information systems B; computer science B; corrections B; creative writing B; dance B; data processing B; dental services B; (pre)dentistry sequence B; dietetics B; early childhood education B; earth science B; ecology/environmental studies B; economics B; education B; electrical engineering B; electrical engineering technology B; elementary education B; engineering technology B; English B; environmental sciences B; European studies B; fashion merchandising B; finance/banking B; food sciences B; food services management B; forestry B; French B; geochemistry B; geography B; geology B; geophysics B; graphic arts B; health education B; history B; home economics B; home economics education B; hotel and restaurant management B; humanities B; illustration B; industrial administration B; industrial arts B; interdisciplinary studies B; interior design B; jazz B; jewelry and metalsmithing B; journalism B; Latin American studies B; law enforcement/police sciences B; (pre)law sequence B; liberal arts/general studies B; linguistics B; literature B; marketing/retailing/merchandising B; mathematics B; mechanical engineering B; mechanical engineering technology B; medical technology B; (pre)medicine sequence B; microbiology B; music B; music education B; music history B; natural resource management B; nursing B; nutrition B; painting/drawing B; philosophy B; photography B; physical education B; physical sciences B; physical therapy B; physics B; piano/organ B; political science/government B; psychology B; public administration B; public relations B; recreation and leisure services B; religious studies B; science education B; sculpture B; secondary education B; social science B; social work B; sociology B; Spanish B; special education B; speech pathology and audiology B; speech/rhetoric/public address/debate B; statistics B; stringed instruments B; studio art B; technical writing B; telecommunications B; textile arts B; theater arts/drama B; tourism and travel B; (pre)veterinary medicine sequence B; voice B; water resources B; wind and percussion instruments B; zoology B. Majors with highest enrollment: business administration/commerce/management, elementary education.

LD Program Information

Name of Program Disabled Student Services.

Availability of Services Began offering services in 1981. Services provided to freshmen, sophomores, juniors, seniors. Program currently serves 13 LD students: 5 freshmen, 5 sophomores, 3 juniors.

Staff 2 part-time staff members, including coordinator. Services provided by tutors, counselors.

Admissions LD applicants evaluated on the basis of high school transcript, standard SAT or ACT, letters of recommendation. LD students may begin taking classes in fall, spring, or summer. Application should be submitted 3 to 5 months in advance of initial anticipated enrollment.

Orientation Optional orientation offered before registration.

Housing College housing (including coed) available. LD students housed randomly. LD students not required to live on campus.

Diagnostic Testing Available in intelligence, reading, math, spelling, work and study habits, personality.

Tutoring Offered one-to-one by professional teachers, peer tutors. Available in all subjects. LD students may receive tutoring in all courses each term.

Basic Skills Remediation Offered one-to-one by LD teachers, regular teachers. Available in reading, math, spelling, work and study habits.

Academic Advisement Help with program planning provided by LD staff members, academic advisers. LD students may take up to 15 semester hours each semester; most take 9 to 12 semester hours; 12 semester hours required to maintain full-time status.

Special Courses Offered in college survival skills, study skills, career planning. All offered for credit; all enter into overall grade point average.

Auxiliary Aids and Services Aids include taped textbooks, tape recorders, typewriters, word processors. Services include alternative exam arrangements, notetakers, advocacy, support group.

Counseling Services Individual counseling, career counseling available.

Contact Ms. Linda L. Price, Coordinator of Disabled Student Services, Northern Arizona University, Box 4107, Flagstaff, AZ 86011, 602-523-2261.

NORTHERN ILLINOIS UNIVERSITY

De Kalb, Illinois

Year Program Began	1979	Special Courses	
Special Fee	None	Taped Textbooks	✓
Special Orientation		Alternative Exam Arrangements	✓
Diagnostic Testing		Notetakers	✓
Subject-Area Tutoring	✓	Staff	6 part-time
Basic Skills Remediation	✓	Number of Students Served	5

General Information State-supported coed university. Founded 1895. Awards B, M, D. Institutionally accredited by regional association; programs accredited by NASAD (art and design), AACSB (business), NLN (nursing), NCATE (teacher education); candidate for program accreditation by NASM (music). Small-town setting, with easy access to Chicago; 589-acre campus. Total enrollment: 23,689. Faculty: 1,230 (1,040 full-time, 190 part-time); 62% have doctoral degrees; graduate assistants teach a few undergraduate courses. Calendar: semesters. Grading system: letters or numbers. Library holdings: 1.4 million bound volumes, 10,000 periodical subscriptions, 33,148 records/tapes.

Undergraduate Profile Fall 1984: 17,650 undergraduates (3,340 freshmen) from 25 states and territories and 52 foreign countries; 10% part-time; 97% state residents; 28% transfers; 67% financial aid recipients; 55% women; 59% blacks; 0% Native Americans; 2% Hispanics; 4% Asian Americans; 1% foreign nationals; 9% of undergraduates over 25 years of age.

Expenses (1985–86) State resident tuition: $996 full-time, $42 per credit hour part-time. Nonresident tuition: $2988 full-time, $125 per credit hour part-time. Mandatory fees: $365. College room and board: $2200.

Financial Aid Fall 1984 full-time freshmen: 86% applied for aid, 91% of those were judged to have need, 88% of those were aided; the average aided freshman received an aid package worth $3096 (41% scholarships/grants, 59% self-help) meeting 80% of need. College-administered aid for all 1984–85 undergraduates: need-based scholarships (average $300); non-need scholarships (average $700); low-interest long-term loans from external sources (average $2500); SEOG; College Work-Study; part-time jobs. Supporting data: FAF, institutional form required; AFSA/SAR acceptable. Priority application deadline: 3/1.

Athletics Member NCAA (Division I), NAIA. Intercollegiate sports: baseball/softball W(I,s); basketball M(I,s), W(I,s); field hockey W(I,s); football M(I-AA,s); golf M(I,s), W(I,s); gymnastics M(I,s), W(I,s); soccer M(I,s); swimming and diving M(I,s), W(I,s); tennis M(I,s), W(I,s); volleyball W(I,s); wrestling M(I,s). Intramural sports: badminton, baseball/softball, basketball, football, golf, racquetball, soccer, swimming and diving, tennis, track and field, volleyball, wrestling.

Majors Accounting B; advertising B; anthropology B; applied mathematics B; art education B; art/fine arts B; art history B; bilingual/bicultural education B; biochemistry B; biology/biological sciences B; broadcasting B; business administration/commerce/management B; business education B; ceramic art and design B; chemistry B; child care/child and family studies B; child psychology/child development B; communication B; computer science B; criminal justice B; dance B; dietetics B; economics B; education B; electrical engineering technology B; elementary education B; engineering design B; English B; family services B; fashion merchandising B; finance/banking B; French B; geography B; geology B; German B; graphic arts B; history B; home economics education B; human resources B; illustration B; industrial administration B; industrial arts B; industrial design B; interior design B; international studies B; jewelry and metalsmithing B; journalism B; labor and industrial relations B; liberal arts/general studies B; machine and tool technologies B; marketing/retailing/merchandising B; mathematics B; mechanical engineering technology B; medical technology B; meteorology B; music B; music education B; music history B; nursing B; nutrition B; painting/drawing B; philosophy B; photography B; physical education B; physical therapy B; physics B; piano/organ B; political science/government B; psychology B; public health B; public relations B; radio and television studies B; Russian B; safety and security technologies B; sculpture B; secondary education B; secretarial studies/office management B; social science B; sociology B; Spanish B; special education B; speech pathology and audiology B; speech therapy B; statistics B; studio art B; textiles and clothing B; theater arts/drama B; urban studies B; vocational education B; voice B. Majors with highest enrollment: art/fine arts, journalism, accounting.

LD Program Information

Name of Program Services for Handicapped Students.

Availability of Services Began offering services in 1979. Services provided to freshmen, sophomores, juniors, seniors. Program currently serves 5 LD students: 2 freshmen, 1 sophomore, 1 junior, 1 senior.

Staff 6 part-time staff members, including co-coordinators. Services provided by tutors, readers, editor/typists.

Admissions LD applicants evaluated on the basis of high school transcript and grade point average, standard or untimed ACT, autobiographical statement, letters of recommendation, psychoeducational report. LD students may begin taking classes in fall, spring, or summer. Application should be submitted at least 1 month in advance of initial anticipated enrollment.

Housing College housing (including coed) available. LD students housed randomly. LD freshmen required to live on campus.

Tutoring Offered one-to-one by professional teachers, peer tutors. Available in all subjects. LD students may receive tutoring in all courses each term.

Basic Skills Remediation Offered one-to-one and in small groups by regular teachers, teacher trainees, peer teachers. Available in reading, math, written language, learning strategies, work and study habits, speech.

Academic Advisement Help with program planning provided by academic advisers. LD students may take up to 18 credit hours each semester; most take 12 credit hours; 12 credit hours required to maintain full-time status.

Auxiliary Aids and Services Aids include taped textbooks, tape recorders, calculators, typewriters. Services include alternative exam arrangements, notetakers, advocacy, readers, editor/typists.

Counseling Services Individual counseling available.

Contact Ms. Linda Sorge, Co-Coordinator, Services for Handicapped Students, Northern Illinois University, Health Service 100, De Kalb, IL 60115, 815-753-1303.

NORTHERN KENTUCKY UNIVERSITY

Highland Heights, Kentucky

Year Program Began	1975	Special Courses	✓
Special Fee	None	Taped Textbooks	✓
Special Orientation	✓	Alternative Exam Arrangements	✓
Diagnostic Testing	✓	Notetakers	✓
Subject-Area Tutoring	✓	Staff	1 part-time
Basic Skills Remediation	✓	Number of Students Served	*Not reported*

General Information State-supported comprehensive coed institution. Founded 1968. Awards A (terminal), B, M. Institutionally accredited by regional association; programs accredited by NLN (nursing). Small-town setting, with easy access to Cincinnati; 300-acre barrier-free campus. Total enrollment: 8,879. Faculty: 480 (270 full-time, 210 part-time); 60% have doctoral degrees; graduate assistants teach no undergraduate courses. Calendar: semesters. Grading system: letters or numbers. Library holdings: 220,665 bound volumes, 723,327 titles on microform, 1,651 periodical subscriptions, 4,607 records/tapes.

Undergraduate Profile Fall 1984: 7,621 undergraduates (1,716 freshmen) from 23 states and territories and 25 foreign countries; 47% part-time; 86% state residents; 4% transfers; 50% financial aid recipients; 54% women; 1% blacks; 0% Native Americans; 0% Hispanics; 1% Asian Americans; 1% foreign nationals; 36% of undergraduates over 25 years of age; 120 legally handicapped students.

Expenses (1985–86) State resident tuition: $944 full-time, $39 per semester hour part-time. Nonresident tuition: $2714 full-time, $113 per semester hour part-time. College room only: $1140.

Financial Aid Fall 1984 full-time freshmen: 92% applied for aid, 50% of those were judged to have need, 100% of those were aided; the average aided freshman received an aid package worth $1687 (28% scholarships/grants, 72% self-help) meeting 50% of need. College-administered aid for all 1984–85 undergraduates: 1,728 need-based scholarships (average $729); 974 non-need scholarships (average $715); low-interest long-term loans from external sources (average $751); SEOG; College Work-Study; 570 part-time jobs. Supporting data: FAF, institutional form required. Priority application deadline: 4/1.

Athletics Member NCAA (Division II). Intercollegiate sports: baseball/softball M(II,s), W(II,s); basketball M(II,s), W(II,s); cross-country running M(II), W(II); golf M(II); soccer M(II,s); tennis M(II,s), W(II,s); volleyball W(II,s). Intramural sports: archery, badminton, baseball/softball, basketball, football, martial arts, soccer, tennis, volleyball, water polo, wrestling.

Majors Accounting B; anthropology B; art education B; art/fine arts B; art history B; aviation administration A; biology/biological sciences B; business administration/commerce/management A, B; business education B; chemical engineering technology A; chemistry B; communication B; computer information systems B; computer science B; construction technologies A; data processing A; economics B; electrical and electronics technologies A; elementary education B; English B; film studies B; fire science A; food marketing B; geography B; geology B; graphic arts B; history B; human services A, B; industrial administration B; industrial engineering technology B; international studies B; journalism B; labor and industrial relations A; labor studies A; law enforcement/police sciences A; manufacturing technology A; marketing/retailing/merchandising B; mathematics B; medical technology B; mental health/rehabilitation counseling B; music B; music education B; nursing A, B; philosophy B; physical education B; physical sciences B; physics B; political science/government B; psychology B; public administration B; radio and television studies B; radiological technology A; real estate A; secretarial studies/office management A, B; social science B; social work B; sociology B; special education B; speech/rhetoric/public address/debate B; theater arts/drama B; urban studies B; vocational education A. Majors with highest enrollment: nursing, business administration/commerce/management, computer science.

LD Program Information

Name of Program Special Services for Disadvantaged Students.

Availability of Services Began offering services in 1975. Services provided to freshmen, sophomores, juniors, seniors.

Staff 1 part-time staff member (director). Services provided by tutors, counselors.

Admissions LD applicants evaluated on the basis of high school transcript, standard or untimed ACT. LD students may begin taking classes in fall, spring, or summer. Application should be submitted 6 months in advance of initial anticipated enrollment.

Orientation Optional orientation offered before registration.

Housing College housing available. LD students housed randomly. LD students not required to live on campus.

Diagnostic Testing Available in reading, math, written language.

Tutoring Offered one-to-one and in small groups by professional teachers, peer tutors. Available in all subjects. LD students may receive tutoring in all courses each term.

Basic Skills Remediation Offered one-to-one and in small groups by regular teachers. Available in reading, math, spelling, written language, work and study habits.

Academic Advisement Help with program planning provided by academic advisers. LD students may take up to 18 semester hours each semester; most take 12 to 15 semester hours; 12 semester hours required to maintain full-time status.

Special Courses Offered in reading, vocabulary development, composition, math, study skills, career planning. All offered for credit; most enter into overall grade point average.

Auxiliary Aids and Services Aids include taped textbooks, word processors. Services include alternative exam arrangements, notetakers, advocacy.

Counseling Services Individual counseling, rap sessions, career counseling available.

Contact Ms. Stephanie Baker, Director, Special Services for Disadvantaged Students, Northern Kentucky University, BEP 209, Highland Heights, KY 41076, 606-572-5189.

NORTHERN MICHIGAN UNIVERSITY

Marquette, Michigan

Year Program Began	1978	Special Courses	✓
Special Fee	None	Taped Textbooks	✓
Special Orientation		Alternative Exam Arrangements	✓
Diagnostic Testing	✓	Notetakers	✓
Subject-Area Tutoring	✓	Staff	3 part-time
Basic Skills Remediation	✓	Number of Students Served	20

General Information State-supported comprehensive coed institution. Founded 1899. Awards A (college transfer and terminal), B, M. Institutionally accredited by regional association; programs accredited by NASM (music), NLN (nursing). Small-town setting; 300-acre campus. Total enrollment: 7,869. Faculty: 309 (275 full-time, 34 part-time); 65% have doctoral degrees; graduate assistants teach a few undergraduate courses. Calendar: semesters. Grading system: letters or numbers. Library holdings: 382,805 bound volumes, 528,000 titles on microform, 2,307 periodical subscriptions, 2,487 records/tapes.

Undergraduate Profile Fall 1984: 7,031 undergraduates (1,492 freshmen) from 28 states and territories and 30 foreign countries; 21% part-time; 94% state residents; 28% transfers; 67% financial aid recipients; 50% women; 1% blacks; 1% Native Americans; 1% Hispanics; 1% foreign nationals; 45 legally handicapped students.

Expenses (1985–86) State resident tuition: $1503 full-time, $48.50 per credit hour part-time. Nonresident tuition: $3456 full-time, $111.50 per credit hour part-time. Mandatory fees: $20. College room and board: $2291 (minimum).

Financial Aid Fall 1984 full-time freshmen: 84% applied for aid, 73% of those were judged to have need, 97% of those were aided; the average aided freshman received an aid package worth $3148 (58% scholarships/grants, 42% self-help) meeting 100% of need. College-administered aid for all 1984–85 undergraduates: 1,600 need-based scholarships (average $1100); 1,600 non-need scholarships (average $200); short-term loans (average $50); low-interest long-term loans from external sources (average $1800); SEOG; College Work-Study; 2,000 part-time jobs. Supporting data: AFSA/SAR required; FFS, FAF acceptable. Priority application deadline: 2/1.

Athletics Member NCAA (Division II). Intercollegiate sports: basketball M(II,s), W(II,s); cross-country running M(II); field hockey W(II,s); football M(II,s); gymnastics W(II,s); ice hockey M(I,s); skiing (cross-country) M; skiing (downhill) M; swimming and diving W(II,s); tennis M(II); volleyball W(II,s); wrestling M(II,s). Intramural sports: baseball/softball, basketball, football, ice hockey, soccer, tennis.

Majors Accounting B; agricultural technologies A; applied art A, B; art education B; art/fine arts A, B; automotive technologies A, B; aviation technology A; biochemistry B; biology/biological sciences A, B; botany/plant sciences A, B; broadcasting A, B; business administration/commerce/management A, B; business education B; carpentry B; ceramic art and design A, B; chemistry A, B; child care/child and family studies A, B; city, community, and regional planning B; commercial art A, B; communication A, B; computer programming A, B; conservation B; construction technologies A, B; corrections B; criminal justice A, B; data processing A, B; (pre)dentistry sequence B; dietetics B; drafting and design A, B; early childhood education B; earth science B; ecology/environmental studies B; economics A, B; education B; electrical and electronics technologies A, B; elementary education B; English A, B; environmental design B; environmental health sciences B; fashion merchandising A; film studies B; finance/banking B; food services management B; food services technology A; French A, B; geography A, B; German A, B; gerontology B; graphic arts A, B; health education B; history A, B; home economics A, B; home economics education B; hotel and restaurant management B; illustration A, B; industrial arts A, B; industrial design B; interior design B; jewelry and metalsmithing A, B; law enforcement/police sciences A, B; (pre)law sequence B; legal secretarial studies A; liberal arts/general studies A; marketing/retailing/merchandising A, B; mathematics A, B; medical laboratory technology A, B; medical secretarial studies A; medical technology A, B; (pre)medicine sequence B; music A, B; music education B; natural resource management B; nursing B; occupational safety and health B; painting/drawing A, B; parks management B; philosophy A, B; photography A, B; physical education B; physics B; piano/organ B; political science/government A, B; psychology B; public administration B; recreation and leisure services A, B; science education B; sculpture B; secondary education B; secretarial studies/office management A, B; social science B; social work B; sociology A, B; Spanish A, B; special education B; speech pathology and audiology B; speech/rhetoric/public address/debate A, B; statistics B; stringed instruments B; studio art B; textile arts B; textiles and clothing B; theater arts/drama A, B; (pre)veterinary medicine sequence B; vocational education B; voice B; water resources B; wildlife biology B; wind and percussion instruments B; zoology B. Majors with highest enrollment: business administration/commerce/management, nursing, criminal justice.

LD Program Information

Name of Program Student Supportive Services.

Availability of Services Began offering services in 1978. Services provided to freshmen, sophomores, juniors, seniors. Program currently serves 20 LD students: 9 freshmen, 5 sophomores, 3 juniors, 3 seniors.

Staff 3 part-time staff members, including director. Services provided by counselor, learning skills specialist.

Admissions LD applicants evaluated on the basis of high school transcript and grade point average, standard or untimed ACT, letters of recommendation. LD students may begin taking classes in fall, spring, or summer. Application should be submitted 4 months in advance of initial anticipated enrollment.

Housing College housing (including coed) available. LD students housed randomly. LD freshmen and sophomores required to live on campus except for veterans, or if 22 or over or married.

Diagnostic Testing Available in reading, math, spelling, spoken language, written language, perceptual skills, work and study habits, speech.

Tutoring Offered one-to-one and in small groups by learning skills specialist. Available in all subjects. LD students may receive tutoring in all courses each term.

Basic Skills Remediation Offered one-to-one and in small groups by peer teachers. Available in reading, math, spelling, written language, learning strategies, work and study habits.

Academic Advisement Help with program planning provided by LD staff members, academic advisers. LD students may take up to 18 credit hours each semester; most take 12 credit hours; 12 credit hours required to maintain full-time status.

Special Courses Offered in college survival skills. None offered for credit; none enter into overall grade point average.

Auxiliary Aids and Services Aids include taped textbooks, tape recorders. Services include alternative exam arrangements, notetakers, advocacy, readers.

Counseling Services Individual counseling, small-group counseling, career counseling available.

Contact Ms. Patti Said, Director, Student Supportive Services/Learning Skills Specialist, Northern Michigan University, 405 Cohodas, Marquette, MI 49855, 906-227-2252.

NORTHWEST MISSOURI STATE UNIVERSITY

Maryville, Missouri

Year Program Began	*Not reported*	Special Courses	✓
Special Fee	None	Taped Textbooks	✓
Special Orientation		Alternative Exam Arrangements	✓
Diagnostic Testing	✓	Notetakers	✓
Subject-Area Tutoring	✓	Staff	20 part-time
Basic Skills Remediation	✓	Number of Students Served	*Not reported*

General Information State-supported comprehensive coed institution. Founded 1905. Awards B, M. Institutionally accredited by regional association; programs accredited by NASM (music), NCATE (teacher education). Small-town setting, with easy access to Kansas City; 170-acre barrier-free campus. Total enrollment: 5,000. Faculty: 238 (all full-time); 52% have doctoral degrees; graduate assistants teach a few undergraduate courses. Calendar: semesters. Grading system: letters or numbers. Library holdings: 237,000 bound volumes, 130,000 titles on microform, 1,648 periodical subscriptions.

Undergraduate Profile Fall 1984: 4,381 undergraduates (1,090 freshmen) from 39 states and territories and 22 foreign countries; 8% part-time; 60% state residents; 6% transfers; 65% financial aid recipients; 51% women; 1% blacks; 0% Native Americans; 0% Hispanics; 2% foreign nationals; 9% of undergraduates over 25 years of age; 8 legally handicapped students.

Expenses (1985–86) State resident tuition: $930 full-time, $30 per semester hour part-time. Nonresident tuition: $1705 full-time, $55 per semester hour part-time. College room and board: $1790.

Financial Aid Fall 1984 full-time freshmen: 83% applied for aid, 72% of those were judged to have need, 99% of those were aided; the average aided freshman received an aid package worth $2695 (42% scholarships/grants, 58% self-help) meeting 80% of need. College-administered aid for all 1984–85 undergraduates: need-based scholarships; non-need scholarships; short-term loans; low-interest long-term loans from external sources; SEOG; College Work-Study; part-time jobs. Supporting data: FFS, IRS, institutional form required; FAF, AFSA/SAR acceptable. Priority application deadline: 4/30.

Athletics Member NCAA (Division II). Intercollegiate sports: baseball/softball M(II,s), W(II,s); basketball M(II,s), W(II,s); cross-country running M(II,s), W(II,s); football M(II,s); tennis M(II,s), W(II,s); track and field M(II,s), W(II,s); volleyball W(II,s); wrestling M(II,s). Intramural sports: badminton, baseball/softball, basketball, bowling, football, racquetball, swimming and diving, tennis, track and field, volleyball, weight lifting, wrestling.

Majors Accounting B; agricultural business B; agricultural economics B; agricultural education B; agricultural sciences B; agricultural technologies B; agronomy/soil and crop sciences B; animal sciences B; art education B; art/fine arts B; behavioral sciences B; biology/biological sciences B; botany/plant sciences B; broadcasting B; business administration/commerce/management B; business education B; chemistry B; child care/child and family studies B; commercial art B; communication B; computer programming B; computer science B; conservation B; dairy sciences B; (pre)dentistry sequence B; dietetics B; early childhood education B; earth science B; ecology/environmental studies B; economics B; education B; elementary education B; English B; family and consumer studies B; farm and ranch management B; fashion merchandising B; finance/banking B; French B; geography B; geology B; German B; health education B; history B; home economics B; home economics education B; horticulture B; humanities B; industrial administration B; industrial arts B; interior design B; international business B; journalism B; (pre)law sequence B; library science B; marketing/retailing/merchandising B; mathematics B; (pre)medicine sequence B; music B; music education B; nursing B; nutrition B; philosophy B; physical education B; physical sciences B; physics B; political science/government B; psychology B; public administration B; public relations B; radio and television studies B; recreation and leisure services B; science B; science education B; secondary education B; secretarial studies/office management B; social science B; sociology B; Spanish B; special education B; speech pathology and audiology B; speech/rhetoric/public address/debate B; theater arts/drama B; (pre)veterinary medicine sequence B; wildlife management B; zoology B. Majors with highest enrollment: business administration/commerce/management, education, agricultural business.

LD Program Information

Name of Program Not specified.

Availability of Services Services provided to freshmen, sophomores, juniors, seniors.

Staff 20 part-time staff members, including coordinator. Services provided by remediation specialists, tutors, counselors, diagnostic specialists.

Admissions LD applicants evaluated on the basis of high school transcript and grade point average, standard or untimed ACT; psychoeducational report recommended. LD students may begin taking classes in fall, spring, or summer. Application should be submitted 1 to 4 months in advance of initial anticipated enrollment.

Housing College housing (including coed) available. LD students housed randomly. LD freshmen required to live on campus.

Diagnostic Testing Available in intelligence, reading, math, spelling, handwriting, spoken language, written language, perceptual skills, work and study habits, personality, social skills, psychoneurology, speech, hearing.

Tutoring Offered one-to-one and in small groups by professional teachers, peer tutors. Available in all subjects. LD students may receive tutoring in 5 courses per term.

Basic Skills Remediation Offered one-to-one and in small groups by regular teachers, teacher trainees, math lab tutor. Available in reading, math, spelling, handwriting, spoken language, written language, learning strategies, work and study habits, speech.

Academic Advisement Help with program planning provided by academic advisers. LD students may take up to 18 semester hours each semester; most take 15 semester hours; 12 semester hours required to maintain full-time status.

Special Courses Offered in reading, math. All offered for credit; all enter into overall grade point average.

Auxiliary Aids and Services Aids include taped textbooks. Services include alternative exam arrangements, notetakers, advocacy.

Counseling Services Individual counseling, small-group counseling, rap sessions, career counseling available.

Contact Dr. W. C. Dizney, Head, Student Specialized Services, Northwest Missouri State University, Maryville, MO 64468, 816-562-1219.

NOTRE DAME COLLEGE

Manchester, New Hampshire

Year Program Began	1982	Special Courses	✓
Special Fee	None	Taped Textbooks	✓
Special Orientation		Alternative Exam Arrangements	✓
Diagnostic Testing		Notetakers	✓
Subject-Area Tutoring	✓	Staff	1 part-time
Basic Skills Remediation		Number of Students Served	10

General Information Roman Catholic comprehensive primarily women's institution. Founded 1950. Awards A (college transfer and terminal), B, M. Institutionally accredited by regional association. City setting, with easy access to Boston; 8-acre campus. Total enrollment: 741. Faculty: 70 (38 full-time, 32 part-time); 27% have doctoral degrees; graduate assistants teach no undergraduate courses. Calendar: semesters. Grading system: letters or numbers. Library holdings: 44,000 bound volumes, 3,052 titles on microform, 278 periodical subscriptions, 2,900 records/tapes.

Undergraduate Profile Fall 1984: 576 undergraduates (155 freshmen) from 9 states and territories and 1 foreign country; 30% part-time; 55% state residents; 17% transfers; 47% financial aid recipients; 87% women; 1% blacks; 3 legally handicapped students.

Expenses (1985–86) Comprehensive fee of $7400 includes full-time tuition ($4260), mandatory fees ($200), and college room and board ($2940). Part-time tuition: $310 per course.

Financial Aid College-administered aid for all 1984–85 undergraduates: 100 need-based scholarships (average $650); low-interest long-term loans from external sources (average $750); SEOG; College Work-Study; 50 part-time jobs. Supporting data: FAF, IRS, institutional form, AFSA/SAR required; FFS acceptable. Application deadline: 3/1.

Athletics Intramural sports: baseball/softball, basketball, tennis, volleyball.

Majors Art education B; art/fine arts B; behavioral sciences B; biology/biological sciences B; business education B; commercial art B; early childhood education A; education B; elementary education B; English B; French B; history B; Latin B; legal secretarial studies A; medical secretarial studies A; medical technology B; music A, B; music education B; paralegal studies B; pharmacy/pharmaceutical sciences A; religious studies B; secretarial studies/office management A, B; Spanish B. Majors with highest enrollment: commercial art, education, behavioral sciences.

LD Program Information

Name of Program Special Needs Assistance Program (SNAP).

Availability of Services Began offering services in 1982. Services provided to freshmen, sophomores, juniors, seniors. Program currently serves 10 LD students: 4 freshmen, 2 sophomores, 4 juniors.

Staff 1 part-time staff member (director).

Admissions LD applicants evaluated on the basis of high school transcript and grade point average, standard or untimed SAT, personal interview, letters of recommendation, IEP. LD students may begin taking classes in fall or winter. Application should be submitted 6 months in advance of initial anticipated enrollment.

Housing College housing available. LD students housed randomly. LD students not required to live on campus.

Tutoring Offered one-to-one and in small groups by professional teachers, peer tutors, professors. Available in some subjects. LD students may receive tutoring in 5 courses per term.

Academic Advisement Help with program planning provided by LD staff member, academic advisers. LD students may take up to 15 credit hours each semester; most take 9 to 15 credit hours; 12 credit hours required to maintain full-time status.

Special Courses Offered in college survival skills, composition, study skills, career planning. Some offered for credit.

Auxiliary Aids and Services Aids include taped textbooks, tape recorders. Services include alternative exam arrangements, notetakers, advocacy.

Counseling Services Individual counseling, small-group counseling, rap sessions, career counseling available.

Contact Dr. Robert Cray-Andrews, Director, Special Needs Assistance Program, Notre Dame College, 2321 Elm Street, Manchester, NH 03104, 603-669-4298 Ext. 151.

OHIO STATE UNIVERSITY

Columbus, Ohio

Year Program Began	1977	Special Courses	✓
Special Fee	None	Taped Textbooks	✓
Special Orientation	✓	Alternative Exam Arrangements	✓
Diagnostic Testing	✓	Notetakers	✓
Subject-Area Tutoring	✓	Staff	2 full-time, 4 part-time
Basic Skills Remediation	✓	Number of Students Served	420

General Information State-supported coed university. Founded 1870. Awards B, M, D. Institutionally accredited by regional association; programs accredited by AACSB (business), ABET (engineering and technology), NASM (music), NLN (nursing), COE (optometry), ACPE (pharmacy), NCATE (teacher education). Metropolitan setting; 3,242-acre barrier-free campus. Total enrollment: 52,434. Faculty: 3,262 (2,849 full-time, 413 part-time); 77% have doctoral degrees; graduate assistants teach about a quarter of the undergraduate courses. Calendar: quarters. Grading system: letters or numbers. Library holdings: 3.9 million bound volumes, 2.2 million titles on microform, 28,594 periodical subscriptions.

Undergraduate Profile Fall 1984: 40,142 undergraduates (6,664 freshmen) from 52 states and territories and 67 foreign countries; 15% part-time; 92% state residents; 5% transfers; 26% financial aid recipients; 45% women; 5% blacks; 1% Native Americans; 1% Hispanics; 2% Asian Americans; 2% foreign nationals; 13% of undergraduates over 25 years of age; 618 legally handicapped students.

Expenses (1985–86) State resident tuition: $1704 full-time. Nonresident tuition: $4416 full-time. Part-time tuition and fees per quarter (1 to 11 quarter hours) range from $94 to $521 for state residents, $169 to $1350 for nonresidents. College room and board: $2814. College room only: $1854.

Financial Aid Fall 1984 full-time freshmen: 93% applied for aid, 80% of those were judged to have need, 96% of those were aided; the average aided freshman received an aid package worth $3000 (25% scholarships/grants, 75% self-help) meeting 90% of need. College-administered aid for all 1984–85 undergraduates: need-based scholarships; 400 non-need scholarships (average $300); short-term loans (average $80); low-interest long-term loans from college funds (average $400), from external sources (average $1600); SEOG; College Work-Study; 5,000 part-time jobs. Supporting data: FAF, institutional form required; FFS acceptable. Priority application deadline: 3/1.

Athletics Member NCAA (Division I). Intercollegiate sports: baseball/softball M(I,s), W(I,s); basketball M(I,s), W(I,s); cross-country running M(I,s), W(I,s); fencing M(I), W(I,s); field hockey W(I,s); football M(I-A,s); golf M(I,s), W(I,s); gymnastics M(I,s), W(I,s); ice hockey M(I,s); lacrosse M(I); riflery M(I), W(I); soccer M(I); swimming and diving M(I,s), W(I,s); tennis M(I,s), W(I,s); track and field M(I,s), W(I,s); volleyball M(I,s), W(I,s); wrestling M(I,s). Intramural sports: archery, badminton, baseball/softball, basketball, bowling, crew, cross-country running, fencing, football, golf, ice hockey, lacrosse, martial arts, racquetball, sailing, soccer, squash, swimming and diving, tennis, track and field, volleyball, water polo, weight lifting, wrestling.

Majors Accounting B; actuarial science B; aerospace engineering B; agricultural economics B; agricultural education B; agricultural engineering B; agronomy/soil and crop sciences B; animal sciences B; anthropology B; applied mathematics B; Arabic B; architecture B; art education B; art/fine arts B; art history B; astronomy B; aviation administration B; aviation technology B; biochemistry B; biology/biological sciences B; black/Afro-American studies B; botany/plant sciences B; broadcasting B; business administration/commerce/management B; business education B; ceramic art and design B; ceramic engineering B; chemical engineering B; chemistry B; Chinese B; civil engineering B; classics B; communication B; computer science B; criminal justice B; dairy sciences B; dance B; dental services B; dietetics B; early childhood education B; economics B; education B; electrical engineering B; elementary education B; engineering physics B; English B; entomology B; environmental education B; family and consumer studies B; film studies B; finance/banking B; fish and game management B; food sciences B; food services technology B; forestry B; French B; genetics B; geodetic sciences B; geography B; geology B; German B; health education B; Hebrew B; history B; home economics education B; horticulture B; hotel and restaurant management B; human development B; human resources B; industrial design B; industrial engineering B; insurance B; interdisciplinary studies B; interior design B; international business B; international studies B; Islamic studies B; Italian B; Japanese B; jazz B; journalism B; labor and industrial relations B; labor studies B; landscape architecture/design B; linguistics B; marketing/retailing/merchandising B; mathematics B; mechanical engineering B; medical illustration B; medical laboratory technology B; medical records services B; medical technology B; medieval studies B; metallurgical engineering B; microbiology B; mining and mineral engineering B; music B; music education B; music history B; natural resource management B; nursing B; nutrition B; occupational therapy B; painting/drawing B; parks management B; pharmacy/pharmaceutical sciences B; philosophy B; photography B; physical education B; physical therapy B; physics B; piano/organ B; political science/government B; poultry sciences B; psychology B; radiological technology B; real estate B; recreation and leisure services B; religious studies B; respiratory therapy B; Romance languages B; science education B; sculpture B; Slavic languages B; social work B; sociology B; Spanish B; speech/rhetoric/public address/debate B; statistics B; surveying engineering B; textiles and clothing B; theater arts/drama B; transportation technologies B; urban studies B; vocational education B; voice B; welding engineering B; wildlife management B; wind and percussion instruments B; women's studies B; zoology B. Majors with highest enrollment: computer science, electrical engineering, mechanical engineering.

LD Program Information

Name of Program Office for Disability Services.

Availability of Services Began offering services in 1977. Services provided to freshmen, sophomores, juniors, seniors. Program currently serves 420 LD students.

Staff 2 full-time, 4 part-time staff members, including director, assistant director, coordinator. Services provided by counselor, diagnostic specialist, psychometrician.

Admissions LD applicants evaluated on the basis of high school transcript and grade point average, standard or untimed SAT or ACT, letters of recommendation, psychoeducational report. LD students may begin taking classes in fall, winter, spring, or summer. Application should be submitted 10 months in advance of initial anticipated enrollment.

Orientation Optional orientation offered before registration.

Housing College housing (including coed) available. LD students housed randomly. LD freshmen required to live on campus except if married or living with relatives.

Diagnostic Testing Available in intelligence, reading, math, spelling, handwriting, written language, perceptual skills, work and study habits, psychoneurology.

Tutoring Offered one-to-one and in small groups by peer tutors. Available in some subjects. LD students may receive tutoring in all courses each term.

Basic Skills Remediation Offered in small groups by regular teachers. Available in reading, math, written language.

Academic Advisement Help with program planning provided by LD staff members, academic advisers. LD students may take up to 21 quarter hours each quarter; most take 12 to 15 quarter hours; 12 quarter hours required to maintain full-time status.

Special Courses Offered in math. All offered for credit; all enter into overall grade point average.

Auxiliary Aids and Services Aids include taped textbooks, tape recorders, typewriters, word processors. Services include alternative exam arrangements, notetakers, advocacy.

Counseling Services Individual counseling, small-group counseling, career counseling available.

Contact Mr. Warren King, Director, Office for Disability Services, Ohio State University, 1971 Neil Avenue, Columbus, OH 43210, 614-422-3307.

OHIO STATE UNIVERSITY–MANSFIELD CAMPUS
Mansfield, Ohio

Year Program Began	1982	Special Courses	
Special Fee	None	Taped Textbooks	
Special Orientation		Alternative Exam Arrangements	✓
Diagnostic Testing		Notetakers	✓
Subject-Area Tutoring	✓	Staff	2 part-time
Basic Skills Remediation	✓	Number of Students Served	8

General Information State-supported 4-year coed college. Part of Ohio State University. Founded 1958. Awards A (college transfer), B (also offers some graduate courses). Institutionally accredited by regional association. City setting; 591-acre barrier-free campus. Total enrollment: 1,089. Faculty: 36 (34 full-time, 2 part-time); 75% have doctoral degrees; graduate assistants teach a few undergraduate courses. Calendar: quarters. Grading system: letters or numbers. Library holdings: 46,153 bound volumes, 13,548 titles on microform, 446 periodical subscriptions.

Undergraduate Profile Fall 1984: 1,051 undergraduates (282 freshmen) from 5 states and territories; 32% part-time; 99% state residents; 10% transfers; 49% financial aid recipients; 61% women; 2% blacks; 0% Native Americans; 1% Hispanics; 1% Asian Americans; 0% foreign nationals; 32% of undergraduates over 25 years of age; 13 legally handicapped students.

Expenses (1985–86) State resident tuition: $1653 full-time. Nonresident tuition: $4365 full-time. Part-time tuition and fees per quarter (1 to 11 quarter hours) range from $92 to $505 for state residents, $167 to $1334 for nonresidents.

Financial Aid Fall 1984 full-time freshmen: 100% applied for aid, 98% of those were judged to have need, 100% of those were aided; the average aided freshman received an aid package worth $2267 (33% scholarships/grants, 67% self-help) meeting 95% of need. College-administered aid for all 1984–85 undergraduates: need-based scholarships; 100 non-need scholarships (average $200); short-term loans (average $50); low-interest long-term loans from college funds (average $300), from external sources (average $700); SEOG; College Work-Study; 20 part-time jobs. Supporting data: FAF, institutional form required; IRS required for some; FFS acceptable. Priority application deadline: 4/1.

Athletics Intramural sports: baseball/softball, basketball, football, golf, racquetball, skiing (downhill), tennis, volleyball.

Majors Elementary education B; liberal arts/general studies A.

LD Program Information

Name of Program Disability Services.

Availability of Services Began offering services in 1982. Services provided to freshmen, sophomores, juniors, seniors. Program currently serves 8 LD students: 4 freshmen, 3 sophomores, 1 junior.

Staff 2 part-time staff members, including coordinator. Services provided by tutors, LD specialist.

Admissions LD applicants evaluated on the basis of high school transcript, standard SAT or ACT. Open admissions policy. LD students may begin taking classes in fall, winter, spring, or summer. Application should be submitted 2 months in advance of initial anticipated enrollment.

Housing College housing not available.

Tutoring Offered one-to-one and in small groups by peer tutors. Available in all subjects. LD students may receive tutoring in all courses each term.

Basic Skills Remediation Offered one-to-one and in small groups by LD teachers, Developmental Education Lab staff. Available in reading, math, spelling, written language, learning strategies, work and study habits.

Academic Advisement Help with program planning provided by academic advisers. LD students may take up to 21 quarter hours each quarter; most take 12 to 15 quarter hours; 12 quarter hours required to maintain full-time status.

Auxiliary Aids and Services Aids include tape recorders. Services include alternative exam arrangements, notetakers, readers.

Counseling Services Individual counseling, career counseling available.

Contact Ms. Ginny Corso, Disability Services Liaison and Academic Adviser, Ohio State University–Mansfield Campus, 1680 University Drive, Mansfield, OH 44906, 419-755-4231.

OHIO STATE UNIVERSITY–MARION CAMPUS

Marion, Ohio

Year Program Began	1984	Special Courses	✓
Special Fee	None	Taped Textbooks	✓
Special Orientation		Alternative Exam Arrangements	✓
Diagnostic Testing	✓	Notetakers	✓
Subject-Area Tutoring	✓	Staff	2 part-time
Basic Skills Remediation		Number of Students Served	5

General Information State-supported 4-year coed college. Part of Ohio State University. Founded 1957. Awards A (college transfer), B (also offers some graduate courses). Institutionally accredited by regional association. Small-town setting, with easy access to Columbus; 180-acre barrier-free campus. Total enrollment: 795. Faculty: 25 (24 full-time, 1 part-time); 75% have doctoral degrees; graduate assistants teach a few undergraduate courses. Calendar: quarters. Grading system: letters or numbers. Library holdings: 32,815 bound volumes, 8,189 titles on microform, 239 periodical subscriptions.

Undergraduate Profile Fall 1984: 739 undergraduates (179 freshmen) from 3 states and territories; 35% part-time; 99% state residents; 16% transfers; 49% financial aid recipients; 53% women; 3% blacks; 1% Native Americans; 1% Hispanics; 1% Asian Americans; 0% foreign nationals; 39% of undergraduates over 25 years of age; 8 legally handicapped students.

Expenses (1985–86) State resident tuition: $1653 full-time. Nonresident tuition: $4365 full-time. Part-time tuition and fees per quarter (1 to 11 quarter hours) range from $92 to $505 for state residents, $167 to $1334 for nonresidents.

Financial Aid Fall 1984 full-time freshmen: 100% applied for aid, 91% of those were judged to have need, 100% of those were aided; the average aided freshman received an aid package worth $2593 (50% scholarships/grants, 50% self-help) meeting 90% of need. College-administered aid for all 1984–85 undergraduates: need-based scholarships; 50 non-need scholarships (average $200); short-term loans (average $50); low-interest long-term loans from college funds (average $300), from external sources (average $1950); SEOG; College Work-Study; 7 part-time jobs. Supporting data: FAF, institutional form required; IRS required for some; FFS acceptable. Priority application deadline: 4/1.

Athletics Intercollegiate sports: golf M, W; track and field M, W. Intramural sports: baseball/softball, basketball, bowling, football, racquetball, soccer, swimming and diving, tennis, track and field, volleyball.

Majors Elementary education B; liberal arts/general studies A.

LD Program Information

Name of Program Office of Disability Services.

Availability of Services Began offering services in 1984. Services provided to freshmen, sophomores, juniors, seniors. Program currently serves 5 LD students: 4 freshmen, 1 senior.

Staff 2 part-time staff members, including coordinator. Services provided by diagnostic specialist.

Admissions LD applicants evaluated on the basis of high school transcript, standard or untimed ACT. LD students may begin taking classes in fall, winter, spring, or summer.

Housing College housing not available.

Diagnostic Testing Available in intelligence, reading, spelling, handwriting, perceptual skills.

Tutoring Offered one-to-one and in small groups by peer tutors. Available in all subjects. LD students may receive tutoring in all courses each term.

Academic Advisement Help with program planning provided by LD staff members, academic advisers. LD students may take up to 23 quarter hours each quarter; most take 12 to 18 quarter hours; 12 quarter hours required to maintain full-time status.

Special Courses Offered in college survival skills. All offered for credit; all enter into overall grade point average.

Auxiliary Aids and Services Aids include taped textbooks, tape recorders. Services include alternative exam arrangements, notetakers, advocacy.

Counseling Services Individual counseling available.

Contact Ms. Melissa Conrath, Academic Adviser and Staff Assistant, Disability Services, Ohio State University–Marion Campus, 1465 Mt. Vernon Avenue, Marion, OH 43302, 614-389-2361.

OHIO STATE UNIVERSITY–NEWARK CAMPUS

Newark, Ohio

Year Program Began	1984	Special Courses	✓
Special Fee	None	Taped Textbooks	✓
Special Orientation		Alternative Exam Arrangements	✓
Diagnostic Testing	✓	Notetakers	✓
Subject-Area Tutoring	✓	Staff	3 part-time
Basic Skills Remediation	✓	Number of Students Served	3

General Information State-supported 4-year coed college. Part of Ohio State University. Founded 1957. Awards A (college transfer), B (also offers some graduate courses). Institutionally accredited by regional association. Small-town setting, with easy access to Columbus; 101-acre barrier-free campus. Total enrollment: 935. Faculty: 27 (all full-time); 63% have doctoral degrees; graduate assistants teach a few undergraduate courses. Calendar: quarters. Grading system: letters or numbers. Library holdings: 42,287 bound volumes, 10,024 titles on microform, 413 periodical subscriptions.

Undergraduate Profile Fall 1984: 896 undergraduates (319 freshmen) from 5 states and territories and 1 foreign country; 35% part-time; 99% state residents; 11% transfers; 80% financial aid recipients; 54% women; 1% blacks; 1% Native Americans; 1% Hispanics; 1% Asian Americans; 1% foreign nationals; 28% of undergraduates over 25 years of age; 10 legally handicapped students.

Expenses (1985–86) State resident tuition: $1653 full-time. Nonresident tuition: $4365 full-time. Part-time tuition and fees per quarter (1 to 11 quarter hours) range from $92 to $505 for state residents, $167 to $1334 for nonresidents.

Financial Aid Fall 1984 full-time freshmen: 93% applied for aid, 90% of those were judged to have need, 95% of those were aided; the average aided freshman received an aid package worth $2150 (28% scholarships/grants, 72% self-help) meeting 90% of need. College-administered aid for all 1984–85 undergraduates: need-based scholarships (average $250); non-need scholarships (average $250); short-term loans (average $50); low-interest long-term loans from college funds (average $300), from external sources (average $1100); College Work-Study; 50 part-time jobs. Supporting data: FAF, institutional form required; IRS required for some; FFS acceptable. Priority application deadline: 4/1.

Athletics Intercollegiate sports: baseball/softball M; basketball M, W; golf M, W; tennis M, W; volleyball W. Intramural sports: badminton, baseball/softball, basketball, bowling, cross-country running, football, golf, racquetball, skiing (cross-country), skiing (downhill), soccer, tennis, volleyball, wrestling.

Majors Elementary education B; liberal arts/general studies A.

LD Program Information

Name of Program Developmental Education.

Availability of Services Began offering services in 1984. Services provided to freshmen, sophomores, juniors, seniors. Program currently serves 3 LD students: 2 freshmen, 1 junior.

Staff 3 part-time staff members, including coordinator. Services provided by tutors, diagnostic specialists.

Admissions LD applicants evaluated on the basis of high school transcript, standard SAT or ACT, personal interview, autobiographical statement, psychoeducational report. LD students may begin taking classes in fall, winter, spring, or summer. Application should be submitted 2 months in advance of initial anticipated enrollment.

Housing College housing not available.

Diagnostic Testing Available in intelligence, reading, math, spelling, handwriting, spoken language, written language, perceptual skills, work and study habits, psychoneurology, speech.

Tutoring Offered one-to-one by professional teachers, peer tutors. Available in all subjects. LD students may receive tutoring in 2 courses per term.

Basic Skills Remediation Offered one-to-one and in small groups by regular teachers. Available in reading, math, spelling, handwriting, written language, learning strategies, work and study habits.

Academic Advisement Help with program planning provided by LD staff members, academic advisers. LD students may take up to 15 quarter hours each quarter; most take 6 quarter hours; 12 quarter hours required to maintain full-time status.

Special Courses Offered in college survival skills, personal psychology, study skills. All offered for credit; all enter into overall grade point average.

Auxiliary Aids and Services Aids include taped textbooks, tape recorders. Services include alternative exam arrangements, notetakers, advocacy.

Counseling Services Individual counseling available.

Contact Ms. Phyllis Thompson, Coordinator of Developmental Education, Ohio State University–Newark Campus, University Drive, Newark, OH 43055, 614-366-9246.

OHIO UNIVERSITY

Athens, Ohio

Year Program Began	*Not reported*
Special Fee	None
Special Orientation	
Diagnostic Testing	
Subject-Area Tutoring	✓
Basic Skills Remediation	✓

Special Courses	✓
Taped Textbooks	✓
Alternative Exam Arrangements	✓
Notetakers	
Staff	1 part-time
Number of Students Served	27

General Information State-supported coed university. Part of Ohio University System. Founded 1804. Awards A (terminal), B, M, D. Institutionally accredited by regional association; programs accredited by AACSB (business), ABET (engineering and technology), NASM (music), NLN (nursing), NCATE (teacher education). Small-town setting; 650-acre campus. Total enrollment: 14,897. Faculty: 778; 65% have doctoral degrees; graduate assistants teach a few undergraduate courses. Calendar: quarters. Grading system: letters or numbers. Library holdings: 1.2 million bound volumes, 1.1 million titles on microform, 20,000 periodical subscriptions, 321,000 records/tapes.

Undergraduate Profile Fall 1984: 11,806 undergraduates (3,025 freshmen) from 52 states and territories and 90 foreign countries; 13% part-time; 80% state residents; 12% transfers; 65% financial aid recipients; 48% women; 7% blacks; 1% Native Americans; 1% Hispanics; 1% Asian Americans; 9% foreign nationals; 7% of undergraduates over 25 years of age.

Expenses (1985–86) State resident tuition: $1992 full-time, $66 per quarter hour part-time. Nonresident tuition: $3993 full-time, $132 per quarter hour part-time. College room and board: $2673. College room only: $1359.

Financial Aid Fall 1984 full-time freshmen: 65% applied for aid, 88% of those were judged to have need, 100% of those were aided; the average aided freshman received an aid package worth $2651 (28% scholarships/grants, 72% self-help) meeting 80% of need. College-administered aid for all 1984–85 undergraduates: 575 need-based scholarships (average $430); 1,565 non-need scholarships (average $500); short-term loans (average $350); low-interest long-term loans from college funds (average $750), from external sources (average $1900); SEOG; College Work-Study; 1,450 part-time jobs. Supporting data: FAF, institutional form required; FFS acceptable. Priority application deadline: 3/15.

Athletics Member NCAA (Division I). Intercollegiate sports: baseball/softball M(I,s), W(I,s); basketball M(I,s), W(I,s); bowling M(c), W(c); cross-country running M(I,s), W(I,s); field hockey W(I,s); football M(I-A,s); golf M(I,s); gymnastics M(c), W(c); ice hockey M(c); lacrosse M(c), W(c); martial arts M(c), W(c); rugby M(c), W(c); sailing M(c), W(c); soccer M(c), W(c); swimming and diving M(I,s), W(I,s); tennis M(I,s), W(I,s); track and field M(I,s), W(I,s); volleyball M(c), W(I,s); weight lifting M(c); wrestling M(I,s). Intramural sports: archery, baseball/softball, basketball, bowling, cross-country running, fencing, football, golf, gymnastics, ice hockey, martial arts, racquetball, riflery, skiing (cross-country), skiing (downhill), soccer, swimming and diving, tennis, track and field, volleyball, water polo, weight lifting, wrestling.

Majors Accounting B; advertising B; anthropology B; applied art B; art education B; art history B; art therapy B; aviation technology A; biology/biological sciences B; biomedical sciences B; black/Afro-American studies B; botany/plant sciences B; broadcasting B; business administration/commerce/management B; business economics B; business education B; cell biology B; ceramic art and design B; chemical engineering B; chemistry B; child care/child and family studies B; child psychology/child development A, B; civil engineering B; commercial art B; communication B; community services B; computer engineering B; computer information systems B; computer science B; creative writing B; criminal justice B; dance B; (pre)dentistry sequence B; dietetics B; early childhood education B; ecology/environmental studies B; economics B; educational media B; electrical engineering B; elementary education B; English B; environmental biology B; environmental health sciences B; environmental sciences B; family services B; fashion merchandising B; finance/banking B; food marketing B; food sciences A, B; food services management B; forensic sciences B; French B; geography B; geology B; German B; gerontology B; graphic arts B; health education B; health services administration B; history B; home economics B; home economics education B; human resources B; industrial arts B; industrial engineering B; industrial engineering technology B; interior design A, B; international business B; international studies B; journalism B; labor and industrial relations B; Latin B; Latin American studies B; (pre)law sequence B; literature B; marketing/retailing/merchandising B; mathematics B; mechanical engineering B; medical illustration B; medical technology B; (pre) medicine sequence B; meteorology B; microbiology B; mining and mineral engineering B; music B; music business B; music education B; music history B; music therapy B; nursing B; nutrition B; occupational safety and health B; operations research B; painting/drawing B; philosophy B; photography B; physical education B; physical fitness/human movement B; physical therapy B; physics B; political science/government B; psychology B; public relations B; radio and television studies B; recreation and leisure services B; recreation therapy B; Russian B; sculpture B; secondary education B; social work B; sociology B; Southeast Asian studies B; Spanish B; special education B; speech pathology and audiology B; speech/rhetoric/public address/debate B; speech therapy B; sports administration B; sports medicine B; stringed instruments B; studio art B; systems engineering B; telecommunications B; textiles and clothing B; theater arts/drama B; (pre)veterinary medicine sequence B; voice B; water resources B; wildlife biology B; wildlife management B; wind and percussion instruments B; zoology B. Majors with highest enrollment: journalism, business administration/commerce/management, telecommunications.

LD Program Information

Name of Program Affirmative Action Office.

Availability of Services Services provided to freshmen, sophomores, juniors, seniors. Program currently serves 27 LD students.

Staff 1 part-time staff member (coordinator).

Admissions LD applicants evaluated on the basis of high school transcript and grade point average, standard or untimed SAT or ACT; personal interview, autobiographical statement, letters of recommendation, psychoeducational report recommended. LD students may begin taking classes in fall, winter, spring, or summer. Application should be submitted 3 months in advance of initial anticipated enrollment.

Housing College housing (including coed) available. LD students housed randomly. LD freshmen and sophomores required to live on campus except for sophomores living in fraternities or sororities.

Tutoring Offered one-to-one and in small groups by peer tutors. Available in all subjects. LD students may receive tutoring in all courses each term.

Basic Skills Remediation Offered in small groups by regular teachers. Available in reading, math, written language, work and study habits.

Academic Advisement Help with program planning provided by academic advisers. LD students may take up to 20 quarter hours each quarter; 12 quarter hours required to maintain full-time status.

Special Courses Offered in college survival skills, reading, math, study skills. All offered for credit; all enter into overall grade point average.

Auxiliary Aids and Services Aids include taped textbooks, tape recorders. Services include alternative exam arrangements, advocacy.

Counseling Services Individual counseling, career counseling available.

Contact Ms. Mary Ann Henry, Assistant Director, Affirmative Action Office, Ohio University, 103 McGuffey Hall, Athens, OH 45701, 614-594-5246.

OLD DOMINION UNIVERSITY
Norfolk, Virginia

Year Program Began	1978	Special Courses	✓
Special Fee	None	Taped Textbooks	✓
Special Orientation		Alternative Exam Arrangements	✓
Diagnostic Testing	✓	Notetakers	✓
Subject-Area Tutoring	✓	Staff	8 part-time
Basic Skills Remediation	✓	Number of Students Served	3

General Information State-supported coed university. Founded 1930. Awards B, M, D. Institutionally accredited by regional association; programs accredited by AACSB (business), ABET (engineering and technology), NLN (nursing), NCATE (teacher education); candidate for program accreditation by NASM (music). City setting; 140-acre campus. Total enrollment: 14,966. Faculty: 717 (579 full-time, 138 part-time); 70% have doctoral degrees; graduate assistants teach a few undergraduate courses. Calendar: semesters. Grading system: letters or numbers. Library holdings: 421,632 bound volumes, 4,632 periodical subscriptions, 31,544 records/tapes.

Undergraduate Profile Fall 1984: 11,673 undergraduates (1,836 freshmen) from 47 states and territories and 63 foreign countries; 24% part-time; 86% state residents; 36% transfers; 18% financial aid recipients; 50% women; 11% blacks; 1% Native Americans; 1% Hispanics; 3% Asian Americans; 3% foreign nationals; 140 legally handicapped students.

Expenses (1985–86) State resident tuition: $1678 full-time, $68 per credit hour part-time. Nonresident tuition: $3118 full-time, $128 per credit hour part-time. College room and board: $3050. College room only: $2030.

Financial Aid Fall 1984 full-time freshmen: 52% applied for aid, 82% of those were judged to have need, 79% of those were aided; the average aided freshman received an aid package worth $3403 (31% scholarships/grants, 69% self-help) meeting 70% of need. College-administered aid for all 1984–85 undergraduates: need-based scholarships (average $370); non-need scholarships (average $585); short-term loans (average $100); low-interest long-term loans from external sources (average $2250); SEOG; College Work-Study; 770 part-time jobs. Supporting data: FAF, institutional form, AFSA/SAR required; IRS, state form required for some. Application deadline: continuous to 3/1.

Athletics Member NCAA (Division I). Intercollegiate sports: baseball/softball M(I,s); basketball M(I,s), W(I,s); cross-country running M(I,s), W(I,s); field hockey W(I,s); golf M(I,s); lacrosse W(I,s); rugby M(c); sailing M, W; soccer M(I,s); swimming and diving M(I,s), W(I,s); tennis M(I,s), W(I,s); wrestling M(I,s). Intramural sports: archery, badminton, baseball/softball, basketball, bowling, cross-country running, field hockey, football, golf, martial arts, rugby, sailing, swimming and diving, tennis, volleyball, wrestling.

Majors Accounting B; anthropology B; applied art B; applied mathematics B; art education B; art/fine arts B; art history B; biochemistry B; biology/biological sciences B; biomedical sciences B; business administration/commerce/management B; chemistry B; child care/child and family studies B; child psychology/child development B; civil engineering B; civil engineering technology B; communication B; computer engineering B; computer information systems B; computer science B; creative writing B; criminal justice B; dance B; dental services B; (pre)dentistry sequence B; earth science B; economics B; education B; electrical engineering B; electrical engineering technology B; elementary education B; engineering (general) B; English B; environmental health sciences B; finance/banking B; French B; geography B; geology B; German B; guidance and counseling B; health education B; history B; human services B; industrial arts B; interdisciplinary studies B; (pre)law sequence B; liberal arts/general studies B; library science B; linguistics B; literature B; management information systems B; marine biology B; marketing/retailing/merchandising B; mathematics B; mechanical engineering B; mechanical engineering technology B; medical assistant technologies B; medical technology B; (pre)medicine sequence B; music B; music education B; music history B; nursing B; oceanography B; philosophy B; physical education B; physical sciences B; physical therapy B; physics B; piano/organ B; political science/government B; psychology B; recreation and leisure services B; Russian B; science education B; secondary education B; secretarial studies/office management B; sociology B; Spanish B; special education B; speech pathology and audiology B; speech/rhetoric/public address/debate B; sports administration B; sports medicine B; studio art B; theater arts/drama B; (pre) veterinary medicine sequence B; voice B; wind and percussion instruments B; women's studies B. Majors with highest enrollment: accounting, mechanical engineering, electrical engineering.

LD Program Information

Name of Program Handicapped Student Services.

Availability of Services Began offering services in 1978. Services provided to freshmen, sophomores, juniors, seniors. Program currently serves 3 LD students: 2 freshmen, 1 sophomore.

Staff 8 part-time staff members, including director, assistant directors. Services provided by remediation specialist, tutors.

Admissions LD applicants evaluated on the basis of high school transcript and grade point average, untimed SAT. LD students may begin taking classes in fall, spring, or summer.

Housing College housing (including coed) available. LD students housed randomly. LD students not required to live on campus.

Diagnostic Testing Available in spelling, written language, French-Orton Association Test.

Tutoring Offered one-to-one and in small groups by professional teachers, peer tutors. Available in some subjects. LD students may receive tutoring in 3 courses per term.

Basic Skills Remediation Offered in small groups by regular teachers. Available in reading, math, spelling, written language.

Academic Advisement Help with program planning provided by LD staff members, academic advisers. LD students may take up to 18 credit hours each semester; 12 credit hours required to maintain full-time status.

Special Courses Offered in reading, composition, math. None offered for credit; none enter into overall grade point average.

Auxiliary Aids and Services Aids include taped textbooks, tape recorders. Services include alternative exam arrangements, notetakers, advocacy.

Counseling Services Individual counseling, small-group counseling, career counseling available.

Contact Ms. Angela M. Blackwell, Assistant Dean of Student Affairs and Director of Handicapped Student Services, Old Dominion University, Webb Center, Room 209, Norfolk, VA 23508, 804-440-4656.

OREGON STATE UNIVERSITY

Corvallis, Oregon

Year Program Began	1985
Special Fee	None
Special Orientation	✓
Diagnostic Testing	
Subject-Area Tutoring	✓
Basic Skills Remediation	
Special Courses	✓
Taped Textbooks	✓
Alternative Exam Arrangements	✓
Notetakers	✓
Staff	1 part-time
Number of Students Served	*Not reported*

General Information State-supported coed university. Founded 1868. Awards B, M, D. Institutionally accredited by regional association; programs accredited by AACSB (business), ABET (engineering and technology), ACPE (pharmacy), NCATE (teacher education); candidate for program accreditation by NASM (music). Small-town setting; 400-acre campus. Total enrollment: 15,624. Faculty: 1,623 (817 full-time, 806 part-time); 52% have doctoral degrees; graduate assistants teach a few undergraduate courses. Calendar: quarters. Grading system: letters or numbers. Library holdings: 965,813 bound volumes, 1 million titles on microform, 17,750 periodical subscriptions.

Undergraduate Profile Fall 1984: 12,886 undergraduates (2,411 freshmen); 5% part-time; 89% state residents; 14% transfers; 65% financial aid recipients; 42% women; 1% blacks; 1% Native Americans; 1% Hispanics; 5% Asian Americans; 3% foreign nationals.

Expenses (1984–85) State resident tuition: $1410 full-time. Nonresident tuition: $4035 full-time. Part-time tuition per quarter (1 to 11 quarter hours) ranges from $95 to $433 for state residents, $168 to $1236 for nonresidents. College room and board: $2120.

Financial Aid Fall 1984 full-time freshmen: 86% applied for aid, 85% of those were judged to have need, 100% of those were aided; the average aided freshman received an aid package worth $2221 (47% scholarships/grants, 53% self-help) meeting 95% of need. College-administered aid for all 1984–85 undergraduates: 5,000 need-based scholarships (average $1000); 900 non-need scholarships (average $2100); short-term loans (average $200); low-interest long-term loans from college funds (average $900), from external sources (average $1500); SEOG; College Work-Study. Supporting data: FAF, AFSA/SAR required. Priority application deadline: 3/1.

Athletics Member NCAA (Division I). Intercollegiate sports: baseball/softball M(I,s), W(I,s); basketball M(I,s), W(I,s); crew M, W; cross-country running M(I,s), W(I,s); football M(I-A,s); golf M(I,s), W(I,s); gymnastics W(I,s); swimming and diving W(I,s); tennis W(I); track and field M(I,s), W(I,s); volleyball W(I,s); wrestling M(I,s). Intramural sports: badminton, baseball/softball, basketball, bowling, crew, cross-country running, football, golf, gymnastics, soccer, squash, swimming and diving, tennis, track and field, volleyball, wrestling.

Majors Adult and continuing education B; agricultural economics B; agricultural engineering B; agronomy/soil and crop sciences B; American studies B; animal sciences B; anthropology B; art/fine arts B; atmospheric sciences B; biochemistry B; biology/biological sciences B; biophysics B; botany/plant sciences B; business administration/commerce/management B; business education B; chemical engineering B; chemistry B; child care/child and family studies B; civil engineering B; computer science B; construction engineering B; early childhood education B; economics B; electrical engineering B; elementary education B; engineering (general) B; engineering physics B; English B; entomology B; family services B; fashion merchandising B; fish and game management B; food sciences B; forestry B; French B; geography B; geology B; German B; health education B; health services administration B; history B; home economics education B; horticulture B; hotel and restaurant management B; human development B; industrial arts B; industrial engineering B; journalism B; liberal arts/general studies B; mathematics B; mechanical engineering B; microbiology B; music B; music education B; nuclear engineering B; nuclear physics B; nutrition B; parks management B; pharmacy/pharmaceutical sciences B; philosophy B; physical education B; physical sciences B; physics B; physiology B; political science/government B; poultry sciences B; range management B; recreation and leisure services B; religious studies B; science education B; secondary education B; sociobiology B; Spanish B; statistics B; technical writing B; vocational education B; zoology B. Major with highest enrollment: business administration/commerce/management.

LD Program Information

Name of Program Services for Disabled Students.

Availability of Services Began offering services in 1985. Services provided to freshmen, sophomores, juniors, seniors.

Staff 1 part-time staff member (director). Services provided by tutors.

Admissions LD applicants evaluated on the basis of high school transcript and grade point average, standard or untimed SAT or ACT, autobiographical statement, letters of recommendation, psychoeducational report. LD students may begin taking classes in fall only. Application should be submitted 1 to 11 months in advance of initial anticipated enrollment.

Orientation Optional orientation offered before registration.

Housing College housing (including coed) available. LD students housed randomly. LD freshmen required to live on campus except if living with relatives.

Tutoring Offered one-to-one by peer tutors. Available in all subjects. LD students may receive tutoring in all courses each term (depending on availability of tutors).

Academic Advisement Help with program planning provided by LD staff member, academic advisers. Most LD students take 9 to 15 quarter hours each quarter; 12 quarter hours required to maintain full-time status.

Special Courses Offered in vocabulary development, communication skills, composition, language development, study skills. Some offered for credit; some enter into overall grade point average.

Auxiliary Aids and Services Aids include taped textbooks, tape recorders, word processors. Services include alternative exam arrangements, notetakers, advocacy, support group.

Counseling Services Individual counseling, rap sessions available.

Contact Ms. Nancy Eldredge, Program Director, Services for Disabled Students, Oregon State University, Administrative Services Building A200, Corvallis, OR 97331, 503-754-3573.

PACIFIC LUTHERAN UNIVERSITY
Tacoma, Washington

Year Program Began	*Not reported*	Special Courses	
Special Fee	None	Taped Textbooks	
Special Orientation		Alternative Exam Arrangements	✓
Diagnostic Testing	✓	Notetakers	✓
Subject-Area Tutoring	✓	Staff	3 part-time
Basic Skills Remediation		Number of Students Served	6

General Information Comprehensive coed institution, affiliated with American Lutheran Church. Founded 1890. Awards B, M. Institutionally accredited by regional association; programs accredited by AACSB (business), NASM (music), NLN (nursing), NCATE (teacher education). City setting, with easy access to Seattle; 138-acre barrier-free campus. Total enrollment: 3,694. Faculty: 291 (216 full-time, 75 part-time); 70% have doctoral degrees; graduate assistants teach no undergraduate courses. Calendar: 4-1-4. Grading system: letters or numbers. Library holdings: 283,131 bound volumes, 1,546 periodical subscriptions, 2,500 records/tapes.

Undergraduate Profile Fall 1984: 3,133 undergraduates (646 freshmen) from 38 states and territories and 34 foreign countries; 9% part-time; 72% state residents; 30% transfers; 70% financial aid recipients; 55% women; 2% blacks; 1% Native Americans; 1% Hispanics; 3% Asian Americans; 5% foreign nationals.

Expenses (1985–86) Comprehensive fee of $9520 includes full-time tuition ($6535) and college room and board ($2985). College room only: $1450. Part-time tuition: $198 per semester hour.

Financial Aid Fall 1984 full-time freshmen: 88% applied for aid, 91% of those were judged to have need, 95% of those were aided; the average aided freshman received an aid package worth $5300 (45% scholarships/grants, 55% self-help) meeting 90% of need. College-administered aid for all 1984–85 undergraduates: 1,500 need-based scholarships (average $1750); 408 non-need scholarships (average $1000); short-term loans (average $250); low-interest long-term loans from external sources (average $2000); SEOG; College Work-Study; 750 part-time jobs. Supporting data: FAF required. Priority application deadline: 3/1.

Athletics Member NAIA. Intercollegiate sports: baseball/softball M(s), W(s); basketball M(s), W(s); crew M, W; cross-country running M(s), W(s); football M(s); golf M(s); skiing (cross-country) M(s), W(s); skiing (downhill) M(s), W(s); soccer M(s), W(s); swimming and diving M(s), W(s); tennis M(s), W(s); track and field M(s), W(s); volleyball W(s); wrestling M(s). Intramural sports: badminton, baseball/softball, basketball, bowling, football, golf, squash, swimming and diving, tennis, track and field, volleyball, water polo.

Majors Accounting B; anthropology B; art education B; art/fine arts B; art history B; biochemistry B; biology/biological sciences B; broadcasting B; business administration/commerce/management B; business education B; chemistry B; classics B; communication B; computer science B; criminal justice B; (pre)dentistry sequence B; early childhood education B; earth science B; ecology/environmental studies B; economics B; education B; elementary education B; engineering physics B; English B; finance/banking B; French B; geology B; German B; history B; international studies B; jazz B; journalism B; (pre)law sequence B; literature B; marketing/retailing/merchandising B; mathematics B; medical technology B; (pre)medicine sequence B; modern languages B; music B; music education B; nursing B; philosophy B; physical education B; physics B; piano/organ B; political science/government B; psychology B; publishing B; radio and television studies B; religious studies B; sacred music B; Scandinavian languages/studies B; secondary education B; social work B; sociology B; Spanish B; special education B; speech/rhetoric/public address/debate B; stringed instruments B; studio art B; (pre)veterinary medicine sequence B; voice B. Majors with highest enrollment: education, business administration/commerce/management, nursing.

LD Program Information

Name of Program Not specified.

Availability of Services Services provided to freshmen, sophomores, juniors, seniors. Program currently serves 6 LD students: 2 freshmen, 2 sophomores, 1 junior, 1 senior.

Staff 3 part-time staff members, including coordinator. Services provided by diagnostic specialists, assistant director of Academic Advising Center.

Admissions LD applicants evaluated on the basis of high school transcript and grade point average, personal interview, autobiographical statement, letters of recommendation, psychoeducational report, physician's report. LD students may begin taking classes in fall, winter, spring, or summer. Application should be submitted 1 year in advance of initial anticipated enrollment.

Housing College housing (including coed) available. LD students housed randomly. LD freshmen, sophomores, juniors, and seniors required to live on campus except if 21 or over, married, or living with relatives, or by special permission.

Diagnostic Testing Available in reading, math, spelling, work and study habits.

Tutoring Offered one-to-one and in small groups by peer tutors, professors. Available in all subjects. LD students may receive tutoring in all courses each term.

Academic Advisement Help with program planning provided by LD staff members, academic advisers. LD students may take up to 16 semester hours each semester; most take 12 semester hours; 10 semester hours required to maintain full-time status.

Auxiliary Aids and Services Aids include tape recorders, typewriters. Services include alternative exam arrangements, notetakers, typing services.

Counseling Services Individual counseling, career counseling available.

Contact Ms. Kathy Olson Mannelly, Associate Dean for Student Life, Pacific Lutheran University, Tacoma, WA 98447, 206-535-7191.

PENNSYLVANIA STATE UNIVERSITY CAPITOL CAMPUS

Middletown, Pennsylvania

Year Program Began	*Not reported*	Special Courses	✓
Special Fee	None	Taped Textbooks	✓
Special Orientation		Alternative Exam Arrangements	
Diagnostic Testing		Notetakers	✓
Subject-Area Tutoring	✓	Staff	1 part-time
Basic Skills Remediation		Number of Students Served	1

General Information State-related upper-level coed institution. Part of Pennsylvania State University. Founded 1966. Awards B, M. Institutionally accredited by regional association; programs accredited by ABET (engineering and technology). Small-town setting; 218-acre campus. Total enrollment: 2,595. Faculty: 149 (121 full-time, 28 part-time); 72% have doctoral degrees. Calendar: semesters. Grading system: letters or numbers. Library holdings: 172,473 bound volumes, 749,122 titles on microform, 1,355 periodical subscriptions, 1,639 records/tapes.

Undergraduate Profile Fall 1984: 1,766 undergraduates (411 in entering class) from 8 states and territories; 38% part-time; 97% state residents; 100% transfers; 72% financial aid recipients; 32% women; 2% blacks; 1% Native Americans; 1% Hispanics; 2% Asian Americans; 1% foreign nationals; 42% of undergraduates over 25 years of age.

Expenses (1984–85) State resident tuition: $2246 full-time, $107 per credit part-time. Nonresident tuition: $5146 full-time, $215 per credit part-time. College room and board: $2750.

Financial Aid College-administered aid for all 1984–85 undergraduates: need-based scholarships; non-need scholarships; low-interest long-term loans; SEOG; College Work-Study; part-time jobs. Supporting data: FAF required. Application deadline: continuous to 2/15.

Athletics Intercollegiate sports: baseball/softball M; basketball M; bowling M, W; golf M, W; soccer M; tennis M, W; volleyball W. Intramural sports: baseball/softball, basketball, bowling, football, ice hockey, tennis, volleyball, wrestling.

Majors Accounting B; behavioral sciences B; business administration/commerce/management B; computer science B; construction technologies B; economics B; electrical engineering technology B; elementary education B; energy management technologies B; finance/banking B; health services administration B; humanities B; human services B; marketing/retailing/merchandising B; mathematics B; mechanical design technology B; psychology B; public affairs and policy studies B; secondary education B; social science B; transportation technologies B; water resources B.

LD Program Information

Name of Program Student Support Center.

Availability of Services Services provided to juniors, seniors. Program currently serves 1 LD senior.

Staff 1 part-time staff member (coordinator).

Admissions LD applicants evaluated on the basis of college transcript. LD students may begin taking classes in fall, spring, or summer. Application should be submitted at least 6 months in advance of initial anticipated enrollment.

Housing College housing available. LD students housed randomly. LD students not required to live on campus.

Tutoring Offered one-to-one by professional teachers, peer tutors. Available in all subjects. LD students may receive tutoring in all courses each term.

Academic Advisement Help with program planning provided by academic advisers. LD students may take up to 19 credits each semester; most take 17 credits; 12 credits required to maintain full-time status.

Special Courses Offered in math, study skills. None offered for credit; none enter into overall grade point average.

Auxiliary Aids and Services Aids include taped textbooks. Services include notetakers.

Counseling Services Individual counseling, small-group counseling, career counseling available.

Contact Mr. David W. Doaty, Coordinator, Student Services, Pennsylvania State University Capitol Campus, Middletown, PA 17057, 717-948-6017.

PENNSYLVANIA STATE UNIVERSITY UNIVERSITY PARK CAMPUS

University Park, Pennsylvania

Year Program Began	*Not reported*	Special Courses	
Special Fee	None	Taped Textbooks	✓
Special Orientation		Alternative Exam Arrangements	✓
Diagnostic Testing	✓	Notetakers	
Subject-Area Tutoring	✓	Staff	1 full-time, 5 part-time
Basic Skills Remediation		Number of Students Served	40 to 80

General Information State-related coed university. Part of Pennsylvania State University. Founded 1855. Awards A (college transfer and terminal), B, M, D. Institutionally accredited by regional association; programs accredited by NAAB (architecture), NASAD (art and design), AACSB (business), ABET (engineering and technology), NASM (music), NLN (nursing), NCATE (teacher education). Small-town setting; 540-acre campus. Total enrollment: 34,401. Faculty: 1,782 (1,519 full-time, 263 part-time); 72% have doctoral degrees; graduate assistants teach a few undergraduate courses. Calendar: semesters. Grading system: letters or numbers. Library holdings: 1.9 million bound volumes, 1.6 million titles on microform, 20,974 periodical subscriptions, 18,808 records/tapes.

Undergraduate Profile Fall 1984: 29,137 undergraduates (3,172 freshmen) from 48 states and territories; 7% part-time; 86% state residents; 2% transfers; 78% financial aid recipients; 44% women; 4% blacks; 1% Native Americans; 1% Hispanics; 3% Asian Americans; 1% foreign nationals; 5% of undergraduates over 25 years of age.

Expenses (1984–85) State resident tuition: $2562 full-time, $107 per credit part-time. Nonresident tuition: $5146 full-time, $215 per credit part-time. College room and board: $2750.

Financial Aid Fall 1984 full-time freshmen: 98% were aided; the average aided freshman received an aid package worth $3187 (44% scholarships/grants, 56% self-help). College-administered aid for all 1984–85 undergraduates: need-based scholarships; non-need scholarships; short-term loans; low-interest long-term loans; SEOG; College Work-Study; part-time jobs. Supporting data: FAF required. Application deadline: continuous to 2/15.

Athletics Member NCAA (Division I). Intercollegiate sports: baseball/softball M(I,s), W(I); basketball M(I,s), W(I,s); cross-country running M(I,s), W(I,s); equestrian sports M(c), W(c); fencing M(I), W(I); field hockey W(I,s); football M(I-A,s); golf M(I), W(I); gymnastics M(I,s), W(I,s); ice hockey M(c); lacrosse M(I,s), W(I,s); rugby M(c), W(c); skiing (downhill) M(c), W(c); soccer M(I,s), W(c); swimming and diving M(I,s), W(I,s); tennis M(I), W(I); track and field M(I,s), W(I,s); volleyball M(I,s), W(I,s); water polo M(c); wrestling M(I,s). Intramural sports: archery, badminton, baseball/softball, basketball, bowling, cross-country running, fencing, field hockey, football, golf, gymnastics, lacrosse, martial arts, racquetball, riflery, sailing, soccer, squash, swimming and diving, tennis, track and field, volleyball, wrestling.

Majors Accounting B; advertising B; aerospace engineering B; agricultural business A, B; agricultural economics B; agricultural education B; agricultural engineering B; agricultural sciences B; agronomy/soil and crop sciences B; American studies B; animal sciences B; anthropology B; architectural engineering B; architecture B; art education B; art/fine arts B; art history B; astronomy B; biochemistry B; biology/biological sciences B; botany/plant sciences B; broadcasting B; business administration/commerce/management B; business economics B; cell biology B; ceramic engineering B; chemical engineering B; chemistry B; child care/child and family studies B; civil engineering B; classics B; communication B; community services B; comparative literature B; computer science B; dairy sciences B; dietetics A; earth science B; East Asian studies B; ecology/environmental studies B; economics B; electrical engineering B; elementary education B; engineering sciences B; English B; entomology B; environmental engineering B; family and consumer studies B; film studies B; finance/banking B; food sciences B; food services management B; forestry B; forest technology B; French B; geography B; geological engineering B; German B; health education B; health services administration B; history B; home economics education B; horticulture B; hotel and restaurant management B; industrial engineering B; insurance B; Italian B; journalism B; labor studies B; landscape architecture/design B; Latin American studies B; law enforcement/police sciences B; (pre)law sequence B; liberal arts/general studies A, B; linguistics B; marketing/retailing/merchandising B; mathematics B; mechanical engineering B; (pre)medicine sequence B; medieval studies B; metallurgy B; meteorology B; microbiology B; mining and mineral engineering B; molecular biology B; music B; music education B; nuclear engineering B; nursing B; nutrition B; parks management B; petroleum/natural gas engineering B; philosophy B; physical education B; physics B; political science/government B; pollution control technologies B; polymer science B; poultry sciences B; psychology B; public affairs and policy studies B; real estate B; recreation and leisure services B; religious studies B; retail management B; Russian B; science B; secondary education B; social work B; sociology B; Spanish B; special education B; speech pathology and audiology B; speech/rhetoric/public address/debate B; telecommunications B; theater arts/drama B; (pre)veterinary medicine sequence B; vocational education B; wildlife management B. Majors with highest enrollment: accounting, electrical engineering, mechanical engineering.

LD Program Information

Name of Program Comprehensive Service Program for LD University Students.

Availability of Services Services provided to freshmen, sophomores, juniors, seniors. Program currently serves 40 to 80 LD students: 10 to 20 freshmen, 10 to 20 sophomores, 10 to 20 juniors, 10 to 20 seniors.

Staff 1 full-time, 5 part-time staff members, including director, assistant director. Services provided by tutors, diagnostic specialists.

Admissions LD applicants evaluated on the basis of high school transcript and grade point average, standard or untimed SAT. LD students may begin taking classes in fall, spring, or summer. Application should be submitted 3 to 4 months in advance of initial anticipated enrollment.

Housing College housing available. LD students housed randomly. LD freshmen required to live on campus except if living with relatives.

Diagnostic Testing Available in intelligence, reading, math, spelling, handwriting, written language, work and study habits, speech, foreign language aptitude.

Tutoring Offered one-to-one by peer tutors. Available in some subjects. LD students may receive tutoring in all courses each term.

Academic Advisement Help with program planning provided by LD staff members, academic advisers. Most LD students take 12 to 15 credits each semester; 12 credits required to maintain full-time status.

Auxiliary Aids and Services Aids include taped textbooks, tape recorders. Services include alternative exam arrangements.

Counseling Services Individual counseling, career counseling available.

Contact Dr. Anna Gajar, Associate Professor of Special Education and Director of Comprehensive Service Program for LD University Students, Pennsylvania State University University Park Campus, 226 B Moore Building, University Park, PA 16802, 814-863-2438.

PHILADELPHIA COLLEGE OF ART
Philadelphia, Pennsylvania

Year Program Began	1983	Special Courses	
Special Fee	None	Taped Textbooks	✓
Special Orientation		Alternative Exam Arrangements	✓
Diagnostic Testing		Notetakers	✓
Subject-Area Tutoring	✓	Staff	3 part-time
Basic Skills Remediation	✓	Number of Students Served	12

General Information Independent comprehensive coed institution. Founded 1876. Awards B, M. Institutionally accredited by regional association; programs accredited by NASAD (art and design). Metropolitan setting. Total enrollment: 1,659. Faculty: 234 (72 full-time, 162 part-time); 10% have doctoral degrees; graduate assistants teach no undergraduate courses. Calendar: semesters. Grading system: letters or numbers. Library holdings: 45,400 bound volumes, 176 periodical subscriptions, 1,003 records/tapes.

Undergraduate Profile Fall 1984: 1,629 undergraduates (267 freshmen) from 35 states and territories and 40 foreign countries; 6% part-time; 36% state residents; 19% transfers; 64% financial aid recipients; 55% women; 8% blacks; 2% Native Americans; 1% Hispanics; 2% Asian Americans; 6% foreign nationals; 70% of undergraduates over 25 years of age.

Expenses (1985–86) Tuition: $6500 full-time, $290 per credit part-time. Mandatory fees: $400. College room only: $2100.

Financial Aid Fall 1984 full-time freshmen: 100% applied for aid, 93% of those were judged to have need, 100% of those were aided; the average aided freshman received an aid package worth $3670 (33% scholarships/grants, 67% self-help) meeting 98% of need. College-administered aid for all 1984–85 undergraduates: 532 need-based scholarships (average $2264); non-need scholarships; low-interest long-term loans from external sources (average $600); SEOG; College Work-Study; part-time jobs. Supporting data: FAF, AFSA/SAR required; state form required for some. Priority application deadline: 2/15.

Majors Applied art B; architecture B; art education B; art/fine arts B; art therapy B; ceramic art and design B; environmental design B; film studies B; graphic arts B; illustration B; industrial design B; interior design B; jewelry and metalsmithing B; painting/drawing B; photography B; sculpture B; textile arts B. Majors with highest enrollment: illustration, graphic arts, industrial design.

LD Program Information

Name of Program Learning Resource Center.

Availability of Services Began offering services in 1983. Services provided to freshmen, sophomores, juniors, seniors. Program currently serves 12 LD students: 4 freshmen, 4 sophomores, 2 juniors, 2 seniors.

Staff 3 part-time staff members, including director. Services provided by tutors, counselor.

Admissions LD applicants evaluated on the basis of high school transcript and grade point average, untimed SAT, personal interview, letters of recommendation, psychoeducational report, art portfolio. LD students may begin taking classes in fall only. Application should be submitted 6 months in advance of initial anticipated enrollment.

Housing College housing (including coed) available. LD students housed randomly. LD freshmen required to live on campus except if living with relatives.

Tutoring Offered one-to-one and in small groups by professional teachers, peer tutors. Available in some subjects. LD students may receive tutoring in all courses each term.

Basic Skills Remediation Offered one-to-one and in small groups by professional tutor, director of Learning Resource Center. Available in reading, spelling, spoken language, written language, learning strategies, work and study habits.

Academic Advisement Help with program planning provided by LD staff members, academic advisers. LD students may take up to 15 credits each semester; 12 credits required to maintain full-time status.

Auxiliary Aids and Services Aids include taped textbooks, tape recorders, typewriters. Services include alternative exam arrangements, notetakers.

Counseling Services Individual counseling, small-group counseling available.

Contact Dr. Eve Orlow, Director, Learning Resource Center, Philadelphia College of Art, Broad and Pine Streets, Philadelphia, PA 19102, 215-893-3113.

PIEDMONT COLLEGE

Demorest, Georgia

Year Program Began	1977	Special Courses	✓
Special Fee	None	Taped Textbooks	✓
Special Orientation	✓	Alternative Exam Arrangements	✓
Diagnostic Testing	✓	Notetakers	✓
Subject-Area Tutoring	✓	Staff	3 part-time
Basic Skills Remediation	✓	Number of Students Served	12

General Information 4-year coed college, affiliated with Congregational Christian Church. Founded 1897. Awards B. Institutionally accredited by regional association. Rural setting; 200-acre campus. Total enrollment: 388. Faculty: 28 (22 full-time, 6 part-time); 60% have doctoral degrees. Calendar: quarters. Grading system: letters or numbers. Library holdings: 71,296 bound volumes, 129 periodical subscriptions, 807 records/tapes.

Undergraduate Profile Fall 1984: 388 undergraduates (124 freshmen) from 7 states and territories and 4 foreign countries; 13% part-time; 90% state residents; 9% transfers; 85% financial aid recipients; 50% women; 5% blacks; 0% Native Americans; 0% Hispanics; 0% Asian Americans; 3% foreign nationals; 15% of undergraduates over 25 years of age; no legally handicapped students.

Expenses (1985–86) Comprehensive fee of $4467 includes full-time tuition ($1890), mandatory fees ($177), and college room and board ($2400). Part-time tuition: $630 per quarter hour.

Financial Aid Fall 1984 full-time freshmen: 69% applied for aid, 80% of those were judged to have need, 100% of those were aided; the average aided freshman received an aid package worth $1066 (69% scholarships/grants, 31% self-help) meeting 95% of need. College-administered aid for all 1984–85 undergraduates: need-based scholarships; 54 non-need scholarships (average $625); low-interest long-term loans from college funds (average $1000), from external sources (average $2000); SEOG; College Work-Study; 100 part-time jobs. Supporting data: FAF, state form, AFSA/SAR required; IRS required for some; FFS acceptable. Priority application deadline: 8/15.

Athletics Member NAIA. Intercollegiate sports: baseball/softball M(s), W(s); basketball M(s), W(s); golf M(s), W(s); tennis M(s), W(s); track and field M(s), W(s). Intramural sports: baseball/softball, basketball, volleyball.

Majors Accounting B; art/fine arts B; biology/biological sciences B; business administration/commerce/management B; chemistry B; early childhood education B; education B; elementary education B; English B; history B; mathematics B; psychology B; secondary education B; sociology B; Spanish B; studio art B. Majors with highest enrollment: business administration/commerce/management, education, sociology.

LD Program Information

Name of Program Special Services.

Availability of Services Began offering services in 1977. Services provided to freshmen, sophomores, juniors, seniors. Program currently serves 12 LD students: 4 freshmen, 3 sophomores, 3 juniors, 2 seniors.

Staff 3 part-time staff members, including director. Services provided by tutors, counselors.

Admissions LD applicants evaluated on the basis of high school transcript and grade point average, untimed SAT, personal interview, autobiographical statement, letters of recommendation, psychoeducational report. LD students may begin taking classes in fall only. Application should be submitted 6 months in advance of initial anticipated enrollment.

Orientation Required orientation held before registration.

Housing College housing available. LD students housed randomly. LD freshmen, sophomores, juniors, and seniors required to live on campus except if married or living with relatives.

Diagnostic Testing Available in reading, math, written language.

Tutoring Offered one-to-one and in small groups by professional teachers, peer tutors. Available in most subjects. LD students may receive tutoring in all courses each term.

Basic Skills Remediation Offered one-to-one and in small groups by LD teachers, peer teachers. Available in reading, math, spelling, spoken language, written language, learning strategies.

Academic Advisement Help with program planning provided by LD staff members, academic advisers. LD students may take up to 15 quarter hours each quarter; most take 15 quarter hours; 10 quarter hours required to maintain full-time status.

Special Courses Offered in reading, vocabulary development, communication skills, composition, language development, math. Some offered for credit; none enter into overall grade point average.

Auxiliary Aids and Services Aids include taped textbooks, tape recorders, typewriters. Services include alternative exam arrangements, notetakers.

Counseling Services Individual counseling, small-group counseling, career counseling available.

Contact Ms. Ellen O'Neal, Special Programs Director, Piedmont College, PO Box 626, Demorest, GA 30535, 404-778-4144.

PIKEVILLE COLLEGE
Pikeville, Kentucky

Year Program Began	1979	Special Courses	✓
Special Fee	None	Taped Textbooks	✓
Special Orientation		Alternative Exam Arrangements	✓
Diagnostic Testing	✓	Notetakers	✓
Subject-Area Tutoring	✓	Staff	6 part-time
Basic Skills Remediation	✓	Number of Students Served	*Not reported*

General Information 4-year coed college, affiliated with Presbyterian Church (U.S.A.) Founded 1889. Awards A (college transfer and terminal), B. Institutionally accredited by regional association. Small-town setting; 25-acre campus. Total enrollment: 453. Faculty: 52 (36 full-time, 16 part-time); 20% have doctoral degrees. Calendar: semesters. Grading system: letters or numbers. Library holdings: 92,100 bound volumes, 14,500 titles on microform, 248 periodical subscriptions, 2,700 records/tapes.

Undergraduate Profile Fall 1984: 453 undergraduates (101 freshmen) from 6 states and territories; 18% part-time; 89% state residents; 18% transfers; 78% financial aid recipients; 71% women; 2% blacks; 0% Native Americans; 0% Hispanics; 0% Asian Americans; 0% foreign nationals; 30% of undergraduates over 25 years of age; 2 legally handicapped students.

Expenses (1985–86) Comprehensive fee of $5400 includes full-time tuition ($3300) and college room and board ($2100). College room only: $770. Part-time tuition: $110 per semester hour.

Financial Aid Fall 1984 full-time freshmen: 95% applied for aid, 81% of those were judged to have need, 100% of those were aided; the average aided freshman received an aid package worth $2557 (66% scholarships/grants, 34% self-help) meeting 91% of need. College-administered aid for all 1984–85 undergraduates: need-based scholarships; 130 non-need scholarships (average $2200); short-term loans (average $500); low-interest long-term loans from college funds (average $1500), from external sources (average $2500); SEOG; College Work-Study; 50 part-time jobs. Supporting data: FAF, IRS, institutional form, AFSA/SAR required. Priority application deadline: 6/1.

Athletics Member NAIA. Intercollegiate sport: basketball M(s), W(s). Intramural sports: badminton, baseball/softball, basketball, bowling, football, golf, gymnastics, tennis, volleyball.

Majors Accounting A, B; art education B; biology/biological sciences B; business administration/commerce/management B; business education B; chemistry B; computer programming B; computer science B; dance A; data processing A; (pre) dentistry sequence B; economics B; education B; elementary education B; (pre) engineering sequence A; English B; history B; (pre)law sequence B; legal secretarial studies A; mathematics B; medical laboratory technology B; medical technology B; (pre)medicine sequence B; mining technology A; music B; music education B; nursing A; physical education B; political science/government B; psychology B; secondary education B; secretarial studies/office management A; sociology B; special education B; (pre)veterinary medicine sequence B. Majors with highest enrollment: business administration/commerce/management, education, computer programming.

LD Program Information

Name of Program Special Services for Disadvantaged Students.

Availability of Services Began offering services in 1979. Services provided to freshmen, sophomores, juniors, seniors.

Staff 6 part-time staff members, including directors of Special Services and Advancement Studies. Services provided by remediation specialists, tutors, counselor, diagnostic specialist.

Admissions LD applicants evaluated on the basis of high school transcript and grade point average, untimed ACT. LD students may begin taking classes in fall, spring, or summer. Application should be submitted 4 months in advance of initial anticipated enrollment.

Housing College housing available. LD students housed randomly. LD students not required to live on campus.

Diagnostic Testing Available in intelligence, reading, math, spelling, handwriting, written language, work and study habits, personality, social skills, career interest inventory.

Tutoring Offered one-to-one and in small groups by professional teachers, peer tutors, occasional community volunteers such as retired teachers. Available in all subjects. LD students may receive tutoring in all courses each term (depending on individual need).

Basic Skills Remediation Offered one-to-one and in small groups by LD teachers, regular teachers, teacher trainees. Available in reading, math, spelling, handwriting, written language, learning strategies, work and study habits, social skills.

Academic Advisement Help with program planning provided by LD staff members. Most LD students take 12 semester hours each semester; 12 semester hours required to maintain full-time status (except by special permission).

Special Courses Offered in college survival skills, reading, vocabulary development, communication skills, composition, language development, math, study skills. Some offered for credit; some enter into overall grade point average.

Auxiliary Aids and Services Aids include taped textbooks, tape recorders, calculators, typewriters, word processors. Services include alternative exam arrangements, notetakers.

Counseling Services Individual counseling, rap sessions, career counseling available.

Contact Ms. C. Kathleen Hall, Director of Special Services for Disadvantaged Students, Pikeville College, CPO Box 12, Pikeville, KY 41501, 606-432-9312.

PONTIFICAL COLLEGE JOSEPHINUM

Columbus, Ohio

Year Program Began	1984	Special Courses	✓
Special Fee	None	Taped Textbooks	
Special Orientation		Alternative Exam Arrangements	✓
Diagnostic Testing	✓	Notetakers	
Subject-Area Tutoring	✓	Staff	3 part-time
Basic Skills Remediation	✓	Number of Students Served	2

General Information Roman Catholic comprehensive primarily men's institution. Founded 1888. Awards B, M. Institutionally accredited by regional association. Metropolitan setting; 100-acre campus. Total enrollment: 192. Faculty: 49 (21 full-time, 28 part-time); 55% have doctoral degrees; graduate assistants teach no undergraduate courses. Calendar: semesters. Grading system: letters or numbers. Library holdings: 90,000 bound volumes, 455 titles on microform, 340 periodical subscriptions, 963 records/tapes.

Undergraduate Profile Fall 1984: 110 undergraduates (30 freshmen) from 15 states and territories; 0% part-time; 50% state residents; 32% transfers; 95% financial aid recipients; 1% women; 0% blacks; 0% Native Americans; 11% Hispanics; no legally handicapped students.

Expenses (1985–86) Comprehensive fee of $4565 includes full-time tuition ($2510) and college room and board ($2055). Part-time tuition: $101 per credit hour.

Financial Aid College-administered aid for all 1984–85 undergraduates: need-based scholarships (average $1700); non-need scholarships (average $1200); low-interest long-term loans; SEOG; College Work-Study; part-time jobs. Supporting data: FAF, institutional form, AFSA/SAR required; IRS required for some; FFS acceptable. Application deadline: continuous.

Athletics Member NLCAA. Intercollegiate sports: basketball M; soccer M; tennis M. Intramural sports: baseball/softball, basketball, bowling, football, gymnastics, martial arts, racquetball, skiing (cross-country), skiing (downhill), soccer, swimming and diving, tennis, track and field, volleyball, weight lifting.

Majors American studies B; English B; history B; Latin American studies B; philosophy B; religious studies B. Majors with highest enrollment: philosophy, religious studies, history.

LD Program Information

Name of Program Not specified.

Availability of Services Began offering services in 1984. Services provided to freshmen, sophomores, juniors, seniors. Program currently serves 2 LD students: 1 sophomore, 1 senior.

Staff 3 part-time staff members, including coordinator. Services provided by tutors, counselor.

Admissions LD applicants evaluated on the basis of high school transcript and grade point average, standard SAT or ACT, personal interview, autobiographical statement, 3 letters of recommendation, psychoeducational report, CLEP tests. LD students may begin taking classes in fall only. Application should be submitted 6 weeks in advance of initial anticipated enrollment.

Housing College housing available. LD students housed randomly. LD freshmen, sophomores, juniors, and seniors required to live on campus.

Diagnostic Testing Available in reading, math, spelling, handwriting, spoken language, written language, motor abilities, perceptual skills.

Tutoring Offered one-to-one by professional teachers, peer tutors. Available in all subjects. LD students may receive tutoring in all courses each term.

Basic Skills Remediation Offered in small groups by regular teachers. Available in reading, math, written language, learning strategies, perceptual skills, work and study habits.

Academic Advisement Help with program planning provided by academic advisers. LD students may take up to 15 credit hours each semester; most take 12 credit hours; 12 credit hours required to maintain full-time status.

Special Courses Offered in composition, math, personal psychology, study skills. All offered for credit; all enter into overall grade point average.

Auxiliary Aids and Services Aids include calculators. Services include alternative exam arrangements, advocacy.

Counseling Services Individual counseling available.

Contact Rev. Dennis P. Ricker, Academic Dean, Pontifical College Josephinum, 7625 North High Street, Columbus, OH 43085, 614-885-5585.

PORTLAND STATE UNIVERSITY

Portland, Oregon

Year Program Began	1977	Special Courses	
Special Fee	None	Taped Textbooks	✓
Special Orientation	✓	Alternative Exam Arrangements	✓
Diagnostic Testing		Notetakers	✓
Subject-Area Tutoring		Staff	1 full-time
Basic Skills Remediation		Number of Students Served	16

General Information State-supported coed university. Founded 1946. Awards B, M, D. Institutionally accredited by regional association; programs accredited by AACSB (business), ABET (engineering and technology), NCATE (teacher education); candidate for program accreditation by NASM (music). Metropolitan setting; 46-acre barrier-free campus. Total enrollment: 14,390. Faculty: 679 (489 full-time, 190 part-time); 70% have doctoral degrees; graduate assistants teach a few undergraduate courses. Calendar: quarters. Grading system: letters or numbers. Library holdings: 694,031 bound volumes, 805,094 titles on microform, 10,723 periodical subscriptions, 19,849 records/tapes.

Undergraduate Profile Fall 1984: 10,245 undergraduates (793 freshmen) from 38 states and territories and 59 foreign countries; 41% part-time; 95% state residents; 49% transfers; 51% financial aid recipients; 50% women; 2% blacks; 1% Native Americans; 1% Hispanics; 9% Asian Americans; 3% foreign nationals; 38% of undergraduates over 25 years of age; 170 legally handicapped students.

Expenses (1984–85) State resident tuition: $1119 full-time. Nonresident tuition: $3744 full-time. Part-time tuition and fees per quarter (1 to 11 credit hours) range from $64 to $433 for state residents, $64 to $1236 for nonresidents. Mandatory fees: $294.

Financial Aid Fall 1984 full-time freshmen: 70% applied for aid, 89% of those were judged to have need, 90% of those were aided; the average aided freshman received an aid package worth $2781 (55% scholarships/grants, 45% self-help) meeting 85% of need. College-administered aid for all 1984–85 undergraduates: 1,203 need-based scholarships (average $670); 139 non-need scholarships (average $433); short-term loans (average $450); low-interest long-term loans from college funds, from external sources (average $1735); SEOG; College Work-Study; 776 part-time jobs. Supporting data: FAF, AFSA/SAR required; IRS required for some. Priority application deadline: 3/1.

Athletics Member NCAA (Division II). Intercollegiate sports: baseball/softball M(I,s), W(II,s); basketball W(I,s); cross-country running M(II,s), W(II,s); football M(II,s); golf M(II,s); tennis W(II,s); track and field M(II,s), W(II,s); volleyball W(II,s); wrestling M(II,s). Intramural sports: baseball/softball, basketball, bowling, crew, cross-country running, fencing, football, martial arts, racquetball, skiing (cross-country), skiing (downhill), soccer, swimming and diving, tennis, volleyball, water polo, weight lifting.

Majors Accounting B; anthropology B; applied art B; art/fine arts B; biology/biological sciences B; business administration/commerce/management B; business education B; ceramic art and design B; chemistry B; civil engineering B; computer engineering B; computer science B; criminal justice B; economics B; electrical engineering B; elementary education B; engineering and applied sciences B; English B; finance/banking B; French B; geography B; geology B; German B; health education B; history B; international studies B; liberal arts/general studies B; marketing/retailing/merchandising B; mathematics B; mechanical engineering B; music B; painting/drawing B; philosophy B; physical education B; physics B; political science/government B; psychology B; Russian B; science B; sculpture B; secondary education B; social science B; social work B; sociology B; Spanish B; speech/rhetoric/public address/debate B; theater arts/drama B. Majors with highest enrollment: business administration/commerce/management, accounting, computer science.

LD Program Information

Name of Program Handicapped Services.

Availability of Services Began offering services in 1977. Services provided to freshmen, sophomores, juniors, seniors. Program currently serves 16 LD students: 6 freshmen, 4 sophomores, 3 juniors, 3 seniors.

Staff 1 full-time staff member (director).

Admissions LD applicants evaluated on the basis of high school transcript, standard or untimed SAT or ACT, personal interview, letters of recommendation. LD students may begin taking classes in fall, winter, spring, or summer. Application should be submitted at least 2 to 3 months in advance of initial anticipated enrollment.

Orientation Required orientation held before registration.

Housing College housing not available.

Academic Advisement Help with program planning provided by LD staff member, academic advisers. LD students may take up to 16 credit hours each quarter; most take 3 to 16 credit hours; 8 credit hours required to maintain full-time status.

Auxiliary Aids and Services Aids include taped textbooks, tape recorders. Services include alternative exam arrangements, notetakers, advocacy.

Counseling Services Individual counseling available.

Contact Ms. Cindy Callis Oberg, Director, Handicapped Services, Portland State University, PO Box 751, Portland, OR 97207, 503-229-4446.

PURDUE UNIVERSITY
West Lafayette, Indiana

Year Program Began	*Not reported*	Special Courses	✓
Special Fee	Varies	Taped Textbooks	✓
Special Orientation		Alternative Exam Arrangements	✓
Diagnostic Testing	✓	Notetakers	
Subject-Area Tutoring	✓	Staff	7 part-time
Basic Skills Remediation	✓	Number of Students Served	17

General Information State-supported coed university. Part of Purdue University System. Founded 1869. Awards A (college transfer), B, M, D. Institutionally accredited by regional association; programs accredited by AACSB (business), ABET (engineering and technology), NLN (nursing), ACPE (pharmacy), NCATE (teacher education); candidate for program accreditation by FIDER (interior design). Small-town setting, with easy access to Indianapolis; 1,565-acre campus. Total enrollment: 31,457. Faculty: 3,100 (2,200 full-time, 900 part-time); 70% have doctoral degrees; graduate assistants teach about a quarter of the undergraduate courses. Calendar: semesters. Grading system: letters or numbers. Library holdings: 1.6 million bound volumes, 1.2 million titles on microform, 18,000 periodical subscriptions.

Undergraduate Profile Fall 1984: 26,529 undergraduates (5,471 freshmen) from 50 states and territories and 90 foreign countries; 4% part-time; 72% state residents; 13% transfers; 55% financial aid recipients; 42% women; 5% blacks; 0% Native Americans; 1% Hispanics; 3% Asian Americans; 1% foreign nationals; 130 legally handicapped students.

Expenses (1985–86) State resident tuition: $0 full-time, $59 per semester hour part-time. Nonresident tuition: $3206 full-time, $159 per semester hour part-time. Mandatory fees: $1629. College room and board: $2600.

Financial Aid Fall 1984 full-time freshmen: the average aided freshman received an aid package meeting 100% of need. College-administered aid for all 1984–85 undergraduates: need-based scholarships; non-need scholarships; low-interest long-term loans; SEOG; College Work-Study; part-time jobs. Supporting data: FAF, IRS, state form required; FFS acceptable. Application deadline: 3/1.

Athletics Member NCAA (Division I). Intercollegiate sports: baseball/softball M(I,s); basketball M(I,s), W(I,s); cross-country running M(I,s), W(I,s); field hockey W(I,s); football M(I-A,s); golf M(I,s), W(I,s); swimming and diving M(I,s), W(I,s); tennis M(I,s), W(I,s); track and field M(I,s), W(I,s); volleyball W(I,s); weight lifting W(c); wrestling M(I,s). Intramural sports: archery, badminton, baseball/softball, basketball, bowling, crew, cross-country running, equestrian sports, fencing, field hockey, golf, gymnastics, ice hockey, lacrosse, martial arts, racquetball, riflery, rugby, sailing, skiing (cross-country), skiing (downhill), soccer, squash, swimming and diving, tennis, track and field, volleyball, water polo, weight lifting, wrestling.

Majors Accounting B; actuarial science B; adult and continuing education B; advertising B; aerospace engineering B; agricultural business B; agricultural economics B; agricultural education B; agricultural engineering B; agricultural sciences B; agronomy/soil and crop sciences B; aircraft and missile maintenance A; air traffic control A; American studies B; animal hospital technology B; animal sciences B; anthropology B; applied art B; applied mathematics B; art education B; art/fine arts B; astrophysics B; atmospheric sciences B; aviation administration B; aviation technology A, B; behavioral sciences B; biochemistry B; bioengineering B; biology/biological sciences B; biomedical engineering B; biomedical sciences B; biometrics B; biophysics B; black/Afro-American studies B; botany/plant sciences B; broadcasting B; business administration/commerce/management B; cell biology B; chemical engineering B; chemistry B; child care/child and family studies B; child psychology/child development B; city, community, and regional planning B; civil engineering B; civil engineering technology A, B; clinical psychology B; commercial art B; communication B; comparative literature B; computer engineering B; computer information systems B; computer programming A, B; computer science B; computer technologies A, B; conservation B; construction engineering B; construction management B; construction technologies A, B; consumer services B; creative writing B; criminal justice B; dairy sciences B; data processing B; (pre)dentistry sequence B; dietetics B; drafting and design B; early childhood education B; earth science B; ecology/environmental studies B; economics B; education B; educational administration B; educational media B; electrical engineering B; electrical engineering technology A, B; electronics engineering B; elementary education B; engineering (general) B; engineering and applied sciences B; engineering management B; engineering physics B; engineering technology A, B; English B; entomology B; environmental biology B; environmental design B; environmental engineering B; environmental health sciences B; evolutionary biology B; experimental psychology B; family services B; farm and ranch management B; fashion design and technology B; fashion merchandising B; film studies B; finance/banking B; fish and game management B; flight training A, B; fluid and thermal sciences B; food marketing B; food sciences B; food services management B; food services technology A; forest engineering B; forestry B; forest technology B; French B; genetics B; geochemistry B; geological engineering B; geology B; geophysical engineering B; geophysics B; German B; graphic arts B; health science B; history B; home economics B; home economics education B; horticulture B; hospitality services B; hotel and restaurant management A, B; illustration A, B; industrial administration B; industrial arts B; industrial design B; industrial engineering B; industrial engineering technology A, B; interior design B; international economics B; international studies B; journalism B; labor and industrial relations B; landscape architecture/design B; (pre)law sequence B; library science B; management engineering B; management information systems B; marine biology B; marketing/retailing/merchandising B; marriage and family counseling B; materials engineering B; materials sciences B; mathematics B; mechanical engineering B; mechanical engineering technology A, B; medical illustration B; medical laboratory technology B; medical technology B; (pre)medicine sequence B; medieval studies B; mental health/rehabilitation counseling B; metallurgical engineering B; meteorology B; microbiology B; modern languages B; molecular biology B; natural resource management B; nuclear engineering B; nuclear medical technology B; nuclear physics B; nursing B; nutrition B; occupational safety and health B; oceanography B; parks management B; pharmacy/pharmaceutical sciences B; philosophy B; physical education B; physical sciences B; physics B; political science/government B; poultry sciences B; psychology B; public administration B; public relations B; radio and television studies B; recreation and leisure services B; robotics B; Russian B; science B; science education B; secondary education B; social science B; sociology B; Spanish B; special education B; speech pathology and audiology B; speech therapy B; sports medicine B; statistics B; surveying engineering B; systems engineering B; technical writing B; telecommunications B; textile arts B; textiles and clothing B; theater arts/drama B; tourism and travel B; transportation engineering B; (pre)veterinary medicine sequence B; veterinary sciences B; vocational education B; wildlife biology B; wildlife management B; wood sciences B; zoology B. Majors with highest enrollment: engineering (general), social science, business administration/commerce/management.

LD Program Information

Name of Program Not specified.

Availability of Services Services provided to freshmen, sophomores, juniors, seniors. Program currently serves 17 LD students: 5 freshmen, 5 sophomores, 4 juniors, 3 seniors.

Fees $4 to $10 per hour for some tutoring services.

Staff 7 part-time staff members. Services provided by clinical psychologist and staffs of Learning Center, Writing Lab, Horizons Program, and Office of Dean of Students.

Admissions LD applicants evaluated on the basis of high school transcript and grade point average, standard or untimed SAT, psychoeducational report. LD students may begin taking classes in fall, spring, or summer. Application should be submitted 3 months in advance of initial anticipated enrollment.

Housing College housing (including coed) available. LD students housed randomly. LD students not required to live on campus.

Diagnostic Testing Available in intelligence, reading, math, perceptual skills, psychoneurology.

Tutoring Offered one-to-one and in small groups by peer tutors. Available in all subjects. LD students may receive tutoring in all courses each term.

Basic Skills Remediation Offered in small groups by teaching assistants. Available in reading, math, written language, learning strategies.

Academic Advisement Help with program planning provided by academic advisers. Most LD students take 12 to 14 semester hours each semester; 8 semester hours required to maintain full-time status (12 for financial aid).

Special Courses Offered in college survival skills. All offered for credit; all enter into overall grade point average.

Auxiliary Aids and Services Aids include taped textbooks, tape recorders, word processors. Services include alternative exam arrangements.

Counseling Services Individual counseling, career counseling available.

Contact Ms. Betty M. Nelson, Associate Dean of Students, Purdue University, Hovde Hall, West Lafayette, IN 47907, 317-494-1252.

RADFORD UNIVERSITY

Radford, Virginia

Year Program Began	*Not reported*	Special Courses	
Special Fee	None	Taped Textbooks	✓
Special Orientation		Alternative Exam Arrangements	✓
Diagnostic Testing	✓	Notetakers	
Subject-Area Tutoring	✓	Staff	7 part-time
Basic Skills Remediation	✓	Number of Students Served	11

General Information State-supported comprehensive coed institution. Founded 1910. Awards B, M. Institutionally accredited by regional association; programs accredited by NLN (nursing), NCATE (teacher education); candidate for program accreditation by NASM (music). Small-town setting; 138-acre campus. Total enrollment: 6,806. Faculty: 341 (300 full-time, 41 part-time); 65% have doctoral degrees; graduate assistants teach a few undergraduate courses. Calendar: semesters. Grading system: letters or numbers. Library holdings: 300,000 bound volumes, 38,000 titles on microform, 3,000 periodical subscriptions, 20,000 records/tapes.

Undergraduate Profile Fall 1984: 5,800 undergraduates (1,444 freshmen) from 39 states and territories and 26 foreign countries; 4% part-time; 89% state residents; 8% transfers; 80% financial aid recipients; 66% women; 3% blacks; 1% Native Americans; 1% Hispanics; 1% Asian Americans; 1% foreign nationals; 25 legally handicapped students.

Expenses (1985–86) State resident tuition: $1726 full-time, $72 per semester hour part-time. Nonresident tuition: $2476 full-time, $103 per semester hour part-time. College room and board: $2936.

Financial Aid Fall 1984 full-time freshmen: 52% applied for aid, 81% of those were judged to have need, 89% of those were aided; the average aided freshman received an aid package worth $1121 (40% scholarships/grants, 60% self-help) meeting 75% of need. College-administered aid for all 1984–85 undergraduates: need-based scholarships (average $675); non-need scholarships (average $1000); low-interest long-term loans; SEOG; College Work-Study; part-time jobs. Supporting data: FAF, institutional form, AFSA/SAR required. Priority application deadline: 4/15.

Athletics Member NCAA (Division I). Intercollegiate sports: baseball/softball M(I,s), W(c); basketball M(I,s), W(I,s); cross-country running M(I,s), W(I,s); equestrian sports W(c); field hockey W(I,s); golf M(I,s); gymnastics M(I,s), W(I,s); lacrosse M(I,s); soccer M(I,s), W(I,s); tennis M(I,s), W(I,s); volleyball W(I,s). Intramural sports: badminton, baseball/softball, basketball, bowling, cross-country running, football, martial arts, racquetball, soccer, swimming and diving, tennis, volleyball, water polo, weight lifting.

Majors Accounting B; applied art B; art education B; art/fine arts B; art history B; art therapy B; biology/biological sciences B; broadcasting B; business administration/commerce/management B; business education B; chemistry B; communication B; computer science B; criminal justice B; dance B; (pre)dentistry sequence B; dietetics B; early childhood education B; economics B; education B; elementary education B; English B; family and consumer studies B; fashion design and technology B; fashion merchandising B; finance/banking B; food sciences B; food services management B; food services technology B; French B; geography B; geology B; German B; health science B; history B; home economics B; home economics education B; illustration B; insurance B; interior design B; journalism B; Latin B; law enforcement/police sciences B; (pre)law sequence B; liberal arts/general studies B; library science B; management information systems B; marketing/retailing/merchandising B; mathematics B; medical technology B; (pre)medicine sequence B; music B; music education B; music therapy B; nursing B; physical education B; political science/government B; psychology B; radio and television studies B; recreation and leisure services B; secondary education B; secretarial studies/office management B; social work B; sociology B; Spanish B; special education B; speech pathology and audiology B; speech/rhetoric/public address/debate B; speech therapy B; statistics B; studio art B; telecommunications B; textiles and clothing B; theater arts/drama B. Majors with highest enrollment: business administration/commerce/management, elementary education, family and consumer studies.

LD Program Information

Name of Program Handicapped Student Services.

Availability of Services Services provided to freshmen, sophomores, juniors, seniors. Program currently serves 11 LD students: 3 freshmen, 2 sophomores, 4 juniors, 2 seniors.

Staff 7 part-time staff members, including coordinator. Services provided by tutors, counselor, diagnostic specialist, academic adviser, directors of Writing Lab and Reading Lab.

Admissions LD applicants evaluated on the basis of high school transcript and grade point average, untimed SAT or ACT, personal interview, letters of recommendation, psychoeducational report. LD students may begin taking classes in fall, spring, or summer. Application should be submitted 6 months in advance of initial anticipated enrollment.

Housing College housing (including coed) available. LD students housed randomly. LD freshmen required to live on campus.

Diagnostic Testing Available in intelligence, reading, math, spelling, handwriting, spoken language, perceptual skills, personality, social skills, speech.

Tutoring Offered one-to-one by professional teachers, peer tutors. Available in all subjects. LD students may receive tutoring in all courses each term.

Basic Skills Remediation Offered one-to-one and in small groups by regular teachers, teacher trainees. Available in reading, spelling, written language, learning strategies, work and study habits.

Academic Advisement Help with program planning provided by LD staff members, academic advisers. LD students may take up to 18 semester hours each semester; most take 12 semester hours; 12 semester hours required to maintain full-time status.

Auxiliary Aids and Services Aids include taped textbooks. Services include alternative exam arrangements.

Counseling Services Individual counseling, career counseling available.

Contact Mr. Michael Walsh, Assistant Director of Residential Life and Coordinator of Handicapped Student Services, Radford University, Box 5897, Radford, VA 24142, 703-731-5375.

RAMAPO COLLEGE OF NEW JERSEY

Mahwah, New Jersey

Year Program Began	1978	Special Courses	
Special Fee	None	Taped Textbooks	✓
Special Orientation	✓	Alternative Exam Arrangements	✓
Diagnostic Testing	✓	Notetakers	✓
Subject-Area Tutoring	✓	Staff	3 full-time
Basic Skills Remediation	✓	Number of Students Served	16

General Information State-supported 4-year coed college. Part of New Jersey State College System. Founded 1969. Awards B. Institutionally accredited by regional association; programs accredited by NCATE (teacher education). Small-town setting, with easy access to New York City; 300-acre barrier-free campus. Total enrollment: 3,961. Faculty: 209 (133 full-time, 76 part-time); 80% have doctoral degrees. Calendar: semesters. Grading system: letters or numbers. Library holdings: 150,000 bound volumes, 5,000 titles on microform, 1,700 periodical subscriptions, 800 records/tapes.

Undergraduate Profile Fall 1984: 3,961 undergraduates (406 freshmen) from 6 states and territories and 28 foreign countries; 43% part-time; 95% state residents; 46% transfers; 50% financial aid recipients; 51% women; 8% blacks; 0% Native Americans; 2% Hispanics; 0% Asian Americans; 1% foreign nationals; 25% of undergraduates over 25 years of age; 60 legally handicapped students.

Expenses (1984–85) State resident tuition: $1326 full-time, $44.20 per credit part-time. Nonresident tuition: $1926 full-time, $64.20 per credit part-time. College room and board: $3185. College room only: $2185.

Financial Aid Fall 1984 full-time freshmen: 57% applied for aid, 75% of those were judged to have need, 100% of those were aided; the average aided freshman received an aid package worth $2500 (33% scholarships/grants, 67% self-help) meeting 70% of need. College-administered aid for all 1984–85 undergraduates: need-based scholarships; 1 non-need scholarship ($1000); SEOG; College Work-Study; 420 part-time jobs. Supporting data: FAF, IRS, state form, institutional form, AFSA/SAR required. Priority application deadline: 5/1.

Athletics Member NCAA (Division III). Intercollegiate sports: archery M, W; baseball/softball M(III), W(III); basketball M(III), W(III); football M(III); golf M(III); soccer M(III); swimming and diving M(III), W(III); tennis M(III), W(III); volleyball W(III). Intramural sports: baseball/softball, basketball, cross-country running, football, volleyball.

Majors Accounting B; American studies B; art/fine arts B; biology/biological sciences B; business administration/commerce/management B; chemistry B; communication B; computer science B; (pre)dentistry sequence B; ecology/environmental studies B; economics B; environmental sciences B; history B; interdisciplinary studies B; international studies B; (pre)law sequence B; literature B; mathematics B; (pre)medicine sequence B; philosophy B; physics B; political science/government B; psychology B; public administration B; secondary education B; social work B; sociology B; (pre)veterinary medicine sequence B. Majors with highest enrollment: business administration/commerce/management, communication, computer science.

LD Program Information

Name of Program Office of Specialized Services.

Availability of Services Began offering services in 1978. Services provided to freshmen, sophomores, juniors, seniors. Program currently serves 16 LD students: 4 freshmen, 2 sophomores, 7 juniors, 3 seniors.

Staff 3 full-time staff members, including director. Services provided by counselors.

Admissions LD applicants evaluated on the basis of high school transcript and grade point average, untimed SAT, personal interview, autobiographical statement, letters of recommendation, psychoeducational report. LD students may begin taking classes in fall, spring, or summer. Application should be submitted 8 months in advance of initial anticipated enrollment.

Orientation Optional orientation offered after classes begin.

Housing College housing (including coed) available. LD students housed randomly. LD students not required to live on campus.

Diagnostic Testing Available in intelligence, reading, math, spelling, written language.

Tutoring Offered one-to-one and in small groups by professional teachers, peer tutors. Available in some subjects. LD students may receive tutoring in all courses each term.

Basic Skills Remediation Offered one-to-one and in small groups by regular teachers, teacher trainees. Available in reading, math, written language, learning strategies, work and study habits.

Academic Advisement Help with program planning provided by LD staff members, academic advisers. LD students may take up to 16 credits each semester; most take 12 credits; 12 credits required to maintain full-time status (except by special permission).

Auxiliary Aids and Services Aids include taped textbooks, tape recorders, calculators, typewriters. Services include alternative exam arrangements, notetakers, advocacy, readers, writers.

Counseling Services Individual counseling, small-group counseling, rap sessions, career counseling available.

Contact Mr. John J. Sarno, Director, Office of Specialized Services, Ramapo College of New Jersey, Mahwah, NJ 07430, 201-825-2800 Ext. 480.

REGIS COLLEGE

Denver, Colorado

Year Program Began	1981	Special Courses	✓
Special Fee	None	Taped Textbooks	
Special Orientation	✓	Alternative Exam Arrangements	✓
Diagnostic Testing	✓	Notetakers	
Subject-Area Tutoring	✓	Staff	3 part-time
Basic Skills Remediation	✓	Number of Students Served	20

General Information Roman Catholic comprehensive coed institution. Founded 1877. Awards B, M. Institutionally accredited by regional association. Metropolitan setting; 90-acre campus. Total enrollment: 1,220. Faculty: 95 (72 full-time, 23 part-time); 85% have doctoral degrees; graduate assistants teach no undergraduate courses. Calendar: semesters. Grading system: letters or numbers. Library holdings: 75,000 bound volumes, 600 periodical subscriptions, 1,500 records/tapes.

Undergraduate Profile Fall 1984: 1,100 undergraduates (276 freshmen) from 35 states and territories and 5 foreign countries; 10% part-time; 54% state residents; 8% transfers; 55% financial aid recipients; 45% women; 5% blacks; 1% Native Americans; 4% Hispanics; 3% foreign nationals; 2% of undergraduates over 25 years of age; 6 legally handicapped students.

Expenses (1985–86) Comprehensive fee of $11,160 includes full-time tuition ($6390), mandatory fees ($200), and college room and board ($4570). Part-time tuition: $203 per credit hour.

Financial Aid Fall 1984 full-time freshmen: 47% applied for aid, 66% of those were judged to have need, 100% of those were aided; the average aided freshman received an aid package worth $6141 (58% scholarships/grants, 42% self-help) meeting 82% of need. College-administered aid for all 1984–85 undergraduates: need-based scholarships; non-need scholarships (average $2000); low-interest long-term loans; College Work-Study; part-time jobs. Supporting data: FFS, IRS, institutional form, AFSA/SAR required; FAF acceptable. Priority application deadline: 3/15.

Athletics Member NCAA (Division II), NAIA. Intercollegiate sports: baseball/softball M(s); basketball M(s), W(s); golf M(s); soccer M(s); swimming and diving M(s), W(s); tennis M(s), W(s); volleyball W(s). Intramural sports: baseball/softball, basketball, football, ice hockey, racquetball, volleyball.

Majors Accounting B; biology/biological sciences B; business administration/commerce/management B; chemistry B; communication B; computer science B; (pre)dentistry sequence B; ecology/environmental studies B; economics B; elementary education B; English B; French B; history B; (pre)law sequence B; mathematics B; medical records services B; (pre)medicine sequence B; philosophy B; political science/government B; psychology B; religious studies B; secondary education B; sociology B; Spanish B; theater arts/drama B. Majors with highest enrollment: business administration/commerce/management, accounting, economics.

LD Program Information

Name of Program Regis Learning Center.

Availability of Services Began offering services in 1981. Services provided to freshmen, sophomores, juniors, seniors. Program currently serves 20 LD students: 5 freshmen, 5 sophomores, 5 juniors, 5 seniors.

Staff 3 part-time staff members, including director. Services provided by tutors, instructors.

Admissions LD applicants evaluated on the basis of high school transcript and grade point average, standard or untimed SAT or ACT, letters of recommendation, psychoeducational report. LD students may begin taking classes in fall or spring. Application should be submitted 8 to 10 months in advance of initial anticipated enrollment.

Orientation Required orientation held before registration.

Housing College housing (including coed) available. LD students housed randomly. LD freshmen and sophomores required to live on campus unless living with parents within commuting distance.

Diagnostic Testing Available in intelligence, reading, math, written language, work and study habits.

Tutoring Offered one-to-one by peer tutors. Available in all subjects. LD students may receive tutoring in all courses each term.

Basic Skills Remediation Offered in small groups by instructors of Regis Learning Center. Available in reading, math, written language, learning strategies, work and study habits.

Academic Advisement Help with program planning provided by LD staff members, academic advisers. LD students may take up to 16 credit hours each semester; most take 12 to 13 credit hours; 12 credit hours required to maintain full-time status.

Special Courses Offered in reading, vocabulary development, composition, study skills. All offered for credit; all enter into overall grade point average.

Auxiliary Aids and Services Aids include tape recorders, calculators, typewriters, word processors. Services include alternative exam arrangements, advocacy.

Counseling Services Individual counseling, career counseling available.

Contact Ms. Carla J. Clements, Director, Regis Learning Center, Regis College, West 50th and Lowell Boulevard, Denver, CO 80221, 303-458-4146.

RHODE ISLAND SCHOOL OF DESIGN

Providence, Rhode Island

Year Program Began	1980	Special Courses	
Special Fee	None	Taped Textbooks	✓
Special Orientation		Alternative Exam Arrangements	✓
Diagnostic Testing		Notetakers	
Subject-Area Tutoring	✓	Staff	2 part-time
Basic Skills Remediation	✓	Number of Students Served	17

General Information Independent comprehensive coed institution. Founded 1877. Awards B, M. Institutionally accredited by regional association; programs accredited by NAAB (architecture), NASAD (art and design), FIDER (interior design). City setting, with easy access to Boston; 12-acre campus. Total enrollment: 1,792. Faculty: 199 (93 full-time, 106 part-time); 12% have doctoral degrees; graduate assistants teach a few undergraduate courses. Calendar: 4-1-4. Grading system: letters or numbers and faculty reports. Library holdings: 69,000 bound volumes, 312 periodical subscriptions, 740 records/tapes.

Undergraduate Profile Fall 1984: 1,702 undergraduates (327 freshmen) from 50 states and territories and 47 foreign countries; 0% part-time; 8% state residents; 45% transfers; 68% financial aid recipients; 56% women; 5% blacks; 1% Native Americans; 2% Hispanics; 2% Asian Americans; 8% foreign nationals; 6 legally handicapped students.

Expenses (1985–86) Comprehensive fee of $12,800 includes full-time tuition ($8930), mandatory fees ($70), and college room and board ($3800).

Financial Aid Fall 1984 full-time freshmen: 52% applied for aid, 85% of those were judged to have need, 70% of those were aided; the average aided freshman received an aid package worth $8000 (40% scholarships/grants, 60% self-help) meeting 50% of need. College-administered aid for all 1984–85 undergraduates: 480 need-based scholarships (average $2200); 4 non-need scholarships (average $1500); short-term loans (average $500); low-interest long-term loans from college funds (average $2500), from external sources (average $2500); SEOG; College Work-Study; part-time jobs. Supporting data: FAF required; IRS required for some; FFS acceptable. Priority application deadline: 2/15.

Athletics Intercollegiate sport: ice hockey M, W. Intramural sports: baseball/softball, equestrian sports, racquetball, sailing, skiing (downhill), soccer, volleyball, weight lifting.

Majors Architecture B; art/fine arts B; ceramic art and design B; commercial art B; fashion design and technology B; film studies B; graphic arts B; illustration B; industrial design B; interior design B; jewelry and metalsmithing B; landscape architecture/design B; painting/drawing B; photography B; radio and television studies B; sculpture B; studio art B; textile arts B; textiles and clothing B.

LD Program Information

Name of Program Not specified.

Availability of Services Began offering services in 1980. Services provided to freshmen, sophomores, juniors, seniors. Program currently serves 17 LD students: 10 freshmen, 2 sophomores, 3 juniors, 2 seniors.

Staff 2 part-time staff members, including director. Services provided by counselors.

Admissions LD applicants evaluated on the basis of high school transcript, untimed SAT or ACT, autobiographical statement, letters of recommendation, portfolio of art work. LD students may begin taking classes in fall only. Application should be submitted 9 to 10 months in advance of initial anticipated enrollment.

Housing College housing (including coed) available. LD students housed randomly. LD freshmen required to live on campus.

Tutoring Offered one-to-one and in small groups by peer tutors. Available in all subjects. LD students may receive tutoring in all courses each term.

Basic Skills Remediation Offered one-to-one by regular teachers. Available in written language.

Academic Advisement Help with program planning provided by LD staff members, academic advisers. LD students may take up to 18 credits each semester; 12 credits required to maintain full-time status.

Auxiliary Aids and Services Aids include taped textbooks. Services include alternative exam arrangements, advocacy.

Counseling Services Individual counseling available.

Contact Ms. Nancy P. Cherico, Acting Director, Student Development and Counseling, Rhode Island School of Design, 2 College Street, Providence, RI 02903, 401-331-3511 Ext. 275.

ROCHESTER INSTITUTE OF TECHNOLOGY

Rochester, New York

Year Program Began	*Not reported*	Special Courses	✓
Special Fee	None	Taped Textbooks	✓
Special Orientation		Alternative Exam Arrangements	✓
Diagnostic Testing	✓	Notetakers	✓
Subject-Area Tutoring	✓	Staff	1 full-time, 4 part-time
Basic Skills Remediation	✓	Number of Students Served	10

General Information Independent comprehensive coed institution. Founded 1829. Awards A (college transfer), B, M. Institutionally accredited by regional association; programs accredited by NASAD (art and design), ABET (engineering and technology). Metropolitan setting; 1,300-acre barrier-free campus. Total enrollment: 15,231. Faculty: 1,241 (680 full-time, 561 part-time); 36% have doctoral degrees; graduate assistants teach no undergraduate courses. Calendar: quarters. Grading system: letters or numbers. Library holdings: 309,000 bound volumes, 218,500 titles on microform, 7,400 periodical subscriptions, 2,000 records/tapes.

Undergraduate Profile Fall 1984: 13,670 undergraduates (1,462 freshmen) from 50 states and territories and 62 foreign countries; 10% part-time; 60% state residents; 45% transfers; 65% financial aid recipients; 42% women; 5% blacks; 2% foreign nationals; 1,000 legally handicapped students.

Expenses (1985–86) Comprehensive fee of $10,671 includes full-time tuition ($7032), mandatory fees ($150), and college room and board ($3489). College room only: $1815. Part-time tuition: $180 per quarter hour.

Financial Aid Fall 1984 full-time freshmen: 45% applied for aid, 100% of those were judged to have need, 100% of those were aided; the average aided freshman received an aid package worth $6274 (45% scholarships/grants, 55% self-help) meeting 100% of need. College-administered aid for all 1984–85 undergraduates: need-based scholarships; non-need scholarships (average $2000); low-interest long-term loans; part-time jobs. Supporting data: FAF, IRS required; FFS, AFSA/SAR acceptable. Application deadline: continuous to 3/1.

Athletics Member NCAA (Division III). Intercollegiate sports: baseball/softball M(III), W(III); basketball M(III); cross-country running M(III), W(III); ice hockey M(III), W; lacrosse M(III); soccer M(III), W(III); swimming and diving M(III), W(III); tennis M(III), W(III); track and field M(III), W(III); volleyball W(III); wrestling M(III). Intramural sports: baseball/softball, basketball, bowling, cross-country running, football, golf, ice hockey, rugby, skiing (downhill), soccer, tennis, volleyball, water polo, weight lifting, wrestling.

Majors Accounting A, B; applied art A, B; applied mathematics B; art/fine arts A, B; biochemistry B; biology/biological sciences A, B; biomedical sciences B; biomedical technologies B; biotechnology B; business administration/commerce/management A, B; carpentry B; ceramic art and design A, B; chemistry A, B; civil engineering technology B; commercial art A, B; communication B; communication equipment technology B; computer engineering B; computer information systems B; computer programming B; computer science B; computer technologies B; construction technologies B; criminal justice B; data processing B; (pre)dentistry sequence B; dietetics A, B; economics B; electrical and electronics technologies B; electrical engineering B; electrical engineering technology B; electronics engineering B; energy management technologies B; engineering technology B; environmental design A, B; fashion merchandising A, B; film studies B; finance/banking B; food services management A, B; graphic arts A, B; hotel and restaurant management A, B; human services B; illustration A, B; industrial design B; industrial engineering B; interior design A, B; jewelry and metalsmithing A, B; law enforcement/police sciences B; (pre)law sequence B; management information systems B; manufacturing technology B; marketing/retailing/merchandising A, B; mathematics A, B; mechanical engineering B; mechanical engineering technology B; medical illustration B; medical technology A, B; (pre)medicine sequence B; nuclear medical technology B; nutrition A, B; painting/drawing A, B; photography A, B; physics B; printing technologies A, B; radio and television studies B; retail management A, B; science education B; social work B; studio art A, B; textile arts B; tourism and travel A, B; (pre)veterinary medicine sequence B.

LD Program Information

Name of Program Office of Special Services.

Availability of Services Services provided to freshmen, sophomores, juniors, seniors. Program currently serves 10 LD students: 5 freshmen, 1 sophomore, 4 juniors.

Staff 1 full-time, 4 part-time staff members, including director, academic coordinator. Services provided by remediation specialists, tutors, counselor, math instructor.

Admissions LD applicants evaluated on the basis of high school transcript and grade point average, untimed SAT or ACT, personal interview, letters of recommendation. LD students may begin taking classes in fall, winter, spring, or summer. Application should be submitted 9 to 12 months in advance of initial anticipated enrollment.

Housing College housing (including coed) available. LD students housed randomly. LD freshmen required to live on campus except if living with relatives.

Diagnostic Testing Available in intelligence, reading, math, spelling, handwriting, spoken language, written language, work and study habits, personality, social skills.

Tutoring Offered one-to-one and in small groups by professional teachers, peer tutors. Available in all subjects. LD students may receive tutoring in all courses each term.

Basic Skills Remediation Offered one-to-one and in small groups by learning development staff, academic coordinator. Available in math, handwriting, written language, learning strategies, work and study habits, social skills.

Academic Advisement Help with program planning provided by LD staff members, academic advisers. LD students may take up to 18 quarter hours each quarter; most take 9 quarter hours; 12 quarter hours required to maintain full-time status.

Special Courses Offered in college survival skills, communication skills, composition, math, personal psychology, study skills, career planning. Some offered for credit; none enter into overall grade point average.

Auxiliary Aids and Services Aids include taped textbooks, tape recorders, calculators, typewriters, word processors. Services include alternative exam arrangements, notetakers, advocacy, readers, scribes.

Counseling Services Individual counseling, small-group counseling, rap sessions, career counseling available.

Contact Ms. Jacqueline L. Czomanske, Academic Coordinator, Office of Special Services, Rochester Institute of Technology, Grace Watson Hall, 1 Lomb Memorial Drive, Rochester, NY 14623-0887, 716-475-2832.

ROCKHURST COLLEGE
Kansas City, Missouri

Year Program Began	1975	Special Courses	✓
Special Fee	None	Taped Textbooks	
Special Orientation		Alternative Exam Arrangements	✓
Diagnostic Testing	✓	Notetakers	
Subject-Area Tutoring	✓	Staff	2 part-time
Basic Skills Remediation	✓	Number of Students Served	2

General Information Roman Catholic comprehensive coed institution. Founded 1910. Awards A (college transfer and terminal), B, M. Institutionally accredited by regional association. Metropolitan setting; 22-acre barrier-free campus. Total enrollment: 2,697. Faculty: 179 (88 full-time, 91 part-time); 44% have doctoral degrees; graduate assistants teach no undergraduate courses. Calendar: semesters. Grading system: letters or numbers. Library holdings: 85,000 bound volumes, 289 titles on microform, 647 periodical subscriptions, 1,740 records/tapes.

Undergraduate Profile Fall 1984: 2,250 undergraduates (375 freshmen) from 29 states and territories; 30% part-time; 75% state residents; 8% transfers; 65% financial aid recipients; 57% women; 7% blacks; 0% Native Americans; 3% Hispanics; 1% Asian Americans; 1% foreign nationals; 7% of undergraduates over 25 years of age.

Expenses (1985–86) Comprehensive fee of $5320 includes full-time tuition ($4900), mandatory fees ($150), and college room and board ($270). Part-time tuition: $170 per credit hour.

Financial Aid Fall 1984 full-time freshmen: 76% applied for aid, 87% of those were judged to have need, 100% of those were aided; the average aided freshman received an aid package worth $4740 (43% scholarships/grants, 57% self-help) meeting 95% of need. College-administered aid for all 1984–85 undergraduates: 725 need-based scholarships (average $1320); 344 non-need scholarships (average $1100); low-interest long-term loans from college funds (average $639), from external sources (average $2399); SEOG; College Work-Study; part-time jobs. Supporting data: FAF, IRS required; state form required for some; FFS, AFSA/SAR acceptable. Priority application deadline: 3/1.

Athletics Member NAIA. Intercollegiate sports: basketball M(s), W(s); soccer M(s); volleyball W(s). Intramural sports: badminton, baseball/softball, basketball, cross-country running, field hockey, football, racquetball, soccer, tennis, volleyball, weight lifting.

Majors Accounting A, B; biology/biological sciences B; business administration/commerce/management A, B; business economics B; chemistry B; communication B; computer information systems B; computer management B; computer science B; (pre) dentistry sequence B; economics B; education B; elementary education B; English B; finance/banking A, B; French B; history B; humanities B; labor and industrial relations A, B; (pre)law sequence B; marketing/retailing/merchandising A, B; mathematics B; medical technology B; (pre)medicine sequence B; nursing B; philosophy B; physical therapy B; physics B; political science/government B; psychology B; public relations B; religious studies B; respiratory therapy B; science education B; secondary education B; social science B; social work B; sociology B; Spanish B; theology B; (pre)veterinary medicine sequence B. Majors with highest enrollment: nursing, accounting, finance/banking.

LD Program Information

Name of Program Learning Center.

Availability of Services Began offering services in 1975. Services provided to freshmen, sophomores, juniors, seniors. Program currently serves 2 LD students (both freshmen).

Staff 2 part-time staff members, including director. Services provided by remediation specialist.

Admissions LD applicants evaluated on the basis of high school transcript and grade point average, standard SAT or ACT, personal interview, autobiographical statement, letters of recommendation, psychoeducational report. LD students may begin taking classes in fall only. Application should be submitted at least 2 months in advance of initial anticipated enrollment.

Housing College housing available. LD students housed randomly. LD freshmen, sophomores, and juniors required to live on campus.

Diagnostic Testing Available in reading, math, spelling, spoken language, written language, perceptual skills, work and study habits, personality, social skills, speech.

Tutoring Offered one-to-one and in small groups by professional teachers, peer tutors. Available in all subjects. LD students may receive tutoring in 4 courses per term.

Basic Skills Remediation Offered one-to-one and in small groups by LD teachers. Available in reading, math, spelling, handwriting, spoken language, written language, learning strategies, perceptual skills, work and study habits, speech.

Academic Advisement Help with program planning provided by academic advisers. Most LD students take 12 to 15 credit hours each semester; 9 credit hours required to maintain full-time status.

Special Courses Offered in college survival skills, reading, vocabulary development, composition, study skills, career planning. All offered for credit; all enter into overall grade point average.

Auxiliary Aids and Services Aids include tape recorders, calculators, typewriters, word processors. Services include alternative exam arrangements, advocacy.

Counseling Services Individual counseling, career counseling available.

Contact Dr. Calvin W. Evans, Director, Learning Center, Rockhurst College, 5225 Troost Avenue, Kansas City, MO 64110, 816-926-4052.

ROCKY MOUNTAIN COLLEGE

Billings, Montana

Year Program Began	1980
Special Fee	None
Special Orientation	
Diagnostic Testing	✓
Subject-Area Tutoring	✓
Basic Skills Remediation	✓
Special Courses	✓
Taped Textbooks	✓
Alternative Exam Arrangements	✓
Notetakers	✓
Staff	1 full-time, 4 part-time
Number of Students Served	7

General Information Interdenominational 4-year coed college. Founded 1878. Awards B. Institutionally accredited by regional association. City setting; 60-acre campus. Total enrollment: 504. Faculty: 45 (30 full-time, 15 part-time); 50% have doctoral degrees. Calendar: 4-4-1. Grading system: letters or numbers. Library holdings: 80,000 bound volumes, 350 titles on microform, 350 periodical subscriptions, 1,707 records/tapes.

Undergraduate Profile Fall 1984: 504 undergraduates (129 freshmen) from 32 states and territories and 7 foreign countries; 16% part-time; 57% state residents; 6% transfers; 75% financial aid recipients; 53% women; 2% blacks; 3% Native Americans; 1% Hispanics; 0% Asian Americans; 5% foreign nationals; 2 legally handicapped students.

Expenses (1985–86) Comprehensive fee of $6565 includes full-time tuition ($4030), mandatory fees ($65), and college room and board ($2470). College room only: $1020. Part-time tuition: $168 per semester hour.

Financial Aid Fall 1984 full-time freshmen: 83% applied for aid, 80% of those were judged to have need, 100% of those were aided; the average aided freshman received an aid package worth $3113 (61% scholarships/grants, 39% self-help) meeting 90% of need. College-administered aid for all 1984–85 undergraduates: need-based scholarships (average $615); non-need scholarships (average $900); low-interest long-term loans from external sources (average $750); SEOG; College Work-Study; 45 part-time jobs. Supporting data: FAF, IRS, state form, institutional form, AFSA/SAR required; FFS acceptable. Priority application deadline: 7/1.

Athletics Member NAIA. Intercollegiate sports: basketball M(s), W(s); football M(s); track and field W(s). Intramural sports: baseball/softball, basketball, cross-country running, football, martial arts, racquetball, skiing (cross-country), skiing (downhill), soccer, swimming and diving, tennis, track and field, volleyball, weight lifting.

Majors Accounting B; anthropology B; art education B; art/fine arts B; biology/biological sciences B; business administration/commerce/management B; chemistry B; computer science B; economics B; education B; elementary education B; English B; geology B; history B; history of philosophy B; land use management and reclamation B; (pre)law sequence B; mathematics B; (pre)medicine sequence B; music B; music education B; philosophy B; physical education B; political science/government B; psychology B; secondary education B; sociology B; Spanish B; theater arts/drama B; theology B. Major with highest enrollment: business administration/commerce/management.

LD Program Information

Name of Program Service for Academic Success.

Availability of Services Began offering services in 1980. Services provided to freshmen, sophomores, juniors, seniors. Program currently serves 7 LD students: 3 freshmen, 1 sophomore, 1 junior, 2 seniors.

Staff 1 full-time, 4 part-time staff members, including director, coordinator. Services provided by instructors.

Admissions LD applicants evaluated on the basis of high school transcript and grade point average, standard SAT or ACT, letters of recommendation; psychoeducational report recommended. LD students may begin taking classes in fall or spring. Application should be submitted 3 months in advance of initial anticipated enrollment.

Housing College housing (including coed) available. LD students housed randomly. LD freshmen, sophomores, juniors, and seniors required to live on campus except if living with relatives.

Diagnostic Testing Available in intelligence, reading, math, work and study habits, personality.

Tutoring Offered one-to-one and in small groups by peer tutors. Available in all subjects. LD students may receive tutoring in all courses each term.

Basic Skills Remediation Offered one-to-one and in small groups by regular teachers. Available in reading, math, written language, work and study habits.

Academic Advisement Help with program planning provided by academic advisers. LD students may take up to 15 semester hours each semester; most take 15 semester hours (12 in first semester); 12 semester hours required to maintain full-time status.

Special Courses Offered in college survival skills, reading, composition, math, study skills. Some offered for credit; some enter into overall grade point average.

Auxiliary Aids and Services Aids include taped textbooks, tape recorders. Services include alternative exam arrangements, notetakers.

Counseling Services Individual counseling, career counseling available.

Contact Mr. Jim B. Bies, Dean of Students and Director of Service for Academic Success, Rocky Mountain College, Billings, MT 59102, 406-657-1018.

ROOSEVELT UNIVERSITY

Chicago, Illinois

Year Program Began	1981	Special Courses	✓
Special Fee	$1200 per year	Taped Textbooks	✓
Special Orientation	✓	Alternative Exam Arrangements	✓
Diagnostic Testing	✓	Notetakers	✓
Subject-Area Tutoring	✓	Staff	1 full-time, 2 part-time
Basic Skills Remediation	✓	Number of Students Served	19

General Information Independent comprehensive coed institution. Founded 1945. Awards B, M. Institutionally accredited by regional association; programs accredited by NASM (music), NCATE (teacher education). Metropolitan setting; barrier-free campus. Total enrollment: 6,061. Faculty: 481 (169 full-time, 312 part-time); 72% have doctoral degrees; graduate assistants teach no undergraduate courses. Calendar: semesters. Grading system: letters or numbers. Library holdings: 365,000 bound volumes, 112,000 titles on microform, 1,500 periodical subscriptions, 10,000 records/tapes.

Undergraduate Profile Fall 1984: 4,129 undergraduates (189 freshmen); 61% part-time; 88% state residents; 60% transfers; 45% financial aid recipients; 54% women; 26% blacks; 1% Native Americans; 3% Hispanics; 4% Asian Americans; 9% foreign nationals; 65% of undergraduates over 25 years of age.

Expenses (1985–86) Comprehensive fee of $8284 includes full-time tuition ($5040), mandatory fees ($34), and college room and board ($3210). Part-time tuition: $168 per semester hour.

Financial Aid Fall 1984 full-time freshmen: 100% applied for aid; the average aided freshman received an aid package meeting 70% of need. College-administered aid for all 1984–85 undergraduates: need-based scholarships; 200 non-need scholarships (average $3000); short-term loans (average $50); low-interest long-term loans from external sources (average $1500); SEOG; College Work-Study. Supporting data: FAF, IRS, state form, institutional form required. Application deadline: continuous to 5/1.

Athletics Member NCAA, NAIA. Intercollegiate sports: basketball M(s), W; golf M(s); soccer M(s); tennis M(s), W. Intramural sports: badminton, baseball/softball, football, soccer, tennis.

Majors Accounting B; actuarial science B; adult and continuing education B; advertising B; African studies B; American studies B; art education B; art/fine arts B; art history B; biology/biological sciences B; black/Afro-American studies B; business administration/commerce/management B; business economics B; business education B; chemistry B; communication B; comparative literature B; computer information systems B; computer science B; criminal justice B; cytotechnology B; data processing B; (pre)dentistry sequence B; early childhood education B; economics B; education B; electronics engineering B; elementary education B; English B; finance/banking B; French B; geography B; gerontology B; health science B; health services administration B; history B; hospitality services B; hotel and restaurant management B; human services B; industrial engineering B; information science B; interior design B; international business B; international studies B; jazz B; journalism B; Judaic studies B; labor and industrial relations B; laboratory technologies B; labor studies B; (pre)law sequence B; legal studies B; liberal arts/general studies B; literature B; marketing/retailing/merchandising B; mathematics B; medical technology B; (pre)medicine sequence B; modern languages B; music B; music education B; music history B; nuclear medical technology B; operations research B; paralegal studies B; philosophy B; physics B; piano/organ B; political science/government B; psychology B; public administration B; public relations B; radiological technology B; real estate B; secondary education B; social science B; sociology B; Spanish B; special education B; speech/rhetoric/public address/debate B; stringed instruments B; telecommunications B; theater arts/drama B; urban studies B; voice B; wind and percussion instruments B; women's studies B. Majors with highest enrollment: accounting, computer science, business administration/commerce/management.

LD Program Information

Name of Program Learning and Support Services Program.

Availability of Services Began offering services in 1981. Services provided to freshmen, sophomores, juniors, seniors. Program currently serves 19 LD students: 16 freshmen, 2 sophomores, 1 senior.

Fees $1200 per year.

Staff 1 full-time, 2 part-time staff members, including director, associate director, assistant director. Services provided by tutors.

Admissions LD applicants evaluated on the basis of high school transcript and grade point average, untimed SAT or ACT, personal interview, autobiographical statement, letters of recommendation, psychoeducational report. LD students may begin taking classes in fall, spring, or summer. Application should be submitted 6 months in advance of initial anticipated enrollment.

Orientation Required orientation held before registration.

Housing College housing (including coed) available. LD students housed randomly. LD students not required to live on campus.

Diagnostic Testing Available in intelligence, reading, math, spelling, handwriting, spoken language, written language, motor abilities, perceptual skills, work and study habits, personality, social skills, psychoneurology, speech.

Tutoring Offered one-to-one and in small groups by professional teachers, peer tutors. Available in all subjects. LD students may receive tutoring in all courses each term.

Basic Skills Remediation Offered one-to-one and in small groups by LD teachers. Available in learning strategies, work and study habits.

Academic Advisement Help with program planning provided by LD staff members, academic advisers. Most LD students take 6 to 9 semester hours each semester; 12 semester hours required to maintain full-time status.

Special Courses Offered in college survival skills, reading, vocabulary development, communication skills, composition, language development, math, personal psychology, study skills, career planning. Some offered for credit; some enter into overall grade point average.

Auxiliary Aids and Services Aids include taped textbooks, tape recorders, calculators, typewriters, word processors. Services include alternative exam arrangements, notetakers, advocacy.

Counseling Services Individual counseling, small-group counseling, career counseling available.

Contact Dr. Margaret Policastro, Director, Learning and Support Services Program and Assistant Professor of Education, Roosevelt University, 430 South Michigan Avenue, Chicago, IL 60605, 312-341-3870.

SAINT FRANCIS COLLEGE

Fort Wayne, Indiana

Year Program Began	1983	Special Courses	✓
Special Fee	None	Taped Textbooks	✓
Special Orientation	✓	Alternative Exam Arrangements	✓
Diagnostic Testing	✓	Notetakers	✓
Subject-Area Tutoring	✓	Staff	3 part-time
Basic Skills Remediation	✓	Number of Students Served	10

General Information Roman Catholic comprehensive coed institution. Founded 1890. Awards A (college transfer), B, M. Institutionally accredited by regional association; programs accredited by NCATE (teacher education). City setting; 73-acre campus. Total enrollment: 1,310. Faculty: 90 (40 full-time, 50 part-time); 67% have doctoral degrees; graduate assistants teach no undergraduate courses. Calendar: semesters. Grading system: letters or numbers. Library holdings: 71,210 bound volumes, 50,000 titles on microform, 565 periodical subscriptions.

Undergraduate Profile Fall 1984: 1,011 undergraduates (100 freshmen) from 16 states and territories and 4 foreign countries; 58% part-time; 80% state residents; 47% transfers; 80% financial aid recipients; 77% women; 2% blacks; 1% Hispanics; 1% foreign nationals; 35% of undergraduates over 25 years of age; 10 legally handicapped students.

Expenses (1985–86) Comprehensive fee of $6172 includes full-time tuition ($3712), mandatory fees ($60), and college room and board ($2400). Part-time tuition: $116 per semester hour.

Financial Aid Fall 1984 full-time freshmen: 80% applied for aid, 91% of those were judged to have need, 100% of those were aided; the average aided freshman received an aid package worth $2191 (53% scholarships/grants, 47% self-help) meeting 95% of need. College-administered aid for all 1984–85 undergraduates: need-based scholarships; 37 non-need scholarships (average $1210); short-term loans (average $500); low-interest long-term loans from external sources (average $2000); SEOG; College Work-Study; 134 part-time jobs. Supporting data: FAF, IRS, AFSA/SAR required; state form required for some. Priority application deadline: 3/1.

Athletics Member NAIA. Intercollegiate sports: baseball/softball M(s), W(s); basketball M(s), W(s); cross-country running M; golf M(s); soccer M(s); tennis M(s), W(s); volleyball W(s). Intramural sports: baseball/softball, basketball, bowling, fencing, volleyball.

Majors Accounting A, B; American studies B; art education B; art/fine arts B; biology/biological sciences B; business administration/commerce/management A, B; business education B; chemistry B; commercial art A, B; computer information systems B; (pre)dentistry sequence B; education B; elementary education B; English B; health services administration A, B; (pre)law sequence B; liberal arts/general studies B; medical laboratory technology A; medical technology B; (pre)medicine sequence B; nursing B; psychology B; radiological technology A; religious studies B; science B; science education B; secondary education B; social work B; special education B; (pre)veterinary medicine sequence B. Majors with highest enrollment: business administration/commerce/management, commercial art, special education.

LD Program Information

Name of Program ACCESS Learning Center.

Availability of Services Began offering services in 1983. Services provided to freshmen, sophomores, juniors, seniors. Program currently serves 10 LD students: 4 freshmen, 3 sophomores, 1 junior, 2 seniors.

Staff 3 part-time staff members, including director. Services provided by remediation specialists.

Admissions LD applicants evaluated on the basis of high school transcript and grade point average, standard or untimed SAT or ACT, personal interview, autobiographical statement, letters of recommendation; psychoeducational report recommended. LD students may begin taking classes in fall or spring. Application should be submitted 1 to 2 weeks in advance of initial anticipated enrollment.

Orientation Optional orientation offered during registration.

Housing College housing available. LD students housed with other LD students and non-LD students. LD freshmen, sophomores, juniors, and seniors required to live on campus except if 21 or over or living with relatives.

Diagnostic Testing Available in intelligence, reading, spelling, written language, perceptual skills, work and study habits, personality.

Tutoring Offered one-to-one and in small groups by professional teachers, peer tutors. Available in some subjects. LD students may receive tutoring in all courses each term (depending on availability of tutors).

Basic Skills Remediation Offered one-to-one and in small groups by regular teachers. Available in reading, math, spelling, written language, learning strategies, perceptual skills, work and study habits.

Academic Advisement Help with program planning provided by LD staff members, academic advisers. Most LD students take 12 to 14 semester hours each semester; 12 semester hours required to maintain full-time status.

Special Courses Offered in college survival skills, reading, vocabulary development, composition, math, study skills, career planning. None offered for credit; none enter into overall grade point average.

Auxiliary Aids and Services Aids include taped textbooks, tape recorders, calculators, typewriters, word processors. Services include alternative exam arrangements, notetakers, advocacy.

Counseling Services Individual counseling, small-group counseling, rap sessions, career counseling available.

Contact Mr. Gregory D. Wible, Director, ACCESS Learning Center, Saint Francis College, 2701 Spring Street, Fort Wayne, IN 46808, 219-432-3551.

SAINT MARY OF THE PLAINS COLLEGE

Dodge City, Kansas

Year Program Began	1985	Special Courses	✓
Special Fee	None	Taped Textbooks	
Special Orientation	✓	Alternative Exam Arrangements	✓
Diagnostic Testing	✓	Notetakers	
Subject-Area Tutoring	✓	Staff	3 part-time
Basic Skills Remediation	✓	Number of Students Served	5

General Information Roman Catholic 4-year coed college. Founded 1952. Awards A (college transfer and terminal), B. Institutionally accredited by regional association; programs accredited by NASM (music), NLN (nursing), NCATE (teacher education). Rural setting; 100-acre campus. Total enrollment: 705. Faculty: 87 (73 full-time, 14 part-time); 20% have doctoral degrees. Calendar: semesters. Grading system: letters or numbers. Library holdings: 80,000 bound volumes, 330 periodical subscriptions, 760 records/tapes.

Undergraduate Profile Fall 1984: 705 undergraduates (113 freshmen) from 22 states and territories and 2 foreign countries; 10% part-time; 50% state residents; 15% transfers; 93% financial aid recipients; 65% women; 3% blacks; 0% Native Americans; 5% Hispanics; 1% foreign nationals; 2% of undergraduates over 25 years of age; 1 legally handicapped student.

Expenses (1985–86) Comprehensive fee of $6310 includes full-time tuition ($4000), mandatory fees ($110), and college room and board ($2200). College room only: $900. Part-time tuition per credit hour: $65 for the first 9 credit hours, 140 for the next 2 credit hours.

Financial Aid College-administered aid for all 1984–85 undergraduates: need-based scholarships (average $500); non-need scholarships (average $200); low-interest long-term loans from external sources; SEOG; College Work-Study. Supporting data: IRS, state form, AFSA/SAR required; FFS, FAF, institutional form acceptable. Priority application deadline: 8/1.

Athletics Member NAIA. Intercollegiate sports: baseball/softball M(s), W(s); basketball M(s), W(s); football M(s); volleyball W(s). Intramural sports: baseball/softball, basketball, football, racquetball, swimming and diving, tennis, volleyball, weight lifting.

Majors Accounting B; agricultural business B; biology/biological sciences B; business administration/commerce/management B; business education B; chemistry B; computer programming B; criminal justice B; (pre)dentistry sequence B; economics B; education B; elementary education B; English B; history B; interdisciplinary studies B; journalism B; mathematics B; medical technology B; (pre) medicine sequence B; music B; music education B; nursing A, B; physical education B; political science/government B; psychology B; radiological technology B; religious studies B; secondary education B; social work B; sociology B; Spanish B; theater arts/drama B. Majors with highest enrollment: business administration/commerce/management, nursing, elementary education.

LD Program Information

Name of Program Learning Lab.

Availability of Services Began offering services in 1985. Services provided to freshmen, sophomores, juniors, seniors. Program currently serves 5 LD students: 3 freshmen, 2 sophomores.

Staff 3 part-time staff members, including director. Services provided by tutors.

Admissions LD applicants evaluated on the basis of high school transcript and grade point average, standard SAT, autobiographical statement, letters of recommendation, parents' statement explaining disability. LD students may begin taking classes in fall only. Application should be submitted 6 months in advance of initial anticipated enrollment.

Orientation Required orientation held during registration.

Housing College housing available. LD students housed with other LD students and non-LD students. LD freshmen and sophomores required to live on campus.

Diagnostic Testing Available in intelligence, reading, math, spelling, written language, work and study habits.

Tutoring Offered one-to-one and in small groups by professional teachers, peer tutors. Available in some subjects. LD students may receive tutoring in all courses each term (for lower level courses only).

Basic Skills Remediation Offered one-to-one and in small groups by regular teachers, peer teachers. Available in reading, math, spelling, written language, learning strategies, work and study habits.

Academic Advisement Help with program planning provided by LD staff members, academic advisers. LD students may take up to 14 credit hours each semester; 12 credit hours required to maintain full-time status.

Special Courses Offered in study skills. None offered for credit; none enter into overall grade point average.

Auxiliary Aids and Services Aids include tape recorders, typewriters, word processors, computers. Services include alternative exam arrangements.

Contact Sister LeAnn Probst, Director of Learning Lab, Saint Mary of the Plains College, San Jose Drive, Dodge City, KS 67801, 316-225-4171 Ext. 210.

ST THOMAS AQUINAS COLLEGE

Sparkill, New York

Year Program Began	1981
Special Fee	$1600 per year
Special Orientation	✓
Diagnostic Testing	✓
Subject-Area Tutoring	✓
Basic Skills Remediation	✓
Special Courses	✓
Taped Textbooks	✓
Alternative Exam Arrangements	✓
Notetakers	✓
Staff	4 full-time, 4 part-time
Number of Students Served	40

General Information Independent 4-year coed college. Founded 1958. Awards B. Institutionally accredited by regional association. Small-town setting, with easy access to New York City; 24-acre campus. Total enrollment: 1,572. Faculty: 67 (47 full-time, 20 part-time); 70% have doctoral degrees. Calendar: 4-1-4. Grading system: letters or numbers. Library holdings: 90,000 bound volumes, 21,000 titles on microform, 600 periodical subscriptions, 2,563 records/tapes.

Undergraduate Profile Fall 1984: 1,572 undergraduates (327 freshmen) from 7 states and territories and 3 foreign countries; 35% part-time; 80% state residents; 35% transfers; 70% financial aid recipients; 50% women; 1% blacks; 0% Native Americans; 4% Hispanics; 1% foreign nationals; 15% of undergraduates over 25 years of age; 4 legally handicapped students.

Expenses (1985–86) Tuition: $3900 full-time, $125 per semester hour part-time. College room only: $1600.

Financial Aid Fall 1984 full-time freshmen: 90% applied for aid, 95% of those were judged to have need, 95% of those were aided; the average aided freshman received an aid package worth $2789 (36% scholarships/grants, 64% self-help) meeting 75% of need. College-administered aid for all 1984–85 undergraduates: need-based scholarships; 20 non-need scholarships (average $600); low-interest long-term loans from external sources (average $1000); SEOG; College Work-Study; 10 part-time jobs. Supporting data: FAF, IRS, institutional form, AFSA/SAR required. Priority application deadline: 3/1.

Athletics Member NAIA. Intercollegiate sports: baseball/softball M(s); basketball M(s), W(s); cross-country running M(s), W(s); volleyball W(s). Intramural sports: baseball/softball, basketball, tennis, volleyball.

Majors Accounting B; applied art B; applied mathematics B; art education B; art/fine arts B; art therapy B; bilingual/bicultural education B; business administration/commerce/management B; commercial art B; communication B; computer information systems B; criminal justice B; early childhood education B; education B; elementary education B; engineering sciences B; English B; finance/banking B; gerontology B; history B; humanities B; journalism B; marketing/retailing/merchandising B; mathematics B; medical laboratory technology B; medical technology B; (pre)medicine sequence B; modern languages B; natural sciences B; philosophy B; psychology B; recreation and leisure services B; religious studies B; Romance languages B; secondary education B; social science B; Spanish B; special education B; studio art B. Majors with highest enrollment: business administration/commerce/management, marketing/retailing/merchandising, special education.

LD Program Information

Name of Program The STAC Exchange (The Program for Learning Disabled Students).

Availability of Services Began offering services in 1981. Services provided to freshmen, sophomores, juniors, seniors. Program currently serves 40 LD students: 20 freshmen, 13 sophomores, 7 juniors.

Fees $1600 per year.

Staff 4 full-time, 4 part-time staff members, including director. Services provided by mentors (counselors/tutors).

Admissions LD applicants evaluated on the basis of high school transcript, untimed SAT or ACT, personal interview, autobiographical statement, letters of recommendation, psychoeducational report, IEP. LD students may begin taking classes in fall or spring. Application should be submitted 8 months in advance of initial anticipated enrollment.

Orientation Required orientation held before registration.

Housing College housing available. LD students housed randomly. LD students not required to live on campus.

Diagnostic Testing Available in reading, spoken language, written language, work and study habits, social skills, cognitive learning styles.

Tutoring Offered one-to-one and in small groups by professional teachers, peer tutors. Available in all subjects. LD students may receive tutoring in all courses each term.

Basic Skills Remediation Offered one-to-one by mentors. Available in spoken language, written language, learning strategies, work and study habits, social skills, speech.

Academic Advisement Help with program planning provided by LD staff members. LD students may take up to 15 semester hours each semester; most take 12 to 15 semester hours (12 in first semester); 12 semester hours required to maintain full-time status.

Special Courses Offered in college survival skills, communication skills, study skills, career planning. None offered for credit; none enter into overall grade point average.

Auxiliary Aids and Services Aids include taped textbooks, tape recorders, calculators, typewriters, word processors, audiovisual aids. Services include alternative exam arrangements, notetakers, advocacy, editorial assistance.

Counseling Services Individual counseling, small-group counseling, rap sessions, career counseling available.

Contact Dr. Marijanet Doonan, Director, The STAC Exchange, St Thomas Aquinas College, Route 340, Sparkill, NY 10976, 914-359-9500 Ext. 275.

SALEM COLLEGE

Salem, West Virginia

Year Program Began	1983	Special Courses	✓
Special Fee	None	Taped Textbooks	✓
Special Orientation	✓	Alternative Exam Arrangements	✓
Diagnostic Testing		Notetakers	
Subject-Area Tutoring	✓	Staff	*Not reported*
Basic Skills Remediation	✓	Number of Students Served	9

General Information Independent comprehensive coed institution. Founded 1888. Awards A (college transfer and terminal), B, M. Institutionally accredited by regional association; programs accredited by AACSB (business). Rural setting; 100-acre campus. Total enrollment: 1,296. Faculty: 68 (52 full-time, 16 part-time); 17% have doctoral degrees; graduate assistants teach no undergraduate courses. Calendar: semesters. Grading system: letters or numbers. Library holdings: 125,000 bound volumes, 94,000 titles on microform, 270 periodical subscriptions, 2,462 records/tapes.

Undergraduate Profile Fall 1984: 1,200 undergraduates (402 freshmen); 33% part-time; 30% state residents; 15% transfers; 90% financial aid recipients; 55% women; 13% blacks; 0% Native Americans; 0% Hispanics; 1% Asian Americans; 2% foreign nationals; 15% of undergraduates over 25 years of age; no legally handicapped students.

Expenses (1985–86) Comprehensive fee of $7814 includes full-time tuition ($4800), mandatory fees ($250), and college room and board ($2764). College room only: $1364. Part-time tuition: $191 per semester hour. Tuition at branch locations: $1408 full-time, $44 per semester hour part-time.

Financial Aid Fall 1984 full-time freshmen: 90% applied for aid, 94% of those were judged to have need, 100% of those were aided; the average aided freshman received an aid package worth $4945 (50% scholarships/grants, 50% self-help) meeting 95% of need. College-administered aid for all 1984–85 undergraduates: need-based scholarships; 313 non-need scholarships (average $770); short-term loans (average $25); low-interest long-term loans from college funds (average $500), from external sources (average $1925); SEOG; College Work-Study; 65 part-time jobs. Supporting data: FAF, IRS, institutional form required; state form required for some; FFS, AFSA/SAR acceptable. Priority application deadline: 4/15.

Athletics Member NAIA. Intercollegiate sports: baseball/softball M(s), W(s); basketball M(s), W(s); equestrian sports M, W; football M(s); golf M; tennis M; volleyball W(s). Intramural sports: baseball/softball, basketball, equestrian sports, football, soccer, swimming and diving, tennis, track and field, volleyball, water polo.

Majors Accounting A, B; applied art A, B; art education B; art therapy B; aviation administration A; biology/biological sciences B; broadcasting A, B; business administration/commerce/management A, B; commercial art B; communication B; community services B; computer science A, B; criminal justice A, B; data processing A; education B; electrical engineering technology A, B; elementary education B; engineering technology A, B; environmental biology B; environmental sciences B; equestrian studies B; finance/banking A; flight training B; industrial arts B; industrial engineering technology B; journalism B; (pre)law sequence B; liberal arts/general studies B; marketing/retailing/merchandising A, B; mathematics B; medical illustration B; medical technology B; (pre)medicine sequence B; mining technology A, B; museum studies A, B; natural sciences B; nursing A, B; occupational safety and health A, B; parks management B; physical education B; political science/government B; psychology B; public administration B; radio and television studies A, B; radiological technology B; real estate A; science A; secondary education B; special education B; speech/rhetoric/public address/debate A, B; sports administration B; sports medicine B; theater arts/drama B; wildlife management B. Majors with highest enrollment: business administration/commerce/management, equestrian studies, nursing.

LD Program Information

Name of Program Not specified.

Availability of Services Began offering services in 1983. Services provided to freshmen, sophomores, juniors, seniors. Program currently serves 9 LD students (all freshmen).

Admissions LD applicants evaluated on the basis of high school transcript and grade point average, untimed SAT or ACT, personal interview, letters of recommendation, psychoeducational report. LD students may begin taking classes in fall only. Application should be submitted 3 months in advance of initial anticipated enrollment.

Orientation Required orientation held before registration.

Housing College housing (including coed) available. LD students housed randomly. LD freshmen, sophomores, juniors, and seniors required to live on campus except if living with relatives or by special permission.

Tutoring Offered one-to-one and in small groups by professional teachers. Available in all subjects. LD students may receive tutoring in all courses each term.

Basic Skills Remediation Offered one-to-one and in small groups by regular teachers. Available in reading, math, spelling, handwriting, spoken language, written language, learning strategies, work and study habits.

Academic Advisement Help with program planning provided by academic advisers. LD students may take up to 20 semester hours each semester; most take 12 to 14 semester hours (12 in first semester); 12 semester hours required to maintain full-time status.

Special Courses Offered in college survival skills, study skills, career planning. Some offered for credit; some enter into overall grade point average.

Auxiliary Aids and Services Aids include taped textbooks, tape recorders, calculators, typewriters, word processors. Services include alternative exam arrangements, advocacy.

Counseling Services Individual counseling, small-group counseling, career counseling available.

Contact Mr. Frank Potter, Director of Admissions, Salem College, Salem, WV 26426, 304-782-5336.

SAM HOUSTON STATE UNIVERSITY

Huntsville, Texas

Year Program Began	1980	Special Courses	✓
Special Fee	None	Taped Textbooks	✓
Special Orientation	✓	Alternative Exam Arrangements	✓
Diagnostic Testing		Notetakers	✓
Subject-Area Tutoring	✓	Staff	1 part-time
Basic Skills Remediation	✓	Number of Students Served	2

General Information State-supported coed university. Founded 1879. Awards B, M, D. Institutionally accredited by regional association; programs accredited by NASM (music), NCATE (teacher education). Small-town setting, with easy access to Houston; 151-acre campus. Total enrollment: 10,492. Faculty: 428 (350 full-time, 78 part-time); 60% have doctoral degrees; graduate assistants teach a few undergraduate courses. Calendar: semesters. Grading system: letters or numbers. Library holdings: 515,000 bound volumes, 108,600 titles on microform, 4,500 periodical subscriptions, 7,260 records/tapes.

Undergraduate Profile Fall 1984: 8,797 undergraduates (1,483 freshmen); 15% part-time; 97% state residents; 12% transfers; 39% financial aid recipients; 49% women; 7% blacks; 0% Native Americans; 4% Hispanics; 0% Asian Americans; 3% foreign nationals; 25% of undergraduates over 25 years of age.

Expenses (1985–86) State resident tuition: $784 full-time. Nonresident tuition: $1920 full-time, $120 per semester hour part-time. State resident part-time tuition (1 to 11 semester hours) ranges from $100 to $136. Mandatory fees: $400. College room and board: $2400 (minimum). College room only: $1000 (minimum).

Financial Aid Fall 1984 full-time freshmen: 47% applied for aid, 82% of those were judged to have need, 86% of those were aided; the average aided freshman received an aid package worth $1900 (33% scholarships/grants, 67% self-help) meeting 70% of need. College-administered aid for all 1984–85 undergraduates: need-based scholarships (average $300); non-need scholarships (average $300); low-interest long-term loans; College Work-Study; part-time jobs. Supporting data: FFS, IRS, institutional form, AFSA/SAR required. Priority application deadline: 7/15.

Athletics Member NCAA (Division II), NAIA. Intercollegiate sports: baseball/softball M(II,s), W(II,s); basketball M(II,s), W(II,s); cross-country running M(II); football M(II,s); golf M(II,s); soccer M(II,s); tennis M(II), W(II); volleyball W(II,s). Intramural sports: baseball/softball, basketball, bowling, football, racquetball, swimming and diving, volleyball, water polo.

Majors Accounting B; advertising B; agricultural business B; agricultural education B; agricultural sciences B; animal sciences B; applied art B; art education B; art/fine arts B; biology/biological sciences B; business administration/commerce/management B; business economics B; business education B; chemistry B; clinical psychology B; commercial art B; computer science B; corrections B; criminal justice B; dance B; ecology/environmental studies B; economics B; electrical and electronics technologies B; elementary education B; English B; environmental sciences B; fashion merchandising B; film studies B; finance/banking B; food sciences B; food services management B; French B; geography B; geology B; German B; health education B; history B; home economics B; home economics education B; humanities B; industrial arts B; industrial engineering technology B; interior design B; journalism B; law enforcement/police sciences B; marketing/retailing/merchandising B; mathematics B; medical technology B; music B; music education B; music therapy B; nutrition B; painting/drawing B; photography B; physical education B; physics B; political science/government B; printing technologies B; psychology B; radio and television studies B; reading education B; sculpture B; secretarial studies/office management B; social work B; sociology B; Spanish B; special education B; speech/rhetoric/public address/debate B; studio art B; theater arts/drama B; vocational education B; voice B.

LD Program Information

Name of Program Academic Assistance for Handicapped Students.

Availability of Services Began offering services in 1980. Services provided to freshmen, sophomores, juniors, seniors. Program currently serves 2 LD students: 1 freshman, 1 senior.

Staff 1 part-time staff member (director).

Admissions LD applicants evaluated on the basis of high school transcript and grade point average, standard or untimed SAT or ACT; psychoeducational report recommended. LD students may begin taking classes in fall, spring, or summer. Application should be submitted 2 to 3 months in advance of initial anticipated enrollment.

Orientation Optional orientation offered after classes begin.

Housing College housing (including coed) available. LD students housed randomly. LD freshmen required to live on campus except by special permission.

Tutoring Offered one-to-one and in small groups by professional teachers, peer tutors. Available in some subjects. LD students may receive tutoring in 2 courses per term.

Basic Skills Remediation Offered in small groups by teacher trainees. Available in reading, math, spelling, written language.

Academic Advisement Help with program planning provided by academic advisers. LD students may take up to 15 semester hours each semester; most take 15 semester hours; 12 semester hours required to maintain full-time status.

Special Courses Offered in reading, vocabulary development, composition, language development, math, typing, career planning. Some offered for credit; some enter into overall grade point average.

Auxiliary Aids and Services Aids include taped textbooks. Services include alternative exam arrangements, notetakers.

Counseling Services Individual counseling, small-group counseling, career counseling available.

Contact Dr. Patsy Copeland, Director, Counseling and Career Placement Center, Sam Houston State University, PO Box 2059, Huntsville, TX 77341, 409-294-1720.

SAN DIEGO STATE UNIVERSITY

San Diego, California

Year Program Began	1981	Special Courses	✓
Special Fee	None	Taped Textbooks	✓
Special Orientation	✓	Alternative Exam Arrangements	✓
Diagnostic Testing	✓	Notetakers	✓
Subject-Area Tutoring	✓	Staff	1 full-time, 2 part-time
Basic Skills Remediation	✓	Number of Students Served	100

General Information State-supported coed university. Part of California State University System. Founded 1897. Awards B, M, D. Institutionally accredited by regional association; programs accredited by NASAD (art and design), AACSB (business), ABET (engineering and technology), NASM (music), NLN (nursing), NCATE (teacher education). Metropolitan setting; 300-acre barrier-free campus. Total enrollment: 33,611. Faculty: 1,935 (1,029 full-time, 906 part-time); 80% have doctoral degrees; graduate assistants teach a few undergraduate courses. Calendar: semesters. Grading system: letters or numbers. Library holdings: 727,730 bound volumes, 8,500 periodical subscriptions, 5,037 records/tapes.

Undergraduate Profile Fall 1984: 27,589 undergraduates (3,448 freshmen); 28% part-time; 92% state residents; 70% transfers; 25% financial aid recipients; 50% women; 4% blacks; 1% Native Americans; 7% Hispanics; 5% Asian Americans; 3% foreign nationals; 436 legally handicapped students.

Expenses (1985–86) State resident tuition: $0 full-time. Nonresident tuition: $3780 full-time, $126 per unit part-time. Mandatory fees: $661 for 6 or more units, $421 for 1 to 5 units. College room and board: $2610.

Financial Aid Fall 1984 full-time freshmen: 91% applied for aid, 72% of those were judged to have need, 36% of those were aided; the average aided freshman received an aid package worth $2337 (40% scholarships/grants, 60% self-help) meeting 62% of need. College-administered aid for all 1984–85 undergraduates: need-based scholarships; non-need scholarships (average $2500); short-term loans; low-interest long-term loans; SEOG; College Work-Study; part-time jobs. Supporting data: IRS, state form, AFSA/SAR required; FAF acceptable. Application deadline: continuous.

Athletics Member NCAA (Division I). Intercollegiate sports: baseball/softball M(I,s), W(I,s); basketball M(I,s), W(I,s); cross-country running M(I,s), W(I,s); football M(I-A,s); golf M(I,s), W(I,s); gymnastics W(I,s); soccer M(I,s); tennis M(I,s), W(I,s); track and field M(I,s), W(I,s); volleyball M(s), W(I,s). Intramural sports: baseball/softball, basketball, crew, fencing, field hockey, football, gymnastics, ice hockey, lacrosse, martial arts, rugby, sailing, skiing (cross-country), skiing (downhill), soccer, swimming and diving, tennis, track and field, volleyball, wrestling.

Majors Accounting B; aerospace engineering B; American studies B; anthropology B; art/fine arts B; Asian/Oriental studies B; astronomy B; biology/biological sciences B; black/Afro-American studies B; botany/plant sciences B; business administration/commerce/management B; chemical engineering B; chemistry B; child care/child and family studies B; child psychology/child development B; civil engineering B; classics B; comparative literature B; computer science B; criminal justice B; (pre)dentistry sequence B; East European and Soviet studies B; economics B; electrical engineering B; engineering (general) B; English B; environmental health sciences B; European studies B; family and consumer studies B; finance/banking B; French B; geography B; geology B; German B; health science B; history B; home economics B; industrial arts B; information science B; insurance B; interdisciplinary studies B; journalism B; Latin American studies B; (pre)law sequence B; liberal arts/general studies B; linguistics B; literature B; marketing/retailing/merchandising B; mathematics B; mechanical engineering B; (pre)medicine sequence B; Mexican-American/Chicano studies B; microbiology B; music B; Native American studies B; nursing B; philosophy B; physical education B; physical sciences B; physics B; political science/government B; psychology B; public administration B; radio and television studies B; real estate B; recreation and leisure services B; religious studies B; Russian B; Russian and Slavic studies B; social science B; social work B; sociology B; Spanish B; speech pathology and audiology B; speech/rhetoric/public address/debate B; statistics B; telecommunications B; theater arts/drama B; vocational education B; women's studies B; zoology B. Majors with highest enrollment: business administration/commerce/management, psychology, accounting.

LD Program Information

Name of Program Disabled Student Services.

Availability of Services Began offering services in 1981. Services provided to freshmen, sophomores, juniors, seniors. Program currently serves 100 LD students: 30 freshmen, 20 sophomores, 20 juniors, 30 seniors.

Staff 1 full-time, 2 part-time staff members, including director. Services provided by remediation specialist, tutors, LD specialist, readers, notetakers, test proctors.

Admissions LD applicants evaluated on the basis of high school transcript and grade point average, untimed SAT or ACT, personal interview, autobiographical statement, letters of recommendation, psychoeducational report. LD students may begin taking classes in fall, spring, or summer. Application should be submitted 1 year in advance of initial anticipated enrollment.

Orientation Optional orientation offered before classes begin.

Housing College housing (including coed) available. LD students housed randomly. LD students not required to live on campus.

Diagnostic Testing Available in intelligence, reading, math, spelling, handwriting, spoken language, written language, perceptual skills.

Tutoring Offered one-to-one and in small groups by professional teachers, peer tutors. Available in all subjects. LD students may receive tutoring in all courses each term.

Basic Skills Remediation Offered in class-size groups by regular teachers. Available in reading, math, written language, speech.

Academic Advisement Help with program planning provided by LD staff members, academic advisers. LD students may take up to 18 units each semester; most take 12 units; 12 units required to maintain full-time status.

Special Courses Offered in reading, math. None offered for credit; none enter into overall grade point average.

Auxiliary Aids and Services Aids include taped textbooks, tape recorders, calculators, typewriters, Visual Tech machine, Kurzweil reading machine. Services include alternative exam arrangements, notetakers, advocacy, readers, peer support group.

Counseling Services Individual counseling, small-group counseling, rap sessions, career counseling available.

Contact Ms. Deirdre Semoff Jordan, Learning Disabilities Specialist, San Diego State University, San Diego, CA 92182, 619-265-6473.

SAN FRANCISCO STATE UNIVERSITY

San Francisco, California

Year Program Began	*Not reported*	Special Courses	✓
Special Fee	None	Taped Textbooks	✓
Special Orientation	✓	Alternative Exam Arrangements	✓
Diagnostic Testing	✓	Notetakers	✓
Subject-Area Tutoring	✓	Staff	7 part-time
Basic Skills Remediation	✓	Number of Students Served	44

General Information State-supported comprehensive coed institution. Part of California State University System. Founded 1899. Awards B, M. Institutionally accredited by regional association; programs accredited by NASAD (art and design), AACSB (business), ABET (engineering and technology), NASM (music), NLN (nursing), NCATE (teacher education). Metropolitan setting; 90-acre barrier-free campus. Total enrollment: 24,170. Faculty: 1,907 (1,202 full-time, 705 part-time); graduate assistants teach a few undergraduate courses. Calendar: semesters. Grading system: letters or numbers. Library holdings: 770,000 bound volumes, 540,000 titles on microform, 4,300 periodical subscriptions.

Undergraduate Profile Fall 1984: 18,339 undergraduates (1,637 freshmen) from 51 states and territories and 111 foreign countries; 33% part-time; 97% state residents; 18% transfers; 57% women; 9% blacks; 2% Native Americans; 7% Hispanics; 28% Asian Americans; 267 legally handicapped students.

Expenses (1985–86) State resident tuition: $0 full-time, $432 per year part-time. Nonresident tuition: $3510 full-time. Nonresident part-time tuition and fees per semester (1 to 11 semester hours) range from $333 to $1623. State residents taking 6 or more semester hours are charged the full-time rate for tuition. Mandatory fees: $672. College room and board: $2800. College room only: $1548.

Financial Aid Fall 1984 full-time freshmen: 51% were aided; the average aided freshman received an aid package worth $5375 (21% scholarships/grants, 79% self-help) meeting 75% of need. College-administered aid for all 1984–85 undergraduates: need-based scholarships; low-interest long-term loans from external sources; SEOG; College Work-Study; part-time jobs. Supporting data: FFS, FAF, institutional form required. Priority application deadline: 4/1.

Athletics Member NCAA (Division II). Intercollegiate sports: baseball/softball M(II), W(II); basketball M(II), W(II); cross-country running M(II), W(II); football M; gymnastics W(II); soccer M(II), W(II); swimming and diving M(II), W(II); tennis M(II), W(II); track and field M(II), W(II); volleyball W(II); wrestling M(II). Intramural sports: badminton, baseball/softball, basketball, cross-country running, fencing, football, martial arts, racquetball, rugby, sailing, soccer, swimming and diving, tennis, track and field, volleyball, weight lifting, wrestling.

Majors Accounting B; American studies B; anthropology B; applied mathematics B; art/fine arts B; astronomy B; biochemistry B; biology/biological sciences B; black/Afro-American studies B; botany/plant sciences B; business administration/commerce/management B; business education B; cell biology B; chemistry B; Chinese B; classics B; comparative literature B; computer information systems B; computer science B; creative writing B; criminal justice B; dance B; data processing B; dietetics B; ecology/environmental studies B; economics B; engineering (general) B; English B; film studies B; finance/banking B; French B; geography B; geological engineering B; geology B; German B; gerontology B; health science B; history B; home economics B; humanities B; industrial arts B; information science B; international business B; international studies B; Italian B; Japanese B; journalism B; labor studies B; liberal arts/general studies B; literature B; marine biology B; marketing/retailing/merchandising B; mathematics B; meteorology B; microbiology B; molecular biology B; music B; nursing B; philosophy B; physical education B; physical sciences B; physics B; physiology B; political science/government B; psychology B; radio and television studies B; real estate B; recreation and leisure services B; religious studies B; retail management B; Russian B; science B; social science B; social work B; sociology B; Spanish B; speech/rhetoric/public address/debate B; statistics B; theater arts/drama B; urban studies B; women's studies B; zoology B.

LD Program Information

Name of Program Project Learn.

Availability of Services Services provided to freshmen, sophomores, juniors, seniors. Program currently serves 44 LD students.

Staff 7 part-time staff members, including director, coordinator. Services provided by remediation specialists, tutors, counselor, diagnostic specialist.

Admissions LD applicants evaluated on the basis of high school transcript and grade point average, standard or untimed SAT or ACT, personal interview, psychoeducational report. LD students may begin taking classes in fall, spring, or summer. Application should be submitted 10 months in advance of initial anticipated enrollment.

Orientation Optional orientation offered before registration.

Housing College housing (including coed) available. LD students housed randomly. LD students not required to live on campus.

Diagnostic Testing Available in intelligence, reading, math, spelling, handwriting, written language, perceptual skills, work and study habits.

Tutoring Offered one-to-one by peer tutors. Available in all subjects. LD students may receive tutoring in all courses each term.

Basic Skills Remediation Offered one-to-one and in small groups by LD teachers. Available in reading, math, spelling, handwriting, spoken language, written language, learning strategies, perceptual skills, work and study habits.

Academic Advisement Help with program planning provided by LD staff members, academic advisers. LD students may take up to 15 semester hours each semester; most take 12 semester hours; 12 semester hours required to maintain full-time status.

Special Courses Offered in college survival skills. All offered for credit; all enter into overall grade point average.

Auxiliary Aids and Services Aids include taped textbooks, tape recorders. Services include alternative exam arrangements, notetakers, advocacy.

Counseling Services Individual counseling, small-group counseling, rap sessions, career counseling available.

Contact Dr. Sarah L. Lovett, Director, Special Services, San Francisco State University, New Administration Building 255, 1600 Holloway Avenue, San Francisco, CA 94132, 415-469-2208.

SANGAMON STATE UNIVERSITY

Springfield, Illinois

Year Program Began	1974	Special Courses	✓
Special Fee	None	Taped Textbooks	
Special Orientation		Alternative Exam Arrangements	✓
Diagnostic Testing	✓	Notetakers	
Subject-Area Tutoring	✓	Staff	5 part-time
Basic Skills Remediation	✓	Number of Students Served	3

General Information State-supported upper-level coed institution. Founded 1969. Awards B, M. Institutionally accredited by regional association; programs accredited by NLN (nursing). City setting; 666-acre barrier-free campus. Total enrollment: 3,027. Faculty: 194 (160 full-time, 34 part-time); 70% have doctoral degrees; graduate assistants teach no undergraduate courses. Calendar: semesters. Grading system: letters or numbers. Library holdings: 279,024 bound volumes, 614,133 titles on microform, 3,112 periodical subscriptions, 25,614 records/tapes.

Undergraduate Profile Fall 1984: 1,606 undergraduates (528 in entering class) from 12 states and territories and 41 foreign countries; 58% part-time; 83% state residents; 100% transfers; 40% financial aid recipients; 54% women; 5% blacks; 0% Native Americans; 1% Hispanics; 0% Asian Americans; 1% foreign nationals; 67% of undergraduates over 25 years of age; 10 legally handicapped students.

Expenses (1984–85) State resident tuition: $864 full-time, $36 per semester hour part-time. Nonresident tuition: $2592 full-time, $108 per semester hour part-time. Mandatory fees: $84. College room only: $766.

Financial Aid College-administered aid for all 1984–85 undergraduates: 6 need-based scholarships (average $300); 14 non-need scholarships (average $500); short-term loans (average $50); low-interest long-term loans; SEOG; College Work-Study; 200 part-time jobs. Supporting data: IRS, state form, institutional form, AFSA/SAR required; FFS acceptable. Priority application deadline: 6/1.

Athletics Member NAIA. Intercollegiate sports: soccer M(s); tennis M(s), W(s). Intramural sports: baseball/softball, basketball, football, tennis, volleyball.

Majors Accounting B; anesthesiology B; anthropology B; art/fine arts B; biology/biological sciences B; business administration/commerce/management B; chemistry B; child care/child and family studies B; communication B; computer science B; criminal justice B; economics B; health services administration B; history B; labor studies B; legal studies B; literature B; mathematics B; medical technology B; nursing B; political science/government B; psychology B; sociology B. Majors with highest enrollment: business administration/commerce/management, accounting, child care/child and family studies.

LD Program Information

Name of Program Learning Center.

Availability of Services Began offering services in 1974. Services provided to juniors, seniors. Program currently serves 3 LD students: 2 juniors, 1 senior.

Staff 5 part-time staff members, including director. Services provided by graduate assistants.

Admissions LD applicants evaluated on the basis of college transcript. LD students may begin taking classes in fall, spring, or summer. Application should be submitted 1 to 2 months in advance of initial anticipated enrollment.

Housing College housing (including coed) available. LD students housed randomly. LD students not required to live on campus.

Diagnostic Testing Available in reading, math, written language.

Tutoring Offered one-to-one and in small groups by professional teachers, peer tutors, graduate assistants. Available in all subjects. LD students may receive tutoring in all courses each term.

Basic Skills Remediation Offered one-to-one and in small groups by LD teachers, teacher trainees, peer teachers. Available in reading, math, spelling, handwriting, spoken language, written language, learning strategies, work and study habits, social skills.

Academic Advisement Help with program planning provided by academic advisers. Most LD students take 8 credits each semester; 12 credits required to maintain full-time status (except by special permission).

Special Courses Offered in reading, vocabulary development, communication skills, composition, language development, math, study skills. None offered for credit; none enter into overall grade point average.

Auxiliary Aids and Services Aids include tape recorders, calculators, typewriters, word processors. Services include alternative exam arrangements, readers.

Counseling Services Individual counseling, career counseling available.

Contact Mr. Miles Woken, Director, Learning Center, Sangamon State University, Springfield, IL 62708, 217-786-6503.

SAN JOSE STATE UNIVERSITY
San Jose, California

Year Program Began	1981	Special Courses	✓
Special Fee	None	Taped Textbooks	✓
Special Orientation	✓	Alternative Exam Arrangements	✓
Diagnostic Testing	✓	Notetakers	✓
Subject-Area Tutoring	✓	Staff	6 part-time
Basic Skills Remediation		Number of Students Served	30

General Information State-supported comprehensive coed institution. Part of California State University System. Founded 1857. Awards B, M. Institutionally accredited by regional association; programs accredited by NASAD (art and design), AACSB (business), ABET (engineering and technology), NASM (music), NLN (nursing), NCATE (teacher education). Metropolitan setting; 104-acre barrier-free campus. Total enrollment: 24,843. Faculty: 1,674 (990 full-time, 684 part-time); 75% have doctoral degrees; graduate assistants teach a few undergraduate courses. Calendar: semesters. Grading system: letters or numbers. Library holdings: 700,000 bound volumes, 5,700 periodical subscriptions, 25,000 records/tapes.

Undergraduate Profile Fall 1984: 20,259 undergraduates (1,539 freshmen) from 48 states and territories and 102 foreign countries; 31% part-time; 97% state residents; 63% transfers; 40% financial aid recipients; 49% women; 5% blacks; 4% Native Americans; 7% Hispanics; 14% Asian Americans; 2% foreign nationals; 30% of undergraduates over 25 years of age; 269 legally handicapped students.

Expenses (1985–86) State resident tuition: $0 full-time. Nonresident tuition: $3627 full-time. Part-time tuition and fees per semester (1 to 11 semester hours) range from $335 to $366 for state residents, $483 to $1653 for nonresidents. Mandatory fees: $731. College room and board: $3034. College room only: $1430.

Financial Aid Fall 1984 full-time freshmen: 61% applied for aid, 76% of those were judged to have need, 100% of those were aided; the average aided freshman received an aid package worth $2674 (22% scholarships/grants, 78% self-help) meeting 95% of need. College-administered aid for all 1984–85 undergraduates: 5,626 need-based scholarships (average $443); non-need scholarships; short-term loans (average $250); low-interest long-term loans from college funds (average $2300), from external sources (average $895); SEOG; College Work-Study. Supporting data: FAF, IRS required. Priority application deadline: 3/1.

Athletics Member NCAA (Division I), NAIA. Intercollegiate sports: baseball/softball M(I,s); basketball M(I,s), W(I,s); cross-country running M(I,s); fencing M(I,s), W(I,s); field hockey W(I,s); football M(I-A,s); golf M(I,s); gymnastics M(I,s), W(I,s); martial arts M(s); soccer M(I,s); swimming and diving M(I,s), W(I,s); tennis M(I,s); track and field M(I,s); volleyball W(I,s); wrestling M(I,s). Intramural sports: baseball/softball, basketball, football, soccer, tennis, volleyball, water polo.

Majors Accounting B; advertising B; aircraft and missile maintenance B; American studies B; anthropology B; applied art B; art education B; art/fine arts B; art history B; aviation administration B; behavioral sciences B; bilingual/bicultural education B; biochemistry B; biology/biological sciences B; black/Afro-American studies B; botany/plant sciences B; broadcasting B; business administration/commerce/management B; cartography B; ceramic art and design B; chemical engineering B; chemistry B; child psychology/child development B; civil engineering B; communication B; computer engineering B; computer information systems B; computer science B; corrections B; criminal justice B; dance B; dietetics B; ecology/environmental studies B; economics B; electrical engineering B; engineering (general) B; English B; entomology B; environmental biology B; environmental health sciences B; environmental sciences B; film studies B; finance/banking B; fish and game management B; French B; geography B; geology B; geophysics B; German B; graphic arts B; health education B; health science B; history B; humanities B; human resources B; human services B; illustration B; industrial administration B; industrial arts B; industrial design B; industrial engineering B; industrial engineering technology B; interdisciplinary studies B; interior design B; international business B; jazz B; journalism B; law enforcement/police sciences B; liberal arts/general studies B; marine biology B; marketing/retailing/merchandising B; materials engineering B; mathematics B; mechanical engineering B; medical laboratory technology B; medical technology B; meteorology B; microbiology B; molecular biology B; music B; music education B; music history B; natural sciences B; nursing B; nutrition B; occupational therapy B; oceanography B; painting/drawing B; parks management B; philosophy B; photography B; physical education B; physical sciences B; physics B; physiology B; political science/government B; psychology B; public administration B; public affairs and policy studies B; public relations B; radio and television studies B; recreation and leisure services B; religious studies B; science B; science education B; sculpture B; secretarial studies/office management B; social science B; social work B; sociology B; Spanish B; speech pathology and audiology B; speech/rhetoric/public address/debate B; statistics B; studio art B; systems engineering B; theater arts/drama B; voice B; wildlife biology B; zoology B. Majors with highest enrollment: accounting, business administration/commerce/management, electrical engineering.

LD Program Information

Name of Program Disabled Services Program.

Availability of Services Began offering services in 1981. Services provided to freshmen, sophomores, juniors, seniors. Program currently serves 30 LD students: 3 freshmen, 3 sophomores, 10 juniors, 14 seniors.

Staff 6 part-time staff members, including director. Services provided by tutors, counselors, diagnostic specialists, reading specialist.

Admissions LD applicants evaluated on the basis of high school transcript and grade point average, standard or untimed SAT or ACT, personal interview, autobiographical statement, letters of recommendation. LD students may begin taking classes in fall, spring, or summer. Application should be submitted 6 months in advance of initial anticipated enrollment.

Orientation Optional orientation offered before registration.

Housing College housing (including coed) available. LD students housed randomly. LD students not required to live on campus.

Diagnostic Testing Available in intelligence, reading, math, spelling, written language, motor abilities, perceptual skills, work and study habits, social skills, speech.

Tutoring Offered one-to-one and in small groups by peer tutors. Available in all subjects. LD students may receive tutoring in all courses each term.

Academic Advisement Help with program planning provided by LD staff members, academic advisers. Most LD students take 9 to 12 semester hours each semester; 12 semester hours required to maintain full-time status.

Special Courses Offered in college survival skills, reading, study skills, career planning. Some offered for credit; some enter into overall grade point average.

Auxiliary Aids and Services Aids include taped textbooks, tape recorders. Services include alternative exam arrangements, notetakers, advocacy, readers.

Counseling Services Individual counseling, small-group counseling, career counseling available.

Contact Mr. Martin B. Schulter, Director, Disabled Services Program, San Jose State University, One Washington Square, San Jose, CA 95192-0168, 408-277-2971.

SCHREINER COLLEGE

Kerrville, Texas

Year Program Began	1979	Special Courses	
Special Fee	$1200 per year	Taped Textbooks	✓
Special Orientation		Alternative Exam Arrangements	✓
Diagnostic Testing		Notetakers	
Subject-Area Tutoring	✓	Staff	2 part-time
Basic Skills Remediation		Number of Students Served	49

General Information Presbyterian 4-year coed college. Founded 1923. Awards A (college transfer and terminal), B. Institutionally accredited by regional association. Small-town setting, with easy access to San Antonio; 141-acre campus. Total enrollment: 489. Faculty: 48 (32 full-time, 16 part-time); 38% have doctoral degrees. Calendar: 4-1-4. Grading system: letters or numbers. Library holdings: 30,000 bound volumes, 8,417 titles on microform, 275 periodical subscriptions, 3,704 records/tapes.

Undergraduate Profile Fall 1984: 489 undergraduates (137 freshmen) from 9 states and territories and 12 foreign countries; 21% part-time; 94% state residents; 9% transfers; 70% financial aid recipients; 50% women; 4% blacks; 0% Native Americans; 10% Hispanics; 0% Asian Americans; 3% foreign nationals; 22% of undergraduates over 25 years of age; 1 legally handicapped student.

Expenses (1985–86) Comprehensive fee of $7530 includes full-time tuition ($4240), mandatory fees ($210), and college room and board ($3080). College room only: $1365. Part-time tuition: $130 per semester hour.

Financial Aid Fall 1984 full-time freshmen: 78% applied for aid, 84% of those were judged to have need, 100% of those were aided; the average aided freshman received an aid package worth $4477 (72% scholarships/grants, 28% self-help) meeting 90% of need. College-administered aid for all 1984–85 undergraduates: need-based scholarships; 300 non-need scholarships (average $1000); College Work-Study; 20 part-time jobs. Supporting data: FFS, FAF acceptable. Priority application deadline: 4/15.

Athletics Intercollegiate sports: baseball/softball M(s); basketball M(s), W(s); golf M(s); tennis M(s), W(s); volleyball W(s). Intramural sports: baseball/softball, basketball, football, racquetball, tennis, track and field, volleyball.

Majors Accounting B; art/fine arts B; business administration/commerce/management A, B; chemistry A; computer information systems B; (pre)engineering sequence A; English B; French B; German B; history B; liberal arts/general studies A, B; literature B; mathematics B; nursing B; philosophy B; physics A; real estate A; secretarial studies/office management A; Spanish B. Majors with highest enrollment: business administration/commerce/management, liberal arts/general studies.

LD Program Information

Name of Program Learning Support Services.

Availability of Services Began offering services in 1979. Services provided to freshmen, sophomores, juniors, seniors. Program currently serves 49 LD students: 27 freshmen, 16 sophomores, 5 juniors, 1 senior.

Fees $1200 per year.

Staff 2 part-time staff members, including codirectors. Services provided by tutors.

Admissions LD applicants evaluated on the basis of high school transcript, untimed SAT or ACT, personal interview, psychoeducational report. LD students may begin taking classes in fall or spring. Application should be submitted 8 months in advance of initial anticipated enrollment.

Housing College housing available. LD students housed with other LD students and non-LD students. LD freshmen, sophomores, juniors, and seniors required to live on campus except if 25 or over, married, or living with relatives.

Tutoring Offered one-to-one and in small groups by professional teachers, peer tutors. Available in all subjects. LD students may receive tutoring in all courses each term.

Academic Advisement Help with program planning provided by LD staff members, academic advisers. LD students may take up to 16 semester hours each semester; most take 13 semester hours; 12 semester hours required to maintain full-time status.

Auxiliary Aids and Services Aids include taped textbooks, tape recorders, word processors. Services include alternative exam arrangements.

Counseling Services Individual counseling, small-group counseling, career counseling available.

Contact Dr. Karen Keefe Dooley, Codirector, Learning Support Services, Schreiner College, Kerrville, TX 78028, 512-896-5411.

SKIDMORE COLLEGE

Saratoga Springs, New York

Year Program Began	1980	Special Courses	✓
Special Fee	None	Taped Textbooks	✓
Special Orientation		Alternative Exam Arrangements	✓
Diagnostic Testing	✓	Notetakers	✓
Subject-Area Tutoring	✓	Staff	2 part-time
Basic Skills Remediation	✓	Number of Students Served	4

General Information Independent 4-year coed college. Founded 1922. Awards B. Institutionally accredited by regional association; programs accredited by NASAD (art and design). Small-town setting; 650-acre campus. Total enrollment: 2,142. Faculty: 228 (170 full-time, 58 part-time); 95% have doctoral degrees. Calendar: semesters. Grading system: letters or numbers. Library holdings: 300,000 bound volumes, 55,000 titles on microform, 1,600 periodical subscriptions, 6,400 records/tapes.

Undergraduate Profile Fall 1984: 2,142 undergraduates (637 freshmen) from 47 states and territories and 31 foreign countries; 1% part-time; 35% state residents; 7% transfers; 25% financial aid recipients; 61% women; 3% blacks; 1% Native Americans; 1% Hispanics; 1% Asian Americans; 3% foreign nationals; 1% of undergraduates over 25 years of age; 4 legally handicapped students.

Expenses (1985–86) Comprehensive fee of $13,765 includes full-time tuition ($9835), mandatory fees ($115), and college room and board ($3815). College room only: $1965. Part-time tuition: $325 per semester hour.

Financial Aid Fall 1984 full-time freshmen: 27% applied for aid, 89% of those were judged to have need, 100% of those were aided; the average aided freshman received an aid package worth $8567 (67% scholarships/grants, 33% self-help) meeting 100% of need. College-administered aid for all 1984–85 undergraduates: 447 need-based scholarships (average $5111); non-need scholarships; low-interest long-term loans from external sources (average $2350); College Work-Study; 133 part-time jobs. Supporting data: FAF, IRS, institutional form required; FFS acceptable. Application deadline: 2/1.

Athletics Member NCAA (Division III), NAIA. Intercollegiate sports: baseball/softball M(c), W(c); basketball M(III), W(III); crew M, W; cross-country running M(c), W(c); equestrian sports M, W; fencing M(c), W(c); field hockey W(III); golf M(III), W(III); gymnastics W(c); ice hockey M(III), W; lacrosse M(III), W(III); sailing M(c), W(c); skiing (downhill) M(III), W(III); soccer M(III), W(III); squash M(c), W(c); swimming and diving W(III); tennis M(III), W(III); volleyball W(III). Intramural sports: badminton, baseball/softball, basketball, crew, cross-country running, equestrian sports, fencing, golf, ice hockey, lacrosse, racquetball, sailing, skiing (cross-country), skiing (downhill), soccer, squash, swimming and diving, tennis, volleyball, water polo.

Majors American studies B; anthropology B; art education B; art/fine arts B; art history B; biochemistry B; biology/biological sciences B; business administration/commerce/management B; chemistry B; classics B; dance B; early childhood education B; economics B; education B; elementary education B; English B; French B; geology B; German B; history B; mathematics B; modern languages B; music B; music education B; philosophy B; physical education B; political science/government B; psychology B; Romance languages B; social work B; sociology B; Spanish B; studio art B; theater arts/drama B. Majors with highest enrollment: art/fine arts, English, business administration/commerce/management.

LD Program Information

Name of Program Not specified.

Availability of Services Began offering services in 1980. Services provided to freshmen, sophomores, juniors, seniors. Program currently serves 4 LD students.

Staff 2 part-time staff members, including director. Services provided by counselor.

Admissions LD applicants evaluated on the basis of high school transcript and grade point average, standard or untimed SAT, personal interview, autobiographical statement, letters of recommendation. LD students may begin taking classes in fall or summer. Application should be submitted 6 months in advance of initial anticipated enrollment.

Housing College housing (including coed) available. LD students housed with other LD students and non-LD students. LD freshmen required to live on campus.

Diagnostic Testing Available in reading, written language, perceptual skills.

Tutoring Offered one-to-one by peer tutors. Available in some subjects. LD students may receive tutoring in all courses each term (depending on availability of tutors).

Basic Skills Remediation Offered one-to-one and in small groups by LD teachers. Available in reading, math, spoken language, written language, learning strategies, perceptual skills, work and study habits, speech.

Academic Advisement Help with program planning provided by LD staff members, academic advisers. LD students may take up to 15 semester hours each semester; most take 15 semester hours; 12 semester hours required to maintain full-time status.

Special Courses Offered in reading, study skills. None offered for credit; none enter into overall grade point average.

Auxiliary Aids and Services Aids include taped textbooks, tape recorders. Services include alternative exam arrangements, notetakers, advocacy.

Counseling Services Individual counseling available.

Contact Dr. Jon R. Ramsey, Associate Dean of Student Affairs, Skidmore College, Saratoga Springs, NY 12866, 518-584-5000 Ext. 2203.

SOUTHEASTERN MASSACHUSETTS UNIVERSITY

North Dartmouth, Massachusetts

Year Program Began	1979	Special Courses	✓
Special Fee	None	Taped Textbooks	✓
Special Orientation		Alternative Exam Arrangements	✓
Diagnostic Testing		Notetakers	✓
Subject-Area Tutoring	✓	Staff	1 full-time
Basic Skills Remediation	✓	Number of Students Served	3

General Information State-supported comprehensive coed institution. Part of Massachusetts State University System. Founded 1895. Awards B, M. Institutionally accredited by regional association; programs accredited by NASAD (art and design), ABET (engineering and technology), NLN (nursing). Small-town setting, with easy access to Boston; 710-acre barrier-free campus. Total enrollment: 5,708. Faculty: 365 (314 full-time, 51 part-time); 75% have doctoral degrees; graduate assistants teach no undergraduate courses. Calendar: semesters. Grading system: letters or numbers. Library holdings: 250,000 bound volumes, 105,000 titles on microform, 1,700 periodical subscriptions, 4,500 records/tapes.

Undergraduate Profile Fall 1984: 5,386 undergraduates (1,547 freshmen) from 17 states and territories and 21 foreign countries; 5% part-time; 99% state residents; 12% transfers; 65% financial aid recipients; 49% women; 1% blacks; 1% Native Americans; 1% Hispanics; 1% Asian Americans; 33 legally handicapped students.

Expenses (1985–86) State resident tuition: $1082 full-time, $64.80 per semester hour part-time. Nonresident tuition: $3432 full-time, $171.30 per semester hour part-time. Mandatory fees: $185. College room and board: $3200.

Financial Aid Fall 1984 full-time freshmen: 65% applied for aid, 88% of those were judged to have need, 89% of those were aided; the average aided freshman received an aid package worth $2571 (45% scholarships/grants, 55% self-help) meeting 98% of need. College-administered aid for all 1984–85 undergraduates: need-based scholarships (average $270); low-interest long-term loans; College Work-Study; part-time jobs. Supporting data: FAF, IRS, institutional form, AFSA/SAR required. Priority application deadline: 5/1.

Athletics Member NCAA (Division III). Intercollegiate sports: baseball/softball M(III), W(III); basketball M(III), W(III); cross-country running M(III), W(III); fencing M(III), W(III); field hockey W(III); golf M(III); ice hockey M(III); soccer M(III); swimming and diving M(III), W(III); tennis M(III), W(III); track and field M(III), W(III); volleyball W(III). Intramural sports: baseball/softball, basketball, football, martial arts, racquetball, tennis, volleyball, water polo, weight lifting.

Majors Accounting B; art education B; art/fine arts B; art history B; biology/biological sciences B; business administration/commerce/management B; chemistry B; civil engineering B; computer engineering B; computer science B; construction engineering B; economics B; electrical engineering B; electrical engineering technology B; engineering (general) B; engineering technology B; English B; finance/banking B; French B; German B; history B; humanities B; human resources B; liberal arts/general studies B; marine biology B; marketing/retailing/merchandising B; mathematics B; mechanical engineering B; mechanical engineering technology B; medical laboratory technology B; modern languages B; music B; nursing B; philosophy B; physics B; political science/government B; Portuguese B; psychology B; social science B; sociology B; Spanish B; textile arts B; textile engineering B; textiles and clothing B. Majors with highest enrollment: liberal arts/general studies, business administration/commerce/management, engineering (general).

LD Program Information

Name of Program Disabled Student Services.

Availability of Services Began offering services in 1979. Services provided to freshmen, sophomores, juniors, seniors. Program currently serves 3 LD students: 2 freshmen, 1 sophomore.

Staff 1 full-time staff member (director).

Admissions LD applicants evaluated on the basis of high school transcript, letters of recommendation. LD students may begin taking classes in fall or spring. Application should be submitted 6 to 9 months in advance of initial anticipated enrollment.

Housing College housing (including coed) available. LD students housed randomly. LD students not required to live on campus.

Tutoring Offered one-to-one by peer tutors. Available in all subjects. LD students may receive tutoring in all courses each term.

Basic Skills Remediation Offered one-to-one by peer teachers. Available in reading, math, spelling, written language, learning strategies, work and study habits.

Academic Advisement Help with program planning provided by LD staff member, academic advisers. Most LD students take 9 to 12 semester hours each semester; 12 semester hours required to maintain full-time status.

Special Courses Offered in career planning. None offered for credit; none enter into overall grade point average.

Auxiliary Aids and Services Aids include taped textbooks, tape recorders, typewriters. Services include alternative exam arrangements, notetakers, advocacy.

Counseling Services Individual counseling, small-group counseling available.

Contact Miss Carole J. Johnson, Director of Disabled Student Services, Southeastern Massachusetts University, North Dartmouth, MA 02747, 617-999-8711.

SOUTHERN ILLINOIS UNIVERSITY AT CARBONDALE

Carbondale, Illinois

Year Program Began	1978
Special Fee	$2600 per year
Special Orientation	✓
Diagnostic Testing	✓
Subject-Area Tutoring	✓
Basic Skills Remediation	✓
Special Courses	✓
Taped Textbooks	✓
Alternative Exam Arrangements	✓
Notetakers	✓
Staff	2 full-time, 10 part-time
Number of Students Served	98

General Information State-supported coed university. Part of Southern Illinois University System. Founded 1869. Awards A (terminal), B, M, D. Institutionally accredited by regional association; programs accredited by NASAD (art and design), AACSB (business), ABET (engineering and technology), ABFSE (funeral service), FIDER (interior design), NASM (music), NCATE (teacher education). Rural setting; 900-acre barrier-free campus. Total enrollment: 22,874. Faculty: 1,478 (1,235 full-time, 243 part-time); 65% have doctoral degrees; graduate assistants teach a few undergraduate courses. Calendar: semesters. Grading system: letters or numbers. Library holdings: 1.5 million bound volumes, 1.6 million titles on microform, 14,800 periodical subscriptions.

Undergraduate Profile Fall 1984: 18,794 undergraduates (2,965 freshmen) from 53 states and territories and 95 foreign countries; 10% part-time; 79% state residents; 39% transfers; 80% financial aid recipients; 36% women; 10% blacks; 0% Native Americans; 1% Hispanics; 1% Asian Americans; 9% foreign nationals; 22% of undergraduates over 25 years of age; 300 legally handicapped students.

Expenses (1985–86) State resident tuition: $1008 full-time, $42 per semester hour part-time. Nonresident tuition: $3024 full-time, $126 per semester hour part-time. Mandatory fees: $520. College room and board: $2484.

Financial Aid Fall 1984 full-time freshmen: 95% applied for aid, 76% of those were judged to have need, 100% of those were aided; the average aided freshman received an aid package worth $4406 (46% scholarships/grants, 54% self-help) meeting 100% of need. College-administered aid for all 1984–85 undergraduates: need-based scholarships; 275 non-need scholarships (average $1000); short-term loans; low-interest long-term loans from external sources (average $500); SEOG; College Work-Study; 3,000 part-time jobs. Supporting data: FFS required. Priority application deadline: 4/1.

Athletics Member NCAA (Division I). Intercollegiate sports: baseball/softball M(I,s), W(I,s); basketball M(I,s), W(I,s); cross-country running M(I,s), W(I,s); field hockey W(I,s); football M(I-AA,s); golf M(I,s), W(I,s); gymnastics M(I,s), W(I,s); swimming and diving M(I,s), W(I,s); tennis M(I,s), W(I,s); track and field M(I,s), W(I,s); volleyball W(I,s). Intramural sports: badminton, baseball/softball, basketball, cross-country running, fencing, field hockey, football, golf, riflery, rugby, sailing, soccer, swimming and diving, tennis, volleyball, weight lifting.

Majors Accounting B; advertising B; agricultural business B; agricultural economics B; agricultural education B; agronomy/soil and crop sciences B; aircraft and missile maintenance A; animal sciences B; anthropology B; applied art B; architectural technologies A; art education B; art/fine arts B; art history B; automotive technologies A; aviation administration B; aviation technology A; biochemistry B; biology/biological sciences B; botany/plant sciences B; broadcasting B; business administration/commerce/management B; business economics B; business education B; cartography B; chemistry B; child care/child and family studies B; civil engineering B; civil engineering technology B; classics B; commercial art A; computer science B; construction technologies A; corrections A; court reporting A; creative writing B; criminal justice B; data processing A; dental services A; (pre)dentistry sequence B; dietetics B; early childhood education B; ecology/environmental studies B; economics B; education B; electrical and electronics technologies A, B; electrical engineering B; electrical engineering technology B; elementary education B; engineering (general) B; engineering mechanics B; engineering technology B; English B; environmental engineering B; family and consumer studies B; fashion merchandising B; film studies B; finance/banking B; fire science B; flight training A; food sciences B; food services management B; forestry B; French B; funeral service A; geography B; geology B; German B; graphic arts A; health education B; health science B; health services administration B; history B; home economics B; home economics education B; horticulture B; hotel and restaurant management B; industrial engineering technology B; interior design B; jewelry and metalsmithing B; journalism B; law enforcement/police sciences A; legal secretarial studies A; legal studies B; liberal arts/general studies B; linguistics B; machine and tool technologies A; marketing/retailing/merchandising B; mathematics B; mechanical engineering technology B; (pre)medicine sequence B; microbiology B; mining and mineral engineering B; mining technology B; music B; music education B; music history B; nutrition B; ornamental horticulture B; paralegal studies B; philosophy B; photography B; physical education B; physical therapy A; physics B; physiology B; political science/government B; psychology B; public relations B; radio and television studies B; radiological technology A; recreation and leisure services B; recreation therapy B; religious studies B; respiratory therapy A; Russian B; science B; secondary education B; secretarial studies/office management A; social science B; social work B; sociology B; Spanish B; special education B; speech pathology and audiology B; speech/rhetoric/public address/debate B; studio art B; systems engineering B; teaching English as a second language B; textiles and clothing B; theater arts/drama B; (pre)veterinary medicine sequence B; vocational education B; wildlife management B; zoology B. Majors with highest enrollment: engineering (general), computer science, business administration/commerce/management.

LD Program Information

Name of Program Clinical Center Achieve Program.

Availability of Services Began offering services in 1978. Services provided to freshmen, sophomores, juniors, seniors. Program currently serves 98 LD students: 49 freshmen, 33 sophomores, 8 juniors, 8 seniors.

Fees $2600 per year for full-time program, $1300 for half-time program.

Staff 2 full-time, 10 part-time staff members, including coordinator, assistant coordinator. Services provided by remediation specialists, tutors, diagnostic specialists, test proctors, microcomputer lab supervisor.

Admissions LD applicants evaluated on the basis of high school transcript, standard or untimed ACT. LD students may begin taking classes in fall only. Application should be submitted 1 to 2 years in advance of initial anticipated enrollment.

Orientation Optional orientation offered during registration.

Housing College housing (including coed) available. LD students housed randomly. LD freshmen and sophomores required to live on campus except if married or 21 or over.

Diagnostic Testing Available in intelligence, reading, math, spelling, spoken language, written language, motor abilities, perceptual skills, personality, psychoneurology, speech, hearing.

Tutoring Offered one-to-one by professional teachers, peer tutors. Available in all subjects. LD students may receive tutoring in all courses each term.

Basic Skills Remediation Offered one-to-one by teacher trainees, graduate assistants. Available in reading, math, spelling, spoken language, written language, learning strategies, work and study habits, social skills.

Academic Advisement Help with program planning provided by LD staff members, academic advisers. LD students may take up to 12 semester hours each semester until adequate grade point average is established; most take 12 to 15 semester hours; 12 semester hours required to maintain full-time status.

Special Courses Offered in reading, vocabulary development, communication skills, composition, math, typing. None offered for credit; none enter into overall grade point average.

Auxiliary Aids and Services Aids include taped textbooks, tape recorders, calculators, word processors, computers. Services include alternative exam arrangements, notetakers, advocacy.

Counseling Services Individual counseling, small-group counseling, rap sessions, career counseling available.

Contact Dr. Barbara Cordoni, Coordinator, Clinical Center Achieve Program, Southern Illinois University at Carbondale, Special Education Department, Carbondale, IL 62901, 618-453-2595 Ext. 42.

Note Services for LD students are also provided through the Disabled Student Services office. These include orientation, tutoring (by peer tutors and graduate students, for $4.50 to $10 per hour), special noncredit courses (college survival skills, career planning), auxiliary aids (taped textbooks, tape recorders, calculators) and services (alternative exam arrangements, advocacy, readers, preadmission and pre-enrollment planning), and individual and career counseling. For information, contact Dr. Ron Blosser, Coordinator, Disabled Student Services, Woody Hall B-150, 618-453-5738.

SOUTHERN OREGON STATE COLLEGE

Ashland, Oregon

Year Program Began	1980	Special Courses	
Special Fee	None	Taped Textbooks	✓
Special Orientation		Alternative Exam Arrangements	✓
Diagnostic Testing	✓	Notetakers	✓
Subject-Area Tutoring	✓	Staff	1 part-time
Basic Skills Remediation		Number of Students Served	*Not reported*

General Information State-supported comprehensive coed institution. Founded 1926. Awards A (terminal), B, M. Institutionally accredited by regional association; programs accredited by NASM (music), NLN (nursing), NCATE (teacher education). Small-town setting; 175-acre campus. Total enrollment: 4,433. Faculty: 240 (210 full-time, 30 part-time); 64% have doctoral degrees; graduate assistants teach a few undergraduate courses. Calendar: quarters. Grading system: letters or numbers. Library holdings: 200,000 bound volumes, 365,000 titles on microform, 4,700 periodical subscriptions.

Undergraduate Profile Fall 1984: 3,891 undergraduates (724 freshmen) from 21 states and territories and 30 foreign countries; 13% part-time; 90% state residents; 30% transfers; 40% financial aid recipients; 51% women; 1% blacks; 1% Native Americans; 1% Hispanics; 2% foreign nationals; 43 legally handicapped students.

Expenses (1985–86) State resident tuition: $1473 full-time. Nonresident tuition: $3786 full-time. Part-time tuition and fees per quarter (1 to 7 credits) range from $68 to $254. Mandatory fees: $25. College room and board: $2407.

Financial Aid Fall 1984 full-time freshmen: 68% applied for aid, 89% of those were judged to have need, 96% of those were aided; the average aided freshman received an aid package worth $3022 (44% scholarships/grants, 56% self-help) meeting 70% of need. College-administered aid for all 1984–85 undergraduates: 1,215 need-based scholarships (average $433); 130 non-need scholarships (average $900); short-term loans (average $100); low-interest long-term loans from college funds (average $300); SEOG; College Work-Study; 425 part-time jobs. Supporting data: FAF, AFSA/SAR, Financial Aid Transcript (for transfers) required; FFS acceptable. Priority application deadline: 3/1.

Athletics Member NAIA. Intercollegiate sports: basketball M(s), W(s); football M(s); track and field M(s), W(s); volleyball W(s); wrestling M(s). Intramural sports: badminton, baseball/softball, basketball, cross-country running, football, gymnastics, sailing, skiing (cross-country), skiing (downhill), soccer, swimming and diving, tennis, track and field, volleyball, water polo, wrestling.

Majors Accounting B; art education B; art/fine arts B; biology/biological sciences B; business administration/commerce/management B; chemistry B; communication B; computer science B; criminal justice B; early childhood education B; economics B; education B; educational administration B; elementary education B; English B; geography B; geology B; health education B; history B; humanities B; interdisciplinary studies B; international studies B; (pre)law sequence B; marketing/retailing/merchandising B; mathematics B; medical secretarial studies A; (pre) medicine sequence B; modern languages B; music B; music education B; nursing A, B; physical education B; physics B; political science/government B; psychology B; science education B; secondary education B; social science B; sociology B; Spanish B; speech/rhetoric/public address/debate B; theater arts/drama A, B. Majors with highest enrollment: business administration/commerce/management, education, psychology.

LD Program Information

Name of Program Services to the Disabled.

Availability of Services Began offering services in 1980. Services provided to freshmen, sophomores, juniors, seniors.

Staff 1 part-time staff member (coordinator). Services provided by tutors, readers, notetakers.

Admissions LD applicants evaluated on the basis of high school transcript and grade point average, standard SAT or ACT; autobiographical statement, psychoeducational report recommended. LD students may begin taking classes in fall, winter, spring, or summer. Application should be submitted 2 to 3 months in advance of initial anticipated enrollment.

Housing College housing (including coed) available. LD students housed randomly. LD freshmen required to live on campus except if living with relatives.

Diagnostic Testing Available in various areas as appropriate.

Tutoring Offered one-to-one and in small groups by peer tutors. Available in some subjects. LD students may receive tutoring in all courses each term (depending on availability of tutors).

Academic Advisement Help with program planning provided by LD staff member, academic advisers. Most LD students take 12 to 15 credits each quarter; 12 credits required to maintain full-time status.

Auxiliary Aids and Services Aids include taped textbooks. Services include alternative exam arrangements, notetakers.

Counseling Services Individual counseling available.

Contact Ms. Judy Lonergan, Handicapped Services Coordinator, Southern Oregon State College, Ashland, OR 97520, 503-482-6213.

SOUTHERN TECHNICAL INSTITUTE

Marietta, Georgia

Year Program Began	1980	Special Courses	
Special Fee	None	Taped Textbooks	✓
Special Orientation	✓	Alternative Exam Arrangements	✓
Diagnostic Testing		Notetakers	✓
Subject-Area Tutoring		Staff	1 part-time
Basic Skills Remediation	✓	Number of Students Served	42

General Information State-supported 4-year coed college. Founded 1948. Awards A (college transfer), B. Institutionally accredited by regional association; programs accredited by ABET (engineering and technology). Small-town setting, with easy access to Atlanta; 160-acre campus. Total enrollment: 3,606. Faculty: 175 (125 full-time, 50 part-time); 35% have doctoral degrees. Calendar: quarters. Grading system: letters or numbers. Library holdings: 75,000 bound volumes, 1,300 periodical subscriptions, 20,000 records/tapes.

Undergraduate Profile Fall 1984: 3,606 undergraduates (437 freshmen) from 48 states and territories and 50 foreign countries; 35% part-time; 92% state residents; 45% transfers; 30% financial aid recipients; 16% women; 9% blacks; 2% foreign nationals; 5 legally handicapped students.

Expenses (1985–86) State resident tuition: $960 full-time, $27 per quarter hour part-time. Nonresident tuition: $2880 full-time, $81 per quarter hour part-time. Mandatory fees: $150. College room only: $825.

Financial Aid Fall 1984 full-time freshmen: 60% applied for aid, 90% of those were judged to have need, 100% of those were aided; the average aided freshman received an aid package worth $288 (23% scholarships/grants, 77% self-help) meeting 80% of need. College-administered aid for all 1984–85 undergraduates: need-based scholarships; 200 non-need scholarships (average $700); short-term loans (average $500); low-interest long-term loans from external sources (average $900); SEOG; College Work-Study; part-time jobs. Supporting data: FAF, state form, institutional form, AFSA/SAR required; IRS required for some. Priority application deadline: 4/1.

Athletics Member NAIA. Intercollegiate sports: baseball/softball M(s); basketball M(s); tennis M, W. Intramural sports: basketball, football, soccer, tennis, volleyball.

Majors Architectural technologies A, B; civil engineering technology A, B; computer engineering B; computer information systems B; computer technologies A, B; electrical engineering technology A, B; engineering technology A, B; industrial engineering technology A, B; mechanical engineering technology A, B; textiles and clothing A, B. Majors with highest enrollment: electrical engineering technology, industrial engineering technology, mechanical engineering technology.

LD Program Information

Name of Program Not specified.

Availability of Services Began offering services in 1980. Services provided to freshmen, sophomores, juniors, seniors. Program currently serves 42 LD students: 15 freshmen, 10 sophomores, 9 juniors, 8 seniors.

Staff 1 part-time staff member (director).

Admissions LD applicants evaluated on the basis of high school transcript, untimed SAT. LD students may begin taking classes in fall, winter, spring, or summer. Application should be submitted 1 month in advance of initial anticipated enrollment.

Orientation Required orientation held before registration.

Housing College housing (including coed) available. LD students housed randomly. LD students not required to live on campus.

Basic Skills Remediation Offered one-to-one and in small groups by regular teachers. Available in reading, math, spelling, written language.

Academic Advisement Help with program planning provided by LD staff member, academic advisers. LD students may take up to 21 quarter hours each quarter; most take 12 to 15 quarter hours; 12 quarter hours required to maintain full-time status.

Auxiliary Aids and Services Aids include taped textbooks. Services include alternative exam arrangements, notetakers.

Counseling Services Individual counseling, career counseling available.

Contact Ms. Barbara N. Anderson, Director of Counseling, Southern Technical Institute, 1112 Clay Street, Marietta, GA 30060, 404-424-7226.

SOUTHERN VERMONT COLLEGE

Bennington, Vermont

Year Program Began	1983	Special Courses	✓
Special Fee	None	Taped Textbooks	✓
Special Orientation	✓	Alternative Exam Arrangements	✓
Diagnostic Testing	✓	Notetakers	
Subject-Area Tutoring	✓	Staff	1 full-time
Basic Skills Remediation	✓	Number of Students Served	*Not reported*

General Information Independent 4-year coed college. Founded 1926. Awards A (college transfer and terminal), B. Institutionally accredited by regional association. Small-town setting; 371-acre campus. Total enrollment: 525. Faculty: 32 (17 full-time, 15 part-time); 50% have doctoral degrees. Calendar: semesters. Grading system: letters or numbers. Library holdings: 25,000 bound volumes, 25 titles on microform, 100 periodical subscriptions, 150 records/tapes.

Undergraduate Profile Fall 1984: 525 undergraduates (244 freshmen) from 19 states and territories and 6 foreign countries; 25% part-time; 40% state residents; 30% transfers; 75% financial aid recipients; 52% women; 5% blacks; 1% Native Americans; 1% Hispanics; 2% Asian Americans; 5% foreign nationals; 20% of undergraduates over 25 years of age.

Expenses (1985–86) Comprehensive fee of $6205 includes full-time tuition ($3540), mandatory fees ($45), and college room and board ($2620). Part-time tuition: $118 per credit.

Financial Aid Fall 1984 full-time freshmen: 69% applied for aid, 92% of those were judged to have need, 100% of those were aided; the average aided freshman received an aid package worth $3894 (48% scholarships/grants, 52% self-help) meeting 96% of need. College-administered aid for all 1984–85 undergraduates: need-based scholarships (average $1000); non-need scholarships (average $1000); SEOG; College Work-Study. Supporting data: institutional form, AFSA/SAR required; FFS, FAF acceptable. Application deadline: continuous.

Athletics Member NAIA, NLCAA. Intercollegiate sports: baseball/softball M, W; basketball M, W; golf M, W; skiing (downhill) M, W; soccer M, W. Intramural sports: cross-country running, golf, skiing (cross-country).

Majors Accounting B; adult and continuing education B; business administration/commerce/management A, B; communication B; criminal justice A, B; ecology/environmental studies A, B; education B; English B; environmental sciences A, B; health science A, B; health services administration B; human services A, B; (pre)law sequence B; legal secretarial studies A; liberal arts/general studies A, B; medical assistant technologies A; nursing B; public administration B; secretarial studies/office management A, B; taxation A. Majors with highest enrollment: business administration/commerce/management, human services, ecology/environmental studies.

LD Program Information

Name of Program Learning Disabilities Program.

Availability of Services Began offering services in 1983. Services provided to freshmen, sophomores, juniors, seniors.

Staff 1 full-time staff member (coordinator).

Admissions LD applicants evaluated on the basis of high school transcript, personal interview, letters of recommendation. LD students may begin taking classes in fall or spring. Application should be submitted 10 to 11 months in advance of initial anticipated enrollment.

Orientation Required orientation held before registration.

Housing College housing (including coed) available. LD students housed randomly. LD students not required to live on campus.

Diagnostic Testing Available in reading, math, written language, work and study habits.

Tutoring Offered one-to-one and in small groups by professional teachers, peer tutors. Available in all subjects. LD students may receive tutoring in all courses each term.

Basic Skills Remediation Offered one-to-one by LD teachers. Available in reading, math, spelling, handwriting, written language, learning strategies, work and study habits.

Academic Advisement Help with program planning provided by LD staff member, academic advisers. LD students may take up to 15 credits each semester; most take 12 credits; 9 credits required to maintain full-time status.

Special Courses Offered in study skills, word processing. None offered for credit; none enter into overall grade point average.

Auxiliary Aids and Services Aids include taped textbooks, tape recorders, calculators, typewriters, word processors. Services include alternative exam arrangements.

Counseling Services Individual counseling, career counseling available.

Contact Dr. Virginia Sturtevant, Learning Disabilities Coordinator, Southern Vermont College, Bennington, VT 05201, 802-442-5427.

SOUTHWESTERN COLLEGE

Winfield, Kansas

Year Program Began	1978	Special Courses	✓
Special Fee	None	Taped Textbooks	
Special Orientation		Alternative Exam Arrangements	✓
Diagnostic Testing	✓	Notetakers	✓
Subject-Area Tutoring	✓	Staff	7 part-time
Basic Skills Remediation	✓	Number of Students Served	3

General Information United Methodist 4-year coed college. Founded 1885. Awards B. Institutionally accredited by regional association; programs accredited by NASM (music). Small-town setting; 38-acre campus. Total enrollment: 586. Faculty: 44 (40 full-time, 4 part-time); 53% have doctoral degrees. Calendar: 4-1-4. Grading system: letters or numbers. Library holdings: 110,000 bound volumes, 500 periodical subscriptions, 200 records/tapes.

Undergraduate Profile Fall 1984: 586 undergraduates (89 freshmen) from 21 states and territories and 7 foreign countries; 13% part-time; 74% state residents; 14% transfers; 92% financial aid recipients; 45% women; 13% blacks; 1% Native Americans; 1% Hispanics; 3% foreign nationals; no legally handicapped students.

Expenses (1985–86) Comprehensive fee of $5467 includes full-time tuition ($2940), mandatory fees ($130), and college room and board ($2397). College room only: $932. Part-time tuition: $123 per semester hour.

Financial Aid Fall 1984 full-time freshmen: 93% applied for aid, 84% of those were judged to have need, 100% of those were aided; the average aided freshman received an aid package worth $5595 (67% scholarships/grants, 33% self-help) meeting 100% of need. College-administered aid for all 1984–85 undergraduates: 350 need-based scholarships (average $1500); 242 non-need scholarships (average $600); short-term loans (average $200); low-interest long-term loans from external sources (average $1000); SEOG; College Work-Study; 120 part-time jobs. Supporting data: IRS, institutional form required; FFS, FAF, AFSA/SAR acceptable. Priority application deadline: 4/1.

Athletics Member NAIA. Intercollegiate sports: basketball M(s), W(s); cross-country running M(s), W(s); football M(s); golf M(s); tennis M(s), W(s); track and field M(s), W(s); volleyball W(s). Intramural sports: baseball/softball, basketball, soccer, swimming and diving, volleyball.

Majors Accounting B; anthropology B; applied art B; art education B; art/fine arts B; biology/biological sciences B; business administration/commerce/management B; business education B; chemistry B; communication B; computer science B; criminal justice B; (pre)dentistry sequence B; economics B; elementary education B; emergency medical technology B; English B; French B; history B; home economics B; home economics education B; humanities B; international business B; (pre)law sequence B; mathematics B; medical technology B; (pre)medicine sequence B; music B; music education B; nursing B; philosophy B; physical education B; physics B; political science/government B; psychology B; religious studies B; secondary education B; social work B; sociology B; Spanish B; speech/rhetoric/public address/debate B; theater arts/drama B; (pre)veterinary medicine sequence B. Majors with highest enrollment: business administration/commerce/management, computer science.

LD Program Information

Name of Program Learning Skills Center.

Availability of Services Began offering services in 1978. Services provided to freshmen, sophomores, juniors, seniors. Program currently serves 3 LD students: 2 freshmen, 1 sophomore.

Staff 7 part-time staff members, including director. Services provided by remediation specialist, tutors, counselor.

Admissions LD applicants evaluated on the basis of high school transcript and grade point average, standard or untimed SAT or ACT, personal interview, letters of recommendation. LD students may begin taking classes in fall, winter, spring, or summer. Application should be submitted 1 month in advance of initial anticipated enrollment.

Housing College housing (including coed) available. LD students housed randomly. LD freshmen and sophomores required to live on campus except if married, 20 or over, or living with relatives.

Diagnostic Testing Available in reading, math, written language.

Tutoring Offered one-to-one and in small groups by professional teachers, peer tutors. Available in all subjects. LD students may receive tutoring in all courses each term.

Basic Skills Remediation Offered one-to-one and in small groups by LD teachers, regular teachers, teacher trainees, peer teachers. Available in reading, math, spelling, handwriting, spoken language, written language, learning strategies, work and study habits, speech.

Academic Advisement Help with program planning provided by academic advisers. LD students may take up to 16 semester hours each semester; most take 13 semester hours; 12 semester hours required to maintain full-time status.

Special Courses Offered in reading, composition, math, personal psychology, study skills, career planning. Most offered for credit; most enter into overall grade point average.

Auxiliary Aids and Services Aids include tape recorders, calculators. Services include alternative exam arrangements, notetakers.

Counseling Services Individual counseling, career counseling available.

Contact Dr. Robert Evans, Director, Learning Skills Center, Southwestern College, Winfield, KS 67156, 316-221-4150.

SOUTHWEST MISSOURI STATE UNIVERSITY

Springfield, Missouri

Year Program Began	1984	Special Courses	✓
Special Fee	None	Taped Textbooks	✓
Special Orientation	✓	Alternative Exam Arrangements	✓
Diagnostic Testing	✓	Notetakers	
Subject-Area Tutoring	✓	Staff	11 part-time
Basic Skills Remediation	✓	Number of Students Served	33

General Information State-supported comprehensive coed institution. Founded 1905. Awards A (terminal), B, M. Institutionally accredited by regional association; programs accredited by NASM (music), NLN (nursing), NCATE (teacher education). City setting; 125-acre barrier-free campus. Total enrollment: 15,121. Faculty: 697 (533 full-time, 164 part-time); 59% have doctoral degrees; graduate assistants teach a few undergraduate courses. Calendar: semesters. Grading system: letters or numbers. Library holdings: 408,325 bound volumes, 519,066 titles on microform, 4,383 periodical subscriptions, 7,223 records/tapes.

Undergraduate Profile Fall 1984: 14,015 undergraduates (2,770 freshmen) from 45 states and territories and 30 foreign countries; 27% part-time; 96% state residents; 7% transfers; 42% financial aid recipients; 53% women; 1% blacks; 1% Asian Americans; 1% foreign nationals; 24% of undergraduates over 25 years of age; 265 legally handicapped students.

Expenses (1985–86) State resident tuition: $1104 full-time, $46 per credit hour part-time. Nonresident tuition: $2208 full-time, $46 per credit hour part-time. College room and board: $1950.

Financial Aid Fall 1984 full-time freshmen: 63% applied for aid, 83% of those were judged to have need, 94% of those were aided; the average aided freshman received an aid package worth $2043 (52% scholarships/grants, 48% self-help) meeting 63% of need. College-administered aid for all 1984–85 undergraduates: 324 need-based scholarships (average $624); 1,546 non-need scholarships (average $826); short-term loans (average $90); low-interest long-term loans from external sources (average $1834); SEOG; College Work-Study; 1,000 part-time jobs. Supporting data: IRS required; FFS, FAF, AFSA/SAR acceptable. Priority application deadline: 3/31.

Athletics Member NCAA (Division I). Intercollegiate sports: baseball/softball M(I,s), W(I,s); basketball M(I,s), W(I,s); cross-country running M(I,s), W(I,s); field hockey W(I,s); football M(I-AA,s); golf M(I,s), W(I,s); riflery M, W; soccer M; swimming and diving M(I,s); tennis M(I,s), W(I,s); track and field M(I,s), W(I,s); volleyball W(I,s); wrestling M(I,s). Intramural sports: archery, badminton, baseball/softball, basketball, bowling, cross-country running, fencing, field hockey, football, golf, racquetball, riflery, rugby, sailing, soccer, swimming and diving, tennis, track and field, volleyball, water polo, weight lifting, wrestling.

Majors Accounting B; agricultural business A, B; agricultural education B; agronomy/soil and crop sciences A, B; anesthesiology B; animal sciences A, B; art education B; art/fine arts A; art history B; atmospheric sciences B; biology/biological sciences B; business administration/commerce/management B; business education B; cartography B; ceramic art and design B; chemistry B; child psychology/child development A, B; commercial art B; communication B; communication equipment technology A; computer information systems B; computer science B; conservation B; construction technologies A; creative writing B; dance B; data processing B; dietetics B; drafting and design A, B; early childhood education B; earth science B; economics B; elementary education B; engineering physics B; English B; finance/banking B; fire science B; food services technology B; French B; geography B; geology B; German B; gerontology B; graphic arts B; history B; home economics B; home economics education B; horticulture A, B; hotel and restaurant management B; industrial arts B; industrial engineering technology B; interior design B; jewelry and metalsmithing B; Latin B; Latin American studies B; liberal arts/general studies A; marketing/retailing/merchandising B; mathematics B; mechanical engineering technology A; medical technology B; music B; music education B; nursing B; painting/drawing B; philosophy B; photography B; physical education B; physics B; political science/government B; printing technologies A; psychology B; public administration B; radiological technology B; recreation and leisure services B; religious studies B; respiratory therapy A, B; retail management A; science education B; sculpture B; secretarial studies/office management A, B; social science B; social work B; sociology B; Spanish B; special education B; speech pathology and audiology B; speech/rhetoric/public address/debate B; studio art B; textiles and clothing B; theater arts/drama B; tourism and travel A; transportation technologies A; urban studies B; vocational education B; wildlife management B. Majors with highest enrollment: elementary education, finance/banking, accounting.

LD Program Information

Name of Program Learning Diagnostic Clinic.

Availability of Services Began offering services in 1984. Services provided to freshmen, sophomores, juniors, seniors. Program currently serves 33 LD students: 14 freshmen, 9 sophomores, 6 juniors, 4 seniors.

Staff 11 part-time staff members, including director. Services provided by remediation specialists, tutors, diagnostic specialists.

Admissions LD applicants evaluated on the basis of high school transcript, standard ACT. LD students may begin taking classes in fall, spring, or summer. Application should be submitted 6 months in advance of initial anticipated enrollment.

Orientation Optional orientation offered before registration.

Housing College housing (including coed) available. LD students housed randomly. LD freshmen and sophomores required to live on campus except if 20 or over (space permitting).

Diagnostic Testing Available in intelligence, reading, math, spelling, handwriting, spoken language, written language, perceptual skills, social skills, psychoneurology, speech.

Tutoring Offered one-to-one and in small groups by professional teachers, peer tutors. Available in all subjects. LD students may receive tutoring in all courses each term.

Basic Skills Remediation Offered one-to-one and in small groups. Available in reading, math, spelling, handwriting, spoken language, written language, learning strategies, work and study habits, social skills.

Academic Advisement Help with program planning provided by LD staff members, academic advisers. LD students may take up to 16 credit hours each semester; most take 12 credit hours; 12 credit hours required to maintain full-time status.

Special Courses Offered in reading, math. All offered for credit; all enter into overall grade point average.

Auxiliary Aids and Services Aids include taped textbooks, tape recorders, calculators, word processors, microcomputers. Services include alternative exam arrangements, advocacy.

Counseling Services Individual counseling, career counseling available.

Contact Dr. Virgil W. McCall, Director, Learning Diagnostic Clinic, Southwest Missouri State University, Springfield, MO 65804, 417-836-5833.

SOUTHWEST TEXAS STATE UNIVERSITY

San Marcos, Texas

Year Program Began	1980	Special Courses	✓
Special Fee	None	Taped Textbooks	✓
Special Orientation		Alternative Exam Arrangements	✓
Diagnostic Testing	✓	Notetakers	✓
Subject-Area Tutoring	✓	Staff	4 part-time
Basic Skills Remediation		Number of Students Served	9

General Information State-supported comprehensive coed institution. Part of Texas State University System. Founded 1899. Awards A (terminal), B, M. Institutionally accredited by regional association; programs accredited by NASM (music), NCATE (teacher education). Small-town setting, with easy access to San Antonio; 317-acre campus. Total enrollment: 19,202. Faculty: 843 (520 full-time, 323 part-time); 74% have doctoral degrees; graduate assistants teach a few undergraduate courses. Calendar: semesters. Grading system: letters or numbers. Library holdings: 690,559 bound volumes, 860,130 titles on microform, 3,941 periodical subscriptions, 3,374 records/tapes.

Undergraduate Profile Fall 1984: 17,381 undergraduates (3,015 freshmen) from 15 states and territories and 10 foreign countries; 18% part-time; 96% state residents; 13% transfers; 17% financial aid recipients; 56% women; 4% blacks; 1% Native Americans; 11% Hispanics; 1% Asian Americans; 1% foreign nationals; 12% of undergraduates over 25 years of age; 150 legally handicapped students.

Expenses (1984–85) State resident tuition: $392 full-time. Nonresident tuition: $1252 full-time. Part-time tuition and fees per semester (1 to 11 semester hours) range from $86 to $190 for state residents, $76 to $580 for nonresidents. Mandatory fees: $328. College room and board: $2023.

Financial Aid Fall 1984 full-time freshmen: 39% applied for aid, 64% of those were judged to have need, 100% of those were aided; the average aided freshman received an aid package worth $2278 (30% scholarships/grants, 70% self-help) meeting 95% of need. College-administered aid for all 1984–85 undergraduates: need-based scholarships; 303 non-need scholarships (average $618); short-term loans (average $200); low-interest long-term loans from external sources (average $2050); SEOG; College Work-Study; 2,000 part-time jobs. Supporting data: FFS, IRS, AFSA/SAR required. Priority application deadline: 5/1.

Athletics Member NCAA (Division II). Intercollegiate sports: basketball M(II,s), W(II,s); cross-country running M(II,s); football M(II,s); golf M(II,s); gymnastics W(II,s); swimming and diving W(s); tennis M(II,s), W(II,s); track and field M(II,s), W(II,s); volleyball W(II,s). Intramural sports: badminton, baseball/softball, basketball, bowling, cross-country running, fencing, racquetball, soccer, water polo, wrestling.

Majors Accounting B; agricultural business B; agricultural education B; agricultural sciences B; agricultural technologies B; agronomy/soil and crop sciences B; animal sciences B; anthropology B; art education B; art/fine arts B; bilingual/bicultural education B; biology/biological sciences B; botany/plant sciences B; business administration/commerce/management B; business education B; cartography B; chemistry B; child care/child and family studies B; city, community, and regional planning B; commercial art B; computer information systems B; computer science B; consumer services B; corrections B; criminal justice B; (pre)dentistry sequence B; economics B; elementary education B; English B; fashion merchandising B; finance/banking B; fish and game management B; French B; geography B; German B; guidance and counseling B; health education B; health services administration B; history B; home economics B; home economics education B; horticulture B; industrial arts B; industrial engineering technology B; interdisciplinary studies B; interior design B; international studies B; journalism B; law enforcement/police sciences B; (pre)law sequence B; manufacturing technology B; marine biology B; marketing/retailing/merchandising B; mathematics B; medical laboratory technology A; medical records services B; medical technology B; (pre)medicine sequence B; microbiology B; music B; music education B; nutrition B; philosophy B; physical education B; physical therapy B; physics B; physiology B; political science/government B; psychology B; range management B; recreation and leisure services B; respiratory therapy A; social science B; social work B; sociology B; Spanish B; speech pathology and audiology B; speech/rhetoric/public address/debate B; studio art B; theater arts/drama B; (pre)veterinary medicine sequence B; vocational education B; wildlife biology B; zoology B. Majors with highest enrollment: elementary education, accounting, business administration/commerce/management.

LD Program Information

Name of Program Student Learning Assistance Center.

Availability of Services Began offering services in 1980. Services provided to freshmen, sophomores, juniors, seniors. Program currently serves 9 LD students: 3 freshmen, 4 sophomores, 1 junior, 1 senior.

Staff 4 part-time staff members, including director. Services provided by tutors, counselors, assistant dean of student affairs.

Admissions LD applicants evaluated on the basis of high school transcript, untimed SAT or ACT, personal interview, psychoeducational report. LD students may begin taking classes in fall, spring, or summer. Application should be submitted 1 semester in advance of initial anticipated enrollment.

Housing College housing (including coed) available. LD students housed randomly. LD freshmen and sophomores required to live on campus except if married, living with relatives, or graduated from high school over 3 years ago.

Diagnostic Testing Available in reading, math, spelling, written language, work and study habits.

Tutoring Offered one-to-one by peer tutors. Available in some subjects. LD students may receive tutoring in all courses each term.

Academic Advisement Help with program planning provided by academic advisers. Most LD students take 9 to 12 semester hours each semester; 12 semester hours required to maintain full-time status.

Special Courses Offered in college survival skills, study skills. Some offered for credit; some enter into overall grade point average.

Auxiliary Aids and Services Aids include taped textbooks, tape recorders, word processors. Services include alternative exam arrangements, notetakers, advocacy.

Counseling Services Individual counseling, career counseling available.

Contact Dr. D. S. Johnson, Director of Student Learning Assistance Center and Assistant Dean of General Studies, Southwest Texas State University, San Marcos, TX 78666, 512-245-2515.

STANFORD UNIVERSITY
Stanford, California

Year Program Began	1985	Special Courses	✓
Special Fee	None	Taped Textbooks	✓
Special Orientation		Alternative Exam Arrangements	✓
Diagnostic Testing		Notetakers	✓
Subject-Area Tutoring	✓	Staff	4 part-time
Basic Skills Remediation	✓	Number of Students Served	*Not reported*

General Information Independent coed university. Founded 1891. Awards B, M, D. Institutionally accredited by regional association; programs accredited by ABET (engineering and technology). City setting, with easy access to San Francisco; 8,800-acre barrier-free campus. Total enrollment: 13,261. Faculty: 1,263 (all full-time); 100% have doctoral degrees; graduate assistants teach a few undergraduate courses. Calendar: quarters. Grading system: letters or numbers. Library holdings: 5.1 million bound volumes, 2.6 million titles on microform, 5,000 periodical subscriptions.

Undergraduate Profile Fall 1984: 6,593 undergraduates (1,610 freshmen) from 52 states and territories and 72 foreign countries; 0% part-time; 42% state residents; 10% transfers; 65% financial aid recipients; 43% women; 8% blacks; 1% Native Americans; 8% Hispanics; 6% Asian Americans; 2% foreign nationals; 14 legally handicapped students.

Expenses (1985–86) Comprehensive fee of $14,893 includes full-time tuition ($10,476) and college room and board ($4417).

Financial Aid Fall 1984 full-time freshmen: 50% applied for aid, 96% of those were judged to have need, 100% of those were aided; the average aided freshman received an aid package worth $10,875 (69% scholarships/grants, 31% self-help) meeting 100% of need. College-administered aid for all 1984–85 undergraduates: need-based scholarships (average $6696); non-need scholarships; short-term loans; low-interest long-term loans; SEOG; College Work-Study; part-time jobs. Supporting data: FAF required. Application deadline: 2/1.

Athletics Member NCAA (Division I), NAIA. Intercollegiate sports: baseball/softball M(I,s); basketball M(I,s), W(I,s); crew M, W; cross-country running M(I,s), W(I,s); fencing M(I,s), W(I,s); field hockey W(I,s); football M(I-A,s); golf M(I,s), W(I,s); gymnastics M(I,s), W(I,s); lacrosse M(c), W(c); rugby M(c), W(c); sailing M, W; skiing (downhill) M(c), W(c); soccer M(c), W(c); swimming and diving M(I,s), W(I,s); tennis M(I,s), W(I,s); track and field M(I,s), W(I,s); volleyball M(I,s), W(I,s); water polo M(I,s); wrestling M(I,s). Intramural sports: archery, badminton, baseball/softball, basketball, bowling, cross-country running, equestrian sports, field hockey, football, golf, gymnastics, ice hockey, martial arts, racquetball, soccer, squash, swimming and diving, tennis, track and field, volleyball, water polo, wrestling.

Majors American studies B; anthropology B; art history B; Asian/Oriental studies B; biology/biological sciences B; black/Afro-American studies B; chemical engineering B; chemistry B; Chinese B; civil engineering B; classics B; communication B; earth science B; East Asian studies B; economics B; electrical engineering B; engineering (general) B; English B; European studies B; French B; geology B; geophysics B; German B; history B; human ecology B; humanities B; industrial engineering B; interdisciplinary studies B; international studies B; Italian B; Japanese B; journalism B; Latin American studies B; linguistics B; materials engineering B; materials sciences B; mathematics B; mechanical engineering B; medieval studies B; music B; music history B; petroleum/natural gas engineering B; philosophy B; physics B; political science/government B; psychology B; public affairs and policy studies B; religious studies B; Russian B; Slavic languages B; sociology B; Spanish B; statistics B; studio art B; theater arts/drama B; urban studies B; women's studies B. Majors with highest enrollment: economics, human ecology, biology/biological sciences.

LD Program Information

Name of Program Disabled Student Services.

Availability of Services Began offering services in 1985. Services provided to freshmen, sophomores, juniors, seniors.

Staff 4 part-time staff members, including director, services coordinator, director and assistant director of Center for Teaching and Learning. Services provided by tutors.

Admissions LD applicants evaluated on the basis of high school transcript and grade point average, standard or untimed SAT or ACT, autobiographical statement, letters of recommendation; psychoeducational report recommended. LD students may begin taking classes in fall, winter, or spring. Application should be submitted at least 10 months in advance of initial anticipated enrollment.

Housing College housing (including coed) available. LD students housed randomly. LD freshmen required to live on campus.

Tutoring Offered one-to-one and in small groups by peer tutors. Available in all subjects. LD students may receive tutoring in all courses each term.

Basic Skills Remediation Offered in small groups by regular teachers. Available in reading, written language, work and study habits.

Academic Advisement Help with program planning provided by academic advisers. LD students may take up to 20 quarter hours each quarter; 12 quarter hours required to maintain full-time status.

Special Courses Offered in reading, composition, study skills. Some offered for credit; none enter into overall grade point average.

Auxiliary Aids and Services Aids include taped textbooks, tape recorders, typewriters, word processors. Services include alternative exam arrangements, notetakers, readers.

Counseling Services Individual counseling, small-group counseling, career counseling available.

Contact Mr. James Bouquin, Director, Disabled Student Services, Stanford University, 307 Old Union, Stanford, CA 94305, 415-497-1039.

STATE UNIVERSITY OF NEW YORK AT ALBANY

Albany, New York

Year Program Began	1980	Special Courses	✓
Special Fee	Varies	Taped Textbooks	✓
Special Orientation	✓	Alternative Exam Arrangements	✓
Diagnostic Testing	✓	Notetakers	
Subject-Area Tutoring	✓	Staff	2 full-time, 1 part-time
Basic Skills Remediation		Number of Students Served	30

General Information State-supported coed university. Part of State University of New York System. Founded 1844. Awards B, M, D. Institutionally accredited by regional association; programs registered by New York State Board of Regents; programs accredited by AACSB (business). City setting; 500-acre barrier-free campus. Total enrollment: 16,000. Faculty: 915 (680 full-time, 235 part-time); 93% have doctoral degrees; graduate assistants teach a few undergraduate courses. Calendar: semesters. Grading system: letters or numbers. Library holdings: 1.1 million bound volumes, 7,241 periodical subscriptions, 4,891 records/tapes.

Undergraduate Profile Fall 1984: 11,500 undergraduates (2,142 freshmen) from 21 states and territories and 28 foreign countries; 4% part-time; 99% state residents; 28% transfers; 50% financial aid recipients; 51% women; 5% blacks; 0% Native Americans; 3% Hispanics; 2% Asian Americans; 1% foreign nationals; 6% of undergraduates over 25 years of age; 102 legally handicapped students.

Expenses (1985–86) State resident tuition: $1350 full-time, $45 per credit part-time. Nonresident tuition: $3200 full-time, $107 per credit part-time. Mandatory fees: $124. College room and board: $2583. College room only: $1550.

Financial Aid Fall 1984 full-time freshmen: 85% applied for aid, 90% of those were judged to have need, 100% of those were aided; the average aided freshman received an aid package worth $2796 (48% scholarships/grants, 52% self-help) meeting 95% of need. College-administered aid for all 1984–85 undergraduates: 1,022 need-based scholarships (average $946); 3,442 non-need scholarships (average $200); short-term loans (average $160); low-interest long-term loans from external sources (average $1470); SEOG; College Work-Study; part-time jobs. Supporting data: FAF, IRS, institutional form required. Application deadline: continuous to 4/15.

Athletics Member NCAA (Division III). Intercollegiate sports: baseball/softball M(III), W(III); basketball M(III), W(III); cross-country running M(III), W(III); football M(III); gymnastics W(III); lacrosse M(III); martial arts M; rugby M; soccer M(III), W(III); swimming and diving M(III), W(III); tennis M(III), W(III); track and field M(III), W(III); volleyball W(III); wrestling M(III). Intramural sports: baseball/softball, basketball, cross-country running, football, golf, riflery, skiing (cross-country), skiing (downhill), soccer, squash, tennis, track and field, volleyball, wrestling.

Majors Accounting B; African studies B; anthropology B; applied mathematics B; art/fine arts B; Asian/Oriental studies B; atmospheric sciences B; biology/biological sciences B; black/Afro-American studies B; business administration/commerce/management B; business education B; chemistry B; Chinese B; classics B; communication B; computer science B; criminal justice B; earth science B; East European and Soviet studies B; economics B; English B; French B; geography B; geology B; German B; Greek B; Hispanic studies B; history B; interdisciplinary studies B; Italian B; Judaic studies B; Latin B; Latin American studies B; linguistics B; mathematics B; medical technology B; meteorology B; modern languages B; music B; philosophy B; physics B; political science/government B; psychology B; public affairs and policy studies B; Romance languages B; Russian B; Russian and Slavic studies B; secondary education B; social work B; sociology B; Spanish B; speech/rhetoric/public address/debate B; studio art B; theater arts/drama B; women's studies B. Majors with highest enrollment: accounting, business administration/commerce/management, psychology.

LD Program Information

Name of Program Disabled Student Services.

Availability of Services Began offering services in 1980. Services provided to freshmen, sophomores, juniors, seniors. Program currently serves 30 LD students: 10 freshmen, 6 sophomores, 8 juniors, 6 seniors.

Fees $3.50 to $15 per hour for tutoring.

Staff 2 full-time, 1 part-time staff members, including director. Services provided by counselors, diagnostic specialists.

Admissions LD applicants evaluated on the basis of high school transcript and grade point average, standard or untimed SAT, autobiographical statement, letters of recommendation, psychoeducational report. LD students may begin taking classes in fall, spring, or summer. Application should be submitted at least 5 months in advance of initial anticipated enrollment.

Orientation Optional orientation offered before registration.

Housing College housing (including coed) available. LD students housed with other LD students and non-LD students. LD students not required to live on campus.

Diagnostic Testing Available in intelligence, motor abilities, perceptual skills, personality, psychoneurology.

Tutoring Offered one-to-one by professional teachers, peer tutors. Available in all subjects. LD students may receive tutoring in all courses each term.

Academic Advisement Help with program planning provided by LD staff members, academic advisers. LD students may take up to 21 credits each semester; most take 12 to 15 credits; 12 credits required to maintain full-time status.

Special Courses Offered in college survival skills, communication skills, composition, career planning. All offered for credit; all enter into overall grade point average.

Auxiliary Aids and Services Aids include taped textbooks, tape recorders, talking calculators. Services include alternative exam arrangements, advocacy.

Counseling Services Individual counseling, small-group counseling, rap sessions, career counseling available.

Contact Ms. Nancy Belowich, Director, Disabled Student Services, State University of New York at Albany, Campus Center 137, 1400 Washington Avenue, Albany, NY 12222, 518-442-3094.

STATE UNIVERSITY OF NEW YORK AT BINGHAMTON

Binghamton, New York

Year Program Began	1983	Special Courses	
Special Fee	None	Taped Textbooks	✓
Special Orientation	✓	Alternative Exam Arrangements	✓
Diagnostic Testing		Notetakers	✓
Subject-Area Tutoring	✓	Staff	1 part-time
Basic Skills Remediation	✓	Number of Students Served	2

General Information State-supported coed university. Part of State University of New York System. Founded 1946. Awards B, M, D. Institutionally accredited by regional association; programs registered by New York State Board of Regents; programs accredited by ABET (engineering and technology), NLN (nursing). City setting; 606-acre barrier-free campus. Total enrollment: 10,788. Faculty: 686 (494 full-time, 192 part-time); 97% have doctoral degrees; graduate assistants teach a few undergraduate courses. Calendar: semesters. Grading system: letters or numbers. Library holdings: 1.1 million bound volumes, 663,007 titles on microform, 13,152 periodical subscriptions, 68,801 records/tapes.

Undergraduate Profile Fall 1984: 8,627 undergraduates (1,601 freshmen) from 23 states and territories and 26 foreign countries; 9% part-time; 96% state residents; 9% transfers; 74% financial aid recipients; 54% women; 4% blacks; 0% Native Americans; 2% Hispanics; 2% Asian Americans; 1% foreign nationals; 7% of undergraduates over 25 years of age; 68 legally handicapped students.

Expenses (1985–86) State resident tuition: $1350 full-time, $45 per credit hour part-time. Nonresident tuition: $3200 full-time, $107 per credit hour part-time. Mandatory fees: $146. College room and board: $2778. College room only: $1550.

Financial Aid Fall 1984 full-time freshmen: 70% applied for aid, 87% of those were judged to have need, 100% of those were aided; the average aided freshman received an aid package meeting 100% of need. College-administered aid for all 1984–85 undergraduates: need-based scholarships; 5 non-need scholarships (average $2000); short-term loans (average $200); low-interest long-term loans from external sources (average $1850); SEOG; College Work-Study; 950 part-time jobs. Supporting data: FAF, IRS, institutional form, AFSA/SAR required; FFS acceptable. Priority application deadline: 4/1.

Athletics Member NCAA (Division III). Intercollegiate sports: baseball/softball M(III), W(III); basketball M(III), W(III); cross-country running M(III), W(III); ice hockey M(c); lacrosse M(c); rugby M(c); skiing (downhill) M(c); soccer M(III); swimming and diving M(III), W(III); tennis M(III), W(III); track and field M(III), W(III); volleyball W(III); wrestling M(III). Intramural sports: badminton, baseball/softball, basketball, bowling, cross-country running, football, golf, lacrosse, martial arts, racquetball, rugby, soccer, squash, swimming and diving, tennis, track and field, volleyball, water polo, wrestling.

Majors Accounting B; African studies B; American studies B; anthropology B; Arabic B; art/fine arts B; art history B; biochemistry B; biology/biological sciences B; black/Afro-American studies B; business administration/commerce/management B; chemistry B; classics B; comparative literature B; computer information systems B; computer science B; (pre)dentistry sequence B; ecology/environmental studies B; economics B; electrical engineering B; electrical engineering technology B; electromechanical technology B; English B; environmental sciences B; film studies B; French B; geography B; geology B; geophysics B; German B; Hebrew B; history B; industrial engineering technology B; Italian B; Judaic studies B; Latin American studies B; (pre)law sequence B; legal studies B; liberal arts/general studies B; linguistics B; literature B; mathematics B; mechanical engineering B; mechanical engineering technology B; (pre)medicine sequence B; medieval studies B; music B; nursing B; philosophy B; physics B; political science/government B; psychology B; social science B; sociology B; Spanish B; studio art B; theater arts/drama B; (pre) veterinary medicine sequence B. Majors with highest enrollment: business administration/commerce/management, psychology, nursing.

LD Program Information

Name of Program Office of Programs for Students with Disabilities.

Availability of Services Began offering services in 1983. Services provided to freshmen, sophomores, juniors, seniors. Program currently serves 2 LD students: 1 freshman, 1 sophomore.

Staff 1 part-time staff member (coordinator). Services provided by tutors.

Admissions LD applicants evaluated on the basis of high school transcript and grade point average, untimed SAT or ACT; personal interview, autobiographical statement, letters of recommendation, psychoeducational report recommended. LD students may begin taking classes in fall, spring, or summer. Application should be submitted 8 to 10 months in advance of initial anticipated enrollment.

Orientation Optional orientation offered before registration.

Housing College housing (including coed) available. LD students housed randomly. LD freshmen required to live on campus unless living within commuting distance, married, or 21 or over.

Tutoring Offered one-to-one and in small groups by peer tutors. Available in all subjects. LD students may receive tutoring in 2 courses per term (additional tutoring available at student's expense).

Basic Skills Remediation Available in reading, math, written language.

Academic Advisement Help with program planning provided by academic advisers. Most LD students take 12 to 16 credit hours each semester; 12 credit hours required to maintain full-time status.

Auxiliary Aids and Services Aids include taped textbooks, tape recorders, talking calculator. Services include alternative exam arrangements, notetakers, advocacy.

Counseling Services Individual counseling, small-group counseling, career counseling available.

Contact Ms. Barbara Jean Fairbairn, Coordinator, Office of Programs for Students with Disabilities, State University of New York at Binghamton, Engineering Building Room 134, Binghamton, NY 13901, 607-777-2686.

STATE UNIVERSITY OF NEW YORK AT BUFFALO

Amherst, New York

Year Program Began	1976	Special Courses	✓
Special Fee	None	Taped Textbooks	✓
Special Orientation	✓	Alternative Exam Arrangements	✓
Diagnostic Testing		Notetakers	✓
Subject-Area Tutoring	✓	Staff	6 part-time
Basic Skills Remediation	✓	Number of Students Served	8 to 10

General Information State-supported coed university. Part of State University of New York System. Founded 1846. Awards B, M, D. Institutionally accredited by regional association; programs accredited by NASAD (art and design), AACSB (business), ABET (engineering and technology), NASM (music), NLN (nursing), ACPE (pharmacy), NCATE (teacher education). Metropolitan setting; 1,376-acre campus. Total enrollment: 26,160. Faculty: 1,853 (1,386 full-time, 467 part-time); 96% have doctoral degrees; graduate assistants teach a few undergraduate courses. Calendar: semesters. Grading system: letters or numbers. Library holdings: 2.3 million bound volumes, 2.7 million titles on microform, 20,710 periodical subscriptions, 20,000 records/tapes.

Undergraduate Profile Fall 1984: 18,282 undergraduates (2,563 freshmen) from 27 states and territories and 64 foreign countries; 23% part-time; 96% state residents; 13% transfers; 53% financial aid recipients; 44% women; 6% blacks; 1% Native Americans; 2% Hispanics; 4% Asian Americans; 3% foreign nationals; 23% of undergraduates over 25 years of age; 73 legally handicapped students.

Expenses (1985–86) State resident tuition: $1350 full-time, $45 per credit hour part-time. Nonresident tuition: $3200 full-time, $107 per credit hour part-time. Mandatory fees: $240. College room and board: $2980. College room only: $1550.

Financial Aid Fall 1984 full-time freshmen: 87% applied for aid, 83% of those were judged to have need, 91% of those were aided; the average aided freshman received an aid package worth $3732 (52% scholarships/grants, 48% self-help) meeting 90% of need. College-administered aid for all 1984–85 undergraduates: 1,000 need-based scholarships (average $3230); 95 non-need scholarships (average $1400); short-term loans (average $250); low-interest long-term loans from college funds (average $1039), from external sources (average $2683); SEOG; College Work-Study; 900 part-time jobs. Supporting data: FAF required; IRS, state form required for some; AFSA/SAR acceptable. Priority application deadline: 3/15.

Athletics Member NCAA (Division III). Intercollegiate sports: baseball/softball M(I), W(III); basketball M(III), W(III); cross-country running M(III), W(III); field hockey W(III); football M(III); golf M(III); ice hockey M(III); soccer M(III), W(III); swimming and diving M(III), W(III); tennis M(III), W(III); track and field M(III), W(III); volleyball W(III); wrestling M(III). Intramural sports: badminton, baseball/softball, basketball, bowling, fencing, football, gymnastics, ice hockey, lacrosse, martial arts, rugby, skiing (downhill), soccer, tennis, volleyball.

Majors Accounting B; aerospace engineering B; American studies B; anthropology B; architecture B; art education B; art/fine arts B; art history B; biochemistry B; biology/biological sciences B; biophysics B; black/Afro-American studies B; business administration/commerce/management B; cell biology B; chemical engineering B; chemistry B; civil engineering B; classics B; communication B; computer science B; dance B; (pre)dentistry sequence B; earth science B; economics B; electrical engineering B; engineering (general) B; engineering sciences B; English B; environmental design B; film studies B; French B; geography B; geology B; German B; health education B; health science B; history B; industrial engineering B; interdisciplinary studies B; Italian B; Judaic studies B; (pre)law sequence B; linguistics B; mathematics B; mechanical engineering B; medical technology B; (pre) medicine sequence B; music B; music education B; Native American studies B; nuclear engineering B; nuclear medical technology B; nursing B; occupational therapy B; pharmacology B; pharmacy/pharmaceutical sciences B; philosophy B; photography B; physical education B; physical therapy B; physics B; political science/government B; psychology B; religious studies B; science education B; social science B; sociology B; Spanish B; speech pathology and audiology B; statistics B; studio art B; theater arts/drama B; (pre)veterinary medicine sequence B; women's studies B. Majors with highest enrollment: engineering (general), business administration/commerce/management, health science.

LD Program Information

Name of Program Office of Services for the Handicapped.

Availability of Services Began offering services in 1976. Services provided to freshmen, sophomores, juniors, seniors. Program currently serves 8 to 10 LD students.

Staff 6 part-time staff members, including coordinator, assistant coordinator. Services provided by remediation specialists, tutors, counselors.

Admissions LD applicants evaluated on the basis of high school transcript and grade point average, standard or untimed SAT or ACT; psychoeducational report recommended. LD students may begin taking classes in fall, spring, or summer. Application should be submitted 8 months in advance of initial anticipated enrollment.

Orientation Optional orientation offered before registration.

Housing College housing (including coed) available. LD students housed randomly. LD students not required to live on campus.

Tutoring Offered one-to-one and in small groups by professional teachers, peer tutors. Available in all subjects. LD students may receive tutoring in all courses each term.

Basic Skills Remediation Offered one-to-one and in small groups by regular teachers, teacher trainees. Available in reading, math, written language.

Academic Advisement Help with program planning provided by academic advisers. LD students may take up to 15 credit hours, plus as many more as individual can handle, each semester; most take 12 credit hours; 12 credit hours required to maintain full-time status.

Special Courses Offered in college survival skills, reading, vocabulary development, communication skills, composition, language development, math, typing, personal psychology, study skills, career planning. Some offered for credit; some enter into overall grade point average.

Auxiliary Aids and Services Aids include taped textbooks, tape recorders, calculators, typewriters, Kurzweil reading machine, talking calculators. Services include alternative exam arrangements, notetakers, advocacy.

Counseling Services Individual counseling, small-group counseling, career counseling available.

Contact Mr. Arthur W. Burke, Coordinator, Office of Services for the Handicapped, State University of New York at Buffalo, 272 Capen Hall, Amherst, NY 14260, 716-636-2608.

STATE UNIVERSITY OF NEW YORK COLLEGE AT NEW PALTZ

New Paltz, New York

Year Program Began	1980	Special Courses	✓
Special Fee	None	Taped Textbooks	✓
Special Orientation		Alternative Exam Arrangements	✓
Diagnostic Testing	✓	Notetakers	
Subject-Area Tutoring	✓	Staff	4 part-time
Basic Skills Remediation	✓	Number of Students Served	35

General Information State-supported comprehensive coed institution. Part of State University of New York System. Founded 1828. Awards B, M. Institutionally accredited by regional association; programs accredited by NASM (music), NCATE (teacher education). Rural setting; 208-acre campus. Total enrollment: 7,344. Faculty: 391 (314 full-time, 77 part-time); 81% have doctoral degrees; graduate assistants teach no undergraduate courses. Calendar: semesters. Grading system: letters or numbers. Library holdings: 350,000 bound volumes, 560,000 titles on microform, 1,560 periodical subscriptions.

Undergraduate Profile Fall 1984: 6,031 undergraduates (816 freshmen) from 22 states and territories and 32 foreign countries; 22% part-time; 89% state residents; 35% transfers; 60% financial aid recipients; 55% women; 12% blacks; 0% Native Americans; 3% Hispanics; 1% Asian Americans; 4% foreign nationals; 125 legally handicapped students.

Expenses (1985–86) State resident tuition: $1350 full-time, $45 per credit part-time. Nonresident tuition: $3200 full-time, $107 per credit part-time. Mandatory fees: $214. College room and board: $2790. College room only: $1550.

Financial Aid Fall 1984 full-time freshmen: 74% applied for aid, 81% of those were judged to have need, 100% of those were aided; the average aided freshman received an aid package worth $5211 (66% scholarships/grants, 34% self-help) meeting 100% of need. College-administered aid for all 1984–85 undergraduates: need-based scholarships; 20 non-need scholarships (average $500); low-interest long-term loans from external sources (average $1500); SEOG; College Work-Study; 885 part-time jobs. Supporting data: FAF required. Priority application deadline: 2/15.

Athletics Member NCAA (Division III). Intercollegiate sports: baseball/softball M(III), W(III); basketball M(III), W(III); cross-country running M(III), W(III); fencing M(c), W(c); golf M(III), W(III); gymnastics W(III); lacrosse M(c); racquetball M(c); soccer M(III), W(c); swimming and diving M(III), W(III); tennis M(III), W(III); track and field M(c), W(c); volleyball M(III), W(III). Intramural sports: archery, badminton, baseball/softball, basketball, bowling, cross-country running, football, golf, racquetball, swimming and diving, tennis, track and field, volleyball, water polo.

Majors Accounting B; anthropology B; applied mathematics B; art education B; art/fine arts B; art history B; bilingual/bicultural education B; biochemistry B; biology/biological sciences B; biophysics B; black/Afro-American studies B; broadcasting B; business administration/commerce/management B; business economics B; ceramic art and design B; chemistry B; city, community, and regional planning B; commercial art B; communication B; comparative literature B; computer engineering B; computer science B; creative writing B; (pre)dentistry sequence B; early childhood education B; economics B; education B; elementary education B; engineering physics B; English B; finance/banking B; French B; geography B; geology B; German B; graphic arts B; history B; international economics B; international studies B; jewelry and metalsmithing B; journalism B; (pre)law sequence B; marketing/retailing/merchandising B; mathematics B; (pre)medicine sequence B; music B; music history B; music therapy B; nursing B; painting/drawing B; philosophy B; photography B; physics B; political science/government B; psychobiology B; psychology B; radio and television studies B; science education B; sculpture B; secondary education B; social work B; sociology B; Spanish B; special education B; speech pathology and audiology B; speech/rhetoric/public address/debate B; speech therapy B; studio art B; theater arts/drama B; (pre)veterinary medicine sequence B; women's studies B. Majors with highest enrollment: business administration/commerce/management, computer science, communication.

LD Program Information

Name of Program Special Student Programs.

Availability of Services Began offering services in 1980. Services provided to freshmen, sophomores, juniors, seniors. Program currently serves 35 LD students: 12 freshmen, 10 sophomores, 7 juniors, 6 seniors.

Staff 4 part-time staff members, including directors of Special Programs and Special Student Programs. Services provided by remediation specialists, tutors.

Admissions LD applicants evaluated on the basis of high school transcript and grade point average, standard or untimed SAT, personal interview, letters of recommendation, psychoeducational report. LD students may begin taking classes in fall or spring. Application should be submitted 3 months in advance of initial anticipated enrollment.

Housing College housing (including coed) available. LD students housed randomly. LD freshmen required to live on campus except if family resides within 25-mile radius.

Diagnostic Testing Available in reading, math, written language.

Tutoring Offered one-to-one and in small groups by peer tutors. Available in all subjects. LD students may receive tutoring in all courses each term (depending on availability of tutors).

Basic Skills Remediation Offered one-to-one and in small groups by LD teachers. Available in reading, math, written language, learning strategies, work and study habits.

Academic Advisement Help with program planning provided by LD staff members, academic advisers. LD students may take up to 18 credits each semester; most take 12 credits; 12 credits required to maintain full-time status.

Special Courses Offered in reading, vocabulary development, composition, language development, math. None offered for credit; none enter into overall grade point average.

Auxiliary Aids and Services Aids include taped textbooks, tape recorders, word processors. Services include alternative exam arrangements, advocacy, writing service, referrals.

Counseling Services Individual counseling, career counseling available.

Contact Ms. Beverly Lavergneau, Director, Special Student Programs, State University of New York College at New Paltz, Hagerty Administration Building 702, New Paltz, NY 12561, 914-257-2467.

STATE UNIVERSITY OF NEW YORK COLLEGE AT PLATTSBURGH

Plattsburgh, New York

Year Program Began	1982	Special Courses	✓
Special Fee	None	Taped Textbooks	✓
Special Orientation	✓	Alternative Exam Arrangements	✓
Diagnostic Testing	✓	Notetakers	✓
Subject-Area Tutoring	✓	Staff	1 full-time, 8 part-time
Basic Skills Remediation	✓	Number of Students Served	10

General Information State-supported comprehensive coed institution. Part of State University of New York System. Founded 1889. Awards B, M. Institutionally accredited by regional association; programs accredited by NLN (nursing), NCATE (teacher education). Small-town setting, with easy access to Montreal; 265-acre barrier-free campus. Total enrollment: 5,624. Faculty: 370 (262 full-time, 108 part-time); 61% have doctoral degrees; graduate assistants teach a few undergraduate courses. Calendar: semesters plus 2 summer sessions. Grading system: letters or numbers. Library holdings: 503,890 bound volumes, 575,000 titles on microform, 2,190 periodical subscriptions, 6,900 records/tapes.

Undergraduate Profile Fall 1984: 5,404 undergraduates (1,008 freshmen) from 18 states and territories and 27 foreign countries; 3% part-time; 96% state residents; 13% transfers; 60% financial aid recipients; 61% women; 2% blacks; 0% Native Americans; 1% Hispanics; 1% Asian Americans; 2% foreign nationals; 8% of undergraduates over 25 years of age; 59 legally handicapped students.

Expenses (1985–86) State resident tuition: $1350 full-time, $45 per credit part-time. Nonresident tuition: $3200 full-time, $107 per credit part-time. Mandatory fees: $118. College room and board: $2864. College room only: $1550.

Financial Aid Fall 1984 full-time freshmen: 84% applied for aid, 91% of those were judged to have need, 100% of those were aided; the average aided freshman received an aid package worth $3413 (44% scholarships/grants, 56% self-help) meeting 100% of need. College-administered aid for all 1984–85 undergraduates: 835 need-based scholarships (average $613); 42 non-need scholarships (average $980); short-term loans (average $25); low-interest long-term loans from external sources (average $930); SEOG; College Work-Study; 500 part-time jobs. Supporting data: FAF, IRS, state form, state income tax form required. Priority application deadline: 4/15.

Athletics Member NCAA (Division III). Intercollegiate sports: basketball M(III), W(III); cross-country running M(III), W(III); ice hockey M(II); soccer M(III), W(III); swimming and diving M(III), W(III); tennis M(III), W(III); track and field M(III), W(III); volleyball W(III). Intramural sports: badminton, baseball/softball, basketball, bowling, football, gymnastics, lacrosse, martial arts, racquetball, rugby, soccer, tennis, volleyball, water polo.

Majors Accounting B; anthropology B; art/fine arts B; art history B; behavioral sciences B; biochemistry B; biology/biological sciences B; biophysics B; biotechnology B; business administration/commerce/management B; business economics B; Canadian studies B; cell biology B; chemistry B; child care/child and family studies B; communication B; computer science B; criminal justice B; dietetics B; ecology/environmental studies B; economics B; education B; elementary education B; engineering sciences B; English B; environmental sciences B; family services B; food services management B; French B; geography B; geology B; health education B; history B; home economics B; home economics education B; human services B; interdisciplinary studies B; international business B; journalism B; Latin American studies B; liberal arts/general studies B; marketing/retailing/merchandising B; mathematics B; medical technology B; music B; natural resource management B; nursing B; nutrition B; philosophy B; physics B; political science/government B; psychology B; radio and television studies B; secondary education B; sociology B; Spanish B; special education B; speech pathology and audiology B; speech/rhetoric/public address/debate B; studio art B; theater arts/drama B. Majors with highest enrollment: business administration/commerce/management, education, nursing.

LD Program Information

Name of Program Special Services Project.

Availability of Services Began offering services in 1982. Services provided to freshmen, sophomores, juniors, seniors. Program currently serves 10 LD students: 4 freshmen, 1 sophomore, 4 juniors, 1 senior.

Staff 1 full-time, 8 part-time staff members, including director. Services provided by remediation specialists, tutors, counselors.

Admissions LD applicants evaluated on the basis of high school transcript and grade point average, standard or untimed SAT or ACT, letters of recommendation, psychoeducational report. LD students may begin taking classes in fall or spring. Application should be submitted 9 months in advance of initial anticipated enrollment.

Orientation Optional orientation offered during registration (optional program also offered during summer prior to enrollment).

Housing College housing (including coed) available. LD students housed randomly. LD freshmen and sophomores required to live on campus except if 21 or over, married, or living with relatives.

Diagnostic Testing Available in intelligence, reading, math, spelling, spoken language, written language, perceptual skills, work and study habits, personality, speech.

Tutoring Offered one-to-one and in small groups by professional teachers, peer tutors. Available in all subjects. LD students may receive tutoring in all courses each term.

Basic Skills Remediation Offered one-to-one and in small groups by regular teachers, Special Services skills specialists, peer teachers, LD counselor. Available in reading, math, written language, learning strategies, work and study habits, speech.

Academic Advisement Help with program planning provided by LD staff members, academic advisers. LD students may take up to 18 credits each semester; most take 12 to 15 credits; 12 credits required to maintain full-time status.

Special Courses Offered in reading, vocabulary development, composition, math, study skills. All offered for credit; some enter into overall grade point average.

Auxiliary Aids and Services Aids include taped textbooks, tape recorders, typewriters, word processors, Visual Tech machine. Services include alternative exam arrangements, notetakers, advocacy.

Counseling Services Individual counseling, career counseling available.

Contact Ms. Elizabeth Pasti, Director, Special Services Project, State University of New York College at Plattsburgh, College Center 110, Plattsburgh, NY 12901, 518-564-2810.

STATE UNIVERSITY OF NEW YORK COLLEGE AT POTSDAM

Potsdam, New York

Year Program Began	1984	Special Courses	✓
Special Fee	None	Taped Textbooks	✓
Special Orientation		Alternative Exam Arrangements	✓
Diagnostic Testing	✓	Notetakers	✓
Subject-Area Tutoring	✓	Staff	2 full-time, 1 part-time
Basic Skills Remediation	✓	Number of Students Served	5

General Information State-supported comprehensive coed institution. Part of State University of New York System. Founded 1816. Awards B, M. Institutionally accredited by regional association; programs accredited by NASM (music). Small-town setting; 240-acre campus. Total enrollment: 4,146. Faculty: 255 (243 full-time, 12 part-time); 66% have doctoral degrees; graduate assistants teach a few undergraduate courses. Calendar: semesters. Grading system: letters or numbers. Library holdings: 331,722 bound volumes, 332,720 titles on microform, 1,584 periodical subscriptions, 13,673 records/tapes.

Undergraduate Profile Fall 1984: 4,035 undergraduates (722 freshmen) from 22 states and territories and 4 foreign countries; 9% part-time; 97% state residents; 6% transfers; 80% financial aid recipients; 52% women; 1% blacks; 1% Native Americans; 1% Hispanics; 1% Asian Americans; 1% foreign nationals; 2% of undergraduates over 25 years of age; 7 legally handicapped students.

Expenses (1985–86) State resident tuition: $1350 full-time, $45 per credit hour part-time. Nonresident tuition: $3200 full-time, $107 per credit hour part-time. Mandatory fees: $115. College room and board: $2750. College room only: $1550.

Financial Aid Fall 1984 full-time freshmen: 78% applied for aid, 86% of those were judged to have need, 100% of those were aided; the average aided freshman received an aid package worth $3802 (35% scholarships/grants, 65% self-help) meeting 90% of need. College-administered aid for all 1984–85 undergraduates: need-based scholarships; 187 non-need scholarships (average $500); low-interest long-term loans from external sources (average $924); SEOG; College Work-Study; 600 part-time jobs. Supporting data: FAF required; IRS required for some. Priority application deadline: 3/1.

Athletics Member NCAA (Division III). Intercollegiate sports: basketball M(III), W(III); cross-country running M(c), W(c); field hockey W(III); ice hockey M(III), W; lacrosse M(III); rugby M(c), W(c); soccer M(III); swimming and diving M(III), W(III); tennis W(III); volleyball W(III); wrestling M(III). Intramural sports: badminton, basketball, equestrian sports, football, golf, martial arts, squash, tennis, volleyball, water polo, wrestling.

Majors Anthropology B; art history B; biochemistry B; biology/biological sciences B; biophysics B; chemistry B; computer science B; dance B; (pre)dentistry sequence B; early childhood education B; economics B; education B; elementary education B; English B; French B; geochemistry B; geography B; geology B; geophysics B; history B; labor and industrial relations B; (pre)law sequence B; mathematics B; (pre) medicine sequence B; music B; music education B; music history B; natural sciences B; painting/drawing B; philosophy B; photography B; physics B; piano/organ B; political science/government B; psychology B; sculpture B; secondary education B; sociology B; Spanish B; stringed instruments B; studio art B; theater arts/drama B; (pre)veterinary medicine sequence B; voice B; wind and percussion instruments B. Majors with highest enrollment: computer science, music education, psychology.

LD Program Information

Name of Program Special Services Program.

Availability of Services Began offering services in 1984. Services provided to freshmen, sophomores, juniors, seniors. Program currently serves 5 LD students: 4 juniors, 1 senior.

Staff 2 full-time, 1 part-time staff members, including director, coordinator. Services provided by remediation specialists, counselors.

Admissions LD applicants evaluated on the basis of high school transcript and grade point average, standard SAT, personal interview, letters of recommendation, psychoeducational report; letter describing support services student will need (from Special Services Program or other agency) required for some. LD students may begin taking classes in fall, spring, or summer. Application should be submitted 6 to 7 months in advance of initial anticipated enrollment.

Housing College housing (including coed) available. LD freshmen and sophomores required to live on campus.

Diagnostic Testing Available in intelligence, reading, math, spelling, handwriting, written language, motor abilities, perceptual skills.

Tutoring Offered one-to-one by professional teachers, peer tutors. Available in all subjects. LD students may receive tutoring in all courses each term.

Basic Skills Remediation Offered one-to-one by LD teachers, teacher trainees. Available in reading, spelling, written language, work and study habits.

Academic Advisement Help with program planning provided by LD staff members, academic advisers. LD students may take up to 18 credit hours each semester; most take 12 credit hours; 12 credit hours required to maintain full-time status.

Special Courses Offered in college survival skills, composition, study skills. Some offered for credit; some enter into overall grade point average.

Auxiliary Aids and Services Aids include taped textbooks, tape recorders, calculators, word processors, Kurzweil reading machine. Services include alternative exam arrangements, notetakers, advocacy, readers.

Counseling Services Individual counseling available.

Contact Ms. Barbara Dillman, Program Director, Special Services, State University of New York College at Potsdam, 135 Sisson Hall, Potsdam, NY 13676, 315-267-2347.

STEPHEN F AUSTIN STATE UNIVERSITY

Nacogdoches, Texas

Year Program Began	1983	Special Courses	
Special Fee	None	Taped Textbooks	
Special Orientation		Alternative Exam Arrangements	✓
Diagnostic Testing		Notetakers	✓
Subject-Area Tutoring	✓	Staff	1 part-time
Basic Skills Remediation	✓	Number of Students Served	3

General Information State-supported comprehensive coed institution. Founded 1923. Awards B, M, D. Institutionally accredited by regional association; programs accredited by AACSB (business), NASM (music), NLN (nursing), NCATE (teacher education). Small-town setting; 400-acre barrier-free campus. Total enrollment: 12,600. Faculty: 517 (470 full-time, 47 part-time); graduate assistants teach a few undergraduate courses. Calendar: semesters. Grading system: letters or numbers. Library holdings: 381,895 bound volumes, 303,818 titles on microform, 3,076 periodical subscriptions, 2,056 records/tapes.

Undergraduate Profile Fall 1984: 10,500 undergraduates (2,200 freshmen) from 36 states and territories and 28 foreign countries; 5% part-time; 97% state residents; 20% transfers; 33% financial aid recipients; 54% women; 4% blacks; 1% foreign nationals; 75 legally handicapped students.

Expenses (1985–86) State resident tuition: $360 full-time. Nonresident tuition: $3600 full-time. Part-time tuition and fees per semester (1 to 11 semester hours) range from $118.50 to $285.50 for state residents, $138.50 to $1473.50 for nonresidents. Mandatory fees: $370. College room and board: $2616.

Financial Aid Fall 1984 full-time freshmen: 29% applied for aid, 92% of those were judged to have need, 85% of those were aided; the average aided freshman received an aid package worth $1200 (61% scholarships/grants, 39% self-help) meeting 75% of need. College-administered aid for all 1984–85 undergraduates: need-based scholarships (average $500); non-need scholarships (average $400); short-term loans (average $400); low-interest long-term loans from external sources (average $800); SEOG; College Work-Study; 450 part-time jobs. Supporting data: FFS, institutional form, AFSA/SAR required. Priority application deadline: 4/1.

Athletics Member NCAA (Division II). Intercollegiate sports: baseball/softball M(II,s), W(II,s); basketball M(II,s), W(I,s); cross-country running M(II,s), W(II,s); football M(I-AA,s); golf M(II,s); rugby M(c), W(c); tennis M(II,s), W(II,s); track and field M(II,s), W(II,s); volleyball W(II,s). Intramural sports: baseball/softball, basketball, cross-country running, football, golf, gymnastics, rugby, soccer, swimming and diving, tennis, track and field, volleyball.

Majors Accounting B; agricultural business B; agricultural economics B; agricultural education B; agricultural sciences B; agronomy/soil and crop sciences B; animal sciences B; applied art B; art education B; art/fine arts B; biology/biological sciences B; botany/plant sciences B; broadcasting B; business administration/commerce/management B; business economics B; business education B; chemistry B; child care/child and family studies B; clinical psychology B; commercial art B; communication B; computer science B; criminal justice B; data processing B; deaf interpreter training B; early childhood education B; earth science B; ecology/environmental studies B; economics B; education B; elementary education B; English B; environmental sciences B; experimental psychology B; farm and ranch management B; fashion merchandising B; finance/banking B; food sciences B; forestry B; forest technology B; French B; geography B; geology B; German B; health education B; history B; home economics B; home economics education B; horticulture B; humanities B; interior design B; journalism B; (pre)law sequence B; marketing/retailing/merchandising B; mathematics B; medical technology B; music B; music education B; nursing B; nutrition B; philosophy B; physical education B; physics B; political science/government B; psychology B; public administration B; radio and television studies B; rehabilitation therapy B; secondary education B; secretarial studies/office management B; social work B; sociology B; Spanish B; special education B; speech pathology and audiology B; speech/rhetoric/public address/debate B; telecommunications B; theater arts/drama B. Majors with highest enrollment: business administration/commerce/management, education, communication.

LD Program Information

Name of Program Handicapped Student Services.

Availability of Services Began offering services in 1983. Services provided to freshmen, sophomores, juniors, seniors. Program currently serves 3 LD students: 1 freshman, 2 sophomores.

Staff 1 part-time staff member (coordinator). Services provided by tutors, readers.

Admissions LD applicants evaluated on the basis of high school transcript and grade point average, standard or untimed SAT or ACT, letters of recommendation, psychoeducational report; personal interview recommended. LD students may begin taking classes in fall, spring, or summer. Application should be submitted 4 months in advance of initial anticipated enrollment.

Housing College housing (including coed) available. LD students housed randomly. LD freshmen, sophomores, and juniors required to live on campus except if married or living with relatives, or by special permission.

Tutoring Offered one-to-one by professional teachers, peer tutors. Available in all subjects. LD students may receive tutoring in 4 courses per term.

Basic Skills Remediation Offered one-to-one by LD teachers, teacher trainees. Available in reading, math, written language, learning strategies, work and study habits.

Academic Advisement Help with program planning provided by academic advisers. LD students may take up to 12 semester hours each semester; 12 semester hours required to maintain full-time status.

Auxiliary Aids and Services Services include alternative exam arrangements, notetakers, readers.

Counseling Services Career counseling available.

Contact Dr. Dale E. Fish, Coordinator, Handicapped Student Services, Stephen F Austin State University, PO Box 13019, SFA Station, Nacogdoches, TX 75961, 409-569-2906.

STEPHENS COLLEGE
Columbia, Missouri

Year Program Began	1979	Special Courses	✓
Special Fee	Varies	Taped Textbooks	✓
Special Orientation		Alternative Exam Arrangements	✓
Diagnostic Testing		Notetakers	✓
Subject-Area Tutoring	✓	Staff	2 part-time
Basic Skills Remediation	✓	Number of Students Served	24

General Information Independent 4-year women's college. Founded 1833. Awards A (college transfer), B. Institutionally accredited by regional association; programs accredited by NASM (music). City setting; 325-acre campus. Total enrollment: 1,047. Faculty: 110 (85 full-time, 25 part-time); 50% have doctoral degrees. Calendar: semesters. Grading system: letters or numbers. Library holdings: 121,000 bound volumes, 475 periodical subscriptions, 4,000 records/tapes.

Undergraduate Profile Fall 1984: 1,047 undergraduates (330 freshmen) from 49 states and territories and 10 foreign countries; 7% part-time; 22% state residents; 7% transfers; 42% financial aid recipients; 100% women; 6% blacks; 1% Native Americans; 1% Hispanics; 0% Asian Americans; 2% foreign nationals; 1% of undergraduates over 25 years of age; 1 legally handicapped student.

Expenses (1985–86) Comprehensive fee of $10,200 includes full-time tuition ($7100) and college room and board ($3100). Part-time tuition: $525 per course.

Financial Aid Fall 1984 full-time freshmen: 41% applied for aid, 97% of those were judged to have need, 94% of those were aided; the average aided freshman received an aid package worth $5292 (57% scholarships/grants, 43% self-help) meeting 95% of need. College-administered aid for all 1984–85 undergraduates: 287 need-based scholarships (average $1808); 66 non-need scholarships (average $1982); low-interest long-term loans from college funds (average $1250), from external sources (average $1343); SEOG; College Work-Study; 500 part-time jobs. Supporting data: institutional form required; AFSA/SAR required for some; FFS, FAF acceptable. Priority application deadline: 3/15.

Athletics Member NCAA (Division II). Intercollegiate sports: golf (I); swimming and diving (III); tennis (II); volleyball (II).

Majors Animal sciences B; applied art B; art/fine arts B; biology/biological sciences B; broadcasting B; business administration/commerce/management B; chemistry B; child care/child and family studies B; child psychology/child development B; clinical psychology B; communication B; computer science B; creative writing B; dance B; (pre)dentistry sequence B; early childhood education B; education B; elementary education B; English B; equestrian studies B; fashion design and technology B; fashion merchandising B; French B; graphic arts B; history B; human development B; human ecology B; humanities B; interdisciplinary studies B; journalism B; (pre)law sequence B; liberal arts/general studies A, B; literature B; marketing/retailing/merchandising B; mathematics B; (pre)medicine sequence B; ministries B; modern languages B; music B; natural sciences B; painting/drawing B; philosophy B; physical education B; physical sciences B; piano/organ B; political science/government B; psychology B; radio and television studies B; religious studies B; Romance languages B; science B; social science B; Spanish B; studio art B; theater arts/drama B; (pre)veterinary medicine sequence B; voice B. Majors with highest enrollment: business administration/commerce/management, fashion design and technology, communication.

LD Program Information

Name of Program Not specified.

Availability of Services Began offering services in 1979. Services provided to freshmen, sophomores, juniors, seniors. Program currently serves 24 LD students: 10 freshmen, 7 sophomores, 4 juniors, 3 seniors.

Fees $5 to $25 per hour for some tutoring services.

Staff 2 part-time staff members, including coordinator. Services provided by librarian.

Admissions LD applicants evaluated on the basis of high school transcript and grade point average, untimed SAT or ACT, personal interview, letters of recommendation. LD students may begin taking classes in fall, winter, or summer. Application should be submitted at least 1 month in advance of initial anticipated enrollment.

Housing College housing available. LD students housed randomly. LD freshmen, sophomores, juniors, and seniors required to live on campus except by special permission after junior year.

Tutoring Offered one-to-one and in small groups by professional teachers, peer tutors. Available in all subjects. LD students may receive tutoring in all courses each term.

Basic Skills Remediation Offered in class-size groups by regular teachers. Available in math, written language, work and study habits. Local clinics provide one-to-one remediation for separate fee.

Academic Advisement Help with program planning provided by academic advisers. Most LD students take 4 courses each semester; 4 courses required to maintain full-time status (except by special permission).

Special Courses Offered in math, personal psychology, study skills. All offered for credit; most enter into overall grade point average.

Auxiliary Aids and Services Aids include taped textbooks, tape recorders. Services include alternative exam arrangements, notetakers, advocacy.

Counseling Services Individual counseling, career counseling available.

Contact Dr. Susan R. Komives, Dean of Student Life, Stephens College, Columbia, MO 65215, 314-876-7212.

SUSQUEHANNA UNIVERSITY

Selinsgrove, Pennsylvania

Year Program Began	*Not reported*	Special Courses	✓
Special Fee	None	Taped Textbooks	
Special Orientation		Alternative Exam Arrangements	✓
Diagnostic Testing	✓	Notetakers	
Subject-Area Tutoring	✓	Staff	2 part-time
Basic Skills Remediation		Number of Students Served	15

General Information 4-year coed college, affiliated with Lutheran Church in America. Founded 1858. Awards A (college transfer and terminal), B. Institutionally accredited by regional association; programs accredited by NASM (music). Small-town setting; 185-acre campus. Total enrollment: 1,456. Faculty: 130 (117 full-time, 13 part-time); 65% have doctoral degrees. Calendar: semesters. Grading system: letters or numbers and pass/fail (limited option). Library holdings: 130,000 bound volumes, 27,000 titles on microform, 1,120 periodical subscriptions, 5,600 records/tapes.

Undergraduate Profile Fall 1984: 1,456 undergraduates (422 freshmen) from 25 states and territories and 6 foreign countries; 1% part-time; 43% state residents; 6% transfers; 60% financial aid recipients; 46% women; 1% blacks; 1% Native Americans; 1% Hispanics; 1% Asian Americans; 1% foreign nationals; 4 legally handicapped students.

Expenses (1985–86) Comprehensive fee of $9970 includes full-time tuition ($6900), mandatory fees ($200), and college room and board ($2870). College room only: $1430. Part-time tuition: $864 per course.

Financial Aid Fall 1984 full-time freshmen: 57% applied for aid, 88% of those were judged to have need, 100% of those were aided; the average aided freshman received an aid package worth $6018 (53% scholarships/grants, 47% self-help) meeting 94% of need. College-administered aid for all 1984–85 undergraduates: 634 need-based scholarships (average $2302); 3 non-need scholarships (average $2000); low-interest long-term loans from college funds (average $1000), from external sources (average $1500); SEOG; College Work-Study. Supporting data: FAF, state form required for some; FFS, AFSA/SAR acceptable. Application deadline: continuous to 5/1.

Athletics Member NCAA (Division III). Intercollegiate sports: baseball/softball M(III), W(III); basketball M(III), W(III); cross-country running M(III); field hockey W(III); football M(III); golf M(III); soccer M(III); swimming and diving M(III), W(III); tennis M(III), W(III); track and field M(III), W(III); volleyball W(III); wrestling M(III). Intramural sports: baseball/softball, basketball, football, ice hockey, lacrosse, racquetball, rugby, skiing (cross-country), skiing (downhill), soccer, volleyball, wrestling.

Majors Accounting A, B; actuarial science B; anesthesiology B; anthropology B; biochemistry B; biology/biological sciences B; business administration/commerce/management A, B; business economics B; chemistry B; classics B; communication A, B; computer science B; cytotechnology A; dental services A; economics B; elementary education B; English B; European studies B; finance/banking B; French B; geology B; German B; Greek B; history B; human services A; Latin B; (pre)law sequence B; liberal arts/general studies A; literature B; marketing/retailing/merchandising B; mathematics B; medical technology A; (pre)medicine sequence B; modern languages B; music B; music education B; nursing A; occupational therapy A; philosophy B; physical therapy A; physics B; political science/government B; psychology B; radiological technology A; religious studies B; sacred music B; sociology B; Spanish B; theater arts/drama B; theology B; (pre)veterinary medicine sequence B. Majors with highest enrollment: business administration/commerce/management, accounting, psychology.

LD Program Information

Name of Program Academic Advancement Program.

Availability of Services Services provided to freshmen, sophomores, juniors, seniors. Program currently serves 15 LD students: 10 freshmen, 4 sophomores, 1 senior.

Staff 2 part-time staff members, including director. Services provided by tutors, counselor.

Admissions LD applicants evaluated on the basis of high school transcript and grade point average, standard or untimed SAT, personal interview, letters of recommendation. LD students may begin taking classes in fall, winter, spring, or summer. Application should be submitted 8 months in advance of initial anticipated enrollment.

Housing College housing (including coed) available. LD students housed randomly. LD freshmen, sophomores, juniors, and seniors required to live on campus except if living with relatives or by special permission.

Diagnostic Testing Available in intelligence, reading, math, spelling, work and study habits.

Tutoring Offered one-to-one by peer tutors. Available in some subjects. LD students may receive tutoring in all courses each term.

Academic Advisement Help with program planning provided by academic advisers. LD students may take up to 3 courses each term; most take 3 courses; 2 courses required to maintain full-time status.

Special Courses Offered in college survival skills, reading, math, study skills. None offered for credit; none enter into overall grade point average.

Auxiliary Aids and Services Services include alternative exam arrangements, advocacy.

Counseling Services Individual counseling available.

Contact Dr. Gary Fincke, Director of Academic Advancement Program and Academic Skills Center, Susquehanna University, Selinsgrove, PA 17870, 717-374-0101 Ext. 164.

SWEET BRIAR COLLEGE

Sweet Briar, Virginia

Year Program Began	1983	Special Courses	✓
Special Fee	None	Taped Textbooks	
Special Orientation		Alternative Exam Arrangements	✓
Diagnostic Testing		Notetakers	
Subject-Area Tutoring	✓	Staff	*Not reported*
Basic Skills Remediation		Number of Students Served	*Not reported*

General Information Independent 4-year women's college. Founded 1901. Awards B. Institutionally accredited by regional association. Rural setting; 3,300-acre barrier-free campus. Total enrollment: 732. Faculty: 87 (68 full-time, 19 part-time); 93% have doctoral degrees. Calendar: 4-1-4. Grading system: letters or numbers. Library holdings: 185,855 bound volumes, 4,800 titles on microform, 894 periodical subscriptions, 2,250 records/tapes.

Undergraduate Profile Fall 1984: 732 undergraduates (213 freshmen) from 41 states and territories and 18 foreign countries; 1% part-time; 18% state residents; 1% transfers; 67% financial aid recipients; 100% women; 4% blacks; 1% Native Americans; 1% Hispanics; 2% Asian Americans; 3% foreign nationals; no legally handicapped students.

Expenses (1985–86) Comprehensive fee of $11,360 includes full-time tuition ($8400), mandatory fees ($60), and college room and board ($2900). Part-time tuition: $884 per course.

Financial Aid Fall 1984 full-time freshmen: 42% applied for aid, 80% of those were judged to have need, 100% of those were aided; the average aided freshman received an aid package worth $6664 (70% scholarships/grants, 30% self-help) meeting 100% of need. College-administered aid for all 1984–85 undergraduates: 203 need-based scholarships (average $3400); 50 non-need scholarships (average $1470); low-interest long-term loans from college funds (average $1500), from external sources (average $2000); SEOG; College Work-Study; 187 part-time jobs. Supporting data: FAF, IRS, institutional form, AFSA/SAR required; state form required for some; FFS acceptable. Priority application deadline: 3/1.

Athletics Member NCAA (Division III). Intercollegiate sports: equestrian sports; field hockey (III); lacrosse (III); soccer (III); swimming and diving (III); tennis (III); volleyball (III). Intramural sports: archery, baseball/softball, basketball, cross-country running, equestrian sports, fencing, field hockey, golf, gymnastics, lacrosse, skiing (cross-country), skiing (downhill), soccer, swimming and diving, tennis, volleyball.

Majors American studies B; anthropology B; art history B; biology/biological sciences B; chemistry B; classics B; computer science B; creative writing B; dance B; ecology/environmental studies B; economics B; English B; European studies B; French B; German B; Greek B; Hispanic studies B; history B; international studies B; Italian B; Latin B; mathematics B; modern languages B; music B; philosophy B; physics B; political science/government B; psychology B; religious studies B; sociology B; Spanish B; studio art B; theater arts/drama B. Majors with highest enrollment: English, economics, mathematics.

LD Program Information

Name of Program Academic Resource Center.

Availability of Services Began offering services in 1983. Services provided to freshmen, sophomores, juniors, seniors.

Staff Includes director. Services provided by tutors.

Admissions LD applicants evaluated on the basis of high school transcript and grade point average, standard or untimed SAT or ACT, personal interview, autobiographical statement, letters of recommendation, psychoeducational report. LD students may begin taking classes in fall, winter, or spring. Application should be submitted 6 months in advance of initial anticipated enrollment.

Housing College housing available. LD students housed with other LD students and non-LD students. LD freshmen, sophomores, juniors, and seniors required to live on campus.

Tutoring Offered one-to-one by professional teachers, peer tutors. Available in all subjects. LD students may receive tutoring in all courses each term.

Academic Advisement Help with program planning provided by academic advisers. LD students may take up to 4 courses each semester; most take 4 courses; 3 courses required to maintain full-time status.

Special Courses Offered in college survival skills, reading, composition, study skills, career planning, word processing. None offered for credit; none enter into overall grade point average.

Auxiliary Aids and Services Aids include typewriters, word processors. Services include alternative exam arrangements.

Counseling Services Individual counseling, career counseling available.

Contact Ms. Mary B. Guthrow, Director, Academic Resource Center, Sweet Briar College, 201 Library, Sweet Briar, VA 24595, 804-381-5708.

SYRACUSE UNIVERSITY

Syracuse, New York

Year Program Began	*Not reported*	Special Courses	✓
Special Fee	None	Taped Textbooks	
Special Orientation		Alternative Exam Arrangements	✓
Diagnostic Testing	✓	Notetakers	✓
Subject-Area Tutoring	✓	Staff	1 full-time
Basic Skills Remediation		Number of Students Served	118

General Information Independent coed university. Founded 1870. Awards B, M, D. Institutionally accredited by regional association; programs accredited by NAAB (architecture), NASAD (art and design), AACSB (business), ABET (engineering and technology), FIDER (interior design), NASM (music), NLN (nursing), NCATE (teacher education). Metropolitan setting; 250-acre campus. Total enrollment: 21,288. Faculty: 1,233 (881 full-time, 352 part-time); 75% have doctoral degrees; graduate assistants teach a few undergraduate courses. Calendar: semesters. Grading system: letters or numbers. Library holdings: 2 million bound volumes, 2.1 million titles on microform, 10,000 periodical subscriptions.

Undergraduate Profile Fall 1984: 14,189 undergraduates (3,059 freshmen) from 38 states and territories and 60 foreign countries; 10% part-time; 53% state residents; 15% transfers; 60% financial aid recipients; 48% women; 10% blacks; 2% Native Americans; 2% Hispanics; 1% Asian Americans; 7% foreign nationals; 150 legally handicapped students.

Expenses (1985–86) Comprehensive fee of $11,700 includes full-time tuition ($7570), mandatory fees ($210), and college room and board ($3920). College room only: $2100. Part-time tuition: $144 per credit hour. Tuition guaranteed not to increase for student's term of enrollment.

Financial Aid Fall 1984 full-time freshmen: 60% applied for aid, 79% of those were judged to have need, 76% of those were aided; the average aided freshman received an aid package worth $8873 (43% scholarships/grants, 57% self-help) meeting 80% of need. College-administered aid for all 1984–85 undergraduates: need-based scholarships; non-need scholarships; short-term loans; low-interest long-term loans from external sources; SEOG; College Work-Study; part-time jobs. Supporting data: FAF required; IRS required for some. Application deadline: 1/31.

Athletics Member NCAA (Division I). Intercollegiate sports: basketball M(I,s), W(I,s); crew M(s), W(s); cross-country running M(I,s), W(I,s); field hockey W(I,s); football M(I-A,s); gymnastics M(I,s); lacrosse M(I,s); soccer M(I,s); swimming and diving M(I,s), W(I,s); tennis W(I,s); track and field M(I,s), W(I,s); volleyball W(I,s); wrestling M(I,s). Intramural sports: badminton, baseball/softball, basketball, bowling, cross-country running, fencing, football, golf, gymnastics, ice hockey, lacrosse, martial arts, racquetball, rugby, skiing (cross-country), skiing (downhill), soccer, squash, swimming and diving, tennis, track and field, volleyball, wrestling.

Majors Accounting B; adult and continuing education B; advertising B; aerospace engineering B; American studies B; anthropology B; applied art B; architecture B; art education B; art/fine arts B; art history B; biblical languages B; biochemistry B; bioengineering B; biology/biological sciences B; biomedical engineering B; biophysics B; black/Afro-American studies B; botany/plant sciences B; broadcasting B; business administration/commerce/management B; ceramic art and design B; chemical engineering B; chemistry B; child care/child and family studies B; child psychology/child development B; civil engineering B; classics B; commercial art B; communication B; community services B; comparative literature B; computer engineering B; computer information systems B; computer science B; conservation B; consumer services B; creative writing B; data processing B; (pre)dentistry sequence B; dietetics B; early childhood education B; East Asian studies B; East European and Soviet studies B; ecology/environmental studies B; economics B; education B; electrical engineering B; elementary education B; engineering (general) B; engineering management B; English B; environmental design B; environmental engineering B; environmental sciences B; family and consumer studies B; family services B; fashion design and technology B; film studies B; finance/banking B; food marketing B; food sciences B; forestry B; French B; geography B; geology B; German B; gerontology B; Greek B; Hebrew B; Hispanic studies B; historic preservation B; history B; home economics B; human development B; humanities B; human services B; illustration B; industrial design B; industrial engineering B; information science B; interdisciplinary studies B; interior design B; international studies B; Italian B; jewelry and metalsmithing B; journalism B; Judaic studies B; labor and industrial relations B; landscape architecture/design B; Latin B; Latin American studies B; (pre)law sequence B; liberal arts/general studies B; library science B; linguistics B; marketing/retailing/merchandising B; materials engineering B; mathematics B; mechanical engineering B; (pre)medicine sequence B; music B; music education B; natural sciences B; nursing B; nutrition B; painting/drawing B; peace studies B; philosophy B; photography B; physical education B; physics B; piano/organ B; political science/government B; psychology B; public relations B; radio and television studies B; real estate B; recreation and leisure services B; rehabilitation therapy B; religious studies B; retail management B; Romance languages B; Russian B; Russian and Slavic studies B; sculpture B; secondary education B; Slavic languages B; social work B; sociology B; Spanish B; special education B; speech pathology and audiology B; stringed instruments B; studio art B; telecommunications B; textile arts B; textiles and clothing B; theater arts/drama B; theology B; urban studies B; (pre)veterinary medicine sequence B; voice B.

LD Program Information

Name of Program Support Services/Academic Support Center.

Availability of Services Services provided to freshmen, sophomores, juniors, seniors. Program currently serves 118 LD students.

Staff 1 full-time staff member (LD specialist).

Admissions LD applicants evaluated on the basis of high school transcript and grade point average, standard or untimed SAT or ACT, personal interview, autobiographical statement, letters of recommendation, psychoeducational report. LD students may begin taking classes in fall only. Application should be submitted 8 to 10 months in advance of initial anticipated enrollment.

Housing College housing (including coed) available. LD students housed randomly. LD freshmen and sophomores required to live on campus.

Diagnostic Testing Available in intelligence, reading, math, spelling, handwriting, spoken language, written language, motor abilities, perceptual skills, work and study habits.

Tutoring Offered one-to-one by peer tutors. Available in some subjects. LD students may receive tutoring in all courses each term.

Academic Advisement Help with program planning provided by LD staff member, academic advisers. LD students may take up to 18 credit hours each semester; most take 12 to 14 credit hours; 12 credit hours required to maintain full-time status.

Special Courses Offered in college survival skills, reading, vocabulary development, study skills. All offered for credit; all enter into overall grade point average.

Auxiliary Aids and Services Services include alternative exam arrangements, notetakers, advocacy, scribes, student support group, proofreaders.

Counseling Services Individual counseling available.

Contact Mrs. Terry M. MacDonald, Diagnostician/LD Specialist, Syracuse University, 804 University Avenue, Syracuse, NY 13210, 315-423-4498.

TAYLOR UNIVERSITY

Upland, Indiana

Year Program Began	*Not reported*	Special Courses	✓
Special Fee	None	Taped Textbooks	✓
Special Orientation		Alternative Exam Arrangements	✓
Diagnostic Testing	✓	Notetakers	✓
Subject-Area Tutoring	✓	Staff	1 part-time
Basic Skills Remediation	✓	Number of Students Served	6

General Information Independent 4-year coed college. Founded 1846. Awards A (terminal), B. Institutionally accredited by regional association; programs accredited by NASM (music), NCATE (teacher education). Rural setting, with easy access to Indianapolis; 250-acre campus. Total enrollment: 1,473. Faculty: 105 (89 full-time, 16 part-time); 56% have doctoral degrees. Calendar: 4-1-4. Grading system: letters or numbers. Library holdings: 134,000 bound volumes, 8,000 titles on microform, 800 periodical subscriptions.

Undergraduate Profile Fall 1984: 1,473 undergraduates (425 freshmen) from 40 states and territories; 5% part-time; 38% state residents; 7% transfers; 70% financial aid recipients; 55% women; 1% blacks; 0% Native Americans; 1% foreign nationals; 2 legally handicapped students.

Expenses (1985–86) Comprehensive fee of $8115 includes full-time tuition ($5759), mandatory fees ($132), and college room and board ($2224). College room only: $1094. Part-time tuition per semester (1 to 11 credit hours) ranges from $167 to $2200.

Financial Aid Fall 1984 full-time freshmen: 68% applied for aid, 80% of those were judged to have need, 100% of those were aided; the average aided freshman received an aid package worth $5700 (57% scholarships/grants, 43% self-help) meeting 95% of need. College-administered aid for all 1984–85 undergraduates: 570 need-based scholarships (average $1490); non-need scholarships; short-term loans (average $60); low-interest long-term loans from college funds (average $800), from external sources (average $2200); 180 part-time jobs. Supporting data: FAF, institutional form required; IRS required for some; FFS acceptable. Priority application deadline: 4/1.

Athletics Member NAIA. Intercollegiate sports: baseball/softball M, W; basketball M, W; cross-country running M, W; football M; track and field M, W; volleyball W. Intramural sports: archery, badminton, baseball/softball, basketball, bowling, cross-country running, football, golf, racquetball, soccer, tennis, track and field, volleyball, weight lifting, wrestling.

Majors Accounting B; art education B; art/fine arts B; biblical languages B; biology/biological sciences B; business administration/commerce/management A, B; chemistry B; communication B; computer science B; (pre)dentistry sequence B; early childhood education A; economics B; education B; elementary education B; English B; French B; history B; (pre)law sequence B; mathematics B; medical technology B; (pre)medicine sequence B; modern languages B; music B; music education B; philosophy B; physical education B; physics B; political science/government B; psychology B; recreation and leisure services B; religious studies B; sacred music B; science education B; secondary education B; social science B; social work B; sociology B; Spanish B; speech/rhetoric/public address/debate B; systems science A; theater arts/drama B; theology B; (pre)veterinary medicine sequence B. Majors with highest enrollment: business administration/commerce/management, education, religious studies.

LD Program Information

Name of Program Learning Skills Center.

Availability of Services Services provided to freshmen, sophomores, juniors, seniors. Program currently serves 6 LD students: 2 freshmen, 2 sophomores, 1 junior, 1 senior.

Staff 1 part-time staff member (director).

Admissions LD applicants evaluated on the basis of high school transcript and grade point average, untimed SAT or ACT, personal interview, autobiographical statement, letters of recommendation. LD students may begin taking classes in fall or summer. Application should be submitted 3 months in advance of initial anticipated enrollment.

Housing College housing available. LD students housed randomly. LD freshmen, sophomores, juniors, and seniors required to live on campus except if married or living with relatives, or by special permission.

Diagnostic Testing Available in intelligence, reading, math, spelling, written language, work and study habits, personality.

Tutoring Offered one-to-one by peer tutors. Available in all subjects. LD students may receive tutoring in all courses each term.

Basic Skills Remediation Offered one-to-one and in small groups by regular teachers. Available in reading, math, spelling, handwriting, written language, learning strategies, work and study habits.

Academic Advisement Help with program planning provided by academic advisers. Most LD students take 16 credit hours each semester; 12 credit hours required to maintain full-time status.

Special Courses Offered in college survival skills, reading, vocabulary development, communication skills, composition, language development, math, study skills, career planning. Most offered for credit; most enter into overall grade point average.

Auxiliary Aids and Services Aids include taped textbooks, word processors. Services include alternative exam arrangements, notetakers, readers.

Counseling Services Individual counseling, small-group counseling, career counseling available.

Contact Mr. Wynn Lembright, Dean of Admissions, Taylor University, Upland, IN 46989, 317-998-2751 Ext. 206.

TEXAS A&M UNIVERSITY

College Station, Texas

Year Program Began	1982	Special Courses	
Special Fee	None	Taped Textbooks	✓
Special Orientation		Alternative Exam Arrangements	✓
Diagnostic Testing		Notetakers	
Subject-Area Tutoring	✓	Staff	1 full-time
Basic Skills Remediation		Number of Students Served	27

General Information State-supported coed university. Part of Texas A&M University System. Founded 1876. Awards B, M, D. Institutionally accredited by regional association; programs accredited by AACSB (business), ABET (engineering and technology), NCATE (teacher education). City setting; 5,142-acre campus. Total enrollment: 36,827. Faculty: 2,218; 68% have doctoral degrees; graduate assistants teach a few undergraduate courses. Calendar: semesters. Grading system: letters or numbers. Library holdings: 1.5 million bound volumes, 2.3 million titles on microform, 16,000 periodical subscriptions, 372 records/tapes.

Undergraduate Profile Fall 1984: 30,077 undergraduates (5,333 freshmen) from 52 states and territories and 100 foreign countries; 7% part-time; 84% state residents; 7% transfers; 30% financial aid recipients; 40% women; 2% blacks; 1% Native Americans; 5% Hispanics; 2% Asian Americans; 2% foreign nationals; 3% of undergraduates over 25 years of age; 235 legally handicapped students.

Expenses (1985–86) State resident tuition: $120 full-time. Nonresident tuition: $1380 full-time. Part-time tuition and fees per semester (1 to 12 semester hours) range from $78.60 to $209.50 for state residents, $74.60 to $711.50 for nonresidents. Mandatory fees: $360. College room and board: $3380. College room only: $2000.

Financial Aid Fall 1984 full-time freshmen: 31% applied for aid, 70% of those were judged to have need, 83% of those were aided; the average aided freshman received an aid package worth $2400 (22% scholarships/grants, 78% self-help) meeting 95% of need. College-administered aid for all 1984–85 undergraduates: 874 need-based scholarships (average $600); 2,042 non-need scholarships (average $961); short-term loans (average $415); low-interest long-term loans from external sources (average $1035); SEOG; College Work-Study; 6,055 part-time jobs. Supporting data: FAF, IRS, AFSA/SAR required; Financial Aid Transcript (for transfers) required for some. Priority application deadline: 4/15.

Athletics Member NCAA (Division I). Intercollegiate sports: baseball/softball M(I,s), W(I,s); basketball M(I,s), W(I,s); cross-country running M(I,s), W(I,s); football M(I-A,s); golf M(I,s), W(I,s); riflery M(I), W(I); soccer W(I); swimming and diving M(I,s), W(I,s); tennis M(I,s), W(I,s); track and field M(I,s), W(I,s); volleyball W(I,s). Intramural sports: archery, badminton, baseball/softball, basketball, bowling, cross-country running, equestrian sports, fencing, field hockey, football, golf, gymnastics, ice hockey, lacrosse, martial arts, racquetball, rugby, sailing, soccer, swimming and diving, tennis, track and field, volleyball, water polo, weight lifting, wrestling.

Majors Accounting B; aerospace engineering B; agricultural economics B; agricultural education B; agricultural engineering B; agronomy/soil and crop sciences B; animal sciences B; anthropology B; applied mathematics B; biochemistry B; bioengineering B; biology/biological sciences B; biomedical sciences B; botany/plant sciences B; business administration/commerce/management B; chemical engineering B; chemistry B; civil engineering B; computer science B; construction management B; construction technologies B; dairy sciences B; economics B; education B; electrical engineering B; engineering technology B; English B; entomology B; environmental design B; finance/banking B; food sciences B; forestry B; geography B; geology B; geophysics B; health education B; history B; horticulture B; industrial arts B; industrial engineering B; journalism B; landscape architecture/design B; marketing/retailing/merchandising B; mathematics B; mechanical engineering B; meteorology B; microbiology B; mining and mineral engineering B; modern languages B; nuclear engineering B; nutrition B; ocean engineering B; ornamental horticulture B; parks management B; petroleum/natural gas engineering B; philosophy B; physical education B; physics B; political science/government B; poultry sciences B; psychology B; range management B; sociology B; theater arts/drama B; vocational education B; wildlife management B; zoology B. Majors with highest enrollment: electrical engineering, education, computer science.

LD Program Information

Name of Program Handicapped and Veterans Services.

Availability of Services Began offering services in 1982. Services provided to freshmen, sophomores, juniors, seniors. Program currently serves 27 LD students: 5 freshmen, 10 sophomores, 10 juniors, 2 seniors.

Staff 1 full-time staff member (coordinator). Services provided by remediation specialists, counselors, diagnostic specialists.

Admissions LD applicants evaluated on the basis of high school transcript and grade point average, standard or untimed SAT, 2 Achievement Tests, English Composition Test (modified). LD students may begin taking classes in fall, spring, or summer. Application should be submitted at least 2 months in advance of initial anticipated enrollment.

Housing College housing available. LD students housed randomly. LD students not required to live on campus.

Tutoring Offered one-to-one by professional teachers, peer tutors. Available in all subjects. LD students may receive tutoring in all courses each term.

Academic Advisement Help with program planning provided by LD staff members, academic advisers. LD students may take up to 16 semester hours each semester; most take 9 to 12 semester hours; 12 semester hours required to maintain full-time status (except by special permission).

Auxiliary Aids and Services Aids include taped textbooks, tape recorders, typewriters, word processors. Services include alternative exam arrangements, advocacy.

Counseling Services Individual counseling, rap sessions, career counseling available.

Contact Mr. Charles W. Powell, Coordinator, Handicapped and Veterans Services, Texas A&M University, College Station, TX 77843, 409-845-1638.

THIEL COLLEGE
Greenville, Pennsylvania

Year Program Began	*Not reported*	Special Courses	✓
Special Fee	None	Taped Textbooks	✓
Special Orientation	✓	Alternative Exam Arrangements	✓
Diagnostic Testing	✓	Notetakers	✓
Subject-Area Tutoring	✓	Staff	2 part-time
Basic Skills Remediation	✓	Number of Students Served	12

General Information 4-year coed college, affiliated with Lutheran Church in America. Founded 1866. Awards A (college transfer), B. Institutionally accredited by regional association. Small-town setting, with easy access to Cleveland; 135-acre campus. Total enrollment: 809. Faculty: 83 (57 full-time, 26 part-time); 45% have doctoral degrees. Calendar: semesters. Grading system: letters or numbers. Library holdings: 117,000 bound volumes, 840 periodical subscriptions.

Undergraduate Profile Fall 1984: 809 undergraduates (335 freshmen); 4% part-time; 75% state residents; 10% transfers; 85% financial aid recipients; 51% women; 3% blacks; 0% Native Americans; 0% Hispanics; 1% foreign nationals; 20 legally handicapped students.

Expenses (1985–86) Comprehensive fee of $9090 includes full-time tuition ($6058), mandatory fees ($100), and college room and board ($2932). Part-time tuition: $176 per semester hour.

Financial Aid Fall 1984 full-time freshmen: 96% applied for aid, 90% of those were judged to have need, 100% of those were aided; the average aided freshman received an aid package meeting 95% of need. College-administered aid for all 1984–85 undergraduates: need-based scholarships; non-need scholarships; low-interest long-term loans; College Work-Study; part-time jobs. Supporting data: FAF, AFSA/SAR required. Priority application deadline: 5/1.

Athletics Member NCAA (Division III). Intercollegiate sports: baseball/softball M(III), W(III); basketball M(III), W(III); cross-country running M(III), W(III); football M(III); golf M(III); tennis M(III), W(III); track and field M(III), W(III); volleyball W(III); wrestling M(III). Intramural sports: baseball/softball, basketball, football, golf, soccer, tennis, volleyball.

Majors Accounting B; actuarial science B; art/fine arts B; biology/biological sciences B; business administration/commerce/management B; chemistry B; computer science A, B; cytotechnology B; (pre)dentistry sequence B; economics B; education B; elementary education B; (pre)engineering sequence A; English B; environmental education B; environmental sciences B; French B; geology B; history B; (pre)law sequence B; liberal arts/general studies A, B; mathematics B; medical technology B; (pre)medicine sequence B; nursing B; philosophy B; physics B; political science/government B; psychology B; religious studies B; science B; science education B; secondary education B; sociology B; Spanish B; speech therapy B; (pre)veterinary medicine sequence B. Majors with highest enrollment: business administration/commerce/management, accounting, biology/biological sciences.

LD Program Information

Name of Program Learning Skills Center.

Availability of Services Services provided to freshmen, sophomores, juniors, seniors. Program currently serves 12 LD students: 4 freshmen, 3 sophomores, 3 juniors, 2 seniors.

Staff 2 part-time staff members, including director. Services provided by remediation specialist.

Admissions LD applicants evaluated on the basis of high school transcript and grade point average, untimed SAT or ACT, personal interview, letters of recommendation, psychoeducational report. LD students may begin taking classes in summer only. Application should be submitted 6 months in advance of initial anticipated enrollment.

Orientation Optional orientation offered before registration.

Housing College housing available. LD students housed randomly. LD freshmen, sophomores, juniors, and seniors required to live on campus.

Diagnostic Testing Available in reading, math, written language, work and study habits, speech.

Tutoring Offered one-to-one by professional teachers, peer tutors. Available in all subjects. LD students may receive tutoring in all courses each term.

Basic Skills Remediation Offered one-to-one and in small groups by regular teachers. Available in reading, math, spelling, written language, learning strategies, work and study habits.

Academic Advisement Help with program planning provided by academic advisers. LD students may take up to 15 semester hours each semester; most take 12 semester hours; 12 semester hours required to maintain full-time status.

Special Courses Offered in college survival skills, reading, communication skills, composition, math. Most offered for credit; most enter into overall grade point average.

Auxiliary Aids and Services Aids include taped textbooks, calculators, typewriters, word processors. Services include alternative exam arrangements, notetakers.

Counseling Services Individual counseling, career counseling available.

Contact Mrs. K. June Dale, Director, Learning Skills Center, Thiel College, Greenville, PA 16125, 412-588-7700 Ext. 459.

THOMAS MORE COLLEGE
Crestview Hills, Kentucky

Year Program Began	1978	Special Courses	✓
Special Fee	None	Taped Textbooks	
Special Orientation	✓	Alternative Exam Arrangements	✓
Diagnostic Testing	✓	Notetakers	✓
Subject-Area Tutoring	✓	Staff	4 full-time, 2 part-time
Basic Skills Remediation	✓	Number of Students Served	48

General Information Roman Catholic 4-year coed college. Founded 1921. Awards A (college transfer), B. Institutionally accredited by regional association; programs accredited by NLN (nursing). Small-town setting, with easy access to Cincinnati; 320-acre barrier-free campus. Total enrollment: 1,319. Faculty: 117 (54 full-time, 63 part-time); 48% have doctoral degrees. Calendar: semesters. Grading system: letters or numbers. Library holdings: 80,000 bound volumes, 654 periodical subscriptions, 1,599 records/tapes.

Undergraduate Profile Fall 1984: 1,319 undergraduates (165 freshmen) from 10 states and territories and 13 foreign countries; 42% part-time; 98% state residents; 3% transfers; 68% financial aid recipients; 56% women; 0% Native Americans; 1% Asian Americans; 1% foreign nationals; 33% of undergraduates over 25 years of age; 7 legally handicapped students.

Expenses (1985–86) Comprehensive fee of $7530 includes full-time tuition ($4470), mandatory fees ($310), and college room and board ($2750). Part-time tuition and fees per credit: $134 for the first 6 credits, $146 for the next 5 credits.

Financial Aid Fall 1984 full-time freshmen: 83% applied for aid, 83% of those were judged to have need, 100% of those were aided; the average aided freshman received an aid package worth $2750 (40% scholarships/grants, 60% self-help) meeting 70% of need. College-administered aid for all 1984–85 undergraduates: need-based scholarships; 85 non-need scholarships (average $750); low-interest long-term loans from external sources (average $1975); SEOG; College Work-Study; 10 part-time jobs. Supporting data: institutional form required; IRS required for some; FFS, FAF, AFSA/SAR acceptable. Priority application deadline: 3/15.

Athletics Member NAIA. Intercollegiate sports: baseball/softball M(s), W(s); basketball M(s), W(s); tennis M(s); volleyball W(s). Intramural sports: baseball/softball, basketball, football, golf, soccer, tennis, volleyball.

Majors Accounting A, B; art education B; art/fine arts A, B; biology/biological sciences B; business administration/commerce/management A, B; chemical engineering technology A; chemistry A, B; computer programming A, B; computer science A, B; criminal justice A, B; data processing A, B; economics A, B; education B; elementary education B; (pre)engineering sequence A; English A, B; finance/banking A, B; history A, B; law enforcement/police sciences B; (pre)law sequence B; liberal arts/general studies B; mathematics A, B; medical technology B; (pre) medicine sequence B; nursing B; philosophy A, B; physics B; political science/government A; psychology A, B; religious studies B; secondary education B; social work B; sociology A, B; theater arts/drama A, B; theology B. Majors with highest enrollment: business administration/commerce/management, data processing, nursing.

LD Program Information

Name of Program Special Services Program.

Availability of Services Began offering services in 1978. Services provided to freshmen, sophomores, juniors, seniors. Program currently serves 48 LD students: 12 freshmen, 12 sophomores, 12 juniors, 12 seniors.

Staff 4 full-time, 2 part-time staff members, including director. Services provided by remediation specialist, tutors, counselor, diagnostic specialist, instructors.

Admissions LD applicants evaluated on the basis of high school transcript and grade point average, standard SAT or ACT, personal interview, autobiographical statement, letters of recommendation, psychoeducational report. LD students may begin taking classes in fall or winter. Application should be submitted 5 to 8 months in advance of initial anticipated enrollment.

Orientation Optional orientation offered during registration.

Housing College housing (including coed) available. LD students housed with other LD students and non-LD students. LD freshmen and sophomores required to live on campus except if 21 or over.

Diagnostic Testing Available in intelligence, reading, math, spelling, handwriting, written language, perceptual skills, work and study habits, personality.

Tutoring Offered one-to-one and in small groups by professional teachers, peer tutors, computer-assisted instruction. Available in all subjects. LD students may receive tutoring in all courses each term.

Basic Skills Remediation Offered one-to-one and in small groups by LD teachers, regular teachers. Available in reading, math, spelling, handwriting, spoken language, written language, learning strategies, work and study habits, social skills.

Academic Advisement Help with program planning provided by LD staff members, academic advisers. Most LD students take 12 credits each semester; 12 credits required to maintain full-time status.

Special Courses Offered in college survival skills, reading, vocabulary development, communication skills, composition, language development, math, personal psychology, study skills, career planning. All offered for credit; all enter into overall grade point average.

Auxiliary Aids and Services Aids include tape recorders, calculators, typewriters, computers. Services include alternative exam arrangements, notetakers, advocacy.

Counseling Services Individual counseling, small-group counseling, rap sessions, career counseling available.

Contact Darryl Mitchell, Director of Special Services, Thomas More College, Crestview Hills, KY 41017, 606-344-3303.

TOWSON STATE UNIVERSITY

Towson, Maryland

Year Program Began	1976	Special Courses	✓
Special Fee	None	Taped Textbooks	✓
Special Orientation	✓	Alternative Exam Arrangements	✓
Diagnostic Testing	✓	Notetakers	✓
Subject-Area Tutoring	✓	Staff	*Not reported*
Basic Skills Remediation	✓	Number of Students Served	37

General Information State-supported comprehensive coed institution. Part of Maryland State Colleges and Universities System. Founded 1866. Awards B, M. Institutionally accredited by regional association; programs accredited by NASM (music), NLN (nursing), NCATE (teacher education). City setting, with easy access to Baltimore and Washington, DC; 326-acre barrier-free campus. Total enrollment: 15,106. Faculty: 866 (474 full-time, 392 part-time); 62% have doctoral degrees; graduate assistants teach a few undergraduate courses. Calendar: 4-1-4. Grading system: letters or numbers. Library holdings: 453,000 bound volumes, 500,000 titles on microform, 2,400 periodical subscriptions, 8,100 records/tapes.

Undergraduate Profile Fall 1984: 13,912 undergraduates (1,778 freshmen) from 26 states and territories and 40 foreign countries; 33% part-time; 95% state residents; 4% transfers; 36% financial aid recipients; 57% women; 12% blacks; 0% Native Americans; 1% Hispanics; 1% Asian Americans; 1% foreign nationals; 24% of undergraduates over 25 years of age; 120 legally handicapped students.

Expenses (1985–86) State resident tuition: $1166 full-time, $49 per credit part-time. Nonresident tuition: $2422 full-time, $49 per credit part-time. Mandatory fees: $343. College room and board: $3433. College room only: $2090.

Financial Aid Fall 1984 full-time freshmen: 95% applied for aid, 84% of those were judged to have need, 77% of those were aided; the average aided freshman received an aid package worth $2173 (43% scholarships/grants, 57% self-help) meeting 100% of need. College-administered aid for all 1984–85 undergraduates: 588 need-based scholarships (average $647); 300 non-need scholarships (average $750); short-term loans (average $100); low-interest long-term loans from external sources (average $1293); SEOG; College Work-Study; 1,050 part-time jobs. Supporting data: FAF, institutional form, AFSA/SAR required; IRS, state form required for some; FFS acceptable. Priority application deadline: 3/15.

Athletics Member NCAA (Division I). Intercollegiate sports: baseball/softball M(I,s), W(I,s); basketball M(I,s), W(I,s); cross-country running M(I), W(I); field hockey W(I,s); football M(II,s); golf M(I); gymnastics M(I), W(I,s); lacrosse M(I,s), W(I,s); soccer M(I,s); swimming and diving M(I,s), W(I); tennis M(I,s), W(I); track and field M(I), W(I); volleyball W(I,s). Intramural sports: archery, badminton, baseball/softball, basketball, bowling, cross-country running, football, ice hockey, racquetball, rugby, soccer, squash, swimming and diving, tennis, track and field, volleyball, wrestling.

Majors Accounting B; actuarial science B; American studies B; anatomy B; anthropology B; applied mathematics B; art education B; art/fine arts B; art history B; Asian/Oriental studies B; biology/biological sciences B; black/Afro-American studies B; botany/plant sciences B; business administration/commerce/management B; business education B; ceramic art and design B; chemistry B; clinical psychology B; communication B; computer science B; corrections B; creative writing B; dance B; (pre)dentistry sequence B; early childhood education B; earth science B; ecology/environmental studies B; economics B; education B; educational media B; elementary education B; English B; environmental sciences B; ethnic studies B; finance/banking B; French B; geography B; geology B; German B; gerontology B; health education B; health science B; health services administration B; history B; human resources B; international business B; international studies B; jazz B; jewelry and metalsmithing B; Latin American studies B; law enforcement/police sciences B; liberal arts/general studies B; library science B; marketing/retailing/merchandising B; mathematics B; medical technology B; (pre)medicine sequence B; medieval studies B; microbiology B; music B; music education B; music history B; natural sciences B; nursing B; occupational therapy B; painting/drawing B; philosophy B; photography B; physical education B; physics B; physiology B; piano/organ B; political science/government B; printing technologies B; psychology B; reading education B; religious studies B; science B; science education B; sculpture B; secondary education B; social science B; sociology B; Spanish B; speech pathology and audiology B; speech/rhetoric/public address/debate B; sports administration B; stringed instruments B; studio art B; technical writing B; textile arts B; theater arts/drama B; voice B; wind and percussion instruments B; women's studies B; zoology B. Majors with highest enrollment: business administration/commerce/management, communication, accounting.

LD Program Information

Name of Program Office of Special Needs.

Availability of Services Began offering services in 1976. Services provided to freshmen, sophomores, juniors, seniors. Program currently serves 37 LD students.

Staff Includes director. Services provided by remediation specialists, tutors, counselors.

Admissions LD applicants evaluated on the basis of high school transcript and grade point average, standard or untimed SAT. LD students may begin taking classes in fall or spring. Application should be submitted 6 to 12 months in advance of initial anticipated enrollment.

Orientation Optional orientation offered before registration.

Housing College housing (including coed) available. LD students housed with other LD students and non-LD students. LD students not required to live on campus.

Diagnostic Testing Available in reading, math, written language.

Tutoring Offered one-to-one and in small groups by peer tutors. Available in all subjects. LD students may receive tutoring in all courses each term.

Basic Skills Remediation Offered in small groups by regular teachers. Available in reading, math, spoken language, written language, learning strategies, work and study habits, speech.

Academic Advisement Help with program planning provided by LD staff members, academic advisers. LD students may take up to 18 credits each semester; 12 credits required to maintain full-time status.

Special Courses Offered in college survival skills, reading, communication skills, composition, language development, math, personal psychology, study skills, career planning. Some offered for credit; some enter into overall grade point average.

Auxiliary Aids and Services Aids include taped textbooks, tape recorders, calculators. Services include alternative exam arrangements, notetakers, readers, priority registration.

Counseling Services Individual counseling, small-group counseling, career counseling available.

Contact Ms. Margaret Warrington, Director, Office of Special Needs, Towson State University, Towson, MD 21204, 301-321-2633.

TRINITY COLLEGE
Hartford, Connecticut

Year Program Began	1976	Special Courses	
Special Fee	None	Taped Textbooks	✓
Special Orientation		Alternative Exam Arrangements	✓
Diagnostic Testing	✓	Notetakers	✓
Subject-Area Tutoring	✓	Staff	1 part-time
Basic Skills Remediation	✓	Number of Students Served	1

General Information Independent comprehensive coed institution. Founded 1823. Awards B, M. Institutionally accredited by regional association. Metropolitan setting; 90-acre barrier-free campus. Total enrollment: 2,082. Faculty: 158 (128 full-time, 30 part-time); 90% have doctoral degrees; graduate assistants teach no undergraduate courses. Calendar: semesters. Grading system: letters or numbers. Library holdings: 706,581 bound volumes, 1,873 periodical subscriptions, 13,000 records/tapes.

Undergraduate Profile Fall 1984: 1,886 undergraduates (516 freshmen); 6% part-time; 30% state residents; 2% transfers; 32% financial aid recipients; 50% women; 3% blacks; 1% Native Americans; 3% Hispanics; 3% Asian Americans; 1% foreign nationals; 6% of undergraduates over 25 years of age; 3 legally handicapped students.

Expenses (1985–86) Comprehensive fee of $13,220 includes full-time tuition ($9370), mandatory fees ($500), and college room and board ($3350). College room only: $1820. Part-time tuition: $1041 per course.

Financial Aid Fall 1984 full-time freshmen: 48% applied for aid, 82% of those were judged to have need, 98% of those were aided; the average aided freshman received an aid package worth $6952 (61% scholarships/grants, 39% self-help) meeting 100% of need. College-administered aid for all 1984–85 undergraduates: 588 need-based scholarships (average $5000); 3 non-need scholarships (average $8600); short-term loans (average $100); low-interest long-term loans from college funds (average $1250), from external sources (average $2200); SEOG; College Work-Study; 150 part-time jobs. Supporting data: FAF, IRS, institutional form, AFSA/SAR required; state form required for some; FFS acceptable. Application deadline: 2/1.

Athletics Member NCAA (Division III), NAIA. Intercollegiate sports: baseball/softball M(III), W(III); basketball M(III), W(III); crew M, W; cross-country running M(III), W(III); fencing M(c), W(c); field hockey W; football M(III); golf M(III); ice hockey M(III); lacrosse M(III), W(III); rugby M(c), W(c); skiing (downhill) M(c), W(c); soccer M(III), W(III); squash M, W; swimming and diving M(III), W(III); tennis M(III), W(III); track and field M(III), W(III); volleyball W(c); water polo M(c), W(c); wrestling M(III). Intramural sports: baseball/softball, basketball, football, martial arts, squash, swimming and diving, tennis, water polo, weight lifting.

Majors American studies B; art/fine arts B; art history B; biochemistry B; biology/biological sciences B; biomedical engineering B; chemistry B; classics B; comparative literature B; computer science B; dance B; ecology/environmental studies B; economics B; education B; engineering (general) B; English B; French B; German B; graphic arts B; Greek B; history B; Italian B; Latin B; mathematics B; music B; philosophy B; physics B; political science/government B; psychology B; religious studies B; Russian and Slavic studies B; sociology B; Spanish B; studio art B; theater arts/drama B; urban studies B. Majors with highest enrollment: history, economics.

LD Program Information

Name of Program Handicapped Services.

Availability of Services Began offering services in 1976. Services provided to freshmen, sophomores, juniors, seniors. Program currently serves 1 LD junior.

Staff 1 part-time staff member (director). Services provided by tutors.

Admissions LD applicants evaluated on the basis of high school transcript and grade point average, standard or untimed SAT or ACT, personal interview, letters of recommendation; psychoeducational report recommended. LD students may begin taking classes in fall only. Application should be submitted 9 months in advance of initial anticipated enrollment.

Housing College housing (including coed) available. LD students housed randomly. LD students not required to live on campus.

Diagnostic Testing Available in intelligence, personality, various other areas as appropriate.

Tutoring Offered one-to-one by peer tutors. Available in all subjects. LD students may receive tutoring in all courses each term.

Basic Skills Remediation Offered one-to-one and in small groups by LD teachers, regular teachers, teacher trainees. Available in reading, math, spelling, handwriting, various other areas as appropriate.

Academic Advisement Help with program planning provided by LD staff member, academic advisers. LD students may take up to 4 courses each semester; most take 3 to 4 courses; 4 courses required to maintain full-time status (or less by special permission).

Auxiliary Aids and Services Aids include taped textbooks, tape recorders, calculators, typewriters. Services include alternative exam arrangements, notetakers, readers.

Counseling Services Individual counseling, career counseling available.

Contact Dr. David Winer, Dean of Students and Director of Handicapped Services, Trinity College, Hartford, CT 06106, 203-527-3151.

TRI-STATE UNIVERSITY
Angola, Indiana

Year Program Began	*Not reported*	Special Courses	✓
Special Fee	None	Taped Textbooks	
Special Orientation		Alternative Exam Arrangements	✓
Diagnostic Testing	✓	Notetakers	✓
Subject-Area Tutoring	✓	Staff	1 part-time
Basic Skills Remediation	✓	Number of Students Served	*Not reported*

General Information Independent 4-year coed college. Founded 1884. Awards A (college transfer and terminal), B. Institutionally accredited by regional association; programs accredited by AACSB (business), ABET (engineering and technology). Small-town setting; 300-acre campus. Total enrollment: 973. Faculty: 76 (73 full-time, 3 part-time); 44% have doctoral degrees. Calendar: quarters. Grading system: letters or numbers. Library holdings: 116,000 bound volumes, 178 titles on microform, 846 periodical subscriptions, 628 records/tapes.

Undergraduate Profile Fall 1984: 973 undergraduates (271 freshmen) from 29 states and territories and 31 foreign countries; 10% part-time; 41% state residents; 39% transfers; 76% financial aid recipients; 19% women; 3% blacks; 0% Native Americans; 1% Hispanics; 2% Asian Americans; 16% foreign nationals; 6 legally handicapped students.

Expenses (1985–86) Comprehensive fee of $7569 includes full-time tuition ($4944), mandatory fees ($225), and college room and board ($2400). Part-time tuition: $103 per credit hour.

Financial Aid Fall 1984 full-time freshmen: 81% applied for aid, 67% of those were judged to have need, 97% of those were aided; the average aided freshman received an aid package worth $4458 (42% scholarships/grants, 58% self-help) meeting 76% of need. College-administered aid for all 1984–85 undergraduates: 350 need-based scholarships (average $625); 175 non-need scholarships (average $1000); low-interest long-term loans from college funds (average $800), from external sources (average $1000); SEOG; College Work-Study; 50 part-time jobs. Supporting data: FAF, IRS, institutional form required; AFSA/SAR required for some; FFS acceptable. Priority application deadline: 3/1.

Athletics Member NCAA (Division III), NAIA. Intercollegiate sports: baseball/softball M(III); basketball M(III), W(III); cross-country running M(III); fencing M(III), W(III); golf M(III); tennis M(III); track and field M(III); volleyball W(III). Intramural sports: baseball/softball, basketball, football, golf, gymnastics, martial arts, riflery, skiing (cross-country), skiing (downhill), soccer, swimming and diving, tennis, track and field, volleyball.

Majors Accounting A, B; aerospace engineering B; business administration/commerce/management B; business education B; chemical engineering B; chemistry B; civil engineering B; communication B; computer information systems B; computer programming A; computer science B; computer technologies A; criminal justice A, B; data processing A; drafting and design A; economics B; education B; electrical engineering B; elementary education B; engineering management B; English A, B; history B; industrial engineering technology A; manufacturing technology A; marketing/retailing/merchandising B; mathematics B; mechanical engineering B; (pre)medicine sequence B; physical education B; physical sciences B; political science/government B; science education B; secondary education B; secretarial studies/office management A; social science B; transportation technologies B; (pre) veterinary medicine sequence B. Majors with highest enrollment: electrical engineering, mechanical engineering, computer science.

LD Program Information

Name of Program Handicapped Services.

Availability of Services Services provided to freshmen, sophomores, juniors, seniors.

Staff 1 part-time staff member (coordinator).

Admissions LD applicants evaluated on the basis of high school transcript and grade point average, standard or untimed SAT or ACT. LD students may begin taking classes in fall, winter, spring, or summer. Application should be submitted 1 month in advance of initial anticipated enrollment.

Housing College housing available. LD students housed randomly. LD freshmen required to live on campus except if living with relatives.

Diagnostic Testing Available in math, written language.

Tutoring Offered one-to-one by peer tutors. Available in all subjects. LD students may receive tutoring in all courses each term.

Basic Skills Remediation Offered in small groups by regular teachers. Available in math.

Academic Advisement Help with program planning provided by academic advisers. LD students may take up to 17 credit hours each quarter; most take 12 credit hours; 12 credit hours required to maintain full-time status.

Special Courses Offered in math. None offered for credit; none enter into overall grade point average.

Auxiliary Aids and Services Services include alternative exam arrangements, notetakers.

Counseling Services Individual counseling, career counseling available.

Contact Ms. Susan Stroh, Assistant Dean of Students/Coordinator of Handicapped Services, Tri-State University, Angola, IN 46703, 219-665-3141.

TUSCULUM COLLEGE
Greeneville, Tennessee

Year Program Began	1981	Special Courses	✓
Special Fee	None	Taped Textbooks	
Special Orientation	✓	Alternative Exam Arrangements	✓
Diagnostic Testing	✓	Notetakers	
Subject-Area Tutoring	✓	Staff	5 part-time
Basic Skills Remediation	✓	Number of Students Served	5

General Information Presbyterian 4-year coed college. Founded 1794. Awards B. Institutionally accredited by regional association. Small-town setting; 140-acre campus. Total enrollment: 394. Faculty: 29 (26 full-time, 3 part-time); 45% have doctoral degrees. Calendar: semesters. Grading system: letters or numbers. Library holdings: 61,000 bound volumes, 8,000 titles on microform, 800 periodical subscriptions, 1,400 records/tapes.

Undergraduate Profile Fall 1984: 394 undergraduates (116 freshmen) from 20 states and territories and 6 foreign countries; 8% part-time; 59% state residents; 21% transfers; 82% financial aid recipients; 50% women; 11% blacks; 0% Native Americans; 0% Hispanics; 0% Asian Americans; 2% foreign nationals; 15% of undergraduates over 25 years of age; no legally handicapped students.

Expenses (1985–86) Comprehensive fee of $6600 includes full-time tuition ($3850), mandatory fees ($160), and college room and board ($2590). College room only: $1100. Part-time tuition: $160 per credit hour.

Financial Aid Fall 1984 full-time freshmen: 100% applied for aid, 88% of those were judged to have need, 100% of those were aided; the average aided freshman received an aid package worth $5600 (69% scholarships/grants, 31% self-help) meeting 90% of need. College-administered aid for all 1984–85 undergraduates: 272 need-based scholarships (average $4000); 120 non-need scholarships (average $2000); low-interest long-term loans from external sources (average $1000); SEOG; College Work-Study. Supporting data: FAF, IRS, AFSA/SAR required; FFS acceptable. Application deadline: continuous.

Athletics Member NAIA. Intercollegiate sports: baseball/softball M(s), W(s); basketball M(s), W(s); golf M, W; soccer M(s); tennis M, W; volleyball W(s). Intramural sports: baseball/softball, basketball, football, soccer, volleyball.

Majors Art/fine arts B; biology/biological sciences B; business administration/commerce/management B; communication B; computer science B; early childhood education B; elementary education B; English B; information science B; medical technology B; music B; physical education B; psychology B; secondary education B; social work B; special education B. Majors with highest enrollment: business administration/commerce/management, special education, physical education.

LD Program Information

Name of Program Developmental Studies.

Availability of Services Began offering services in 1981. Services provided to freshmen, sophomores, juniors, seniors. Program currently serves 5 LD students: 2 freshmen, 2 sophomores, 1 junior.

Staff 5 part-time staff members. Services provided by remediation specialists, counselor, diagnostic specialist.

Admissions LD applicants evaluated on the basis of high school transcript and grade point average, standard SAT or ACT, personal interview, letters of recommendation. LD students may begin taking classes in fall only. Application should be submitted 3 months in advance of initial anticipated enrollment.

Orientation Required orientation held during registration.

Housing College housing available. LD students housed with other LD students and non-LD students. LD freshmen, sophomores, and juniors required to live on campus except if married or living with relatives.

Diagnostic Testing Available in reading, math, spelling, handwriting, spoken language, written language, perceptual skills, work and study habits.

Tutoring Offered one-to-one and in small groups by professional teachers, peer tutors. Available in all subjects. LD students may receive tutoring in all courses each term.

Basic Skills Remediation Offered one-to-one and in small groups by regular teachers. Available in reading, math, spelling, handwriting, spoken language, written language, learning strategies, perceptual skills, work and study habits.

Academic Advisement Help with program planning provided by LD staff members, academic advisers. LD students may take up to 15 credit hours each semester; most take 14 credit hours; 12 credit hours required to maintain full-time status.

Special Courses Offered in college survival skills, study skills, career planning. Some offered for credit; some enter into overall grade point average.

Auxiliary Aids and Services Aids include tape recorders, calculators, typewriters, word processors. Services include alternative exam arrangements, advocacy.

Counseling Services Individual counseling, small-group counseling, rap sessions, career counseling available.

Contact Mr. William D. Smith, Assistant Professor of Special Education, Tusculum College, PO Box 5078, Greeneville, TN 37743, 615-638-1111 Ext. 293.

UNITY COLLEGE

Unity, Maine

Year Program Began	1978	Special Courses	✓
Special Fee	None	Taped Textbooks	
Special Orientation	✓	Alternative Exam Arrangements	✓
Diagnostic Testing	✓	Notetakers	
Subject-Area Tutoring	✓	Staff	1 full-time, 5 part-time
Basic Skills Remediation	✓	Number of Students Served	28

General Information Independent 4-year coed college. Founded 1965. Awards A (college transfer and terminal), B. Institutionally accredited by regional association. Rural setting; 185-acre campus. Total enrollment: 274. Faculty: 32 (22 full-time, 10 part-time); 50% have doctoral degrees. Calendar: 4-1-4. Grading system: letters or numbers. Library holdings: 40,000 bound volumes, 440 titles on microform, 400 periodical subscriptions, 534 records/tapes.

Undergraduate Profile Fall 1984: 274 undergraduates (123 freshmen); 3% part-time; 18% state residents; 10% transfers; 80% financial aid recipients; 30% women; 1% blacks; 0% Native Americans; 1% Hispanics; 0% Asian Americans; 1% foreign nationals; 4% of undergraduates over 25 years of age; 1 legally handicapped student.

Expenses (1985–86) Comprehensive fee of $8448 includes full-time tuition ($5175), mandatory fees ($300), and college room and board ($2973). College room only: $1373. Part-time tuition: $166 per semester hour. Tuition guaranteed not to increase for student's term of enrollment.

Financial Aid Fall 1984 full-time freshmen: 81% applied for aid, 91% of those were judged to have need, 100% of those were aided; the average aided freshman received an aid package worth $5799 (44% scholarships/grants, 56% self-help) meeting 90% of need. College-administered aid for all 1984–85 undergraduates: 272 need-based scholarships (average $800); 80 non-need scholarships (average $1000); low-interest long-term loans from external sources (average $2100); SEOG; College Work-Study; 1 part-time job. Supporting data: FAF, IRS, state form, institutional form, AFSA/SAR required; FFS acceptable. Priority application deadline: 6/1.

Athletics Member NAIA. Intercollegiate sports: basketball M(s); cross-country running M, W; soccer M(s), W(s); volleyball W(s). Intramural sports: baseball/softball, basketball, cross-country running, football, ice hockey, lacrosse, skiing (cross-country), skiing (downhill), tennis, volleyball, weight lifting.

Majors Conservation B; ecology/environmental studies A, B; environmental sciences B; fish and game management B; forestry B; forest technology A; land use management and reclamation B; liberal arts/general studies A; natural resource management B; parks management B; recreation and leisure services B; wildlife biology B; wildlife management B. Majors with highest enrollment: wildlife biology, forestry, recreation and leisure services.

LD Program Information

Name of Program Learning Resource Center.

Availability of Services Began offering services in 1978. Services provided to freshmen, sophomores, juniors, seniors. Program currently serves 28 LD students: 16 freshmen, 8 sophomores, 4 juniors.

Staff 1 full-time, 5 part-time staff members, including director. Services provided by remediation specialists, tutors, counselor, LD specialist.

Admissions LD applicants evaluated on the basis of high school transcript and grade point average, personal interview, letters of recommendation, psychoeducational report; untimed SAT or ACT recommended. LD students may begin taking classes in fall, spring, or summer. Application should be submitted 4 months in advance of initial anticipated enrollment.

Orientation Orientation (required for some) held before registration.

Housing College housing (including coed) available. LD students housed randomly. LD freshmen and sophomores required to live on campus except if 21 or over.

Diagnostic Testing Available in reading, math, written language, work and study habits.

Tutoring Offered one-to-one and in small groups by professional teachers, peer tutors. Available in all subjects. LD students may receive tutoring in all courses each term.

Basic Skills Remediation Offered one-to-one and in small groups by LD teachers, regular teachers. Available in reading, math, spelling, written language, work and study habits.

Academic Advisement Help with program planning provided by LD staff members, academic advisers. LD students may take up to 16 semester hours each semester; most take 12 semester hours; 12 semester hours required to maintain full-time status.

Special Courses Offered in college survival skills, reading, composition, math, study skills, career planning. Some offered for credit; some enter into overall grade point average.

Auxiliary Aids and Services Aids include tape recorders, calculators, typewriters. Services include alternative exam arrangements, advocacy.

Counseling Services Individual counseling, small-group counseling, rap sessions, career counseling available.

Contact Mr. James J. Horan, Director, Learning Resource Center, Unity College, Quaker Hill Road, Unity, ME 04988, 207-948-3131.

UNIVERSITY OF ALABAMA

University, Alabama

Year Program Began	1981	Special Courses	✓
Special Fee	Varies	Taped Textbooks	✓
Special Orientation		Alternative Exam Arrangements	✓
Diagnostic Testing		Notetakers	✓
Subject-Area Tutoring	✓	Staff	1 part-time
Basic Skills Remediation		Number of Students Served	9

General Information State-supported coed university. Part of University of Alabama System. Founded 1831. Awards B, M, D. Institutionally accredited by regional association; programs accredited by AACSB (business), ABET (engineering and technology), NASM (music), NLN (nursing), NCATE (teacher education); candidate for program accreditation by FIDER (interior design). City setting, with easy access to Birmingham; 900-acre campus. Total enrollment: 15,145. Faculty: 919 (802 full-time, 117 part-time); graduate assistants teach a few undergraduate courses. Calendar: semesters. Grading system: letters or numbers. Library holdings: 1.5 million bound volumes, 13,000 periodical subscriptions, 13,380 records/tapes.

Undergraduate Profile Fall 1984: 12,528 undergraduates (2,126 freshmen); 6% part-time; 76% state residents; 8% transfers; 35% financial aid recipients; 48% women; 10% blacks; 1% foreign nationals; 116 legally handicapped students.

Expenses (1984–85) State resident tuition: $1206 full-time. Nonresident tuition: $2587 full-time. Part-time tuition and fees per semester (1 to 11 semester hours) range from $155.50 to $630.50 for state residents, $213.50 to $1268.50 for nonresidents. College room and board: $2400. College room only: $1100.

Financial Aid Fall 1984 full-time freshmen: 59% applied for aid, 84% of those were judged to have need, 95% of those were aided; the average aided freshman received an aid package worth $3930 (61% scholarships/grants, 39% self-help) meeting 96% of need. College-administered aid for all 1984–85 undergraduates: need-based scholarships (average $500); non-need scholarships (average $800); low-interest long-term loans from external sources (average $600); 1,100 part-time jobs. Supporting data: FFS, institutional form, AFSA/SAR required; IRS acceptable. Application deadline: continuous to 3/1.

Athletics Member NCAA (Division I). Intercollegiate sports: baseball/softball M(I,s); basketball M(I,s), W(I,s); cross-country running M(I,s), W(I,s); football M(I-A,s); golf M(I,s), W(I,s); gymnastics W(I,s); swimming and diving M(I,s), W(I,s); tennis M(I,s), W(I,s); track and field M(I,s), W(I). Intramural sports: baseball/softball, basketball, football, golf, rugby, soccer, swimming and diving, tennis, track and field, volleyball.

Majors Accounting B; advertising B; aerospace engineering B; American studies B; anthropology B; archaeology B; art education B; art/fine arts B; art history B; biochemistry B; biology/biological sciences B; broadcasting B; business administration/commerce/management B; business education B; chemical engineering B; chemistry B; child care/child and family studies B; civil engineering B; civil engineering technology B; communication B; computer science B; creative writing B; criminal justice B; dance B; (pre)dentistry sequence B; dietetics B; early childhood education B; economics B; education B; electrical engineering B; electrical engineering technology B; elementary education B; engineering (general) B; engineering technology B; English B; environmental engineering B; fashion design and technology B; film studies B; finance/banking B; food sciences B; food services management B; French B; geography B; geology B; German B; health education B; health services administration B; history B; home economics B; human resources B; industrial engineering B; insurance B; interior design B; international economics B; international studies B; journalism B; Latin American studies B; (pre)law sequence B; library science B; literature B; marine biology B; marine sciences B; marketing/retailing/merchandising B; mathematics B; mechanical engineering B; (pre)medicine sequence B; metallurgical engineering B; microbiology B; mining and mineral engineering B; music B; music education B; nursing B; nutrition B; petroleum/natural gas engineering B; philosophy B; physical education B; physics B; piano/organ B; political science/government B; psychology B; public administration B; public relations B; real estate B; recreation and leisure services B; religious studies B; Romance languages B; secondary education B; secretarial studies/office management B; social work B; sociology B; Spanish B; special education B; speech pathology and audiology B; speech/rhetoric/public address/debate B; statistics B; textiles and clothing B; theater arts/drama B; transportation technologies B; urban studies B. Majors with highest enrollment: accounting, marketing/retailing/merchandising, nursing.

LD Program Information

Name of Program Disabled Student Office.

Availability of Services Began offering services in 1981. Services provided to freshmen, sophomores, juniors, seniors. Program currently serves 9 LD students.

Fees $5 to $8 per hour for tutoring.

Staff 1 part-time staff member (director).

Admissions LD applicants evaluated on the basis of high school transcript and grade point average, standard SAT or ACT; personal interview, autobiographical statement, letters of recommendation, psychoeducational report recommended. LD students may begin taking classes in fall, spring, or summer. Application should be submitted at least 2 months in advance of initial anticipated enrollment.

Housing College housing available. LD students housed randomly. LD students not required to live on campus.

Tutoring Offered one-to-one and in small groups by professional teachers, peer tutors, graduate students. Available in some subjects. LD students may receive tutoring in all courses each term (depending on individual need).

Academic Advisement Help with program planning provided by academic advisers. LD students required to take 12 semester hours each semester to maintain full-time status.

Special Courses Offered in college survival skills, reading, vocabulary development, communication skills, composition, language development, study skills. All offered for credit; all enter into overall grade point average.

Auxiliary Aids and Services Aids include taped textbooks, tape recorders. Services include alternative exam arrangements, notetakers, advocacy.

Counseling Services Individual counseling, career counseling available.

Contact Mr. Tom Tumlin, Director of Disabled Student Office, University of Alabama, PO Box 9347, University, AL 35486, 205-348-5306.

UNIVERSITY OF ARIZONA

Tucson, Arizona

Year Program Began	1981	Special Courses	✓
Special Fee	$500 to $850 per year	Taped Textbooks	✓
Special Orientation	✓	Alternative Exam Arrangements	✓
Diagnostic Testing	✓	Notetakers	✓
Subject-Area Tutoring	✓	Staff	3 full-time, 2 part-time
Basic Skills Remediation		Number of Students Served	223

General Information State-supported coed university. Founded 1885. Awards B, M, D. Institutionally accredited by regional association; programs accredited by NAAB (architecture), AACSB (business), ABET (engineering and technology), NASM (music), NLN (nursing), ACPE (pharmacy), NCATE (teacher education). Metropolitan setting; 325-acre barrier-free campus. Total enrollment: 30,306. Faculty: 1,652 (1,390 full-time, 262 part-time); 83% have doctoral degrees; graduate assistants teach about a quarter of the undergraduate courses. Calendar: semesters. Grading system: letters or numbers. Library holdings: 1.6 million bound volumes, 2.1 million titles on microform, 39,982 periodical subscriptions, 132,318 records/tapes.

Undergraduate Profile Fall 1984: 20,712 undergraduates (3,746 freshmen) from 57 states and territories and 111 foreign countries; 19% part-time; 79% state residents; 42% transfers; 61% financial aid recipients; 48% women; 2% blacks; 1% Native Americans; 9% Hispanics; 2% Asian Americans; 5% foreign nationals; 33% of undergraduates over 25 years of age; 625 legally handicapped students.

Expenses (1985–86) State resident tuition: $0 full-time, $53 per semester hour part-time. Nonresident tuition: $2844 full-time. All students taking 6 or more credits are charged the full-time mandatory fee. Nonresident part-time tuition per semester (1 to 11 semester hours) ranges from $53 to $1804. Mandatory fees: $990. College room and board: $2400. College room only: $800.

Financial Aid Fall 1984 full-time freshmen: 98% applied for aid, 80% of those were judged to have need, 92% of those were aided; the average aided freshman received an aid package worth $1527 (54% scholarships/grants, 46% self-help) meeting 80% of need. College-administered aid for all 1984–85 undergraduates: 9,200 need-based scholarships (average $800); 1,200 non-need scholarships (average $800); short-term loans (average $200); low-interest long-term loans from college funds (average $1000), from external sources (average $2500); SEOG; College Work-Study; 1,000 part-time jobs. Supporting data: FFS required; FAF acceptable. Priority application deadline: 5/1.

Athletics Member NCAA (Division I). Intercollegiate sports: baseball/softball M(I,s), W(I,s); basketball M(I,s), W(I,s); cross-country running M(I,s), W(I,s); football M(I-A,s); golf M(I,s), W(I,s); gymnastics W(I,s); swimming and diving M(I,s), W(I,s); tennis M(I,s), W(I,s); track and field M(I,s), W(I,s); volleyball W(I,s). Intramural sports: badminton, baseball/softball, basketball, bowling, cross-country running, football, golf, racquetball, soccer, swimming and diving, tennis, track and field, volleyball, water polo, wrestling.

Majors Accounting B; aerospace engineering B; agricultural economics B; agricultural education B; agricultural engineering B; agricultural technologies B; agronomy/soil and crop sciences B; animal sciences B; anthropology B; architecture B; art education B; art/fine arts B; art history B; Asian/Oriental studies B; astronomy B; atmospheric sciences B; biochemistry B; biology/biological sciences B; botany/plant sciences B; business administration/commerce/management B; business economics B; business education B; cell biology B; chemical engineering B; chemistry B; child care/child and family studies B; city, community, and regional planning B; civil engineering B; classics B; communication B; computer engineering B; computer information systems B; consumer services B; creative writing B; criminal justice B; dance B; early childhood education B; earth science B; ecology/environmental studies B; economics B; education B; electrical engineering B; elementary education B; energy management technologies B; engineering physics B; English B; entomology B; evolutionary biology B; family and consumer studies B; farm and ranch management B; fashion merchandising B; finance/banking B; fish and game management B; food sciences B; food services management B; French B; geography B; geological engineering B; geology B; German B; Greek B; health education B; health services administration B; history B; home economics B; home economics education B; horticulture B; human resources B; human services B; industrial engineering B; interior design B; Italian B; jazz B; journalism B; landscape architecture/design B; Latin B; Latin American studies B; liberal arts/general studies B; linguistics B; management information systems B; marketing/retailing/merchandising B; mathematics B; mechanical engineering B; medical technology B; metallurgical engineering B; Mexican-American/Chicano studies B; microbiology B; mining and mineral engineering B; music B; music education B; music history B; natural resource management B; nuclear engineering B; nursing B; nutrition B; occupational safety and health B; parks management B; pharmacy/pharmaceutical sciences B; philosophy B; physical education B; physics B; piano/organ B; political science/government B; Portuguese B; psychology B; public administration B; radio and television studies B; range management B; real estate B; recreation and leisure services B; rehabilitation therapy B; religious studies B; Romance languages B; Russian B; secondary education B; social science B; sociology B; Spanish B; speech pathology and audiology B; speech/rhetoric/public address/debate B; stringed instruments B; studio art B; systems engineering B; textiles and clothing B; theater arts/drama B; (pre)veterinary medicine sequence B; veterinary sciences B; voice B; water resources B; wildlife management B; wind and percussion instruments B; women's studies B. Majors with highest enrollment: business administration/commerce/management, electrical engineering, accounting.

LD Program Information

Name of Program Special Academic Learning Techniques (SALT).

Availability of Services Began offering services in 1981. Services provided to freshmen, sophomores, juniors, seniors. Program currently serves 223 LD students: 65 freshmen, 78 sophomores, 65 juniors, 15 seniors.

Fees Range from $500 to $850 per year according to level of services required.

Staff 3 full-time, 2 part-time staff members, including coordinator. Services provided by tutors, LD language specialist, directors of Writing Lab and Math/Science Lab, tutoring coordinator.

Admissions LD applicants evaluated on the basis of high school transcript and grade point average, untimed SAT or ACT, personal interview, autobiographical statement, letters of recommendation, psychoeducational report. LD students may begin taking classes in fall or spring. Application should be submitted 6 to 12 months in advance of initial anticipated enrollment.

Orientation Required orientation held during registration.

Housing College housing (including coed) available. LD students housed randomly. LD students not required to live on campus.

Diagnostic Testing Available in reading, math, spelling, spoken language, written language, perceptual skills, work and study habits, personality, social skills, career instruments.

Tutoring Offered in small groups by professional teachers, peer tutors. Available in most subjects. LD students may receive tutoring in all courses each term (depending on level of courses and availability of tutors).

Academic Advisement Help with program planning provided by LD staff members, academic advisers. LD students may take up to 18 semester hours each semester; most take 12 semester hours; 12 semester hours required to maintain full-time status.

Special Courses Offered in college survival skills, reading, vocabulary development, communication skills, composition, math, study skills, career planning. None offered for credit; none enter into overall grade point average.

Auxiliary Aids and Services Aids include taped textbooks. Services include alternative exam arrangements, notetakers, advocacy.

Counseling Services Individual counseling, small-group counseling, rap sessions, career counseling available.

Contact Mrs. Eleanor V. Harner, Coordinator, SALT Program, University of Arizona, Student Resource Center, Tucson, AZ 85721, 602-621-1171.

UNIVERSITY OF CALIFORNIA, BERKELEY

Berkeley, California

Year Program Began	1980	Special Courses	✓
Special Fee	None	Taped Textbooks	✓
Special Orientation		Alternative Exam Arrangements	✓
Diagnostic Testing	✓	Notetakers	✓
Subject-Area Tutoring	✓	Staff	1 full-time
Basic Skills Remediation		Number of Students Served	45

General Information State-supported coed university. Part of University of California System. Founded 1868. Awards B, M, D. Institutionally accredited by regional association; programs accredited by AACSB (business), ABET (engineering and technology), COE (optometry). City setting, with easy access to San Francisco; 1,200-acre barrier-free campus. Total enrollment: 30,008. Faculty: 3,800; 94% have doctoral degrees; graduate assistants teach a few undergraduate courses. Calendar: semesters. Grading system: letters or numbers. Library holdings: 6.3 million bound volumes, 2.7 million titles on microform, 101,584 periodical subscriptions, 44,000 records/tapes.

Undergraduate Profile Fall 1984: 21,907 undergraduates (4,630 freshmen) from 53 states and territories and 100 foreign countries; 90% state residents; 27% transfers; 40% financial aid recipients; 45% women; 4% blacks; 1% Native Americans; 5% Hispanics; 24% Asian Americans; 2% foreign nationals; 8% of undergraduates over 25 years of age; 236 legally handicapped students.

Expenses (1985–86) State resident tuition: $0 full-time. Nonresident tuition: $3816 full-time. Mandatory fees: $1346. College room and board: $3685.

Financial Aid Fall 1984 full-time freshmen: the average aided freshman received an aid package meeting 100% of need. College-administered aid for all 1984–85 undergraduates: need-based scholarships; non-need scholarships; short-term loans; low-interest long-term loans from external sources; College Work-Study; part-time jobs. Supporting data: FAF, IRS, state form, institutional form, AFSA/SAR required. Priority application deadline: 2/1.

Athletics Member NCAA (Division I). Intercollegiate sports: baseball/softball M(I,s), W(I,s); basketball M(I,s), W(I,s); crew M, W; cross-country running M(I,s), W(I); fencing M(c), W(c); field hockey W(I); football M(I-A,s); golf M(I,s), W(I); gymnastics M(I,s), W(I); lacrosse M(c); racquetball M(c), W(c); rugby M(c); skiing (downhill) M(c), W(c); soccer M(I), W(I); squash M(c), W(c); swimming and diving M(I,s), W(I,s); tennis M(I,s), W(I); track and field M(I,s), W(I,s); volleyball M(I), W(I); water polo M(I,s), W(c). Intramural sports: archery, badminton, baseball/softball, basketball, bowling, martial arts, sailing, weight lifting.

Majors Accounting B; aerospace sciences B; anatomy B; anthropology B; applied mathematics B; Arabic B; architectural engineering B; architecture B; art/fine arts B; art history B; Asian/Oriental studies B; astronomy B; biochemistry B; bioengineering B; biology/biological sciences B; biophysics B; black/Afro-American studies B; botany/plant sciences B; business administration/commerce/management B; cell biology B; chemical engineering B; chemistry B; Chinese B; civil engineering B; classics B; communication B; computer engineering B; computer science B; conservation B; dance B; data processing B; dietetics B; East Asian studies B; ecology/environmental studies B; economics B; education B; electrical engineering B; engineering physics B; English B; entomology B; environmental design B; environmental engineering B; ethnic studies B; evolutionary biology B; film studies B; forestry B; forest technology B; French B; genetics B; geography B; geology B; German B; Greek B; Hebrew B; history B; history of science B; humanities B; industrial engineering B; Italian B; Japanese B; landscape architecture/design B; Latin B; Latin American studies B; legal studies B; library science B; linguistics B; literature B; marine biology B; materials sciences B; mathematics B; mechanical engineering B; metallurgical engineering B; Mexican-American/Chicano studies B; mining and mineral engineering B; molecular biology B; music B; Native American studies B; natural resource management B; naval architecture B; Near and Middle Eastern studies B; neurosciences B; nuclear engineering B; nutrition B; optometry B; paleontology B; peace studies B; petroleum/natural gas engineering B; philosophy B; physical education B; physics B; physiology B; political science/government B; Portuguese B; psychology B; religious studies B; Scandinavian languages/studies B; Slavic languages B; social science B; sociology B; Southeast Asian studies B; Spanish B; speech/rhetoric/public address/debate B; statistics B; theater arts/drama B; urban studies B; women's studies B; wood sciences B; zoology B. Majors with highest enrollment: political science/government, architecture, English.

LD Program Information

Name of Program Learning Disabilities Services.

Availability of Services Began offering services in 1980. Services provided to freshmen, sophomores, juniors, seniors. Program currently serves 45 LD students.

Staff 1 full-time staff member (coordinator). Services provided by tutors.

Admissions LD applicants evaluated on the basis of high school transcript and grade point average, standard or untimed SAT or ACT, personal interview, autobiographical statement, psychoeducational report, 3 Achievement Tests (untimed), English Composition Test. LD students may begin taking classes in fall, spring, or summer. Application should be submitted 6 to 12 months in advance of initial anticipated enrollment.

Housing College housing (including coed) available. LD students housed with other LD students and non-LD students. LD students not required to live on campus.

Diagnostic Testing Available in intelligence, reading, math, spelling, handwriting, written language, perceptual skills.

Tutoring Offered one-to-one and in small groups by peer tutors. Available in all subjects. LD students may receive tutoring in all courses each term.

Academic Advisement Help with program planning provided by LD staff member, academic advisers. Most LD students take 12 to 15 credits each semester; 12 credits required to maintain full-time status (except by special permission).

Special Courses Offered in communication skills, study skills. Some offered for credit; some enter into overall grade point average.

Auxiliary Aids and Services Aids include taped textbooks, tape recorders, calculators. Services include alternative exam arrangements, notetakers, advocacy, secretarial services.

Counseling Services Individual counseling available.

Contact Ms. M. Kay Runyan-Brown, Coordinator of Learning Disabilities Services, University of California, Berkeley, 2515 Channing Way, Berkeley, CA 94720, 415-642-0518.

UNIVERSITY OF CALIFORNIA, IRVINE

Irvine, California

Year Program Began	1978	Special Courses	✓
Special Fee	None	Taped Textbooks	✓
Special Orientation	✓	Alternative Exam Arrangements	✓
Diagnostic Testing		Notetakers	✓
Subject-Area Tutoring	✓	Staff	5 part-time
Basic Skills Remediation		Number of Students Served	9

General Information State-supported coed university. Part of University of California System. Founded 1960. Awards B, M, D. Institutionally accredited by regional association; programs accredited by ABET (engineering and technology). City setting, with easy access to Los Angeles; 1,510-acre barrier-free campus. Total enrollment: 12,684. Faculty: 805 (642 full-time, 163 part-time); 99% have doctoral degrees; graduate assistants teach a few undergraduate courses. Calendar: quarters. Grading system: letters or numbers. Library holdings: 1.1 million bound volumes, 1.3 million titles on microform, 15,264 periodical subscriptions, 7,690 records/tapes.

Undergraduate Profile Fall 1984: 10,211 undergraduates (2,544 freshmen) from 36 states and territories and 38 foreign countries; 0% part-time; 97% state residents; 23% transfers; 45% financial aid recipients; 50% women; 3% blacks; 1% Native Americans; 7% Hispanics; 26% Asian Americans; 2% foreign nationals; 8% of undergraduates over 25 years of age; 110 legally handicapped students.

Expenses (1985–86) State resident tuition: $0 full-time, $975 per year part-time. Nonresident tuition: $3816 full-time, $2883 per year part-time. Mandatory fees: $1336. College room and board: $3868.

Financial Aid Fall 1984 full-time freshmen: the average aided freshman received an aid package meeting 100% of need. College-administered aid for all 1984–85 undergraduates: 2,344 need-based scholarships (average $1474); 322 non-need scholarships (average $941); short-term loans (average $100); low-interest long-term loans from college funds (average $1437), from external sources (average $2181); SEOG; College Work-Study; 1,200 part-time jobs. Supporting data: FAF, IRS, state form, AFSA/SAR required. Priority application deadline: 2/9.

Athletics Member NCAA (Division I). Intercollegiate sports: baseball/softball M(I,s); basketball M(I,s), W(I,s); crew M; cross-country running M(I,s), W(I); golf M(I); sailing M; swimming and diving M(I,s), W(I,s); tennis M(I,s), W(I,s); track and field M(I,s), W(I,s); volleyball W(I,s). Intramural sports: baseball/softball, basketball, fencing, football, golf, ice hockey, martial arts, rugby, sailing, skiing (cross-country), skiing (downhill), soccer, swimming and diving, tennis, volleyball.

Majors Anthropology B; art/fine arts B; art history B; biology/biological sciences B; chemistry B; civil engineering B; classics B; comparative literature B; computer engineering B; computer information systems B; computer science B; dance B; ecology/environmental studies B; economics B; education B; electrical engineering B; engineering (general) B; English B; environmental biology B; evolutionary biology B; French B; geography B; German B; history B; human ecology B; humanities B; information science B; interdisciplinary studies B; Italian B; legal studies B; linguistics B; literature B; mathematics B; mechanical engineering B; microbiology B; molecular biology B; music B; philosophy B; physics B; political science/government B; Portuguese B; psychobiology B; psychology B; Russian B; social science B; sociology B; Spanish B; studio art B; theater arts/drama B; urban studies B.

LD Program Information

Name of Program Disabled Student Services.

Availability of Services Began offering services in 1978. Services provided to freshmen, sophomores, juniors, seniors. Program currently serves 9 LD students: 3 freshmen, 4 sophomores, 1 junior, 1 senior.

Staff 5 part-time staff members, including director. Services provided by tutors, counselor, notetaking specialist, testing specialist.

Admissions LD applicants evaluated on the basis of high school transcript and grade point average, standard or untimed SAT, autobiographical statement, letters of recommendation. LD students may begin taking classes in fall, winter, spring, or summer. Application should be submitted 10 months in advance of initial anticipated enrollment.

Orientation Optional orientation offered before registration.

Housing College housing (including coed) available. LD students housed randomly. LD students not required to live on campus.

Tutoring Offered one-to-one and in small groups by professional teachers, peer tutors. Available in some subjects. LD students may receive tutoring in all courses each term.

Academic Advisement Help with program planning provided by LD staff members, academic advisers. Most LD students take 12 to 16 quarter hours each quarter; 12 quarter hours required to maintain full-time status.

Special Courses Offered in college survival skills, reading, vocabulary development, composition, math, study skills, career planning. None offered for credit; none enter into overall grade point average.

Auxiliary Aids and Services Aids include taped textbooks, tape recorders, calculators, typewriters, word processors. Services include alternative exam arrangements, notetakers, advocacy.

Counseling Services Individual counseling, small-group counseling, rap sessions, career counseling available.

Contact Dr. Patricia L. Romero, Director, Disabled Student Services, University of California, Irvine, Irvine, CA 92717, 714-856-7494.

UNIVERSITY OF CALIFORNIA, RIVERSIDE

Riverside, California

Year Program Began	Early 1970's	Special Courses	✓
Special Fee	None	Taped Textbooks	✓
Special Orientation		Alternative Exam Arrangements	✓
Diagnostic Testing	✓	Notetakers	✓
Subject-Area Tutoring	✓	Staff	3 part-time
Basic Skills Remediation	✓	Number of Students Served	5

General Information State-supported coed university. Part of University of California System. Founded 1954. Awards B, M, D. Institutionally accredited by regional association. City setting, with easy access to Los Angeles; 1,200-acre barrier-free campus. Total enrollment: 4,855. Faculty: 375 (307 full-time, 68 part-time); 99% have doctoral degrees; graduate assistants teach a few undergraduate courses. Calendar: quarters. Grading system: letters or numbers. Library holdings: 1.2 million bound volumes, 952,769 titles on microform, 14,000 periodical subscriptions, 22,463 records/tapes.

Undergraduate Profile Fall 1984: 3,519 undergraduates (833 freshmen) from 27 states and territories and 30 foreign countries; 10% part-time; 98% state residents; 11% transfers; 65% financial aid recipients; 51% women; 7% blacks; 1% Native Americans; 10% Hispanics; 12% Asian Americans; 1% foreign nationals; 78 legally handicapped students.

Expenses (1985–86) State resident tuition: $0 full-time, $955 per year part-time. Nonresident tuition: $3816 full-time, $2854 per year part-time. Mandatory fees: $1307. College room and board: $3145. College room only: $1385.

Financial Aid Fall 1984 full-time freshmen: the average aided freshman received an aid package meeting 100% of need. College-administered aid for all 1984–85 undergraduates: 1,694 need-based scholarships (average $1040); 305 non-need scholarships (average $300); short-term loans (average $409); low-interest long-term loans from college funds (average $1067), from external sources (average $1915); SEOG; College Work-Study; 1,369 part-time jobs. Supporting data: IRS, state form, AFSA/SAR, Financial Aid Transcript (for transfers) required. Priority application deadline: 7/1.

Athletics Member NCAA (Division II), NAIA. Intercollegiate sports: baseball/softball M(II,s), W(II); basketball M(II,s), W(II,s); cross-country running M(II,s), W(II,s); martial arts M, W; tennis M(II,s), W(II); track and field M(II,s), W(II,s); volleyball W(II,s); water polo M(II). Intramural sports: baseball/softball, basketball, bowling, fencing, football, martial arts, racquetball, rugby, skiing (cross-country), skiing (downhill), soccer, tennis, volleyball, water polo.

Majors Agronomy/soil and crop sciences B; anthropology B; art/fine arts B; art history B; biochemistry B; biology/biological sciences B; biomedical sciences B; black/Afro-American studies B; botany/plant sciences B; business administration/commerce/management B; business economics B; chemistry B; classics B; comparative literature B; computer science B; dance B; economics B; engineering and applied sciences B; English B; entomology B; environmental sciences B; French B; geography B; geology B; geophysics B; German B; history B; human development B; humanities B; Latin American studies B; (pre)law sequence B; liberal arts/general studies B; linguistics B; mathematics B; Mexican-American/Chicano studies B; modern languages B; music B; philosophy B; physical sciences B; physics B; political science/government B; psychobiology B; psychology B; religious studies B; Russian and Slavic studies B; sociology B; Spanish B; statistics B; studio art B; theater arts/drama B. Majors with highest enrollment: business administration/commerce/management, biology/biological sciences, biomedical sciences.

LD Program Information

Name of Program Disabled Student Services.

Availability of Services Began offering services in early 1970's. Services provided to freshmen, sophomores, juniors, seniors. Program currently serves 5 LD students: 3 freshmen, 1 sophomore, 1 junior.

Staff 3 part-time staff members, including coordinator. Services provided by learning skills counselor, Disabled Services assistant.

Admissions LD applicants evaluated on the basis of high school transcript and grade point average, standard or untimed SAT or ACT; personal interview, autobiographical statement, letters of recommendation, psychoeducational report required for some. LD students may begin taking classes in fall, winter, spring, or summer (special action admission restricted to fall). Application should be submitted 10 months in advance of initial anticipated enrollment.

Housing College housing (including coed) available. LD students housed randomly. LD students not required to live on campus.

Diagnostic Testing Available in intelligence, reading, math, spelling, written language, work and study habits, personality.

Tutoring Offered one-to-one and in small groups by peer tutors. Available in all subjects. LD students may receive tutoring in all courses each term.

Basic Skills Remediation Offered one-to-one and in small groups by learning skills counselors. Available in reading, math, written language, learning strategies, work and study habits.

Academic Advisement Help with program planning provided by LD staff members, academic advisers. LD students may take up to 16 quarter hours each quarter; most take 12 quarter hours; 12 quarter hours required to maintain full-time status.

Special Courses Offered in reading, vocabulary development, composition, math, study skills, career planning. None offered for credit; none enter into overall grade point average.

Auxiliary Aids and Services Aids include taped textbooks, tape recorders, calculators, typewriters. Services include alternative exam arrangements, notetakers, advocacy, limited secretarial services.

Counseling Services Individual counseling, small-group counseling, career counseling available.

Contact Ms. Marcia Theise Schiffer, Coordinator, Disabled Student Services, University of California, Riverside, Special Services Office, Riverside, CA 92521, 714-787-4538.

UNIVERSITY OF CALIFORNIA, SAN DIEGO

La Jolla, California

Year Program Began	1978	Special Courses	
Special Fee	None	Taped Textbooks	✓
Special Orientation		Alternative Exam Arrangements	✓
Diagnostic Testing		Notetakers	✓
Subject-Area Tutoring	✓	Staff	2 part-time
Basic Skills Remediation		Number of Students Served	6

General Information State-supported coed university. Part of University of California System. Founded 1964. Awards B, M, D. Institutionally accredited by regional association; programs accredited by ABET (engineering and technology). Metropolitan setting; 1,200-acre barrier-free campus. Total enrollment: 13,950. Faculty: 947; 98% have doctoral degrees; graduate assistants teach a few undergraduate courses. Calendar: quarters. Grading system: letters or numbers and pass/fail. Library holdings: 1.6 million bound volumes, 1 million titles on microform, 29,852 periodical subscriptions.

Undergraduate Profile Fall 1984: 11,422 undergraduates (2,672 freshmen) from 57 states and territories and 56 foreign countries; 1% part-time; 90% state residents; 6% transfers; 40% financial aid recipients; 44% women; 4% blacks; 1% Native Americans; 6% Hispanics; 16% Asian Americans; 2% foreign nationals; 7% of undergraduates over 25 years of age; 100 legally handicapped students.

Expenses (1985–86) State resident tuition: $0 full-time, $986 per year part-time. Nonresident tuition: $3816 full-time, $2894 per year part-time. Mandatory fees: $1347. College room and board: $3840.

Financial Aid Fall 1984 full-time freshmen: 53% applied for aid, 55% of those were judged to have need, 95% of those were aided; the average aided freshman received an aid package worth $3812 (60% scholarships/grants, 40% self-help) meeting 100% of need. College-administered aid for all 1984–85 undergraduates: 2,877 need-based scholarships (average $1000); 75 non-need scholarships (average $300); short-term loans (average $150); low-interest long-term loans from college funds (average $1200), from external sources (average $2500); SEOG; College Work-Study; part-time jobs. Supporting data: FAF, IRS, state form, AFSA/SAR, Financial Aid Transcript (for transfers) required. Priority application deadline: 2/11.

Athletics Member NCAA (Division III). Intercollegiate sports: badminton M, W; baseball/softball M(III), W(III); basketball M(III), W(III); crew M, W; cross-country running M(III), W(III); fencing M(III), W(III); golf M(III), W(III); sailing M, W; skiing (downhill) M(c), W(c); soccer M(III), W(III); swimming and diving M(III), W(III); tennis M(III), W(III); track and field M(III), W(III); volleyball M(III), W(III); water polo M(III), W. Intramural sports: baseball/softball, basketball, bowling, football, soccer, tennis, track and field, volleyball, water polo.

Majors Anthropology B; applied mathematics B; art/fine arts B; art history B; biochemistry B; bioengineering B; biology/biological sciences B; biophysics B; cell biology B; chemical engineering B; chemistry B; Chinese B; classics B; communication B; computer engineering B; computer science B; creative writing B; (pre)dentistry sequence B; economics B; electrical engineering B; engineering (general) B; engineering and applied sciences B; engineering physics B; engineering sciences B; English B; experimental psychology B; French B; Germanic languages and literature B; history B; information science B; interdisciplinary studies B; Italian B; Judaic studies B; (pre)law sequence B; linguistics B; literature B; mathematics B; mechanical engineering B; (pre)medicine sequence B; Mexican-American/Chicano studies B; microbiology B; molecular biology B; music B; music history B; philosophy B; physics B; political science/government B; psychology B; sociology B; Spanish B; studio art B; systems engineering B; systems science B; theater arts/drama B; urban studies B; (pre)veterinary medicine sequence B. Majors with highest enrollment: biology/biological sciences, engineering sciences, computer science.

LD Program Information

Name of Program Disabled Student Services.

Availability of Services Began offering services in 1978. Services provided to freshmen, sophomores, juniors, seniors. Program currently serves 6 LD students: 2 sophomores, 1 junior, 3 seniors.

Staff 2 part-time staff members, including director, assistant directors.

Admissions LD applicants evaluated on the basis of high school transcript and grade point average, standard SAT or ACT, autobiographical statement, 3 Achievement Tests. LD students may begin taking classes in fall, winter, spring, or summer. Application should be submitted 10 months in advance of initial anticipated enrollment.

Housing College housing (including coed) available. LD students housed randomly. LD students not required to live on campus.

Tutoring Offered one-to-one and in small groups by peer tutors. Available in some subjects. LD students may receive tutoring in all courses each term.

Academic Advisement Help with program planning provided by academic advisers. Most LD students take 9 to 12 quarter hours each quarter; 12 quarter hours required to maintain full-time status.

Auxiliary Aids and Services Aids include taped textbooks, tape recorders, calculators. Services include alternative exam arrangements, notetakers, advocacy, readers.

Counseling Services Individual counseling, career counseling available.

Contact Ms. Constance A. Wilbur, Director, Disabled Student Services, University of California, San Diego, Q-019, La Jolla, CA 92093, 619-452-4382.

UNIVERSITY OF CALIFORNIA, SANTA CRUZ

Santa Cruz, California

Year Program Began	1971
Special Fee	None
Special Orientation	
Diagnostic Testing	
Subject-Area Tutoring	✓
Basic Skills Remediation	
Special Courses	
Taped Textbooks	
Alternative Exam Arrangements	✓
Notetakers	✓
Staff	3 part-time
Number of Students Served	7

General Information State-supported coed university. Part of University of California System. Founded 1965. Awards B, M, D. Institutionally accredited by regional association. Small-town setting, with easy access to San Francisco and San Jose; 2,000-acre campus. Total enrollment: 7,137. Faculty: 640 (310 full-time, 330 part-time); 95% have doctoral degrees; graduate assistants teach a few undergraduate courses. Calendar: quarters. Grading system: letters or numbers, pass/fail, and faculty reports. Library holdings: 739,374 bound volumes, 245,703 titles on microform, 11,358 periodical subscriptions, 8,592 records/tapes.

Undergraduate Profile Fall 1984: 6,556 undergraduates (1,480 freshmen) from 39 states and territories and 21 foreign countries; 9% part-time; 97% state residents; 31% transfers; 60% financial aid recipients; 51% women; 3% blacks; 1% Native Americans; 6% Hispanics; 9% Asian Americans; 2% foreign nationals; 12% of undergraduates over 25 years of age; 192 legally handicapped students.

Expenses (1985–86) State resident tuition: $0 full-time, $1029 per year part-time. Nonresident tuition: $3816 full-time, $2937 per year part-time. Mandatory fees: $1388. College room and board: $3305.

Financial Aid Fall 1984 full-time freshmen: 55% applied for aid, 73% of those were judged to have need, 100% of those were aided; the average aided freshman received an aid package worth $3569 (58% scholarships/grants, 42% self-help) meeting 100% of need. College-administered aid for all 1984–85 undergraduates: 1,076 need-based scholarships (average $765); 105 non-need scholarships (average $645); short-term loans (average $100); low-interest long-term loans from college funds (average $1000), from external sources (average $1200); SEOG; College Work-Study; 2,037 part-time jobs. Supporting data: FAF, IRS, AFSA/SAR required. Priority application deadline: 2/9.

Athletics Member NCAA (Division III). Intercollegiate sports: basketball M(III), W(III); cross-country running M(III), W(III); fencing M(c), W(c); martial arts M(c), W(c); rugby M(c); sailing M, W; soccer M(III), W(c); tennis M(III), W(III); volleyball M(III), W(III). Intramural sports: baseball/softball, basketball, cross-country running, fencing, football, martial arts, racquetball, rugby, sailing, skiing (cross-country), skiing (downhill), soccer, tennis, track and field, volleyball.

Majors American studies B; anthropology B; applied mathematics B; art/fine arts B; art history B; biochemistry B; biology/biological sciences B; botany/plant sciences B; business administration/commerce/management B; business economics B; ceramic art and design B; classics B; communication B; computer engineering B; computer science B; creative writing B; dance B; earth science B; East Asian studies B; ecology/environmental studies B; economics B; English B; environmental sciences B; evolutionary biology B; experimental psychology B; film studies B; French B; geology B; geophysics B; German B; Greek B; history B; information science B; Italian B; Latin B; Latin American studies B; legal studies B; liberal arts/general studies B; linguistics B; literature B; marine biology B; mathematics B; (pre)medicine sequence B; medieval studies B; molecular biology B; music B; philosophy B; photography B; physics B; political science/government B; psychobiology B; psychology B; religious studies B; Russian B; Russian and Slavic studies B; social science B; sociology B; South Asian studies B; Southeast Asian studies B; Spanish B; studio art B; theater arts/drama B; women's studies B. Majors with highest enrollment: biology/biological sciences, psychology, literature.

LD Program Information

Name of Program Office of Disabled Student Services.

Availability of Services Began offering services in 1971. Services provided to freshmen, sophomores, juniors, seniors. Program currently serves 7 LD students: 1 freshman, 2 sophomores, 2 juniors, 2 seniors.

Staff 3 part-time staff members, including coordinators. Services provided by readers, notetakers.

Admissions LD applicants evaluated on the basis of high school transcript and grade point average, standard or untimed SAT or ACT, 3 letters of recommendation, 3 Achievement Tests, English Composition Test (with essay); psychoeducational report recommended; personal interview required for some. LD students may begin taking classes in fall, winter, spring, or summer. Application should be submitted at least 9 months in advance of initial anticipated enrollment.

Housing College housing (including coed) available. LD students housed randomly. LD students not required to live on campus.

Tutoring Offered one-to-one by peer tutors. Available in all subjects. LD students may receive tutoring in all courses each term.

Academic Advisement Help with program planning provided by LD staff members, academic advisers. LD students may take up to 3 courses each quarter (more only by special permission); 3 courses required to maintain full-time status (except by special permission).

Auxiliary Aids and Services Aids include tape recorders, calculators, computers. Services include alternative exam arrangements, notetakers, advocacy, readers.

Counseling Services Individual counseling, career counseling available.

Contact Ms. S. Lea Van Meter, Coordinator, Office of Disabled Student Services, University of California, Santa Cruz, 140 Hahn Student Services, Santa Cruz, CA 95064, 408-429-2294.

UNIVERSITY OF CENTRAL FLORIDA
Orlando, Florida

Year Program Began	1978	Special Courses	
Special Fee	None	Taped Textbooks	✓
Special Orientation		Alternative Exam Arrangements	✓
Diagnostic Testing		Notetakers	
Subject-Area Tutoring	✓	Staff	1 part-time
Basic Skills Remediation		Number of Students Served	*Not reported*

General Information State-supported coed university. Part of State University System of Florida. Founded 1963. Awards A (college transfer), B, M, D. Institutionally accredited by regional association; programs accredited by AACSB (business), ABET (engineering and technology), NLN (nursing); candidate for program accreditation by NASM (music). Metropolitan setting; 1,227-acre barrier-free campus. Total enrollment: 15,846. Faculty: 658 (487 full-time, 171 part-time); 75% have doctoral degrees; graduate assistants teach a few undergraduate courses. Calendar: semesters. Grading system: letters or numbers. Library holdings: 401,668 bound volumes, 369,309 titles on microform, 3,476 periodical subscriptions, 6,830 records/tapes.

Undergraduate Profile Fall 1984: 12,619 undergraduates (1,067 freshmen); 37% part-time; 95% state residents; 72% transfers; 56% financial aid recipients; 50% women; 4% blacks; 0% Native Americans; 4% Hispanics; 2% Asian Americans; 2% foreign nationals; 26% of undergraduates over 25 years of age.

Expenses (1985–86) State resident tuition: $927 full-time, $30.89 per semester hour part-time. Nonresident tuition: $3297 full-time, $109.89 per semester hour part-time. Mandatory fees: $66. College room and board: $2600. College room only: $1200.

Financial Aid Fall 1984 full-time freshmen: 73% applied for aid, 90% of those were judged to have need, 99% of those were aided; the average aided freshman received an aid package worth $1309 (51% scholarships/grants, 49% self-help) meeting 50% of need. College-administered aid for all 1984–85 undergraduates: need-based scholarships; non-need scholarships; short-term loans; low-interest long-term loans; College Work-Study; part-time jobs. Supporting data: FAF, institutional form, AFSA/SAR required; IRS required for some; FFS acceptable. Priority application deadline: 4/1.

Athletics Member NCAA (Division II). Intercollegiate sports: baseball/softball M(I,s); basketball M(I,s), W(I,s); cross-country running M(I,s), W(I,s); football M(II,s); golf M(I,s), W(I,s); riflery M(I,s), W(I,s); soccer M(I,s), W(I,s); tennis M(I,s), W(I,s); volleyball W(I,s); wrestling M(I,s). Intramural sports: baseball/softball, basketball, crew, cross-country running, fencing, field hockey, football, golf, skiing (cross-country), skiing (downhill), soccer, swimming and diving, tennis, track and field, volleyball.

Majors Accounting B; anthropology B; art education B; art/fine arts B; biology/biological sciences B; botany/plant sciences B; business administration/commerce/management B; business education B; chemistry B; civil engineering B; communication B; computer engineering B; computer science B; computer technologies B; construction technologies B; criminal justice B; early childhood education B; ecology/environmental studies B; economics B; educational media B; electrical and electronics technologies B; electrical engineering B; elementary education B; engineering design B; engineering technology B; English B; environmental engineering B; film studies B; finance/banking B; forensic sciences B; French B; history B; hotel and restaurant management B; humanities B; industrial engineering B; journalism B; liberal arts/general studies A, B; marketing/retailing/merchandising B; mathematics B; mechanical engineering B; medical records services B; medical technology B; microbiology B; music B; music education B; nursing B; philosophy B; physical education B; physics B; political science/government B; psychology B; public administration B; radio and television studies B; radiological sciences B; respiratory therapy B; science education B; secondary education B; social work B; sociology B; Spanish B; speech pathology and audiology B; speech/rhetoric/public address/debate B; statistics B; theater arts/drama B; (pre)veterinary medicine sequence B; zoology B. Majors with highest enrollment: computer science, accounting, business administration/commerce/management.

LD Program Information

Name of Program Handicapped Student Services.

Availability of Services Began offering services in 1978. Services provided to freshmen, sophomores, juniors, seniors.

Staff 1 part-time staff member (coordinator).

Admissions LD applicants evaluated on the basis of high school transcript and grade point average, standard or untimed SAT or ACT, letters of recommendation. LD students may begin taking classes in fall, spring, or summer. Application should be submitted up to 1 year in advance of initial anticipated enrollment.

Housing College housing available. LD students housed randomly. LD students not required to live on campus.

Tutoring Offered one-to-one by peer tutors. Available in some subjects.

Academic Advisement Help with program planning provided by academic advisers. LD students required to take 12 semester hours each semester to maintain full-time status.

Auxiliary Aids and Services Aids include taped textbooks. Services include alternative exam arrangements.

Counseling Services Individual counseling, career counseling available.

Contact Ms. Louise Friderici, Coordinator of Handicapped Student Services, University of Central Florida, Orlando, FL 32816, 305-275-2371.

UNIVERSITY OF COLORADO AT BOULDER

Boulder, Colorado

Year Program Began	1979	Special Courses	
Special Fee	None	Taped Textbooks	
Special Orientation	✓	Alternative Exam Arrangements	✓
Diagnostic Testing	✓	Notetakers	
Subject-Area Tutoring	✓	Staff	2 full-time, 1 part-time
Basic Skills Remediation	✓	Number of Students Served	65

General Information State-supported coed university. Part of University of Colorado System. Founded 1876. Awards B, M, D. Institutionally accredited by regional association; programs accredited by AACSB (business), ABET (engineering and technology), NASM (music), ACPE (pharmacy), NCATE (teacher education). City setting, with easy access to Denver; 650-acre barrier-free campus. Total enrollment: 22,285. Faculty: 1,151 (968 full-time, 183 part-time); 90% have doctoral degrees; graduate assistants teach a few undergraduate courses. Calendar: semesters. Grading system: letters or numbers. Library holdings: 2 million bound volumes, 2.6 million titles on microform, 21,000 periodical subscriptions, 50,000 records/tapes.

Undergraduate Profile Fall 1984: 18,153 undergraduates (3,338 freshmen) from 52 states and territories and 74 foreign countries; 10% part-time; 68% state residents; 7% transfers; 55% financial aid recipients; 46% women; 1% blacks; 1% Native Americans; 3% Hispanics; 3% Asian Americans; 3% foreign nationals; 8% of undergraduates over 25 years of age; 30 legally handicapped students.

Expenses (1985–86) State resident tuition: $1194 full-time. Nonresident tuition: $5272 full-time. Part-time tuition and fees per semester (1 to 10 semester hours) range from $217 to $597 for state residents, $1211 to $2638 for nonresidents. Mandatory fees: $243. College room and board: $2606.

Financial Aid Fall 1984 full-time freshmen: 51% applied for aid, 71% of those were judged to have need, 89% of those were aided; the average aided freshman received an aid package worth $1747 (65% scholarships/grants, 35% self-help) meeting 75% of need. College-administered aid for all 1984–85 undergraduates: 7,000 need-based scholarships (average $2200); 2,150 non-need scholarships (average $600); short-term loans (average $200); low-interest long-term loans from college funds (average $2500), from external sources (average $1500); SEOG; College Work-Study; 2,500 part-time jobs. Supporting data: FFS, IRS required; FAF acceptable. Application deadline: continuous to 3/1.

Athletics Member NCAA (Division I). Intercollegiate sports: basketball M(I,s), W(I,s); cross-country running M(I,s), W(I,s); fencing M(c), W(c); field hockey W(c); football M(I-A,s); golf M(s); skiing (cross-country) M(I,s), W(I,s); skiing (downhill) M(I,s), W(I,s); tennis M(I,s), W(I,s); track and field M(I,s), W(I,s). Intramural sports: baseball/softball, basketball, cross-country running, football, golf, ice hockey, lacrosse, martial arts, racquetball, riflery, rugby, skiing (cross-country), skiing (downhill), soccer, squash, swimming and diving, tennis, volleyball, water polo, weight lifting.

Majors Accounting B; advertising B; aerospace engineering B; African studies B; American studies B; anthropology B; applied mathematics B; architectural engineering B; art education B; art/fine arts B; art history B; Asian/Oriental studies B; biology/biological sciences B; black/Afro-American studies B; broadcasting B; business administration/commerce/management B; cell biology B; chemical engineering B; chemistry B; Chinese B; civil engineering B; classics B; communication B; computer engineering B; computer information systems B; computer management B; computer science B; conservation B; dance B; (pre) dentistry sequence B; East European and Soviet studies B; ecology/environmental studies B; economics B; electrical engineering B; engineering physics B; English B; environmental biology B; environmental design B; evolutionary biology B; film studies B; finance/banking B; French B; geography B; geology B; geophysics B; German B; history B; humanities B; international business B; international studies B; Italian B; Japanese B; journalism B; labor and industrial relations B; land use management and reclamation B; Latin American studies B; linguistics B; marketing/retailing/merchandising B; mathematics B; mechanical engineering B; medical technology B; (pre)medicine sequence B; molecular biology B; music B; music education B; Near and Middle Eastern studies B; nursing B; pharmacy/pharmaceutical sciences B; philosophy B; physical education B; physical therapy B; physics B; political science/government B; Portuguese B; psychology B; public administration B; public relations B; radio and television studies B; real estate B; recreation and leisure services B; religious studies B; Russian B; Russian and Slavic studies B; sociology B; Spanish B; speech pathology and audiology B; studio art B; theater arts/drama B; transportation engineering B; women's studies B.

LD Program Information

Name of Program Learning Disabilities Program.

Availability of Services Began offering services in 1979. Services provided to freshmen, sophomores, juniors, seniors. Program currently serves 65 LD students: 25 freshmen, 20 sophomores, 10 juniors, 10 seniors.

Staff 2 full-time, 1 part-time staff members, including coordinator. Services provided by remediation specialist, diagnostic specialist.

Admissions LD applicants evaluated on the basis of high school transcript and grade point average, standard or untimed SAT or ACT, personal interview, letters of recommendation, psychoeducational report. LD students may begin taking classes in fall only. Application should be submitted 7 to 8 months in advance of initial anticipated enrollment.

Orientation Required orientation held before registration.

Housing College housing (including coed) available. LD students housed randomly. LD freshmen required to live on campus.

Diagnostic Testing Available in intelligence, reading, math, spelling, handwriting, spoken language, written language, perceptual skills, work and study habits.

Tutoring Offered by peer tutors. Available in some subjects.

Basic Skills Remediation Offered one-to-one and in small groups by LD teachers. Available in reading, spelling, written language, learning strategies, work and study habits.

Academic Advisement Help with program planning provided by LD staff members, academic advisers. Most LD students take 12 to 15 semester hours each semester (12 in first semester); 12 semester hours required to maintain full-time status.

Auxiliary Aids and Services Aids include typewriters, word processors, computers. Services include alternative exam arrangements, advocacy.

Counseling Services Individual counseling, small-group counseling, career counseling available.

Contact Ms. Laura Fischer, Coordinator, Learning Disabilities Program, University of Colorado at Boulder, Campus Box 133, Boulder, CO 80309, 303-492-1591.

UNIVERSITY OF CONNECTICUT

Storrs, Connecticut

Year Program Began	1984	Special Courses	
Special Fee	None	Taped Textbooks	✓
Special Orientation		Alternative Exam Arrangements	✓
Diagnostic Testing	✓	Notetakers	
Subject-Area Tutoring	✓	Staff	6 part-time
Basic Skills Remediation	✓	Number of Students Served	14

General Information State-supported coed university. Founded 1881. Awards B, M, D. Institutionally accredited by regional association; programs accredited by NASAD (art and design), AACSB (business), ABET (engineering and technology), NASM (music), NLN (nursing), ACPE (pharmacy), NCATE (teacher education). Rural setting, with easy access to Hartford; 3,000-acre campus. Total enrollment: 17,170. Faculty: 1,244 (1,208 full-time, 36 part-time); 88% have doctoral degrees; graduate assistants teach a few undergraduate courses. Calendar: semesters. Grading system: letters or numbers. Library holdings: 1.4 million bound volumes, 1.3 million titles on microform, 17,400 periodical subscriptions.

Undergraduate Profile Fall 1984: 12,691 undergraduates (2,387 freshmen); 5% part-time; 90% state residents; 12% transfers; 50% financial aid recipients; 52% women; 3% blacks; 1% Native Americans; 2% Hispanics; 1% Asian Americans; 1% foreign nationals; 2% of undergraduates over 25 years of age; 146 legally handicapped students.

Expenses (1985–86) State resident tuition: $1801 full-time, $70 per credit part-time. Nonresident tuition: $4971 full-time, $120 per credit part-time. College room and board: $2466. College room only: $1320.

Financial Aid Fall 1984 full-time freshmen: 56% applied for aid, 87% of those were judged to have need, 100% of those were aided; the average aided freshman received an aid package worth $1576 (73% scholarships/grants, 27% self-help) meeting 70% of need. College-administered aid for all 1984–85 undergraduates: need-based scholarships (average $300); non-need scholarships; low-interest long-term loans from external sources (average $500); SEOG; College Work-Study; part-time jobs. Supporting data: FAF, IRS, AFSA/SAR required; institutional form required for some. Priority application deadline: 2/15.

Athletics Member NCAA (Division I). Intercollegiate sports: baseball/softball M(I,s), W(I,s); basketball M(I,s), W(I,s); cross-country running M(I,s), W(I,s); field hockey W(I,s); football M(I-AA,s); golf M(I,s); gymnastics W(I,s); ice hockey M(II,s); soccer M(I,s), W(I,s); swimming and diving M(I,s), W(I,s); tennis M(I,s), W(I,s); track and field M(I,s), W(I,s); volleyball W(I,s). Intramural sports: archery, badminton, baseball/softball, basketball, football, ice hockey, riflery, rugby, sailing.

Majors Accounting B; actuarial science B; agricultural economics B; agricultural education B; agronomy/soil and crop sciences B; animal sciences B; anthropology B; art/fine arts B; art history B; biology/biological sciences B; biophysics B; business administration/commerce/management B; business education B; ceramic art and design B; chemical engineering B; chemistry B; child care/child and family studies B; child psychology/child development B; civil engineering B; classics B; computer engineering B; computer science B; cytotechnology B; (pre)dentistry sequence B; dietetics B; early childhood education B; East European and Soviet studies B; economics B; education B; educational administration B; electrical engineering B; elementary education B; English B; environmental engineering B; family and consumer studies B; fashion design and technology B; fashion merchandising B; finance/banking B; French B; geography B; geology B; geophysics B; German B; graphic arts B; health services administration B; history B; home economics B; horticulture B; insurance B; Italian B; journalism B; Latin B; Latin American studies B; (pre)law sequence B; linguistics B; management information systems B; marketing/retailing/merchandising B; materials engineering B; mathematics B; mechanical engineering B; mechanical engineering technology B; medical technology B; (pre)medicine sequence B; music B; music education B; music history B; natural resource management B; nursing B; nutrition B; painting/drawing B; pharmacy/pharmaceutical sciences B; philosophy B; photography B; physical education B; physical therapy B; physics B; piano/organ B; political science/government B; Portuguese B; psychology B; real estate B; recreation and leisure services B; rehabilitation therapy B; Russian B; Russian and Slavic studies B; sculpture B; secondary education B; social work B; sociology B; Spanish B; special education B; speech pathology and audiology B; speech therapy B; sports medicine B; statistics B; studio art B; textiles and clothing B; theater arts/drama B; urban studies B; (pre) veterinary medicine sequence B; voice B; wind and percussion instruments B; zoology B.

LD Program Information

Name of Program Program for the Learning Disabled College Student.

Availability of Services Began offering services in 1984. Services provided to freshmen, sophomores, juniors, seniors. Program currently serves 14 LD students: 3 freshmen, 6 sophomores, 4 juniors, 1 senior.

Staff 6 part-time staff members, including director, assistant director. Services provided by remediation specialists, tutors, diagnostic specialist.

Admissions LD applicants evaluated on the basis of high school transcript and grade point average, standard or untimed SAT, personal interview, autobiographical statement, letters of recommendation, psychoeducational report, writing sample, Achievement Tests (modified). LD students may begin taking classes in fall, spring, or summer. Application should be submitted 9 months in advance of initial anticipated enrollment.

Housing College housing (including coed) available. LD students housed randomly. LD students not required to live on campus.

Diagnostic Testing Available in intelligence, reading, math, spelling, handwriting, spoken language, written language, perceptual skills, work and study habits, personality, social skills, speech.

Tutoring Offered one-to-one and in small groups by professional teachers, peer tutors. Available in all subjects. LD students may receive tutoring in all courses each term.

Basic Skills Remediation Offered one-to-one and in small groups by LD teachers. Available in reading, math, spelling, handwriting, spoken language, written language, learning strategies, motor abilities, perceptual skills, work and study habits, social skills, speech.

Academic Advisement Help with program planning provided by LD staff members, academic advisers. Most LD students take 9 to 12 credits each semester.

Auxiliary Aids and Services Aids include taped textbooks, word processors, Kurzweil reading machine, special study rooms, computers. Services include alternative exam arrangements.

Counseling Services Individual counseling, small-group counseling, rap sessions, career counseling available.

Contact Dr. Stan Shaw, Professor of Special Education and Director of LD College Program, University of Connecticut, School of Education, Box U-64, Storrs, CT 06268, 203-486-4031.

UNIVERSITY OF DAYTON
Dayton, Ohio

Year Program Began	*Not reported*	Special Courses	
Special Fee	None	Taped Textbooks	✓
Special Orientation		Alternative Exam Arrangements	✓
Diagnostic Testing	✓	Notetakers	✓
Subject-Area Tutoring	✓	Staff	2 part-time
Basic Skills Remediation	✓	Number of Students Served	6

General Information Roman Catholic coed university. Founded 1850. Awards B, M, D. Institutionally accredited by regional association; programs accredited by AACSB (business), ABET (engineering and technology), NASM (music), NCATE (teacher education). Metropolitan setting; 80-acre barrier-free campus. Total enrollment: 10,555. Faculty: 678 (375 full-time, 303 part-time); 71% have doctoral degrees; graduate assistants teach a few undergraduate courses. Calendar: trimesters. Grading system: letters or numbers. Library holdings: 640,759 bound volumes, 202,890 titles on microform, 4,598 periodical subscriptions, 2,500 records/tapes.

Undergraduate Profile Fall 1984: 7,152 undergraduates (1,693 freshmen) from 43 states and territories and 39 foreign countries; 13% part-time; 64% state residents; 14% transfers; 85% financial aid recipients; 44% women; 4% blacks; 0% Native Americans; 1% Hispanics; 1% Asian Americans; 1% foreign nationals; 9% of undergraduates over 25 years of age; 19 legally handicapped students.

Expenses (1985–86) Comprehensive fee of $7992 includes full-time tuition ($4980), mandatory fees ($280), and college room and board ($2732). College room only: $1320. Part-time tuition: $136 per semester hour.

Financial Aid Fall 1984 full-time freshmen: 87% applied for aid, 58% of those were judged to have need, 100% of those were aided; the average aided freshman received an aid package worth $4462 (48% scholarships/grants, 52% self-help) meeting 100% of need. College-administered aid for all 1984–85 undergraduates: 2,258 need-based scholarships (average $1200); 763 non-need scholarships (average $2100); short-term loans (average $605); low-interest long-term loans from external sources (average $2260); SEOG; College Work-Study; 1,166 part-time jobs. Supporting data: institutional form required; FFS, FAF, IRS, state form, AFSA/SAR acceptable. Priority application deadline: 3/31.

Athletics Member NCAA (Division I). Intercollegiate sports: baseball/softball M(I), W(I); basketball M(I,s), W(I,s); cross-country running M(I), W(I); field hockey W(I); football M(III); golf M(I); ice hockey M(I); soccer M(I), W(I); tennis M(I), W(I); volleyball W(I); water polo M(I); wrestling M(I). Intramural sports: badminton, baseball/softball, basketball, bowling, cross-country running, field hockey, football, golf, ice hockey, lacrosse, martial arts, racquetball, riflery, rugby, skiing (cross-country), skiing (downhill), soccer, squash, swimming and diving, tennis, track and field, volleyball, water polo, weight lifting, wrestling.

Majors Accounting B; American studies B; applied art B; art education B; art/fine arts B; biology/biological sciences B; biomedical technologies B; broadcasting B; business administration/commerce/management B; business economics B; business education B; chemical engineering B; chemical engineering technology B; chemistry B; civil engineering B; commercial art B; communication B; computer science B; corrections B; criminal justice B; cytotechnology B; (pre)dentistry sequence B; dietetics B; early childhood education B; economics B; education B; electrical and electronics technologies B; electrical engineering B; elementary education B; engineering (general) B; engineering technology B; English B; environmental engineering technology B; finance/banking B; food services management B; French B; geology B; German B; Greek B; health education B; history B; home economics B; home economics education B; industrial engineering technology B; interdisciplinary studies B; interior design B; international studies B; journalism B; Latin B; law enforcement/police sciences B; (pre)law sequence B; liberal arts/general studies B; management information systems B; marketing/retailing/merchandising B; mathematics B; mechanical engineering B; mechanical engineering technology B; medical technology B; (pre)medicine sequence B; modern languages B; music B; music education B; music therapy B; nuclear medical technology B; nutrition B; philosophy B; photography B; physical education B; physical sciences B; physics B; political science/government B; psychology B; public relations B; radio and television studies B; religious education B; religious studies B; retail management B; science education B; secondary education B; social work B; sociology B; Spanish B; special education B; speech/rhetoric/public address/debate B; theater arts/drama B; theology B; (pre)veterinary medicine sequence B. Majors with highest enrollment: communication, business administration/commerce/management.

LD Program Information

Name of Program Handicapped Student Services.

Availability of Services Services provided to freshmen, sophomores, juniors, seniors. Program currently serves 6 LD students: 5 freshmen, 1 senior.

Staff 2 part-time staff members, including coordinator, assistant coordinator. Services provided by tutors, counselors, diagnostic specialists.

Admissions LD applicants evaluated on the basis of high school transcript and grade point average, standard SAT or ACT. LD students may begin taking classes in fall, winter, spring, or summer. Application should be submitted 6 to 8 weeks in advance of initial anticipated enrollment.

Housing College housing (including coed) available. LD students housed randomly. LD freshmen required to live on campus except if 21 or over or living with relatives.

Diagnostic Testing Available in intelligence, reading, perceptual skills, work and study habits.

Tutoring Offered one-to-one by peer tutors. Available in all subjects. LD students may receive tutoring in 2 courses per term.

Basic Skills Remediation Offered in small groups by regular teachers. Available in reading, math, written language, work and study habits.

Academic Advisement Help with program planning provided by academic advisers. LD students may take up to 18 credit hours each trimester; most take 12 to 15 credit hours; 12 credit hours required to maintain full-time status.

Auxiliary Aids and Services Aids include taped textbooks, tape recorders. Services include alternative exam arrangements, notetakers.

Counseling Services Individual counseling, career counseling available.

Contact Mrs. Susan M. Iwinski, Coordinator, Handicapped Student Services, University of Dayton, Center for Psychological Services, 412 St. Mary's Hall, Dayton, OH 45469, 513-229-3141.

UNIVERSITY OF DENVER

Denver, Colorado

Year Program Began	1982	Special Courses	✓
Special Fee	Varies	Taped Textbooks	✓
Special Orientation		Alternative Exam Arrangements	✓
Diagnostic Testing	✓	Notetakers	✓
Subject-Area Tutoring	✓	Staff	1 full-time, 1 part-time
Basic Skills Remediation	✓	Number of Students Served	25

General Information Independent coed university. Founded 1864. Awards B, M, D. Institutionally accredited by regional association; programs accredited by NASAD (art and design), AACSB (business), NASM (music). Metropolitan setting; 125-acre campus. Total enrollment: 7,875. Faculty: 486 (462 full-time, 24 part-time); 89% have doctoral degrees; graduate assistants teach a few undergraduate courses. Calendar: quarters. Grading system: letters or numbers. Library holdings: 1.2 million bound volumes, 985,707 titles on microform, 5,127 periodical subscriptions.

Undergraduate Profile Fall 1984: 4,058 undergraduates (593 freshmen); 16% part-time; 42% state residents; 30% transfers; 65% financial aid recipients; 50% women; 4% blacks; 1% Native Americans; 5% Hispanics; 2% Asian Americans; 9% foreign nationals; 7% of undergraduates over 25 years of age.

Expenses (1985–86) Comprehensive fee of $11,175 includes full-time tuition ($7560), mandatory fees ($360), and college room and board ($3255). Part-time tuition: $210 per quarter hour.

Financial Aid Fall 1984 full-time freshmen: 50% applied for aid, 93% of those were judged to have need, 100% of those were aided; the average aided freshman received an aid package worth $7725 (58% scholarships/grants, 42% self-help) meeting 100% of need. College-administered aid for all 1984–85 undergraduates: 1,158 need-based scholarships (average $3024); 966 non-need scholarships (average $2758); low-interest long-term loans from college funds (average $1404), from external sources (average $2380); SEOG; College Work-Study; part-time jobs. Supporting data: IRS, AFSA/SAR required; FFS, FAF acceptable. Priority application deadline: 4/1.

Athletics Member NCAA (Division II), NAIA. Intercollegiate sports: baseball/softball M(II,s); basketball M(II,s), W(II,s); gymnastics W(I,s); ice hockey M(I,s); lacrosse M(II,s); soccer M(II,s), W(II,s); swimming and diving M(II,s), W(III); tennis M(II,s), W(II,s); volleyball W(II,s). Intramural sports: badminton, baseball/softball, basketball, bowling, football, golf, ice hockey, martial arts, racquetball, skiing (downhill), soccer, swimming and diving, tennis, track and field, volleyball, water polo, wrestling.

Majors Accounting B; American studies B; animal hospital technology B; anthropology B; art education B; art/fine arts B; art history B; biology/biological sciences B; business administration/commerce/management B; chemistry B; classics B; communication B; comparative literature B; computer engineering B; computer science B; construction management B; creative writing B; (pre)dentistry sequence B; economics B; education B; electrical engineering B; engineering (general) B; English B; environmental sciences B; finance/banking B; French B; geography B; German B; graphic arts B; history B; hotel and restaurant management B; Latin American studies B; (pre)law sequence B; marketing/retailing/merchandising B; mathematics B; mechanical engineering B; (pre)medicine sequence B; music B; music education B; music history B; nursing B; philosophy B; physical education B; physics B; political science/government B; psychology B; public affairs and policy studies B; real estate B; religious studies B; Russian B; science B; secondary education B; social science B; sociology B; Spanish B; speech/rhetoric/public address/debate B; sports medicine B; statistics B; studio art B; (pre)veterinary medicine sequence B. Majors with highest enrollment: hotel and restaurant management, political science/government, communication.

LD Program Information

Name of Program Learning Effectiveness Program.

Availability of Services Began offering services in 1982. Services provided to freshmen, sophomores, juniors, seniors. Program currently serves 25 LD students.

Fees $175 for testing; $25 per hourly session with learning specialist; $10 to $15 per hour for tutoring in subjects other than English.

Staff 1 full-time, 1 part-time staff members, including director. Services provided by learning specialist, paraprofessional.

Admissions LD applicants evaluated on the basis of high school transcript, untimed SAT or ACT, personal interview, autobiographical statement, letters of recommendation. LD students may begin taking classes in fall, winter, spring, or summer. Application should be submitted 6 months in advance of initial anticipated enrollment.

Housing College housing (including coed) available. LD students housed randomly. LD freshmen required to live on campus.

Diagnostic Testing Available in intelligence, reading, math, spelling, spoken language, written language, perceptual skills, personality, speech.

Tutoring Offered one-to-one by professional teachers, peer tutors. Available in all subjects. LD students may receive tutoring in all courses each term.

Basic Skills Remediation Offered one-to-one by LD teachers. Available in reading, spelling, spoken language, written language, learning strategies, work and study habits.

Academic Advisement Help with program planning provided by LD staff members, academic advisers. LD students may take up to 18 quarter hours each quarter; most take 12 to 14 quarter hours; 12 quarter hours required to maintain full-time status.

Special Courses Offered in study skills. None offered for credit; none enter into overall grade point average.

Auxiliary Aids and Services Aids include taped textbooks. Services include alternative exam arrangements, notetakers, advocacy, library assistance, priority registration, editorial services.

Counseling Services Individual counseling, small-group counseling, career counseling available.

Contact Ms. Maria Armstrong, Director of Learning Effectiveness Program, University of Denver, Driscoll Center South, Denver, CO 80208, 303-871-2278.

UNIVERSITY OF FLORIDA
Gainesville, Florida

Year Program Began	1975	Special Courses	✓
Special Fee	None	Taped Textbooks	✓
Special Orientation		Alternative Exam Arrangements	✓
Diagnostic Testing		Notetakers	✓
Subject-Area Tutoring	✓	Staff	1 part-time
Basic Skills Remediation	✓	Number of Students Served	*Not reported*

General Information State-supported coed university. Part of State University System of Florida. Founded 1853. Awards B, M, D. Institutionally accredited by regional association; programs accredited by NAAB (architecture), AACSB (business), ABET (engineering and technology), FIDER (interior design), NASM (music), NLN (nursing), ACPE (pharmacy), NCATE (teacher education). City setting, with easy access to Jacksonville; 2,000-acre campus. Total enrollment: 35,496. Faculty: 3,405 (3,179 full-time, 226 part-time); 70% have doctoral degrees; graduate assistants teach a few undergraduate courses. Calendar: semesters. Grading system: letters or numbers. Library holdings: 2.3 million bound volumes, 1.6 million titles on microform, 24,000 periodical subscriptions, 3,650 records/tapes.

Undergraduate Profile Fall 1984: 26,965 undergraduates (3,036 freshmen) from 52 states and territories and 105 foreign countries; 11% part-time; 93% state residents; 52% transfers; 60% financial aid recipients; 47% women; 6% blacks; 1% Native Americans; 6% Hispanics; 2% Asian Americans; 2% foreign nationals; 7% of undergraduates over 25 years of age; 198 legally handicapped students.

Expenses (1985–86) State resident tuition ranges from $889 to $1017 full-time, $28.67 to $32.80 per semester hour part-time, according to course level. Nonresident tuition ranges from $2549 to $3588 full-time, $82.22 to $115.75 per semester hour part-time, according to course level. Mandatory fees: $84. College room and board: $2769. College room only: $1194.

Financial Aid Fall 1984 full-time freshmen: 81% applied for aid, 68% of those were judged to have need, 95% of those were aided; the average aided freshman received an aid package worth $2901 (50% scholarships/grants, 50% self-help). College-administered aid for all 1984–85 undergraduates: need-based scholarships; non-need scholarships; short-term loans; low-interest long-term loans; SEOG; College Work-Study; part-time jobs. Supporting data: FAF, IRS, institutional form, AFSA/SAR required. Priority application deadline: 3/1.

Athletics Member NCAA (Division I). Intercollegiate sports: baseball/softball M(I,s), W(s); basketball M(I,s), W(I,s); cross-country running M(I,s), W(I,s); football M(I-A,s); golf M(I,s), W(I,s); gymnastics W(I,s); swimming and diving M(I,s), W(I,s); tennis M(I,s), W(I,s); track and field M(I,s), W(I,s); volleyball W(s). Intramural sports: archery, badminton, baseball/softball, basketball, bowling, cross-country running, fencing, field hockey, football, golf, gymnastics, martial arts, racquetball, soccer, swimming and diving, tennis, track and field, volleyball, weight lifting.

Majors Accounting B; advertising B; aerospace engineering B; agricultural engineering B; agronomy/soil and crop sciences B; American studies B; animal sciences B; anthropology B; architecture B; art education B; art/fine arts B; Asian/Oriental studies B; astronomy B; botany/plant sciences B; broadcasting B; business administration/commerce/management B; ceramic art and design B; ceramic engineering B; chemical engineering B; chemistry B; civil engineering B; classics B; communication B; computer science B; conservation B; construction technologies B; criminal justice B; dairy sciences B; dance B; dietetics B; early childhood education B; economics B; education B; educational administration B; electrical engineering B; elementary education B; engineering (general) B; engineering and applied sciences B; engineering sciences B; English B; entomology B; environmental engineering B; finance/banking B; food sciences B; forestry B; French B; geography B; geology B; German B; health education B; health science B; history B; horticulture B; industrial engineering B; insurance B; interior design B; journalism B; landscape architecture/design B; marketing/retailing/merchandising B; materials engineering B; mathematics B; mechanical engineering B; medical technology B; metallurgical engineering B; microbiology B; music B; music education B; nuclear engineering B; nursing B; nutrition B; occupational therapy B; ornamental horticulture B; painting/drawing B; pharmacy/pharmaceutical sciences B; philosophy B; physical education B; physical therapy B; physician's assistant studies B; physics B; political science/government B; poultry sciences B; psychology B; public relations B; radio and television studies B; real estate B; recreation and leisure services B; religious studies B; Romance languages B; Russian B; sacred music B; science education B; sculpture B; secondary education B; sociology B; Spanish B; special education B; speech/rhetoric/public address/debate B; statistics B; studio art B; systems engineering B; technical writing B; theater arts/drama B; zoology B. Majors with highest enrollment: engineering (general), business administration/commerce/management, journalism.

LD Program Information

Name of Program Services for Disabled Students.

Availability of Services Began offering services in 1975. Services provided to freshmen, sophomores, juniors, seniors.

Staff 1 part-time staff member (coordinator). Services provided by tutors.

Admissions LD applicants evaluated on the basis of high school transcript and grade point average, standard or untimed SAT or ACT; autobiographical statement, letters of recommendation, psychoeducational report recommended. LD students may begin taking classes in fall, spring, or summer. Application should be submitted 6 months in advance of initial anticipated enrollment.

Housing College housing (including coed) available. LD students housed randomly. LD students not required to live on campus.

Tutoring Offered one-to-one and in small groups by professional teachers, peer tutors. Available in some subjects. LD students may receive tutoring in all courses each term (depending on availability of tutors, level of courses, and individual need).

Basic Skills Remediation Offered one-to-one and in small groups by regular teachers, teacher trainees. Available in reading, math, spelling, handwriting, spoken language, written language, learning strategies, motor abilities, perceptual skills, work and study habits, social skills.

Academic Advisement Help with program planning provided by academic advisers. LD students may take up to 18 semester hours each semester; 12 semester hours required to maintain full-time status.

Special Courses Offered in college survival skills, reading, vocabulary development, communication skills, composition, language development, math, personal psychology, study skills, career planning. Some offered for credit; some enter into overall grade point average.

Auxiliary Aids and Services Aids include taped textbooks, tape recorders, calculators, typewriters, word processors. Services include alternative exam arrangements, notetakers, advocacy.

Counseling Services Individual counseling, small-group counseling, rap sessions, career counseling available.

Contact Ms. Mary Skorheim, Coordinator of Programs and Services for Disabled Students, University of Florida, 124 Tigert Hall, Gainesville, FL 32612, 904-392-1261.

UNIVERSITY OF GEORGIA

Athens, Georgia

Year Program Began	1982	Special Courses	
Special Fee	Varies	Taped Textbooks	✓
Special Orientation	✓	Alternative Exam Arrangements	✓
Diagnostic Testing	✓	Notetakers	✓
Subject-Area Tutoring	✓	Staff	1 full-time, 3 part-time
Basic Skills Remediation	✓	Number of Students Served	63

General Information State-supported coed university. Part of University System of Georgia. Founded 1785. Awards A (college transfer and terminal), B, M, D. Institutionally accredited by regional association; programs accredited by NASAD (art and design), AACSB (business), ABET (engineering and technology), FIDER (interior design), NASM (music), ACPE (pharmacy), NCATE (teacher education). Small-town setting, with easy access to Atlanta; 1,502-acre campus. Total enrollment: 25,230. Faculty: 1,895 (1,795 full-time, 100 part-time); 80% have doctoral degrees; graduate assistants teach a few undergraduate courses. Calendar: quarters. Grading system: letters or numbers. Library holdings: 2.3 million bound volumes, 2.8 million titles on microform, 49,599 periodical subscriptions, 35,000 records/tapes.

Undergraduate Profile Fall 1984: 19,680 undergraduates (2,814 freshmen) from 51 states and territories and 67 foreign countries; 8% part-time; 81% state residents; 10% transfers; 41% financial aid recipients; 46% women; 5% blacks; 1% Native Americans; 1% Hispanics; 1% Asian Americans; 2% foreign nationals; 6% of undergraduates over 25 years of age; 340 legally handicapped students.

Expenses (1985–86) State resident tuition: $1272 full-time, $36 per quarter hour part-time. Nonresident tuition: $3816 full-time, $108 per quarter hour part-time. Mandatory fees: $282. College room and board: $2205.

Financial Aid Fall 1984 full-time freshmen: the average aided freshman received an aid package meeting 90% of need. College-administered aid for all 1984–85 undergraduates: need-based scholarships (average $625); non-need scholarships (average $870); short-term loans (average $150); low-interest long-term loans from college funds (average $1000), from external sources (average $1500); SEOG; College Work-Study; part-time jobs. Supporting data: institutional form, AFSA/SAR required; state form required for some; FFS acceptable. Priority application deadline: 4/15.

Athletics Member NCAA (Division I). Intercollegiate sports: baseball/softball M(I,s); basketball M(I,s), W(I,s); cross-country running M(I), W(I); football M(I-A,s); golf M(I,s), W(I,s); gymnastics M(s), W(s); swimming and diving M(I,s), W(I,s); tennis M(I,s), W(I,s); track and field M(I,s), W(I,s); volleyball W(I,s). Intramural sports: archery, badminton, baseball/softball, basketball, bowling, cross-country running, field hockey, football, golf, lacrosse, racquetball, riflery, rugby, soccer, swimming and diving, tennis, volleyball.

Majors Accounting B; advertising B; agricultural economics B; agricultural education B; agricultural engineering B; agricultural sciences B; agricultural technologies B; agronomy/soil and crop sciences B; animal sciences B; anthropology B; applied art B; art education B; art/fine arts B; art history B; art therapy B; astronomy B; biochemistry B; biology/biological sciences B; botany/plant sciences B; broadcasting B; business administration/commerce/management B; business education B; ceramic art and design B; chemistry B; child care/child and family studies B; child psychology/child development B; classics B; comparative literature B; computer science B; criminal justice B; dairy sciences B; dance B; (pre)dentistry sequence B; dietetics B; early childhood education B; economics B; education B; elementary education B; English B; entomology B; environmental health sciences B; family and consumer studies B; fashion merchandising B; film studies B; finance/banking B; fish and game management B; food sciences B; food services management B; forestry B; forest technology B; French B; genetics B; geography B; geology B; German B; Germanic languages and literature B; graphic arts B; Greek B; health education B; history B; home economics B; home economics education B; horticulture B; industrial arts B; insurance B; interdisciplinary studies B; interior design B; international business B; international studies B; journalism B; labor and industrial relations B; landscape architecture/design B; Latin B; Latin American studies B; (pre)law sequence B; literature B; management information systems B; marketing/retailing/merchandising B; mathematics B; (pre)medicine sequence B; medieval studies B; microbiology B; music B; music education B; music history B; music therapy B; nutrition B; painting/drawing B; pharmacy/pharmaceutical sciences B; philosophy B; photography B; physical education B; physics B; piano/organ B; political science/government B; poultry sciences B; psychology B; public relations B; publishing B; radio and television studies B; real estate B; recreation and leisure services B; religious studies B; Romance languages B; sacred music B; science education B; sculpture B; secondary education B; secretarial studies/office management A; Slavic languages B; social science B; social work B; sociology B; Spanish B; special education B; speech pathology and audiology B; speech/rhetoric/public address/debate B; statistics B; stringed instruments B; studio art B; systems science B; telecommunications B; textiles and clothing B; theater arts/drama B; (pre) veterinary medicine sequence B; voice B; water resources B; wildlife biology B; wind and percussion instruments B; women's studies B; zoology B. Majors with highest enrollment: biology/biological sciences, chemistry, history.

LD Program Information

Name of Program LD Adult Clinic.

Availability of Services Began offering services in 1982. Services provided to freshmen, sophomores, juniors, seniors. Program currently serves 63 LD students.

Fees $175 for initial assessment; additional fees based on services provided.

Staff 1 full-time, 3 part-time staff members, including director. Services provided by remediation specialists, diagnostic specialists.

Admissions LD applicants evaluated on the basis of high school transcript, untimed SAT. LD students may begin taking classes in fall, winter, spring, or summer. Application should be submitted 6 months in advance of initial anticipated enrollment.

Orientation Optional orientation offered before registration.

Housing College housing (including coed) available. LD students housed randomly. LD students not required to live on campus.

Diagnostic Testing Available in intelligence, reading, math, spelling, handwriting, spoken language, written language, motor abilities, perceptual skills, work and study habits, personality, social skills, psychoneurology, speech.

Tutoring Offered one-to-one by professional teachers, peer tutors. Available in all subjects. LD students may receive tutoring in all courses each term.

Basic Skills Remediation Offered one-to-one and in small groups by LD teachers, regular teachers. Available in reading, math, spelling, handwriting, spoken language, written language, learning strategies, motor abilities, perceptual skills, work and study habits, social skills, speech.

Academic Advisement Help with program planning provided by LD staff members, academic advisers. LD students may take up to 20 quarter hours each quarter; most take 10 to 17 quarter hours; 12 quarter hours required to maintain full-time status.

Auxiliary Aids and Services Aids include taped textbooks. Services include alternative exam arrangements, notetakers, advocacy.

Counseling Services Individual counseling, small-group counseling, rap sessions available.

Contact Dr. Noel Gregg, Director, LD Adult Clinic, University of Georgia, 528 Aderhold Hall, Athens, GA 30602, 404-542-1685.

UNIVERSITY OF HAWAII AT MANOA

Honolulu, Hawaii

Year Program Began	1966	Special Courses	
Special Fee	Varies	Taped Textbooks	✓
Special Orientation	✓	Alternative Exam Arrangements	✓
Diagnostic Testing		Notetakers	✓
Subject-Area Tutoring	✓	Staff	4 part-time
Basic Skills Remediation	✓	Number of Students Served	7

General Information State-supported coed university. Part of University of Hawaii System. Founded 1907. Awards A (terminal), B, M, D. Institutionally accredited by regional association; programs accredited by NAAB (architecture), AACSB (business), ABET (engineering and technology), NASM (music), NLN (nursing). Metropolitan setting; 300-acre campus. Total enrollment: 20,023. Faculty: 1,615 (1,149 full-time, 466 part-time); graduate assistants teach a few undergraduate courses. Calendar: semesters. Grading system: letters or numbers. Library holdings: 1.9 million bound volumes, 77,069 titles on microform, 28,619 periodical subscriptions, 5,000 records/tapes.

Undergraduate Profile Fall 1984: 14,645 undergraduates (2,294 freshmen); 18% part-time; 81% state residents; 11% transfers; 22% financial aid recipients; 53% women; 1% blacks; 5% Native Americans; 1% Hispanics; 66% Asian Americans; 12% foreign nationals; 15% of undergraduates over 25 years of age.

Expenses (1985–86) State resident tuition: $850 full-time, $36 per credit part-time. Nonresident tuition: $3060 full-time, $128 per credit part-time. Mandatory fees: $31. College room and board: $2442.

Financial Aid Fall 1984 full-time freshmen: 78% applied for aid, 30% of those were judged to have need, 100% of those were aided; the average aided freshman received an aid package worth $2478 (61% scholarships/grants, 39% self-help) meeting 100% of need. College-administered aid for all 1984–85 undergraduates: 1,897 need-based scholarships (average $594); 345 non-need scholarships (average $800); short-term loans (average $99); low-interest long-term loans from college funds (average $1800), from external sources (average $2500); SEOG; College Work-Study; 4,215 part-time jobs. Supporting data: FAF, IRS, institutional form required; validation form required for some; AFSA/SAR acceptable. Priority application deadline: 3/1.

Athletics Member NCAA (Division I). Intercollegiate sports: baseball/softball M(I,s), W(I); basketball M(I,s), W(I,s); cross-country running W(I,s); football M(I-A,s); golf M(I,s), W(I,s); sailing M, W; swimming and diving M(I,s), W(I,s); tennis M(I,s), W(I,s); volleyball M(I,s), W(I,s). Intramural sports: baseball/softball, basketball, football, golf, gymnastics, swimming and diving, tennis, track and field, volleyball.

Majors Accounting B; agricultural economics B; agricultural technologies B; agronomy/soil and crop sciences B; American studies B; animal sciences B; anthropology B; architecture B; art/fine arts B; Asian/Oriental studies B; biology/biological sciences B; botany/plant sciences B; business administration/commerce/management B; chemistry B; Chinese B; civil engineering B; classics B; communication B; computer information systems B; computer science B; dance B; dental services A, B; economics B; electrical engineering B; elementary education B; engineering (general) B; English B; entomology B; fashion design and technology B; fashion merchandising B; finance/banking B; food sciences B; French B; geography B; geology B; geophysics B; German B; Greek B; history B; home economics B; horticulture B; human development B; international economics B; Japanese B; journalism B; labor and industrial relations B; Latin B; marketing/retailing/merchandising B; mathematics B; mechanical engineering B; medical technology B; meteorology B; microbiology B; music B; nursing A, B; nutrition B; philosophy B; physics B; political science/government B; psychology B; real estate B; recreation and leisure services B; religious studies B; Russian B; secondary education B; social work B; sociology B; Spanish B; speech pathology and audiology B; speech/rhetoric/public address/debate B; theater arts/drama B; tourism and travel B; zoology B. Majors with highest enrollment: tourism and travel, electrical engineering, accounting.

LD Program Information

Name of Program KOKUA Program.

Availability of Services Began offering services in 1966. Services provided to freshmen, sophomores, juniors, seniors. Program currently serves 7 LD students: 1 freshman, 4 sophomores, 1 junior, 1 senior.

Fees $3.80 to $4 per hour for services provided by peers.

Staff 4 part-time staff members, including director. Services provided by tutor, counselor, auxiliary aids specialist.

Admissions LD applicants evaluated on the basis of high school transcript and grade point average, standard or untimed SAT or ACT, personal interview, letters of recommendation. LD students may begin taking classes in fall, spring, or summer. Application should be submitted 3 months in advance of initial anticipated enrollment.

Orientation Optional orientation offered before registration.

Housing College housing (including coed) available. LD students housed randomly. LD students not required to live on campus.

Tutoring Offered one-to-one by peer tutors. Available in some subjects. LD students may receive tutoring in all courses each term.

Basic Skills Remediation Offered one-to-one and in small groups by regular teachers. Available in reading, math, spelling, written language, learning strategies, work and study habits, social skills, speech.

Academic Advisement Help with program planning provided by LD staff members, academic advisers. Most LD students take 6 credits each semester; 12 credits required to maintain full-time status.

Auxiliary Aids and Services Aids include taped textbooks, tape recorders, typewriters, word processors. Services include alternative exam arrangements, notetakers, transcribers, readers.

Counseling Services Individual counseling available.

Contact Mrs. Ann Ito, Director, KOKUA Program, University of Hawaii at Manoa, Bachman Annex 13, Honolulu, HI 96822, 808-948-7511.

UNIVERSITY OF HOUSTON–UNIVERSITY PARK

Houston, Texas

Year Program Began	*Not reported*	Special Courses	
Special Fee	Varies	Taped Textbooks	✓
Special Orientation		Alternative Exam Arrangements	✓
Diagnostic Testing	✓	Notetakers	✓
Subject-Area Tutoring	✓	Staff	20 part-time
Basic Skills Remediation		Number of Students Served	2

General Information State-supported coed university. Part of University of Houston System. Founded 1927. Awards B, M, D. Institutionally accredited by regional association; programs accredited by NAAB (architecture), AACSB (business), ABET (engineering and technology), NASM (music), COE (optometry), ACPE (pharmacy), NCATE (teacher education). Metropolitan setting; 525-acre barrier-free campus. Total enrollment: 31,095. Faculty: 2,710 (1,082 full-time, 1,628 part-time); 80% have doctoral degrees; graduate assistants teach a few undergraduate courses. Calendar: semesters. Grading system: letters or numbers. Library holdings: 1.4 million bound volumes, 1.5 million titles on microform, 13,400 periodical subscriptions.

Undergraduate Profile Fall 1984: 20,000 undergraduates (2,050 freshmen); 48% part-time; 88% state residents; 16% transfers; 50% financial aid recipients; 45% women; 9% blacks; 1% Native Americans; 6% Hispanics; 6% Asian Americans; 7% foreign nationals; 267 legally handicapped students.

Expenses (1985–86) State resident tuition: $720 full-time, $12 per semester hour part-time. Nonresident tuition: $3960 full-time, $120 per semester hour part-time. College room and board: $3000.

Financial Aid Fall 1984 full-time freshmen: the average aided freshman received an aid package meeting 70% of need. College-administered aid for all 1984–85 undergraduates: need-based scholarships; non-need scholarships; short-term loans (average $300); low-interest long-term loans; College Work-Study; part-time jobs. Supporting data: FFS, FAF, state form, institutional form, AFSA/SAR required; IRS required for some. Priority application deadline: 3/1.

Athletics Member NCAA (Division I). Intercollegiate sports: baseball/softball M(I,s); basketball M(I,s), W(I,s); cross-country running M(I,s), W(I,s); football M(I-A,s); golf M(I,s); swimming and diving W(I,s); tennis M(I,s), W(I,s); track and field M(I,s), W(I,s); volleyball W(I,s). Intramural sports: badminton, baseball/softball, basketball, bowling, cross-country running, football, golf, lacrosse, racquetball, soccer, swimming and diving, tennis, track and field, volleyball, water polo, weight lifting.

Majors Accounting B; American studies B; anthropology B; applied art B; architecture B; art education B; art/fine arts B; art history B; bilingual/bicultural education B; biochemistry B; biology/biological sciences B; biophysics B; broadcasting B; business administration/commerce/management B; business education B; business machine technologies B; ceramic art and design B; chemical engineering B; chemical engineering technology B; chemistry B; civil engineering B; civil engineering technology B; communication B; computer engineering B; computer science B; computer technologies B; construction management B; construction technologies B; consumer services B; economics B; education B; electrical and electronics technologies B; electrical engineering B; elementary education B; engineering (general) B; English B; environmental design B; family and consumer studies B; fashion merchandising B; finance/banking B; French B; geography B; geology B; geophysics B; German B; health education B; heating/refrigeration/air conditioning B; history B; home economics B; home economics education B; hotel and restaurant management B; human development B; humanities B; industrial engineering B; jewelry and metalsmithing B; journalism B; manufacturing technology B; marketing/retailing/merchandising B; mathematics B; mechanical engineering B; mechanical engineering technology B; music B; music education B; natural sciences B; optometry B; painting/drawing B; pharmacy/pharmaceutical sciences B; philosophy B; photography B; physical education B; physics B; political science/government B; psychology B; radio and television studies B; science B; science education B; sculpture B; secondary education B; secretarial studies/office management B; social science B; sociology B; Spanish B; special education B; speech pathology and audiology B; speech therapy B; surveying technology B; theater arts/drama B. Majors with highest enrollment: business administration/commerce/management, biology/biological sciences, computer science.

LD Program Information

Name of Program Handicapped Services.

Availability of Services Services provided to freshmen, sophomores, juniors, seniors. Program currently serves 2 LD students: 1 freshman, 1 sophomore.

Fees $5 to $10 for testing and evaluation.

Staff 20 part-time staff members, including coordinator. Services provided by remediation specialists, tutors, counselors, diagnostic specialists, amanuenses, readers.

Admissions LD applicants evaluated on the basis of high school transcript and grade point average, standard or untimed SAT or ACT. LD students may begin taking classes in fall, spring, or summer. Application should be submitted 2 months in advance of initial anticipated enrollment.

Housing College housing (including coed) available. LD students housed randomly. LD students not required to live on campus.

Diagnostic Testing Available in intelligence, reading, math, written language, perceptual skills, work and study habits, personality, social skills, speech.

Tutoring Offered one-to-one and in small groups by peer tutors. Available in some subjects. LD students may receive tutoring in all courses each term.

Academic Advisement Help with program planning provided by academic advisers. LD students may take up to 18 semester hours each semester; 12 semester hours required to maintain full-time status.

Auxiliary Aids and Services Aids include taped textbooks, tape recorders, calculators, typewriters, word processors. Services include alternative exam arrangements, notetakers, advocacy.

Counseling Services Individual counseling, small-group counseling, career counseling available.

Contact Coordinator of Handicapped Services, University of Houston–University Park, Houston, TX 77004, 713-749-1527.

UNIVERSITY OF IDAHO
Moscow, Idaho

Year Program Began	1981	Special Courses	✓
Special Fee	None	Taped Textbooks	✓
Special Orientation		Alternative Exam Arrangements	✓
Diagnostic Testing	✓	Notetakers	✓
Subject-Area Tutoring	✓	Staff	9 part-time
Basic Skills Remediation	✓	Number of Students Served	17

General Information State-supported coed university. Founded 1889. Awards B, M, D. Institutionally accredited by regional association; programs accredited by NAAB (architecture), ABET (engineering and technology), NASM (music), NCATE (teacher education). Small-town setting; 1,200-acre campus. Total enrollment: 8,970. Faculty: 589 (561 full-time, 28 part-time); 71% have doctoral degrees; graduate assistants teach a few undergraduate courses. Calendar: semesters. Grading system: letters or numbers. Library holdings: 625,833 bound volumes, 347,253 titles on microform, 5,426 periodical subscriptions.

Undergraduate Profile Fall 1984: 7,267 undergraduates (1,151 freshmen) from 49 states and territories and 32 foreign countries; 19% part-time; 72% state residents; 36% transfers; 60% financial aid recipients; 38% women; 1% blacks; 1% Native Americans; 1% Hispanics; 1% Asian Americans; 2% foreign nationals; 27% of undergraduates over 25 years of age; 64 legally handicapped students.

Expenses (1985–86) State resident tuition: $0 full-time, $53.25 per credit part-time. Nonresident tuition: $2000 full-time, $53.25 per credit part-time. Mandatory fees: $1010. College room and board: $2224. College room only: $785 (minimum).

Financial Aid Fall 1984 full-time freshmen: 60% applied for aid, 75% of those were judged to have need, 100% of those were aided; the average aided freshman received an aid package worth $3500 (34% scholarships/grants, 66% self-help) meeting 75% of need. College-administered aid for all 1984–85 undergraduates: 622 need-based scholarships (average $610); 1,058 non-need scholarships (average $610); short-term loans (average $300); low-interest long-term loans from college funds (average $892), from external sources (average $2365); SEOG; College Work-Study; 2,500 part-time jobs. Supporting data: FAF, institutional form, AFSA/SAR required; IRS required for some; FFS acceptable. Priority application deadline: 3/8.

Athletics Member NCAA (Division I). Intercollegiate sports: basketball M(I,s), W(I,s); cross-country running M(I,s), W(I,s); football M(I-AA,s); golf M(s), W(s); swimming and diving M(I,s), W(II,s); tennis M(I,s), W(I,s); track and field M(I,s), W(I,s); volleyball W(I,s). Intramural sports: baseball/softball, basketball, bowling, cross-country running, equestrian sports, fencing, football, golf, gymnastics, martial arts, riflery, rugby, skiing (cross-country), skiing (downhill), soccer, squash, swimming and diving, tennis, track and field, volleyball, weight lifting.

Majors Accounting B; agricultural business B; agricultural economics B; agricultural education B; agricultural engineering B; agricultural sciences B; agronomy/soil and crop sciences B; anthropology B; applied art B; applied mathematics B; architecture B; art education B; art/fine arts B; art history B; bacteriology B; biochemistry B; biology/biological sciences B; botany/plant sciences B; broadcasting B; business administration/commerce/management B; business education B; cartography B; ceramic art and design B; chemical engineering B; chemistry B; child care/child and family studies B; child psychology/child development B; civil engineering B; classics B; commercial art B; communication B; computer science B; creative writing B; dance B; earth science B; economics B; education B; electrical engineering B; elementary education B; engineering (general) B; English B; entomology B; farm and ranch management B; finance/banking B; fish and game management B; food sciences B; forestry B; French B; geography B; geological engineering B; geology B; German B; history B; home economics B; home economics education B; horticulture B; industrial arts B; interdisciplinary studies B; interior design B; journalism B; landscape architecture/design B; Latin B; Latin American studies B; liberal arts/general studies B; marketing/retailing/merchandising B; mathematics B; mechanical engineering B; medical technology B; metallurgical engineering B; metallurgy B; mining and mineral engineering B; museum studies B; music B; music education B; music history B; natural resource management B; naval sciences B; nuclear engineering B; ornamental horticulture B; parks management B; philosophy B; photography B; physical education B; physics B; political science/government B; poultry sciences B; psychology B; radio and television studies B; range management B; recreation and leisure services B; secondary education B; secretarial studies/office management B; social science B; sociology B; soil conservation B; Spanish B; special education B; speech/rhetoric/public address/debate B; statistics B; stringed instruments B; teaching English as a second language B; telecommunications B; textiles and clothing B; theater arts/drama B; veterinary sciences B; vocational education B; wildlife biology B; wildlife management B; wind and percussion instruments B; wood sciences B; zoology B. Majors with highest enrollment: education, architecture, computer science.

LD Program Information

Name of Program Special Services for Disadvantaged Students.

Availability of Services Began offering services in 1981. Services provided to freshmen, sophomores, juniors, seniors. Program currently serves 17 LD students: 6 freshmen, 2 sophomores, 4 juniors, 5 seniors.

Staff 9 part-time staff members, including director, program consultant. Services provided by remediation specialists, tutors, counselor, diagnostic specialists, handicapped student adviser.

Admissions LD applicants evaluated on the basis of high school transcript and grade point average, standard or untimed SAT or ACT; personal interview, autobiographical statement, letters of recommendation, psychoeducational report required for some. LD students may begin taking classes in fall, spring, or summer. Application should be submitted 6 to 9 months in advance of initial anticipated enrollment.

Housing College housing (including coed) available. LD students housed randomly. LD students not required to live on campus.

Diagnostic Testing Available in intelligence, reading, math, spelling, written language, motor abilities, perceptual skills, work and study habits, personality, social skills, psychoneurology, memory.

Tutoring Offered one-to-one and in small groups by professional teachers, peer tutors. Available in all subjects. LD students may receive tutoring in all courses each term.

Basic Skills Remediation Offered one-to-one and in small groups by regular teachers, teacher trainees. Available in reading, math, spelling, written language, learning strategies, work and study habits.

Academic Advisement Help with program planning provided by LD staff members, academic advisers. LD students may take up to 21 credits each semester; most take 12 credits; 12 credits required to maintain full-time status.

Special Courses Offered in college survival skills, reading, vocabulary development, composition, math, study skills. None offered for credit; none enter into overall grade point average.

Auxiliary Aids and Services Aids include taped textbooks, tape recorders, typewriters, word processors, Kurzweil reading machine, Visual Tech machine. Services include alternative exam arrangements, notetakers, advocacy, referral to vocational rehabilitation and other services.

Counseling Services Individual counseling, small-group counseling, career counseling available.

Contact Ms. Mary L. Morris, Director, Special Services for Disadvantaged Students, University of Idaho, Phinney 302, Moscow, ID 83843, 208-885-6746.

UNIVERSITY OF KANSAS

Lawrence, Kansas

Year Program Began	1979	Special Courses	
Special Fee	None	Taped Textbooks	✓
Special Orientation		Alternative Exam Arrangements	✓
Diagnostic Testing	✓	Notetakers	✓
Subject-Area Tutoring	✓	Staff	1 part-time
Basic Skills Remediation		Number of Students Served	*Not reported*

General Information State-supported coed university. Founded 1866. Awards B, M, D. Institutionally accredited by regional association; programs accredited by NAAB (architecture), NASAD (art and design), AACSB (business), ABET (engineering and technology), NASM (music), ACPE (pharmacy), NCATE (teacher education). City setting, with easy access to Kansas City; 1,000-acre campus. Total enrollment: 24,436. Faculty: 1,143; 76% have doctoral degrees; graduate assistants teach a few undergraduate courses. Calendar: semesters. Grading system: letters or numbers. Library holdings: 2.2 million bound volumes, 1.2 million titles on microform, 25,900 periodical subscriptions, 37,000 records/tapes.

Undergraduate Profile Fall 1984: 17,874 undergraduates (3,812 freshmen) from 53 states and territories and 97 foreign countries; 12% part-time; 72% state residents; 72% financial aid recipients; 47% women; 4% blacks; 1% Native Americans; 1% Hispanics; 1% Asian Americans; 5% foreign nationals.

Expenses (1985–86) State resident tuition: $990 full-time, $50 per credit hour part-time. Nonresident tuition: $2794 full-time, $110 per credit hour part-time. Mandatory fees: $240. College room and board: $2071.

Financial Aid Fall 1984 full-time freshmen: 62% applied for aid, 80% of those were judged to have need, 92% of those were aided; the average aided freshman received an aid package worth $2434 (24% scholarships/grants, 76% self-help) meeting 84% of need. College-administered aid for all 1984–85 undergraduates: 696 need-based scholarships (average $1074); 381 non-need scholarships (average $376); short-term loans (average $350); low-interest long-term loans from external sources (average $1200); SEOG; College Work-Study; 1,400 part-time jobs. Supporting data: FFS, IRS, institutional form, AFSA/SAR required. Priority application deadline: 3/1.

Athletics Member NCAA (Division I). Intercollegiate sports: baseball/softball M(I,s), W(I,s); basketball M(I,s), W(I,s); crew M, W; cross-country running M(I,s), W(I,s); football M(I-A,s); golf M(I,s), W(I,s); rugby M(c); soccer M(c); swimming and diving M(I,s), W(I,s); tennis M(I,s), W(I,s); track and field M(I,s), W(I,s); volleyball W(I,s). Intramural sports: archery, badminton, baseball/softball, basketball, bowling, crew, cross-country running, fencing, football, golf, martial arts, racquetball, rugby, sailing, soccer, squash, swimming and diving, tennis, track and field, volleyball, water polo, weight lifting, wrestling.

Majors Accounting B; advertising B; aerospace engineering B; African studies B; American studies B; anthropology B; applied art B; architectural engineering B; architecture B; art education B; art/fine arts B; art history B; Asian/Oriental studies B; astronomy B; atmospheric sciences B; biochemistry B; biology/biological sciences B; biophysics B; broadcasting B; business administration/commerce/management B; cell biology B; ceramic art and design B; chemical engineering B; chemistry B; child care/child and family studies B; child psychology/child development B; Chinese B; civil engineering B; classics B; commercial art B; communication B; computer engineering B; computer science B; dance B; early childhood education B; East Asian studies B; East European and Soviet studies B; ecology/environmental studies B; economics B; education B; educational administration B; electrical engineering B; elementary education B; emergency medical technology B; engineering physics B; engineering sciences B; English B; entomology B; environmental design B; environmental sciences B; film studies B; French B; geography B; geological engineering B; geology B; geophysics B; German B; Germanic languages and literature B; graphic arts B; health education B; history B; history of science B; human development B; humanities B; illustration B; industrial design B; interior design B; Italian B; Japanese B; jewelry and metalsmithing B; journalism B; Latin American studies B; liberal arts/general studies B; linguistics B; mathematics B; mechanical engineering B; medical records services B; medical technology B; meteorology B; microbiology B; music B; music education B; music history B; music therapy B; nursing B; occupational therapy B; painting/drawing B; petroleum/natural gas engineering B; pharmacy/pharmaceutical sciences B; philosophy B; photography B; physical education B; physical therapy B; physics B; physiology B; piano/organ B; political science/government B; psychology B; public relations B; radio and television studies B; recreation and leisure services B; religious studies B; respiratory therapy B; Russian and Slavic studies B; science education B; sculpture B; secondary education B; Slavic languages B; social work B; sociology B; Spanish B; speech pathology and audiology B; stringed instruments B; textile arts B; theater arts/drama B; toxicology B; voice B; wind and percussion instruments B; women's studies B. Majors with highest enrollment: business administration/commerce/management, communication.

LD Program Information

Name of Program Student Assistance Center.

Availability of Services Began offering services in 1979. Services provided to freshmen, sophomores, juniors, seniors.

Staff 1 part-time staff member (assistant director).

Admissions LD applicants evaluated on the basis of high school transcript and grade point average, standard or untimed ACT. LD students may begin taking classes in fall, spring, or summer.

Housing College housing (including coed) available. LD students housed randomly. LD students not required to live on campus.

Diagnostic Testing Available in intelligence, reading, math, spelling, spoken language, written language, perceptual skills, personality, speech, hearing.

Tutoring Offered one-to-one and in small groups by peer tutors. Available in all subjects. LD students may receive tutoring in all courses each term.

Academic Advisement Help with program planning provided by academic advisers. LD students may take up to 18 credit hours each semester; 12 credit hours required to maintain full-time status.

Auxiliary Aids and Services Aids include taped textbooks, tape recorders, calculators. Services include alternative exam arrangements, notetakers, advocacy.

Counseling Services Individual counseling available.

Contact Dr. Lorraine I. Michel, Assistant Director, Student Assistance Center, University of Kansas, 121 Strong Hall, Lawrence, KS 66045, 913-864-4064.

UNIVERSITY OF KENTUCKY
Lexington, Kentucky

Year Program Began	1975	Special Courses	
Special Fee	None	Taped Textbooks	✓
Special Orientation		Alternative Exam Arrangements	✓
Diagnostic Testing	✓	Notetakers	✓
Subject-Area Tutoring	✓	Staff	2 part-time
Basic Skills Remediation	✓	Number of Students Served	*Not reported*

General Information State-supported coed university. Founded 1865. Awards B, M, D. Institutionally accredited by regional association; programs accredited by NAAB (architecture), AACSB (business), ABET (engineering and technology), FIDER (interior design), NASM (music), NLN (nursing), ACPE (pharmacy), NCATE (teacher education). City setting, with easy access to Cincinnati and Louisville; 750-acre campus. Total enrollment: 21,300. Faculty: 1,842 (1,524 full-time, 318 part-time); 95% have doctoral degrees; graduate assistants teach a few undergraduate courses. Calendar: semesters. Grading system: letters or numbers. Library holdings: 1.8 million bound volumes, 1.9 million titles on microform, 33,000 periodical subscriptions, 10,000 records/tapes.

Undergraduate Profile Fall 1984: 16,076 undergraduates (2,336 freshmen) from 50 states and territories and 55 foreign countries; 13% part-time; 89% state residents; 40% transfers; 58% financial aid recipients; 47% women; 4% blacks; 1% Native Americans; 1% Hispanics; 1% Asian Americans; 1% foreign nationals; 20% of undergraduates over 25 years of age; 300 legally handicapped students.

Expenses (1985–86) State resident tuition: $1228 full-time, $50 per semester hour part-time. Nonresident tuition: $3518 full-time, $145 per semester hour part-time. College room and board: $2456.

Financial Aid Fall 1984 full-time freshmen: 70% applied for aid, 86% of those were judged to have need, 96% of those were aided; the average aided freshman received an aid package worth $3654 (51% scholarships/grants, 49% self-help) meeting 85% of need. College-administered aid for all 1984–85 undergraduates: 5,599 need-based scholarships (average $1080); 1,500 non-need scholarships (average $500); short-term loans (average $155); low-interest long-term loans from college funds (average $594), from external sources (average $2300); SEOG; College Work-Study; 1,800 part-time jobs. Supporting data: FAF, institutional form, AFSA/SAR required. Priority application deadline: 4/15.

Athletics Member NCAA (Division I). Intercollegiate sports: baseball/softball M(I,s); basketball M(I,s), W(I,s); cross-country running M(I,s), W(I,s); football M(I-A,s); golf M(I,s), W(I,s); gymnastics W(I,s); riflery M(I), W(I); swimming and diving M(I,s), W(I); tennis M(I,s), W(I,s); track and field M(I,s), W(I,s); volleyball W(I,s); water polo M(I,s). Intramural sports: badminton, baseball/softball, basketball, cross-country running, fencing, field hockey, football, golf, martial arts, rugby, soccer, squash, swimming and diving, tennis, track and field, volleyball.

Majors Accounting B; advertising B; agricultural business B; agricultural economics B; agricultural education B; agricultural engineering B; agricultural sciences B; agronomy/soil and crop sciences B; animal sciences B; anthropology B; architecture B; art education B; art/fine arts B; art history B; astronomy B; biology/biological sciences B; botany/plant sciences B; business administration/commerce/management B; business education B; chemical engineering B; chemistry B; child care/child and family studies B; civil engineering B; classics B; communication B; comparative literature B; computer science B; dairy sciences B; (pre)dentistry sequence B; dietetics B; early childhood education B; economics B; educational media B; electrical engineering B; elementary education B; English B; entomology B; family and consumer studies B; finance/banking B; food sciences B; forestry B; French B; geography B; geology B; German B; Greek B; health education B; history B; home economics education B; horticulture B; industrial administration B; interior design B; Italian B; journalism B; labor and industrial relations B; landscape architecture/design B; Latin B; Latin American studies B; liberal arts/general studies B; linguistics B; literature B; marketing/retailing/merchandising B; mathematics B; mechanical engineering B; medical technology B; (pre)medicine sequence B; metallurgical engineering B; microbiology B; mining and mineral engineering B; modern languages B; music B; music education B; music history B; Near and Middle Eastern studies B; nursing B; nutrition B; pest control technology B; pharmacy/pharmaceutical sciences B; philosophy B; physical education B; physical therapy B; physics B; political science/government B; psychology B; public health B; public relations B; radiological sciences B; recreation and leisure services B; Russian B; Russian and Slavic studies B; science education B; secondary education B; social science B; social work B; sociology B; Spanish B; special education B; speech/rhetoric/public address/debate B; studio art B; telecommunications B; textiles and clothing B; theater arts/drama B; (pre)veterinary medicine sequence B; vocational education B; zoology B. Majors with highest enrollment: business administration/commerce/management, accounting, biology/biological sciences.

LD Program Information

Name of Program Handicapped Student Services.

Availability of Services Began offering services in 1975. Services provided to freshmen, sophomores, juniors, seniors.

Staff 2 part-time staff members, including directors of Handicapped Student Services and Educational Assessment Clinic.

Admissions LD applicants evaluated on the basis of high school transcript and grade point average, untimed SAT or ACT, personal interview, psychoeducational report. LD students may begin taking classes in fall, winter, spring, or summer. Application should be submitted at least 7 months in advance of initial anticipated enrollment.

Housing College housing (including coed) available. LD students housed randomly. LD students not required to live on campus.

Diagnostic Testing Available in various areas through University Counseling and Testing Center.

Tutoring Offered one-to-one and in small groups by staff of departmental resource centers. Available in some subjects. LD students may receive tutoring in all courses each term.

Basic Skills Remediation Offered one-to-one and in small groups by regular teachers. Available in reading, math, spelling, handwriting, learning strategies, work and study habits.

Academic Advisement Help with program planning provided by academic advisers. LD students may take up to 18 semester hours each semester; 12 semester hours required to maintain full-time status.

Auxiliary Aids and Services Aids include taped textbooks, tape recorders, calculators, typewriters. Services include alternative exam arrangements, notetakers.

Counseling Services Individual counseling, small-group counseling, rap sessions available.

Contact Mr. Jacob Karnes, Director, Handicapped Student Services, University of Kentucky, 8 Alumni Gym, Lexington, KY 40506-0291, 606-257-2754.

UNIVERSITY OF LOUISVILLE
Louisville, Kentucky

Year Program Began	1980	Special Courses	✓
Special Fee	None	Taped Textbooks	✓
Special Orientation		Alternative Exam Arrangements	✓
Diagnostic Testing	✓	Notetakers	✓
Subject-Area Tutoring	✓	Staff	2 full-time, 4 part-time
Basic Skills Remediation	✓	Number of Students Served	50

General Information State-supported coed university. Founded 1798. Awards A (college transfer and terminal), B, M, D. Institutionally accredited by regional association; programs accredited by AACSB (business), ABET (engineering and technology), NASM (music), NLN (nursing), NCATE (teacher education). Metropolitan setting; 140-acre campus. Total enrollment: 19,794. Faculty: 1,363 (994 full-time, 369 part-time); 81% have doctoral degrees; graduate assistants teach a few undergraduate courses. Calendar: semesters. Grading system: letters or numbers. Library holdings: 923,294 bound volumes, 820,287 titles on microform, 9,208 periodical subscriptions.

Undergraduate Profile Fall 1984: 15,132 undergraduates (2,354 freshmen) from 48 states and territories and 61 foreign countries; 42% part-time; 93% state residents; 35% transfers; 45% financial aid recipients; 48% women; 8% blacks; 1% Hispanics; 1% Asian Americans; 1% foreign nationals; 339 legally handicapped students.

Expenses (1985–86) State resident tuition: $1239 full-time. Nonresident tuition: $3529 full-time. Part-time tuition and fees per semester (1 to 11 credit hours) range from $58 to $570.50 for state residents, $153.50 to $1621 for nonresidents. College room and board: $2100. College room only: $800.

Financial Aid Fall 1984 full-time freshmen: 84% applied for aid, 79% of those were judged to have need, 100% of those were aided; the average aided freshman received an aid package worth $1179 (70% scholarships/grants, 30% self-help) meeting 66% of need. College-administered aid for all 1984–85 undergraduates: 3,700 need-based scholarships (average $947); non-need scholarships (average $500); short-term loans (average $200); low-interest long-term loans from college funds (average $800), from external sources (average $1850); SEOG; College Work-Study; 575 part-time jobs. Supporting data: FAF, institutional form, AFSA/SAR required; IRS required for some; FFS acceptable. Priority application deadline: 4/15.

Athletics Member NCAA (Division I). Intercollegiate sports: baseball/softball M(I,s); basketball M(I,s), W(I,s); cross-country running M(I,s), W(I,s); field hockey W(I,s); football M(I-A,s); golf M(I,s); soccer M(I,s); swimming and diving M(I,s), W(I,s); tennis M(I,s), W(I,s); track and field M(I,s), W(I,s); volleyball W(I,s). Intramural sports: archery, badminton, baseball/softball, basketball, bowling, cross-country running, fencing, field hockey, football, golf, martial arts, racquetball, riflery, rugby, soccer, swimming and diving, tennis, track and field, volleyball, water polo, weight lifting, wrestling.

Majors Accounting B; American studies B; anthropology B; applied art B; applied mathematics B; art education B; art/fine arts B; art history B; biology/biological sciences A, B; botany/plant sciences B; business administration/commerce/management B; chemical engineering B; chemical engineering technology A; chemistry B; civil engineering B; classics B; communication B; computer science B; corrections B; cytotechnology B; data processing A; dental services A, B; (pre) dentistry sequence B; early childhood education B; economics B; education B; electrical engineering B; electrical engineering technology A; elementary education B; engineering management B; engineering technology A; English B; environmental engineering B; finance/banking B; French B; geography B; geology B; German B; Greek A, B; guidance and counseling B; health education B; history B; humanities B; industrial design A; industrial engineering B; interior design B; Latin B; law enforcement/police sciences B; (pre)law sequence B; liberal arts/general studies B; linguistics B; management engineering B; marketing/retailing/merchandising B; mathematics B; mechanical engineering B; mechanical engineering technology A; medical laboratory technology B; medical technology B; (pre)medicine sequence B; music B; music education B; music history B; nursing B; nutrition B; paralegal studies A; pharmacy/pharmaceutical sciences B; philosophy B; physical education B; physical therapy B; physics B; piano/organ B; political science/government B; psychology B; radiological technology A; recreation and leisure services B; respiratory therapy A; Russian B; Russian and Slavic studies B; science B; secondary education B; sociology B; Spanish B; speech therapy B; telecommunications B; theater arts/drama B; urban studies B; vocational education B; voice B; zoology B. Majors with highest enrollment: accounting, business administration/commerce/management, communication.

LD Program Information

Name of Program Special Student Services.

Availability of Services Began offering services in 1980. Services provided to freshmen, sophomores, juniors, seniors. Program currently serves 50 LD students.

Staff 2 full-time, 4 part-time staff members, including director. Services provided by remediation specialists, tutors, counselors.

Admissions LD applicants evaluated on the basis of high school transcript and grade point average, standard or untimed ACT. LD students may begin taking classes in fall, spring, or summer. Application should be submitted 2 to 3 months in advance of initial anticipated enrollment.

Housing College housing (including coed) available. LD students housed with other LD students and non-LD students. LD students not required to live on campus.

Diagnostic Testing Available in reading, math, written language.

Tutoring Offered one-to-one by professional teachers, peer tutors. Available in all subjects. LD students may receive tutoring in all courses each term.

Basic Skills Remediation Offered one-to-one and in small groups by regular teachers. Available in reading, math, spelling, written language.

Academic Advisement Help with program planning provided by academic advisers. LD students may take up to 12 credit hours each semester; 12 credit hours required to maintain full-time status.

Special Courses Offered in communication skills, career planning. None offered for credit; none enter into overall grade point average.

Auxiliary Aids and Services Aids include taped textbooks, tape recorders. Services include alternative exam arrangements, notetakers, advocacy.

Counseling Services Individual counseling, career counseling available.

Contact Mr. William J. Cox, Director, Special Student Services, University of Louisville, Robbins Hall, Louisville, KY 40292, 502-588-6927.

UNIVERSITY OF MARYLAND COLLEGE PARK

College Park, Maryland

Year Program Began	1978	Special Courses	
Special Fee	None	Taped Textbooks	✓
Special Orientation		Alternative Exam Arrangements	✓
Diagnostic Testing		Notetakers	✓
Subject-Area Tutoring	✓	Staff	2 part-time
Basic Skills Remediation		Number of Students Served	*Not reported*

General Information State-supported coed university. Part of University of Maryland System. Founded 1856. Awards B, M, D. Institutionally accredited by regional association; programs accredited by NAAB (architecture), AACSB (business), ABET (engineering and technology), NASM (music), NCATE (teacher education). Small-town setting, with easy access to Washington, DC; 1,378-acre campus. Total enrollment: 38,307. Faculty: 2,346 (1,870 full-time, 476 part-time); 80% have doctoral degrees; graduate assistants teach a few undergraduate courses. Calendar: semesters. Grading system: letters or numbers. Library holdings: 1.6 million bound volumes, 1.7 million titles on microform, 19,441 periodical subscriptions, 26,000 records/tapes.

Undergraduate Profile Fall 1984: 30,231 undergraduates (5,133 freshmen) from 51 states and territories and 90 foreign countries; 16% part-time; 75% state residents; 13% transfers; 46% financial aid recipients; 46% women; 8% blacks; 0% Native Americans; 2% Hispanics; 6% Asian Americans; 2% foreign nationals; 11% of undergraduates over 25 years of age; 200 legally handicapped students.

Expenses (1985–86) State resident tuition: $1496 full-time. Nonresident tuition: $4002 full-time. Part-time tuition per semester (1 to 8 semester hours) ranges from $123 to $627. College room and board: $3345. College room only: $1842.

Financial Aid Fall 1984 full-time freshmen: 60% applied for aid, 90% of those were judged to have need, 86% of those were aided; the average aided freshman received an aid package worth $2106 (41% scholarships/grants, 59% self-help) meeting 90% of need. College-administered aid for all 1984–85 undergraduates: 2,200 need-based scholarships (average $590); 450 non-need scholarships (average $900); short-term loans (average $100); low-interest long-term loans from external sources (average $1500); SEOG; College Work-Study; 1,000 part-time jobs. Supporting data: FAF, institutional form, AFSA/SAR, Financial Aid Transcript (for transfers) required; state form required for some; FFS, IRS acceptable. Priority application deadline: 2/15.

Athletics Member NCAA (Division I). Intercollegiate sports: baseball/softball M(I,s); basketball M(I,s), W(I,s); bowling M; cross-country running M(I,s), W(I,s); field hockey W(I,s); football M(I-A,s); golf M(I,s); gymnastics W(I,s); lacrosse M(I,s), W(I,s); soccer M(I,s); swimming and diving M(I,s), W(I,s); tennis M(I,s), W(I,s); track and field M(I,s), W(I,s); volleyball W(I,s); wrestling M(I,s). Intramural sports: badminton, baseball/softball, basketball, bowling, cross-country running, equestrian sports, football, golf, lacrosse, racquetball, soccer, squash, swimming and diving, tennis, track and field, volleyball, weight lifting, wrestling.

Majors Accounting B; advertising B; aerospace engineering B; agricultural economics B; agricultural education B; agricultural engineering B; agricultural sciences B; agronomy/soil and crop sciences B; American studies B; animal sciences B; anthropology B; architecture B; art education B; art/fine arts B; art history B; astronomy B; biochemistry B; biology/biological sciences B; black/Afro-American studies B; botany/plant sciences B; broadcasting B; business administration/commerce/management B; business education B; chemical engineering B; chemistry B; child care/child and family studies B; civil engineering B; classics B; community services B; computer science B; conservation B; consumer services B; criminal justice B; dairy sciences B; dance B; (pre)dentistry sequence B; dietetics B; early childhood education B; East Asian studies B; economics B; education B; educational administration B; electrical engineering B; elementary education B; engineering (general) B; English B; entomology B; family and consumer studies B; finance/banking B; fire protection engineering B; fire science B; food sciences B; French B; geography B; geology B; German B; Germanic languages and literature B; health education B; history B; home economics B; home economics education B; horticulture B; human ecology B; industrial arts B; interior design B; journalism B; Judaic studies B; labor and industrial relations B; Latin B; law enforcement/police sciences B; (pre)law sequence B; liberal arts/general studies B; library science B; marketing/retailing/merchandising B; mathematics B; mechanical engineering B; (pre)medicine sequence B; microbiology B; music B; music education B; music history B; nuclear engineering B; nutrition B; philosophy B; photography B; physical education B; physical fitness/human movement B; physical sciences B; physics B; political science/government B; poultry sciences B; psychology B; public relations B; radio and television studies B; recreation and leisure services B; Russian B; Russian and Slavic studies B; science education B; secondary education B; Slavic languages B; sociology B; Spanish B; special education B; speech pathology and audiology B; speech/rhetoric/public address/debate B; speech therapy B; statistics B; studio art B; technical writing B; textiles and clothing B; theater arts/drama B; transportation technologies B; urban studies B; (pre)veterinary medicine sequence B; wildlife management B; zoology B. Majors with highest enrollment: accounting, computer science, electrical engineering.

LD Program Information

Name of Program Disabled Student Services.

Availability of Services Began offering services in 1978. Services provided to freshmen, sophomores, juniors, seniors.

Staff 2 part-time staff members, including coordinator. Services provided by tutors, graduate assistant.

Admissions LD applicants evaluated on the basis of high school transcript and grade point average, untimed SAT or ACT, autobiographical statement, letters of recommendation. LD students may begin taking classes in fall, spring, or summer. Application should be submitted 5 to 10 months in advance of initial anticipated enrollment.

Housing College housing (including coed) available. LD students housed randomly. LD students not required to live on campus.

Tutoring Offered one-to-one and in small groups by peer tutors, graduate students. Available in some subjects. LD students may receive tutoring in all courses each term.

Academic Advisement Help with program planning provided by academic advisers. LD students may take up to 12 semester hours each semester; 9 semester hours required to maintain full-time status.

Auxiliary Aids and Services Aids include taped textbooks. Services include alternative exam arrangements, notetakers, advocacy.

Counseling Services Individual counseling, career counseling available.

Contact Ms. Carol J. Wilde, Coordinator, Disabled Student Services, University of Maryland College Park, 0126 Shoemaker Hall, College Park, MD 20742, 301-454-6701.

UNIVERSITY OF MARYLAND EASTERN SHORE

Princess Anne, Maryland

Year Program Began	1983	Special Courses	✓
Special Fee	None	Taped Textbooks	
Special Orientation	✓	Alternative Exam Arrangements	✓
Diagnostic Testing	✓	Notetakers	✓
Subject-Area Tutoring	✓	Staff	4 full-time, 12 part-time
Basic Skills Remediation	✓	Number of Students Served	1

General Information State-supported coed university. Part of University of Maryland System. Founded 1886. Awards B, M, D. Institutionally accredited by regional association. Rural setting; 540-acre campus. Total enrollment: 1,230. Faculty: 94 (79 full-time, 15 part-time); 56% have doctoral degrees; graduate assistants teach no undergraduate courses. Calendar: semesters. Grading system: letters or numbers. Library holdings: 106,050 bound volumes, 840 periodical subscriptions, 1,564 records/tapes.

Undergraduate Profile Fall 1984: 1,160 undergraduates (301 freshmen) from 17 states and territories and 31 foreign countries; 15% part-time; 73% state residents; 25% transfers; 85% financial aid recipients; 54% women; 68% blacks; 2% Hispanics; 2% Asian Americans; 7% foreign nationals; 20% of undergraduates over 25 years of age; 1 legally handicapped student.

Expenses (1985–86) State resident tuition: $1350 full-time, $72 per credit part-time. Nonresident tuition: $3804 full-time, $72 per credit part-time. College room and board: $2810 (minimum). College room only: $1620.

Financial Aid Fall 1984 full-time freshmen: 93% applied for aid, 95% of those were judged to have need, 99% of those were aided; the average aided freshman received an aid package worth $3600 (47% scholarships/grants, 53% self-help) meeting 90% of need. College-administered aid for all 1984–85 undergraduates: need-based scholarships; non-need scholarships; short-term loans; low-interest long-term loans from external sources; SEOG; College Work-Study. Supporting data: FAF, institutional form, AFSA/SAR required. Priority application deadline: 4/15.

Athletics Member NCAA (Division I). Intercollegiate sports: baseball/softball M(I); basketball M(I,s), W(I,s); cross-country running M(I), W(I); tennis M(I,s), W(I); track and field M(I), W(I); volleyball W(I); wrestling M(I). Intramural sports: baseball/softball, basketball, bowling, cross-country running, gymnastics, martial arts, soccer, swimming and diving, tennis, track and field, volleyball, wrestling.

Majors Accounting B; agricultural education B; art education B; biology/biological sciences B; business administration/commerce/management B; business education B; chemistry B; computer science B; construction management B; construction technologies B; (pre)dentistry sequence B; ecology/environmental studies B; education B; electrical and electronics technologies B; electrical engineering technology B; elementary education B; engineering technology B; English B; environmental sciences B; fashion merchandising B; food services management B; history B; home economics B; home economics education B; hotel and restaurant management B; industrial arts B; (pre)law sequence B; liberal arts/general studies B; marine biology B; mathematics B; medical laboratory technology B; medical technology B; (pre)medicine sequence B; music education B; physical education B; physical therapy B; poultry sciences B; radiological technology B; secondary education B; social science B; sociology B; special education B.

LD Program Information

Name of Program Student Special Services.

Availability of Services Began offering services in 1983. Services provided to freshmen. Program currently serves 1 LD freshman.

Staff 4 full-time, 12 part-time staff members, including director. Services provided by remediation specialists, tutors, counselor.

Admissions LD applicants evaluated on the basis of high school transcript, standard or untimed SAT, personal interview, letters of recommendation, psychoeducational report. LD students may begin taking classes in fall, spring, or summer. Application should be submitted 2 months in advance of initial anticipated enrollment.

Orientation Optional orientation offered before registration.

Housing College housing (including coed) available. LD students housed randomly. LD students not required to live on campus.

Diagnostic Testing Available in reading, math, spelling, written language, perceptual skills, work and study habits, personality, speech.

Tutoring Offered one-to-one and in small groups by professional teachers, peer tutors. Available in some subjects. LD students may receive tutoring in 4 courses per term.

Basic Skills Remediation Offered in small groups by regular teachers. Available in reading, math, written language, work and study habits.

Academic Advisement Help with program planning provided by academic advisers. LD students may take up to 18 credits each semester; most take 13 to 14 credits; 12 credits required to maintain full-time status.

Special Courses Offered in college survival skills, communication skills, study skills, career planning. None offered for credit; none enter into overall grade point average.

Auxiliary Aids and Services Aids include tape recorders, word processors. Services include alternative exam arrangements, notetakers.

Counseling Services Individual counseling, small-group counseling, career counseling available.

Contact Dr. Diann R. Showell, Director, Student Special Services, University of Maryland Eastern Shore, PO Box 1088, Princess Anne, MD 21853, 301-651-2200 Ext. 654.

UNIVERSITY OF MASSACHUSETTS AT BOSTON

Boston, Massachusetts

Year Program Began	1978	Special Courses	✓
Special Fee	None	Taped Textbooks	✓
Special Orientation	✓	Alternative Exam Arrangements	✓
Diagnostic Testing	✓	Notetakers	✓
Subject-Area Tutoring	✓	Staff	1 full-time, 6 part-time
Basic Skills Remediation	✓	Number of Students Served	20

General Information State-supported comprehensive coed institution. Part of University of Massachusetts. Founded 1965. Awards B, M, D. Institutionally accredited by regional association; programs accredited by NLN (nursing). Metropolitan setting; 90-acre barrier-free campus. Total enrollment: 11,725. Faculty: 594 (376 full-time, 218 part-time); 84% have doctoral degrees; graduate assistants teach no undergraduate courses. Calendar: semesters. Grading system: letters or numbers. Library holdings: 325,000 bound volumes, 3,000 periodical subscriptions, 1,162 records/tapes.

Undergraduate Profile Fall 1984: 10,833 undergraduates (910 freshmen) from 37 states and territories and 61 foreign countries; 19% part-time; 96% state residents; 43% transfers; 60% financial aid recipients; 54% women; 10% blacks; 1% Native Americans; 4% Hispanics; 3% Asian Americans; 3% foreign nationals; 36% of undergraduates over 25 years of age; 35 legally handicapped students.

Expenses (1985–86) State resident tuition: $1296 full-time, $54 per credit part-time. Nonresident tuition: $4320 full-time, $180 per credit part-time. Mandatory fees: $280.

Financial Aid Fall 1984 full-time freshmen: 94% applied for aid, 91% of those were judged to have need, 100% of those were aided; the average aided freshman received an aid package worth $2967 (60% scholarships/grants, 40% self-help) meeting 60% of need. College-administered aid for all 1984–85 undergraduates: need-based scholarships; non-need scholarships; short-term loans; low-interest long-term loans from external sources; SEOG; College Work-Study; part-time jobs. Supporting data: FAF, IRS required; AFSA/SAR acceptable. Priority application deadline: 3/31.

Athletics Member NCAA (Division III). Intercollegiate sports: baseball/softball M(III), W(III); basketball M(III), W(III); cross-country running M(III), W(III); football M(c); ice hockey M(III); lacrosse M(III); rugby M(c); soccer M(III); swimming and diving M(III), W(III); tennis M(III); track and field M(III), W(III); volleyball W(III); wrestling M(III). Intramural sports: badminton, baseball/softball, basketball, cross-country running, gymnastics, ice hockey, martial arts, racquetball, sailing, soccer, squash, swimming and diving, tennis, volleyball, water polo, weight lifting.

Majors Accounting B; adult and continuing education B; anthropology B; applied mathematics B; art/fine arts B; biology/biological sciences B; black/Afro-American studies B; business administration/commerce/management B; chemistry B; classics B; community services B; computer science B; criminal justice B; (pre)dentistry sequence B; early childhood education B; earth science B; economics B; elementary education B; engineering (general) B; English B; French B; geography B; German B; gerontology B; Greek B; history B; human services B; Italian B; Latin B; (pre)law sequence B; legal studies B; mathematics B; (pre)medicine sequence B; music B; nursing B; philosophy B; physical education B; physics B; psychology B; Russian B; sociology B; Spanish B; theater arts/drama B; (pre)veterinary medicine sequence B.

LD Program Information

Name of Program Learning Disabilities Program.

Availability of Services Began offering services in 1978. Services provided to freshmen, sophomores, juniors, seniors. Program currently serves 20 LD students: 7 freshmen, 9 sophomores, 2 juniors, 2 seniors.

Staff 1 full-time, 6 part-time staff members, including director, LD coordinator. Services provided by tutors.

Admissions LD applicants evaluated on the basis of high school transcript and grade point average, standard or untimed SAT, autobiographical statement, letters of recommendation. Diagnostic evaluation or IEP may be submitted in lieu of SAT. LD students may begin taking classes in fall, spring, or summer. Application should be submitted at least 1 month in advance of initial anticipated enrollment.

Orientation Optional orientation offered after classes begin.

Housing College housing not available.

Diagnostic Testing Available in reading, math, spelling, handwriting, spoken language, written language, perceptual skills, work and study habits.

Tutoring Offered one-to-one and in small groups by professional teachers, peer tutors. Available in some subjects. LD students may receive tutoring in all courses each term (depending on individual need, course level, tutor availability).

Basic Skills Remediation Offered one-to-one and in small groups by LD teachers, regular teachers. Available in reading, math, spelling, handwriting, spoken language, written language, learning strategies, perceptual skills, work and study habits, social skills.

Academic Advisement Help with program planning provided by LD staff members, academic advisers. LD students may take up to 15 credits each semester; most take 9 to 12 credits; 12 credits required to maintain full-time status.

Special Courses Offered in college survival skills, reading, communication skills, composition, math. Some offered for credit; some enter into overall grade point average.

Auxiliary Aids and Services Aids include taped textbooks. Services include alternative exam arrangements, notetakers, advocacy.

Counseling Services Individual counseling, small-group counseling, rap sessions, career counseling available.

Contact Ms. Linda Dugas, Learning Disabilities Coordinator, University of Massachusetts at Boston, 020-3/435, Harbor Campus, Boston, MA 02125, 617-929-7870.

UNIVERSITY OF MINNESOTA, TWIN CITIES CAMPUS

Minneapolis, Minnesota

Year Program Began	1979	Special Courses	✓
Special Fee	None	Taped Textbooks	✓
Special Orientation		Alternative Exam Arrangements	✓
Diagnostic Testing		Notetakers	✓
Subject-Area Tutoring	✓	Staff	3 part-time
Basic Skills Remediation		Number of Students Served	75

General Information State-supported coed university. Part of University of Minnesota System. Founded 1851. Awards A (college transfer), B, M, D. Institutionally accredited by regional association; programs accredited by NAAB (architecture), AACSB (business), ABET (engineering and technology), ABFSE (funeral service), FIDER (interior design), NASM (music), NLN (nursing), ACPE (pharmacy), NCATE (teacher education). Metropolitan setting; 1,000-acre campus. Total enrollment: 44,659. Faculty: 5,800; 95% have doctoral degrees; graduate assistants teach about a quarter of the undergraduate courses. Calendar: quarters. Grading system: letters or numbers and pass/fail. Library holdings: 4.1 million bound volumes, 1.8 million titles on microform, 45,946 periodical subscriptions, 253,599 records/tapes.

Undergraduate Profile Fall 1984: 33,375 undergraduates (4,740 freshmen); 26% part-time; 88% state residents; 8% transfers; 60% financial aid recipients; 46% women; 2% blacks; 1% Native Americans; 1% Hispanics; 4% Asian Americans; 3% foreign nationals; 18% of undergraduates over 25 years of age.

Expenses (1985–86) State resident tuition ranges from $1633 to $1702 full-time, $38.90 to $40.54 part-time, according to class level. Nonresident tuition ranges from $4493 to $4682 full-time, $106.98 to $111.49 part-time, according to class level. Wisconsin residents pay tuition at the rate they would pay if attending a comparable state-supported institution in Wisconsin. Mandatory fees: $273. College room and board: $2496 (minimum).

Financial Aid Fall 1984 full-time freshmen: 56% applied for aid, 95% of those were judged to have need. College-administered aid for all 1984–85 undergraduates: need-based scholarships; 200 non-need scholarships (average $700); short-term loans (average $300); low-interest long-term loans from college funds (average $1100), from external sources (average $1200); SEOG; College Work-Study; 9,000 part-time jobs. Supporting data: FFS, AFSA/SAR required. Application deadline: continuous.

Athletics Member NCAA (Division I). Intercollegiate sports: baseball/softball M(I,s), W(I,s); basketball M(I,s), W(I,s); cross-country running M(I,s), W(I,s); football M(I-A,s); golf M(I,s), W(I,s); gymnastics M(I,s), W(I,s); ice hockey M(I,s); swimming and diving M(I,s), W(I,s); tennis M(I,s), W(I,s); track and field M(I,s), W(I,s); volleyball M(I), W(I,s); wrestling M(I,s). Intramural sports: archery, badminton, baseball/softball, basketball, bowling, crew, equestrian sports, fencing, football, golf, gymnastics, ice hockey, martial arts, riflery, rugby, sailing, skiing (cross-country), skiing (downhill), soccer, swimming and diving, tennis, volleyball, water polo, wrestling.

Majors Accounting B; advertising B; aerospace engineering B; African studies B; agricultural business B; agricultural economics B; agricultural education B; agricultural engineering B; agronomy/soil and crop sciences B; American studies B; anesthesiology B; animal sciences B; anthropology B; Arabic B; archaeology B; architecture B; art education B; art/fine arts B; art history B; Asian/Oriental studies B; astronomy B; astrophysics B; biochemistry B; biology/biological sciences B; biometrics B; black/Afro-American studies B; botany/plant sciences B; broadcasting B; business administration/commerce/management B; business education B; cell biology B; chemical engineering B; chemistry B; child psychology/child development B; Chinese B; civil engineering B; classics B; commercial art A; communication B; comparative literature B; computer science B; consumer services B; creative writing B; dental services B; dietetics B; early childhood education B; earth science B; East Asian studies B; economics B; electrical engineering B; elementary education B; English B; entomology B; environmental design B; family services B; fashion design and technology B; fashion merchandising B; fish and game management B; food sciences B; food services management B; food services technology B; forestry B; forest technology B; French B; funeral service B; genetics B; geography B; geological engineering B; geology B; geophysics B; German B; graphic arts B; Greek B; Hebrew B; Hispanic studies B; history B; home economics B; home economics education B; horticulture B; humanities B; human services A; interdisciplinary studies B; interior design B; international studies B; Italian B; Japanese B; journalism B; Judaic studies B; landscape architecture/design B; Latin B; Latin American studies B; law enforcement/police sciences A; liberal arts/general studies A; linguistics B; marketing/retailing/merchandising B; mathematics B; mechanical engineering B; medical technology B; metallurgical engineering B; Mexican-American/Chicano studies B; microbiology B; mining and mineral engineering B; music B; music education B; music history B; music therapy B; Native American studies B; Near and Middle Eastern studies B; nursing B; nutrition B; occupational therapy B; paper and pulp sciences B; paralegal studies A; parks management B; pharmacy/pharmaceutical sciences B; philosophy B; photography B; physical education B; physical sciences B; physical therapy B; physics B; physiology B; political science/government B; Portuguese B; psychology B; radio and television studies B; recreation and leisure services B; religious studies B; retail management B; Russian B; Scandinavian languages/studies B; science education B; secondary education B; Slavic languages B; social work B; sociology B; Southeast Asian studies B; Spanish B; speech pathology and audiology B; speech/rhetoric/public address/debate B; statistics B; studio art B; technical writing B; textiles and clothing B; theater arts/drama B; urban studies B; veterinary sciences B; vocational education B; wildlife biology B; wildlife management B; women's studies B. Majors with highest enrollment: journalism, psychology, business administration/commerce/management.

LD Program Information

Name of Program Office for Students with Disabilities.

Availability of Services Began offering services in 1979. Services provided to freshmen, sophomores, juniors, seniors. Program currently serves 75 LD students.

Staff 3 part-time staff members, including director. Services provided by remediation specialists, counselors.

Admissions LD applicants evaluated on the basis of high school transcript and grade point average, standard or untimed SAT or ACT; psychoeducational report recommended. LD students may begin taking classes in fall, winter, spring, or summer. Application should be submitted at least 2 months in advance of initial anticipated enrollment.

Housing College housing (including coed) available. LD students housed randomly. LD students not required to live on campus.

Tutoring Offered one-to-one and in small groups by professional teachers, peer tutors. Available in some subjects. LD students may receive tutoring in all courses each term (depending on availability of tutors).

Academic Advisement Help with program planning provided by LD staff members, academic advisers. Most LD students take 8 to 12 credits each quarter; 12 credits required to maintain full-time status.

Special Courses Offered in college survival skills, study skills. All offered for credit; all enter into overall grade point average.

Auxiliary Aids and Services Aids include taped textbooks, tape recorders, word processors. Services include alternative exam arrangements, notetakers, advocacy, early syllabus, extra time to complete coursework, adapted library use, adapted paper-writing, support group.

Counseling Services Individual counseling, small-group counseling, rap sessions, career counseling available.

Contact Dr. Robert Seybold, Director, Office for Students with Disabilities, University of Minnesota, Twin Cities Campus, 12 Johnston Hall, 101 Pleasant Street, SE, Minneapolis, MN 55455, 612-376-2727.

UNIVERSITY OF MISSISSIPPI

University, Mississippi

Year Program Began	1978	Special Courses	✓
Special Fee	None	Taped Textbooks	
Special Orientation		Alternative Exam Arrangements	✓
Diagnostic Testing	✓	Notetakers	
Subject-Area Tutoring	✓	Staff	1 part-time
Basic Skills Remediation	✓	Number of Students Served	15

General Information State-supported coed university. Founded 1844. Awards B, M, D. Institutionally accredited by regional association; programs accredited by NASAD (art and design), AACSB (business), ABET (engineering and technology), NASM (music), ACPE (pharmacy), NCATE (teacher education). Small-town setting, with easy access to Memphis; 2,300-acre campus. Total enrollment: 8,715. Faculty: 574 (421 full-time, 153 part-time); 73% have doctoral degrees; graduate assistants teach a few undergraduate courses. Calendar: semesters. Grading system: letters or numbers. Library holdings: 750,000 bound volumes, 4,696 periodical subscriptions, 400 records/tapes.

Undergraduate Profile Fall 1984: 7,088 undergraduates (1,707 freshmen) from 50 states and territories and 58 foreign countries; 13% part-time; 72% state residents; 9% transfers; 56% financial aid recipients; 47% women; 7% blacks; 4% foreign nationals; 100 legally handicapped students.

Expenses (1985–86) State resident tuition: $1517 full-time, $53 per semester hour part-time. Nonresident tuition: $2699 full-time, $102 per semester hour part-time. Students taking 7 or more semester hours are charged the full-time rate for tuition. College room and board: $2328 (minimum). College room only: $1078 (minimum).

Financial Aid Fall 1984 full-time freshmen: the average aided freshman received an aid package meeting 95% of need. College-administered aid for all 1984–85 undergraduates: need-based scholarships (average $1000); non-need scholarships (average $1000); short-term loans (average $300); low-interest long-term loans from college funds (average $1000), from external sources (average $800); SEOG; College Work-Study; 1,200 part-time jobs. Supporting data: FAF required. Priority application deadline: 4/1.

Athletics Member NCAA (Division I), NAIA. Intercollegiate sports: baseball/softball M(I,s); basketball M(I,s), W(I,s); cross-country running M(I); football M(I-A,s); golf M(I,s); rugby M, W; tennis M(I,s), W(I,s); track and field M(I,s); volleyball W(I,s). Intramural sports: baseball/softball, basketball, cross-country running, equestrian sports, field hockey, football, golf, gymnastics, martial arts, racquetball, riflery, rugby, soccer, swimming and diving, tennis, track and field, volleyball.

Majors Accounting B; advertising B; anthropology B; applied art B; archaeology B; art education B; art/fine arts B; art history B; arts administration B; biology/biological sciences B; biomedical sciences B; botany/plant sciences B; broadcasting B; business administration/commerce/management B; business education B; ceramic art and design B; chemical engineering B; chemistry B; city, community, and regional planning B; civil engineering B; classics B; communication B; computer science B; corrections B; court reporting B; creative writing B; criminal justice B; dance B; (pre) dentistry sequence B; early childhood education B; economics B; education B; educational administration B; electrical engineering B; elementary education B; engineering (general) B; English B; fashion merchandising B; finance/banking B; forensic sciences B; French B; geological engineering B; geology B; German B; Greek B; guidance and counseling B; health education B; history B; home economics B; home economics education B; insurance B; interior design B; Italian B; journalism B; Latin B; law enforcement/police sciences B; (pre)law sequence B; liberal arts/general studies B; library science B; literature B; marketing/retailing/merchandising B; mathematics B; mechanical engineering B; medical laboratory technology B; medical records services B; medical technology B; (pre)medicine sequence B; military science B; music B; music education B; music history B; naval sciences B; nursing B; painting/drawing B; paralegal studies B; pharmacology B; pharmacy/pharmaceutical sciences B; philosophy B; physical education B; physical therapy B; physics B; piano/organ B; political science/government B; psychology B; public administration B; public relations B; radio and television studies B; real estate B; religious studies B; retail management B; secondary education B; social science B; social work B; sociology B; Spanish B; special education B; speech pathology and audiology B; speech/rhetoric/public address/debate B; speech therapy B; theater arts/drama B; urban studies B; zoology B. Majors with highest enrollment: (pre)medicine sequence, (pre)law sequence, accounting.

LD Program Information

Name of Program Handicapped Services.

Availability of Services Began offering services in 1978. Services provided to freshmen, sophomores, juniors, seniors. Program currently serves 15 LD students: 5 freshmen, 3 sophomores, 4 juniors, 3 seniors.

Staff 1 part-time staff member. Services provided by counselor.

Admissions LD applicants evaluated on the basis of high school transcript, untimed SAT or ACT, psychoeducational report. LD students may begin taking classes in fall, spring, or summer. Application should be submitted 2 weeks in advance of initial anticipated enrollment.

Housing College housing available. LD students housed randomly. LD freshmen required to live on campus.

Diagnostic Testing Available in intelligence, perceptual skills.

Tutoring Offered in small groups by professional teachers, peer tutors. Available in some subjects. LD students may receive tutoring in 2 courses per term.

Basic Skills Remediation Offered in small groups by regular teachers, teacher trainees. Available in reading, math, written language, work and study habits, speech.

Academic Advisement Help with program planning provided by LD staff members, academic advisers. LD students may take up to 15 semester hours each semester; most take 12 semester hours; 12 semester hours required to maintain full-time status.

Special Courses Offered in study skills, career planning. All offered for credit; all enter into overall grade point average.

Auxiliary Aids and Services Services include alternative exam arrangements.

Counseling Services Individual counseling, small-group counseling, career counseling available.

Contact Dr. Judy Trott, Director of Student Services, University of Mississippi, Room 200 Lyceum, University, MS 38677, 601-232-7247.

UNIVERSITY OF MISSOURI–COLUMBIA
Columbia, Missouri

Year Program Began	1980	Special Courses	✓
Special Fee	None	Taped Textbooks	✓
Special Orientation		Alternative Exam Arrangements	✓
Diagnostic Testing	✓	Notetakers	✓
Subject-Area Tutoring	✓	Staff	8 part-time
Basic Skills Remediation	✓	Number of Students Served	*Not reported*

General Information State-supported coed university. Part of University of Missouri System. Founded 1839. Awards B, M, D. Institutionally accredited by regional association; programs accredited by AACSB (business), ABET (engineering and technology), FIDER (interior design), NASM (music), NLN (nursing), NCATE (teacher education). City setting; 692-acre barrier-free campus. Total enrollment: 23,410. Faculty: 2,485 (2,031 full-time, 454 part-time); 80% have doctoral degrees; graduate assistants teach a few undergraduate courses. Calendar: semesters. Grading system: letters or numbers. Library holdings: 2 million bound volumes, 2 million titles on microform, 20,000 periodical subscriptions.

Undergraduate Profile Fall 1984: 17,806 undergraduates (3,671 freshmen) from 51 states and territories and 34 foreign countries; 6% part-time; 91% state residents; 8% transfers; 50% financial aid recipients; 49% women; 4% blacks; 1% Native Americans; 1% Hispanics; 1% Asian Americans; 2% foreign nationals; 5% of undergraduates over 25 years of age; 314 legally handicapped students.

Expenses (1985–86) State resident tuition: $1457 full-time, $52.50 per credit hour part-time. Nonresident tuition: $4214 full-time, $151 per credit hour part-time. College room and board: $2111.

Financial Aid Fall 1984 full-time freshmen: 46% applied for aid, 51% of those were judged to have need, 85% of those were aided; the average aided freshman received an aid package worth $3077 (50% scholarships/grants, 50% self-help) meeting 94% of need. College-administered aid for all 1984–85 undergraduates: need-based scholarships; non-need scholarships; low-interest long-term loans from external sources; SEOG; College Work-Study; part-time jobs. Supporting data: IRS required for some; FFS, FAF, AFSA/SAR acceptable. Priority application deadline: 3/15.

Athletics Member NCAA (Division I). Intercollegiate sports: baseball/softball M(I,s), W(I,s); basketball M(I,s), W(I,s); cross-country running M(I,s), W(I,s); football M(I-A,s); golf M(I,s), W(I,s); gymnastics W(I,s); swimming and diving M(I,s), W(I,s); track and field M(I,s), W(I,s); volleyball W(I,s); wrestling M(I,s). Intramural sports: badminton, baseball/softball, basketball, bowling, cross-country running, football, golf, gymnastics, racquetball, soccer, swimming and diving, tennis, track and field, volleyball, wrestling.

Majors Accounting B; advertising B; agricultural economics B; agricultural education B; agricultural engineering B; agronomy/soil and crop sciences B; animal sciences B; anthropology B; archaeology B; art education B; art/fine arts B; art history B; atmospheric sciences B; behavioral sciences B; biochemistry B; biology/biological sciences B; black/Afro-American studies B; broadcasting B; business administration/commerce/management B; business education B; chemical engineering B; chemistry B; child psychology/child development B; civil engineering B; classics B; community services B; computer engineering B; computer science B; cytotechnology B; dairy sciences B; (pre)dentistry sequence B; dietetics B; early childhood education B; earth science B; economics B; education B; educational administration B; electrical engineering B; elementary education B; English B; entomology B; fashion merchandising B; film studies B; finance/banking B; fish and game management B; food sciences B; forestry B; French B; geography B; geology B; German B; health education B; health services administration B; history B; home economics B; home economics education B; horticulture B; industrial engineering B; insurance B; interior design B; Italian B; journalism B; laboratory technologies B; liberal arts/general studies B; library science B; linguistics B; marketing/retailing/merchandising B; mathematics B; mechanical engineering B; medical technology B; (pre)medicine sequence B; microbiology B; music B; music education B; nursing B; nutrition B; occupational therapy B; parks management B; peace studies B; philosophy B; photography B; physical education B; physical therapy B; physics B; political science/government B; poultry sciences B; psychology B; public administration B; publishing B; radio and television studies B; radiological sciences B; recreation and leisure services B; respiratory therapy B; Russian B; Russian and Slavic studies B; science education B; secondary education B; social work B; sociology B; South Asian studies B; Spanish B; special education B; speech pathology and audiology B; speech/rhetoric/public address/debate B; speech therapy B; statistics B; technical writing B; textiles and clothing B; (pre)veterinary medicine sequence B; vocational education B; wood sciences B. Majors with highest enrollment: business administration/commerce/management, electrical engineering, journalism.

LD Program Information

Name of Program Learning Center.

Availability of Services Began offering services in 1980. Services provided to freshmen, sophomores, juniors, seniors.

Staff 8 part-time staff members, including director, assistant director. Services provided by remediation specialists, tutors.

Admissions LD applicants evaluated on the basis of high school transcript, standard or untimed SAT or ACT. LD students may begin taking classes in fall, winter, or summer. Application should be submitted at least 5 months in advance of initial anticipated enrollment.

Housing College housing (including coed) available. LD students housed randomly. LD students not required to live on campus.

Diagnostic Testing Available in intelligence, reading, math, spelling, handwriting, written language, work and study habits, hearing.

Tutoring Offered one-to-one and in small groups by professional teachers, peer tutors. Available in all subjects. LD students may receive tutoring in all courses each term.

Basic Skills Remediation Offered one-to-one and in small groups by peer teachers. Available in reading, written language, learning strategies.

Academic Advisement Help with program planning provided by academic advisers. Most LD students take 15 credit hours each semester; 14 credit hours required to maintain full-time status.

Special Courses Offered in reading. All offered for credit; none enter into overall grade point average.

Auxiliary Aids and Services Aids include taped textbooks, tape recorders, calculators, typewriters, word processors. Services include alternative exam arrangements, notetakers, advocacy.

Counseling Services Individual counseling, career counseling available.

Contact Ms. Bonnie Zelenak, Director of Learning Center, University of Missouri–Columbia, 204 Watson Place, Columbia, MO 65211, 314-882-2493.

UNIVERSITY OF MONTANA

Missoula, Montana

Year Program Began	1979	Special Courses	✓
Special Fee	None	Taped Textbooks	✓
Special Orientation	✓	Alternative Exam Arrangements	✓
Diagnostic Testing	✓	Notetakers	✓
Subject-Area Tutoring	✓	Staff	3 part-time
Basic Skills Remediation	✓	Number of Students Served	7

General Information State-supported coed university. Founded 1893. Awards A (college transfer), B, M, D. Institutionally accredited by regional association; programs accredited by AACSB (business), NASM (music), ACPE (pharmacy), NCATE (teacher education). City setting; 200-acre campus. Total enrollment: 9,213. Faculty: 487 (459 full-time, 28 part-time); 82% have doctoral degrees; graduate assistants teach a few undergraduate courses. Calendar: quarters. Grading system: letters or numbers and pass/fail. Library holdings: 700,000 bound volumes, 19,200 titles on microform, 4,500 periodical subscriptions, 7,135 records/tapes.

Undergraduate Profile Fall 1984: 7,305 undergraduates (1,270 freshmen); 15% part-time; 72% state residents; 40% transfers; 50% financial aid recipients; 47% women; 1% blacks; 3% Native Americans; 1% Hispanics; 1% Asian Americans; 2% foreign nationals; 36% of undergraduates over 25 years of age; 140 legally handicapped students.

Expenses (1984–85) State resident tuition: $975 full-time. Nonresident tuition: $2745 full-time. Part-time tuition and fees per quarter (1 to 11 credits) range from $92 to $229 for state residents, $135 to $772 for nonresidents. College room and board: $2283. College room only: $957.

Financial Aid Fall 1984 full-time freshmen: 98% applied for aid, 81% of those were judged to have need, 100% of those were aided; the average aided freshman received an aid package worth $1561 (46% scholarships/grants, 54% self-help) meeting 76% of need. College-administered aid for all 1984–85 undergraduates: 1,012 need-based scholarships (average $846); non-need scholarships (average $800); short-term loans (average $200); low-interest long-term loans from external sources (average $900); SEOG; College Work-Study; 1,100 part-time jobs. Supporting data: FAF required; IRS, institutional form, AFSA/SAR required for some. Priority application deadline: 3/1.

Athletics Member NCAA (Division I). Intercollegiate sports: basketball M(I,s), W(I,s); cross-country running M(I,s), W(I,s); football M(I-AA,s); golf M(I,s); gymnastics W(I,s); swimming and diving W(II,s); tennis M(I,s), W(I,s); track and field M(I,s), W(I,s); volleyball W(I,s); wrestling M(I,s). Intramural sports: baseball/softball, basketball, football, martial arts, racquetball, rugby, skiing (cross-country), skiing (downhill), soccer, swimming and diving, tennis, track and field, volleyball, wrestling.

Majors Accounting B; anthropology B; applied mathematics B; art education B; art/fine arts B; Asian/Oriental studies B; astronomy B; behavioral sciences B; biology/biological sciences B; botany/plant sciences B; broadcasting B; business administration/commerce/management B; business education B; ceramic art and design B; chemistry B; city, community, and regional planning B; classics B; communication B; comparative literature B; computer science B; conservation B; dance B; East Asian studies B; East European and Soviet studies B; economics B; education B; educational media B; elementary education B; English B; environmental biology B; finance/banking B; fish and game management B; forestry B; French B; geography B; geology B; German B; Germanic languages and literature B; health education B; history B; home economics B; home economics education B; humanities B; Italian B; journalism B; Latin B; liberal arts/general studies A, B; mathematics B; medical technology B; (pre)medicine sequence B; microbiology B; military science B; modern languages B; music B; music education B; Native American studies B; parks management B; pharmacy/pharmaceutical sciences B; philosophy B; physical education B; physical therapy B; physics B; piano/organ B; political science/government B; psychology B; radio and television studies B; range management B; reading education B; recreation and leisure services B; religious studies B; Russian B; science education B; secondary education B; secretarial studies/office management B; social work B; sociology B; Spanish B; speech pathology and audiology B; speech/rhetoric/public address/debate B; statistics B; stringed instruments B; studio art B; telecommunications B; theater arts/drama B; (pre)veterinary medicine sequence B; wildlife biology B; zoology B.

LD Program Information

Name of Program Special Services.

Availability of Services Began offering services in 1979. Services provided to freshmen, sophomores, juniors, seniors. Program currently serves 7 LD students.

Staff 3 part-time staff members, including director. Services provided by remediation specialist, tutors, counselor.

Admissions LD applicants evaluated on the basis of high school transcript and grade point average, standard or untimed SAT or ACT; psychoeducational report recommended. LD students may begin taking classes in fall, winter, spring, or summer. Application should be submitted 1 to 2 months in advance of initial anticipated enrollment.

Orientation Optional orientation offered during registration.

Housing College housing (including coed) available. LD students housed randomly. LD students not required to live on campus.

Diagnostic Testing Available in intelligence, reading, math, spelling, handwriting, spoken language, written language, motor abilities, perceptual skills, work and study habits.

Tutoring Offered one-to-one and in small groups by peer tutors. Available in all subjects. LD students may receive tutoring in 2 courses per term.

Basic Skills Remediation Offered in class-size groups by regular teachers. Available in reading, math, work and study habits.

Academic Advisement Help with program planning provided by academic advisers. Most LD students take 12 credits each quarter; 12 credits required to maintain full-time status.

Special Courses Offered in college survival skills, reading, vocabulary development, composition, math, study skills, career planning. Some offered for credit; some enter into overall grade point average.

Auxiliary Aids and Services Aids include taped textbooks, tape recorders. Services include alternative exam arrangements, notetakers, advocacy.

Counseling Services Individual counseling, small-group counseling, career counseling available.

Contact Mr. Ray Carlisle, Director, Special Services, University of Montana, 600 East Beckwith, Missoula, MT 59812, 406-243-5033.

UNIVERSITY OF MONTEVALLO

Montevallo, Alabama

Year Program Began	1979	Special Courses	✓
Special Fee	None	Taped Textbooks	
Special Orientation		Alternative Exam Arrangements	
Diagnostic Testing	✓	Notetakers	
Subject-Area Tutoring	✓	Staff	2 part-time
Basic Skills Remediation		Number of Students Served	13

General Information State-supported comprehensive coed institution. Founded 1896. Awards B, M. Institutionally accredited by regional association; programs accredited by NASM (music), NCATE (teacher education). Small-town setting, with easy access to Birmingham; 106-acre barrier-free campus. Total enrollment: 2,782. Faculty: 170 (147 full-time, 23 part-time); 62% have doctoral degrees; graduate assistants teach no undergraduate courses. Calendar: semesters. Grading system: letters or numbers. Library holdings: 170,339 bound volumes, 358,918 titles on microform, 1,300 periodical subscriptions, 2,000 records/tapes.

Undergraduate Profile Fall 1984: 2,270 undergraduates (559 freshmen) from 25 states and territories and 10 foreign countries; 10% part-time; 94% state residents; 25% transfers; 55% financial aid recipients; 63% women; 10% blacks; 0% Native Americans; 0% Hispanics; 0% Asian Americans; 3% foreign nationals; 10% of undergraduates over 25 years of age; 14 legally handicapped students.

Expenses (1985–86) State resident tuition: $1090 full-time, $39 per semester hour part-time. Nonresident tuition: $1904 full-time, $68 per semester hour part-time. Mandatory fees: $110. College room and board: $2060. College room only: $900.

Financial Aid Fall 1984 full-time freshmen: 45% applied for aid, 100% of those were judged to have need, 100% of those were aided; the average aided freshman received an aid package meeting 100% of need. College-administered aid for all 1984–85 undergraduates: need-based scholarships (average $1000); non-need scholarships (average $500); low-interest long-term loans from college funds, from external sources; part-time jobs. Supporting data: FFS, FAF, institutional form, AFSA/SAR required. Application deadline: continuous.

Athletics Member NAIA. Intercollegiate sports: baseball/softball M(s); basketball M(s), W(s); golf M(s); volleyball W(s). Intramural sports: archery, badminton, baseball/softball, basketball, bowling, cross-country running, football, golf, racquetball, tennis, volleyball.

Majors Accounting B; art education B; art/fine arts B; art history B; biology/biological sciences B; broadcasting B; business administration/commerce/management B; chemistry B; communication B; (pre)dentistry sequence B; early childhood education B; education B; elementary education B; English B; fashion merchandising B; finance/banking B; French B; guidance and counseling B; health education B; history B; home economics B; home economics education B; interdisciplinary studies B; interior design B; international studies B; (pre)law sequence B; liberal arts/general studies B; maritime sciences B; marketing/retailing/merchandising B; mathematics B; medical technology B; (pre)medicine sequence B; music B; music education B; physical education B; piano/organ B; political science/government B; psychology B; radio and television studies B; sacred music B; science B; secondary education B; social science B; social work B; sociology B; Spanish B; speech pathology and audiology B; speech/rhetoric/public address/debate B; studio art B; theater arts/drama B; voice B. Majors with highest enrollment: business administration/commerce/management, communication, elementary education.

LD Program Information

Name of Program Special Services.

Availability of Services Began offering services in 1979. Services provided to freshmen, sophomores. Program currently serves 13 LD students.

Staff 2 part-time staff members. Services provided by tutor, counselor.

Admissions LD applicants evaluated on the basis of high school transcript and grade point average, standard or untimed ACT; psychoeducational report recommended. LD students may begin taking classes in fall, spring, or summer. Application should be submitted 3 months in advance of initial anticipated enrollment.

Housing College housing (including coed) available. LD students housed randomly. LD freshmen required to live on campus except if married, living with relatives, or 19 or over.

Diagnostic Testing Available in reading, math, work and study habits.

Tutoring Offered one-to-one and in small groups by peer tutors. Available in some subjects. LD students may receive tutoring in 3 courses per term.

Academic Advisement Help with program planning provided by LD staff members. LD students may take up to 16 semester hours each semester; most take 12 semester hours; 12 semester hours required to maintain full-time status.

Special Courses Offered in study skills, career planning. None offered for credit; none enter into overall grade point average.

Counseling Services Individual counseling, career counseling available.

Contact Ms. Elaine Elledge, Director of Special Services, University of Montevallo, Station 281, Montevallo, AL 35115, 205-665-6307.

UNIVERSITY OF NEBRASKA–LINCOLN

Lincoln, Nebraska

Year Program Began	1980
Special Fee	Varies
Special Orientation	✓
Diagnostic Testing	✓
Subject-Area Tutoring	✓
Basic Skills Remediation	✓
Special Courses	
Taped Textbooks	✓
Alternative Exam Arrangements	✓
Notetakers	✓
Staff	1 full-time, 11 part-time
Number of Students Served	38

General Information State-supported coed university. Part of University of Nebraska System. Founded 1869. Awards B, M, D. Institutionally accredited by regional association; programs accredited by AACSB (business), ABET (engineering and technology), FIDER (interior design), NASM (music), NCATE (teacher education). City setting, with easy access to Omaha; 552-acre campus. Total enrollment: 24,228. Faculty: 1,025; 81% have doctoral degrees; graduate assistants teach a few undergraduate courses. Calendar: semesters. Grading system: letters or numbers. Library holdings: 1.6 million bound volumes, 17,583 titles on microform, 19,216 periodical subscriptions.

Undergraduate Profile Fall 1984: 20,083 undergraduates (3,572 freshmen) from 48 states and territories and 82 foreign countries; 22% part-time; 91% state residents; 12% transfers; 62% financial aid recipients; 43% women; 2% blacks; 1% Native Americans; 1% Hispanics; 1% Asian Americans; 5% foreign nationals; 271 legally handicapped students.

Expenses (1985–86) State resident tuition: $1312 full-time, $43.75 per credit hour part-time. Nonresident tuition: $3570 full-time, $119 per credit hour part-time. Mandatory fees: $200. College room and board: $2010.

Financial Aid Fall 1984 full-time freshmen: 85% applied for aid, 64% of those were judged to have need, 77% of those were aided; the average aided freshman received an aid package worth $2837 (44% scholarships/grants, 56% self-help) meeting 70% of need. College-administered aid for all 1984–85 undergraduates: 3,420 need-based scholarships (average $900); 2,644 non-need scholarships (average $750); short-term loans (average $500); low-interest long-term loans from external sources (average $500); SEOG; College Work-Study; 1,700 part-time jobs. Supporting data: FAF required; FFS acceptable. Priority application deadline: 2/15.

Athletics Member NCAA (Division I). Intercollegiate sports: baseball/softball M(I,s), W(I,s); basketball M(I,s), W(I,s); bowling M, W; crew M, W; cross-country running M(I,s), W(I,s); football M(I-A,s); golf M(I,s), W(I,s); gymnastics M(I,s), W(I,s); riflery M(c); soccer M(c), W(c); swimming and diving M(I,s), W(I,s); tennis M(I,s), W(I,s); track and field M(I,s), W(I,s); volleyball W(I,s); wrestling M(I,s). Intramural sports: archery, badminton, baseball/softball, basketball, bowling, crew, fencing, field hockey, football, golf, lacrosse, martial arts, racquetball, riflery, rugby, soccer, tennis, track and field, volleyball, water polo, weight lifting, wrestling.

Majors Accounting B; actuarial science B; advertising B; agricultural business B; agricultural economics B; agricultural engineering B; agronomy/soil and crop sciences B; American studies B; animal sciences B; anthropology B; architecture B; art education B; art/fine arts B; art history B; astronomy B; biology/biological sciences B; botany/plant sciences B; broadcasting B; business administration/commerce/management B; business economics B; business education B; chemical engineering B; chemistry B; child care/child and family studies B; civil engineering B; classics B; communication B; comparative literature B; computer science B; construction management B; consumer services B; criminal justice B; dairy sciences B; dance B; dental services B; (pre)dentistry sequence B; early childhood education B; ecology/environmental studies B; economics B; electrical engineering B; elementary education B; English B; entomology B; environmental health sciences B; family and consumer studies B; fashion merchandising B; fish and game management B; food sciences B; food services management B; French B; geography B; geology B; German B; Greek B; health education B; history B; home economics B; horticulture B; human development B; industrial engineering B; interior design B; international studies B; journalism B; Latin B; Latin American studies B; (pre)law sequence B; linguistics B; literature B; marketing/retailing/merchandising B; mathematics B; mechanical engineering B; (pre)medicine sequence B; metallurgical engineering B; microbiology B; molecular biology B; music B; music education B; natural sciences B; nursing B; nutrition B; philosophy B; physical education B; physics B; physiology B; political science/government B; psychology B; radio and television studies B; range management B; recreation and leisure services B; Russian B; science education B; secondary education B; social work B; sociology B; Spanish B; special education B; speech pathology and audiology B; textiles and clothing B; theater arts/drama B; urban studies B; (pre)veterinary medicine sequence B; voice B; water resources B; wildlife management B; women's studies B; zoology B. Majors with highest enrollment: agronomy/soil and crop sciences, accounting, (pre)medicine sequence.

LD Program Information

Name of Program Postsecondary Intervention Model for Learning Disabilities (PS IM LD).

Availability of Services Began offering services in 1980. Services provided to freshmen, sophomores, juniors, seniors. Program currently serves 38 LD students: 11 freshmen, 11 sophomores, 8 juniors, 8 seniors.

Fees $15 for evaluation.

Staff 1 full-time, 11 part-time staff members, including director, co-administrators. Services provided by remediation specialist, tutors, diagnostic specialists.

Admissions LD applicants evaluated on the basis of high school transcript, standard or untimed SAT. LD students may begin taking classes in fall, spring, or summer. Application should be submitted 2 months in advance of initial anticipated enrollment.

Orientation Optional orientation offered during registration.

Housing College housing (including coed) available. LD students housed randomly. LD freshmen and sophomores required to live on campus except by special permission.

Diagnostic Testing Available in intelligence, reading, math, spelling, handwriting, spoken language, written language, work and study habits, speech.

Tutoring Offered one-to-one and in small groups by professional teachers, peer tutors. Available in all subjects. LD students may receive tutoring in all courses each term.

Basic Skills Remediation Offered one-to-one and in small groups by LD teachers, teacher trainees. Available in reading, math, spelling, handwriting, spoken language, written language, learning strategies, work and study habits, social skills, speech.

Academic Advisement Help with program planning provided by LD staff members, academic advisers. LD students may take up to 18 credit hours each semester; most take 12 credit hours; 12 credit hours required to maintain full-time status.

Auxiliary Aids and Services Aids include taped textbooks, tape recorders, word processors. Services include alternative exam arrangements, notetakers, advocacy.

Counseling Services Individual counseling, small-group counseling, rap sessions, career counseling available.

Contact Ms. Janice Leuenberger, Co-Administrator, Postsecondary Intervention Model for Learning Disabilities, University of Nebraska–Lincoln, 250A Barkley Memorial Center, Lincoln, NE 68583-0731, 402-472-5530.

UNIVERSITY OF NEVADA, LAS VEGAS

Las Vegas, Nevada

Year Program Began	1981	Special Courses	✓
Special Fee	None	Taped Textbooks	✓
Special Orientation		Alternative Exam Arrangements	✓
Diagnostic Testing	✓	Notetakers	
Subject-Area Tutoring	✓	Staff	1 full-time, 3 part-time
Basic Skills Remediation	✓	Number of Students Served	27

General Information State-supported coed university. Part of University of Nevada System. Founded 1957. Awards A (terminal), B, M, D. Institutionally accredited by regional association; programs accredited by NLN (nursing), NCATE (teacher education); candidate for program accreditation by NASM (music). City setting; 335-acre barrier-free campus. Total enrollment: 10,989. Faculty: 451; 62% have doctoral degrees; graduate assistants teach a few undergraduate courses. Calendar: 4-1-4. Grading system: letters or numbers. Library holdings: 439,071 bound volumes, 500,000 titles on microform, 5,300 periodical subscriptions, 21,000 records/tapes.

Undergraduate Profile Fall 1984: 8,944 undergraduates (1,519 freshmen); 33% part-time; 87% state residents; 11% transfers; 39% financial aid recipients; 49% women; 6% blacks; 1% Native Americans; 4% Hispanics; 3% Asian Americans; 1% foreign nationals; 61% of undergraduates over 25 years of age.

Expenses (1985–86) State resident tuition: $1152 full-time, $36 per credit hour part-time. Nonresident tuition: $3352 full-time. Nonresident part-time tuition and fees per semester (1 to 11 credit hours) range from $36 to $2596. College room and board: $2515.

Financial Aid Fall 1984 full-time freshmen: 60% applied for aid, 81% of those were judged to have need, 87% of those were aided; the average aided freshman received an aid package worth $1478 (31% scholarships/grants, 69% self-help) meeting 100% of need. College-administered aid for all 1984–85 undergraduates: 740 need-based scholarships (average $655); 748 non-need scholarships (average $1209); short-term loans (average $67); low-interest long-term loans from external sources (average $1244); SEOG; College Work-Study; part-time jobs. Supporting data: FFS, state form required; FAF, IRS, AFSA/SAR acceptable. Priority application deadline: 3/1.

Athletics Member NCAA (Division I). Intercollegiate sports: baseball/softball M(I,s), W(I,s); basketball M(I,s), W(I,s); cross-country running M(I,s); football M(I-A,s); golf M(I,s); soccer M(I,s); swimming and diving M(I,s), W(I,s); tennis M(I,s); track and field W(I,s); volleyball W(I,s). Intramural sports: baseball/softball, basketball, bowling, football, tennis, volleyball.

Majors Accounting B; advertising B; American studies B; anthropology B; applied mathematics B; art/fine arts B; art history B; Asian/Oriental studies B; biochemistry B; biology/biological sciences B; broadcasting B; business administration/commerce/management B; chemistry B; civil engineering B; communication B; comparative literature B; computer engineering B; computer science B; criminal justice B; dance B; (pre)dentistry sequence B; earth science B; East Asian studies B; economics B; education B; electrical engineering B; elementary education B; engineering (general) B; engineering sciences B; English B; ethnic studies B; film studies B; finance/banking B; food services management B; French B; geology B; German B; gerontology B; health education B; history B; hotel and restaurant management B; human services B; industrial administration B; insurance B; interdisciplinary studies B; journalism B; Latin American studies B; liberal arts/general studies B; linguistics B; marketing/retailing/merchandising B; mathematics B; mechanical engineering B; (pre)medicine sequence B; music B; music education B; nuclear medical technology B; nursing A, B; philosophy B; physical education B; physics B; political science/government B; psychology B; public administration B; public relations B; radiological sciences A, B; real estate B; recreation and leisure services B; Romance languages B; secondary education B; social science B; social work B; sociology B; Spanish B; special education B; sports medicine B; statistics B; theater arts/drama B; (pre) veterinary medicine sequence B; vocational education B; women's studies B. Majors with highest enrollment: hotel and restaurant management, accounting, nursing.

LD Program Information

Name of Program Learning Abilities Program.

Availability of Services Began offering services in 1981. Services provided to freshmen, sophomores, juniors, seniors. Program currently serves 27 LD students: 9 freshmen, 7 sophomores, 6 juniors, 5 seniors.

Staff 1 full-time, 3 part-time staff members, including director, assistant director. Services provided by counselors.

Admissions LD applicants evaluated on the basis of high school transcript and grade point average, standard or untimed ACT; testing and evaluation by Reading Center and Clinic recommended. LD students may begin taking classes in fall, winter, spring, or summer. Application should be submitted 1 month in advance of initial anticipated enrollment.

Housing College housing (including coed) available. LD students housed randomly. LD students not required to live on campus.

Diagnostic Testing Available in intelligence, reading, math, spelling, handwriting, spoken language, written language, motor abilities, perceptual skills.

Tutoring Offered one-to-one by peer tutors. Available in all subjects. LD students may receive tutoring in all courses each term.

Basic Skills Remediation Offered one-to-one and in small groups by LD teachers. Available in reading, spelling, handwriting, work and study habits.

Academic Advisement Help with program planning provided by LD staff members, academic advisers. LD students may take up to 15 credit hours each semester; most take 12 credit hours; 12 credit hours required to maintain full-time status.

Special Courses Offered in college survival skills, reading, vocabulary development, study skills. All offered for credit; all enter into overall grade point average.

Auxiliary Aids and Services Aids include taped textbooks, tape recorders, typewriters, word processors. Services include alternative exam arrangements, advocacy.

Counseling Services Individual counseling, career counseling available.

Contact Dr. Judith Dettre, Director of Reading Center and Clinic, University of Nevada, Las Vegas, 4505 Maryland Parkway, Las Vegas, NV 89154, 702-739-3781.

UNIVERSITY OF NEVADA RENO

Reno, Nevada

Year Program Began	*Not reported*	Special Courses	✓
Special Fee	None	Taped Textbooks	
Special Orientation	✓	Alternative Exam Arrangements	✓
Diagnostic Testing	✓	Notetakers	✓
Subject-Area Tutoring	✓	Staff	3 full-time, 1 part-time
Basic Skills Remediation	✓	Number of Students Served	*Not reported*

General Information State-supported coed university. Part of University of Nevada System. Founded 1874. Awards B, M, D. Institutionally accredited by regional association; programs accredited by AACSB (business), ABET (engineering and technology), NLN (nursing), NCATE (teacher education); candidate for program accreditation by NASM (music). City setting; 200-acre campus. Total enrollment: 8,862. Faculty: 430 (395 full-time, 35 part-time); 74% have doctoral degrees; graduate assistants teach a few undergraduate courses. Calendar: semesters. Grading system: letters or numbers. Library holdings: 750,000 bound volumes, 393,263 titles on microform, 5,540 periodical subscriptions, 62,599 records/tapes.

Undergraduate Profile Fall 1984: 7,064 undergraduates (1,422 freshmen) from 45 states and territories and 58 foreign countries; 30% part-time; 84% state residents; 25% transfers; 60% financial aid recipients; 49% women; 2% blacks; 1% Native Americans; 2% Hispanics; 2% Asian Americans; 4% foreign nationals; 34% of undergraduates over 25 years of age; 47 legally handicapped students.

Expenses (1985–86) State resident tuition: $1152 full-time, $36 per credit part-time. Nonresident tuition: $2200 full-time, $36 per credit part-time. College room and board: $2445. College room only: $1412.

Financial Aid Fall 1984 full-time freshmen: 50% applied for aid, 48% of those were judged to have need, 80% of those were aided; the average aided freshman received an aid package worth $4100 (39% scholarships/grants, 61% self-help) meeting 80% of need. College-administered aid for all 1984–85 undergraduates: 2,000 need-based scholarships (average $500); 1,839 non-need scholarships (average $606); short-term loans (average $500); low-interest long-term loans from college funds (average $500), from external sources (average $2000); SEOG; College Work-Study; 1,100 part-time jobs. Supporting data: FFS, institutional form required; FAF, AFSA/SAR acceptable. Application deadline: continuous to 2/15.

Athletics Member NCAA (Division I). Intercollegiate sports: baseball/softball M(I,s), W(I,s); basketball M(I,s), W(I,s); cross-country running M(I,s), W(I,s); football M(I-AA,s); golf M(I,s); skiing (cross-country) M(I,s); skiing (downhill) M(I,s); swimming and diving W(II,s); tennis M(I,s), W(I,s); track and field M(I,s); volleyball W(I,s). Intramural sports: basketball, cross-country running, football, golf, skiing (cross-country), skiing (downhill), soccer, swimming and diving, tennis, track and field, volleyball, water polo.

Majors Accounting B; agricultural economics B; agricultural education B; animal sciences B; anthropology B; art/fine arts B; biochemistry B; biology/biological sciences B; botany/plant sciences B; business administration/commerce/management B; business economics B; chemical engineering B; chemistry B; child care/child and family studies B; civil engineering B; computer information systems B; computer science B; criminal justice B; (pre)dentistry sequence B; economics B; education B; electrical engineering B; elementary education B; engineering sciences B; English B; fashion merchandising B; finance/banking B; French B; geography B; geological engineering B; geology B; geophysics B; German B; health education B; history B; home economics B; home economics education B; journalism B; liberal arts/general studies B; marketing/retailing/merchandising B; mathematics B; mechanical engineering B; medical technology B; (pre)medicine sequence B; metallurgical engineering B; mining and mineral engineering B; music B; natural resource management B; nursing B; nutrition B; philosophy B; physical education B; physics B; political science/government B; psychology B; public relations B; radio and television studies B; recreation and leisure services B; secondary education B; social work B; sociology B; Spanish B; special education B; speech pathology and audiology B; speech/rhetoric/public address/debate B; textiles and clothing B; theater arts/drama B; veterinary sciences B; zoology B. Majors with highest enrollment: business administration/commerce/management, accounting, electrical engineering.

LD Program Information

Name of Program Special Services.

Availability of Services Services provided to freshmen, sophomores, juniors, seniors.

Staff 3 full-time, 1 part-time staff members, including director, tutoring coordinator. Services provided by tutors, counselor, diagnostic specialist.

Admissions LD applicants evaluated on the basis of high school transcript and grade point average, standard or untimed SAT or ACT. LD students may begin taking classes in fall, spring, or summer. Application should be submitted 2 months in advance of initial anticipated enrollment.

Orientation Optional orientation offered before registration.

Housing College housing (including coed) available. LD students housed with other LD students and non-LD students. LD students not required to live on campus.

Diagnostic Testing Available in various areas through counseling and testing office.

Tutoring Offered one-to-one and in small groups by professional teachers, peer tutors. Available in some subjects. LD students may receive tutoring in all courses each term.

Basic Skills Remediation Offered one-to-one and in small groups by writing specialist. Available in spelling, written language, learning strategies, work and study habits.

Academic Advisement Help with program planning provided by LD staff members, academic advisers. LD students may take up to 18 credits each semester; most take 12 credits; 12 credits required to maintain full-time status.

Special Courses Offered in college survival skills, vocabulary development, communication skills, composition, math, typing, study skills, career planning. Some offered for credit; some enter into overall grade point average.

Auxiliary Aids and Services Aids include tape recorders, calculators, typewriters. Services include alternative exam arrangements, notetakers, advocacy.

Counseling Services Individual counseling, small-group counseling, rap sessions, career counseling available.

Contact Ms. Hazel Ralston, Counselor, Special Services, University of Nevada Reno, Special Programs/Academic Skills Center, Room 107 TSS, Reno, NV 89557, 702-784-6901.

UNIVERSITY OF NEW ENGLAND

Biddeford, Maine

Year Program Began	1983	Special Courses	✓
Special Fee	$2200 per year	Taped Textbooks	✓
Special Orientation		Alternative Exam Arrangements	✓
Diagnostic Testing	✓	Notetakers	✓
Subject-Area Tutoring	✓	Staff	2 full-time
Basic Skills Remediation	✓	Number of Students Served	40

General Information Independent comprehensive coed institution. Founded 1939. Awards B, D. Institutionally accredited by regional association. Small-town setting; 122-acre campus. Total enrollment: 750. Faculty: 49 (38 full-time, 11 part-time); 53% have doctoral degrees; graduate assistants teach no undergraduate courses. Calendar: 4-1-4. Grading system: letters or numbers. Library holdings: 70,000 bound volumes, 495 periodical subscriptions, 500 records/tapes.

Undergraduate Profile Fall 1984: 470 undergraduates (187 freshmen); 20% part-time; 38% state residents; 15% transfers; 75% financial aid recipients; 64% women; 6% blacks; 1% Native Americans; 1% Hispanics; 1% Asian Americans; 2% foreign nationals; 5% of undergraduates over 25 years of age; 2 legally handicapped students.

Expenses (1985–86) Comprehensive fee of $9015 includes full-time tuition ($5900), mandatory fees ($65), and college room and board ($3050). Part-time tuition per credit hour ranges from $150 (for 1 to 6 credit hours) to $190 (for 7 to 11 credit hours).

Financial Aid Fall 1984 full-time freshmen: 89% applied for aid, 94% of those were judged to have need, 100% of those were aided; the average aided freshman received an aid package worth $4673 (30% scholarships/grants, 70% self-help) meeting 70% of need. College-administered aid for all 1984–85 undergraduates: 233 need-based scholarships (average $1100); 48 non-need scholarships (average $600); low-interest long-term loans from external sources (average $2350); College Work-Study; 20 part-time jobs. Supporting data: FAF, institutional form required. Priority application deadline: 4/1.

Athletics Member NAIA. Intercollegiate sports: baseball/softball M(s), W(s); basketball M(s), W(s); golf M(s); ice hockey M(s); lacrosse M(s); soccer M(s); tennis M(s), W(s); volleyball W(s). Intramural sports: baseball/softball, basketball, martial arts, skiing (cross-country), skiing (downhill), soccer, tennis, volleyball.

Majors Accounting B; adult and continuing education B; biology/biological sciences B; business administration/commerce/management B; computer information systems B; education B; elementary education B; environmental biology B; human services B; liberal arts/general studies B; marine biology B; medical laboratory technology B; (pre)medicine sequence B; nursing B; occupational therapy B; pharmacy/pharmaceutical sciences B; physical therapy B; psychology B; science education B. Majors with highest enrollment: physical therapy, occupational therapy, marine biology.

LD Program Information

Name of Program Individual Learning Program.

Availability of Services Began offering services in 1983. Services provided to freshmen (full-time program), sophomores, juniors, seniors. Program currently serves 40 LD students: 20 freshmen, 20 sophomores.

Fees $2200 per year for full-time program, $550 per semester for half-time program.

Staff 2 full-time staff members, including director, assistant director.

Admissions LD applicants evaluated on the basis of high school transcript, personal interview, letters of recommendation, psychoeducational report. LD students may begin taking classes in fall, winter, or spring. Application should be submitted at least 6 months in advance of initial anticipated enrollment.

Housing College housing (including coed) available. LD students housed with other LD students and non-LD students. LD freshmen, sophomores, juniors, and seniors required to live on campus except by special permission.

Diagnostic Testing Available in reading, math, written language.

Tutoring Offered one-to-one and in small groups by peer tutors. Available in all subjects. LD students may receive tutoring in all courses each term.

Basic Skills Remediation Offered in small groups by regular teachers. Available in reading, math, written language.

Academic Advisement Help with program planning provided by LD staff members, academic advisers. LD students may take up to 15 credit hours each semester; 12 credit hours required to maintain full-time status.

Special Courses Offered in college survival skills, study skills, career planning. None offered for credit; none enter into overall grade point average.

Auxiliary Aids and Services Aids include taped textbooks, typewriters, word processors. Services include alternative exam arrangements, notetakers.

Counseling Services Individual counseling, career counseling available.

Contact Dr. Barbara Berkovich, Director, Individual Learning Program, University of New England, Biddeford, ME 04005, 207-283-0171 Ext. 242.

UNIVERSITY OF NEW HAMPSHIRE

Durham, New Hampshire

Year Program Began	1979	Special Courses	✓
Special Fee	None	Taped Textbooks	✓
Special Orientation		Alternative Exam Arrangements	✓
Diagnostic Testing	✓	Notetakers	✓
Subject-Area Tutoring	✓	Staff	4 part-time
Basic Skills Remediation	✓	Number of Students Served	30

General Information State-supported coed university. Part of University System of New Hampshire. Founded 1866. Awards A (terminal), B, M, D. Institutionally accredited by regional association; programs accredited by ABET (engineering and technology), NASM (music), NLN (nursing), NCATE (teacher education). Small-town setting, with easy access to Boston; 188-acre campus. Total enrollment: 10,500. Faculty: 639 (538 full-time, 101 part-time); 85% have doctoral degrees; graduate assistants teach a few undergraduate courses. Calendar: semesters. Grading system: letters or numbers. Library holdings: 850,000 bound volumes, 24,000 titles on microform, 8,301 periodical subscriptions, 6,923 records/tapes.

Undergraduate Profile Fall 1984: 9,646 undergraduates (2,408 freshmen) from 26 states and territories and 45 foreign countries; 9% part-time; 56% state residents; 16% transfers; 83% financial aid recipients; 54% women; 1% blacks; 1% foreign nationals; 18 legally handicapped students.

Expenses (1984–85) State resident tuition: $2080 full-time, $55 per credit part-time. Nonresident tuition: $5650 full-time, $65 per credit part-time. Mandatory fees: $320. College room and board: $2614.

Financial Aid Fall 1984 full-time freshmen: 68% applied for aid, 80% of those were judged to have need, 97% of those were aided; the average aided freshman received an aid package worth $5055 (42% scholarships/grants, 58% self-help) meeting 90% of need. College-administered aid for all 1984–85 undergraduates: need-based scholarships; non-need scholarships; low-interest long-term loans from external sources (average $2518); SEOG; College Work-Study; part-time jobs. Supporting data: FAF, institutional form required. Priority application deadline: 2/15.

Athletics Member NCAA (Division I). Intercollegiate sports: baseball/softball M(I); basketball M(I,s), W(I,s); cross-country running M(I), W(I); field hockey W(I,s); football M(I-AA,s); golf M(I); gymnastics W(I,s); ice hockey M(I,s), W(s); lacrosse M(I), W(I); skiing (cross-country) M(I), W(I); skiing (downhill) M(I), W(I); soccer M(I), W(I); swimming and diving M(I), W(II); tennis M(I), W(I); track and field M(I), W(I); wrestling M(I). Intramural sports: baseball/softball, basketball, bowling, crew, equestrian sports, fencing, football, golf, ice hockey, martial arts, racquetball, rugby, sailing, soccer, squash, tennis, volleyball, water polo, weight lifting, wrestling.

Majors Accounting A; animal sciences A, B; anthropology B; art/fine arts B; art history B; biochemistry B; biology/biological sciences B; botany/plant sciences B; business administration/commerce/management A, B; business economics B; chemical engineering B; chemistry B; child care/child and family studies B; city, community, and regional planning B; civil engineering B; civil engineering technology A; classics B; communication B; computer engineering B; computer science B; conservation B; consumer services B; criminal justice A; culinary arts A; dietetics B; earth science B; economics B; electrical engineering B; engineering technology B; English B; entomology B; family and consumer studies B; finance/banking A; food services management A; forestry B; forest technology A; French B; geography B; geology B; German B; Greek B; health services administration B; history B; home economics education B; hotel and restaurant management B; humanities B; insurance A; Latin B; liberal arts/general studies A; library science A; linguistics B; marketing/retailing/merchandising A; mathematics B; mechanical engineering B; medical technology B; microbiology B; music B; music education B; music history B; nursing B; occupational therapy B; parks management B; philosophy B; physical education B; physics B; piano/organ B; political science/government B; psychology B; real estate A; recreation and leisure services B; Russian B; science B; social work B; sociology B; Spanish B; speech pathology and audiology B; stringed instruments B; theater arts/drama B; (pre)veterinary medicine sequence B; voice B; water resources B; wildlife management B; zoology B. Majors with highest enrollment: business administration/commerce/management, psychology, English.

LD Program Information

Name of Program Handicapped Services.

Availability of Services Began offering services in 1979. Services provided to freshmen, sophomores, juniors, seniors. Program currently serves 30 LD students.

Staff 4 part-time staff members, including codirectors. Services provided by tutor, diagnostic specialist.

Admissions LD applicants evaluated on the basis of high school transcript and grade point average, standard or untimed SAT, personal interview, letters of recommendation, psychoeducational report, application essay questions. LD students may begin taking classes in fall, spring, or summer. Application should be submitted at least 7 months in advance of initial anticipated enrollment.

Housing College housing (including coed) available. LD students housed with other LD students and non-LD students. LD students not required to live on campus.

Diagnostic Testing Available in intelligence, reading, math, spelling, spoken language, written language, work and study habits, personality, speech.

Tutoring Offered one-to-one by peer tutors. Available in all subjects. LD students may receive tutoring in 2 courses per term.

Basic Skills Remediation Offered one-to-one by peer teachers. Available in reading, spelling, spoken language, written language, learning strategies, perceptual skills, work and study habits, social skills.

Academic Advisement Help with program planning provided by LD staff members, academic advisers. LD students may take up to 21 credits each semester; most take 12 credits; 8 credits (with approval) required to maintain full-time status.

Special Courses Offered in college survival skills. None offered for credit; none enter into overall grade point average.

Auxiliary Aids and Services Aids include taped textbooks, tape recorders. Services include alternative exam arrangements, notetakers, advocacy.

Counseling Services Individual counseling, small-group counseling, rap sessions available.

Contact Ms. Sharon Kraft-Lund, Coordinator, Handicapped Services, University of New Hampshire, Memorial Union Building 200, Durham, NH 03824, 603-862-2607.

UNIVERSITY OF NORTH CAROLINA AT CHAPEL HILL

Chapel Hill, North Carolina

Year Program Began	1980	Special Courses	✓
Special Fee	None	Taped Textbooks	✓
Special Orientation	✓	Alternative Exam Arrangements	✓
Diagnostic Testing	✓	Notetakers	✓
Subject-Area Tutoring	✓	Staff	*Not reported*
Basic Skills Remediation	✓	Number of Students Served	30

General Information State-supported coed university. Part of University of North Carolina System. Founded 1795. Awards B, M, D. Institutionally accredited by regional association; programs accredited by AACSB (business), NLN (nursing), ACPE (pharmacy), NCATE (teacher education). Small-town setting; 474-acre campus. Total enrollment: 21,612. Faculty: 2,301 (2,150 full-time, 151 part-time); 87% have doctoral degrees; graduate assistants teach a few undergraduate courses. Calendar: semesters. Grading system: letters or numbers. Library holdings: 3 million bound volumes, 1.8 million titles on microform, 38,510 periodical subscriptions, 32,001 records/tapes.

Undergraduate Profile Fall 1984: 13,719 undergraduates (3,390 freshmen) from 38 states and territories and 7 foreign countries; 7% part-time; 85% state residents; 16% transfers; 30% financial aid recipients; 57% women; 9% blacks; 1% Native Americans; 1% Hispanics; 1% Asian Americans; 1% foreign nationals; 125 legally handicapped students.

Expenses (1984–85) State resident tuition: $772 full-time. Nonresident tuition: $3100 full-time. Part-time tuition per semester (1 to 8 credits) ranges from $60 to $180 for state residents, $355 to $1066 for nonresidents. Mandatory fees: $285. College room and board: $2535. College room only: $1220.

Financial Aid Fall 1984 full-time freshmen: 39% applied for aid, 65% of those were judged to have need, 96% of those were aided; the average aided freshman received an aid package worth $2967 (63% scholarships/grants, 37% self-help) meeting 95% of need. College-administered aid for all 1984–85 undergraduates: 2,300 need-based scholarships (average $775); non-need scholarships; short-term loans (average $110); low-interest long-term loans from college funds (average $1500), from external sources (average $2000); SEOG; College Work-Study; 4,500 part-time jobs. Supporting data: FAF required; IRS required for some; FFS acceptable. Priority application deadline: 3/1.

Athletics Member NCAA (Division I). Intercollegiate sports: baseball/softball M(I,s), W(I,s); basketball M(I,s), W(I,s); cross-country running M(I,s), W(I,s); fencing M(I,s), W(I,s); field hockey W(I,s); football M(I-A,s); golf M(I,s), W(I,s); gymnastics W(I,s); lacrosse M(I,s); soccer M(I,s), W(I,s); swimming and diving M(I,s), W(I,s); tennis M(I,s), W(I,s); track and field M(I,s), W(I,s); volleyball W(I,s); wrestling M(I,s). Intramural sports: archery, badminton, baseball/softball, basketball, bowling, crew, cross-country running, football, golf, gymnastics, ice hockey, lacrosse, racquetball, rugby, soccer, squash, swimming and diving, tennis, track and field, volleyball, water polo, wrestling.

Majors Accounting B; African studies B; American studies B; anthropology B; art/fine arts B; art history B; astronomy B; biology/biological sciences B; black/Afro-American studies B; business administration/commerce/management B; chemistry B; classics B; criminal justice B; dental services B; early childhood education B; East Asian studies B; economics B; education B; elementary education B; English B; film studies B; French B; geography B; geology B; Germanic languages and literature B; Greek B; history B; industrial administration B; interdisciplinary studies B; international studies B; Italian B; journalism B; Latin B; Latin American studies B; linguistics B; literature B; mathematics B; medical technology B; music B; naval sciences B; nursing B; peace studies B; pharmacy/pharmaceutical sciences B; philosophy B; physical education B; physical therapy B; physics B; political science/government B; Portuguese B; psychology B; public affairs and policy studies B; public health B; radio and television studies B; radiological technology B; recreation and leisure services B; religious studies B; Russian B; secondary education B; sociology B; Spanish B; speech/rhetoric/public address/debate B; theater arts/drama B; urban studies B; women's studies B. Majors with highest enrollment: business administration/commerce/management, industrial administration, psychology.

LD Program Information

Name of Program Handicapped Student Services.

Availability of Services Began offering services in 1980. Services provided to freshmen, sophomores, juniors, seniors. Program currently serves 30 LD students: 12 freshmen, 10 sophomores, 4 juniors, 4 seniors.

Staff Includes coordinator. Services provided by remediation specialists, tutors, diagnostic specialists.

Admissions LD applicants evaluated on the basis of high school transcript and grade point average, untimed SAT, autobiographical statement, letters of recommendation, psychoeducational report. LD students may begin taking classes in fall, spring, or summer. Application should be submitted 9 to 10 months in advance of initial anticipated enrollment.

Orientation Optional orientation offered before registration.

Housing College housing (including coed) available. LD students housed randomly. LD students not required to live on campus.

Diagnostic Testing Available in intelligence, reading, math, spelling, spoken language, written language, perceptual skills, work and study habits, personality, social skills, speech.

Tutoring Offered one-to-one and in small groups by professional teachers, peer tutors. Available in all subjects. LD students may receive tutoring in all courses each term.

Basic Skills Remediation Offered one-to-one and in small groups by LD teachers, teacher trainees. Available in math, written language, learning strategies, work and study habits.

Academic Advisement Help with program planning provided by LD staff members, academic advisers. LD students may take up to 17 credits each semester; most take 12 credits; 9 credits required to maintain full-time status.

Special Courses Offered in reading, composition, math, study skills, career planning, metacognitive development. Some offered for credit; some enter into overall grade point average.

Auxiliary Aids and Services Aids include taped textbooks, tape recorders, calculators, word processors. Services include alternative exam arrangements, notetakers.

Counseling Services Individual counseling, career counseling available.

Contact Ms. Laura L. D. Thomas, Coordinator for Handicapped Student Services, University of North Carolina at Chapel Hill, 05 Steele Building 050A, Chapel Hill, NC 27514, 919-966-4041.

UNIVERSITY OF NORTH CAROLINA AT CHARLOTTE

Charlotte, North Carolina

Year Program Began	1983	Special Courses	✓
Special Fee	None	Taped Textbooks	✓
Special Orientation	✓	Alternative Exam Arrangements	✓
Diagnostic Testing	✓	Notetakers	✓
Subject-Area Tutoring	✓	Staff	2 part-time
Basic Skills Remediation	✓	Number of Students Served	14

General Information State-supported comprehensive coed institution. Part of University of North Carolina System. Founded 1946. Awards B, M. Institutionally accredited by regional association; programs accredited by NAAB (architecture), AACSB (business), ABET (engineering and technology), NLN (nursing), NCATE (teacher education). City setting; 1,000-acre barrier-free campus. Total enrollment: 10,459. Faculty: 689 (484 full-time, 205 part-time); 72% have doctoral degrees; graduate assistants teach no undergraduate courses. Calendar: semesters. Grading system: letters or numbers. Library holdings: 362,080 bound volumes, 110,443 titles on microform, 5,205 periodical subscriptions, 32,387 records/tapes.

Undergraduate Profile Fall 1984: 9,120 undergraduates (1,367 freshmen) from 45 states and territories and 61 foreign countries; 23% part-time; 87% state residents; 13% transfers; 40% financial aid recipients; 47% women; 8% blacks; 1% Native Americans; 1% Hispanics; 2% Asian Americans; 4% foreign nationals; 22% of undergraduates over 25 years of age.

Expenses (1984–85) State resident tuition: $410 full-time. Nonresident tuition: $2968 full-time. Part-time tuition and fees per semester (1 to 11 semester hours) range from $76 to $229 for state residents, $396 to $1258 for nonresidents. Mandatory fees: $290. College room and board: $2096. College room only: $1052.

Financial Aid Fall 1984 full-time freshmen: 60% applied for aid, 97% of those were judged to have need, 90% of those were aided; the average aided freshman received an aid package worth $1739 (40% scholarships/grants, 60% self-help) meeting 90% of need. College-administered aid for all 1984–85 undergraduates: 1,180 need-based scholarships (average $510); 290 non-need scholarships (average $780); short-term loans (average $275); low-interest long-term loans from external sources (average $1950); SEOG; College Work-Study; 780 part-time jobs. Supporting data: FAF, IRS, institutional form, AFSA/SAR required; FFS acceptable. Priority application deadline: 4/15.

Athletics Member NCAA (Division I). Intercollegiate sports: baseball/softball M(I,s), W(I,s); basketball M(I,s), W(I,s); cross-country running M(I,s); golf M(I,s); riflery M(I), W(I); soccer M(I,s); swimming and diving M(I), W(I); tennis M(I,s), W(I,s); volleyball W(I,s). Intramural sports: badminton, baseball/softball, basketball, bowling, football, golf, racquetball, soccer, swimming and diving, tennis, track and field, volleyball.

Majors Accounting B; anthropology B; architecture B; art education B; art/fine arts B; biology/biological sciences B; black/Afro-American studies B; business administration/commerce/management B; chemistry B; child care/child and family studies B; civil engineering B; civil engineering technology B; computer science B; criminal justice B; dance B; early childhood education B; earth science B; economics B; electrical engineering B; electrical engineering technology B; elementary education B; English B; French B; geography B; German B; history B; human services B; mathematics B; mechanical engineering B; mechanical engineering technology B; medical technology B; music B; nursing B; philosophy B; physics B; political science/government B; psychology B; religious studies B; science education B; secondary education B; social science B; sociology B; Spanish B; theater arts/drama B. Majors with highest enrollment: business administration/commerce/management, mathematics, accounting.

LD Program Information

Name of Program Disabled Student Services.

Availability of Services Began offering services in 1983. Services provided to freshmen, sophomores, juniors, seniors. Program currently serves 14 LD students: 4 freshmen, 4 sophomores, 4 juniors, 2 seniors.

Staff 2 part-time staff members, including coordinator, assistant coordinator. Services provided by tutors.

Admissions LD applicants evaluated on the basis of high school transcript and grade point average, untimed SAT or ACT, psychoeducational report. LD students may begin taking classes in fall, spring, or summer. Application should be submitted 4 to 6 months in advance of initial anticipated enrollment.

Orientation Optional orientation offered during registration (individual orientation for some services after classes begin).

Housing College housing (including coed) available. LD students housed randomly. LD students not required to live on campus.

Diagnostic Testing Available in intelligence, reading, math, spelling, handwriting, spoken language, written language, motor abilities, perceptual skills, work and study habits, personality, social skills.

Tutoring Offered one-to-one by peer tutors. Available in some subjects. LD students may receive tutoring in all courses each term by special request.

Basic Skills Remediation Offered one-to-one by LD teachers. Available in reading, math, spelling, handwriting, spoken language, written language, learning strategies, motor abilities, perceptual skills, work and study habits, social skills.

Academic Advisement Help with program planning provided by LD staff members, academic advisers. LD students may take up to 18 semester hours each semester; most take 12 semester hours; 12 semester hours required to maintain full-time status.

Special Courses Offered in college survival skills, vocabulary development, personal psychology, study skills, career planning. Some offered for credit; some enter into overall grade point average.

Auxiliary Aids and Services Aids include taped textbooks, tape recorders, calculators, typewriters, word processors. Services include alternative exam arrangements, notetakers, advocacy, proofreading.

Counseling Services Individual counseling, career counseling available.

Contact Mrs. Janet D. Daniel, Coordinator of Disabled Student Services Counseling Center, University of North Carolina at Charlotte, Charlotte, NC 28223, 704-597-2162.

UNIVERSITY OF NORTH CAROLINA AT WILMINGTON

Wilmington, North Carolina

Year Program Began	1984	Special Courses	✓
Special Fee	None	Taped Textbooks	
Special Orientation	✓	Alternative Exam Arrangements	✓
Diagnostic Testing	✓	Notetakers	✓
Subject-Area Tutoring	✓	Staff	3 part-time
Basic Skills Remediation		Number of Students Served	4

General Information State-supported comprehensive coed institution. Part of University of North Carolina System. Founded 1947. Awards B, M. Institutionally accredited by regional association; programs accredited by AACSB (business), NASM (music), NLN (nursing), NCATE (teacher education). City setting; 600-acre campus. Total enrollment: 5,566. Faculty: 315 (281 full-time, 34 part-time); 66% have doctoral degrees; graduate assistants teach no undergraduate courses. Calendar: semesters. Grading system: letters or numbers. Library holdings: 223,403 bound volumes, 1,828 titles on microform, 3,511 periodical subscriptions, 5,296 records/tapes.

Undergraduate Profile Fall 1984: 5,320 undergraduates (1,163 freshmen) from 32 states and territories and 16 foreign countries; 20% part-time; 92% state residents; 10% transfers; 50% financial aid recipients; 53% women; 7% blacks; 0% Native Americans; 1% Hispanics; 1% Asian Americans; 1% foreign nationals; 17% of undergraduates over 25 years of age; 15 legally handicapped students.

Expenses (1984–85) State resident tuition: $716 full-time. Nonresident tuition: $2966 full-time. Part-time tuition and fees per semester (1 to 11 credits) range from $84.50 to $314 for state residents, $365.50 to $1158 for nonresidents. Mandatory fees: $327. College room and board: $2090.

Financial Aid Fall 1984 full-time freshmen: 65% applied for aid, 74% of those were judged to have need, 94% of those were aided; the average aided freshman received an aid package worth $1682 (44% scholarships/grants, 56% self-help) meeting 51% of need. College-administered aid for all 1984–85 undergraduates: 417 need-based scholarships (average $300); 746 non-need scholarships (average $400); low-interest long-term loans from external sources (average $1000); SEOG; College Work-Study; 300 part-time jobs. Supporting data: institutional form, AFSA/SAR, Financial Aid Transcript (for transfers) required; IRS required for some; FFS, FAF, state form acceptable. Priority application deadline: 3/15.

Athletics Member NCAA (Division I), NAIA. Intercollegiate sports: baseball/softball M(I,s), W(s); basketball M(I,s), W(s); cross-country running M(I), W; golf M(I,s), W(I,s); soccer M(I,s); swimming and diving M(I,s), W(I,s); tennis M(I,s), W(s); volleyball W(s); water polo M(I). Intramural sports: archery, baseball/softball, basketball, bowling, cross-country running, football, golf, racquetball, soccer, swimming and diving, tennis, volleyball, water polo.

Majors Accounting B; art/fine arts B; biology/biological sciences B; business administration/commerce/management B; business economics B; chemistry B; computer science B; earth science B; education B; English B; environmental sciences B; French B; geography B; geology B; history B; marine biology B; marketing/retailing/merchandising B; mathematics B; medical technology B; music B; nursing B; parks management B; philosophy B; physical education B; physics B; political science/government B; psychology B; religious studies B; social science B; sociology B; Spanish B; special education B; speech/rhetoric/public address/debate B; theater arts/drama B. Majors with highest enrollment: business administration/commerce/management, computer science, accounting.

LD Program Information

Name of Program Student Development.

Availability of Services Began offering services in 1984. Services provided to freshmen, sophomores, juniors, seniors. Program currently serves 4 LD students (all freshmen).

Staff 3 part-time staff members, including director. Services provided by counselors.

Admissions LD applicants evaluated on the basis of high school transcript and grade point average, standard or untimed SAT or ACT, psychoeducational report. LD students may begin taking classes in fall, spring, or summer. Application should be submitted 3 months in advance of initial anticipated enrollment.

Orientation Optional orientation offered before registration.

Housing College housing (including coed) available. LD students housed randomly. LD students not required to live on campus.

Diagnostic Testing Available in intelligence, reading, math, spoken language, motor abilities, perceptual skills, work and study habits, personality, social skills.

Tutoring Offered one-to-one and in small groups by professional teachers, peer tutors. Available in all subjects. LD students may receive tutoring in all courses each term.

Academic Advisement Help with program planning provided by LD staff members, academic advisers. LD students may take up to 16 credits each semester; most take 9 to 12 credits; 10 credits required to maintain full-time status.

Special Courses Offered in college survival skills, reading, communication skills, composition, language development, math, personal psychology, study skills, career planning. None offered for credit; none enter into overall grade point average.

Auxiliary Aids and Services Aids include tape recorders, calculators, typewriters. Services include alternative exam arrangements, notetakers, advocacy, readers.

Counseling Services Individual counseling, small-group counseling, career counseling available.

Contact Ms. Linda Shaddix, Counselor, Student Development, University of North Carolina at Wilmington, 601 South College Road, Wilmington, NC 28403, 919-395-3280.

UNIVERSITY OF NORTH DAKOTA

Grand Forks, North Dakota

Year Program Began	1978	Special Courses	✓
Special Fee	None	Taped Textbooks	✓
Special Orientation		Alternative Exam Arrangements	✓
Diagnostic Testing	✓	Notetakers	✓
Subject-Area Tutoring	✓	Staff	7 part-time
Basic Skills Remediation	✓	Number of Students Served	73

General Information State-supported coed university. Founded 1883. Awards A (college transfer), B, M, D. Institutionally accredited by regional association; programs accredited by NASAD (art and design), AACSB (business), ABET (engineering and technology), NLN (nursing), NCATE (teacher education); candidate for program accreditation by NASM (music). Rural setting; 470-acre barrier-free campus. Total enrollment: 11,060. Faculty: 650 (450 full-time, 200 part-time); 70% have doctoral degrees; graduate assistants teach a few undergraduate courses. Calendar: semesters. Grading system: letters or numbers. Library holdings: 460,000 bound volumes, 720,000 titles on microform, 4,300 periodical subscriptions, 2,000 records/tapes.

Undergraduate Profile Fall 1984: 9,358 undergraduates (1,706 freshmen) from 52 states and territories and 39 foreign countries; 5% part-time; 63% state residents; 25% transfers; 75% financial aid recipients; 47% women; 438 legally handicapped students.

Expenses (1985–86) State resident tuition: $1166 full-time, $48.63 per credit hour part-time. Nonresident tuition: $2160 full-time, $90 per credit hour part-time. Minnesota resident tuition: $1374 full-time, $57.25 per credit hour part-time. College room and board: $1882.

Financial Aid Fall 1984 full-time freshmen: 91% applied for aid, 52% of those were judged to have need, 100% of those were aided; the average aided freshman received an aid package worth $3212 (35% scholarships/grants, 65% self-help) meeting 93% of need. College-administered aid for all 1984–85 undergraduates: need-based scholarships; non-need scholarships; short-term loans; low-interest long-term loans from external sources; SEOG; part-time jobs. Supporting data: FFS, institutional form required. Priority application deadline: 3/15.

Athletics Member NCAA (Division II). Intercollegiate sports: baseball/softball M(II), W(II); basketball M(II,s), W(II,s); cross-country running M(II), W(II); field hockey W(III); football M(II); golf M(II), W(II); gymnastics W(II); ice hockey M(I,s); swimming and diving M(II), W(II); tennis M(II), W(II); track and field M(II,s), W(II,s); volleyball W(II,s); wrestling M(II,s). Intramural sports: baseball/softball, basketball, cross-country running, golf, racquetball, riflery, swimming and diving, track and field, volleyball, wrestling.

Majors Accounting B; advertising B; aerospace sciences B; air traffic control B; anthropology B; art education B; art/fine arts B; aviation administration B; biology/biological sciences B; broadcasting B; business administration/commerce/management B; business economics B; business education B; chemical engineering B; chemistry B; civil engineering B; communication B; computer science B; criminal justice B; (pre) dentistry sequence B; dietetics B; early childhood education B; economics B; education B; electrical engineering B; elementary education B; engineering management B; English B; flight training A; French B; geography B; geological engineering B; geology B; German B; history B; home economics B; home economics education B; industrial arts B; journalism B; library science B; linguistics B; management information systems B; marketing/retailing/merchandising B; mathematics B; mechanical engineering B; medical technology B; (pre)medicine sequence B; meteorology B; modern languages B; music B; music education B; natural sciences B; nursing B; nutrition B; occupational therapy B; philosophy B; physical education B; physical sciences B; physical therapy B; physics B; political science/government B; psychology B; public administration B; public relations B; recreation and leisure services B; religious studies B; Romance languages B; Russian B; Scandinavian languages/studies B; science education B; secondary education B; social science B; social work B; sociology B; Spanish B; special education B; speech pathology and audiology B; textiles and clothing B; theater arts/drama B; (pre) veterinary medicine sequence B; wildlife biology B; zoology B. Majors with highest enrollment: accounting, computer science, business administration/commerce/management.

LD Program Information

Name of Program Disabled Student Services.

Availability of Services Began offering services in 1978. Services provided to freshmen, sophomores, juniors, seniors. Program currently serves 73 LD students: 19 freshmen, 24 sophomores, 18 juniors, 12 seniors.

Staff 7 part-time staff members, including director. Services provided by remediation specialist, tutors, counselors, diagnostic specialist, career development counselor.

Admissions LD applicants evaluated on the basis of high school transcript and grade point average, standard or untimed ACT; psychoeducational report recommended. LD students may begin taking classes in fall, spring, or summer. Application should be submitted 3 months in advance of initial anticipated enrollment.

Housing College housing (including coed) available. LD students housed randomly. LD students not required to live on campus.

Diagnostic Testing Available in intelligence, reading, math, spelling, handwriting, spoken language, written language, motor abilities, perceptual skills, work and study habits, personality, social skills, speech, hearing.

Tutoring Offered one-to-one by professional teachers, peer tutors. Available in all subjects. LD students may receive tutoring in all courses each term.

Basic Skills Remediation Offered one-to-one and in small groups by LD teachers. Available in reading, math, spelling, handwriting, spoken language, written language, learning strategies, motor abilities, perceptual skills, work and study habits, social skills, speech.

Academic Advisement Help with program planning provided by LD staff members, academic advisers. LD students may take up to 21 credit hours each semester; most take 14 credit hours; 12 credit hours required to maintain full-time status.

Special Courses Offered in college survival skills, reading, vocabulary development, communication skills, composition, language development, math, typing, personal psychology, study skills, career planning. Some offered for credit; none enter into overall grade point average.

Auxiliary Aids and Services Aids include taped textbooks, tape recorders, calculators, typewriters, word processors, Kurzweil reading machine, talking computer. Services include alternative exam arrangements, notetakers, advocacy, typing services, proofreaders.

Counseling Services Individual counseling, small-group counseling, rap sessions, career counseling available.

Contact Ms. Kaye Becker, Coordinator, Disabled Student Services, University of North Dakota, Box 8256, University Station, Grand Forks, ND 58202, 701-777-3425.

UNIVERSITY OF NORTHERN IOWA

Cedar Falls, Iowa

Year Program Began	1983	Special Courses	✓
Special Fee	None	Taped Textbooks	✓
Special Orientation	✓	Alternative Exam Arrangements	✓
Diagnostic Testing	✓	Notetakers	✓
Subject-Area Tutoring	✓	Staff	1 full-time, 1 part-time
Basic Skills Remediation	✓	Number of Students Served	15

General Information State-supported comprehensive coed institution. Founded 1876. Awards B, M, D. Institutionally accredited by regional association; programs accredited by NASAD (art and design), NASM (music), NCATE (teacher education). Small-town setting; 723-acre barrier-free campus. Total enrollment: 11,161. Faculty: 720 (616 full-time, 104 part-time); 53% have doctoral degrees; graduate assistants teach a few undergraduate courses. Calendar: semesters. Grading system: letters or numbers. Library holdings: 600,146 bound volumes, 407,298 titles on microform, 2,799 periodical subscriptions, 13,255 records/tapes.

Undergraduate Profile Fall 1984: 10,124 undergraduates (1,775 freshmen) from 39 states and territories and 31 foreign countries; 18% part-time; 97% state residents; 33% transfers; 66% financial aid recipients; 55% women; 2% blacks; 1% Hispanics; 1% Asian Americans; 369 legally handicapped students.

Expenses (1985–86) State resident tuition: $1612 full-time, $52 per semester hour part-time. Nonresident tuition: $2998 full-time, $125 per semester hour part-time. College room and board: $1902.

Financial Aid Fall 1984 full-time freshmen: 89% applied for aid, 66% of those were judged to have need, 100% of those were aided; the average aided freshman received an aid package worth $1316 (77% scholarships/grants, 23% self-help) meeting 70% of need. College-administered aid for all 1984–85 undergraduates: 1,766 need-based scholarships (average $575); 1,305 non-need scholarships (average $540); low-interest long-term loans from college funds (average $400), from external sources (average $2200); SEOG; College Work-Study; 1,500 part-time jobs. Supporting data: IRS required; FFS, FAF, AFSA/SAR acceptable. Priority application deadline: 3/15.

Athletics Member NCAA (Division I). Intercollegiate sports: baseball/softball M(I), W(I,s); basketball M(I,s), W(I,s); cross-country running M(I,s); football M(I-AA,s); golf M(I), W(I); swimming and diving M(I), W(I); tennis M(I), W(I); track and field M(I,s), W(I,s); volleyball W(I,s); wrestling M(I,s). Intramural sports: baseball/softball, basketball, cross-country running, football, golf, gymnastics, rugby, soccer, swimming and diving, tennis, track and field, volleyball, wrestling.

Majors Accounting B; American studies B; anthropology B; applied art B; art education B; art/fine arts B; art history B; arts administration B; Asian/Oriental studies B; automotive technologies B; behavioral sciences B; biology/biological sciences B; broadcasting B; business administration/commerce/management B; business education B; ceramic art and design B; chemistry B; child care/child and family studies B; child psychology/child development B; clinical psychology B; communication B; computer information systems B; computer programming B; computer science B; conservation B; construction technologies B; creative writing B; (pre)dentistry sequence B; dietetics B; drafting and design B; early childhood education B; earth science B; ecology/environmental studies B; economics B; education B; educational administration B; educational media B; electrical and electronics technologies B; elementary education B; English B; environmental biology B; fashion merchandising B; finance/banking B; food marketing B; food sciences B; French B; geography B; geology B; German B; graphic arts B; health education B; history B; home economics B; home economics education B; humanities B; industrial arts B; industrial engineering technology B; interdisciplinary studies B; interior design B; Latin American studies B; (pre)law sequence B; liberal arts/general studies B; linguistics B; marketing/retailing/merchandising B; mathematics B; mechanical engineering technology B; medical technology B; (pre)medicine sequence B; modern languages B; music B; music education B; music history B; natural sciences B; nutrition B; philosophy B; physical education B; physical sciences B; physical therapy B; physics B; political science/government B; psychology B; public administration B; public health B; public relations B; quality control technology B; radio and television studies B; reading education B; recreation and leisure services B; recreation therapy B; religious studies B; retail management B; Russian and Slavic studies B; science B; science education B; secondary education B; secretarial studies/office management B; social science B; social work B; sociology B; Spanish B; special education B; speech pathology and audiology B; speech/rhetoric/public address/debate B; speech therapy B; studio art B; teaching English as a second language B; textiles and clothing B; theater arts/drama B; (pre)veterinary medicine sequence B; vocational education B. Majors with highest enrollment: elementary education, accounting, business administration/commerce/management.

LD Program Information

Name of Program Handicapped Student Services.

Availability of Services Began offering services in 1983. Services provided to freshmen, sophomores, juniors, seniors. Program currently serves 15 LD students: 5 freshmen, 5 sophomores, 3 juniors, 2 seniors.

Staff 1 full-time, 1 part-time staff members, including director. Services provided by LD specialist.

Admissions LD applicants evaluated on the basis of high school transcript and grade point average, standard or untimed ACT. LD students may begin taking classes in fall, spring, or summer. Application should be submitted 2 months in advance of initial anticipated enrollment.

Orientation Optional orientation offered before registration (individual orientation for some services offered during registration and after classes begin).

Housing College housing (including coed) available. LD students housed randomly. LD students not required to live on campus.

Diagnostic Testing Available in intelligence, reading, math, spelling, handwriting, spoken language, written language, work and study habits, personality.

Tutoring Offered one-to-one and in small groups by professional teachers, peer tutors. Available in some subjects. LD students may receive tutoring in all courses each term.

Basic Skills Remediation Offered one-to-one and in small groups by LD teachers. Available in reading, math, spelling, handwriting, spoken language, written language, learning strategies, motor abilities, perceptual skills, work and study habits, social skills, speech.

Academic Advisement Help with program planning provided by LD staff members, academic advisers. LD students may take up to 16 semester hours each semester; most take 12 semester hours; 12 semester hours required to maintain full-time status.

Special Courses Offered in reading, vocabulary development, communication skills, composition, language development, typing, study skills, career planning. None offered for credit; none enter into overall grade point average.

Auxiliary Aids and Services Aids include taped textbooks, tape recorders, calculators, typewriters, word processors. Services include alternative exam arrangements, notetakers, advocacy.

Counseling Services Individual counseling, small-group counseling, rap sessions, career counseling available.

Contact Dr. Larry Steinhauser, Coordinator of Handicapped Student Services, University of Northern Iowa, Cedar Falls, IA 50614, 319-273-2676.

UNIVERSITY OF OKLAHOMA

Norman, Oklahoma

Year Program Began	*Not reported*	Special Courses	✓
Special Fee	None	Taped Textbooks	✓
Special Orientation	✓	Alternative Exam Arrangements	✓
Diagnostic Testing	✓	Notetakers	
Subject-Area Tutoring	✓	Staff	2 part-time
Basic Skills Remediation	✓	Number of Students Served	22

General Information State-supported coed university. Founded 1890. Awards B, M, D. Institutionally accredited by regional association; programs accredited by NAAB (architecture), AACSB (business), ABET (engineering and technology), NASM (music), NLN (nursing), NCATE (teacher education). City setting, with easy access to Oklahoma City; 1,000-acre campus. Total enrollment: 19,931. Faculty: 882 (788 full-time, 94 part-time); 81% have doctoral degrees; graduate assistants teach a few undergraduate courses. Calendar: semesters. Grading system: letters or numbers. Library holdings: 2 million bound volumes, 1.5 million titles on microform, 16,000 periodical subscriptions.

Undergraduate Profile Fall 1984: 15,395 undergraduates (2,563 freshmen) from 51 states and territories and 69 foreign countries; 17% part-time; 84% state residents; 10% transfers; 55% financial aid recipients; 42% women; 4% blacks; 2% Native Americans; 1% Hispanics; 2% Asian Americans; 4% foreign nationals; 15% of undergraduates over 25 years of age; 59 legally handicapped students.

Expenses (1985–86) State resident tuition ranges from $700 to $803 full-time, $22.60 to $25.90 per credit hour part-time, according to course level. Nonresident tuition ranges from $2257 to $2607 full-time, $72.80 to $84.10 per credit hour part-time, according to course level. Mandatory fees: $130. College room and board: $2542.

Financial Aid Fall 1984 full-time freshmen: 47% applied for aid, 48% of those were judged to have need, 100% of those were aided; the average aided freshman received an aid package worth $2976 (55% scholarships/grants, 45% self-help) meeting 100% of need. College-administered aid for all 1984–85 undergraduates: 2,883 need-based scholarships (average $432); 2,365 non-need scholarships (average $989); short-term loans (average $150); low-interest long-term loans from college funds (average $552), from external sources (average $1465); SEOG; College Work-Study; 2,815 part-time jobs. Supporting data: FAF, AFSA/SAR required. Application deadline: continuous to 3/1.

Athletics Member NCAA (Division I). Intercollegiate sports: baseball/softball M(I,s), W(I,s); basketball M(I,s), W(I,s); cross-country running M(I,s), W(I,s); football M(I-A,s); golf M(I,s), W(I,s); gymnastics M(I,s), W(I,s); swimming and diving M(I,s), W(I,s); tennis M(I,s), W(I,s); track and field M(I,s), W(I,s); volleyball W(I,s); wrestling M(I,s). Intramural sports: badminton, baseball/softball, basketball, bowling, football, golf, racquetball, swimming and diving, tennis, track and field, volleyball, water polo, weight lifting.

Majors Accounting B; advertising B; aerospace engineering B; American studies B; anthropology B; architectural engineering B; architecture B; art/fine arts B; art history B; Asian/Oriental studies B; astronomy B; astrophysics B; botany/plant sciences B; broadcasting B; business administration/commerce/management B; business economics B; ceramic art and design B; chemical engineering B; chemistry B; civil engineering B; classics B; commercial art B; communication B; community services B; computer engineering B; computer science B; construction technologies B; creative writing B; dance B; (pre)dentistry sequence B; dietetics B; early childhood education B; economics B; education B; electrical engineering B; elementary education B; engineering (general) B; engineering physics B; English B; environmental design B; environmental engineering B; environmental sciences B; European studies B; fashion design and technology B; fashion merchandising B; film studies B; finance/banking B; French B; geography B; geological engineering B; geology B; geophysics B; German B; graphic arts B; health education B; history B; human development B; industrial engineering B; interior design B; journalism B; laboratory technologies B; land use management and reclamation B; Latin American studies B; law enforcement/police sciences B; liberal arts/general studies B; linguistics B; marketing/retailing/merchandising B; mathematics B; mechanical engineering B; medical assistant technologies B; (pre)medicine sequence B; meteorology B; microbiology B; music B; music education B; music history B; nursing B; nutrition B; occupational therapy B; painting/drawing B; petroleum/natural gas engineering B; petroleum technology B; pharmacy/pharmaceutical sciences B; philosophy B; physical education B; physical therapy B; physician's assistant studies B; physics B; piano/organ B; political science/government B; psychology B; public administration B; public affairs and policy studies B; public relations B; radio and television studies B; radiological technology B; real estate B; recreation and leisure services B; religious studies B; Russian B; Russian and Slavic studies B; science education B; sculpture B; secretarial studies/office management B; social work B; sociology B; Spanish B; special education B; speech/rhetoric/public address/debate B; stringed instruments B; studio art B; systems engineering B; technical writing B; theater arts/drama B; urban studies B; (pre)veterinary medicine sequence B; voice B; wind and percussion instruments B; zoology B. Majors with highest enrollment: accounting, business administration/commerce/management, computer science.

LD Program Information

Name of Program Handicapped Student Services.

Availability of Services Services provided to freshmen, sophomores, juniors, seniors. Program currently serves 22 LD students.

Staff 2 part-time staff members, including coordinator. Services provided by tutors, diagnostic specialist.

Admissions LD applicants evaluated on the basis of high school transcript and grade point average, standard or untimed SAT or ACT, psychoeducational report. LD students may begin taking classes in fall, spring, or summer. Application should be submitted 3 months in advance of initial anticipated enrollment.

Orientation Optional orientation offered during registration.

Housing College housing (including coed) available. LD students housed randomly. LD freshmen required to live on campus.

Diagnostic Testing Available in intelligence, reading, math, spelling, written language, perceptual skills, social skills.

Tutoring Offered one-to-one by peer tutors. Available in some subjects. LD students may receive tutoring in all courses each term (depending on availability of tutors).

Basic Skills Remediation Offered in class-size groups by regular teachers. Available in spelling, written language, learning strategies, work and study habits.

Academic Advisement Help with program planning provided by LD staff members, academic advisers. Most LD students take 12 semester hours each semester; 12 semester hours required to maintain full-time status.

Special Courses Offered in college survival skills, reading, language development, study skills. Most offered for credit; most enter into overall grade point average.

Auxiliary Aids and Services Aids include taped textbooks. Services include alternative exam arrangements, advocacy.

Counseling Services Individual counseling, career counseling available.

Contact Ms. Linda Zinner, Coordinator, Handicapped Student Services, University of Oklahoma, 731 Elm Street, Room 218, Norman, OK 73019, 405-325-1459.

UNIVERSITY OF OREGON
Eugene, Oregon

Year Program Began	1977	Special Courses	✓
Special Fee	None	Taped Textbooks	
Special Orientation		Alternative Exam Arrangements	✓
Diagnostic Testing		Notetakers	✓
Subject-Area Tutoring	✓	Staff	7 part-time
Basic Skills Remediation	✓	Number of Students Served	9

General Information State-supported coed university. Founded 1876. Awards B, M, D. Institutionally accredited by regional association; programs accredited by NAAB (architecture), AACSB (business), FIDER (interior design), NASM (music), NCATE (teacher education). City setting; 250-acre campus. Total enrollment: 15,840. Faculty: 1,287 (1,049 full-time, 238 part-time); 85% have doctoral degrees; graduate assistants teach about a quarter of the undergraduate courses. Calendar: quarters. Grading system: letters or numbers and pass/fail. Library holdings: 1.8 million bound volumes, 960,000 titles on microform, 20,000 periodical subscriptions, 4,000 records/tapes.

Undergraduate Profile Fall 1984: 11,948 undergraduates (2,095 freshmen) from 52 states and territories and 70 foreign countries; 14% part-time; 79% state residents; 34% transfers; 50% financial aid recipients; 49% women; 1% blacks; 1% Native Americans; 1% Hispanics; 4% Asian Americans; 7% foreign nationals.

Expenses (1984–85) State resident tuition: $1432 full-time. Nonresident tuition: $4057 full-time. Part-time tuition per quarter (1 to 11 credit hours) ranges from $101 to $441 for state residents, $174 to $1244 for nonresidents. Mandatory fees: $50. College room and board: $2340.

Financial Aid Fall 1984 full-time freshmen: 76% applied for aid, 85% of those were judged to have need, 100% of those were aided; the average aided freshman received an aid package worth $3525 (41% scholarships/grants, 59% self-help) meeting 90% of need. College-administered aid for all 1984–85 undergraduates: need-based scholarships (average $500); non-need scholarships (average $500); short-term loans (average $250); low-interest long-term loans from external sources; SEOG; College Work-Study; part-time jobs. Supporting data: FAF, AFSA/SAR required. Priority application deadline: 3/1.

Athletics Member NCAA (Division I). Intercollegiate sports: baseball/softball W(I,s); basketball M(I,s), W(I,s); cross-country running M(I,s), W(I,s); football M(I-A,s); golf M(I,s); gymnastics W(I,s); swimming and diving M(I,s), W(I,s); tennis M(I,s), W(I); track and field M(I,s), W(I,s); volleyball W(I); wrestling M(I,s). Intramural sports: badminton, baseball/softball, basketball, bowling, crew, cross-country running, equestrian sports, fencing, field hockey, football, golf, gymnastics, martial arts, racquetball, rugby, skiing (cross-country), skiing (downhill), soccer, squash, swimming and diving, tennis, track and field, volleyball, wrestling.

Majors Accounting B; advertising B; American studies B; anthropology B; architecture B; art education B; art/fine arts B; art history B; biochemistry B; biology/biological sciences B; broadcasting B; business administration/commerce/management B; chemistry B; child psychology/child development B; Chinese B; classics B; communication B; community services B; comparative literature B; computer information systems B; computer programming B; computer science B; creative writing B; dance B; (pre)dentistry sequence B; East Asian studies B; East European and Soviet studies B; ecology/environmental studies B; economics B; education B; educational administration B; elementary education B; English B; film studies B; finance/banking B; French B; genetics B; geography B; geology B; German B; Germanic languages and literature B; gerontology B; Greek B; health education B; history B; humanities B; interior design B; international studies B; Italian B; Japanese B; jewelry and metalsmithing B; journalism B; labor and industrial relations B; landscape architecture/design B; Latin B; Latin American studies B; linguistics B; marine biology B; mathematics B; (pre)medicine sequence B; music B; music education B; philosophy B; physical education B; physical sciences B; physics B; political science/government B; psychology B; public administration B; public affairs and policy studies B; public relations B; radio and television studies B; real estate B; recreation and leisure services B; religious studies B; Romance languages B; Russian B; secondary education B; sociology B; Spanish B; speech pathology and audiology B; speech/rhetoric/public address/debate B; telecommunications B; theater arts/drama B; urban studies B; voice B; women's studies B. Majors with highest enrollment: business administration/commerce/management, architecture, journalism.

LD Program Information

Name of Program Educational Opportunities Program.

Availability of Services Began offering services in 1977. Services provided to freshmen, sophomores, juniors, seniors. Program currently serves 9 LD students: 2 freshmen, 1 sophomore, 4 juniors, 2 seniors.

Staff 7 part-time staff members, including director, assistant director. Services provided by tutors.

Admissions LD applicants evaluated on the basis of high school transcript and grade point average, standard or untimed SAT or ACT; autobiographical statement, letters of recommendation, psychoeducational report, medical certification recommended. LD students may begin taking classes in fall, winter, spring, or summer. Application should be submitted 1 to 2 months in advance of initial anticipated enrollment.

Housing College housing (including coed) available. LD students housed randomly. LD students not required to live on campus.

Tutoring Offered one-to-one by peer tutors. Available in all subjects. LD students may receive tutoring in 3 courses per term.

Basic Skills Remediation Offered in small groups by regular teachers. Available in written language, learning strategies, work and study habits.

Academic Advisement Help with program planning provided by academic advisers. LD students may take up to 21 credit hours each quarter; most take 12 credit hours; 9 credit hours required to maintain full-time status.

Special Courses Offered in college survival skills, vocabulary development, communication skills, composition, personal psychology, study skills, career planning. All offered for credit; all enter into overall grade point average.

Auxiliary Aids and Services Aids include tape recorders. Services include alternative exam arrangements, notetakers, advocacy.

Counseling Services Individual counseling, career counseling available.

Contact Ms. Jacquie Bonner, Director, Educational Opportunities Program, University of Oregon, 207 Emerald Hall, Eugene, OR 97403, 503-686-3232.

UNIVERSITY OF PENNSYLVANIA

Philadelphia, Pennsylvania

Year Program Began	1978	Special Courses	
Special Fee	None	Taped Textbooks	✓
Special Orientation	✓	Alternative Exam Arrangements	✓
Diagnostic Testing		Notetakers	✓
Subject-Area Tutoring	✓	Staff	1 part-time
Basic Skills Remediation	✓	Number of Students Served	6

General Information Independent coed university. Founded 1740. Awards A (college transfer), B, M, D. Institutionally accredited by regional association; programs accredited by AACSB (business), ABET (engineering and technology), NLN (nursing). Metropolitan setting; 260-acre campus. Total enrollment: 22,000. Faculty: 2,500 (2,000 full-time, 500 part-time); 90% have doctoral degrees; graduate assistants teach a few undergraduate courses. Calendar: semesters plus 2 summer sessions. Grading system: letters or numbers. Library holdings: 3.1 million bound volumes, 1.4 million titles on microform, 44,000 periodical subscriptions, 26,000 records/tapes.

Undergraduate Profile Fall 1984: 9,200 undergraduates (2,070 freshmen) from 52 states and territories and 100 foreign countries; 25% state residents; 7% transfers; 55% financial aid recipients; 40% women; 8% blacks; 1% Native Americans; 4% Hispanics; 2% foreign nationals; 50 legally handicapped students.

Expenses (1985–86) Comprehensive fee of $14,835 includes full-time tuition ($9525), mandatory fees ($875), and college room and board ($4435). College room only: $2050. Part-time tuition: $400 per course. Tuition prepayment plan available.

Financial Aid Fall 1984 full-time freshmen: 56% applied for aid, 86% of those were judged to have need, 100% of those were aided; the average aided freshman received an aid package worth $9286 (71% scholarships/grants, 29% self-help) meeting 100% of need. College-administered aid for all 1984–85 undergraduates: 3,810 need-based scholarships (average $5385); short-term loans (average $500); low-interest long-term loans from college funds (average $640), from external sources (average $1980); SEOG; College Work-Study. Supporting data: FAF, IRS, state form, institutional form, AFSA/SAR required. Application deadline: 1/1.

Athletics Member NCAA (Division I). Intercollegiate sports: baseball/softball M(I), W(I); basketball M(I), W(I); crew M, W; cross-country running M(I), W(I); fencing M(I), W(I); field hockey W(I); football M(I-AA); gymnastics W(I); lacrosse M(I), W(I); soccer M(I); squash M, W; swimming and diving M(I), W(I); tennis M(I), W(I); track and field M(I), W(I); volleyball W(I); wrestling M(I). Intramural sports: badminton, baseball/softball, basketball, bowling, cross-country running, football, golf, ice hockey, martial arts, riflery, rugby, sailing, skiing (cross-country), skiing (downhill), soccer, squash, swimming and diving, tennis, track and field, volleyball, water polo, wrestling.

Majors Accounting B; actuarial science B; adult and continuing education B; African studies B; American studies B; anthropology B; applied art B; Arabic B; art/fine arts B; art history B; Asian/Oriental studies B; astronomy B; astrophysics B; biochemistry B; bioengineering B; biology/biological sciences B; biomedical engineering B; biophysics B; black/Afro-American studies B; chemical engineering B; chemistry B; Chinese B; city, community, and regional planning B; civil engineering B; classics B; communication B; comparative literature B; computer engineering B; computer programming B; computer science B; (pre)dentistry sequence B; drafting and design B; East Asian studies B; ecology/environmental studies B; economics B; education B; electrical engineering B; electrical engineering technology B; elementary education B; engineering (general) B; engineering and applied sciences B; English B; environmental design B; environmental sciences B; ethnic studies B; European studies B; finance/banking B; folklore B; French B; geography B; geology B; German B; Germanic languages and literature B; Greek B; Hebrew B; Hispanic studies B; history B; history of science B; insurance B; international business B; international economics B; international studies B; Italian B; Japanese B; labor and industrial relations B; landscape architecture/design B; Latin B; Latin American studies B; (pre)law sequence B; liberal arts/general studies A; linguistics B; literature B; management engineering B; marketing/retailing/merchandising B; materials engineering B; materials sciences B; mathematics B; mechanical engineering B; mechanical engineering technology B; (pre)medicine sequence B; military science B; modern languages B; museum studies B; music B; natural sciences B; naval sciences B; Near and Middle Eastern studies B; nursing B; peace studies B; philosophy B; physics B; political science/government B; Portuguese B; psychobiology B; psychology B; religious studies B; Romance languages B; Russian B; Russian and Slavic studies B; Scandinavian languages/studies B; secondary education B; Slavic languages B; sociology B; South Asian studies B; Southeast Asian studies B; Spanish B; statistics B; systems engineering B; systems science B; theater arts/drama B; theology B; transportation engineering B; urban studies B; women's studies B.

LD Program Information

Name of Program Programs for the Handicapped.

Availability of Services Began offering services in 1978. Services provided to freshmen, sophomores, juniors, seniors. Program currently serves 6 LD students: 1 freshman, 4 juniors, 1 senior.

Staff 1 part-time staff member (coordinator). Services provided by tutors, counselors.

Admissions LD applicants evaluated on the basis of high school transcript and grade point average, standard or untimed SAT or ACT, personal interview, autobiographical statement, letters of recommendation, psychoeducational report, 3 Achievement Tests, English Composition Test. LD students may begin taking classes in fall, spring, or summer. Application should be submitted 9 to 12 months in advance of initial anticipated enrollment.

Orientation Optional orientation offered before registration or later by individual arrangement.

Housing College housing (including coed) available. LD students housed randomly. LD students not required to live on campus.

Tutoring Offered one-to-one and in small groups by professional teachers, peer tutors. Available in all subjects. LD students may receive tutoring in all courses each term.

Basic Skills Remediation Offered one-to-one and in small groups by writing lab and reading clinic instructors. Available in reading, written language.

Academic Advisement Help with program planning provided by LD staff member, academic advisers. LD students may take up to 4 courses each semester; most take 2 to 4 courses; 3 courses required to maintain full-time status.

Auxiliary Aids and Services Aids include taped textbooks, tape recorders, calculators, typewriters, word processors, Kurzweil reading machine. Services include alternative exam arrangements, notetakers, advocacy, research, editorial, and typing services.

Counseling Services Individual counseling, small-group counseling, rap sessions, career counseling available.

Contact Ms. Alice Nagle, Coordinator, Programs for the Handicapped, University of Pennsylvania, 4 Bennett Hall, 3340 Walnut Street, Philadelphia, PA 19104, 215-898-6993.

UNIVERSITY OF PITTSBURGH

Pittsburgh, Pennsylvania

Year Program Began	1980	Special Courses	
Special Fee	None	Taped Textbooks	✓
Special Orientation		Alternative Exam Arrangements	✓
Diagnostic Testing		Notetakers	
Subject-Area Tutoring	✓	Staff	5 part-time
Basic Skills Remediation	✓	Number of Students Served	5

General Information State-related coed university. Part of University of Pittsburgh System. Founded 1787. Awards B, M, D. Institutionally accredited by regional association; programs accredited by AACSB (business), ABET (engineering and technology), NLN (nursing), ACPE (pharmacy), NCATE (teacher education). Metropolitan setting; 131-acre barrier-free campus. Total enrollment: 29,197. Faculty: 2,765 (2,176 full-time, 589 part-time); 86% have doctoral degrees; graduate assistants teach a few undergraduate courses. Calendar: three 15-week terms. Grading system: letters or numbers. Library holdings: 2.6 million bound volumes, 1.8 million titles on microform, 20,012 periodical subscriptions.

Undergraduate Profile Fall 1984: 19,295 undergraduates (2,707 freshmen) from 41 states and territories and 42 foreign countries; 34% part-time; 94% state residents; 67% financial aid recipients; 48% women; 10% blacks; 0% Native Americans; 1% Hispanics; 2% Asian Americans; 1% foreign nationals; 200 legally handicapped students.

Expenses (1985–86) State resident tuition: $2890 full-time, $97 per credit part-time. Nonresident tuition: $5780 full-time, $194 per credit part-time. Mandatory fees: $120. College room and board: $2836. College room only: $1698.

Financial Aid Fall 1984 full-time freshmen: 98% applied for aid, 86% of those were judged to have need, 100% of those were aided; the average aided freshman received an aid package worth $4600 (34% scholarships/grants, 66% self-help) meeting 77% of need. College-administered aid for all 1984–85 undergraduates: 1,830 need-based scholarships (average $960); 1,233 non-need scholarships (average $1628); short-term loans (average $100); low-interest long-term loans from external sources (average $856); SEOG; College Work-Study; 1,648 part-time jobs. Supporting data: FAF, IRS, state form, institutional form, AFSA/SAR, Financial Aid Transcript (for transfers) required. Priority application deadline: 3/1.

Athletics Member NCAA (Division I). Intercollegiate sports: baseball/softball M(I,s); basketball M(I,s), W(I,s); cross-country running M(I,s), W(I,s); football M(I-A,s); gymnastics M(I,s), W(I,s); soccer M(I,s); swimming and diving M(I,s), W(I,s); tennis M(I), W(I); track and field M(I,s), W(I,s); volleyball W(I,s); wrestling M(I,s). Intramural sports: baseball/softball, basketball, bowling, fencing, football, ice hockey, martial arts, racquetball, riflery, sailing, skiing (downhill), soccer, squash, swimming and diving, tennis, track and field, volleyball, water polo, wrestling.

Majors Accounting B; anthropology B; applied mathematics B; architectural technologies B; art/fine arts B; astronomy B; biochemistry B; biology/biological sciences B; biophysics B; black/Afro-American studies B; business administration/commerce/management B; business education B; chemical engineering B; chemistry B; child care/child and family studies B; child psychology/child development B; Chinese B; civil engineering B; classics B; communication B; computer science B; creative writing B; criminal justice B; dietetics B; early childhood education B; economics B; electrical engineering B; elementary education B; English B; film studies B; French B; geology B; German B; health education B; health science B; health services administration B; history B; history of philosophy B; history of science B; home economics education B; humanities B; industrial engineering B; information science B; Italian B; Japanese B; legal studies B; liberal arts/general studies B; linguistics B; literature B; mathematics B; mechanical engineering B; medical technology B; metallurgical engineering B; microbiology B; mining and mineral engineering B; music B; natural sciences B; neurosciences B; nursing B; nutrition B; occupational therapy B; pharmacy/pharmaceutical sciences B; philosophy B; physical education B; physical therapy B; physics B; political science/government B; psychology B; public administration B; reading education B; religious studies B; Russian B; secondary education B; Slavic languages B; social science B; social work B; sociology B; Spanish B; speech/rhetoric/public address/debate B; statistics B; studio art B; theater arts/drama B; urban studies B; vocational education B. Majors with highest enrollment: nursing, computer science, business administration/commerce/management.

LD Program Information

Name of Program Disabled Student Services.

Availability of Services Began offering services in 1980. Services provided to freshmen, sophomores, juniors, seniors. Program currently serves 5 LD students: 2 freshmen, 1 sophomore, 1 junior, 1 senior.

Staff 5 part-time staff members, including coordinator. Services provided by counselors, director of Learning Skills Center.

Admissions LD applicants evaluated on the basis of high school transcript and grade point average, untimed SAT or ACT, autobiographical statement, letters of recommendation. LD students may begin taking classes in fall, winter, spring, or summer.

Housing College housing (including coed) available. LD students housed randomly. LD students not required to live on campus.

Tutoring Offered one-to-one and in small groups by peer tutors. LD students may receive tutoring in lower level mathematics only.

Basic Skills Remediation Offered in small groups by paraprofessionals. Available in reading, learning strategies, work and study habits.

Academic Advisement Help with program planning provided by LD staff members, academic advisers. LD students may take up to 15 credits each term; most take 9 to 12 credits; 12 credits required to maintain full-time status.

Auxiliary Aids and Services Aids include taped textbooks. Services include alternative exam arrangements.

Counseling Services Individual counseling, career counseling available.

Contact Mr. Tom Galante, Coordinator, Disabled Student Services, University of Pittsburgh, 731 William Pitt Union, Pittsburgh, PA 15260, 412-624-6738.

UNIVERSITY OF SOUTH CAROLINA

Columbia, South Carolina

Year Program Began	1979	Special Courses	
Special Fee	Varies	Taped Textbooks	✓
Special Orientation		Alternative Exam Arrangements	✓
Diagnostic Testing		Notetakers	✓
Subject-Area Tutoring	✓	Staff	2 part-time
Basic Skills Remediation	✓	Number of Students Served	7

General Information State-supported coed university. Part of University of South Carolina System. Founded 1801. Awards B, M, D. Institutionally accredited by regional association; programs accredited by AACSB (business), ABET (engineering and technology), NASM (music), NLN (nursing), ACPE (pharmacy), NCATE (teacher education). City setting; 242-acre barrier-free campus. Total enrollment: 23,301. Faculty: 1,247 (1,040 full-time, 207 part-time); 77% have doctoral degrees; graduate assistants teach a few undergraduate courses. Calendar: semesters. Grading system: letters or numbers. Library holdings: 2.1 million bound volumes, 2.1 million titles on microform, 16,800 periodical subscriptions, 5,689 records/tapes.

Undergraduate Profile Fall 1984: 15,295 undergraduates (2,332 freshmen) from 53 states and territories and 68 foreign countries; 18% part-time; 83% state residents; 20% transfers; 51% women; 15% blacks; 0% Native Americans; 1% Hispanics; 1% Asian Americans; 2% foreign nationals; 16% of undergraduates over 25 years of age; 200 legally handicapped students.

Expenses (1985–86) State resident tuition: $1440 full-time, $58 per semester hour part-time. Nonresident tuition: $2970 full-time, $125 per semester hour part-time. College room and board: $2300. College room only: $1150.

Financial Aid Fall 1984 full-time freshmen: the average aided freshman received an aid package meeting 80% of need. College-administered aid for all 1984–85 undergraduates: need-based scholarships; 1,556 non-need scholarships (average $769); low-interest long-term loans from external sources; SEOG; College Work-Study; 1,242 part-time jobs. Supporting data: FFS required. Priority application deadline: 4/15.

Athletics Member NCAA (Division I). Intercollegiate sports: baseball/softball M(I,s), W(I,s); basketball M(I,s), W(I,s); cross-country running M(I,s); football M(I-A,s); golf M(I,s), W(I,s); soccer M(I,s); swimming and diving M(I,s), W(I,s); tennis M(I,s), W(I,s); track and field M(I,s); volleyball W(I,s). Intramural sports: badminton, baseball/softball, basketball, bowling, equestrian sports, fencing, football, golf, lacrosse, martial arts, racquetball, rugby, sailing, skiing (cross-country), skiing (downhill), soccer, squash, swimming and diving, tennis, track and field, volleyball, water polo, weight lifting, wrestling.

Majors Accounting B; advertising B; anthropology B; applied mathematics B; art education B; art/fine arts B; art history B; biology/biological sciences B; black/Afro-American studies B; broadcasting B; business administration/commerce/management B; business economics B; chemical engineering B; chemistry B; civil engineering B; classics B; computer engineering B; computer science B; criminal justice B; economics B; electrical engineering B; English B; experimental psychology B; finance/banking B; French B; geography B; geology B; German B; Greek B; history B; hotel and restaurant management B; insurance B; interdisciplinary studies B; international studies B; Italian B; journalism B; Latin B; Latin American studies B; liberal arts/general studies B; marine sciences B; marketing/retailing/merchandising B; mathematics B; mechanical engineering B; medical technology B; music B; music education B; music history B; nursing B; pharmacy/pharmaceutical sciences B; philosophy B; physical education B; physics B; political science/government B; psychology B; public relations B; radio and television studies B; real estate B; religious studies B; secretarial studies/office management B; sociology B; Spanish B; statistics B; studio art B; theater arts/drama B; tourism and travel B. Majors with highest enrollment: business administration/commerce/management, accounting, computer science.

LD Program Information

Name of Program PROCESS.

Availability of Services Began offering services in 1979. Services provided to freshmen, sophomores, juniors, seniors. Program currently serves 7 LD students: 3 freshmen, 2 sophomores, 1 junior, 1 senior.

Fees $5 per hour for tutoring.

Staff 2 part-time staff members, including director, coordinator.

Admissions LD applicants evaluated on the basis of high school transcript, standard or untimed SAT or ACT; psychoeducational report recommended. LD students may begin taking classes in fall, spring, or summer. Application should be submitted at least 1 month in advance of initial anticipated enrollment.

Housing College housing (including coed) available. LD students housed randomly. LD students not required to live on campus.

Tutoring Offered one-to-one by peer tutors. Available in some subjects. LD students may receive tutoring in all courses each term.

Basic Skills Remediation Offered one-to-one and in small groups by learning specialist. Available in reading, math, spelling, handwriting, written language, learning strategies, perceptual skills, work and study habits.

Academic Advisement Help with program planning provided by academic advisers. LD students may take up to 18 semester hours each semester; most take 12 semester hours; 12 semester hours required to maintain full-time status.

Auxiliary Aids and Services Aids include taped textbooks. Services include alternative exam arrangements, notetakers, advocacy.

Counseling Services Individual counseling, career counseling available.

Contact Mr. Doug Craven, Assistant Director of Disabled Student Services and Coordinator of PROCESS, University of South Carolina, 1625 College Street, Columbia, SC 29208, 803-777-6742.

UNIVERSITY OF SOUTH CAROLINA AT SPARTANBURG

Spartanburg, South Carolina

Year Program Began	1984	Special Courses	✓
Special Fee	None	Taped Textbooks	
Special Orientation		Alternative Exam Arrangements	✓
Diagnostic Testing	✓	Notetakers	✓
Subject-Area Tutoring	✓	Staff	2 full-time, 2 part-time
Basic Skills Remediation	✓	Number of Students Served	6

General Information State-supported 4-year coed college. Part of University of South Carolina System. Founded 1967. Awards A (terminal), B. Institutionally accredited by regional association; programs accredited by NLN (nursing), NCATE (teacher education). City setting; 70-acre barrier-free campus. Total enrollment: 2,610. Faculty: 170 (135 full-time, 35 part-time); 75% have doctoral degrees. Calendar: semesters. Grading system: letters or numbers. Library holdings: 125,000 bound volumes, 4,000 titles on microform.

Undergraduate Profile Fall 1984: 2,610 undergraduates (487 freshmen) from 15 states and territories and 7 foreign countries; 42% part-time; 95% state residents; 35% transfers; 42% financial aid recipients; 60% women; 11% blacks; 1% Native Americans; 1% Hispanics; 3% foreign nationals; 35% of undergraduates over 25 years of age; 10 legally handicapped students.

Expenses (1985–86) State resident tuition: $1250 full-time, $55 per semester hour part-time. Nonresident tuition: $2500 full-time, $110 per semester hour part-time. College room only: $1170.

Financial Aid Fall 1984 full-time freshmen: 47% were judged to have need, 88% of those were aided; the average aided freshman received an aid package meeting 70% of need. College-administered aid for all 1984–85 undergraduates: need-based scholarships; 20 non-need scholarships (average $800); short-term loans (average $50); low-interest long-term loans; SEOG; College Work-Study; 120 part-time jobs. Supporting data: FFS, FAF, AFSA/SAR acceptable. Priority application deadline: 4/15.

Athletics Member NAIA. Intercollegiate sports: baseball/softball W(s); basketball M(s), W(s); cross-country running M(s); golf M(s); soccer M(s); tennis M(s); volleyball W(s). Intramural sports: baseball/softball, basketball, bowling, cross-country running, football, golf, martial arts, racquetball, riflery, skiing (cross-country), skiing (downhill), soccer, tennis, volleyball, weight lifting, wrestling.

Majors Accounting B; applied mathematics B; behavioral sciences B; biology/biological sciences B; business administration/commerce/management B; chemistry B; computer information systems B; computer science B; criminal justice B; (pre) dentistry sequence B; early childhood education B; economics B; education B; elementary education B; English B; history B; management information systems B; marketing/retailing/merchandising B; mathematics B; medical technology B; nursing A, B; physical education B; political science/government B; psychology B; secondary education B; sociology B. Majors with highest enrollment: business administration/commerce/management, computer science, nursing.

LD Program Information

Name of Program Special Services/CORE.

Availability of Services Began offering services in 1984. Services provided to freshmen, sophomores, juniors, seniors. Program currently serves 6 LD students.

Staff 2 full-time, 2 part-time staff members, including director. Services provided by counselors, diagnostic specialist.

Admissions LD applicants evaluated on the basis of high school transcript, standard or untimed SAT or ACT. LD students may begin taking classes in fall or spring. Application should be submitted 1 month in advance of initial anticipated enrollment.

Housing College housing (including coed) available.

Diagnostic Testing Available in intelligence, reading, math, spelling.

Tutoring Offered one-to-one by peer tutors. Available in all subjects. LD students may receive tutoring in all courses each term.

Basic Skills Remediation Offered one-to-one and in small groups by regular teachers. Available in reading, math, spelling, work and study habits.

Academic Advisement Help with program planning provided by LD staff members, academic advisers. LD students may take up to 16 credit hours each semester; most take 12 credit hours first semester, 12 to 16 thereafter; 12 credit hours required to maintain full-time status.

Special Courses Offered in reading, vocabulary development, composition, language development, math. Most offered for credit; most enter into overall grade point average.

Auxiliary Aids and Services Aids include tape recorders, typewriters. Services include alternative exam arrangements, notetakers.

Counseling Services Individual counseling, small-group counseling, career counseling available.

Contact Ms. Janice Lipscomb, Director, Special Services, University of South Carolina at Spartanburg, Spartanburg, SC 29303, 803-578-1800 Ext. 2651.

UNIVERSITY OF SOUTH CAROLINA–COASTAL CAROLINA COLLEGE

Conway, South Carolina

Year Program Began	1982	Special Courses	✓
Special Fee	None	Taped Textbooks	✓
Special Orientation	✓	Alternative Exam Arrangements	✓
Diagnostic Testing		Notetakers	✓
Subject-Area Tutoring		Staff	4 part-time
Basic Skills Remediation	✓	Number of Students Served	14

General Information State-supported 4-year coed college. Part of University of South Carolina System. Founded 1954. Awards A (college transfer and terminal), B. Institutionally accredited by regional association; programs accredited by NLN (nursing). Rural setting; 185-acre barrier-free campus. Total enrollment: 2,631. Faculty: 174 (130 full-time, 44 part-time); 60% have doctoral degrees. Calendar: semesters. Grading system: letters or numbers. Library holdings: 80,000 bound volumes, 75,656 titles on microform, 8,608 periodical subscriptions, 4,000 records/tapes.

Undergraduate Profile Fall 1984: 2,631 undergraduates (1,211 freshmen) from 28 states and territories and 10 foreign countries; 31% part-time; 82% state residents; 8% transfers; 60% financial aid recipients; 52% women; 8% blacks; 0% Native Americans; 1% Hispanics; 0% Asian Americans; 1% foreign nationals; 24% of undergraduates over 25 years of age; 4 legally handicapped students.

Expenses (1984–85) State resident tuition: $1000 full-time, $42 per semester hour part-time. Nonresident tuition: $2140 full-time, $84 per semester hour part-time.

Financial Aid Fall 1984 full-time freshmen: 43% applied for aid, 88% of those were judged to have need, 86% of those were aided; the average aided freshman received an aid package worth $2213 (35% scholarships/grants, 65% self-help) meeting 75% of need. College-administered aid for all 1984–85 undergraduates: need-based scholarships; non-need scholarships (average $850); short-term loans; low-interest long-term loans from external sources; College Work-Study; part-time jobs. Supporting data: FFS, FAF, IRS, institutional form, AFSA/SAR required. Priority application deadline: 4/1.

Athletics Member NAIA. Intercollegiate sports: baseball/softball M(s), W(s); basketball M(s), W(s); cross-country running M(s); golf M(s); soccer M(s); tennis M(s), W(s); volleyball W(s). Intramural sports: baseball/softball, basketball, rugby, soccer, tennis, track and field, volleyball.

Majors Accounting B; applied mathematics B; art education B; biology/biological sciences B; business administration/commerce/management B; business education B; computer science B; (pre)dentistry sequence B; early childhood education B; education B; elementary education B; English B; finance/banking B; history B; interdisciplinary studies B; (pre)law sequence B; liberal arts/general studies A, B; marine sciences B; marketing/retailing/merchandising B; (pre)medicine sequence B; music education B; nursing A; philosophy B; physical education B; physical sciences B; political science/government B; psychology B; real estate B; recreation and leisure services B; religious studies B; science education B; secondary education B. Majors with highest enrollment: business administration/commerce/management, education, psychology.

LD Program Information

Name of Program Not specified.

Availability of Services Began offering services in 1982. Services provided to freshmen, sophomores, juniors, seniors. Program currently serves 14 LD students: 7 freshmen, 3 sophomores, 2 juniors, 2 seniors.

Staff 4 part-time staff members. Services provided by remediation specialists, counselor, graduate assistant.

Admissions LD applicants evaluated on the basis of high school transcript and grade point average, standard SAT or ACT, personal interview, letters of recommendation. LD students may begin taking classes in fall, spring, or summer. Application should be submitted 6 months in advance of initial anticipated enrollment.

Orientation Optional orientation offered before registration.

Housing College housing not available.

Basic Skills Remediation Offered one-to-one and in small groups by regular teachers. Available in reading, math, spoken language, written language, work and study habits.

Academic Advisement Help with program planning provided by academic advisers. Most LD students take 12 semester hours each semester; 12 semester hours required to maintain full-time status.

Special Courses Offered in college survival skills, reading, vocabulary development, composition, math, personal psychology, study skills, career planning. Some offered for credit; some enter into overall grade point average.

Auxiliary Aids and Services Aids include taped textbooks, tape recorders, typewriters, word processors. Services include alternative exam arrangements, notetakers, advocacy.

Counseling Services Individual counseling, career counseling available.

Contact Ms. Cynthia Terres, Director of Counseling, University of South Carolina–Coastal Carolina College, PO Box 1954, Conway, SC 29526, 803-347-3161.

UNIVERSITY OF SOUTHERN CALIFORNIA

Los Angeles, California

Year Program Began	1982	Special Courses	
Special Fee	None	Taped Textbooks	✓
Special Orientation	✓	Alternative Exam Arrangements	✓
Diagnostic Testing	✓	Notetakers	
Subject-Area Tutoring	✓	Staff	6 part-time
Basic Skills Remediation	✓	Number of Students Served	14

General Information Independent coed university. Founded 1880. Awards B, M, D. Institutionally accredited by regional association; programs accredited by NAAB (architecture), AACSB (business), ABET (engineering and technology), NASM (music), NCATE (teacher education). Metropolitan setting; 165-acre campus. Total enrollment: 26,621. Faculty: 2,441 (1,591 full-time, 850 part-time); 87% have doctoral degrees; graduate assistants teach a few undergraduate courses. Calendar: semesters. Grading system: letters or numbers. Library holdings: 2.3 million bound volumes, 38,598 periodical subscriptions.

Undergraduate Profile Fall 1984: 16,078 undergraduates (3,066 freshmen); 10% part-time; 71% state residents; 11% transfers; 65% financial aid recipients; 41% women; 8% blacks; 0% Native Americans; 7% Hispanics; 14% Asian Americans; 13% foreign nationals; 8% of undergraduates over 25 years of age; 150 legally handicapped students.

Expenses (1985–86) Comprehensive fee of $13,325 includes full-time tuition ($9400), mandatory fees ($175), and college room and board ($3750). College room only: $1950. Part-time tuition: $318 per unit. Tuition prepayment plan available.

Financial Aid Fall 1984 full-time freshmen: 65% applied for aid, 80% of those were judged to have need, 100% of those were aided; the average aided freshman received an aid package worth $8678 (68% scholarships/grants, 32% self-help) meeting 100% of need. College-administered aid for all 1984–85 undergraduates: 4,100 need-based scholarships (average $3100); 1,190 non-need scholarships (average $2039); low-interest long-term loans from college funds (average $400), from external sources (average $1150); SEOG; College Work-Study; part-time jobs. Supporting data: FAF, IRS, state form, institutional form, AFSA/SAR required. Priority application deadline: 12/31.

Athletics Member NCAA (Division I). Intercollegiate sports: baseball/softball M(I,s); basketball M(I,s), W(I,s); crew M, W; cross-country running W(I); football M(I-A,s); golf M(I,s), W(I,s); gymnastics W(I,s); lacrosse M(c); rugby M(c); sailing M, W; skiing (cross-country) M, W; skiing (downhill) M, W; soccer M(c); swimming and diving M(I,s), W(I,s); tennis M(I,s), W(I,s); track and field M(I,s), W(I,s); volleyball M(I,s), W(I,s); water polo M(I,s). Intramural sports: badminton, baseball/softball, basketball, bowling, equestrian sports, field hockey, football, golf, gymnastics, ice hockey, lacrosse, martial arts, racquetball, riflery, rugby, sailing, skiing (cross-country), skiing (downhill), soccer, squash, swimming and diving, tennis, track and field, volleyball, water polo, weight lifting, wrestling.

Majors Accounting B; aerospace engineering B; American studies B; anthropology B; architecture B; art education B; art/fine arts B; art history B; astronomy B; biology/biological sciences B; biomedical engineering B; broadcasting B; business administration/commerce/management B; chemical engineering B; chemistry B; civil engineering B; classics B; communication B; comparative literature B; computer science B; creative writing B; dance B; dental services B; East Asian studies B; economics B; education B; electrical engineering B; engineering (general) B; English B; ethnic studies B; film studies B; food marketing B; French B; geography B; geology B; German B; gerontology B; Greek B; history B; humanities B; industrial engineering B; interdisciplinary studies B; international studies B; jazz B; journalism B; linguistics B; mathematics B; mechanical engineering B; metallurgical engineering B; music B; music education B; natural sciences B; nursing B; occupational therapy B; petroleum/natural gas engineering B; philosophy B; physical education B; physical sciences B; physics B; piano/organ B; political science/government B; psychobiology B; psychology B; public administration B; public affairs and policy studies B; public relations B; radio and television studies B; religious studies B; Russian B; safety and security technologies B; Slavic languages B; social science B; sociology B; Spanish B; stringed instruments B; studio art B; systems engineering B; theater arts/drama B; urban studies B; voice B; wind and percussion instruments B; women's studies B. Majors with highest enrollment: business administration/commerce/management, engineering (general), social science.

LD Program Information

Name of Program Learning Disabilities Assistance Program.

Availability of Services Began offering services in 1982. Services provided to freshmen, sophomores, juniors, seniors. Program currently serves 14 LD students: 4 sophomores, 7 juniors, 3 seniors.

Staff 6 part-time staff members, including director. Services provided by tutors, counselors, learning specialists.

Admissions LD applicants evaluated on the basis of high school transcript and grade point average, standard or untimed SAT or ACT, personal interview, autobiographical statement, letters of recommendation, psychoeducational report. LD students may begin taking classes in fall, spring, or summer. Application should be submitted 3 months in advance of initial anticipated enrollment.

Orientation Optional orientation offered before registration.

Housing College housing (including coed) available. LD students housed randomly. LD students not required to live on campus.

Diagnostic Testing Available in intelligence, reading, math, spelling, spoken language, written language, perceptual skills, work and study habits.

Tutoring Offered one-to-one by professional teachers, peer tutors. Available in some subjects. LD students may receive tutoring in all courses each term.

Basic Skills Remediation Offered one-to-one by LD teachers, learning skills counselors. Available in reading, math, spelling, written language, learning strategies, perceptual skills, work and study habits.

Academic Advisement Help with program planning provided by LD staff members, academic advisers. Most LD students take 12 units each semester; 12 units required to maintain full-time status.

Auxiliary Aids and Services Aids include taped textbooks, tape recorders, word processors. Services include alternative exam arrangements, advocacy.

Counseling Services Individual counseling, career counseling available.

Contact Mrs. Janet Ewart Eddy, Learning Specialist, The Learning Center, University of Southern California, University Village, Suite E, 3375 South Hoover Street, Los Angeles, CA 90007, 213-743-6544.

UNIVERSITY OF SOUTHERN MISSISSIPPI
Hattiesburg, Mississippi

Year Program Began	*Not reported*	Special Courses	
Special Fee	None	Taped Textbooks	
Special Orientation		Alternative Exam Arrangements	✓
Diagnostic Testing	✓	Notetakers	✓
Subject-Area Tutoring	✓	Staff	2 part-time
Basic Skills Remediation	✓	Number of Students Served	*Not reported*

General Information State-supported coed university. Founded 1910. Awards B, M, D. Institutionally accredited by regional association; programs accredited by AACSB (business), ABET (engineering and technology), NASM (music), NLN (nursing), NCATE (teacher education). Small-town setting; 220-acre barrier-free campus. Total enrollment: 11,169. Faculty: 646 (547 full-time, 99 part-time); 64% have doctoral degrees; graduate assistants teach a few undergraduate courses. Calendar: semesters. Grading system: letters or numbers. Library holdings: 548,660 bound volumes, 754,303 titles on microform, 4,652 periodical subscriptions, 15,428 records/tapes.

Undergraduate Profile Fall 1984: 9,602 undergraduates (1,229 freshmen) from 44 states and territories and 47 foreign countries; 12% part-time; 88% state residents; 35% transfers; 51% financial aid recipients; 54% women; 14% blacks; 1% Native Americans; 1% Hispanics; 1% Asian Americans; 1% foreign nationals; 26% of undergraduates over 25 years of age; 32 legally handicapped students.

Expenses (1984–85) State resident tuition: $1266 full-time, $54 per semester hour part-time. Nonresident tuition: $2342 full-time, $99 per semester hour part-time. Mandatory fees: $8. College room and board: $1910. College room only: $1120.

Financial Aid Fall 1984 full-time freshmen: the average aided freshman received an aid package worth $85. College-administered aid for all 1984–85 undergraduates: need-based scholarships; non-need scholarships (average $300); low-interest long-term loans; College Work-Study; part-time jobs. Supporting data: FFS, institutional form, AFSA/SAR required; FAF acceptable. Priority application deadline: 3/15.

Athletics Member NCAA (Division I). Intercollegiate sports: baseball/softball M(I,s), W(I); basketball M(I,s), W(I,s); cross-country running M(I), W(I); football M(I-A,s); golf M(I,s); swimming and diving M(I), W(I); tennis M(I,s), W(I,s); track and field M(I), W(I); volleyball W(I). Intramural sports: badminton, baseball/softball, basketball, bowling, cross-country running, equestrian sports, football, golf, gymnastics, soccer, squash, swimming and diving, tennis, track and field, volleyball, water polo.

Majors Accounting B; advertising B; American studies B; anthropology B; architectural technologies B; art education B; art/fine arts B; Asian/Oriental studies B; biology/biological sciences B; broadcasting B; business administration/commerce/management B; business economics B; business education B; chemistry B; child care/child and family studies B; child psychology/child development B; city, community, and regional planning B; classics B; communication B; computer science B; computer technologies B; construction technologies B; criminal justice B; dance B; data processing B; (pre)dentistry sequence B; dietetics B; economics B; educational media B; electrical and electronics technologies B; elementary education B; English B; environmental engineering technology B; environmental sciences B; fashion merchandising B; film studies B; finance/banking B; food sciences B; geography B; geology B; health education B; history B; home economics education B; hotel and restaurant management B; industrial arts B; industrial engineering technology B; insurance B; interior design B; journalism B; Latin American studies B; library science B; linguistics B; marketing/retailing/merchandising B; mathematics B; mechanical engineering technology B; medical technology B; (pre)medicine sequence B; microbiology B; music B; music education B; nursing B; paralegal studies B; philosophy B; physical education B; physics B; political science/government B; polymer science B; psychology B; radio and television studies B; real estate B; recreation and leisure services B; science education B; secondary education B; social work B; sociology B; special education B; speech pathology and audiology B; speech/rhetoric/public address/debate B; speech therapy B; statistics B; textiles and clothing B; theater arts/drama B; (pre)veterinary medicine sequence B; vocational education B. Majors with highest enrollment: business administration/commerce/management, computer science, industrial engineering technology.

LD Program Information

Name of Program Disabled Student Services.

Availability of Services Services provided to freshmen, sophomores, juniors, seniors.

Staff 2 part-time staff members, including coordinator. Services provided by counselor.

Admissions LD applicants evaluated on the basis of high school transcript and grade point average, standard ACT. LD students may begin taking classes in fall, spring, or summer. Application should be submitted at least 2 months in advance of initial anticipated enrollment.

Housing College housing available. LD students housed randomly. LD students not required to live on campus.

Diagnostic Testing Available in intelligence, reading, math, work and study habits, personality, speech.

Tutoring Offered one-to-one and in small groups by peer tutors. Available in some subjects. LD students may receive tutoring in 2 courses per term.

Basic Skills Remediation Offered in small groups by regular teachers. Available in reading, math, spelling, handwriting, spoken language, written language, learning strategies, perceptual skills, work and study habits, social skills, speech.

Academic Advisement Help with program planning provided by academic advisers. LD students may take up to 19 semester hours each semester; 12 semester hours required to maintain full-time status.

Auxiliary Aids and Services Aids include tape recorders, calculators, typewriters. Services include alternative exam arrangements, notetakers, advocacy.

Counseling Services Individual counseling, small-group counseling, career counseling available.

Contact Mr. Mike Dobbins, Assistant Dean of Student Development and Coordinator of Disabled Student Services, University of Southern Mississippi, Southern Station, Box 5067, Hattiesburg, MS 39406-5067, 601-266-4403.

UNIVERSITY OF TENNESSEE AT CHATTANOOGA

Chattanooga, Tennessee

Year Program Began	1985	Special Courses	✓
Special Fee	None	Taped Textbooks	✓
Special Orientation	✓	Alternative Exam Arrangements	✓
Diagnostic Testing	✓	Notetakers	✓
Subject-Area Tutoring	✓	Staff	4 full-time, 2 part-time
Basic Skills Remediation	✓	Number of Students Served	12

General Information State-supported comprehensive coed institution. Part of University of Tennessee System. Founded 1886. Awards B, M. Institutionally accredited by regional association; programs accredited by AACSB (business), ABET (engineering and technology), NASM (music), NLN (nursing), NCATE (teacher education). City setting; 60-acre campus. Total enrollment: 7,474. Faculty: 415 (265 full-time, 150 part-time); 70% have doctoral degrees; graduate assistants teach no undergraduate courses. Calendar: semesters. Grading system: letters or numbers. Library holdings: 316,485 bound volumes, 592,604 titles on microform, 3,000 periodical subscriptions, 4,253 records/tapes.

Undergraduate Profile Fall 1984: 6,164 undergraduates (972 freshmen) from 40 states and territories and 39 foreign countries; 25% part-time; 86% state residents; 11% transfers; 50% financial aid recipients; 49% women; 14% blacks; 1% Native Americans; 1% Hispanics; 1% foreign nationals.

Expenses (1985–86) State resident tuition: $960 full-time, $47 per semester hour part-time. Nonresident tuition: $3106 full-time, $130 per semester hour part-time. College room only: $1260.

Financial Aid College-administered aid for all 1984–85 undergraduates: 350 need-based scholarships (average $800); 350 non-need scholarships (average $600); short-term loans (average $100); low-interest long-term loans from college funds (average $750), from external sources (average $1750); SEOG; College Work-Study; 1,000 part-time jobs. Supporting data: FFS, institutional form, AFSA/SAR required; IRS, state form required for some; FAF acceptable. Priority application deadline: 3/1.

Athletics Member NCAA (Division I). Intercollegiate sports: basketball M(I,s), W(I,s); cross-country running M(I,s); football M(I-AA,s); golf M(I,s), W(I); riflery M(I); soccer M(I,s); tennis M(I,s), W(II,s); volleyball W(I,s); wrestling M(I,s). Intramural sports: baseball/softball, basketball, cross-country running, fencing, football, golf, swimming and diving, tennis, volleyball, wrestling.

Majors Accounting B; American studies B; anthropology B; art education B; art/fine arts B; biology/biological sciences B; business administration/commerce/management B; chemical engineering B; chemistry B; civil engineering B; communication B; computer science B; criminal justice B; early childhood education B; ecology/environmental studies B; economics B; education B; elementary education B; engineering and applied sciences B; engineering management B; English B; environmental sciences B; French B; geology B; German B; Greek B; history B; home economics B; home economics education B; humanities B; human services B; industrial engineering B; Latin B; marketing/retailing/merchandising B; mathematics B; mechanical engineering B; medical technology B; (pre)medicine sequence B; music B; music education B; nursing B; philosophy B; physical education B; physics B; piano/organ B; political science/government B; psychology B; science education B; sculpture B; secondary education B; secretarial studies/office management B; social work B; sociology B; Spanish B; special education B; theater arts/drama B; urban studies B; (pre)veterinary medicine sequence B. Majors with highest enrollment: engineering and applied sciences, business administration/commerce/management, accounting.

LD Program Information

Name of Program College Access Program.

Availability of Services Began offering services in 1985. Services provided to freshmen, sophomores, juniors, seniors. Program currently serves 12 LD students: 3 freshmen, 4 sophomores, 4 juniors, 1 senior.

Staff 4 full-time, 2 part-time staff members, including coordinator. Services provided by tutors, counselor, diagnostic specialist, psychologist, tutoring service coordinator, testing service coordinator.

Admissions LD applicants evaluated on the basis of high school transcript and grade point average, standard or untimed SAT or ACT, personal interview, autobiographical statement, letters of recommendation, psychoeducational report. LD students may begin taking classes in fall, spring, or summer.

Orientation Optional orientation offered before registration (individual orientation for some services during registration or after classes begin).

Housing College housing (including coed) available. LD students housed randomly. LD students not required to live on campus.

Diagnostic Testing Available in intelligence, reading, math, spelling, handwriting.

Tutoring Offered one-to-one by peer tutors. Available in all subjects. LD students may receive tutoring in all courses each term (but limited to 6 hourly sessions per week).

Basic Skills Remediation Offered one-to-one by peer teachers. Available in reading, math, spelling, handwriting, spoken language, written language, learning strategies, work and study habits.

Academic Advisement Help with program planning provided by LD staff members, academic advisers. LD students may take up to 19 semester hours each semester; most take 9 to 12 semester hours; 12 semester hours required to maintain full-time status.

Special Courses Offered in college survival skills, reading, vocabulary development, communication skills, composition, language development, math, study skills, career planning. Some offered for credit; some enter into overall grade point average.

Auxiliary Aids and Services Aids include taped textbooks, tape recorders, calculators, typewriters, word processors. Services include alternative exam arrangements, notetakers, advocacy, "buddy-system" tutoring.

Counseling Services Individual counseling, rap sessions, career counseling available.

Contact Dr. Patricia Snowden, Coordinator of College Access Program, University of Tennessee at Chattanooga, 311 Holt Hall, Chattanooga, TN 37403, 615-755-4006.

UNIVERSITY OF TEXAS AT ARLINGTON

Arlington, Texas

Year Program Began	1982	Special Courses	✓
Special Fee	None	Taped Textbooks	✓
Special Orientation		Alternative Exam Arrangements	✓
Diagnostic Testing	✓	Notetakers	
Subject-Area Tutoring	✓	Staff	1 full-time
Basic Skills Remediation	✓	Number of Students Served	5

General Information State-supported coed university. Part of University of Texas System. Founded 1895. Awards B, M, D. Institutionally accredited by regional association; programs accredited by NAAB (architecture), AACSB (business), ABET (engineering and technology), NASM (music), NLN (nursing); candidate for program accreditation by FIDER (interior design). City setting, with easy access to Dallas–Fort Worth; 300-acre campus. Total enrollment: 23,397. Faculty: 1,269 (869 full-time, 400 part-time); 55% have doctoral degrees; graduate assistants teach a few undergraduate courses. Calendar: semesters. Grading system: letters or numbers. Library holdings: 875,000 bound volumes, 3,500 periodical subscriptions.

Undergraduate Profile Fall 1984: 20,200 undergraduates (2,008 freshmen); 45% part-time; 87% state residents; 17% transfers; 30% financial aid recipients; 43% women; 7% blacks; 1% Native Americans; 4% Hispanics; 5% Asian Americans; 4% foreign nationals; 46% of undergraduates over 25 years of age; 150 legally handicapped students.

Expenses (1985–86) State resident tuition: $954 full-time. Nonresident tuition: $3994 full-time. Part-time tuition and fees per semester (1 to 11 semester hours) range from $122.25 to $296.75 for state residents, $142.25 to $1484.75 for nonresidents. College room and board: $3156. College room only: $990.

Financial Aid Fall 1984 full-time freshmen: 21% applied for aid, 58% of those were judged to have need, 100% of those were aided; the average aided freshman received an aid package worth $3753 (28% scholarships/grants, 72% self-help) meeting 100% of need. College-administered aid for all 1984–85 undergraduates: need-based scholarships; non-need scholarships; short-term loans; low-interest long-term loans from external sources; SEOG; College Work-Study; part-time jobs. Supporting data: FAF required; IRS, institutional form, AFSA/SAR acceptable. Priority application deadline: 5/15.

Athletics Member NCAA (Division I). Intercollegiate sports: baseball/softball M(I,s), W(I,s); basketball M(I,s), W(I,s); football M(I-AA,s); golf M(I,s); riflery M(I), W(I); tennis M(I,s), W(I,s); track and field M(I,s), W(I,s); volleyball W(I,s). Intramural sports: baseball/softball, basketball, bowling, fencing, football, golf, gymnastics, martial arts, racquetball, riflery, soccer, swimming and diving, tennis, track and field, volleyball, weight lifting, wrestling.

Majors Accounting B; aerospace engineering B; anthropology B; architecture B; art education B; art/fine arts B; biochemistry B; biology/biological sciences B; business administration/commerce/management B; chemistry B; civil engineering B; communication B; computer science B; criminal justice B; economics B; electrical engineering B; elementary education B; English B; finance/banking B; French B; geology B; German B; history B; industrial engineering B; interdisciplinary studies B; interior design B; journalism B; landscape architecture/design B; marketing/retailing/merchandising B; mathematics B; mechanical engineering B; medical technology B; microbiology B; music B; music education B; nursing B; paralegal studies B; philosophy B; physical education B; physics B; political science/government B; psychology B; radio and television studies B; real estate B; Russian B; social work B; sociology B; Spanish B; speech/rhetoric/public address/debate B; theater arts/drama B. Majors with highest enrollment: business administration/commerce/management, accounting, architecture.

LD Program Information

Name of Program Not specified.

Availability of Services Began offering services in 1982. Services provided to freshmen, sophomores, juniors, seniors. Program currently serves 5 LD students: 2 freshmen, 1 sophomore, 2 juniors.

Staff 1 full-time staff member (learning specialist).

Admissions LD applicants evaluated on the basis of high school transcript and grade point average, standard or untimed SAT or ACT, psychoeducational report. LD students may begin taking classes in fall, spring, or summer. Application should be submitted 1 year in advance of initial anticipated enrollment.

Housing College housing (including coed) available. LD students housed randomly. LD students not required to live on campus.

Diagnostic Testing Available in intelligence, reading, math, spelling, handwriting, written language, perceptual skills, work and study habits.

Tutoring Offered one-to-one by professional teachers, peer tutors. Available in some subjects. LD students may receive tutoring in all courses each term.

Basic Skills Remediation Offered one-to-one by LD teachers. Available in reading, spelling, learning strategies, perceptual skills, work and study habits.

Academic Advisement Help with program planning provided by LD staff member, academic advisers. LD students may take up to 18 semester hours each semester; most take 6 to 12 semester hours; 12 semester hours required to maintain full-time status.

Special Courses Offered in college survival skills, reading, vocabulary development, communication skills, career planning. Some offered for credit; some enter into overall grade point average.

Auxiliary Aids and Services Aids include taped textbooks, tape recorders, typewriters. Services include alternative exam arrangements, advocacy.

Counseling Services Individual counseling, small-group counseling, rap sessions, career counseling available.

Contact Mr. Richard Massie, Learning Specialist, University of Texas at Arlington, Box 19156, Arlington, TX 76019, 817-273-3671.

UNIVERSITY OF TEXAS AT AUSTIN
Austin, Texas

Year Program Began	1977	Special Courses	✓
Special Fee	None	Taped Textbooks	✓
Special Orientation		Alternative Exam Arrangements	✓
Diagnostic Testing	✓	Notetakers	
Subject-Area Tutoring	✓	Staff	2 part-time
Basic Skills Remediation		Number of Students Served	4

General Information State-supported coed university. Part of University of Texas System. Founded 1883. Awards B, M, D. Institutionally accredited by regional association; programs accredited by NAAB (architecture), AACSB (business), ABET (engineering and technology), FIDER (interior design), NASM (music), NLN (nursing), ACPE (pharmacy), NCATE (teacher education). City setting; 300-acre campus. Total enrollment: 47,973. Faculty: 2,337 (1,460 full-time, 877 part-time); 80% have doctoral degrees; graduate assistants teach about a quarter of the undergraduate courses. Calendar: semesters. Grading system: letters or numbers. Library holdings: 5.1 million bound volumes, 2.2 million titles on microform, 60,000 periodical subscriptions, 5,000 records/tapes.

Undergraduate Profile Fall 1984: 36,687 undergraduates (6,079 freshmen) from 47 states and territories and 45 foreign countries; 12% part-time; 81% state residents; 12% transfers; 45% financial aid recipients; 47% women; 3% blacks; 3% Native Americans; 9% Hispanics; 3% Asian Americans; 4% foreign nationals; 12% of undergraduates over 25 years of age.

Expenses (1984–85) State resident tuition: $120 full-time. Nonresident tuition: $1200 full-time. Part-time tuition and fees per semester (1 to 11 semester hours) range from $106.75 to $194.25 for state residents, $96.75 to $584.25 for nonresidents. Mandatory fees: $300. College room and board: $3600.

Financial Aid Fall 1984 full-time freshmen: 24% applied for aid, 79% of those were judged to have need, 94% of those were aided; the average aided freshman received an aid package worth $3006 (60% scholarships/grants, 40% self-help) meeting 90% of need. College-administered aid for all 1984–85 undergraduates: need-based scholarships; non-need scholarships; short-term loans (average $75); low-interest long-term loans from college funds (average $1000); SEOG; College Work-Study; part-time jobs. Supporting data: FFS, IRS, institutional form, AFSA/SAR required; FAF acceptable. Priority application deadline: 3/15.

Athletics Member NCAA (Division I). Intercollegiate sports: baseball/softball M(I,s); basketball M(I,s), W(I,s); cross-country running M(I,s), W(I,s); football M(I-A,s); golf M(I,s), W(I,s); soccer M(c); swimming and diving M(I,s), W(I,s); tennis M(I,s), W(I,s); track and field M(I,s), W(I,s); volleyball W(I,s). Intramural sports: archery, baseball/softball, basketball, crew, cross-country running, fencing, football, golf, lacrosse, martial arts, racquetball, riflery, rugby, sailing, skiing (cross-country), skiing (downhill), soccer, squash, swimming and diving, tennis, track and field, volleyball, wrestling.

Majors Accounting B; advertising B; aerospace engineering B; African languages B; African studies B; American studies B; anthropology B; applied art B; Arabic B; archaeology B; architectural engineering B; architecture B; art education B; art/fine arts B; art history B; Asian/Oriental studies B; astronomy B; bilingual/bicultural education B; biochemistry B; bioengineering B; biology/biological sciences B; biomedical engineering B; black/Afro-American studies B; botany/plant sciences B; broadcasting B; business administration/commerce/management B; chemical engineering B; chemical engineering technology B; chemistry B; child psychology/child development B; Chinese B; civil engineering B; classics B; communication B; computer engineering B; computer science B; dance B; data processing B; (pre) dentistry sequence B; early childhood education B; East Asian studies B; East European and Soviet studies B; ecology/environmental studies B; economics B; education B; electrical engineering B; elementary education B; engineering (general) B; engineering management B; engineering physics B; engineering sciences B; engineering technology B; English B; environmental engineering B; ethnic studies B; European studies B; fashion merchandising B; film studies B; finance/banking B; French B; geography B; geological engineering B; geology B; geophysical engineering B; German B; Germanic languages and literature B; Greek B; Hebrew B; Hispanic studies B; history B; home economics B; home economics education B; insurance B; interior design B; international business B; international studies B; Italian B; Japanese B; journalism B; Latin B; Latin American studies B; (pre)law sequence B; liberal arts/general studies B; linguistics B; literature B; marine biology B; marine engineering B; marketing/retailing/merchandising B; mathematics B; mechanical engineering B; (pre)medicine sequence B; metallurgical engineering B; meteorology B; Mexican-American/Chicano studies B; microbiology B; music B; music education B; music history B; Near and Middle Eastern studies B; nuclear engineering B; nuclear physics B; nursing B; petroleum/natural gas engineering B; pharmacology B; pharmacy/pharmaceutical sciences B; philosophy B; photography B; physical education B; physics B; piano/organ B; political science/government B; Portuguese B; psychology B; public relations B; radio and television studies B; real estate B; Russian B; Russian and Slavic studies B; Scandinavian languages/studies B; science education B; secondary education B; Slavic languages B; social science B; social work B; sociology B; South Asian studies B; Spanish B; special education B; speech pathology and audiology B; speech/rhetoric/public address/debate B; speech therapy B; statistics B; textiles and clothing B; theater arts/drama B; (pre)veterinary medicine sequence B; voice B; zoology B. Majors with highest enrollment: electrical engineering, computer science, accounting.

LD Program Information

Name of Program Disabled Student Services.

Availability of Services Began offering services in 1977. Services provided to freshmen, sophomores, juniors, seniors. Program currently serves 4 LD students: 1 sophomore, 2 juniors, 1 senior.

Staff 2 part-time staff members. Services provided by diagnostic specialist, student development specialist.

Admissions LD applicants evaluated on the basis of high school transcript and grade point average, standard or untimed SAT or ACT; psychoeducational report recommended. LD students may begin taking classes in fall, spring, or summer. Application should be submitted 3 to 4 months in advance of initial anticipated enrollment.

Housing College housing (including coed) available. LD students housed randomly. LD students not required to live on campus.

Diagnostic Testing Available in perceptual skills, personality, speech.

Tutoring Offered one-to-one. Available in some subjects. LD students may receive tutoring in all courses each term.

Academic Advisement Help with program planning provided by academic advisers. LD students may take up to 15 semester hours each semester; most take 12 semester hours; 12 semester hours required to maintain full-time status.

Special Courses Offered in college survival skills, study skills, career planning. None offered for credit; none enter into overall grade point average.

Auxiliary Aids and Services Aids include taped textbooks, carbonless notepaper. Services include alternative exam arrangements, readers.

Counseling Services Individual counseling, career counseling available.

Contact Ms. Suzzanna Cortez Currier, Student Development Specialist, University of Texas at Austin, Dorothy Gebauer Building 2.116, Austin, TX 78712, 512-471-1205.

UNIVERSITY OF UTAH

Salt Lake City, Utah

Year Program Began	1982	Special Courses	✓
Special Fee	None	Taped Textbooks	✓
Special Orientation		Alternative Exam Arrangements	✓
Diagnostic Testing		Notetakers	✓
Subject-Area Tutoring	✓	Staff	2 part-time
Basic Skills Remediation	✓	Number of Students Served	*Not reported*

General Information State-supported coed university. Founded 1850. Awards B, M, D. Institutionally accredited by regional association; programs accredited by AACSB (business), ABET (engineering and technology), NASM (music), NLN (nursing), ACPE (pharmacy), NCATE (teacher education). Metropolitan setting; 1,500-acre barrier-free campus. Total enrollment: 24,600. Faculty: 2,734 (1,373 full-time, 1,361 part-time); 90% have doctoral degrees; graduate assistants teach a few undergraduate courses. Calendar: quarters. Grading system: letters or numbers. Library holdings: 2 million bound volumes, 2 million titles on microform, 14,300 periodical subscriptions, 5,000 records/tapes.

Undergraduate Profile Fall 1984: 20,500 undergraduates (3,100 freshmen) from 50 states and territories and 90 foreign countries; 31% part-time; 91% state residents; 33% transfers; 56% financial aid recipients; 41% women; 1% blacks; 1% Native Americans; 2% Hispanics; 3% Asian Americans; 3% foreign nationals; 50% of undergraduates over 25 years of age; 325 legally handicapped students.

Expenses (1985–86) State resident tuition: $1272 full-time. Nonresident tuition: $3630 full-time. Part-time tuition and fees per quarter (1 to 14 credit hours) range from $135 to $405 for state residents, $325 to $1150 for nonresidents. College room and board: $3217. College room only: $1648.

Financial Aid Fall 1984 full-time freshmen: 22% applied for aid, 78% of those were judged to have need, 83% of those were aided; the average aided freshman received an aid package worth $1617 (89% scholarships/grants, 11% self-help) meeting 90% of need. College-administered aid for all 1984–85 undergraduates: 1,412 need-based scholarships (average $575); 2,330 non-need scholarships (average $608); short-term loans (average $350); low-interest long-term loans from college funds (average $1134), from external sources (average $2400); SEOG; College Work-Study; part-time jobs. Supporting data: FAF, IRS, institutional form, AFSA/SAR required; state form acceptable. Priority application deadline: 4/1.

Athletics Member NCAA (Division I). Intercollegiate sports: baseball/softball M(I,s), W(s); basketball M(I,s), W(s); cross-country running M(I,s), W(s); football M(I-A,s); golf M(I,s); gymnastics W(I,s); skiing (cross-country) M(I,s), W(I,s); skiing (downhill) M(I,s), W(I,s); swimming and diving M(I,s), W(I,s); tennis M(I,s), W(I,s); track and field M(I,s), W(I,s); volleyball W(I,s); water polo M(I,s). Intramural sports: baseball/softball, basketball, bowling, cross-country running, field hockey, football, golf, martial arts, racquetball, rugby, skiing (cross-country), skiing (downhill), soccer, squash, swimming and diving, tennis, track and field, volleyball, wrestling.

Majors Accounting B; anthropology B; Arabic B; archaeology B; art/fine arts B; art history B; biology/biological sciences B; biomedical sciences B; broadcasting B; business administration/commerce/management B; chemical engineering B; chemistry B; child psychology/child development B; civil engineering B; classics B; communication B; computer science B; dance B; economics B; electrical engineering B; elementary education B; English B; family and consumer studies B; film studies B; finance/banking B; food sciences B; French B; geography B; geological engineering B; geology B; geophysics B; German B; Greek B; health education B; history B; industrial engineering B; journalism B; Latin B; liberal arts/general studies B; linguistics B; marketing/retailing/merchandising B; materials engineering B; materials sciences B; mathematics B; mechanical engineering B; metallurgical engineering B; meteorology B; mining and mineral engineering B; music B; music education B; Near and Middle Eastern studies B; nursing B; nutrition B; pharmacy/pharmaceutical sciences B; philosophy B; physical education B; physical therapy B; physics B; political science/government B; psychology B; public relations B; radio and television studies B; recreation and leisure services B; Russian B; secondary education B; social science B; sociology B; Spanish B; special education B; speech pathology and audiology B; speech/rhetoric/public address/debate B; theater arts/drama B; urban studies B. Majors with highest enrollment: psychology, accounting, nursing.

LD Program Information

Name of Program Center for Handicapped Student Services.

Availability of Services Began offering services in 1982. Services provided to freshmen, sophomores, juniors, seniors.

Staff 2 part-time staff members, including coordinator. Services provided by counselors.

Admissions LD applicants evaluated on the basis of high school transcript, standard or untimed ACT. Open admissions policy for state residents. LD students may begin taking classes in fall, winter, spring, or summer. Application should be submitted at least 1 month in advance of initial anticipated enrollment.

Housing College housing (including coed) available. LD students housed randomly. LD students not required to live on campus.

Tutoring Offered one-to-one by peer tutors. Available in some subjects. LD students may receive tutoring in all courses each term.

Basic Skills Remediation Offered in small groups by regular teachers. Available in math.

Academic Advisement Help with program planning provided by LD staff members, academic advisers. LD students may take up to 18 credit hours each quarter; most take 8 to 10 credit hours; 12 credit hours required to maintain full-time status.

Special Courses Offered in math, study skills. Some offered for credit; some enter into overall grade point average.

Auxiliary Aids and Services Aids include taped textbooks, tape recorders. Services include alternative exam arrangements, notetakers.

Counseling Services Individual counseling, small-group counseling available.

Contact Ms. Olga Nadeau, Coordinator, Center for Handicapped Student Services, University of Utah, 160 Olpin Union, Salt Lake City, UT 84112, 801-581-5020.

UNIVERSITY OF VERMONT

Burlington, Vermont

Year Program Began	1981	Special Courses	
Special Fee	None	Taped Textbooks	✓
Special Orientation		Alternative Exam Arrangements	✓
Diagnostic Testing	✓	Notetakers	✓
Subject-Area Tutoring	✓	Staff	2 full-time, 3 part-time
Basic Skills Remediation	✓	Number of Students Served	41

General Information State-supported coed university. Founded 1791. Awards A (terminal), B, M, D. Institutionally accredited by regional association; programs accredited by ABET (engineering and technology), NASM (music), NLN (nursing), NCATE (teacher education). Small-town setting; 424-acre barrier-free campus. Total enrollment: 8,860. Faculty: 877 (774 full-time, 103 part-time); 81% have doctoral degrees; graduate assistants teach a few undergraduate courses. Calendar: semesters. Grading system: letters or numbers. Library holdings: 800,000 bound volumes, 500,000 titles on microform, 8,500 periodical subscriptions, 8,600 records/tapes.

Undergraduate Profile Fall 1984: 7,818 undergraduates (2,002 freshmen) from 39 states and territories and 43 foreign countries; 5% part-time; 45% state residents; 14% transfers; 59% financial aid recipients; 59% women; 1% blacks; 0% Native Americans; 1% Hispanics; 1% Asian Americans; 1% foreign nationals; 5% of undergraduates over 25 years of age; 17 legally handicapped students.

Expenses (1985–86) State resident tuition: $2680 full-time, $112 per credit part-time. Nonresident tuition: $7438 full-time, $310 per credit part-time. Mandatory fees: $268. College room and board: $3326. College room only: $2032.

Financial Aid Fall 1984 full-time freshmen: 65% applied for aid, 75% of those were judged to have need, 100% of those were aided; the average aided freshman received an aid package worth $5560 (49% scholarships/grants, 51% self-help) meeting 91% of need. College-administered aid for all 1984–85 undergraduates: 3,175 need-based scholarships (average $980); 127 non-need scholarships (average $4700); low-interest long-term loans from college funds (average $485), from external sources (average $690); SEOG; College Work-Study; part-time jobs. Supporting data: IRS required; FFS, FAF acceptable. Application deadline: 3/1.

Athletics Member NCAA (Division I), NAIA. Intercollegiate sports: baseball/softball M(I), W(I); basketball M(I,s), W(I,s); cross-country running M(I), W(I); field hockey W(I); golf M(I); gymnastics M(I), W(I); ice hockey M(I,s); lacrosse M(I), W(I); rugby M; skiing (cross-country) M(I,s), W(I,s); skiing (downhill) M(I,s), W(I,s); soccer M(I), W(I); swimming and diving M(I), W(I); tennis M(I), W(I); track and field M(I), W(I,s); volleyball W(I). Intramural sports: archery, badminton, baseball/softball, basketball, fencing, gymnastics, ice hockey, racquetball, rugby, skiing (cross-country), skiing (downhill), soccer, squash, swimming and diving, tennis, track and field, volleyball, wrestling.

Majors Accounting B; agricultural economics B; agricultural technologies B; agronomy/soil and crop sciences B; animal sciences B; anthropology B; applied mathematics B; art education B; art/fine arts B; art history B; biochemistry B; bioengineering B; biology/biological sciences B; biomedical engineering B; botany/plant sciences B; business administration/commerce/management B; Canadian studies B; chemistry B; child care/child and family studies B; civil engineering B; classics B; computer science B; dairy sciences B; dental services A; (pre)dentistry sequence B; dietetics B; early childhood education B; East European and Soviet studies B; ecology/environmental studies B; economics B; education B; electrical engineering B; elementary education B; engineering (general) B; engineering and applied sciences B; engineering physics B; engineering sciences B; English B; environmental biology B; environmental education B; environmental sciences B; European studies B; fashion merchandising B; finance/banking B; fish and game management B; food sciences B; forestry B; French B; geography B; geology B; German B; Greek B; health education B; history B; home economics B; home economics education B; horticulture B; human development B; industrial arts B; Latin B; Latin American studies B; (pre)law sequence B; marketing/retailing/merchandising B; mathematics B; mechanical engineering B; medical laboratory technology B; (pre)medicine sequence B; microbiology B; modern languages B; music B; music education B; music history B; natural resource management B; nursing A, B; nutrition B; parks management B; philosophy B; physical education B; physical sciences B; physical therapy B; physics B; political science/government B; psychology B; radiological technology A; recreation and leisure services B; religious studies B; Romance languages B; Russian B; Russian and Slavic studies B; science education B; secondary education B; social work B; sociology B; soil conservation B; Spanish B; special education B; speech pathology and audiology B; speech/rhetoric/public address/debate B; statistics B; studio art B; textiles and clothing B; theater arts/drama B; (pre)veterinary medicine sequence B; vocational education B; wildlife biology B; zoology B. Majors with highest enrollment: business administration/commerce/management, political science/government, biology/biological sciences.

LD Program Information

Name of Program Specialized Student Services.

Availability of Services Began offering services in 1981. Services provided to freshmen, sophomores, juniors, seniors. Program currently serves 41 LD students: 10 freshmen, 5 sophomores, 14 juniors, 12 seniors.

Staff 2 full-time, 3 part-time staff members, including director. Services provided by diagnostic specialist, English, reading, and math skills instructors of Learning Cooperative.

Admissions LD applicants evaluated on the basis of high school transcript and grade point average, untimed SAT, autobiographical statement, letters of recommendation; personal interview recommended. LD students may begin taking classes in fall, spring, or summer. Application should be submitted at least 7 to 10 months in advance of initial anticipated enrollment.

Housing College housing (including coed) available. LD students housed randomly. LD freshmen required to live on campus.

Diagnostic Testing Available in intelligence, reading, math, spelling, handwriting, written language, work and study habits.

Tutoring Offered one-to-one and in small groups by professional teachers, peer tutors. Available in all subjects. LD students may receive tutoring in all courses each term.

Basic Skills Remediation Offered one-to-one and in small groups by LD teachers, regular teachers, peer teachers. Available in reading, math, written language, learning strategies, work and study habits, speech.

Academic Advisement Help with program planning provided by LD staff members, academic advisers. LD students may take up to 18 credits each semester; most take 9 to 15 credits; 12 credits required to maintain full-time status.

Auxiliary Aids and Services Aids include taped textbooks, tape recorders, word processors, talking computer terminal. Services include alternative exam arrangements, notetakers, advocacy.

Counseling Services Individual counseling, career counseling available.

Contact Ms. Nancy Oliker, Coordinator, Office of Specialized Student Services, University of Vermont, 146 South William Street, Burlington, VT 05405, 802-656-3340.

UNIVERSITY OF VIRGINIA

Charlottesville, Virginia

Year Program Began	Early 1980's	Special Courses	✓
Special Fee	None	Taped Textbooks	✓
Special Orientation		Alternative Exam Arrangements	✓
Diagnostic Testing	✓	Notetakers	✓
Subject-Area Tutoring	✓	Staff	11 part-time
Basic Skills Remediation		Number of Students Served	*Not reported*

General Information State-related coed university. Founded 1819. Awards B, M, D. Institutionally accredited by regional association; programs accredited by AACSB (business), ABET (engineering and technology), NLN (nursing), NCATE (teacher education). Small-town setting, with easy access to Richmond; 2,000-acre barrier-free campus. Total enrollment: 16,379. Faculty: 1,579 (1,377 full-time, 202 part-time); 95% have doctoral degrees; graduate assistants teach a few undergraduate courses. Calendar: semesters. Grading system: letters or numbers. Library holdings: 2.5 million bound volumes, 8 million titles on microform, 25,197 periodical subscriptions, 10,362 records/tapes.

Undergraduate Profile Fall 1984: 10,967 undergraduates (2,634 freshmen) from 50 states and territories; 0% part-time; 60% state residents; 4% transfers; 34% financial aid recipients; 49% women; 9% blacks; 2% Asian Americans; 2% foreign nationals; 125 legally handicapped students.

Expenses (1985–86) State resident tuition: $2050 full-time. Nonresident tuition: $4950 full-time. Mandatory fees: $16. College room and board: $2600. College room only: $1150.

Financial Aid Fall 1984 full-time freshmen: 53% applied for aid, 64% of those were judged to have need, 100% of those were aided; the average aided freshman received an aid package worth $2850 (65% scholarships/grants, 35% self-help) meeting 90% of need. College-administered aid for all 1984–85 undergraduates: need-based scholarships (average $1950); 390 non-need scholarships (average $3725); low-interest long-term loans from external sources (average $1000); College Work-Study; part-time jobs. Supporting data: FAF, AFSA/SAR required; IRS required for some. Priority application deadline: 3/1.

Athletics Member NCAA (Division I). Intercollegiate sports: baseball/softball M(I,s), W(I,s); basketball M(I,s), W(I,s); cross-country running M(I,s), W(I,s); field hockey W(I,s); football M(I-A,s); golf M(I,s); lacrosse M(I,s), W(I,s); soccer M(I,s), W(I); swimming and diving M(I,s), W(I,s); tennis M(I,s), W(I,s); track and field M(I,s), W(I,s); volleyball W(I,s); wrestling M(I,s). Intramural sports: archery, badminton, baseball/softball, basketball, bowling, crew, cross-country running, equestrian sports, fencing, field hockey, football, golf, gymnastics, lacrosse, martial arts, racquetball, riflery, rugby, sailing, skiing (cross-country), skiing (downhill), soccer, squash, swimming and diving, tennis, track and field, volleyball, water polo, weight lifting, wrestling.

Majors Accounting B; aerospace engineering B; African studies B; anthropology B; applied mathematics B; architecture B; art history B; Asian/Oriental studies B; astronomy B; astrophysics B; biology/biological sciences B; business administration/commerce/management B; chemical engineering B; chemistry B; civil engineering B; classics B; comparative literature B; computer information systems B; computer science B; economics B; electrical engineering B; elementary education B; engineering sciences B; English B; environmental sciences B; finance/banking B; French B; German B; health education B; history B; interdisciplinary studies B; international studies B; Latin B; Latin American studies B; linguistics B; marketing/retailing/merchandising B; mathematics B; mechanical engineering B; music B; nuclear engineering B; nursing B; philosophy B; physical education B; physics B; political science/government B; psychology B; religious studies B; Russian B; Russian and Slavic studies B; secondary education B; Slavic languages B; sociology B; Spanish B; special education B; speech pathology and audiology B; speech/rhetoric/public address/debate B; studio art B; systems engineering B; systems science B; theater arts/drama B.

LD Program Information

Name of Program Learning Needs and Evaluation Center.

Availability of Services Began offering services in early 1980's. Services provided to freshmen, sophomores, juniors, seniors.

Staff 11 part-time staff members, including director. Services provided by tutors, counselors, diagnostic specialists.

Admissions LD applicants evaluated on the basis of high school transcript and grade point average, untimed SAT, autobiographical statement, letters of recommendation, psychoeducational report, 3 Achievement Tests, English Composition Test. LD students may begin taking classes in fall or spring. Application should be submitted 9 to 12 months in advance of initial anticipated enrollment.

Housing College housing (including coed) available. LD students housed randomly. LD freshmen required to live on campus.

Diagnostic Testing Available in intelligence, reading, math, spelling, spoken language, motor abilities, perceptual skills, work and study habits, psychoneurology.

Tutoring Offered one-to-one and in small groups by professional teachers, peer tutors. Available in all subjects. LD students may receive tutoring in all courses each term.

Academic Advisement Help with program planning provided by LD staff members, academic advisers. LD students may take up to 18 semester hours each semester; 12 semester hours required to maintain full-time status.

Special Courses Offered in reading, typing. None offered for credit; none enter into overall grade point average.

Auxiliary Aids and Services Aids include taped textbooks, tape recorders, typewriters. Services include alternative exam arrangements, notetakers, advocacy.

Counseling Services Individual counseling, small-group counseling, career counseling available.

Contact Dr. Eleanor Westhead, Director, Learning Needs and Evaluation Center, University of Virginia, Randall Hall, Charlottesville, VA 22903, 804-924-3139.

UNIVERSITY OF WASHINGTON

Seattle, Washington

Year Program Began	1981
Special Fee	None
Special Orientation	✓
Diagnostic Testing	
Subject-Area Tutoring	
Basic Skills Remediation	✓
Special Courses	
Taped Textbooks	✓
Alternative Exam Arrangements	✓
Notetakers	✓
Staff	2 part-time
Number of Students Served	13

General Information State-supported coed university. Founded 1861. Awards B, M, D. Institutionally accredited by regional association; programs accredited by NAAB (architecture), NASAD (art and design), AACSB (business), ABET (engineering and technology), NASM (music), NLN (nursing), ACPE (pharmacy), NCATE (teacher education). Metropolitan setting; 680-acre campus. Total enrollment: 26,380. Faculty: 2,600 (all full-time); 82% have doctoral degrees; graduate assistants teach about a quarter of the undergraduate courses. Calendar: quarters. Grading system: letters or numbers. Library holdings: 4 million bound volumes, 3 million titles on microform, 39,500 periodical subscriptions.

Undergraduate Profile Fall 1984: 25,928 undergraduates (4,920 freshmen) from 52 states and territories and 90 foreign countries; 20% part-time; 88% state residents; 36% transfers; 35% financial aid recipients; 48% women; 4% blacks; 1% Native Americans; 2% Hispanics; 14% Asian Americans; 2% foreign nationals; 19% of undergraduates over 25 years of age; 400 legally handicapped students.

Expenses (1985–86) State resident tuition: $1308 full-time, $46 per quarter hour part-time. Nonresident tuition: $3624 full-time, $122 per quarter hour part-time. College room and board: $2462.

Financial Aid Fall 1984 full-time freshmen: 80% applied for aid, 62% of those were judged to have need, 72% of those were aided; the average aided freshman received an aid package worth $3522 (43% scholarships/grants, 57% self-help) meeting 88% of need. College-administered aid for all 1984–85 undergraduates: need-based scholarships; 280 non-need scholarships (average $1300); short-term loans; low-interest long-term loans from external sources; SEOG; College Work-Study; part-time jobs. Supporting data: FAF, AFSA/SAR required; institutional form required for some. Priority application deadline: 3/1.

Athletics Member NCAA (Division I). Intercollegiate sports: archery M(c), W(c); badminton M(c), W(c); baseball/softball M(I,s), W(c); basketball M, W; crew M, W; cross-country running M(I,s), W(I,s); football M(I-A,s); golf M(I), W(I); gymnastics M(I), W(I,s); ice hockey M(I); soccer M(I); swimming and diving M(I,s), W(I,s); tennis M(I,s), W(I,s); track and field M(I,s), W(I,s); volleyball M(c), W(I); wrestling M(c). Intramural sports: baseball/softball, basketball, crew, football, golf, gymnastics, ice hockey, racquetball, rugby, sailing, skiing (cross-country), skiing (downhill), soccer, swimming and diving, tennis, track and field, volleyball, wrestling.

Majors Accounting B; advertising B; aerospace engineering B; anthropology B; architecture B; art/fine arts B; art history B; Asian/Oriental studies B; astronomy B; atmospheric sciences B; biology/biological sciences B; black/Afro-American studies B; botany/plant sciences B; broadcasting B; business administration/commerce/management B; ceramic engineering B; chemical engineering B; chemistry B; Chinese B; city, community, and regional planning B; civil engineering B; classics B; communication B; comparative literature B; computer science B; criminal justice B; dance B; (pre)dentistry sequence B; East Asian studies B; East European and Soviet studies B; ecology/environmental studies B; economics B; education B; electrical engineering B; elementary education B; engineering (general) B; English B; environmental health sciences B; ethnic studies B; food sciences B; forestry B; French B; geography B; geology B; Germanic languages and literature B; Greek B; history B; industrial engineering B; interdisciplinary studies B; international studies B; Italian B; Japanese B; Judaic studies B; landscape architecture/design B; Latin B; Latin American studies B; (pre)law sequence B; liberal arts/general studies B; linguistics B; mathematics B; mechanical engineering B; medical technology B; (pre)medicine sequence B; medieval studies B; metallurgical engineering B; Mexican-American/Chicano studies B; mining and mineral engineering B; music B; music education B; Native American studies B; Near and Middle Eastern studies B; nursing B; occupational therapy B; ocean engineering B; oceanography B; paper and pulp sciences B; pharmacy/pharmaceutical sciences B; philosophy B; physical therapy B; physics B; political science/government B; psychology B; Russian B; Russian and Slavic studies B; Scandinavian languages/studies B; secondary education B; social work B; sociology B; Spanish B; speech pathology and audiology B; statistics B; technical writing B; theater arts/drama B; (pre)veterinary medicine sequence B; women's studies B; wood sciences B; zoology B. Majors with highest enrollment: business administration/commerce/management, economics, English.

LD Program Information

Name of Program Disabled Student Services.

Availability of Services Began offering services in 1981. Services provided to freshmen, sophomores, juniors, seniors. Program currently serves 13 LD students: 1 freshman, 3 sophomores, 5 juniors, 4 seniors.

Staff 2 part-time staff members, including coordinator, assistant coordinator.

Admissions LD applicants evaluated on the basis of high school transcript and grade point average, standard or untimed SAT or ACT, personal interview, psychoeducational report, standard or untimed WPCT (in lieu of SAT or ACT). LD students may begin taking classes in fall, winter, spring, or summer. Application should be submitted at least 4 months in advance of initial anticipated enrollment.

Orientation Optional orientation offered before registration.

Housing College housing (including coed) available. LD students housed randomly. LD students not required to live on campus.

Basic Skills Remediation Offered in small groups by regular teachers. Available in math, written language, work and study habits.

Academic Advisement Help with program planning provided by LD staff members, academic advisers. Most LD students take 12 to 15 quarter hours each quarter; 12 quarter hours required to maintain full-time status.

Auxiliary Aids and Services Aids include taped textbooks, tape recorders, typewriters. Services include alternative exam arrangements, notetakers, advocacy.

Counseling Services Individual counseling, small-group counseling, rap sessions, career counseling available.

Contact Ms. Roxanne Baker, Program Coordinator, Disabled Student Services (PB-07), University of Washington, Seattle, WA 98195, 206-543-8924.

UNIVERSITY OF WISCONSIN–EAU CLAIRE

Eau Claire, Wisconsin

Year Program Began	1978	Special Courses	✓
Special Fee	None	Taped Textbooks	✓
Special Orientation		Alternative Exam Arrangements	✓
Diagnostic Testing	✓	Notetakers	✓
Subject-Area Tutoring	✓	Staff	3 part-time
Basic Skills Remediation	✓	Number of Students Served	8

General Information State-supported comprehensive coed institution. Part of University of Wisconsin System. Founded 1916. Awards A (college transfer), B, M. Institutionally accredited by regional association; programs accredited by AACSB (business), NASM (music), NLN (nursing). City setting; 333-acre campus. Total enrollment: 10,757. Faculty: 572 (518 full-time, 54 part-time); 65% have doctoral degrees; graduate assistants teach no undergraduate courses. Calendar: semesters. Grading system: letters or numbers. Library holdings: 473,676 bound volumes, 2,320 periodical subscriptions, 6,971 records/tapes.

Undergraduate Profile Fall 1984: 10,260 undergraduates (2,355 freshmen) from 24 states and territories and 44 foreign countries; 9% part-time; 87% state residents; 6% transfers; 70% financial aid recipients; 56% women; 1% blacks; 1% Native Americans; 1% Hispanics; 1% Asian Americans; 1% foreign nationals; 12% of undergraduates over 25 years of age; 127 legally handicapped students.

Expenses (1985–86) State resident tuition: $1309 full-time, $54.70 per credit part-time. Nonresident tuition: $3942 full-time, $164.20 per credit part-time. Minnesota residents pay tuition at the rate they would pay if attending a comparable state-supported institution in Minnesota. College room and board: $2040. College room only: $940.

Financial Aid Fall 1984 full-time freshmen: 77% applied for aid, 88% of those were judged to have need, 93% of those were aided; the average aided freshman received an aid package worth $1819 (38% scholarships/grants, 62% self-help) meeting 100% of need. College-administered aid for all 1984–85 undergraduates: 1,316 need-based scholarships (average $486); 437 non-need scholarships (average $711); low-interest long-term loans from college funds (average $500), from external sources (average $1223); SEOG; College Work-Study; 750 part-time jobs. Supporting data: institutional form required; IRS required for some; FFS, FAF, AFSA/SAR acceptable. Priority application deadline: 4/15.

Athletics Member NAIA. Intercollegiate sports: baseball/softball M; basketball M, W; cross-country running M, W; football M; golf M; gymnastics W; ice hockey M; swimming and diving M, W; tennis M, W; track and field M, W; volleyball W; wrestling M. Intramural sports: archery, badminton, baseball/softball, basketball, bowling, cross-country running, field hockey, football, golf, ice hockey, martial arts, skiing (cross-country), skiing (downhill), soccer, swimming and diving, tennis, track and field, volleyball, weight lifting.

Majors Accounting B; advertising B; applied art B; art education B; art/fine arts B; biology/biological sciences B; botany/plant sciences B; business administration/commerce/management A, B; business economics B; business education B; ceramic art and design B; chemistry B; commercial art B; communication B; computer information systems B; computer science B; criminal justice B; data processing B; economics B; education B; elementary education B; English B; environmental health sciences B; finance/banking B; French B; geography B; geology B; German B; health services administration B; history B; journalism B; Latin American studies B; liberal arts/general studies A; management information systems B; marketing/retailing/merchandising B; mathematics B; medical technology B; music B; music education B; music therapy B; nursing B; philosophy B; physical education B; physical sciences B; physics B; political science/government B; psychology B; public health B; radio and television studies B; religious studies B; secondary education B; secretarial studies/office management B; social science B; social work B; sociology B; Spanish B; special education B; speech pathology and audiology B; speech therapy B; theater arts/drama B; zoology B. Majors with highest enrollment: business administration/commerce/management, accounting, management information systems.

LD Program Information

Name of Program Disabled Student Services.

Availability of Services Began offering services in 1978. Services provided to freshmen, sophomores, juniors, seniors. Program currently serves 8 LD students: 3 freshmen, 2 sophomores, 2 juniors, 1 senior.

Staff 3 part-time staff members, including coordinator, assistant coordinator. Services provided by tutors, reading/study skills specialist.

Admissions LD applicants evaluated on the basis of high school transcript and grade point average, standard or untimed ACT. LD students may begin taking classes in fall, spring, or summer. Application should be submitted at least 6 months in advance of initial anticipated enrollment.

Housing College housing (including coed) available. LD students housed randomly. LD freshmen and sophomores required to live on campus except if living with relatives.

Diagnostic Testing Available in reading, math, spelling, written language, work and study habits.

Tutoring Offered one-to-one and in small groups by peer tutors. Available in some subjects. LD students may receive tutoring in 4 courses per term.

Basic Skills Remediation Offered one-to-one and in small groups by reading/study skills specialist, peer teachers. Available in reading, math, spelling, written language, learning strategies, work and study habits, vocabulary development.

Academic Advisement Help with program planning provided by LD staff members, academic advisers. LD students may take up to 18 credits each semester; most take 12 credits; 12 credits required to maintain full-time status.

Special Courses Offered in college survival skills, reading, vocabulary development, communication skills, composition, language development, math, study skills. Some offered for credit; some enter into overall grade point average.

Auxiliary Aids and Services Aids include taped textbooks, tape recorders. Services include alternative exam arrangements, notetakers.

Counseling Services Individual counseling, small-group counseling, career counseling available.

Contact Mr. Joseph C. Hisrich, Coordinator of Services for Disabled Students, University of Wisconsin–Eau Claire, Library 2058, Eau Claire, WI 54701, 715-836-4542.

UNIVERSITY OF WISCONSIN–LA CROSSE

La Crosse, Wisconsin

Year Program Began	1982	Special Courses	✓
Special Fee	None	Taped Textbooks	✓
Special Orientation	✓	Alternative Exam Arrangements	✓
Diagnostic Testing	✓	Notetakers	✓
Subject-Area Tutoring	✓	Staff	2 part-time
Basic Skills Remediation		Number of Students Served	17

General Information State-supported comprehensive coed institution. Part of University of Wisconsin System. Founded 1909. Awards A (college transfer), B, M. Institutionally accredited by regional association; programs accredited by AACSB (business), NASM (music), NCATE (teacher education). City setting; 108-acre barrier-free campus. Total enrollment: 9,800. Faculty: 380; graduate assistants teach no undergraduate courses. Calendar: semesters. Grading system: letters or numbers. Library holdings: 486,637 bound volumes, 6,881 titles on microform, 1,926 periodical subscriptions, 837 records/tapes.

Undergraduate Profile Fall 1984: 9,112 undergraduates (2,095 freshmen) from 33 states and territories and 30 foreign countries; 4% part-time; 84% state residents; 19% transfers; 55% financial aid recipients; 55% women; 2% foreign nationals; 11% of undergraduates over 25 years of age; 400 legally handicapped students.

Expenses (1984–85) State resident tuition: $1212 full-time, $50.45 per credit part-time. Nonresident tuition: $3694 full-time, $153.95 per credit part-time. Minnesota residents pay tuition at the rate they would pay if attending a comparable state-supported institution in Minnesota. Mandatory fees: $232. College room and board: $1730. College room only: $830.

Financial Aid Fall 1984 full-time freshmen: 73% applied for aid, 55% of those were judged to have need, 100% of those were aided; the average aided freshman received an aid package worth $3010 (32% scholarships/grants, 68% self-help) meeting 72% of need. College-administered aid for all 1984–85 undergraduates: need-based scholarships; 56 non-need scholarships (average $700); short-term loans (average $100); low-interest long-term loans from external sources (average $2100); SEOG; College Work-Study; 1,200 part-time jobs. Supporting data: FAF, IRS, institutional form required; FFS, AFSA/SAR acceptable. Priority application deadline: 3/1.

Athletics Member NCAA (Division III), NAIA. Intercollegiate sports: baseball/softball M, W; basketball M, W; cross-country running M, W; field hockey W; football M; golf M, W; gymnastics M, W; ice hockey M; swimming and diving M, W; tennis M, W; track and field M, W; volleyball W; wrestling M. Intramural sports: badminton, baseball/softball, basketball, bowling, cross-country running, football, ice hockey, martial arts, racquetball, riflery, rugby, sailing, skiing (cross-country), skiing (downhill), soccer, tennis, volleyball, water polo, wrestling.

Majors Accounting B; art education B; art/fine arts B; biology/biological sciences B; business administration/commerce/management B; chemistry B; communication B; computer science B; (pre)dentistry sequence B; early childhood education B; economics B; elementary education B; engineering (general) B; English B; finance/banking B; French B; geography B; health education B; history B; (pre)law sequence B; liberal arts/general studies A; marketing/retailing/merchandising B; mathematics B; medical technology B; (pre)medicine sequence B; microbiology B; music B; music education B; nuclear medical technology B; philosophy B; physical education B; physical therapy B; physics B; political science/government B; psychology B; public administration B; recreation and leisure services B; recreation therapy B; secondary education B; social science B; social work B; sociology B; Spanish B; speech/rhetoric/public address/debate B; theater arts/drama B; (pre)veterinary medicine sequence B. Majors with highest enrollment: business administration/commerce/management, computer science, physical education.

LD Program Information

Name of Program Handicapped Student Services.

Availability of Services Began offering services in 1982. Services provided to freshmen, sophomores, juniors, seniors. Program currently serves 17 LD students.

Staff 2 part-time staff members, including coordinator. Services provided by tutors, diagnostic specialist, notetakers, textbook tapers.

Admissions LD applicants evaluated on the basis of high school transcript and grade point average, standard or untimed ACT, autobiographical statement, letters of recommendation, psychoeducational report. LD students may begin taking classes in fall, spring, or summer. Application should be submitted 9 months in advance of initial anticipated enrollment.

Orientation Optional orientation offered before registration.

Housing College housing (including coed) available. LD students housed randomly. LD freshmen and sophomores required to live on campus except for veterans, or if married or living with relatives.

Diagnostic Testing Available in intelligence, reading, math, spelling.

Tutoring Offered one-to-one and in small groups by professional teachers, peer tutors. Available in all subjects. LD students may receive tutoring in all courses each term.

Academic Advisement Help with program planning provided by LD staff members. Most LD students take 12 to 13 credits each semester; 12 credits required to maintain full-time status.

Special Courses Offered in college survival skills, reading, composition, math, study skills, career planning. Some offered for credit; some enter into overall grade point average.

Auxiliary Aids and Services Aids include taped textbooks, tape recorders, word processors, computers. Services include alternative exam arrangements, notetakers, advocacy, pre-registration.

Counseling Services Individual counseling, small-group counseling, career counseling available.

Contact Ms. Linda Kerrigan, Coordinator of Handicapped Student Services, University of Wisconsin–La Crosse, 1725 State Street, La Crosse, WI 54601, 608-785-8535.

UNIVERSITY OF WISCONSIN–OSHKOSH

Oshkosh, Wisconsin

Year Program Began	1979	Special Courses	✓
Special Fee	None	Taped Textbooks	
Special Orientation	✓	Alternative Exam Arrangements	✓
Diagnostic Testing	✓	Notetakers	
Subject-Area Tutoring	✓	Staff	1 full-time, 1 part-time
Basic Skills Remediation	✓	Number of Students Served	114

General Information State-supported comprehensive coed institution. Part of University of Wisconsin System. Founded 1871. Awards A (college transfer), B, M. Institutionally accredited by regional association; programs accredited by AACSB (business), NASM (music), NLN (nursing), NCATE (teacher education). City setting; 192-acre barrier-free campus. Total enrollment: 11,200. Faculty: 600; 70% have doctoral degrees; graduate assistants teach no undergraduate courses. Calendar: semesters. Grading system: letters or numbers. Library holdings: 600,000 bound volumes, 1,800 periodical subscriptions.

Undergraduate Profile Fall 1984: 9,200 undergraduates (1,886 freshmen); 19% part-time; 97% state residents; 9% transfers; 50% financial aid recipients; 52% women; 2% blacks; 1% Native Americans; 1% Hispanics; 1% Asian Americans; 1% foreign nationals; 7% of undergraduates over 25 years of age; 100 legally handicapped students.

Expenses (1984–85) State resident tuition: $1170 full-time, $49.16 per semester hour part-time. Nonresident tuition: $3653 full-time, $152.66 per semester hour part-time. Minnesota residents pay tuition at the rate they would pay if attending a comparable state-supported institution in Minnesota. College room and board: $1880. College room only: $1030.

Financial Aid Fall 1984 full-time freshmen: 55% applied for aid, 82% of those were judged to have need, 96% of those were aided; the average aided freshman received an aid package worth $3000 (44% scholarships/grants, 56% self-help) meeting 85% of need. College-administered aid for all 1984–85 undergraduates: 1,800 need-based scholarships (average $556); 50 non-need scholarships (average $450); short-term loans (average $50); low-interest long-term loans from external sources (average $1726); SEOG; College Work-Study; 1,250 part-time jobs. Supporting data: FAF, institutional form, AFSA/SAR required; FFS acceptable. Application deadline: continuous.

Athletics Member NCAA (Division III). Intercollegiate sports: baseball/softball M(III), W(III); basketball M(III), W(III); cross-country running M(III), W(III); football M; golf M(III); gymnastics M(III), W(III); riflery M(III), W(III); soccer M(III); tennis M(III), W(III); track and field M(III), W(III); volleyball W(III); wrestling M(III). Intramural sports: badminton, baseball/softball, basketball, bowling, cross-country running, football, golf, ice hockey, rugby, sailing, skiing (cross-country), skiing (downhill), swimming and diving, tennis, volleyball, wrestling.

Majors Accounting B; advertising B; anthropology B; art education B; art/fine arts B; biology/biological sciences B; broadcasting B; business administration/commerce/management B; chemistry B; commercial art B; communication B; computer science B; criminal justice B; early childhood education B; earth science B; economics B; education B; elementary education B; engineering sciences B; English B; finance/banking B; French B; geography B; geology B; German B; health education B; history B; human services B; journalism B; law enforcement/police sciences A; (pre) law sequence B; liberal arts/general studies A; library science B; marketing/retailing/merchandising B; mathematics B; medical technology B; (pre)medicine sequence B; microbiology B; music B; music education B; music therapy B; natural sciences B; nursing B; philosophy B; physical education B; physics B; physiology B; political science/government B; psychology B; public relations B; radio and television studies B; secondary education B; social science B; social work B; sociology B; Spanish B; special education B; speech pathology and audiology B; urban studies B; (pre) veterinary medicine sequence B. Majors with highest enrollment: computer science, psychology, journalism.

LD Program Information

Name of Program Project Success.

Availability of Services Began offering services in 1979. Services provided to freshmen, sophomores, juniors, seniors. Program currently serves 114 LD students: 46 freshmen, 36 sophomores, 22 juniors, 10 seniors.

Staff 1 full-time, 1 part-time staff members, including director, assistant director. Services provided by tutors.

Admissions LD applicants evaluated on the basis of high school transcript and grade point average, personal interview, psychoeducational report; standard or untimed ACT, family interview recommended. LD students may begin taking classes in summer only. Application should be submitted 2 to 3 years in advance of initial anticipated enrollment.

Orientation Required orientation held after classes begin.

Housing College housing (including coed) available. LD students housed randomly. LD freshmen and sophomores required to live on campus.

Diagnostic Testing Available in reading, spelling, handwriting, spoken language, written language, ability to use phonemic structure of English for encoding and decoding.

Tutoring Offered one-to-one and in small groups by professional teachers, peer tutors. Available in all subjects. LD students may receive tutoring in all courses each term.

Basic Skills Remediation Offered one-to-one and in small groups by regular teachers, peer teachers. Available in reading, math, spelling, handwriting, written language, learning strategies, work and study habits, social skills.

Academic Advisement Help with program planning provided by LD staff members, academic advisers. LD students may take up to 15 semester hours each semester; most take 12 to 13 semester hours; 12 semester hours required to maintain full-time status.

Special Courses Offered in reading, composition, language development, math, study skills. All offered for credit; all enter into overall grade point average.

Auxiliary Aids and Services Services include alternative exam arrangements, advocacy.

Counseling Services Individual counseling, small-group counseling, rap sessions, career counseling available.

Contact Dr. Robert T. Nash, Director, Project Success, University of Wisconsin–Oshkosh, Box 52, Nursing/Education Building, Oshkosh, WI 54901, 414-424-1033.

UNIVERSITY OF WISCONSIN–PLATTEVILLE

Platteville, Wisconsin

Year Program Began	*Not reported*
Special Fee	None
Special Orientation	
Diagnostic Testing	✓
Subject-Area Tutoring	✓
Basic Skills Remediation	✓
Special Courses	✓
Taped Textbooks	✓
Alternative Exam Arrangements	✓
Notetakers	✓
Staff	4 part-time
Number of Students Served	12

General Information State-supported comprehensive coed institution. Part of University of Wisconsin System. Founded 1866. Awards A (college transfer), B, M. Institutionally accredited by regional association; programs accredited by ABET (engineering and technology). Small-town setting; 380-acre campus. Total enrollment: 5,305. Faculty: 244 (236 full-time, 8 part-time); 54% have doctoral degrees; graduate assistants teach a few undergraduate courses. Calendar: semesters. Grading system: letters or numbers. Library holdings: 180,000 bound volumes, 1,600 periodical subscriptions, 2,400 records/tapes.

Undergraduate Profile Fall 1984: 5,105 undergraduates (1,063 freshmen) from 19 states and territories and 23 foreign countries; 10% part-time; 89% state residents; 7% transfers; 63% financial aid recipients; 45% women; 3% blacks; 1% Native Americans; 1% Hispanics; 12% Asian Americans; 1% foreign nationals; 5% of undergraduates over 25 years of age; 9 legally handicapped students.

Expenses (1985–86) State resident tuition: $1391 full-time, $58 per credit part-time. Nonresident tuition: $3963 full-time, $186 per credit part-time. Minnesota residents pay tuition at the rate they would pay if attending a comparable state-supported institution in Minnesota. Mandatory fees: $135. College room and board: $2330. College room only: $1240.

Financial Aid Fall 1984 full-time freshmen: 80% applied for aid, 75% of those were judged to have need, 100% of those were aided; the average aided freshman received an aid package worth $3394 (29% scholarships/grants, 71% self-help) meeting 94% of need. College-administered aid for all 1984–85 undergraduates: need-based scholarships (average $150); non-need scholarships (average $150); short-term loans (average $100); low-interest long-term loans; SEOG; College Work-Study; 950 part-time jobs. Supporting data: FFS, FAF, institutional form, AFSA/SAR acceptable. Priority application deadline: 3/1.

Athletics Member NCAA (Division III), NAIA. Intercollegiate sports: baseball/softball M(III), W(III); basketball M(III); cross-country running M(III); field hockey W(III); football M(III); golf M(III); gymnastics M(III), W(III); ice hockey M(c); soccer M(III); tennis M(III); track and field M(III), W(III); volleyball W(III); wrestling M(III). Intramural sports: basketball, bowling, football, martial arts, volleyball.

Majors Accounting B; agricultural business B; agricultural economics B; agricultural engineering B; agricultural technologies B; agronomy/soil and crop sciences B; animal sciences B; applied art B; art education B; biology/biological sciences B; botany/plant sciences B; broadcasting B; business administration/commerce/management B; chemistry B; civil engineering B; computer science B; construction management B; construction technologies B; criminal justice B; drafting and design B; early childhood education B; economics B; electrical and electronics technologies B; electrical engineering B; elementary education B; English B; environmental engineering technology B; farm and ranch management B; finance/banking B; French B; geography B; geology B; German B; graphic arts B; history B; industrial arts B; industrial design B; industrial engineering B; industrial engineering technology B; labor and industrial relations B; land use management and reclamation B; liberal arts/general studies A, B; marketing/retailing/merchandising B; mathematics B; mechanical engineering B; mining and mineral engineering B; music B; music education B; occupational safety and health B; petroleum/natural gas engineering B; philosophy B; photography B; physical education B; physics B; political science/government B; printing technologies B; psychology B; radio and television studies B; science B; science education B; secondary education B; social science B; sociology B; Spanish B; speech/rhetoric/public address/debate B; telecommunications B; (pre)veterinary medicine sequence B; vocational education B; zoology B.

LD Program Information

Name of Program Special Services.

Availability of Services Services provided to freshmen, sophomores, juniors, seniors. Program currently serves 12 LD students: 5 freshmen, 2 sophomores, 3 juniors, 2 seniors.

Staff 4 part-time staff members, including director. Services provided by remediation specialists, counselor.

Admissions LD applicants evaluated on the basis of high school transcript and grade point average, standard or untimed SAT or ACT, personal interview, autobiographical statement, letters of recommendation, psychoeducational report. LD students may begin taking classes in fall, spring, or summer. Application should be submitted 3 months in advance of initial anticipated enrollment.

Housing College housing (including coed) available. LD students housed randomly. LD freshmen and sophomores required to live on campus.

Diagnostic Testing Available in intelligence, reading, math, spelling, handwriting, spoken language, written language, motor abilities, perceptual skills, work and study habits, personality, social skills.

Tutoring Offered one-to-one and in small groups by professional teachers, peer tutors. Available in all subjects. LD students may receive tutoring in all courses each term.

Basic Skills Remediation Offered one-to-one and in small groups by regular teachers, teacher trainees. Available in reading, math, spelling, written language, learning strategies, perceptual skills, work and study habits, social skills.

Academic Advisement Help with program planning provided by LD staff members, academic advisers. LD students may take up to 18 credits each semester; most take 12 to 15 credits; 12 credits required to maintain full-time status.

Special Courses Offered in college survival skills, reading, vocabulary development, communication skills, composition, language development, math, personal psychology, study skills, career planning. None offered for credit; none enter into overall grade point average.

Auxiliary Aids and Services Aids include taped textbooks. Services include alternative exam arrangements, notetakers, advocacy.

Counseling Services Individual counseling, small-group counseling, rap sessions, career counseling available.

Contact Mr. Bernie Bernhardt, Director of Special Services, University of Wisconsin–Platteville, 449 Gardner Hall, Platteville, WI 53818, 608-342-1816.

UNIVERSITY OF WISCONSIN–SUPERIOR

Superior, Wisconsin

Year Program Began	1982	Special Courses	✓
Special Fee	None	Taped Textbooks	✓
Special Orientation	✓	Alternative Exam Arrangements	✓
Diagnostic Testing	✓	Notetakers	✓
Subject-Area Tutoring	✓	Staff	5 part-time
Basic Skills Remediation	✓	Number of Students Served	6

General Information State-supported comprehensive coed institution. Part of University of Wisconsin System. Founded 1893. Awards A (college transfer), B, M. Institutionally accredited by regional association; programs accredited by NASM (music). Small-town setting; 230-acre campus. Total enrollment: 2,096. Faculty: 144; 65% have doctoral degrees; graduate assistants teach no undergraduate courses. Calendar: quarters. Grading system: letters or numbers. Library holdings: 230,000 bound volumes, 6,100 titles on microform, 850 periodical subscriptions, 1,500 records/tapes.

Undergraduate Profile Fall 1984: 1,728 undergraduates (321 freshmen) from 19 states and territories and 15 foreign countries; 17% part-time; 73% state residents; 6% transfers; 59% financial aid recipients; 50% women; 1% blacks; 1% Native Americans; 3% foreign nationals; 29% of undergraduates over 25 years of age.

Expenses (1984–85) State resident tuition: $1165 full-time. Nonresident tuition: $3647 full-time. Part-time tuition and fees per quarter (1 to 11 credit hours) range from $33 to $329 for state residents, $99 to $1061 for nonresidents. Minnesota residents pay tuition at the rate they would pay if attending a comparable state-supported institution in Minnesota. College room and board: $2220. College room only: $975.

Financial Aid Fall 1984 full-time freshmen: 59% applied for aid, 83% of those were judged to have need, 100% of those were aided; the average aided freshman received an aid package worth $1836 (33% scholarships/grants, 67% self-help) meeting 95% of need. College-administered aid for all 1984–85 undergraduates: need-based scholarships; 194 non-need scholarships (average $464); short-term loans (average $100); low-interest long-term loans from external sources (average $700); SEOG; College Work-Study; 150 part-time jobs. Supporting data: FAF, IRS, institutional form required; state form required for some; FFS, AFSA/SAR acceptable. Priority application deadline: 5/1.

Athletics Member NCAA (Division III), NAIA. Intercollegiate sports: baseball/softball M(III), W(III); basketball M(III), W(III); cross-country running M(III), W(III); football M(III); golf M(III); gymnastics W(III); ice hockey M(III); track and field M(III), W(III); volleyball W(III); wrestling M(III). Intramural sports: badminton, baseball/softball, basketball, bowling, ice hockey, martial arts, racquetball, skiing (cross-country), skiing (downhill), soccer, swimming and diving.

Majors Accounting B; art education B; art/fine arts B; art history B; arts administration B; art therapy B; biology/biological sciences B; broadcasting B; business administration/commerce/management B; business education B; chemistry B; commercial art B; communication B; computer information systems B; computer science B; criminal justice B; (pre)dentistry sequence B; economics B; education B; elementary education B; (pre)engineering sequence A; English B; environmental sciences B; fish and game management B; history B; human resources B; international studies B; (pre)law sequence B; liberal arts/general studies A; marketing/retailing/merchandising B; mathematics B; medical laboratory technology B; (pre)medicine sequence B; music B; music education B; nursing B; photography B; physical education B; physics B; political science/government B; psychology B; radio and television studies B; science B; science education B; secondary education B; secretarial studies/office management B; social work B; sociology B; special education B; speech/rhetoric/public address/debate B; studio art B; theater arts/drama B; (pre)veterinary medicine sequence B; women's studies B. Majors with highest enrollment: accounting, elementary education, computer information systems.

LD Program Information

Name of Program Special Services.

Availability of Services Began offering services in 1982. Services provided to freshmen, sophomores, juniors, seniors. Program currently serves 6 LD students: 2 freshmen, 1 sophomore, 1 junior, 2 seniors.

Staff 5 part-time staff members, including director. Services provided by remediation specialist, tutors, counselor, diagnostic specialists, graduate assistants.

Admissions LD applicants evaluated on the basis of high school transcript and grade point average, standard SAT or ACT, personal interview, letters of recommendation, psychoeducational report. LD students may begin taking classes in fall, spring, or summer.

Orientation Optional orientation offered before registration or during registration.

Housing College housing (including coed) available. LD students housed randomly. LD freshmen and sophomores required to live on campus.

Diagnostic Testing Available in intelligence, reading, math, spelling, spoken language, written language, motor abilities, perceptual skills, personality.

Tutoring Offered one-to-one and in small groups by peer tutors, graduate assistants. Available in all subjects. LD students may receive tutoring in 3 courses per term (or more by special arrangement).

Basic Skills Remediation Offered one-to-one and in small groups by LD teachers. Available in reading, math, spelling, written language, learning strategies, perceptual skills, work and study habits, social skills.

Academic Advisement Help with program planning provided by LD staff members, academic advisers. Most LD students take up to 15 credit hours each quarter; 12 credit hours required to maintain full-time status.

Special Courses Offered in reading, language development, math, study skills. Some offered for credit; some enter into overall grade point average.

Auxiliary Aids and Services Aids include taped textbooks, tape recorders. Services include alternative exam arrangements, notetakers, advocacy.

Counseling Services Individual counseling, small-group counseling, career counseling available.

Contact Mr. T. Reilly O'Halloran, Director/Counselor, Special Services, University of Wisconsin–Superior, Erlanson 107, 1800 Grand Avenue, Superior, WI 54880, 715-394-8185.

UNIVERSITY OF WISCONSIN–WHITEWATER

Whitewater, Wisconsin

Year Program Began	1977	Special Courses	✓
Special Fee	None	Taped Textbooks	✓
Special Orientation	✓	Alternative Exam Arrangements	✓
Diagnostic Testing	✓	Notetakers	✓
Subject-Area Tutoring	✓	Staff	1 full-time, 5 part-time
Basic Skills Remediation	✓	Number of Students Served	39

General Information State-supported comprehensive coed institution. Part of University of Wisconsin System. Founded 1868. Awards A (college transfer), B, M. Institutionally accredited by regional association; programs accredited by AACSB (business), NASM (music), NCATE (teacher education). Small-town setting, with easy access to Milwaukee; 380-acre barrier-free campus. Total enrollment: 10,737. Faculty: 636 (554 full-time, 82 part-time); 62% have doctoral degrees; graduate assistants teach no undergraduate courses. Calendar: semesters. Grading system: letters or numbers. Library holdings: 302,000 bound volumes, 617,000 titles on microform, 1,884 periodical subscriptions, 22,000 records/tapes.

Undergraduate Profile Fall 1984: 9,441 undergraduates (2,197 freshmen) from 23 states and territories and 28 foreign countries; 10% part-time; 92% state residents; 6% transfers; 42% financial aid recipients; 52% women; 2% blacks; 1% Native Americans; 1% Hispanics; 1% Asian Americans; 1% foreign nationals; 21% of undergraduates over 25 years of age; 150 legally handicapped students.

Expenses (1984–85) State resident tuition: $1197 full-time, $49.85 per credit part-time. Nonresident tuition: $3679 full-time, $153.35 per credit part-time. Minnesota residents pay tuition at the rate they would pay if attending a comparable state-supported institution in Minnesota. College room and board: $1730. College room only: $924.

Financial Aid Fall 1984 full-time freshmen: the average aided freshman received an aid package meeting 100% of need. College-administered aid for all 1984–85 undergraduates: need-based scholarships (average $400); non-need scholarships (average $100); low-interest long-term loans; SEOG; College Work-Study; part-time jobs. Supporting data: FFS, AFSA/SAR required; FAF acceptable. Priority application deadline: 3/1.

Athletics Member NCAA (Division III). Intercollegiate sports: baseball/softball M(III), W(III); basketball M(III), W(III); cross-country running M(III); football M(III); golf M(III), W(III); gymnastics W(III); soccer M(III); swimming and diving M(III), W(III); tennis M(III), W(III); track and field M(III), W(III); volleyball W(III); wrestling M(III). Intramural sports: baseball/softball, basketball, bowling, cross-country running, football, gymnastics, ice hockey, skiing (cross-country), skiing (downhill), soccer, swimming and diving, tennis, track and field, volleyball, water polo.

Majors Accounting B; American studies B; art education B; art/fine arts A, B; art history B; biology/biological sciences B; business administration/commerce/management A, B; chemistry B; computer science B; early childhood education B; economics B; education A; elementary education B; English B; finance/banking B; French B; geography B; German B; history B; journalism B; (pre)law sequence B; liberal arts/general studies A, B; marketing/retailing/merchandising B; mathematics B; music B; music education B; physics B; political science/government B; psychology B; secondary education B; social work B; sociology B; Spanish B; special education B; speech/rhetoric/public address/debate B; speech therapy B; theater arts/drama B; (pre)veterinary medicine sequence B. Majors with highest enrollment: accounting, computer science, education.

LD Program Information

Name of Program Project ASSIST.

Availability of Services Began offering services in 1977. Services provided to freshmen, sophomores, juniors, seniors. Program currently serves 39 LD students: 14 freshmen, 18 sophomores, 3 juniors, 4 seniors.

Staff 1 full-time, 5 part-time staff members, including coordinator. Services provided by remediation specialists.

Admissions LD applicants evaluated on the basis of high school transcript, standard or untimed SAT or ACT, personal interview, letters of recommendation, psychoeducational report; individual testing by Project ASSIST staff required for some. LD students may begin taking classes in fall, spring, or summer. Application should be submitted 2 months in advance of initial anticipated enrollment.

Orientation Optional orientation offered before registration.

Housing College housing (including coed) available. LD students housed randomly. LD freshmen and sophomores required to live on campus.

Diagnostic Testing Available in intelligence, reading, math, spelling, handwriting, spoken language, written language, motor abilities, perceptual skills, work and study habits, personality, social skills, speech.

Tutoring Offered one-to-one and in small groups by professional teachers, peer tutors. Available in all subjects. LD students may receive tutoring in all courses each term.

Basic Skills Remediation Offered one-to-one and in small groups by LD teachers, teacher trainees. Available in reading, math, spelling, handwriting, spoken language, written language, learning strategies, motor abilities, perceptual skills, work and study habits, social skills, speech.

Academic Advisement Help with program planning provided by LD staff members, academic advisers. LD students may take up to 12 credits each semester; most take 10 to 12 credits.

Special Courses Offered in college survival skills, reading, vocabulary development, composition, math, study skills. None offered for credit; none enter into overall grade point average.

Auxiliary Aids and Services Aids include taped textbooks. Services include alternative exam arrangements, notetakers, advocacy.

Counseling Services Individual counseling, small-group counseling, rap sessions, career counseling available.

Contact Dr. Connie Dalke, Coordinator, Project ASSIST, University of Wisconsin–Whitewater, Roseman 2023, Whitewater, WI 53190, 414-472-4788.

UNIVERSITY OF WYOMING

Laramie, Wyoming

Year Program Began	1983	Special Courses	✓
Special Fee	None	Taped Textbooks	✓
Special Orientation		Alternative Exam Arrangements	✓
Diagnostic Testing	✓	Notetakers	✓
Subject-Area Tutoring	✓	Staff	6 part-time
Basic Skills Remediation	✓	Number of Students Served	32

General Information State-supported coed university. Founded 1886. Awards B, M, D. Institutionally accredited by regional association; programs accredited by AACSB (business), ABET (engineering and technology), NASM (music), NLN (nursing), ACPE (pharmacy), NCATE (teacher education). Small-town setting; 753-acre barrier-free campus. Total enrollment: 10,075. Faculty: 868 (823 full-time, 45 part-time); 85% have doctoral degrees; graduate assistants teach a few undergraduate courses. Calendar: semesters. Grading system: letters or numbers. Library holdings: 800,000 bound volumes, 1.4 million titles on microform, 9,723 periodical subscriptions, 6,114 records/tapes.

Undergraduate Profile Fall 1984: 8,264 undergraduates (1,482 freshmen) from 51 states and territories and 59 foreign countries; 15% part-time; 77% state residents; 24% transfers; 82% financial aid recipients; 44% women; 1% blacks; 1% Native Americans; 1% Hispanics; 1% Asian Americans; 3% foreign nationals; 34% of undergraduates over 25 years of age; 212 legally handicapped students.

Expenses (1985–86) State resident tuition: $721 full-time, $30 per semester hour part-time. Nonresident tuition: $2233 full-time, $93 per semester hour part-time. College room and board: $2500. College room only: $1037.

Financial Aid Fall 1984 full-time freshmen: 75% applied for aid, 47% of those were judged to have need, 92% of those were aided; the average aided freshman received an aid package worth $2371 (37% scholarships/grants, 63% self-help) meeting 94% of need. College-administered aid for all 1984–85 undergraduates: need-based scholarships (average $600); non-need scholarships (average $700); short-term loans (average $500); low-interest long-term loans from college funds (average $791), from external sources (average $1006); SEOG; College Work-Study; 1,765 part-time jobs. Supporting data: FAF, institutional form, AFSA/SAR required; IRS required for some; FFS acceptable. Priority application deadline: 3/1.

Athletics Member NCAA (Division I). Intercollegiate sports: baseball/softball M(I,s); basketball M(I,s), W(I,s); cross-country running M(I,s), W(I,s); equestrian sports M(s), W(s); football M(I-A,s); golf M(I,s), W(I,s); ice hockey M(c), W(c); lacrosse M(c); riflery M(I), W(I); rugby M(c), W(c); skiing (cross-country) M(I,s), W(I,s); skiing (downhill) M(I,s), W(I,s); soccer M(c), W(c); swimming and diving M(I,s), W(I,s); tennis M(c), W(c); track and field M(I,s), W(I,s); volleyball W(I,s); wrestling M(I,s). Intramural sports: archery, badminton, baseball/softball, basketball, bowling, cross-country running, equestrian sports, fencing, football, golf, gymnastics, ice hockey, lacrosse, martial arts, racquetball, riflery, rugby, skiing (cross-country), skiing (downhill), soccer, squash, swimming and diving, tennis, track and field, volleyball, water polo, weight lifting, wrestling.

Majors Accounting B; agricultural business B; agricultural economics B; agricultural education B; agricultural engineering B; agricultural sciences B; agronomy/soil and crop sciences B; American studies B; animal sciences B; anthropology B; architectural engineering B; art education B; art/fine arts B; astronomy B; astrophysics B; biochemistry B; bioengineering B; biology/biological sciences B; botany/plant sciences B; broadcasting B; business administration/commerce/management B; business education B; chemical engineering B; chemistry B; civil engineering B; communication B; computer engineering B; computer information systems B; computer science B; construction engineering B; criminal justice B; dance B; dental services B; (pre)dentistry sequence B; dietetics B; early childhood education B; earth science B; economics B; education B; educational administration B; electrical engineering B; elementary education B; English B; entomology B; family and consumer studies B; farm and ranch management B; fashion merchandising B; finance/banking B; fish and game management B; food sciences B; French B; geography B; geology B; geophysics B; German B; Greek B; health education B; history B; home economics B; home economics education B; humanities B; industrial administration B; industrial arts B; international studies B; journalism B; labor and industrial relations B; Latin B; law enforcement/police sciences B; (pre)law sequence B; liberal arts/general studies B; marketing/retailing/merchandising B; mathematics B; mechanical engineering B; medical technology B; (pre)medicine sequence B; microbiology B; mining and mineral engineering B; modern languages B; music B; music education B; natural sciences B; nursing B; nutrition B; paleontology B; parks management B; petroleum/natural gas engineering B; pharmacy/pharmaceutical sciences B; philosophy B; physical education B; physics B; physiology B; piano/organ B; political science/government B; psychology B; public administration B; range management B; reading education B; recreation and leisure services B; Romance languages B; Russian B; science education B; secondary education B; secretarial studies/office management B; social science B; social work B; sociology B; Spanish B; special education B; speech pathology and audiology B; speech therapy B; statistics B; telecommunications B; theater arts/drama B; (pre) veterinary medicine sequence B; vocational education B; voice B; wildlife management B; wind and percussion instruments B; zoology B. Majors with highest enrollment: accounting, geology, petroleum/natural gas engineering.

LD Program Information

Name of Program Handicapped Student Services.

Availability of Services Began offering services in 1983. Services provided to freshmen, sophomores, juniors, seniors. Program currently serves 32 LD students: 16 freshmen, 10 sophomores, 2 juniors, 4 seniors.

Staff 6 part-time staff members, including coordinator. Services provided by tutor, counselors.

Admissions LD applicants evaluated on the basis of high school transcript and grade point average, standard or untimed ACT, psychoeducational report. LD students may begin taking classes in fall, spring, or summer. Application should be submitted 4 to 6 months in advance of initial anticipated enrollment.

Housing College housing (including coed) available. LD students housed randomly. LD students not required to live on campus.

Diagnostic Testing Available in intelligence, reading, math, spelling, spoken language, written language, motor abilities, perceptual skills, personality, psychoneurology, speech.

Tutoring Offered one-to-one and in small groups by professional teachers, peer tutors. Available in all subjects. LD students may receive tutoring in all courses each term.

Basic Skills Remediation Offered one-to-one and in small groups by regular teachers, teacher trainees. Available in reading, math, handwriting, spoken language, written language, work and study habits, social skills, speech.

Academic Advisement Help with program planning provided by LD staff members, academic advisers. LD students may take up to 19 semester hours each semester; most take 14 semester hours; 12 semester hours required to maintain full-time status (except by special permission).

Special Courses Offered in college survival skills, reading, math, study skills, career planning. Most offered for credit; most enter into overall grade point average.

Auxiliary Aids and Services Aids include taped textbooks, tape recorders, word processors, Kurzweil reading machine, Phonic Ears, Talking Book Machine. Services include alternative exam arrangements, notetakers, advocacy.

Counseling Services Individual counseling, small-group counseling, career counseling available.

Contact Ms. Chris Primus, Coordinator, Handicapped Student Services, University of Wyoming, Box 3808, University Station, Laramie, WY 82071, 307-766-6189.

UTAH STATE UNIVERSITY

Logan, Utah

Year Program Began	1980	Special Courses	✓
Special Fee	Varies	Taped Textbooks	✓
Special Orientation		Alternative Exam Arrangements	✓
Diagnostic Testing	✓	Notetakers	✓
Subject-Area Tutoring	✓	Staff	2 part-time
Basic Skills Remediation		Number of Students Served	4

General Information State-supported coed university. Founded 1888. Awards B, M, D. Institutionally accredited by regional association; programs accredited by AACSB (business), ABET (engineering and technology), NLN (nursing), NCATE (teacher education); candidate for program accreditation by NASM (music). Small-town setting; 332-acre campus. Total enrollment: 11,544. Faculty: 504; graduate assistants teach a few undergraduate courses. Calendar: quarters. Grading system: letters or numbers. Library holdings: 981,225 bound volumes, 782,204 titles on microform, 6,787 periodical subscriptions, 17,669 records/tapes.

Undergraduate Profile Fall 1984: 9,460 undergraduates (1,964 freshmen) from 51 states and territories and 82 foreign countries; 22% part-time; 81% state residents; 9% transfers; 40% financial aid recipients; 43% women; 1% blacks; 1% Native Americans; 1% Hispanics; 1% Asian Americans; 8% foreign nationals; 51% of undergraduates over 25 years of age; 49 legally handicapped students.

Expenses (1985–86) State resident tuition: $1071 full-time. Nonresident tuition: $3051 full-time. Part-time tuition and fees per quarter (1 to 12 quarter hours) range from $69 to $306 for state residents, $183 to $849 for nonresidents. College room and board: $2180.

Financial Aid Fall 1984 full-time freshmen: 59% applied for aid, 100% of those were judged to have need, 83% of those were aided; the average aided freshman received an aid package worth $2926 (53% scholarships/grants, 47% self-help) meeting 80% of need. College-administered aid for all 1984–85 undergraduates: 2,500 need-based scholarships (average $400); 1,000 non-need scholarships (average $900); low-interest long-term loans; SEOG; College Work-Study; part-time jobs. Supporting data: FFS, institutional form, AFSA/SAR required; IRS required for some; FAF acceptable. Priority application deadline: 4/15.

Athletics Member NCAA (Division I). Intercollegiate sports: baseball/softball W(I,s); basketball M(I,s), W(I,s); cross-country running M(I,s), W(I,s); football M(I-A,s); golf M(I,s); gymnastics W(I,s); tennis M(I,s); track and field M(I,s), W(I,s); volleyball W(I,s); wrestling M(I,s). Intramural sports: baseball/softball, basketball, bowling, cross-country running, football, golf, gymnastics, lacrosse, martial arts, skiing (cross-country), skiing (downhill), soccer, swimming and diving, tennis, track and field, volleyball, wrestling.

Majors Accounting B; agricultural business B; agricultural economics B; agricultural education B; agricultural engineering B; agricultural sciences B; agronomy/soil and crop sciences B; American studies B; animal sciences B; art education B; art/fine arts B; bacteriology B; biochemistry B; biology/biological sciences B; botany/plant sciences B; business administration/commerce/management B; business education B; business machine technologies B; cell biology B; chemistry B; child care/child and family studies B; child psychology/child development B; city, community, and regional planning B; civil engineering B; communication B; computer science B; consumer services B; dairy sciences B; dance B; (pre)dentistry sequence B; early childhood education B; ecology/environmental studies B; economics B; education B; educational media B; electrical engineering B; elementary education B; engineering (general) B; engineering technology B; English B; entomology B; environmental biology B; environmental design B; environmental engineering B; environmental sciences B; family services B; finance/banking B; fish and game management B; food marketing B; food sciences B; forestry B; forest technology B; French B; geography B; geology B; German B; health education B; history B; home economics B; home economics education B; human development B; industrial engineering technology B; journalism B; labor and industrial relations B; landscape architecture/design B; (pre)law sequence B; liberal arts/general studies B; manufacturing engineering B; marketing/retailing/merchandising B; mathematics B; mechanical engineering B; medical assistant technologies B; medical laboratory technology B; medical technology B; (pre)medicine sequence B; meteorology B; military science B; molecular biology B; music B; music therapy B; Native American studies B; natural resource management B; nursing B; nutrition B; occupational safety and health B; parks management B; philosophy B; physical education B; physical sciences B; physics B; physiology B; political science/government B; psychology B; public affairs and policy studies B; public health B; range management B; recreation and leisure services B; secondary education B; secretarial studies/office management B; social science B; social work B; sociology B; Spanish B; special education B; speech pathology and audiology B; speech/rhetoric/public address/debate B; speech therapy B; statistics B; textiles and clothing B; theater arts/drama B; toxicology B; (pre)veterinary medicine sequence B; veterinary sciences B; vocational education B; water resources B; welding technology B; wildlife management B; zoology B. Majors with highest enrollment: business administration/commerce/management, elementary education, biology/biological sciences.

LD Program Information

Name of Program Disabled Student Center.

Availability of Services Began offering services in 1980. Services provided to freshmen, sophomores, juniors, seniors. Program currently serves 4 LD students: 1 freshman, 1 sophomore, 2 juniors.

Fees $3.35 to $3.50 per hour for tutoring.

Staff 2 part-time staff members, including assistant director, coordinator.

Admissions LD applicants evaluated on the basis of high school transcript, standard ACT. LD students may begin taking classes in fall, winter, spring, or summer.

Housing College housing available. LD students not required to live on campus.

Diagnostic Testing Available in reading, various other areas as appropriate.

Tutoring Offered one-to-one by peer tutors. Available in all subjects. LD students may receive tutoring in all courses each term (depending on need).

Academic Advisement Help with program planning provided by LD staff members, academic advisers. LD students may take up to 25 quarter hours each quarter; most take 10 to 15 quarter hours; 12 quarter hours required to maintain full-time status.

Special Courses Offered in college survival skills, reading, vocabulary development, communication skills, composition, math, typing, study skills, career planning. Some offered for credit; some enter into overall grade point average.

Auxiliary Aids and Services Aids include taped textbooks, tape recorders. Services include alternative exam arrangements, notetakers, advocacy, support group.

Counseling Services Individual counseling, career counseling available.

Contact Ms. Diane Baum, Assistant Director, Disabled Student Center, Utah State University, UMC 46, Logan, UT 84322, 801-750-1104.

VIRGINIA INTERMONT COLLEGE

Bristol, Virginia

Year Program Began	1978	Special Courses	✓
Special Fee	None	Taped Textbooks	✓
Special Orientation		Alternative Exam Arrangements	✓
Diagnostic Testing		Notetakers	
Subject-Area Tutoring	✓	Staff	6 part-time
Basic Skills Remediation	✓	Number of Students Served	19

General Information 4-year coed college, affiliated with Baptist Church. Founded 1884. Awards A (college transfer and terminal), B. Institutionally accredited by regional association. City setting; 16-acre campus. Total enrollment: 517. Faculty: 63 (45 full-time, 18 part-time); 30% have doctoral degrees. Calendar: semesters. Grading system: letters or numbers. Library holdings: 58,033 bound volumes, 407 periodical subscriptions.

Undergraduate Profile Fall 1984: 517 undergraduates (152 freshmen) from 35 states and territories and 18 foreign countries; 8% part-time; 45% state residents; 9% transfers; 67% financial aid recipients; 83% women; 6% blacks; 2% Hispanics; 8% foreign nationals; 2 legally handicapped students.

Expenses (1985–86) Comprehensive fee of $6700 includes full-time tuition ($4200) and college room and board ($2500). Part-time tuition per semester (1 to 11 semester hours) ranges from $100 to $1375.

Financial Aid Fall 1984 full-time freshmen: 87% applied for aid, 100% of those were judged to have need, 100% of those were aided; the average aided freshman received an aid package worth $1668 (53% scholarships/grants, 47% self-help) meeting 75% of need. College-administered aid for all 1984–85 undergraduates: need-based scholarships; 20 non-need scholarships (average $625); short-term loans (average $500); low-interest long-term loans from college funds (average $1200), from external sources (average $1000); SEOG; College Work-Study; 50 part-time jobs. Supporting data: IRS, institutional form required; FAF, state form, AFSA/SAR acceptable. Priority application deadline: 8/15.

Athletics Intercollegiate sports: equestrian sports M, W; tennis W. Intramural sports: archery, badminton, basketball, equestrian sports, swimming and diving, tennis, volleyball.

Majors Art education B; art/fine arts B; biology/biological sciences B; business administration/commerce/management B; communication B; computer management B; creative writing B; dance B; early childhood education B; education B; elementary education B; English B; equestrian studies B; fashion merchandising B; graphic arts A; journalism B; (pre)law sequence B; liberal arts/general studies B; medical laboratory technology A; medical technology B; music B; music education B; paralegal studies B; philosophy B; photography B; psychology B; religious studies B; sacred music B; science B; secondary education B; secretarial studies/office management B; social science B; social work B; sociology B; (pre)veterinary medicine sequence B. Majors with highest enrollment: equestrian studies, business administration/commerce/management, fashion merchandising.

LD Program Information

Name of Program Special Services.

Availability of Services Began offering services in 1978. Services provided to freshmen, sophomores, juniors, seniors. Program currently serves 19 LD students: 7 freshmen, 5 sophomores, 4 juniors, 3 seniors.

Staff 6 part-time staff members, including director, assistant director. Services provided by tutors, counselors, basic skills teachers.

Admissions LD applicants evaluated on the basis of high school transcript and grade point average, standard or untimed SAT or ACT, personal interview, autobiographical statement, letters of recommendation, psychoeducational report. LD students may begin taking classes in fall or spring.

Housing College housing available. LD students housed with other LD students and non-LD students. LD freshmen, sophomores, juniors, and seniors required to live on campus except if living with relatives.

Tutoring Offered one-to-one by peer tutors. Available in all subjects. LD students may receive tutoring in all courses each term.

Basic Skills Remediation Offered one-to-one and in small groups by regular teachers. Available in reading, math, spelling, written language, learning strategies, work and study habits.

Academic Advisement Help with program planning provided by LD staff members, academic advisers. LD students may take up to 16 semester hours each semester; most take 12 to 16 semester hours (12 in first semester); 12 semester hours required to maintain full-time status.

Special Courses Offered in reading, composition, math, study skills. Some offered for credit; some enter into overall grade point average.

Auxiliary Aids and Services Aids include taped textbooks, tape recorders, calculators. Services include alternative exam arrangements.

Counseling Services Individual counseling, career counseling available.

Contact Ms. Donna S. Cowan, Director/Counselor, Department of Special Services, Virginia Intermont College, Moore Street, Bristol, VA 24201, 703-669-6101.

VIRGINIA POLYTECHNIC INSTITUTE AND STATE UNIVERSITY

Blacksburg, Virginia

Year Program Began	1979	Special Courses	✓
Special Fee	None	Taped Textbooks	✓
Special Orientation		Alternative Exam Arrangements	✓
Diagnostic Testing	✓	Notetakers	✓
Subject-Area Tutoring	✓	Staff	1 part-time
Basic Skills Remediation	✓	Number of Students Served	12

General Information State-related coed university. Founded 1872. Awards B, M, D. Institutionally accredited by regional association; programs accredited by NAAB (architecture), AACSB (business), ABET (engineering and technology), NCATE (teacher education). Small-town setting; 2,600-acre campus. Total enrollment: 21,455. Faculty: 1,942 (1,836 full-time, 106 part-time); 76% have doctoral degrees; graduate assistants teach a few undergraduate courses. Calendar: quarters. Grading system: letters or numbers. Library holdings: 1.4 million bound volumes, 3.6 million titles on microform, 23,000 periodical subscriptions, 6,500 records/tapes.

Undergraduate Profile Fall 1984: 18,091 undergraduates (4,127 freshmen) from 52 states and territories and 33 foreign countries; 3% part-time; 75% state residents; 5% transfers; 55% financial aid recipients; 42% women; 4% blacks; 1% Native Americans; 1% Hispanics; 1% Asian Americans; 1% foreign nationals; 4% of undergraduates over 25 years of age; 52 legally handicapped students.

Expenses (1985–86) State resident tuition: $1875 full-time. Nonresident tuition: $3885 full-time. Part-time tuition per quarter (1 to 9 credit hours) ranges from $198.50 to $584.50 for state residents, $399.50 to $1187.50 for nonresidents. Mandatory fees: $144. College room and board: $1758.

Financial Aid Fall 1984 full-time freshmen: 71% applied for aid, 59% of those were judged to have need, 93% of those were aided; the average aided freshman received an aid package worth $1675 (66% scholarships/grants, 34% self-help) meeting 70% of need. College-administered aid for all 1984–85 undergraduates: 3,096 need-based scholarships (average $977); 868 non-need scholarships (average $878); short-term loans (average $300); low-interest long-term loans from college funds (average $388), from external sources (average $1879); SEOG; College Work-Study; 3,735 part-time jobs. Supporting data: FAF, IRS required; AFSA/SAR acceptable. Priority application deadline: 3/15.

Athletics Member NCAA (Division I). Intercollegiate sports: baseball/softball M(I,s); basketball M(I,s), W(I,s); cross-country running M(I,s); football M(I-A,s); golf M(I,s); soccer M(I,s); swimming and diving M(I,s), W(I,s); tennis M(I,s), W(I,s); track and field M(I,s), W(I,s); volleyball W(I,s); wrestling M(I,s). Intramural sports: archery, badminton, baseball/softball, basketball, bowling, cross-country running, fencing, field hockey, football, golf, gymnastics, lacrosse, martial arts, racquetball, rugby, soccer, squash, swimming and diving, tennis, track and field, volleyball, water polo, weight lifting, wrestling.

Majors Accounting B; aerospace engineering B; agricultural economics B; agricultural education B; agricultural engineering B; agronomy/soil and crop sciences B; animal sciences B; architecture B; art/fine arts B; biochemistry B; biology/biological sciences B; business administration/commerce/management B; business economics B; business education B; chemical engineering B; chemistry B; child care/child and family studies B; civil engineering B; communication B; community services B; computer science B; construction management B; dairy sciences B; (pre) dentistry sequence B; dietetics B; early childhood education B; economics B; education B; electrical engineering B; elementary education B; engineering sciences B; English B; family and consumer studies B; fashion design and technology B; fashion merchandising B; finance/banking B; food sciences B; forestry B; French B; geography B; geology B; geophysics B; German B; gerontology B; health education B; history B; home economics B; home economics education B; horticulture B; hotel and restaurant management B; human services B; industrial arts B; industrial engineering B; interior design B; landscape architecture/design B; (pre)law sequence B; liberal arts/general studies B; marketing/retailing/merchandising B; materials engineering B; mathematics B; mechanical engineering B; (pre)medicine sequence B; mining and mineral engineering B; music B; music education B; nutrition B; ocean engineering B; pest control technology B; philosophy B; physical education B; physics B; political science/government B; poultry sciences B; psychology B; public administration B; science education B; secondary education B; sociology B; Spanish B; statistics B; textiles and clothing B; theater arts/drama B; urban studies B; (pre) veterinary medicine sequence B; vocational education B; wildlife management B. Majors with highest enrollment: electrical engineering, biology/biological sciences, accounting.

LD Program Information

Name of Program Not specified.

Availability of Services Began offering services in 1979. Services provided to freshmen, sophomores, juniors, seniors. Program currently serves 12 LD students: 3 freshmen, 3 sophomores, 3 juniors, 3 seniors.

Staff 1 part-time staff member (handicap concerns officer). Services provided by tutors.

Admissions LD applicants evaluated on the basis of high school transcript and grade point average, standard or untimed SAT, letters of recommendation, 2 Achievement Tests, English Composition Test. LD students may begin taking classes in fall, winter, spring, or summer. Application should be submitted 7 months in advance of initial anticipated enrollment.

Housing College housing (including coed) available. LD students housed randomly. LD freshmen required to live on campus.

Diagnostic Testing Available in reading, spelling.

Tutoring Offered one-to-one and in small groups by peer tutors. Available in some subjects. LD students may receive tutoring in all courses each term.

Basic Skills Remediation Offered one-to-one and in small groups by regular teachers, peer teachers. Available in reading, math, spelling, written language.

Academic Advisement Help with program planning provided by academic advisers. Most LD students take 12 to 15 credit hours each quarter; 12 quarter hours required to maintain full-time status.

Special Courses Offered in reading, composition, study skills. None offered for credit; none enter into overall grade point average.

Auxiliary Aids and Services Aids include taped textbooks, tape recorders, word processors. Services include alternative exam arrangements, notetakers.

Counseling Services Individual counseling, small-group counseling, career counseling available.

Contact Mr. Wayne E. Speer, Handicap Concerns Officer, Virginia Polytechnic Institute and State University, Smith House, Blacksburg, VA 24061, 703-961-7500.

WASHBURN UNIVERSITY OF TOPEKA

Topeka, Kansas

Year Program Began	1978	Special Courses	✓
Special Fee	None	Taped Textbooks	✓
Special Orientation		Alternative Exam Arrangements	✓
Diagnostic Testing		Notetakers	✓
Subject-Area Tutoring	✓	Staff	1 part-time
Basic Skills Remediation	✓	Number of Students Served	3

General Information City-supported comprehensive coed institution. Founded 1865. Awards A (college transfer and terminal), B, M, D. Institutionally accredited by regional association; programs accredited by NASM (music), NLN (nursing), NCATE (teacher education). City setting, with easy access to Kansas City; 160-acre barrier-free campus. Total enrollment: 7,088. Faculty: 258 (183 full-time, 75 part-time); 65% have doctoral degrees; graduate assistants teach no undergraduate courses. Calendar: semesters. Grading system: letters or numbers. Library holdings: 232,000 bound volumes, 250,045 titles on microform, 1,688 periodical subscriptions.

Undergraduate Profile Fall 1984: 6,211 undergraduates (1,105 freshmen) from 35 states and territories and 17 foreign countries; 51% part-time; 97% state residents; 31% transfers; 45% financial aid recipients; 52% women; 6% blacks; 1% Native Americans; 3% Hispanics; 1% foreign nationals; 42% of undergraduates over 25 years of age.

Expenses (1985–86) State resident tuition: $1590 full-time, $53 per credit hour part-time. Nonresident tuition: $2340 full-time, $78 per credit hour part-time. Mandatory fees: $24. College room and board: $2430.

Financial Aid Fall 1984 full-time freshmen: 89% applied for aid, 62% of those were judged to have need, 98% of those were aided; the average aided freshman received an aid package worth $2211 (41% scholarships/grants, 59% self-help) meeting 90% of need. College-administered aid for all 1984–85 undergraduates: 1,468 need-based scholarships (average $530); 1,725 non-need scholarships (average $600); short-term loans (average $100); low-interest long-term loans from external sources (average $2526); SEOG; College Work-Study; 350 part-time jobs. Supporting data: FFS, FAF, institutional form, AFSA/SAR acceptable. Priority application deadline: 3/15.

Athletics Member NAIA. Intercollegiate sports: baseball/softball M(s), W(s); basketball M(s), W(s); crew M(c), W(c); football M(s); golf M(s); tennis M(s), W(s); volleyball W(s); wrestling M(c). Intramural sports: baseball/softball, basketball, bowling, crew, football, golf, racquetball, tennis, volleyball, wrestling.

Majors Accounting B; anthropology B; art/fine arts B; aviation technology A; biology/biological sciences B; business administration/commerce/management B; chemistry B; child care/child and family studies A; communication B; computer information systems A, B; corrections A, B; court reporting A; criminal justice A, B; economics B; education B; electrical and electronics technologies A; elementary education B; (pre)engineering sequence A; English B; finance/banking A, B; food services management A; French B; German B; health education B; history B; home economics B; hospitality services A; journalism B; law enforcement/police sciences A, B; (pre)law sequence B; legal secretarial studies A; liberal arts/general studies A, B; marketing/retailing/merchandising B; mathematics B; medical records services A; medical secretarial studies A; medical technology B; (pre)medicine sequence B; music B; nursing B; occupational safety and health A; paralegal studies A; philosophy B; physical education B; physical therapy A; physics B; political science/government B; postal management A; psychology B; radio and television studies B; radiological sciences A; radiological technology A; real estate B; respiratory therapy B; science B; secretarial studies/office management A; social work B; sociology B; Spanish B; speech/rhetoric/public address/debate B; studio art B; theater arts/drama B. Majors with highest enrollment: business administration/commerce/management, computer information systems.

LD Program Information

Name of Program Handicapped Student Services.

Availability of Services Began offering services in 1978. Services provided to freshmen, sophomores, juniors, seniors. Program currently serves 3 LD students: 2 freshmen, 1 sophomore.

Staff 1 part-time staff member (assistant dean of students).

Admissions LD applicants evaluated on the basis of high school transcript and grade point average, standard or untimed ACT, autobiographical statement, letters of recommendation, psychoeducational report. LD students may begin taking classes in fall, spring, or summer. Application should be submitted 3 months in advance of initial anticipated enrollment.

Housing College housing (including coed) available. LD students housed randomly. LD students not required to live on campus.

Tutoring Offered one-to-one and in small groups by professional teachers, peer tutors. Available in most subjects. LD students may receive tutoring in all courses each term (depending on availability of tutors).

Basic Skills Remediation Offered in small groups by counselors. Available in learning strategies, work and study habits.

Academic Advisement Help with program planning provided by LD staff member. LD students may take up to 16 credit hours each semester; most take 12 credit hours; 12 credit hours required to maintain full-time status.

Special Courses Offered in college survival skills, study skills, career planning. Some offered for credit; some enter into overall grade point average.

Auxiliary Aids and Services Aids include taped textbooks, tape recorders. Services include alternative exam arrangements, notetakers, advocacy, readers.

Counseling Services Individual counseling, small-group counseling, career counseling available.

Contact Mr. Greg Moore, Assistant Dean of Students, Washburn University of Topeka, Morgan Hall 123, Topeka, KS 66621, 913-295-6625.

WASHINGTON STATE UNIVERSITY

Pullman, Washington

Year Program Began	1980	Special Courses	✓
Special Fee	None	Taped Textbooks	✓
Special Orientation		Alternative Exam Arrangements	✓
Diagnostic Testing	✓	Notetakers	
Subject-Area Tutoring	✓	Staff	4 part-time
Basic Skills Remediation	✓	Number of Students Served	60

General Information State-supported coed university. Founded 1892. Awards B, M, D. Institutionally accredited by regional association; programs accredited by NAAB (architecture), AACSB (business), ABET (engineering and technology), NASM (music), NLN (nursing), ACPE (pharmacy), NCATE (teacher education); candidate for program accreditation by FIDER (interior design). Rural setting; 620-acre barrier-free campus. Total enrollment: 16,459. Faculty: 1,017 (941 full-time, 76 part-time); 80% have doctoral degrees; graduate assistants teach a few undergraduate courses. Calendar: semesters. Grading system: letters or numbers. Library holdings: 1.1 million bound volumes, 20,000 periodical subscriptions.

Undergraduate Profile Fall 1984: 14,579 undergraduates (2,691 freshmen) from 55 states and territories and 53 foreign countries; 3% part-time; 85% state residents; 40% transfers; 45% financial aid recipients; 42% women; 3% blacks; 1% Native Americans; 1% Hispanics; 3% Asian Americans; 6% foreign nationals; 3% of undergraduates over 25 years of age; 100 legally handicapped students.

Expenses (1985–86) State resident tuition: $1606 full-time, $80 per credit part-time. Nonresident tuition: $4462 full-time, $223 per credit part-time. College room and board: $2400.

Financial Aid Fall 1984 full-time freshmen: 47% applied for aid, 75% of those were judged to have need, 100% of those were aided; the average aided freshman received an aid package worth $3400 (29% scholarships/grants, 71% self-help) meeting 100% of need. College-administered aid for all 1984–85 undergraduates: need-based scholarships (average $500); non-need scholarships; short-term loans (average $250); low-interest long-term loans; SEOG; part-time jobs. Supporting data: FAF, IRS, AFSA/SAR required. Priority application deadline: 4/1.

Athletics Member NCAA (Division I). Intercollegiate sports: baseball/softball M(I,s); basketball M(I,s), W(I,s); crew M(c), W(c); cross-country running M(I,s); football M(I-A,s); golf M(I,s), W(I); gymnastics W(I,s); skiing (cross-country) W(I,s); skiing (downhill) W(I,s); soccer M(c); swimming and diving W(I,s); tennis M(I,s), W(I,s); track and field M(I,s), W(I,s); volleyball W(I,s); wrestling M(I,s). Intramural sports: badminton, baseball/softball, basketball, bowling, cross-country running, equestrian sports, fencing, field hockey, football, golf, martial arts, racquetball, riflery, rugby, skiing (cross-country), skiing (downhill), soccer, swimming and diving, tennis, track and field, volleyball, water polo, wrestling.

Majors Accounting B; advertising B; agricultural economics B; agricultural education B; agricultural engineering B; agronomy/soil and crop sciences B; animal sciences B; anthropology B; architecture B; art education B; art/fine arts B; Asian/Oriental studies B; bacteriology B; biochemistry B; biology/biological sciences B; biophysics B; black/Afro-American studies B; botany/plant sciences B; broadcasting B; business administration/commerce/management B; chemical engineering B; chemistry B; child care/child and family studies B; civil engineering B; communication B; computer engineering B; computer science B; construction management B; criminal justice B; dietetics B; early childhood education B; economics B; education B; electrical engineering B; engineering (general) B; English B; environmental sciences B; fashion merchandising B; finance/banking B; food sciences B; forestry B; French B; geology B; German B; health education B; history B; home economics B; home economics education B; horticulture B; hotel and restaurant management B; industrial arts B; insurance B; interior design B; journalism B; landscape architecture/design B; (pre)law sequence B; liberal arts/general studies B; marketing/retailing/merchandising B; materials sciences B; mathematics B; mechanical engineering B; medical technology B; (pre)medicine sequence B; metallurgy B; Mexican-American/Chicano studies B; microbiology B; music B; music education B; Native American studies B; nursing B; nutrition B; ornamental horticulture B; painting/drawing B; parks management B; pharmacy/pharmaceutical sciences B; philosophy B; photography B; physical education B; physical sciences B; physics B; political science/government B; poultry sciences B; psychology B; public administration B; public health B; public relations B; radio and television studies B; range management B; real estate B; recreation and leisure services B; Russian B; secondary education B; secretarial studies/office management B; social work B; sociology B; Spanish B; special education B; speech/rhetoric/public address/debate B; speech therapy B; sports medicine B; textiles and clothing B; theater arts/drama B; (pre)veterinary medicine sequence B; veterinary sciences B; vocational education B; wildlife biology B; women's studies B; zoology B. Majors with highest enrollment: business administration/commerce/management, engineering (general).

LD Program Information

Name of Program Disabled Student Services.

Availability of Services Began offering services in 1980. Services provided to freshmen, sophomores, juniors, seniors. Program currently serves 60 LD students.

Staff 4 part-time staff members, including coordinator. Services provided by program assistants.

Admissions LD applicants evaluated on the basis of high school transcript and grade point average, psychoeducational report, WPCT. LD students may begin taking classes in fall, spring, or summer. Application should be submitted 2 months in advance of initial anticipated enrollment.

Housing College housing (including coed) available. LD students housed with other LD students and non-LD students. LD freshmen required to live on campus.

Diagnostic Testing Available in intelligence, reading, math, spelling, spoken language, written language, perceptual skills, work and study habits, personality, psychoneurology, speech.

Tutoring Offered one-to-one and in small groups by professional teachers, peer tutors. Available in some subjects. LD students may receive tutoring in 5 courses per term.

Basic Skills Remediation Offered one-to-one and in small groups by regular teachers. Available in reading, math, spelling, spoken language, written language, learning strategies, work and study habits, speech.

Academic Advisement Help with program planning provided by LD staff member, academic advisers. LD students may take up to 16 credits each semester; most take 12 credits; 10 credits required to maintain full-time status.

Special Courses Offered in reading, composition, language development, study skills, career planning. Some offered for credit; some enter into overall grade point average.

Auxiliary Aids and Services Aids include taped textbooks, tape recorders, word processors. Services include alternative exam arrangements, advocacy.

Counseling Services Individual counseling, small-group counseling, career counseling available.

Contact Dr. Kathy Jane Garretson, Coordinator, Disabled Student Services, Washington State University, 461 Holland Library, Pullman, WA 99164, 509-335-1565.

WASHINGTON UNIVERSITY

St Louis, Missouri

Year Program Began	1979	Special Courses	✓
Special Fee	None	Taped Textbooks	
Special Orientation	✓	Alternative Exam Arrangements	✓
Diagnostic Testing		Notetakers	✓
Subject-Area Tutoring	✓	Staff	8 part-time
Basic Skills Remediation	✓	Number of Students Served	6

General Information Independent coed university. Founded 1853. Awards B, M, D. Institutionally accredited by regional association; programs accredited by NAAB (architecture), NASAD (art and design), AACSB (business), ABET (engineering and technology), NASM (music), NCATE (teacher education). Metropolitan setting; 169-acre campus. Total enrollment: 10,709. Faculty: 2,590 (1,340 full-time, 1,250 part-time); 95% have doctoral degrees; graduate assistants teach a few undergraduate courses. Calendar: semesters. Grading system: letters or numbers. Library holdings: 1.2 million bound volumes, 1.4 million titles on microform, 154,000 periodical subscriptions, 26,462 records/tapes.

Undergraduate Profile Fall 1984: 4,499 undergraduates (986 freshmen) from 50 states and territories and 100 foreign countries; 13% part-time; 23% state residents; 24% transfers; 66% financial aid recipients; 41% women; 5% blacks; 0% Native Americans; 1% Hispanics; 6% Asian Americans; 4% foreign nationals; 6 legally handicapped students.

Expenses (1985–86) Comprehensive fee of $13,021 includes full-time tuition ($9200), mandatory fees ($40), and college room and board ($3781). College room only: $2104. Part-time tuition: $110 per semester hour. Tuition prepayment plan available.

Financial Aid Fall 1984 full-time freshmen: 65% applied for aid, 91% of those were judged to have need, 100% of those were aided; the average aided freshman received an aid package worth $8883 (67% scholarships/grants, 33% self-help) meeting 100% of need. College-administered aid for all 1984–85 undergraduates: 2,359 need-based scholarships (average $4985); 238 non-need scholarships (average $3572); short-term loans (average $250); low-interest long-term loans from college funds (average $1200), from external sources (average $2200); SEOG; College Work-Study; 380 part-time jobs. Supporting data: FAF required; institutional form acceptable. Priority application deadline: 2/1.

Athletics Member NCAA (Division III). Intercollegiate sports: baseball/softball M(III); basketball M(III), W(III); cross-country running M(III), W(III); football M(III); golf M(III); soccer M(III); swimming and diving M(III), W(III); tennis M(III), W(III); track and field M(III), W(III); volleyball W(III); wrestling M(III). Intramural sports: badminton, baseball/softball, basketball, bowling, cross-country running, football, golf, racquetball, soccer, swimming and diving, tennis, track and field, volleyball, wrestling.

Majors Accounting B; anthropology B; applied art B; applied mathematics B; archaeology B; architectural technologies B; architecture B; art/fine arts B; art history B; Asian/Oriental studies B; biology/biological sciences B; black/Afro-American studies B; botany/plant sciences B; business administration/commerce/management B; ceramic art and design B; chemical engineering B; chemistry B; Chinese B; civil engineering B; civil engineering technology B; classics B; comparative literature B; computer engineering B; computer science B; computer technologies B; dance B; data processing B; early childhood education B; earth science B; economics B; education B; electrical engineering B; elementary education B; engineering (general) B; engineering and applied sciences B; engineering physics B; engineering sciences B; engineering technology B; English B; fashion design and technology B; finance/banking B; French B; geodetic sciences B; geology B; German B; Germanic languages and literature B; graphic arts B; Greek B; Hebrew B; Hispanic studies B; history B; human services B; interdisciplinary studies B; international economics B; Japanese B; jewelry and metalsmithing B; Judaic studies B; Latin B; Latin American studies B; (pre)law sequence B; liberal arts/general studies B; linguistics B; literature B; marketing/retailing/merchandising B; mathematics B; mechanical engineering B; (pre)medicine sequence B; modern languages B; music B; occupational therapy B; painting/drawing B; paleontology B; philosophy B; photography B; physical sciences B; physical therapy B; physics B; planetary and space sciences B; political science/government B; psychology B; public administration B; religious studies B; Romance languages B; Russian B; Scandinavian languages/studies B; science B; science education B; sculpture B; secondary education B; social science B; sociology B; Spanish B; speech pathology and audiology B; studio art B; systems engineering B; systems science B; technology and public affairs B; theater arts/drama B; urban studies B; (pre)veterinary medicine sequence B; women's studies B. Majors with highest enrollment: engineering (general), (pre)medicine sequence, business administration/commerce/management.

LD Program Information

Name of Program Student Educational Service.

Availability of Services Began offering services in 1979. Services provided to freshmen, sophomores, juniors, seniors. Program currently serves 6 LD students: 2 freshmen, 3 sophomores, 1 senior.

Staff 8 part-time staff members, including director, assistant director. Services provided by remediation specialists, counselors.

Admissions LD applicants evaluated on the basis of high school transcript and grade point average, standard or untimed SAT or ACT, personal interview, autobiographical statement, letters of recommendation, psychoeducational report. LD students may begin taking classes in fall or spring. Application should be submitted 4 to 5 months in advance of initial anticipated enrollment.

Orientation Optional orientation offered before registration (individual orientation offered during registration).

Housing College housing (including coed) available. LD students housed randomly. LD freshmen required to live on campus.

Tutoring Offered one-to-one and in small groups by professional teachers, peer tutors. Available in all subjects. LD students may receive tutoring in all courses each term.

Basic Skills Remediation Offered one-to-one and in small groups by regular teachers. Available in reading, math, spelling, written language, learning strategies, work and study habits, social skills.

Academic Advisement Help with program planning provided by LD staff members, academic advisers. LD students may take up to 18 credit hours each semester; most take 15 credit hours; 12 credit hours required to maintain full-time status.

Special Courses Offered in college survival skills, reading, vocabulary development, communication skills, composition, language development, study skills, career planning. None offered for credit; none enter into overall grade point average.

Auxiliary Aids and Services Aids include tape recorders, typewriters, Kurzweil reading machine. Services include alternative exam arrangements, notetakers.

Counseling Services Individual counseling, small-group counseling, rap sessions, career counseling available.

Contact Mr. Leon Ashford, Director of Student Educational Service, Washington University, Campus Box 1134, St Louis, MO 63130, 314-889-5970.

WEBER STATE COLLEGE

Ogden, Utah

Year Program Began	*Not reported*	Special Courses	
Special Fee	None	Taped Textbooks	✓
Special Orientation		Alternative Exam Arrangements	
Diagnostic Testing		Notetakers	
Subject-Area Tutoring	✓	Staff	2 part-time
Basic Skills Remediation	✓	Number of Students Served	5

General Information State-supported comprehensive coed institution. Part of Utah System of Higher Education. Founded 1889. Awards A (college transfer and terminal), B, M. Institutionally accredited by regional association; programs accredited by ABET (engineering and technology), NASM (music), NLN (nursing), NCATE (teacher education). City setting, with easy access to Salt Lake City; 375-acre barrier-free campus. Total enrollment: 10,198. Faculty: 560 (432 full-time, 128 part-time); 62% have doctoral degrees; graduate assistants teach no undergraduate courses. Calendar: quarters. Grading system: letters or numbers. Library holdings: 239,894 bound volumes, 2,400 periodical subscriptions, 2,502 records/tapes.

Undergraduate Profile Fall 1984: 10,164 undergraduates (1,612 freshmen); 20% part-time; 93% state residents; 20% transfers; 29% financial aid recipients; 42% women; 3% blacks; 2% Native Americans; 5% Hispanics; 4% foreign nationals; 46% of undergraduates over 25 years of age; 314 legally handicapped students.

Expenses (1985–86) State resident tuition: $738 full-time. Nonresident tuition: $2361 full-time. Part-time tuition and fees per quarter (1 to 11 credits) range from $86 to $314 for state residents, $225 to $851 for nonresidents. Mandatory fees: $213. College room and board: $2280. College room only: $1125.

Financial Aid Fall 1984 full-time freshmen: 47% applied for aid, 52% of those were judged to have need, 100% of those were aided; the average aided freshman received an aid package worth $2632 (37% scholarships/grants, 63% self-help) meeting 75% of need. College-administered aid for all 1984–85 undergraduates: need-based scholarships; 850 non-need scholarships (average $678); short-term loans (average $226); SEOG; College Work-Study; part-time jobs. Supporting data: institutional form, AFSA/SAR required; FFS acceptable. Priority application deadline: 2/1.

Athletics Member NCAA (Division I). Intercollegiate sports: basketball M(I,s), W(I,s); cross-country running M(I,s), W(I,s); football M(I-AA,s); golf M(I,s), W(II,s); tennis M(I,s), W(I,s); track and field M(I,s), W(I,s); volleyball W(I,s); wrestling M(I,s). Intramural sports: archery, baseball/softball, basketball, bowling, cross-country running, football, golf, racquetball, skiing (cross-country), skiing (downhill), soccer, squash, swimming and diving, tennis, track and field, volleyball, weight lifting, wrestling.

Majors Accounting B; advertising B; anthropology A; applied art B; art education B; art/fine arts B; Asian/Oriental studies A; automotive engineering B; automotive technologies A; bilingual/bicultural education B; biology/biological sciences B; botany/plant sciences B; broadcasting B; business administration/commerce/management B; business education B; carpentry A; chemical engineering technology A; chemistry B; child care/child and family studies B; child psychology/child development A, B; commercial art B; communication B; computer information systems B; computer science A, B; computer technologies A; construction engineering B; construction technologies A; corrections B; cosmetology A; dance A; data processing A, B; dental services A; (pre)dentistry sequence B; drafting and design A, B; early childhood education B; earth science B; economics B; education B; electrical and electronics technologies A, B; electrical engineering technology B; elementary education B; emergency medical technology A; (pre)engineering sequence A; English B; family and consumer studies A, B; fashion merchandising A; finance/banking B; food services management A; food services technology A; French B; geography B; geology B; German B; gerontology B; graphic arts B; health education A; health science B; history B; humanities B; illustration B; industrial administration A; industrial and heavy equipment maintenance A; insurance A; interior design A; journalism A, B; law enforcement/police sciences A, B; (pre)law sequence B; liberal arts/general studies B; machine and tool technologies A; manufacturing engineering B; manufacturing technology A, B; marketing/retailing/merchandising A; mathematics B; mechanical engineering B; mechanical engineering technology B; medical laboratory technology A, B; medical technology A, B; (pre)medicine sequence B; microbiology B; military science B; music B; music education B; nursing A, B; painting/drawing B; photography B; physical education B; physical sciences B; physics B; piano/organ B; political science/government B; practical nursing A; psychology B; public relations B; radiological sciences A, B; radiological technology A; real estate B; recreation and leisure services A; respiratory therapy A; retail management A; science education B; sculpture B; secretarial studies/office management A, B; social science B; social work B; sociology B; Spanish B; speech/rhetoric/public address/debate B; theater arts/drama B; transportation technologies A; (pre)veterinary medicine sequence B; voice B; welding technology A; zoology B. Majors with highest enrollment: nursing, elementary education, accounting.

LD Program Information

Name of Program Services for the Physically Challenged.

Availability of Services Services provided to freshmen, sophomores, juniors, seniors. Program currently serves 5 LD students: 1 freshman, 3 sophomores, 1 junior.

Staff 2 part-time staff members, including director. Services provided by remediation specialists, tutors.

Admissions LD applicants evaluated on the basis of high school transcript, untimed ACT. LD students may begin taking classes in fall, winter, spring, or summer. Application should be submitted 1 month in advance of initial anticipated enrollment.

Housing College housing (including coed) available. LD students housed randomly. LD students not required to live on campus.

Tutoring Offered one-to-one by peer tutors. Available in all subjects. LD students may receive tutoring in all courses each term.

Basic Skills Remediation Offered one-to-one by regular teachers. Available in reading, math, spelling, work and study habits.

Academic Advisement Help with program planning provided by academic advisers. LD students may take up to 18 credits each quarter; 12 credits required to maintain full-time status.

Auxiliary Aids and Services Aids include taped textbooks, tape recorders, typewriters.

Counseling Services Individual counseling, career counseling available.

Contact Mr. La Mar "C" Kap, Director of Services for the Physically Challenged, Weber State College, 3750 Harrison Boulevard, Ogden, UT 84408, 801-626-6413.

WESTERN ILLINOIS UNIVERSITY

Macomb, Illinois

Year Program Began	1982	Special Courses	✓
Special Fee	Varies	Taped Textbooks	✓
Special Orientation		Alternative Exam Arrangements	✓
Diagnostic Testing		Notetakers	✓
Subject-Area Tutoring	✓	Staff	1 part-time
Basic Skills Remediation	✓	Number of Students Served	8

General Information State-supported comprehensive coed institution. Founded 1899. Awards B, M. Institutionally accredited by regional association; programs accredited by AACSB (business), NASM (music), NCATE (teacher education). Small-town setting; 1,056-acre barrier-free campus. Total enrollment: 11,751. Faculty: 693 (622 full-time, 71 part-time); 67% have doctoral degrees; graduate assistants teach no undergraduate courses. Calendar: semesters. Grading system: letters or numbers. Library holdings: 515,695 bound volumes, 30,000 titles on microform, 3,600 periodical subscriptions, 4,100 records/tapes.

Undergraduate Profile Fall 1984: 9,369 undergraduates (2,043 freshmen) from 25 states and territories and 25 foreign countries; 11% part-time; 96% state residents; 27% transfers; 90% financial aid recipients; 47% women; 10% blacks; 1% Hispanics; 1% Asian Americans; 4% foreign nationals; 1% of undergraduates over 25 years of age; 40 legally handicapped students.

Expenses (1985–86) State resident tuition ranges from $1020 to $1068 full-time, $84 to $86 per semester hour part-time, according to class level. Nonresident tuition ranges from $2665 to $3204 full-time, $169 to $175 per semester hour part-time, according to class level. Mandatory fees: $395. College room and board: $2170.

Financial Aid Fall 1984 full-time freshmen: 90% applied for aid, 90% of those were judged to have need, 100% of those were aided; the average aided freshman received an aid package worth $1719 (50% scholarships/grants, 50% self-help) meeting 80% of need. College-administered aid for all 1984–85 undergraduates: 250 need-based scholarships (average $516); 283 non-need scholarships (average $662); short-term loans (average $75); low-interest long-term loans from external sources; SEOG; College Work-Study; 2,000 part-time jobs. Supporting data: FFS, IRS required; AFSA/SAR acceptable. Priority application deadline: 3/15.

Athletics Member NCAA (Division I). Intercollegiate sports: baseball/softball M(I,s), W(I,s); basketball M(I,s), W(I,s); bowling W; crew W; cross-country running M(I), W(I,s); field hockey W(I,s); football M(I-AA,s); golf M(I,s); gymnastics W(I,s); soccer M(I,s); swimming and diving M(I,s), W(I,s); tennis M(I,s), W(I,s); track and field M(I,s), W(I,s); volleyball W(I,s); wrestling M(I,s). Intramural sports: archery, badminton, baseball/softball, basketball, bowling, cross-country running, fencing, field hockey, football, golf, gymnastics, lacrosse, martial arts, riflery, rugby, skiing (cross-country), soccer, swimming and diving, tennis, track and field, volleyball, water polo, wrestling.

Majors Accounting B; agricultural sciences B; anthropology B; art/fine arts B; bilingual/bicultural education B; biology/biological sciences B; business administration/commerce/management B; business education B; chemistry B; communication B; computer science B; earth science B; economics B; educational media B; elementary education B; English B; finance/banking B; French B; geography B; geology B; German B; health science B; history B; home economics B; human resources B; industrial arts B; industrial engineering technology B; information science B; law enforcement/police sciences B; marketing/retailing/merchandising B; mathematics B; medical technology B; music B; philosophy B; physical education B; physics B; political science/government B; psychology B; recreation and leisure services B; secretarial studies/office management B; sociology B; Spanish B; special education B; speech pathology and audiology B; speech/rhetoric/public address/debate B; theater arts/drama B; transportation technologies B. Majors with highest enrollment: business administration/commerce/management, accounting, law enforcement/police sciences.

LD Program Information

Name of Program Not specified.

Availability of Services Began offering services in 1982. Services provided to freshmen, sophomores, juniors, seniors. Program currently serves 8 LD students: 3 sophomores, 5 juniors.

Fees $4 to $7 per hour for tutoring and notetaking services.

Staff 1 part-time staff member (adviser).

Admissions LD applicants evaluated on the basis of high school transcript and grade point average, standard or untimed SAT or ACT. LD students may begin taking classes in fall, spring, or summer. Application should be submitted 6 to 8 months in advance of initial anticipated enrollment.

Housing College housing (including coed) available. LD students housed randomly. LD freshmen and sophomores required to live on campus.

Tutoring Offered one-to-one by peer tutors, graduate students. Available in some subjects. LD students may receive tutoring in all courses each term (depending on availability of tutors and level of courses).

Basic Skills Remediation Offered in small groups by regular teachers. Available in reading, math, written language, learning strategies, work and study habits.

Academic Advisement Help with program planning provided by LD staff member, academic advisers. LD students may take up to 15 semester hours each semester; most take 12 to 15 semester hours; 12 semester hours required to maintain full-time status.

Special Courses Offered in reading, vocabulary development, study skills, career planning. All offered for credit; all enter into overall grade point average.

Auxiliary Aids and Services Aids include taped textbooks, tape recorders. Services include alternative exam arrangements, notetakers, priority registration.

Counseling Services Individual counseling, career counseling available.

Contact Ms. Candace McLaughlin, Adviser to the Handicapped, Western Illinois University, University Advising Center, Memorial Hall, Macomb, IL 61455, 309-298-1846.

WESTERN WASHINGTON UNIVERSITY

Bellingham, Washington

Year Program Began	1981	Special Courses	✓
Special Fee	None	Taped Textbooks	✓
Special Orientation	✓	Alternative Exam Arrangements	✓
Diagnostic Testing	✓	Notetakers	
Subject-Area Tutoring	✓	Staff	1 part-time
Basic Skills Remediation		Number of Students Served	60

General Information State-supported comprehensive coed institution. Founded 1893. Awards B, M. Institutionally accredited by regional association; programs accredited by NLN (nursing), NCATE (teacher education); candidate for program accreditation by NASM (music). Small-town setting, with easy access to Vancouver (BC, Canada); 225-acre campus. Total enrollment: 9,144. Faculty: 527 (383 full-time, 144 part-time); 77% have doctoral degrees; graduate assistants teach a few undergraduate courses. Calendar: quarters. Grading system: letters or numbers. Library holdings: 456,119 bound volumes, 98,312 titles on microform, 4,255 periodical subscriptions, 9,650 records/tapes.

Undergraduate Profile Fall 1984: 8,314 undergraduates (1,408 freshmen) from 46 states and territories and 27 foreign countries; 4% part-time; 93% state residents; 45% transfers; 51% financial aid recipients; 51% women; 1% blacks; 1% Native Americans; 1% Hispanics; 2% Asian Americans; 2% foreign nationals; 21% of undergraduates over 25 years of age; 70 legally handicapped students.

Expenses (1985–86) State resident tuition: $1200 full-time, $40 per quarter hour part-time. Nonresident tuition: $4194 full-time, $140 per quarter hour part-time. Mandatory fees: $27. College room and board: $2339.

Financial Aid Fall 1984 full-time freshmen: 60% applied for aid, 75% of those were judged to have need, 89% of those were aided; the average aided freshman received an aid package worth $1892 (40% scholarships/grants, 60% self-help) meeting 100% of need. College-administered aid for all 1984–85 undergraduates: 2,102 need-based scholarships (average $500); 247 non-need scholarships (average $545); short-term loans (average $350); low-interest long-term loans from college funds (average $850), from external sources (average $2100); SEOG; College Work-Study. Supporting data: FAF, institutional form, AFSA/SAR required; IRS required for some; FFS acceptable. Priority application deadline: 4/1.

Athletics Member NAIA. Intercollegiate sports: basketball M, W; crew M, W; cross-country running M, W; football M; golf M; soccer M, W; track and field M, W; volleyball W. Intramural sports: badminton, baseball/softball, basketball, racquetball, swimming and diving, tennis, volleyball, wrestling.

Majors Accounting B; American studies B; anthropology B; applied mathematics B; art education B; art/fine arts B; art history B; astronomy B; biochemistry B; biology/biological sciences B; broadcasting B; business administration/commerce/management B; business education B; Canadian studies B; ceramic art and design B; chemistry B; child care/child and family studies B; city, community, and regional planning B; classics B; computer science B; creative writing B; dance B; (pre) dentistry sequence B; earth science B; ecology/environmental studies B; economics B; education B; elementary education B; engineering technology B; English B; environmental education B; environmental health sciences B; environmental sciences B; ethnic studies B; family services B; fashion design and technology B; fashion merchandising B; French B; geography B; geology B; geophysics B; German B; graphic arts B; health education B; history B; home economics B; home economics education B; human services B; industrial arts B; industrial design B; industrial engineering technology B; interdisciplinary studies B; interior design B; jazz B; jewelry and metalsmithing B; journalism B; (pre)law sequence B; liberal arts/general studies B; manufacturing technology B; marine biology B; mathematics B; (pre) medicine sequence B; music B; music education B; music history B; nursing B; nutrition B; painting/drawing B; parks management B; philosophy B; physical education B; physical sciences B; physics B; political science/government B; psychology B; public administration B; recreation and leisure services B; Russian B; science B; science education B; sculpture B; secondary education B; secretarial studies/office management B; social science B; sociology B; Spanish B; special education B; speech pathology and audiology B; speech/rhetoric/public address/debate B; studio art B; textile arts B; theater arts/drama B; urban studies B; (pre) veterinary medicine sequence B; water resources B. Majors with highest enrollment: business administration/commerce/management, accounting, elementary education.

LD Program Information

Name of Program Not specified.

Availability of Services Began offering services in 1981. Services provided to freshmen, sophomores, juniors, seniors. Program currently serves 60 LD students.

Staff 1 part-time staff member (coordinator). Services provided by tutors, counselors, diagnostic specialists.

Admissions LD applicants evaluated on the basis of high school transcript and grade point average; standard or untimed SAT or ACT, autobiographical statement, psychoeducational report, WPCT required for some. LD students may begin taking classes in fall, winter, spring, or summer. Application should be submitted 10 months in advance of initial anticipated enrollment.

Orientation Optional orientation offered before registration.

Housing College housing (including coed) available. LD students housed randomly. LD students not required to live on campus.

Diagnostic Testing Available in intelligence, reading, math, spelling, handwriting, spoken language, written language.

Tutoring Offered one-to-one. Available in all subjects. LD students may receive tutoring in all courses each term.

Academic Advisement Help with program planning provided by LD staff member, academic advisers. Most LD students take 12 quarter hours each quarter; 10 quarter hours required to maintain full-time status.

Special Courses Offered in math, typing, study skills, career planning. Some offered for credit; some enter into overall grade point average.

Auxiliary Aids and Services Aids include taped textbooks, tape recorders, word processors. Services include alternative exam arrangements, advocacy.

Counseling Services Individual counseling, small-group counseling, career counseling available.

Contact Ms. Dorothy Crow, Learning Disabilities Coordinator, Western Washington University, 262 Miller Hall, Bellingham, WA 98225, 206-676-3187.

WEST GEORGIA COLLEGE

Carrollton, Georgia

Year Program Began	1979	Special Courses	✓
Special Fee	None	Taped Textbooks	✓
Special Orientation		Alternative Exam Arrangements	✓
Diagnostic Testing	✓	Notetakers	✓
Subject-Area Tutoring	✓	Staff	5 part-time
Basic Skills Remediation	✓	Number of Students Served	10

General Information State-supported comprehensive coed institution. Part of University System of Georgia. Founded 1933. Awards A (terminal), B, M. Institutionally accredited by regional association; programs accredited by AACSB (business), NASM (music), NLN (nursing), NCATE (teacher education). Small-town setting, with easy access to Atlanta; 400-acre barrier-free campus. Total enrollment: 6,250. Faculty: 278 (244 full-time, 34 part-time); 67% have doctoral degrees; graduate assistants teach a few undergraduate courses. Calendar: quarters. Grading system: letters or numbers. Library holdings: 248,657 bound volumes, 675,834 titles on microform, 1,400 periodical subscriptions, 457 records/tapes.

Undergraduate Profile Fall 1984: 5,058 undergraduates (1,502 freshmen) from 30 states and territories and 17 foreign countries; 16% part-time; 97% state residents; 7% transfers; 40% financial aid recipients; 55% women; 13% blacks; 0% Native Americans; 1% Hispanics; 1% Asian Americans; 1% foreign nationals; 5% of undergraduates over 25 years of age; 13 legally handicapped students.

Expenses (1985–86) State resident tuition: $960 full-time. Nonresident tuition: $2880 full-time. Part-time tuition and fees per quarter (1-11 credits) range from $27 to $389 for state residents, $81 to $983 for nonresidents. Mandatory fees: $276. College room and board: $1581. College room only: $711.

Financial Aid Fall 1984 full-time freshmen: the average aided freshman received an aid package meeting 81% of need. College-administered aid for all 1984–85 undergraduates: 1,023 need-based scholarships (average $441); 310 non-need scholarships (average $575); short-term loans (average $200); low-interest long-term loans from external sources (average $2300); SEOG; College Work-Study; 389 part-time jobs. Supporting data: FAF, state form, institutional form required; IRS, AFSA/SAR required for some. Priority application deadline: 4/1.

Athletics Member NCAA (Division II), NAIA. Intercollegiate sports: baseball/softball M(II,s); basketball M(II,s), W(s); cross-country running M(II,s), W; football M(II,s); golf M(II,s); tennis M(II), W(s); track and field M(II,s), W; volleyball W(s). Intramural sports: baseball/softball, basketball, football, tennis, track and field, volleyball.

Majors Accounting B; anthropology B; art/fine arts B; biology/biological sciences B; business administration/commerce/management B; business economics B; business education B; chemistry B; communication B; computer science A, B; criminal justice A, B; early childhood education B; earth science B; economics B; education A; elementary education B; (pre)engineering sequence A; English B; finance/banking B; French B; geography B; geology B; history B; (pre)law sequence B; management information systems B; marketing/retailing/merchandising B; mathematics B; (pre) medicine sequence B; music B; music education B; nursing A; philosophy B; physical education B; physics B; political science/government B; psychology B; recreation and leisure services B; science education B; secondary education B; secretarial studies/office management A, B; social science B; sociology B; Spanish B; special education B; speech pathology and audiology B; speech/rhetoric/public address/debate B; theater arts/drama B; (pre)veterinary medicine sequence B. Majors with highest enrollment: business administration/commerce/management, accounting, computer science.

LD Program Information

Name of Program Learning Disabled Program.

Availability of Services Began offering services in 1979. Services provided to freshmen, sophomores, juniors, seniors. Program currently serves 10 LD students: 4 freshmen, 4 sophomores, 2 juniors.

Staff 5 part-time staff members, including coordinator, advisory committee members. Services provided by tutors, academic adviser, graduate assistant specializing in LD.

Admissions LD applicants evaluated on the basis of high school transcript and grade point average, untimed SAT, personal interview, letters of recommendation. LD students may begin taking classes in fall, winter, spring, or summer. Application should be submitted 1 month in advance of initial anticipated enrollment.

Housing College housing (including coed) available. LD students housed randomly. LD freshmen and sophomores required to live on campus.

Diagnostic Testing Available in intelligence, reading, math, spelling, written language, perceptual skills.

Tutoring Offered one-to-one and in small groups by peer tutors, graduate assistant. Available in all subjects. LD students may receive tutoring in 6 courses per term.

Basic Skills Remediation Offered one-to-one by teacher trainees, graduate assistant. Available in reading, math, spelling, spoken language, written language, learning strategies, perceptual skills, work and study habits, social skills, speech.

Academic Advisement Help with program planning provided by LD staff members, academic advisers. LD students may take up to 17 credits each quarter; most take 10 to 12 credits; 12 credits required to maintain full-time status.

Special Courses Offered in reading, vocabulary development, composition, language development, math, study skills. All offered for credit; none enter into overall grade point average.

Auxiliary Aids and Services Aids include taped textbooks, tape recorders. Services include alternative exam arrangements, notetakers, advocacy, LD peer group, provision for auditing courses before taking for credit.

Counseling Services Individual counseling, career counseling available.

Contact Dr. Ann Phillips, Coordinator of Special Services for Disabled Students, West Georgia College, Student Development Center, 136 Mandeville Hall, Carrollton, GA 30118, 404-834-1416.

WESTMINSTER COLLEGE

Fulton, Missouri

Year Program Began	1974	Special Courses	✓
Special Fee	$1500 per year	Taped Textbooks	✓
Special Orientation	✓	Alternative Exam Arrangements	✓
Diagnostic Testing	✓	Notetakers	✓
Subject-Area Tutoring	✓	Staff	3 part-time
Basic Skills Remediation	✓	Number of Students Served	33

General Information 4-year coed college, affiliated with Presbyterian Church. Founded 1851. Awards B. Institutionally accredited by regional association. Small-town setting; 252-acre campus. Total enrollment: 600. Faculty: 60 (57 full-time, 3 part-time); 65% have doctoral degrees. Calendar: 5-4-1. Grading system: letters or numbers. Library holdings: 150,000 bound volumes, 7,500 titles on microform, 11,700 periodical subscriptions, 11,000 records/tapes.

Undergraduate Profile Fall 1984: 600 undergraduates (165 freshmen) from 27 states and territories and 3 foreign countries; 0% part-time; 54% state residents; 12% transfers; 75% financial aid recipients; 25% women; 3% blacks; 1% Native Americans; 1% Hispanics; 1% Asian Americans; 1% foreign nationals; 1% of undergraduates over 25 years of age; 1 legally handicapped student.

Expenses (1985–86) Comprehensive fee of $7800 includes full-time tuition ($5200), mandatory fees ($100), and college room and board ($2500). College room only: $900.

Financial Aid Fall 1984 full-time freshmen: 76% applied for aid, 65% of those were judged to have need, 100% of those were aided; the average aided freshman received an aid package worth $5526 (66% scholarships/grants, 34% self-help) meeting 98% of need. College-administered aid for all 1984–85 undergraduates: need-based scholarships (average $963); non-need scholarships (average $1500); SEOG; College Work-Study; 200 part-time jobs. Supporting data: IRS, institutional form, AFSA/SAR required; FFS, FAF acceptable. Application deadline: continuous to 4/15.

Athletics Member NAIA. Intercollegiate sports: baseball/softball M(s); basketball M(s); cross-country running M(s), W(s); golf M(s); riflery M, W; soccer M(s); tennis M(s), W(s); track and field M(s), W(s); volleyball W(s). Intramural sports: baseball/softball, basketball, football, golf, racquetball, swimming and diving, tennis, track and field, volleyball, wrestling.

Majors Accounting B; anthropology B; applied art B; art/fine arts B; biology/biological sciences B; business administration/commerce/management B; chemistry B; computer science B; (pre)dentistry sequence B; economics B; English B; French B; history B; (pre)law sequence B; mathematics B; (pre)medicine sequence B; music B; philosophy B; physical education B; physics B; political science/government B; psychology B; religious studies B; sociology B; Spanish B; speech/rhetoric/public address/debate B; theater arts/drama B. Majors with highest enrollment: business administration/commerce/management, (pre)medicine sequence, (pre)law sequence.

LD Program Information

Name of Program Learning Disabilities Program.

Availability of Services Began offering services in 1974. Services provided to freshmen, sophomores, juniors, seniors (full-time program for freshmen; half-time program for those who have completed full-time program). Program currently serves 33 LD students: 18 freshmen, 7 sophomores, 5 juniors, 3 seniors.

Fees $1500 per year for full-time program, $750 for half-time program.

Staff 3 part-time staff members, including director, associate directors.

Admissions LD applicants evaluated on the basis of high school transcript and grade point average, untimed SAT or ACT, personal interview, letters of recommendation, psychoeducational report. LD students may begin taking classes in fall only. Application should be submitted 3 to 8 months in advance of initial anticipated enrollment.

Orientation Required orientation held during registration.

Housing College housing available. LD students housed randomly. LD freshmen, sophomores, and juniors required to live on campus except if married, living with relatives, or 21 or over.

Diagnostic Testing Available in intelligence, reading, handwriting, written language, work and study habits, personality.

Tutoring Offered one-to-one by professional teachers, peer tutors. Available in all subjects. LD students may receive tutoring in all courses each term.

Basic Skills Remediation Offered one-to-one and in small groups by LD teachers. Available in reading.

Academic Advisement Help with program planning provided by LD staff members, academic advisers. LD students may take up to 15 credits each semester; most take 12 credits in first semester; 10 credits required to maintain full-time status.

Special Courses Offered in college survival skills, reading, vocabulary development, composition, study skills. All offered for credit; all enter into overall grade point average.

Auxiliary Aids and Services Aids include taped textbooks, tape recorders, word processors. Services include alternative exam arrangements, notetakers, advocacy.

Counseling Services Individual counseling available.

Contact Mr. Henry F. Ottinger, Director of Learning Disabilities Program, Westminster College, Fulton, MO 65251, 314-642-3361.

WESTMINSTER COLLEGE OF SALT LAKE CITY

Salt Lake City, Utah

Year Program Began	1983	Special Courses	✓
Special Fee	None	Taped Textbooks	✓
Special Orientation		Alternative Exam Arrangements	✓
Diagnostic Testing		Notetakers	✓
Subject-Area Tutoring	✓	Staff	2 part-time
Basic Skills Remediation	✓	Number of Students Served	*Not reported*

General Information Independent comprehensive coed institution. Founded 1875. Awards B, M. Institutionally accredited by regional association; programs accredited by NLN (nursing). Metropolitan setting; 27-acre campus. Total enrollment: 1,234. Faculty: 79 (50 full-time, 29 part-time); 48% have doctoral degrees; graduate assistants teach no undergraduate courses. Calendar: 4-4-1. Grading system: letters or numbers. Library holdings: 61,000 bound volumes, 150 titles on microform, 320 periodical subscriptions, 2,000 records/tapes.

Undergraduate Profile Fall 1984: 1,138 undergraduates (136 freshmen) from 35 states and territories and 23 foreign countries; 54% part-time; 81% state residents; 40% transfers; 65% financial aid recipients; 54% women; 2% blacks; 1% Native Americans; 5% Hispanics; 4% Asian Americans; 4% foreign nationals; 45% of undergraduates over 25 years of age; 6 legally handicapped students.

Expenses (1985–86) Comprehensive fee of $7450 includes full-time tuition ($4440), mandatory fees ($110), and college room and board ($2900). Part-time tuition: $148 per semester hour.

Financial Aid Fall 1984 full-time freshmen: 87% applied for aid, 75% of those were judged to have need, 100% of those were aided; the average aided freshman received an aid package worth $4718 (53% scholarships/grants, 47% self-help) meeting 90% of need. College-administered aid for all 1984–85 undergraduates: need-based scholarships; 350 non-need scholarships (average $1000); short-term loans (average $200); low-interest long-term loans from external sources (average $2200); SEOG; College Work-Study. Supporting data: FFS, IRS, institutional form required; FAF, AFSA/SAR acceptable. Priority application deadline: 6/1.

Athletics Member NAIA. Intercollegiate sports: soccer M; tennis M, W. Intramural sports: baseball/softball, basketball, football, golf, skiing (cross-country), skiing (downhill), soccer, volleyball.

Majors Accounting B; aerospace sciences B; art/fine arts B; behavioral sciences B; biology/biological sciences B; business administration/commerce/management B; chemistry B; communication B; computer science B; (pre)dentistry sequence B; early childhood education B; economics B; education B; elementary education B; English B; finance/banking B; history B; humanities B; human resources B; (pre)law sequence B; liberal arts/general studies B; marketing/retailing/merchandising B; mathematics B; (pre)medicine sequence B; nursing B; philosophy B; physical sciences B; physics B; religious studies B; science B; secondary education B; theater arts/drama B; (pre)veterinary medicine sequence B. Majors with highest enrollment: business administration/commerce/management, education, behavioral sciences.

LD Program Information

Name of Program Student Services.

Availability of Services Began offering services in 1983. Services provided to freshmen, sophomores, juniors, seniors.

Staff 2 part-time staff members, including director. Services provided by tutors, counselor.

Admissions LD applicants evaluated on the basis of high school transcript and grade point average, standard or untimed SAT or ACT, personal interview, letters of recommendation. LD students may begin taking classes in fall or spring. Application should be submitted 6 months in advance of initial anticipated enrollment.

Housing College housing available. LD students housed randomly. LD freshmen required to live on campus except if living with relatives.

Tutoring Offered one-to-one and in small groups by peer tutors. Available in some subjects. LD students may receive tutoring in all courses each term.

Basic Skills Remediation Offered one-to-one and in small groups by regular teachers. Available in reading, math, spelling, written language, learning strategies, work and study habits.

Academic Advisement Help with program planning provided by LD staff members, academic advisers. LD students may take up to 16 semester hours each semester; most take 13 semester hours; 12 semester hours required to maintain full-time status.

Special Courses Offered in college survival skills, reading, vocabulary development, composition, language development, math, study skills, career planning. All offered for credit; all enter into overall grade point average.

Auxiliary Aids and Services Aids include taped textbooks, tape recorders, typewriters, word processors. Services include alternative exam arrangements, notetakers, advocacy, proofreaders.

Counseling Services Individual counseling, career counseling available.

Contact Mr. Gary Fitzer, Dean of Students, Westminster College of Salt Lake City, 1840 South 1300 East, Salt Lake City, UT 84105, 801-484-7651.

WEST VIRGINIA UNIVERSITY
Morgantown, West Virginia

Year Program Began	*Not reported*	Special Courses	✓
Special Fee	None	Taped Textbooks	✓
Special Orientation		Alternative Exam Arrangements	✓
Diagnostic Testing	✓	Notetakers	✓
Subject-Area Tutoring	✓	Staff	15 part-time
Basic Skills Remediation	✓	Number of Students Served	*Not reported*

General Information State-supported coed university. Founded 1867. Awards B, M, D. Institutionally accredited by regional association; programs accredited by NASAD (art and design), AACSB (business), ABET (engineering and technology), NASM (music), NLN (nursing), ACPE (pharmacy), NCATE (teacher education). Small-town setting, with easy access to Pittsburgh; 800-acre campus. Total enrollment: 19,071. Faculty: 2,346 (1,307 full-time, 1,039 part-time); 55% have doctoral degrees; graduate assistants teach a few undergraduate courses. Calendar: semesters. Grading system: letters or numbers. Library holdings: 1 million bound volumes, 921,113 titles on microform, 9,425 periodical subscriptions, 11,454 records/tapes.

Undergraduate Profile Fall 1984: 13,915 undergraduates (2,647 freshmen) from 45 states and territories and 45 foreign countries; 7% part-time; 61% state residents; 4% transfers; 55% financial aid recipients; 45% women; 3% blacks; 0% Native Americans; 0% Hispanics; 1% Asian Americans; 3% foreign nationals; 7% of undergraduates over 25 years of age.

Expenses (1985–86) State resident tuition: $1160 full-time, $31 per credit hour part-time. Nonresident tuition: $3140 full-time, $114 per credit hour part-time. College room and board: $2886. College room only: $1476.

Financial Aid Fall 1984 full-time freshmen: 65% applied for aid, 75% of those were judged to have need, 89% of those were aided; the average aided freshman received an aid package worth $2927 (45% scholarships/grants, 55% self-help) meeting 87% of need. College-administered aid for all 1984–85 undergraduates: 834 need-based scholarships (average $769); 413 non-need scholarships (average $1680); short-term loans (average $83); low-interest long-term loans from college funds (average $510), from external sources (average $1700); SEOG; College Work-Study; 1,500 part-time jobs. Supporting data: FAF required. Priority application deadline: 3/1.

Athletics Member NCAA (Division I). Intercollegiate sports: baseball/softball M(I,s); basketball M(I,s), W(I,s); cross-country running M(I,s), W(I,s); football M(I-A,s); gymnastics W(I,s); riflery M(I,s), W(I,s); soccer M(I,s); swimming and diving M(I,s), W(I,s); tennis M(I,s), W(I,s); track and field M(I,s), W(I,s); volleyball W(I,s); wrestling M(I,s). Intramural sports: baseball/softball, basketball, crew, cross-country running, field hockey, football, ice hockey, lacrosse, racquetball, riflery, rugby, soccer, swimming and diving, tennis, track and field, volleyball, wrestling.

Majors Accounting B; aerospace engineering B; agricultural business B; agricultural economics B; agricultural education B; agronomy/soil and crop sciences B; animal sciences B; anthropology B; art education B; art/fine arts B; biology/biological sciences B; botany/plant sciences B; business administration/commerce/management B; chemical engineering B; chemistry B; civil engineering B; computer science B; dental services B; economics B; electrical engineering B; elementary education B; English B; farm and ranch management B; finance/banking B; fish and game management B; forestry B; French B; geography B; geology B; German B; history B; home economics B; home economics education B; horticulture B; industrial engineering B; interdisciplinary studies B; interior design B; international studies B; journalism B; landscape architecture/design B; linguistics B; marketing/retailing/merchandising B; mathematics B; mechanical engineering B; medical technology B; mining and mineral engineering B; music B; natural resource management B; nursing B; painting/drawing B; parks management B; petroleum/natural gas engineering B; pharmacy/pharmaceutical sciences B; philosophy B; physical education B; physical therapy B; physics B; political science/government B; psychology B; Russian B; secondary education B; social work B; sociology B; Spanish B; speech pathology and audiology B; speech/rhetoric/public address/debate B; statistics B; theater arts/drama B; veterinary sciences B; wildlife management B. Majors with highest enrollment: electrical engineering, nursing, accounting.

LD Program Information

Name of Program Disabled Student Services.

Availability of Services Services provided to freshmen, sophomores, juniors, seniors.

Staff 15 part-time staff members, including director. Services provided by remediation specialists, tutors, counselors, diagnostic specialists.

Admissions LD applicants evaluated on the basis of high school transcript, standard ACT. LD students may begin taking classes in fall, spring, or summer.

Housing College housing (including coed) available. LD students housed randomly. LD freshmen required to live on campus.

Diagnostic Testing Available in intelligence, reading, math, spelling, perceptual skills, personality, psychoneurology.

Tutoring Offered one-to-one and in small groups by peer tutors. Available in some subjects.

Basic Skills Remediation Offered one-to-one and in small groups by LD teachers, regular teachers, teacher trainees. Available in reading, math, spelling, spoken language, written language, learning strategies, work and study habits.

Academic Advisement Help with program planning provided by academic advisers. LD students may take up to 18 credit hours each semester; 12 credit hours required to maintain full-time status.

Special Courses Offered in college survival skills, reading, vocabulary development, composition, study skills, career planning. None offered for credit; none enter into overall grade point average.

Auxiliary Aids and Services Aids include taped textbooks. Services include alternative exam arrangements, notetakers.

Counseling Services Individual counseling, small-group counseling, rap sessions, career counseling available.

Contact Dr. Gordon Kent, Director of Disabled Student Services, West Virginia University, Student Services Center, Morgantown, WV 26506, 304-293-4431.

WEST VIRGINIA WESLEYAN COLLEGE
Buckhannon, West Virginia

Year Program Began	1978	Special Courses	✓
Special Fee	$1000 per year	Taped Textbooks	✓
Special Orientation	✓	Alternative Exam Arrangements	✓
Diagnostic Testing	✓	Notetakers	
Subject-Area Tutoring	✓	Staff	5 part-time
Basic Skills Remediation	✓	Number of Students Served	52

General Information Methodist comprehensive coed institution. Founded 1890. Awards B, M. Institutionally accredited by regional association; programs accredited by NASM (music), NLN (nursing). Small-town setting; 80-acre barrier-free campus. Total enrollment: 1,392. Faculty: 111 (92 full-time, 19 part-time); 47% have doctoral degrees; graduate assistants teach no undergraduate courses. Calendar: 4-1-4. Grading system: letters or numbers. Library holdings: 135,000 bound volumes, 4,390 titles on microform, 667 periodical subscriptions.

Undergraduate Profile Fall 1984: 1,374 undergraduates (367 freshmen) from 32 states and territories and 18 foreign countries; 6% part-time; 39% state residents; 10% transfers; 90% financial aid recipients; 54% women; 3% blacks; 1% Native Americans; 1% Hispanics; 1% Asian Americans; 3% foreign nationals; 5% of undergraduates over 25 years of age; 5 legally handicapped students.

Expenses (1985–86) Comprehensive fee of $8337 includes full-time tuition ($4900), mandatory fees ($550), and college room and board ($2887). College room only: $1397. Part-time tuition: $210 per credit hour.

Financial Aid Fall 1984 full-time freshmen: 94% applied for aid, 91% of those were judged to have need, 65% of those were aided; the average aided freshman received an aid package worth $3748 (56% scholarships/grants, 44% self-help) meeting 93% of need. College-administered aid for all 1984–85 undergraduates: need-based scholarships (average $900); 578 non-need scholarships (average $941); low-interest long-term loans from external sources (average $600); SEOG; College Work-Study; 220 part-time jobs. Supporting data: FAF, institutional form, AFSA/SAR required; FFS, IRS acceptable. Priority application deadline: 2/15.

Athletics Member NAIA. Intercollegiate sports: baseball/softball M; basketball M(s), W(s); cross-country running M; field hockey W; football M; golf M; soccer M(s); tennis M, W(s); track and field M, W. Intramural sports: baseball/softball, basketball, bowling, football, racquetball, swimming and diving, track and field, volleyball.

Majors Accounting B; American studies B; art education B; art/fine arts B; biology/biological sciences B; business administration/commerce/management B; business education B; chemistry B; communication B; computer science B; (pre) dentistry sequence B; dietetics B; early childhood education B; economics B; education B; electrical engineering B; elementary education B; engineering physics B; English B; fashion merchandising B; French B; guidance and counseling B; health education B; history B; home economics B; home economics education B; interdisciplinary studies B; international studies B; (pre)law sequence B; library science B; management information systems B; marketing/retailing/merchandising B; mathematics B; medical technology B; (pre)medicine sequence B; music B; music education B; nursing B; nutrition B; philosophy B; physical education B; physics B; political science/government B; psychology B; rehabilitation therapy B; religious education B; religious studies B; secondary education B; secretarial studies/office management B; social science B; social work B; sociology B; special education B; speech/rhetoric/public address/debate B; studio art B; theater arts/drama B; (pre) veterinary medicine sequence B. Majors with highest enrollment: business administration/commerce/management, nursing, elementary education.

LD Program Information

Name of Program Supportive Services.

Availability of Services Began offering services in 1978. Services provided to freshmen, sophomores, juniors, seniors. Program currently serves 52 LD students: 15 freshmen, 20 sophomores, 14 juniors, 3 seniors.

Fees $1000 per year.

Staff 5 part-time staff members, including director. Services provided by remediation specialists.

Admissions LD applicants evaluated on the basis of high school transcript and grade point average, untimed SAT or ACT, personal interview, autobiographical statement, letters of recommendation, WAIS or WISC; psychoeducational report recommended. LD students may begin taking classes in fall only. Application should be submitted 6 months to 1 year in advance of initial anticipated enrollment.

Orientation Required orientation held before registration.

Housing College housing available. LD students housed randomly. LD freshmen, sophomores, juniors, and seniors required to live on campus.

Diagnostic Testing Available in intelligence, reading, math, perceptual skills, work and study habits, personality.

Tutoring Offered one-to-one by peer tutors. Available in all subjects. LD students may receive tutoring in all courses each term.

Basic Skills Remediation Offered one-to-one and in small groups by regular teachers. Available in reading, math, spelling, handwriting, written language, work and study habits.

Academic Advisement Help with program planning provided by LD staff members, academic advisers. LD students may take up to 16 credit hours each semester; most take 12 to 13 credit hours; 12 credit hours required to maintain full-time status.

Special Courses Offered in reading, vocabulary development, composition, math, typing, study skills, career planning. All offered for credit; all enter into overall grade point average.

Auxiliary Aids and Services Aids include taped textbooks, tape recorders. Services include alternative exam arrangements, pre-registration (in freshman year).

Counseling Services Individual counseling, small-group counseling, career counseling available.

Contact Mrs. Phyllis Coston, Director of Learning Center, West Virginia Wesleyan College, Buckhannon, WV 26201, 304-473-8498.

WILMINGTON COLLEGE OF OHIO
Wilmington, Ohio

Year Program Began	*Not reported*	Special Courses	✓
Special Fee	None	Taped Textbooks	
Special Orientation		Alternative Exam Arrangements	✓
Diagnostic Testing	✓	Notetakers	
Subject-Area Tutoring	✓	Staff	3 part-time
Basic Skills Remediation	✓	Number of Students Served	3

General Information Friends 4-year coed college. Founded 1870. Awards B. Institutionally accredited by regional association; programs accredited by NCATE (teacher education). Rural setting, with easy access to Cincinnati; 65-acre campus. Total enrollment: 832. Faculty: 59 (49 full-time, 10 part-time); 64% have doctoral degrees. Calendar: quarters. Grading system: letters or numbers. Library holdings: 100,145 bound volumes, 500 periodical subscriptions, 2,555 records/tapes.

Undergraduate Profile Fall 1984: 832 undergraduates (310 freshmen) from 13 states and territories and 21 foreign countries; 5% part-time; 91% state residents; 24% transfers; 73% financial aid recipients; 39% women; 6% blacks; 0% Hispanics; 5% foreign nationals; no legally handicapped students.

Expenses (1985–86) Comprehensive fee of $8226 includes full-time tuition ($5550), mandatory fees ($285), and college room and board ($2391). College room only: $990. Part-time tuition: $155 per credit.

Financial Aid Fall 1984 full-time freshmen: 91% applied for aid, 89% of those were judged to have need, 90% of those were aided; the average aided freshman received an aid package worth $5939 (61% scholarships/grants, 39% self-help) meeting 90% of need. College-administered aid for all 1984–85 undergraduates: 495 need-based scholarships (average $1974); 245 non-need scholarships (average $1200); low-interest long-term loans from college funds (average $1000), from external sources (average $1000); SEOG; College Work-Study; 200 part-time jobs. Supporting data: FAF, IRS, institutional form, AFSA/SAR required; state form acceptable. Priority application deadline: 3/31.

Athletics Member NAIA. Intercollegiate sports: baseball/softball M, W; basketball M, W; cross-country running M; football M; golf M; soccer M, W; tennis M, W; track and field M, W; volleyball W; wrestling M. Intramural sports: baseball/softball, basketball, football, racquetball, squash, tennis, volleyball.

Majors Accounting B; agricultural business B; agricultural economics B; agricultural education B; agricultural sciences B; agronomy/soil and crop sciences B; American studies B; animal sciences B; art education B; art/fine arts B; biology/biological sciences B; business administration/commerce/management B; business economics B; business education B; chemistry B; classics B; communication B; community services B; comparative literature B; computer information systems B; computer science B; conservation B; corrections B; criminal justice B; (pre)dentistry sequence B; ecology/environmental studies B; economics B; education B; elementary education B; English B; environmental sciences B; European studies B; finance/banking B; French B; German B; graphic arts B; health education B; history B; humanities B; human services B; industrial administration B; industrial arts B; interdisciplinary studies B; international business B; international economics B; international studies B; journalism B; (pre)law sequence B; liberal arts/general studies B; literature B; marketing/retailing/merchandising B; mathematics B; medical laboratory technology B; medical technology B; (pre)medicine sequence B; modern languages B; music B; music education B; natural resource management B; peace studies B; philosophy B; physical education B; physical sciences B; physician's assistant studies B; political science/government B; psychology B; public administration B; public relations B; recreation and leisure services B; religious studies B; science B; science education B; secondary education B; social science B; social work B; sociology B; Spanish B; special education B; sports medicine B; teaching English as a second language B; technical writing B; theater arts/drama B; theology B; (pre)veterinary medicine sequence B; vocational education B. Majors with highest enrollment: business administration/commerce/management, agricultural business, education.

LD Program Information

Name of Program Not specified.

Availability of Services Services provided to freshmen, sophomores, juniors, seniors. Program currently serves 3 LD students: 2 freshmen, 1 junior.

Staff 3 part-time staff members. Services provided by professor of English, reading specialist, writing specialist.

Admissions LD applicants evaluated on the basis of high school transcript and grade point average, standard or untimed SAT or ACT, letters of recommendation; personal interview, autobiographical statement, psychoeducational report recommended. LD students may begin taking classes in fall, winter, or spring. Application should be submitted 1 to 3 months in advance of initial anticipated enrollment.

Housing College housing (including coed) available. LD students housed randomly. LD freshmen required to live on campus except if family resides within 30-mile radius.

Diagnostic Testing Available in reading, math, spelling, written language, personality.

Tutoring Offered one-to-one by professional teachers, peer tutors. Available in all subjects. LD students may receive tutoring in all courses each term.

Basic Skills Remediation Offered one-to-one and in small groups by regular teachers. Available in reading, math, spelling, written language, learning strategies, work and study habits.

Academic Advisement Help with program planning provided by academic advisers. LD students may take up to 17 credits each quarter; most take 14 to 15 credits; 12 credits required to maintain full-time status.

Special Courses Offered in college survival skills, composition, study skills, career planning. Some offered for credit; some enter into overall grade point average.

Auxiliary Aids and Services Services include alternative exam arrangements.

Counseling Services Individual counseling, career counseling available.

Contact Dr. William Guthrie, Professor of English, Wilmington College of Ohio, Department of English, Wilmington, OH 45177, 513-382-6661 Ext. 351.

WRIGHT STATE UNIVERSITY

Dayton, Ohio

Year Program Began	1974	Special Courses	✓
Special Fee	Varies	Taped Textbooks	✓
Special Orientation	✓	Alternative Exam Arrangements	✓
Diagnostic Testing	✓	Notetakers	✓
Subject-Area Tutoring	✓	Staff	4 part-time
Basic Skills Remediation	✓	Number of Students Served	70

General Information State-supported coed university. Founded 1964. Awards A (terminal), B, M, D. Institutionally accredited by regional association; programs accredited by AACSB (business), ABET (engineering and technology), NASM (music), NLN (nursing), NCATE (teacher education). Metropolitan setting; 618-acre barrier-free campus. Total enrollment: 15,517. Faculty: 875 (629 full-time, 246 part-time); 64% have doctoral degrees; graduate assistants teach a few undergraduate courses. Calendar: quarters. Grading system: letters or numbers. Library holdings: 345,332 bound volumes, 700,407 titles on microform, 3,948 periodical subscriptions.

Undergraduate Profile Fall 1984: 12,292 undergraduates (1,835 freshmen) from 52 states and territories and 36 foreign countries; 40% part-time; 95% state residents; 7% transfers; 50% financial aid recipients; 50% women; 6% blacks; 1% Native Americans; 1% Hispanics; 1% Asian Americans; 1% foreign nationals; 45% of undergraduates over 25 years of age; 371 legally handicapped students.

Expenses (1985–86) State resident tuition: $1686 full-time, $53 per credit hour part-time. Nonresident tuition: $3372 full-time, $106 per credit hour part-time. College room and board: $2727. College room only: $1635.

Financial Aid Fall 1984 full-time freshmen: 72% applied for aid, 55% of those were judged to have need, 87% of those were aided; the average aided freshman received an aid package worth $3118 (39% scholarships/grants, 61% self-help) meeting 86% of need. College-administered aid for all 1984–85 undergraduates: 700 need-based scholarships (average $335); 700 non-need scholarships (average $815); short-term loans (average $150); low-interest long-term loans from college funds (average $1623), from external sources (average $1000); SEOG; College Work-Study; part-time jobs. Supporting data: FAF, state form, institutional form required; IRS required for some; FFS acceptable. Priority application deadline: 4/15.

Athletics Member NCAA (Division II). Intercollegiate sports: baseball/softball M(II,s), W(II,s); basketball M(II,s), W(II,s); cross-country running M(II,s), W(II); golf M(II,s); soccer M(II,s); swimming and diving M(II,s), W(II,s); tennis M(II,s), W(II,s); volleyball W(II,s); wrestling M(II,s). Intramural sports: archery, baseball/softball, basketball, cross-country running, football, golf, racquetball, soccer, squash, tennis, volleyball, wrestling.

Majors Accounting A, B; anthropology B; applied mathematics B; art education B; art/fine arts B; art history B; automotive technologies A; biology/biological sciences A, B; biomedical engineering B; business administration/commerce/management A, B; business economics B; business education B; chemistry A, B; city, community, and regional planning B; classics B; communication A, B; community services A; computer engineering B; computer science B; criminal justice B; dance B; data processing A; drafting and design A; early childhood education B; economics A, B; educational media B; electrical and electronics technologies A; electrical engineering B; electrical engineering technology A; elementary education A, B; engineering physics B; English A, B; environmental health sciences B; environmental sciences B; film studies B; finance/banking B; fire science B; French B; geography A, B; geological engineering B; geology A, B; geophysics B; German B; Greek B; health education B; history A, B; Latin B; law enforcement/police sciences A; legal secretarial studies A; manufacturing technology A; marketing/retailing/merchandising A, B; materials engineering B; mathematics A, B; mechanical design technology A; mechanical engineering B; medical secretarial studies A; medical technology B; mental health/rehabilitation counseling B; modern languages B; music B; music education B; music history B; nursing B; painting/drawing B; philosophy B; photography B; physical education B; physics B; political science/government B; psychology A, B; reading education B; rehabilitation therapy B; religious studies B; science education B; secondary education B; secretarial studies/office management A; social work A, B; sociology A, B; Spanish B; special education B; statistics B; systems engineering B; theater arts/drama B; urban studies B; water resources A, B. Majors with highest enrollment: accounting, computer science, nursing.

LD Program Information

Name of Program Learning Disabilities Program.

Availability of Services Began offering services in 1974. Services provided to freshmen, sophomores, juniors, seniors. Program currently serves 70 LD students.

Fees $400 plus room and board for Pre-College Assessment Program (PCAP).

Staff 4 part-time staff members, including assistant director. Services provided by remediation specialist, reading specialist, supervisor of tutoring.

Admissions LD applicants evaluated on the basis of high school transcript, standard or untimed SAT or ACT, GED (in lieu of high school diploma); personal interview, letters of recommendation, psychoeducational report recommended. LD students may begin taking classes in fall, winter, spring, or summer. Application should be submitted 6 to 8 months in advance of initial anticipated enrollment.

Orientation Optional orientation offered during registration.

Housing College housing (including coed) available. LD students housed randomly. LD students not required to live on campus.

Diagnostic Testing Available in reading, math, written language, work and study habits. Offered through PCAP during summer prior to enrollment.

Tutoring Offered one-to-one by peer tutors. Available in all subjects. LD students may receive tutoring in all courses each term.

Basic Skills Remediation Offered one-to-one by developmental education instructors. Available in reading, math, spelling, written language, learning strategies, work and study habits, social skills.

Academic Advisement Help with program planning provided by LD staff members, academic advisers. LD students may take up to 18 credit hours each quarter; 12 credit hours required to maintain full-time status.

Special Courses Offered in college survival skills, reading, vocabulary development, communication skills, composition, math, study skills, career planning. Some offered for credit; some enter into overall grade point average.

Auxiliary Aids and Services Aids include taped textbooks. Services include alternative exam arrangements, notetakers, advocacy, LD support group.

Counseling Services Individual counseling, small-group counseling, rap sessions, career counseling available.

Contact Mrs. Patricia E. Schlaerth, Assistant Director, Handicapped Student Services, Wright State University, Dayton, OH 45435, 513-873-2141.

XAVIER UNIVERSITY
Cincinnati, Ohio

Year Program Began	1981	Special Courses	✓
Special Fee	None	Taped Textbooks	
Special Orientation	✓	Alternative Exam Arrangements	✓
Diagnostic Testing		Notetakers	✓
Subject-Area Tutoring	✓	Staff	20 part-time
Basic Skills Remediation	✓	Number of Students Served	8

General Information Roman Catholic comprehensive coed institution. Founded 1831. Awards A (college transfer and terminal), B, M. Institutionally accredited by regional association; programs registered by New York State Board of Regents; programs accredited by NLN (nursing). Metropolitan setting; 104-acre campus. Total enrollment: 6,850. Faculty: 343 (219 full-time, 124 part-time); 70% have doctoral degrees; graduate assistants teach no undergraduate courses. Calendar: semesters. Grading system: letters or numbers. Library holdings: 300,000 bound volumes, 2,000 periodical subscriptions, 2,000 records/tapes.

Undergraduate Profile Fall 1984: 4,038 undergraduates (566 freshmen) from 34 states and territories and 45 foreign countries; 18% part-time; 80% state residents; 5% transfers; 68% financial aid recipients; 52% women; 7% blacks; 0% Native Americans; 1% Hispanics; 3% foreign nationals.

Expenses (1985–86) Comprehensive fee of $8370 includes full-time tuition ($5400) and college room and board ($2970). College room only: $1470. Part-time tuition: $180 per semester hour.

Financial Aid Fall 1984 full-time freshmen: 90% applied for aid, 72% of those were judged to have need, 100% of those were aided; the average aided freshman received an aid package worth $4680 (50% scholarships/grants, 50% self-help) meeting 90% of need. College-administered aid for all 1984–85 undergraduates: need-based scholarships; non-need scholarships; low-interest long-term loans from external sources (average $2200); SEOG; College Work-Study; 150 part-time jobs. Supporting data: FAF, institutional form, Financial Aid Transcript (for transfers) required; IRS required for some; FFS, AFSA/SAR acceptable. Priority application deadline: 4/15.

Athletics Member NCAA (Division I). Intercollegiate sports: baseball/softball M(I,s); basketball M(I,s), W(I,s); cross-country running M(I), W(I); golf M(I,s); ice hockey M(c); martial arts M(c), W(c); riflery M(I), W(I); rugby M(c); sailing M(c), W(c); soccer M(I,s), W(I,s); swimming and diving M(I), W(I); tennis M(I,s), W(I,s); volleyball W(II,s). Intramural sports: baseball/softball, basketball, bowling, crew, field hockey, football, ice hockey, martial arts, racquetball, riflery, rugby, sailing, skiing (cross-country), skiing (downhill), soccer, tennis, volleyball, water polo, weight lifting.

Majors Accounting A, B; adult and continuing education B; art education B; art/fine arts B; art history B; art therapy B; biology/biological sciences B; broadcasting B; business administration/commerce/management A, B; chemistry A, B; child care/child and family studies A; classics B; communication A, B; computer information systems B; computer programming A; computer science B; criminal justice B; data processing A; (pre)dentistry sequence B; economics A, B; education B; elementary education B; English A, B; finance/banking B; French B; funeral service A, B; history A, B; international studies B; journalism B; labor and industrial relations A, B; (pre)law sequence B; marketing/retailing/merchandising A, B; mathematics B; medical technology B; (pre)medicine sequence B; modern languages A; music B; music education B; natural sciences B; nuclear medical technology A, B; nursing B; philosophy B; physical education B; physics B; political science/government A, B; psychology A, B; radio and television studies B; radiological technology A; secondary education B; social work B; sociology A, B; Spanish B; special education B; theater arts/drama B; theology A, B. Majors with highest enrollment: marketing/retailing/merchandising, accounting, (pre)medicine sequence.

LD Program Information

Name of Program Special Students Assistance Program.

Availability of Services Began offering services in 1981. Services provided to freshmen, sophomores, juniors, seniors. Program currently serves 8 LD students: 2 freshmen, 3 sophomores, 2 juniors, 1 senior.

Staff 20 part-time staff members, including chairman. Services provided by remediation specialists, tutors, counselors.

Admissions LD applicants evaluated on the basis of high school transcript and grade point average, untimed SAT or ACT, letters of recommendation; psychoeducational report recommended. LD students may begin taking classes in fall or spring. Application should be submitted 4 to 6 months in advance of initial anticipated enrollment.

Orientation Optional orientation offered during registration.

Housing College housing (including coed) available. LD students housed randomly. LD freshmen, sophomores, and juniors required to live on campus.

Tutoring Offered one-to-one by professional teachers, peer tutors. Available in some subjects. LD students may receive tutoring in all courses each term.

Basic Skills Remediation Offered one-to-one by regular teachers, peer teachers. Available in reading, math, spoken language, written language, learning strategies, work and study habits.

Academic Advisement Help with program planning provided by academic advisers. LD students may take up to 18 semester hours each semester; 12 semester hours required to maintain full-time status.

Special Courses Offered in reading, communication skills, composition, math, study skills. All offered for credit; most enter into overall grade point average.

Auxiliary Aids and Services Aids include tape recorders, typewriters. Services include alternative exam arrangements, notetakers, advocacy.

Counseling Services Individual counseling available.

Contact Dr. Sally Pruden, Director of Special Education and Chairman of Committee for Special Students Assistance, Xavier University, 3800 Victory Parkway, Cincinnati, OH 45207, 513-745-3655.

Geographical Index to Colleges

Alphabetical Index to Colleges

Sources of Additional Information

More information about programs and services for learning-disabled young adults may be obtained from these organizations.

Association for Children and Adults with Learning Disabilities (ACLD)
4156 Library Road
Pittsburgh, PA 15234
412-341-1515 or 8077

Association of Learning Disabled Adults
P.O. Box 9722
Friendship Station
Washington, DC 20016

Association on Handicapped Student Service Programs in Post-Secondary Education
P.O. Box 21192
Columbus, OH 43221
614-488-4972

Closer Look/Parents' Campaign for Handicapped Children and Youth
1201 16th Street, NW
Washington, DC 20036
202-822-7900
LD Teenline toll-free number: 800-522-3458

Council for Exceptional Children (CEC)
1920 Association Drive
Reston, VA 22091-1589
703-620-3660

Council for Learning Disabilities (CLD)
GR 4.1
University of Texas at Dallas
P.O. Box 830688
Richardson, TX 75083-0688
214-690-2065

Foundation for Children with Learning Disabilities (FCLD)
99 Park Avenue
New York, NY 10016
212-687-7211

HEATH Resource Center (Higher Education and the Handicapped)
One Dupont Circle, Suite 670
Washington, DC 20036-1193
202-833-4707

Information Center for Individuals with Disabilities
20 Park Plaza, Room 330
Boston, MA 02116
617-727-5540

International Reading Association (IRA)
800 Barksdale Road
P.O. Box 8139
Newark, DE 19714
302-731-1600

National Easter Seal Society
2023 West Ogden Avenue
Chicago, IL 60612
312-243-8400

National Information Center for Handicapped Children and Youth (NICHCY)
P.O. Box 1492
Washington, DC 20013
703-528-8480

National Rehabilitation Information Center (NARIC)
Catholic University of America
4407 8th Street, NE
Washington, DC 20017
202-635-5822

Orton Dyslexia Society
724 York Road
Baltimore, MD 21204
301-296-0232

Parent Information Center
P.O. Box 1422
Concord, NH 03301
603-224-7005

President's Committee on Employment of the Handicapped
1111 20th Street, NW, Room 600
Washington, DC 20036
202-653-5010

The Puzzle People
1368 Lincoln Avenue, Suite 105
San Rafael, CA 94901
415-453-4006

Time Out to Enjoy
715 West Lake Street, Suite 100
Oak Park, IL 60301
312-383-9017

help: ROTC programs, the service academies, and direct enlistment (during which money is accumulated for college enrollment). Directories show all colleges that host ROTC programs or have cooperative agreements with programs at nearby institutions. The book also contains charts and comparison tables that help students determine which program will be the most beneficial.

6" x 9", about 120 pages — Stock no. 3622
ISBN 0-87866-362-2 — **$5.95** paperback

Summer Jobs:
Finding Them, Getting Them, Enjoying Them
Sandra Schocket

Designed especially for high school and college students, this valuable guide shows how to find and get good summer jobs. It covers topics such as the process of finding a summer job, specific fields of employment that have summer jobs for students, options for students who want nontraditional types of employment (volunteer work, internships, working abroad, self-employment), and additional resources that might aid students in their summer job search.

6" x 9", 170 pages — Stock no. 3258
ISBN 0-87866-325-8 — **$5.95** paperback

How to Order

These publications are available from all good booksellers, or you may order direct from **Peterson's Guides, Dept. 5626, P.O. Box 2123, Princeton, New Jersey 08540.** Please note that prices are necessarily subject to change without notice.

- Enclose full payment for each book, plus postage and handling charges as follows:

Amount of Order	*4th-Class Postage and Handling Charges*
$1–$10	$1.25
$10.01–$20	$2.00
$20.01–$40	$3.00
$40.01 +	Add $1.00 shipping and handling for every additional $20 worth of books ordered.

Place your order TOLL-FREE by calling 800-225-0261 between 8:30 A.M. and 4:30 P.M. Eastern time, Monday through Friday. From New Jersey, Alaska, Hawaii, and outside the United States, call 609-924-5338. Telephone orders over $15 may be charged to your charge card; institutional and trade orders over $20 may be billed.

- For faster shipment via United Parcel Service (UPS), add $2.00 over and above the appropriate fourth-class book-rate charges listed.
- Bookstores and tax-exempt organizations should contact us for appropriate discounts.
- You may charge your order to VISA, MasterCard, or American Express. Minimum charge order: $15. Please include the name, account number, and validation and expiration dates for charge orders.
- New Jersey residents should add 6% sales tax to the cost of the books, excluding the postage and handling charge.
- Write for a free catalog describing all of our latest publications.